P9-DEH-582

AMERICAN
POLITICS

AMERICAN POLITICS

POLICIES, POWER, AND CHANGE

FIFTH
EDITION

KENNETH M. DOLBEARE / Evergreen State College
MURRAY J. EDELMAN / University of Wisconsin

assisted by
LINDA J. MEDCALF / Olympia Technical Community College

D.C. HEATH and Company
Lexington, Massachusetts / Toronto

Copyright © 1985 by D. C. Heath and Company.
Previous editions copyright © 1971, 1974, 1977, 1979, and 1981 by D. C. Heath and Company.

All rights reserved. No part of this publication may be reproduced or transmitted in any form or by any means, electronic or mechanical, including photocopy, recording, or any information storage or retrieval system, without permission in writing from the publisher.

Published simultaneously in Canada.

Printed in the United States of America.

International Standard Book Number: 0-669-07323-7

Library of Congress Catalog Card Number: 84-81190

Preface

This is the fifth edition of a book originally conceived and written in the late 1960s. We are gratified that its two most distinguishing features—its political economy framework and its critical nature—have stood the test of more than a decade.

Our framework integrates politics and government with the private economy and its dynamics. The influence of economic conditions on politics and public policy could hardly be clearer than it is today. Neither politics nor economics can be fully understood separately, and the connections between them must be made explicit, rather than left to the coincidental combination of courses from several departments or a fortunate intellectual leap by a determined student.

This revision retains the political economy framework while more fully delivering on its promise. We have shifted the emphasis from the now-dated debate between the power-elite and pluralist schools of political science to a simple acknowledgment of the existence of an "establishment." We believe that most students of today know instinctively that the wealthy and powerful are in charge. Therefore, the questions addressed change slightly. Students need more careful and complete understanding and analysis, in order to deal effectively with their instinctual reactions. What are the implications for Americans of the current state of affairs? Is it systemic, unchangeable, bad, or not so bad? In other words, we try to make clear that we are dealing with a system that is neither democracy, as generally understood, nor despotism. The main question for students is Why, how, and to what purpose can the individual participate?

We have incorporated into the political economy framework a comprehensively updated set of facts and circumstances from the 1980 census and the 1982 and 1984 elections. We have carefully revised the entire text to update the data, and we have added extensive material on the nature of current economic problems and their implications for politics and public policy. The United States is presently undergoing an economic transformation that will mean transformations and consequences for the whole political economy. We have added several examples to illustrate the disagreements regarding the policies necessary for economic recovery. We have removed the chapter focused exclusively on the military and national security, and present these issues in this new edition as part of the problem of managing the interdependent, international economy and the domestic population.

We have made other substantive changes to the descriptions of institutions and processes. For example, we have updated and expanded the abortion case study, so that it can stand by itself. We also have updated the chapters on the judiciary, the Congress, and the presidency, as well, to include changes brought about by the 1970s and 1980s reforms and the "Reagan revolution." Acknowledging its importance as a policy-shaping tool, we have added a chapter on the budgetary process. New public policy examples, including much analysis of the Reagan administration, illustrate the various facets of American politics. Similarly, in keeping with our theme of transformation, we have increased our emphasis on political participation *in all its guises*. Finally, we have included and discussed questions about political action committees, the role of the media, the decline of the parties, and so forth. But the fundamental political economy framework and its central questions remain.

This book is critical, not in the sense of being a negative polemic or proceeding from an alternative ideology, but rather in the classical liberal arts sense. To be critical is to be self-conscious about one's own values, assumptions, and way of thinking. It clarifies concepts, rigorously examines evidence, and looks beyond the way that institutions and events present themselves, to search for underlying causes and relationships. With this sort of critical approach, people learn analytical and evaluative skills, not just facts. On this basis, we frankly encourage readers to make their own judgments and interpretations.

This fifth edition is accompanied by a very useful Instructor's Guide, prepared by Janna Merrick of St. Cloud State University. It, too, has been thoroughly updated to fit with this edition. Professor Merrick has as much experience teaching with this book as anyone else we know and is ideally qualified to provide instructors with test questions and other assistance.

We acknowledge the immensely helpful assistance of Linda Medcalf in revising and updating this edition. Valuable research assistance for the fifth edition was provided by Steve Hodes of The Evergreen State College in Olympia, Washington. As always, we invite comments and suggestions from teachers and students.

K.M.D.
M.J.E.

Contents

AMERICAN POLITICS

PART I

Why and How to Study Politics

What is American politics? And who cares? These questions may occur to students confronting a new textbook with the prospect of eighteen chapters to go. *American Politics,* when properly used, will help to explain why our political system works as it does and how its workings affect people and problems. Most importantly, we need to be able to understand where our political system—and therefore all of us—might be going. If our efforts are successful, this text should also help readers ask the right questions, evaluate the answers, and act in an effective way. This is not a book for those who think they can avoid or transcend the effects of politics. Moral dilemmas, the failures and successes of human efforts to build a decent world, and the opportunities of our times deserve our best understanding and response. We think this book can help.

Our primary purposes are to help people see their political system more clearly, to develop their skills of analysis and evaluation, and to enable them to act more effectively to gain their ends in politics—whether through, around, or in spite of the established political system. To do these things honestly forces us to look critically at many of the revered institutions and values of the United States, to challenge some familiar myths, and to expand on some standard approaches to political science.

Unfortunately, in today's world, the American reaction to the mention of "politics" is often one of general distaste, if not revulsion. Politics conjures up visions of unfulfilled promises, cheating, manipulation, and the use of power for private ends rather than public good. Politics implies general all-around corruption at its worst, and general bungling at its best. The word *politician* is a term of opprobrium, whether it is used as a professional term or as a way to describe someone's behavior. What was once an honorable calling—to serve the public—has fallen just about as low as it can go.

1

In today's terms, much of the general American feeling is probably justified. Analyzing the reasons and uses for such distaste forms an important part of the discussion in this text. Historically, politics had a much broader base than the narrow world to which it now has been consigned. Politics was, and is, a necessary and possibly highly moral part of human existence. In pure American self-interest terms, to leave politics to the politicians, especially in these times, is to give away any possibility for truly choosing our own future. If freedom is to have any meaning and democracy is to be realized in any meaningful way, then politics that are consistent with freedom and democracy must be undertaken.

The main problem with this derogatory vision of politics and Americans' withdrawal from the political arena is that this is one of those rare times when popular participation can make a significant difference in our future. Fundamental political economic change is on the agenda; we cannot keep what we have had or presently have, even if we want to. The choice is not *whether or not* to change anything; the choice is *what* changes, in what directions, and under whose leadership and values. If we do not engage in politics, those choices will be left to others.

In these first two chapters, we begin to assemble the ingredients of a conceptual framework—including key definitions—that will enable us to understand what is going on in American politics. We shall try to be explicit about our purposes, the themes that we see as important in the 1980s, and the techniques of analysis and evaluation that we believe will be most helpful.

CHAPTER 1

Politics as Political Economy: Designing an Approach

What you see in the world depends upon what you are looking for. How you understand it depends upon the concepts you use as you undertake your inquiry. All concepts reflect assumptions and suggest conclusions. For example, many people conceive of "politics" as a distinct compartment of social life, set apart from "economics" and "society." "Politics" has to do with Democrats and Republicans, the President on television, and occasional elections. People choose their elected officials and that is "democracy." "Economics" involves a complicated system of production and distribution upon which one depends for material survival; it is a private activity. "Society" is an independent area with distinct forces at work. People have unequal status and prestige, mostly as a result of differences in talent and effort. Customs and values from the past are steadily modified by changing relationships within the family, among racial and ethnic groups, and among men, women, and children.

There are two vitally important factors to consider and resolve in an open and explicit manner before undertaking the task of trying to understand politics. Both of them have been suggested in the introductory paragraph above:

1. *Key definitions*—how we define the major terms we use will shape what we see and how we understand it.
2. *A conceptual framework*—these definitions form part of a larger approach, a way of looking at the "picture" we want to see and understand.

In the next two sections, we shall define some key terms and describe what we believe to be the most informative conceptual approach to understanding American politics. After that, we shall illustrate our approach in two different ways.

KEY DEFINITIONS: POLITICS, POWER, AND PARTICIPATION

Politics. A leading political scientist once characterized politics as "who gets what, when, and how."[1] Though it requires some refinement, this is a good general definition, because it points well beyond "government" or "the state" to focus on other holders of power in the society and the ways that they achieve their goals and affect others' lives. In order to get to our refinement, however, we need to spell out more fully what is included in our definition.

In order to live together on a continuing basis, and to achieve various goals in life, people seek and employ power in ways that affect the lives of others. In other words, they engage in politics. They erect governments to maintain order, further mutual goals, and promote general well-being. Around and within that framework, people continue to seek their individual and group goals. People can no more live without politics in this sense than they can forego food, love, or other basic human needs and desires. Politics is the activity by which people define themselves and their world and publicly seek their goals. By means of politics, people can create, maintain, or adapt the context that allows them to pursue their goals and/ or defend what they have already gained. For many people, of course, political activity serves all of these purposes.

In the broadest sense of the term, politics occurs whenever an individual or group brings resources of power to bear on any other individual, group, or institution whose behavior it desires to change. Interaction with governmental bodies is only the most obvious possibility. If tenants withhold rent in order to induce a landlord to make needed improvements on a building, they are engaging in political activity. Regardless of how often, or seldom, individuals employ their own political resources to influence the actions of others, they cannot escape from the consequences of political decisions. We are all engaged in politics, if only as consumers of the political products generated by the actions of others. Like it or not, inevitably and permanently, politics is a part of our lives.

We must also include in this definition extragovernmental activity that bears on who rules, who benefits, and how change comes about, because government is only one of several channels through which vital goals are obtained. The use of government therefore implies change in, or confirmation of, preexisting patterns of benefits. Fundamentally revealing uses of power are more often prompted by the question of *whether* government should act than by the *way* in which government is to act. For example, in

---

[1] Harold Lasswell, *Politics: Who Gets What, When, How* (New York: McGraw-Hill, 1936).

recent years, a number of manufacturing plants in the midwest and northeast have closed for a variety of reasons, but always amid controversy. Their communities suffered unemployment, tax-base loss, and a general decline in their ability to maintain essential services. Plant owners argue that closure is a *private* decision that is based on economic necessity or desirability. The public consequences are unfortunate, but. . . . Should there be governmental involvement in this area? The consequences for ordinary people, who inevitably feel the impact of this struggle in one form or another, are very great.

Further, a concern for the nature of problems and the character of extragovernmental activity will alert us to the processes by which an issue becomes recognized as a possible subject for public debate. Some matters are routinely understood as being appropriate for governmental action; others, such as poverty and racial discrimination, are seen as such only at very late stages. Still other issues, such as the nationalization of major industries, are not at all viewed as being public issues (at least in the United States). Sometimes a subject initially appears to be quite outside the range of "practical" political consideration; after a period of struggle, however, it moves into the field of political debate and eventually takes a place among accepted governmental policies. Such was the case with medical care for the aged, for example.

Throughout the period when some political actors are trying to move a subject from the unthinkable stage to the stage of debate and action, many forces are at work to shape opinion about whether or not the issue should be a subject for public resolution. These initial shaping forces reach deep into the underpinnings of our politics. Our understanding of what is proper for government action is strongly affected by the cultural values and assumptions we acquire while growing up. These shaping assumptions and values are not coincidental; they have been taught to us. Some issues and problems automatically elicit public attention and government action, but some continue to be purely private matters. Which issues become "public" issues? Why and under what conditions? When they do, *who* acts, and *how* do they act to shape our understanding of the nature of these issues?

The point is that the relationship of the individual to politics *never* ends. Every contact with politics implies a prior history of choices made in keeping with the preferences of those with the greatest amount of power at a particular time over a particular issue. The individual exists in a world shaped by the decisions of others. Not even the most determined effort to extricate oneself from such effects can be successful. You might as well learn the rules, problems, and possibilities, and join the game more fully informed and ready to play.

The temptation is strong to try to understand too much, to treat almost every pattern of social and economic activity as if it had political implications. The fact is, of course, that almost everything does. For the purposes of this textbook, however, we must exclude much of this activity in order to cope concretely with *some* of it. We shall limit ourselves to matters that have a direct and immediate relation to the present character or future prospect of American governmental action. Our definition of politics then becomes: *the process by which power is employed to affect whether and how government will act on any given matter.*

Power. Power is derived from the possession of resources. Obviously such resources would include money, prestige, and official position, but things such as numbers of people, moral suasion, or acts of individual conscience are also resources. It is the possession of a resource that causes other political actors to modify their behavior and conform to what they perceive the possessor of the resources to prefer. Such resources need not be tangible or direct, although they can be; one would be foolish to discount guns and money. However, often what counts is others' perceptions of one's resources. These resources need not be actually mobilized and employed in any particular situation because others may act in anticipation or expectation, or even fear, of such use. Indeed, much politically significant behavior occurs because of "voluntary" conformity with the perceived expectations of others.

One of the major resources of power is legitimacy. Legitimacy is a status *conferred by people* on other people or on institutions. When people believe, for example, that their government is the right one, and that it works properly and for desirable ends, they place their trust in it and grant it their obedience. Elected officials, bureaucrats, and law enforcement personnel all acquire some of this special status by virtue of their institutional positions. We then say that the government has authority. This authority enables higher officials to exert considerable influence over what people believe, to draw support for their actions, and to shape the agenda of politics so as to gain their ends more easily.

Legitimacy and authority are fluid and intangible attributes however, and can be undermined by frequent requests for uncritical support. They are endangered by actions that are inconsistent with expectations or traditions, and, of course, by extreme misconduct. Once undermined, voluntary compliance with the acts of government and normal cooperation on the part of the general public may cease. At this point, legitimacy and authority have been lost. If this occurs among a large proportion of the population, people in government may have to fall back on outright coercion to achieve their ends. The shift to this form of power, of course, means that the existing political system is close to breaking down.

Participation. In light of the foregoing, our definition of political participation is broader than merely voting, running for, or holding public office. Further, it is very difficult to *choose* not to participate. The very act of withdrawal or denial is a form of participation. It leaves the decisions in the hands of others and grants them that power. For example, we emphasized in the discussion of legitimacy that it is a status *conferred* by people. Power that is not actively countered or denied will be exercised, nevertheless. Participation may come in various degrees of passivity or activity, but it cannot be foregone altogether.

A second major component to be considered in defining political participation is its degree of self-consciousness. In other words, the very simple act of voting can be any number of different versions of participation. It could be that the voter is responding solely to the televised commercial that insists that all "good" Americans vote. In this case, participation is limited to supporting the status quo and symbolically reaffirming that one is a "good" American. Conversely, the decision *not* to vote could be a decision based on a well-thought-out and completely rational conclusion that voting serves no purpose *other* than legitimating the status quo, which one chooses not to do. The form, degree, and self-consciousness of political participation often are derived from one's place in the current order, as well as the opportunities that are both perceived to be, and realistically are, available.

Thus, "politics" is a vast interactive process of *power* applications, which nearly always has consequences for others. From the ideology learned as a child to the present process of defining a "problem" and perhaps acting on it, we are participants in this process—or at least in its effects. Fortunately, our limited definition of politics as those uses of power that bear directly on whether or how the American government will be employed makes it unnecessary to trace the entire web of power transactions in society. The focus on what bears "directly" on the use of government will not always be clearcut, but we can keep our definition manageable, without losing its scope, by using a political economy framework of analysis.

THE CONCEPT OF POLITICAL ECONOMY

An old—and new—conceptual approach to political analysis is to see economic and political life, as well as the society and its culture, as one integrated whole. All areas are connected to one another so closely that they become mutually supportive and interdependent (in more technical terms, "coherent"). In the eighteenth century, people such as the framers of our Constitution regularly thought and talked in terms of a single economy-government-society unit, within which they saw the economy as the principal dynamic. We use their term, *political economy,* to refer to the web of political and social institutions and human activity that are interwoven with the contemporary economy. We include society and culture as well as government and politics in this conceptual approach. However, we do not mean to suggest that all areas are merely reflective of economic conditions or forces; each area has independent characteristics and causes of change that affect all the others. Rather than seeing the "areas" as either reflections or causes, we want to stress their continuing relationship and interdependence, as well as the centrality of economics to each.

What difference does it make how we conceive of the interaction between economy and government? In social analysis, the most useful concepts are usually those that take the most factors into account. We want to be able to look beyond mere facts in search of relationships, connections, and explanations. A compartmentalized approach to politics and economics obscures many such vital connections. The integrated political economy approach is deliberately inclusive.

We consider the political economy concept valuable and rewarding, but it is not always easy to think (or write or read) in that framework. We are so used to the idea of separate compartments that it takes deliberate effort for each of us to abandon familiar habits of thought. In this and subsequent chapters, for example, we characterize our political economy in a preliminary way, but this material should not evoke images of "government" managing the "economy." Conversely, to see it as the "economy" managing the "government" also oversimplifies the situation. Either approach means a return to the two-compartments concept. Instead, we should be searching for interests, trends, power, and potential actions wherever they exist within the single entity under analysis. Our focus will shift from one sector of the political economy to another, but the entire inquiry proceeds within the integrated political economy framework. Let us take an obvious example.

The United States is a capitalist society. This pronouncement is one of the most meaningful statements that can be made about American politics. It is not a very startling or original observation, but Americans react to it in sharply contrasting ways. Most people never understand its implications, and often not even its meaning. Others are so shocked by the discovery and its implications that they believe there is nothing more to be said.

Neither of these two responses satisfies the demands of sophisticated political analysis. Both result from a lack of understanding of the interrelationship of economic, social, cultural, and ideological factors in shaping politics. We must develop concepts, methods, and other tools of analysis that enable us to transcend these responses to the point of understanding, for example, how much of our politics is traceable to the capitalist nature of the American social order and how much is due to other factors.

What does it mean that the United States is a capitalist society? First, it means that the productive resources of the society—farms, factories, mines, and so on—are all owned by private individuals or corporations, and operated so as to produce profits for their owners. Services such as transportation, advertising, communications, and the like are also privately owned and operated for profit. Most people are not owners and must earn their livelihoods by working for those who are.

Next, it means that the social structure is shaped in important ways by patterns of wealth and income distribution that are created by that economic system. A relatively few people—mostly owners, but also some salaried managers and other persons—receive a large share of all the wealth and income produced in this economy. A larger group of people with especially useful skills—engineers, lawyers, accountants, doctors—also receive a substantial proportion. A still larger number of people, mostly low-skill workers, females, and minorities, receive a smaller proportion of income. Status and power in the society are distributed in the same stratified manner, thereby giving rise to a class system.

A capitalist society also has certain cultural and ideological characteristics. The values of the society support behavior that is consistent with the economic system and social structure. Individual self-seeking, materialism, the work ethic or profit motive, and respect for private property are at once basic American values and necessary principles of behavior in a capitalist society. The characteristic American way of thinking is also (but less obviously) consistent with a capitalist social order. It assumes the continuity of existing patterns of ownership, social structure, and values, and unconsciously tries to fit all it sees or imagines into that mold. It asks only questions that are answerable in these terms and employs only words that express attitudes appropriate to such a society. For example, it looks at higher education chiefly as a means to prepare young people for jobs and income in a technological society. It either cannot imagine other purposes or considers them uneconomical "frills"—or possibly even subversive.

Finally, although all societies generate self-congratulatory and justifying ideologies, the ideology that is associated with a capitalist society has certain special features. It holds that economic activity is separate from (and morally superior to) politics. It teaches that human nature itself is the basis of capitalism: people are naturally competitive and self-seeking, and thus, capitalism is the "natural" economic system. American ideology includes many other beliefs as well, as we shall see in later chapters, but the outlooks just identified are especially linked to the capitalist nature of the American system.

In the foregoing example, we have seen in a general way how the economy, society, culture, and politics are all understandable as one integrated whole. Now let us turn to two more concrete examples of how to see these important factors together. The first is the forces working to transform the American economy—and society, and politics—in the 1980s. The second is the enduring relationship between the American social structure, or "pyramid," as we shall refer to it, and the political leadership, or "elite level," of American politics. These examples of seeing things in a political economy framework will also introduce two important themes that run through this entire book:

1. The American political economy is undergoing a major transformation that makes political participation by ordinary people both vital and potentially much more effective than at other times.
2. The American system has historically been managed by a relatively small body of leaders, drawn from the upper levels of the American social pyramid. This elite sector may now be split and subject to more control from below—by ordinary citizens—than is usually the case.

THE TRANSFORMATION UNDER WAY IN THE AMERICAN ECONOMY

We have stressed the concept of *political economy*—the integration of economy, politics, and society into one coherent social order whose nature and dynamics are powerfully, but not wholly, shaped by the character and needs of the economic system. We presently face an era in which the character and needs of our economic system are changing. What *needs* to be done has, and is, debated heatedly. What is less frequently discussed is that a monumental change in the economy, and thus in the society and our politics, is under way. As John Naisbitt, author of the bestseller *Megatrends,* stated:

> The United States is rapidly shifting from a mass industrial society to an information society, and the final impact will be more profound than the nineteenth century shift from an agricultural to an industrial society.[2]

What we are producing, as well as where and how we produce it, is in the process of transformation, and therefore, the American political, economic, and social orders are also in flux. We shall look first at economic changes and then at the associated changes in social structure, and conclude with a discussion of the political implications.

Economic Changes. The first factor to be particularly noted is the one alluded to by Naisbitt—the "information explosion," or the technological developments associated with the "computer revolution." The development of computers with microprocessor chips is a growth industry in and of itself. Most of the major new businesses are related to this development in one way or another. Just as important, if not more so, is that the development of this technology has led to automated production in every area of the economy. Industries that have taken advantage of this capability use fewer workers, much-expanded data processing, and generally lighter materials. This process is what is meant by the shift from "heavy" to "light" industry.

Second, a major portion of profits, sales, and assets are derived internationally. We have a global economy, with products and capital moving rapidly and easily (partly because of the computer revolution) around the world. The component parts of any particular end product may have been manufactured in a dozen countries, shipped separately to another country for assembly, and the assembled product shipped to a final country for sale. "American" firms overseas produce items for sale in Europe *and* import into the United States. We must also add that other countries' products are imported into U.S. markets, where they are often competitively superior. The U.S. imports a much larger volume of products than it exports. One of the major reasons that the U.S. balance of trade is not even worse is that profits from services rendered abroad and overseas investments flowing into the U.S. offset the bad import/export balance. American capital investment overseas returns a handsome profit to those investors but does little to help Americans in search of work.

The results of this developing global, high-technology, and information-industry economy affect industries and people differently. Obviously, industries damaged by imports or whose capital investment is locked into

---

[2] John Naisbitt, speech in Stockholm, Sweden, September, 1979.

now-outmoded production techniques are going to suffer. These "smoke-stack" industries—our traditional heavy industries—are in rapid decline, causing the loss of thousands of jobs as an occupational shift to high technology and services production occurs. Unemployment among the older industries, most particularly the traditional blue-collar industries, soars. In other words, the economic transformation is costing some and benefiting others and generally reverberating not only throughout the American political and economic structure but also the rest of the world.

Changes in the Social Pyramid. Some changes in American society result from changes in the economic structure, and some from other factors, such as cultural or population shifts. Most of the changes in occupational structure are obviously responses to the economic changes. Occupation translates directly into other areas of social and cultural life. Other changes in the social structure may be quite independent of the economic transformation and, in turn, affect it. Analysis of recent demographic, or population, information reveals some important changes that translate into social, political, and economic impacts.

The obvious result of occupational shifts is changes in income and opportunity for large numbers of people. One of the enduring myths about the United States regards the importance of its "middle class" core. Even if the data are not completely accurate, a disturbing portion of the job shift appears to indicate a significant decline among the stable middle class. Jobs are increasing at the upper and lower levels of income and responsibility, and declining in the middle. Table 1.1 gives a composite picture of the shifting job market. One of the most important facts to notice is the great increase in the total number of jobs in the American economy between 1950 and 1980. The largest share of this increase came from women entering the labor force, perhaps partly out of necessity and partly because of their increased desire for such opportunities. There were also major changes in the makeup of the work force in those three decades. Professional and managerial jobs increased in proportion, as did clerical jobs, but blue-collar opportunities dropped substantially—and farm workers were particularly subject to replacement by machines.

Where were the jobs created most recently, in the 1970s? Seventy percent of the new jobs created between 1970 and 1980 were in service and retail industries. The vast majority of them were in food service, particularly the fast-food industry. The service needs of business expanded with a percentage increase in jobs for data processors, janitorial workers, temporary office personnel, and lower-level clerks. The health-service industry also expanded, but not with professionals. Nursing-home personnel, doctor and dentist office personnel, and private hospital staff positions increased. Many (*not* teachers) found jobs in the public sector as what are often termed "low-level bureaucrats." Although many of these positions were filled by men and younger (teenage) workers, they traditionally had been regarded as "women's jobs."

Projections for the future, shown in the second and third sections of Table 1.1, require that we distinguish between high *percentage* increases and large *numbers* of new jobs. The list at the left contains several of the romantic, high-technology occupations about which much is heard today. The actual numbers of new jobs involved are quite small, however, because the base on which the percentage rests was tiny to begin with. The contrasting list on the right, which ranks occupations by the number of new jobs to be produced by 1990, contains no such romance. For the most part, it is a list of relatively familiar and rather unglamorous occupations. Only two occupations on the fastest growing list also appear on the largest job categories list—fast-food workers and nurses' aides and orderlies.

The majority of the new jobs are concentrated at the lower levels of the social and status pyramid. What they have in common is low pay, low security, poor working conditions, and, most importantly, no union. Although older industries still provide many jobs, there is a decided lack of fit between those who are unemployed because of the decline of older industries and the jobs created by the transformation. These shifts in occupation mean major changes in income and opportunity for large numbers of people, and they obviously arise out of the ongoing economic transformation.

Overlapping with the changing occupational picture are shifts in social structure caused by population changes. Several things are happening at once. One is that the U.S. population is getting older. The median age of Americans rose from 28 in 1970 to 30 in 1980. By the year 2000, 25.1 percent of the population will be below 18 while 13.1 percent will be over 65 years of age. In 1980, 27.5 percent were under 18 and only 11.3 percent over 65. This means that fewer people will be entering the labor market at the same time that more are retiring and living longer. Many of those retirees seek easier retirement climates, such as the Sun Belt.

Many other people are also moving to the Sun Belt, that group of states that stretches from North Carolina on the Atlantic Ocean across the bottom half of the U.S. to California. Table 1.2 shows the official projections for continued movement between 1980 and 2000. For convenience, the table follows the standard classifications of states, in which the South and West categories represent the Sun Belt states and the Northeast and North Central groups represent the Snow Belt states. According to these projections, the population shift that characterized the last two decades is far from over. Population is moving and jobs are shifting in mutually reinforcing ways. The Northeast and North Central will lose in shares of the U.S. population, but they will also lose a larger proportion of the country's jobs—and an even larger share of the country's *manufacturing* jobs, the jobs that are thought to be the keys to further economic growth. The South and West are catching up quickly, and in the process are pulling ahead of the older states in all the important economic dimensions.

Not surprisingly, this continuing pattern of job and population changes means that some states are growing very rapidly in population, whereas others are stagnating. In the first set of comparisons, Table 1.3 shows the populations and growth rates of leading high- and low-growth states for the period 1970–2000. The high-growth states will grow at roughly the same rapid rates as they have been, and the low-growth states will grow more slowly than the nation as a whole.

TABLE
1.1

The Changing American Occupational Structure
The Past: Evolution of the Work Force, 1950–80

	1950	1980
Work force (millions)	62.2	106.9
Men	43.8	61.4
Women	18.4	45.5
Participation rate*	59.2%	63.8%
Men	86.4	77.4
Women	33.9	51.5
Occupations (share of total)**		
White collar	35.9%	52.2%
Professional, technical	8.4	16.1
Managers, administrators	8.6	11.2
Clerical	12.0	18.6
Sales workers	6.8	6.3
Blue collar	40.1%	31.6%
Craftsmen, foremen	13.9	12.8
Operatives	19.8	14.2
Laborers	6.4	4.6
Service workers	10.2%	13.3%
Farm workers	11.6%	2.8%

* Proportion of noninstitutional population 16 and over in the labor force.
** Excludes the unemployed in 1950.

The Future:

THE 20 FASTEST-GROWING JOBS

	1980 Employment	Projected Growth, 1980–90	Percentage of Growth
Paralegal personnel	32,000	35,000	108.9
Data processing mechanics	83,000	77,000	92.3
Computer operators	185,000	133,000	71.6
Computer analysts	205,000	139,000	67.8
Office machine servicers	55,000	33,000	59.8
Physical therapists	34,000	17,000	50.9
Fast-food workers	806,000	400,000	49.6
Computer programmers	228,000	112,000	48.9
Tax preparers	31,000	15,000	48.6
Employment interviewers	58,000	27,000	47.0
Speech, hearing clinicians	35,000	16,000	46.6
Correction officials	103,000	45,000	46.5
EDP equipment operators	49,000	21,000	44.0
Aero-astronautical engineers	68,000	29,000	43.4
Travel agents	52,000	22,000	43.4
Nurses' aides, orderlies	1,175,000	508,000	43.2
Insurance claims examiners	40,000	17,000	43.0
Economists	29,000	12,000	42.0
Brickmasons	146,000	58,000	40.2
Psychiatric aides	82,000	33,000	39.9

TABLE   **The Changing American Occupational Structure**
1.1   **The Future** (*cont.*)

THE 20 LARGEST JOB CATEGORIES

	1980 Employment	Projected Growth, 1980–90	Percentage of Growth
Secretaries	2,469,000	700,000	28.3
Nurses' aides, orderlies	1,175,000	508,000	43.2
Janitors and sextons	2,751,000	501,000	18.2
Sales clerks	2,880,000	479,000	16.7
Cashiers	1,597,000	452,000	28.4
Professional nurses	1,104,000	437,000	39.6
Truck drivers	1,696,000	415,000	24.5
Fast-food workers	806,000	400,000	49.6
General office clerks	2,395,000	377,000	15.8
Waiters, waitresses	1,711,000	360,000	21.1
Elementary teachers	1,286,000	251,000	19.5
Kitchen helpers	839,000	231,000	27.6
Accountants, auditors	833,000	221,000	26.5
Construction helpers	955,000	212,000	22.2
Automotive mechanics	846,000	206,000	24.4
Blue-collar supervisors	1,297,000	206,000	15.9
Typists	1,067,000	187,000	17.5
Licensed practical nurses	522,000	185,000	35.5
Carpenters	970,000	173,000	17.9
Bookkeepers, hand	975,000	167,000	17.2

SOURCE: U.S. Bureau of Labor Statistics.

TABLE
1.2   **U.S. Regional Changes, 1980–2000**

	Northeast	North Central	South	West
Percentage of U.S. population, 1980	22.7	26.6	32.5	18.3
Net change in percentage of U.S. pop., 1980–2000	− 1.6	− 1.3	+ 1.5	+ 1.3
Percentage of U.S. jobs, 1973	23.5	27.5	30.6	17.6
Net change in percentage of U.S. jobs, 1973–2000	− 4.4	− 2.1	+ 3.2	+ 3.6
Percentage of U.S. manufacturing jobs, 1973	26.5	32.5	28.1	12.9
Net change in percentage of U.S. manufacturing jobs, 1973–2000	− 7.0	− 3.2	+ 5.8	+ 6.2

SOURCE: U.S. Department of Commerce, Bureau of Economic Analysis, *BEA Regional Projections, 1981.*

TABLE 1.3
Contrasting Patterns of Population Change

	TOTAL POPULATION INCREASE				MINORITY INCREASE (All Minorities)	
	Total Population, 1970 (in thousands)	Percentage of Increase, 1970–1980	Total Population, 2000 (in thousands)	Percentage of Increase, 1980–2000	Minority Percentage of, 1980	Minority Percentage of, 2000
HIGH-GROWTH STATES						
California	19,971	19	29,002	22	33	51
Texas	11,199	27	18,790	32	34	45
Florida	6,791	43	13,260	35	24	26
Colorado	2,209	31	3,869	34	18	26
Arizona	1,775	53	4,080	50	26	38
LOW-GROWTH STATES						
New York	18,241	–4	18,166	3	25	32
New Jersey	7,171	3	8,098	10	21	26
Pennsylvania	11,801	1	12,830	8	11	11
Ohio	10,657	1	11,742	9	11	12
Illinois	11,110	3	12,546	10	22	26
Michigan	8,882	4	10,361	12	16	17

SOURCE: U.S. Census Bureau Current Population Reports Series, *Illustrative Projections of State Populations, 1983*, p. 25, and U.S. Census Bureau Current Population Reports Series *Characteristics of the Population, 1980*. p. 60.

This brings us to some vitally important patterns of change involving minorities. The minority population (here defined as Asian, black, Native American, and of Spanish origin) is rapidly increasing, both naturally and as a result of immigration. Approximately 1,000,000 people now enter the U.S. legally each year. About 42 percent of our immigrants are of Spanish origin (Mexican, Puerto Rican, and Latin), and another 40 percent are Asians. The minority population, both as a whole and as a percentage of the entire population, is increasing. It tends, however, to be concentrated in the declining cities of the Snow Belt and the fastest-booming Sun Belt states of California, Florida, and Texas.

The last two columns of Table 1.3 show that the minority proportion of *both* the high- and low-growth states will rise—in some cases quite sharply—between 1980 and 2000. Hispanic immigration, legal and illegal, accounts for most of this increase in the high-growth states. The rise in the low-growth states results from *whites* moving to the Sun Belt and obtaining jobs in the newer industries, whereas blacks are being left behind in the states with declining older industries.

Political Implications. For lifestyle, occupational, economic, and basic demographic reasons, there is a decidedly sharp contrast between the Snow Belt and the Sun Belt. It reflects the very sharp regional migration of both *population* and *jobs.* This combination has obvious public-policy implications, as well as basic political consequences. The most obvious political consequence is the power shift that this population change will cause in Washington, D.C. Because representation in the electoral college is based on population, the regional population shift will show up in those numbers. Seventeen seats in the House of Representatives, and therefore seventeen electoral college ballots, were lost by the Snow Belt to the Sun Belt following the 1980 census. It is projected that they will lose ten more in 1990 and another eight to ten in 2000. The minority concentration in Snow Belt cities leads to marked shifts in urban political power, such as the election of black mayors in several major northern cities. Although presently unpredictable, these population trends will show up sooner or later as changes in political structures and practices, and in public policies.

Public policies have historically supported and encouraged a growing national commercial economy. We are now facing a period in which the economic and social transformations require political support of a new kind. There is a contrast between the needs of old and new industries. New and old workers must retrain and relocate even while unemployment remains a serious problem. Do we protect domestic markets against imports while promoting export markets? Do we encourage investment in new industries, which are mostly in the Sun Belt, or do we modernize existing industries, which are mostly in the Snow Belt? Or should we do nothing, which benefits whoever happens to be favored under current conditions? Who will pay, and who will benefit, is an insistent value question.

A similar example, which has already had wide and immediate impact, is the problem occasioned by Social Security. As elder citizens became more numerous and politically significant, Congress increased eligibility and benefits, finally indexing it to inflation in 1972. As inflation took off and the number of retirees increased, benefit payments ballooned, and Congress raised worker and employer taxes. Then the recession reduced receipts, and the Social Security system presented a crisis—"outgo" increasing faster than income. We are still faced with pressing public policy questions. Should the young be taxed to pay for the old, and if so, how much? Who should benefit and who should pay? No matter which way we turn, we are confronted by value-based policy choices.

All these questions arise from and have implications for the economic *and* social *and* political arenas. Whatever the "answers," the economic problems and the political solutions are interconnected. Our difficulty is not only how to understand and analyze the situation but also how to evaluate and thus make judgments about how and under what conditions to proceed. The following section illustrates the interconnections between the political arena and other arenas. The political economy works together to form a total context. In order to understand what is happening in American politics today, and in order to be able to act effectively, we must examine the whole. The political economy framework helps.

LEADERSHIP IN AMERICAN POLITICS

As we shall see in exhaustive detail when we analyze the American social pyramid in Chapter 4, a relatively few people hold the greatest amounts of wealth, status, and power in the United States. Many more people with much less wealth, status, or power make up the lower and bottom layers of our society, thus justifying our use of the term "pyramid" as a shorthand characterization. One crucial question that results from recognition of the differences within this social pyramid is whether those with the most wealth, status, and power are also dominant in politics. The disproportionate income, wealth, and status levels in this pyramid, it might be assumed, are likely to result in economic, social, and political leadership being held by those same few people. We cannot take this for granted, no matter how obvious it might seem to be, because it is so crucial to the question of whether our system can fairly be called democratic. This is a complex issue, and we will have to clarify concepts carefully and analyze data thoroughly throughout this book. For the moment, we shall simply present the findings of the two leading studies in this field.

In a carefully researched study that starts with the key *institutional* positions of power and leadership in the U.S., political scientist Thomas Dye identified 7,314 "top" positions, occupied by a total of 5,778 people.[3] These institutions, and the number of leading companies, firms, or other

---

[3] Thomas R. Dye, *Who's Running America? The Reagan Years,* 3rd ed. (Englewood Cliffs, N.J.: Prentice-Hall, Inc., 1976, 1979, 1983), p. 12.

units included in each category, are shown in the left column of Table 1.4. The number of top leadership positions involved are shown in the next column of the table. Dye characterizes the elite thus identified as follows:

> These top positions, taken collectively, control half of the nation's indus-trial assets; half of all assets in communication, transportation, and utilities; half of all banking assets; two thirds of all insurance assets; and they direct Wall Street's largest investment firms. They control the televi-sion networks, the influential news agencies, and the major newspaper chains. They control nearly 40 percent of all the assets of private founda-tions and half of all private university endowments. They direct the na-tion's largest and best-known New York and Washington law firms as well as the nation's major civic and cultural organizations. They occupy key federal governmental positions in the executive, legislative, and judi-cial branches. And they occupy all the top command positions in the Army, Navy, Air Force, and Marines.[4]

Table 1.4 summarizes certain of the social background characteristics of the people who occupy the institutional positions of power from data presented in Dye's work. Immediately apparent is that they are nearly all older white males. In a population in which only 20 percent of those over twenty-five years of age have college degrees, 94 percent of these elites have graduated with at least a bachelor's degree. Fifty-six percent of those are from a "prestige" college or university—one of the Ivy League schools or Johns Hopkins, Chicago, Stanford, Northwestern, or the University of California at Berkeley. Those with law or business degrees from the presti-gious universities do not show up separately on this table, but among the very high proportions who have such degrees are certainly many more from these prestigious universities. On almost any characteristic, down to membership in social clubs (over one-third belong to one of the exclusive private social clubs of the country), the power/leadership roles in Ameri-can society are concentrated in the very highest strata of the social pyra-mid.[5]

More central to our immediate concerns are the positions of leadership in the federal government. Public positions are slightly less "elite" than private ones, but only slightly. Moreover, many of the top government positions are filled from the other elite positions—the famous "revolving door" theory. This movement in and out of government service by the top layer of the social pyramid is not a new phenomenon; it has been a con-stant in American political history. Table 1.5, drawn from a meticulous three-volume study of all American administrations since 1789, lists the principal backgrounds of the secretaries of the various executive depart-ments of the national government in post–World War II administrations. It shows that such cabinet appointees have regularly come from the highest levels of the economic, social, and political structures of the American

---

[4] Ibid., p. 14.
[5] Ibid., Chapter 6.

TABLE 1.4
Social Background Characteristics, U.S. Institutional Elites, 1980–1981

INSTITUTIONAL LOCATIONS	NUMBER OF LEADERSHIP POSITIONS	AVERAGE AGE	PERCENTAGE FEMALE	HIGHER EDUCATION LEVELS (IN PERCENTAGES)				
				No Degree	Bachelor's Degree Only	Law Degree	Other Advanced Degree	Bachelor's Degree from "Prestige" College or University
Industrial corporations (100)	1,475	61	2.4	3	43	23	30	55
Utilities, communications, transportation companies (50)	668	61	4.3	8	41	25	27	51
Banks (50)	1,092	61	2.3	6	43	22	29	50
Insurance (50)	611	62	1.1	5	43	23	30	55
Investments (15)	479	58	.9	1	51	9	39	61
Mass media (18)	220	61	6.8	18	39	21	22	52
Education (25)	892	62	10.6	4	33	28	35	74
Foundations (50)	402	62	14.7	5	25	27	43	67
Law (25)	758	64	1.8	0	0	100	5	83
Civic and cultural organizations (12)	433	60	9.0	4	37	25	35	60
Government: Exec., Legis., & Judicial	236	56	7.7	9	11	41	34	42
Government: Military	48	56	0	5	30	9	56	21
Totals or Averages:	7,314	60	4.3	6	37	26	31	56

SOURCE: Derived from Thomas R. Dye, Who's Running America? The Reagan Years (Englewood Cliffs, N.J.: Prentice-Hall, 1983), tables on pp. 14 and 196. For definitions, see accompanying text.

TABLE 1.5
Principal Backgrounds of Cabinet Appointees for Post–World War II Administrations

	Corporate Law firms	Large Industrial or Retail Corporations	Banks or Other Financial Enterprises	High Appointed U.S. Govt. Offices	Elective Offices, State or Congress	Other
Truman	12	4	3	7	3	
Eisenhower	5	13	6	0	4	1
Kennedy	5	2	2	2	3	
Johnson	11	5	3	4	1	
Nixon	7	9	2	0	3	5
Ford	5	0	3	0	3	2
Carter	7	4	2	1	3	1
Reagan	3	5	2	1	3	4

SOURCE: Derived from Philip H. Burch. *Elites in American History*, Volume III (New York: Holmes & Meier, 1981), Appendix A, pp. 399–517. Non-Cabinet appointees eliminated. Reagan data has been added by authors.

DEFINITIONS: Cabinet appointees only (currently 13 secretaries), for purposes of comparability. For Presidents Johnson and Ford, only new appointments are included.

"Corporate law firms" are major New York, Washington, or regionally prominent firms specializing in work for large corporations and banks.

social order. There are minor differences in preference between Democratic and Republican administrations, although Republicans tend to draw more from the business world. Up until the Nixon administration, most cabinet officers were drawn from the "Eastern Establishment" ("old" money); later appointments begin to reflect the divergence in interests of the large economic units, but the point is *all come from the highest strata.*

The image of the American social structure that emerges is one of stratification and inequality in all the relevant categories. Of course, this pattern may be a totally random product of differences in talent, effort, or luck. However, the fact that it exists poses such questions as its relative permanence across generations, whether and how it may be related to the economic system, and whether and how it may translate itself into political power.

Our posing of the political economy concept, in which society and economy are connected and together affect politics, brings such questions up for analysis. The suspicion grows that there may be an empirically demonstrable connection among the position people occupy in the social pyramid, what their values and ideology are, what their relationship to the economic system is, and how they think and act in politics. Such conceptualization helps to focus basic questions more sharply.

SUMMARY AND PREVIEW

We began this chapter by asserting that American politics could be understood best by seeing it embedded in its economic, social, and cultural context—with the whole moving together through time as one integrated unit. We offered some key definitions and then sketched our approach to understanding an integrated "political economy" in a general way. In the last two sections, we have seen how our economy, society, and politics are intertwined in practice. Economic changes, for example, result in social and political changes in such a closely connected way that it is not really possible to say which comes first. The second example showed how closely the wealth gained through the economy translates into social status, but perhaps the reverse is also true; in any event, the result is that political leadership is drawn from the highest levels of the society.

One implication that should be drawn from these two examples is that our analysis must be directed at all sectors simultaneously. We cannot look simply at who does what in politics and expect to understand either the *reasons* behind such actions or their *implications* for people, problems, or the nature of American democracy.

Another purpose in employing these particular illustrations was to establish two themes that we consider to be particularly important. American politics is in the process of being reshaped, in part by the powerful effects of the combined economic and social transformation under way. Basic values and beliefs, the distribution of wealth and power, and the directions of public policy today and tomorrow are all changing as the way we earn our living and lead our lives changes. The dominance of the upper levels of our political system by people drawn from the upper strata of our society may also be changing. Long-established elites may have to make room for new people with different priorities, people who come from other regions of the country and different sectors of the economy. Whether this means that the shift will be only from one group of wealthy and powerful people to another, or whether the millions of ordinary people who individually have less wealth and power will gain greater influence, is one of the central questions of the 1980s—and of this book.

Perhaps most important, these examples should serve to illustrate our need for the most careful kind of inquiry. We need to address the issues raised by these and many other similar situations we shall encounter in this book with the utmost concern for evidence and its thoughtful evaluation. The validity and utility of our inquiry depend entirely on how well we conduct our analysis. We shall consider both the techniques of careful analysis and the procedures of responsible evaluation in the next chapter.

CHAPTER 2

Political Economy: Analysis
and Evaluation

The last chapter illustrated the many links between social and economic factors, as well as their political implications at any given time. But we also need to recognize that political institutions themselves are inherently linked to what is happening in the economy and society by their origins, present structural characteristics, and the impact of the public policies they produce. It would be very difficult to overstate the intimacy of these connections. In order for our political economy framework to be complete, it must include the structural ties between the economy and political institutions, as well as the way in which the policies produced bind political institutions to the economy. Let us take as an example one of the politically "independent" agencies of the U.S. government, the Federal Reserve System. When we have completed this final illustration, we can move on to consider the methods by which we can analyze and evaluate within the political economy framework.

THE FEDERAL RESERVE SYSTEM

Most of the important features of the American political economy are illustrated by this vital independent agency and its actions. The Federal Reserve System was created in 1913 after extended negotiations among the banking industry, corporate lawyers, and government experts. It functions as a kind of government central bank, and is able to regulate the amount and value of money as economic conditions dictate. Naturally, people's opinions differ sharply as to exactly what sort of actions should be taken at any given time.

Beginning in the 1880s, many small farmers and entrepreneurs found it extremely difficult to get the credit that they needed from private bankers. The idea of a government bank that would provide such funds increasingly became part of the platforms of political reformers.[1] As enacted, the Fed was a system with the appearance and powers of a government body and the reality of domination by the values, priorities, and personnel of the private banking industry. Despite the vast scope of its powers, the Fed is not directly accountable to the electorate or its representatives in any way. Monetary policy is a vital component of public policy. Let us now explore how such policies are made and implemented and how they affect both the United States and world economies.

The Fed is headed by a seven-member Board of Governors who are appointed by the President to fourteen-year terms and are subject to confirmation by the Senate. The Chair is designated by the President from among the Governors for a four-year term. Almost all major banks are members of the Federal Reserve System and their needs are served by twelve Federal Reserve banks in various districts of the country. The Board has the power to set the "discount rate," or the rate of interest that Federal Reserve banks charge for loans to their member banks. This rate is widely recognized as a basic signal about how high or low interest rates should be and whether they should be headed up or down. The Board also has the power to set the reserve requirements for member banks. (The reserve requirement specifies the proportion of deposits that must be kept on hand to the share that can be loaned.) The higher the reserve requirement, the less money available for loans, and thus the higher the interest rates for borrowing it.

The key decision-making unit of the Fed is the Federal Open Market Committee (FOMC). FOMC consists of all seven Governors, the president of the New York Federal Reserve Bank, and four other presidents of Reserve banks on a rotating basis. This group meets regularly and secretly to decide on Fed policy with respect to expansion or contraction of the money supply. Such decisions are implemented by buying or selling government securities, such as Treasury bills and notes. The Fed does all it can to mask its strategy in the complex securities market so that it can work its will effectively. If the Fed buys, it pays by crediting the selling banks with new reserves in their accounts at the Fed; this transaction in effect creates new money. The selling banks, which are only the very largest, are now able to make more loans to their borrower banks, which can, in turn, make more loans, and thus, the supply of "money" multiplies. As this new money circulates, the economy picks up speed. If the Fed sells government securities, it reduces the reserves in the biggest banks, makes money more difficult to acquire, pushes interest rates up, and slows the economy down.

---

[1] For a history of this process, see Gabriel Kolko, *The Triumph of Conservatism: A Reinterpretation of American History, 1900–1916* (New York: The Free Press, 1963).

TABLE
2.1   **The Federal Reserve System**

Entity	Membership	Function
Board of Governors	Seven Governors, appointed by President for 14-year terms, confirmed by Senate. Chair designated by President for 4-year term.	Set discount rate. Set reserve requirements.
Fed. Open Market Committee	Seven Governors, President of N.Y. Federal Reserve Bank, four other Presidents of Reserve Banks. Chair is Chair of Board of Governors.	Expand or contract money supply through buying or selling U.S. securities.
Reserve Banks (12)	Nine Directors, elected and appointed from both banking and non-banking sources.	Service member banks in area.

Table 2.1 summarizes the formal makeup of the decision-making units of the Fed. In practice, the Board of Governors and the system as a whole are dominated by the Chair, who also serves as Chair at meetings of the FOMC. With fourteen-year terms, some members of the Board may hold views that are at odds with the current President and the Chair of the Board, but the other members normally will defer to the Chair, who is traditionally a strong personality. The Chair represents the Board in such political arenas as the White House, Congress, and various international conferences. The Chair is also more likely to be sympathetic to the President's priorities and view of the economic world. The other Governors are better known for their technical competence than their political positions. Many of them have risen through the ranks of the Fed itself or have gained their appointments as political concessions to important senators or representatives.

The Fed is closely interlocked with other units of the financial community, particularly the major banks and the U.S. Department of Treasury. Staff and officers move back and forth between leading positions. A generally shared ethos of concern for the stable value of money permeates the whole. The current Chair, Paul Volcker, exhibits these features clearly. His career includes periods at the New York Fed, the Treasury, and Chase Manhattan Bank. He came to the Board and the position of Chair from the presidency of the New York Federal Reserve bank.

Of course there are arguments in favor of having money controlled by an independent agency, but in recent years, many voices in Congress and elsewhere have been raised on behalf of greater political accountability.

The recession of the early 1980s, for example, was a deliberate choice of one man, Paul Volcker, and perhaps the banking constituency that he represents. Although President Reagan also sought to control inflation, he did not support the full vigor of the attack mounted by Volcker and the Fed; many in Congress also preferred a lower priority for control of inflation, or at least a different mix of measures to do the job that would spread the costs more evenly. The point is that there was no opportunity for debate or choice—the Fed acted, on its own, with profound social consequences. The concentration of such vast powers, and its insulation from popular accountability, seems likely to lead to continuing controversy.

Concerns about the actions and independence of the Fed are not limited to the United States. Foreign countries are profoundly affected by the level of interest rates in the United States. When U.S. interest rates are high, foreign countries lose capital to investments in the United States and Third World debtors have trouble obtaining dollars, with which to repay their loans, through international trade. A strong and sustained U.S. recovery is needed to help both all foreign countries in general and specifically the Third World economies toward recovery, growth, and the easing of the Third World debt crisis. All of these concerns depend, not on U.S. political leaders, or even on Congress and the President together, but on the one person whose powers are both independent and specifically addressed to the crucial needs that they have.

The Fed faces a real dilemma in trying to meet these needs. In order to bring interest rates down in the context of the massive federal deficits, the Fed would have to increase the money supply rather sharply. If it did so, it would certainly create inflationary expectations among investors, bankers, and the general public. Such expectations already exist because of the deficits, and any confirmation would be likely to set off a wave of self-fulfilling behaviors, such as consumer buying sprees or the cancellation of long-term investments in favor of short-term speculation. In order to prevent "inflationary psychology" and maintain its own credibility, the Fed is almost obliged to restrict the money supply and push interest rates up at the first sign of returning inflation.

Restricting the money supply, however, would inhibit the recovery and worsen the interest rate situation. There is no way out of this dilemma other than to walk a tightrope between preventing inflation and encouraging recovery for several years. Meanwhile, unemployment will continue to be high, and there is always the possibility that the whole enterprise will fail for some extraneous reason that is not now visible. The only real cure is a period of sustained high growth, which is perhaps the least likely of the various alternatives in view. This dilemma recurs in future chapters, but probably nowhere in as acute a form as when it confronts the powerful, politically insulated Federal Reserve Board. We are starting, however, to come to grips with the complexity of the interconnections that make up the world as seen from a political economy perspective. It is now time to be more precise about the analytic techniques that we employ in trying to understand the large and complicated entity we call the American political economy.

TECHNIQUES OF ANALYSIS AND EVALUATION

As we illustrated in Chapter 1, economic and social characteristics play a significant part in our politics. We have just seen that political institutions themselves are thoroughly interlaced with the economy and its needs, and these are not the only factors to be included in an effort to understand American politics. At this point an important question should occur to the reader: How do we find and identify the parts played by all these different factors? Clearly we must cast our analytical net wide enough to include all the major factors, and we must be alert enough to see them after we have caught them.

By trying to cast our analytical net as widely and as skeptically as possible, we affect the interpretation that we ultimately reach. If we reject the idea of separate compartments for "politics," "economics," and "society," we force ourselves to be alert to their interconnections—and we might find some. If we are skeptical about the familiar images of an affluent, classless, conflict-free society, we might find reasons to doubt each of these. Our approach then, is biased, both in its commitments to scope and skepticism, and in its ways of transcending ideology in search of truth.

The distinguishing features of an analysis that claims to be trustworthy are a *framework* whose components are made clear and an *approach* that permits contrasting interpretations to be tested against the evidence. In other words, *are conclusions left open by the assumptions and procedures of the inquiry?* We think that this is the case here. We shall pose two beginning questions that will shape our inquiry throughout this book. They are "Who rules?" and "What difference does it make?" We shall first discuss our premises, clarify some of the components of our political economy approach to inquiry, and then take up the implications of these two central questions.

Our premise, as we have stated, is that understanding is best achieved by looking at an integrated political economy and trying to identify the fundamental sources of its dynamics. We will first look at the needs and circumstances of the economy, but basic values, social conflicts, and external pressures also play important parts. The most basic factors, such as societal values or economic imperatives, are the tools for explanation in this approach, and *not* the personalities of individual officeholders or the characteristics of individual institutions.

The political economy approach argues that government, *no matter who the people holding office may be*, generally acts in ways that serve the needs of the dominant units of the economic system. Whatever the social origins and political beliefs of officeholders, they traditionally act to defend investments and open up markets abroad. At home, they encourage profitability, defend inequality of wealth and income, and prevent social unrest.

One weakness of the political economic approach is that it may seem to explain things too mechanically (*everything* happens because the needs of the economic system dictate it). After all, there is much conflict about proposed government actions, and at times, the policies implemented appear to be at odds with the interests of the dominant economic units. Three observations need to be offered here:

1. Much of what government does is not of fundamental importance to the maintenance of the economic system itself, its major imperatives, or the basic established pattern of burdens and benefits. Such nonfundamental issues may well be subjects of controversy among components of the economy or social groups in general.

2. The shared commitment of major units to the maintenance and continued profitability of the total system should not obscure the existence of ongoing rivalries among component elements. For example, the divergence in interest between multinational corporations and small businesses, or the Snow Belt and the Sun Belt, is likely to require different *policies* from the federal government. These differences may be over rather crucial public policy choices, such as protectionism or free trade, military buildup or reduction of the deficit, or full employment or control of inflation. When differences between the dominant units over major economic policies are on the agenda, more fundamental questions, such as the desirability of maintaining the total system as is, often also are opened up, in spite of efforts to contain them. It is at these times that public impact is greatest and inevitably, considerable political conflict results.

3. The policies that appear to be contrary to the immediate interests of dominant elements may actually serve their long-range interests. The Federal Reserve System is a celebrated example of this. As we have seen, it initially had the appearance of reform and government control over the banking system, but it was drafted and accepted by the banking industry itself, and now operates with concern for that industry's needs. The Marshall Plan, through which the United States invested tens of billions of dollars in the reconstruction of European industries after World War II, is often cited as an example of American generosity, but U.S. industries *required* export markets and investment opportunities, and the only possible market of the necessary size and scope was a revived Europe. Moreover, the investment of vast public funds provided many opportunities for profitable investment of private funds. The American investment was provided by tax revenues from the entire population, and not just from the corporate-banking beneficiaries of a revived Europe.

These observations make the political economy approach appear to be less mechanical and more open to contending forces whose efforts often succeed in shaping particular outcomes. All such conflict, however, can be seen as occurring within the basic framework created by the structure and imperatives of the total political economy. Where fundamental questions are concerned, the range of choice is often very narrow. However, during eras of transformation, such as the 1970s and 1980s, the political possibilities widen. The strengths of the political economy approach lie in its scope and its search for the most fundamental causes and explanations. When filled in with evidence, it provides a satisfyingly comprehensive interpretation of what is happening and why. Let's return now to the two central questions and show what kinds of evidence and interpretation are in store for us.

The Focus of Analysis: Who Rules? We must look comprehensively at the acts of all (or at least most) of the powerholders who are active in any given area. We cannot direct our analyses exclusively at the acts or words of leaders or the official decisions, laws, and regulations of governmental institutions. Unfortunately, the easiest way to "study" politics is to look at the public acts and words of political leaders on the assumption that they make the key decisions. Political leaders often act in public; indeed, one of their chief functions is to make a strong and widespread impression that will make good copy for journalists. Journalistic accounts of politics consist largely of descriptions of the statements, actions, and interactions of political leaders.

In the political economy approach, however, the answer to the question "Who rules?" or "Who holds power?" is not found solely by analyzing government officeholders or even their policies. It lies more fundamentally in the structure of ownership and control of the major private economic units and the identification of those whose interests are served by the workings of the *total* system. For many years, very little evidence was available to connect directly the interests of the owners and managers of the dominant private units with the actual decision making of government officials. However, recent studies of the makeup of governing elites and the agenda-shaping role of prestigious policy-planning groups have gone a long way toward filling this gap. We touched on some of this work in the second illustration in Chapter 1, and will develop the point much more fully in Chapter 5.

What configuration of powerholders effectively shapes the actions of the U.S. government? Our view is that power is extracted from both public and private resources by a more or less continuing body of elites (or "establishment") that seeks to shape popular preferences into forms that can be used to support both its own basic goals and the system itself. On major issues involving the basic structure of the economic and political order and the permanence of the established patterns of distribution of wealth and social status, a *relatively* unified power structure comes into being. Various holders of power coalesce to form a coherent and nearly single-minded force that is capable of managing major sources of private power, the government, and the general public alike.

The "glue" that holds this coalition together and enables it to work so effectively in defense of the status quo comes from two primary sources.

One is the class-originated shared values and interests of the establishment, which is essentially a circulating group of persons moving freely among the upper echelons of the economic, social, and political systems. These people are accustomed to holding and exercising power from their "command post" positions. Their life experiences and current interests have bred in them a strong commitment to orthodoxy and defense of the integrated economic and political structure. They see these values as being synonymous with the public interest, and not as self-serving.

The other source is the willingness of the general public—or at least the majority of its visible, audible, and active members—to endorse and support the actions of the major officials of their government. This acquiescence has many sources: faith in the institutions established by the Constitution, lack of alternatives, political party loyalties, or feelings of powerlessness. One of its major sources, however, is the wide dissemination of effective inculcation of the familiar American political values and ideology. After twelve or more years of schooling, patriotic rituals, and media messages, the individual lives in a context of symbolic assurances and benevolent rationalizations about how the government does and should operate. Embedded in this body of myth are the clear grounds of establishment dominance. At least some fragments of this belief system become implanted in peoples' minds, and are thus available to be drawn on in times of stress by the status- and legitimacy-exuding establishment.

What Difference Does It Make? A second basic question that helps shape inquiry builds on the first: What difference does it make? For example, does our answer to "Who rules?" bear upon the character of American democracy or the probable directions of change in the near future? Most Americans share a belief in representative democracy and they also believe that our system, although improvable, amounts to a rough approximation of that kind of democracy. But what if the evidence leads us to conclude that the patterns of who wins and who loses through American public policies are *not* in the interests of majorities of people? What if we find that, over and over again, the interests of a relative few at the top of the economic and social pyramids are reflected in public policies? We are clearly faced with the problem of why so many Americans continue to cling to the idea of a "democratic" America. Or perhaps we need to modify our definition of "democracy" to fit what we actually find to exist. Along the same lines, our estimation of the probable directions of future change are going to be very different, depending upon our analysis of who rules and how. In any event, our analytic conclusions regarding who rules and how ultimately influence our actions.

There is a tendency in American politics to either pronouce the system democratic, with full popular participation, and a responsiveness to public pressure, or to denounce it as being despotic, and totally dominated by a small elite exclusively for their benefit. Although we admit that within our framework it is possible to conclude that one or the other of these statements is true, it is more likely that we will find the American system to be more complicated than either of those conclusions. In other words, the framework *does* suggest certain conclusions. One of them is that the system, *as it presently exists and has existed*, is neither as democratic as its staunch defenders would have us believe nor as despotic as its most radical critics maintain.

Under ordinary circumstances, few major issues arise. Most public policies and private practices fit snugly within the approved contours of the established economic, social, and political systems. Special interests are free to seek their narrow ends within this context. However, sometimes conditions change in such a way that more basic questions are forced to the fore. The establishment begins to rally to the defense of the systems that have served it so well, but the normal consensus is lacking. Action then occurs simultaneously on many fronts to mobilize public support for particular forms of governmental action to meet and "solve" the crisis. Let us reiterate what is at stake in this inquiry. Neither masses nor elites are powerless. We know that *each* can initiate change and constrain the other under particular circumstances, and that generally, those circumstances arise at times like the present, when basic questions are on the agenda.

Thus our questions press further: How much power of initiative and constraint characteristically lies on each side? Under what conditions is the normal balance disrupted? Not all of these questions can be answered but they suggest the direction and goals of our inquiry. They help to remind us that a focus on governmental elites and processes is narrow. We can escape the effects of the premise that everything important is encompassed within the institutions of government by constantly recognizing that this premise is a form of tunnel vision. Along with that recognition, however, we have much to gain from understanding the part played by governmental institutions in the American political economy.

This second question also can be stated as, "In what ways is the American political economy democratic, and in what ways despotic?" This is, of course, a political question with major implications for effective and informed political action. In other words, the question of democracy or despotism is a summary of all the questions we have been discussing up to this point. It is a simultaneously factual and value-based issue that implies several specific questions:

- Should people seek to expand the democratic possibilities in the American political economy?
- If so, what current institutions and practices would contribute to such expansion?
- What actions can one take?
- What policies should one advocate?
- What has a "real" chance of winning?

To answer these questions, one must make *value* choices encompassing a definition based on assumptions about human nature, the proper goals of a social and political and economic order, and the relationships between them. Those fundamental questions and problems in *evaluation* are the subject of the next section.

PROBLEMS IN ANALYSIS AND EVALUATION

How can we assure ourselves that the understanding of American politics that we acquire consists of valid interpretations and not merely uncritical projections of our assumptions, hopes, or fears? We shall consider the technical problems of data collection and interpretation as they arise in later chapters. The more serious problems of nonobjectivity and misinterpretation, however, are conceptual in character. Before discussing the fundamental questions that are necessary for effective evaluation, let us try to identify some of the barriers to clear understanding.

Culture-Bound or Ideological Premises and Assumptions

The first pitfall is the assumption that everything important in politics and policy formation takes place in the formal institutions and organs of government. A high proportion of decisions are made outside the corridors of government buildings. The actions that can be observed taking place within governmental institutions often convey a very superficial, and even misleading, notion of what is going on. What goes on in courts, legislatures, bureaus, and United Nations meetings certainly has to be observed, but merely observing it usually reveals little about its *meaning*. In order to understand the significance of formal governmental actions, the political analyst has to observe many other activities as well; he or she must also have in mind a theoretical framework that describes how the observed activities are related to one another.

More fundamentally, we are all more or less captives of our culture and products of years of indoctrination in its values and assumptions about what is right and good. What is, is right. And what exists in the United States is necessary, desirable, or at least the best that is practical under the circumstances. Every person who would be an objective analyst must go through a process of wrenching loose from such premises, assumptions, and conceptual blinders. The process is a lengthy and difficult one. Ideology reaches deep into the culture, stereotypes, symbols, and even the language we use. We will discuss these at length in Chapter 6. Positive images are conjured up in most of us by such phrases as "Constitution," "free enterprise," "the rule of law," "free speech," and "democracy." The use of such terms to describe what exists may lead us to believe that reality fits into such "good" patterns. Sometimes reality may indeed be what the words suggest, but reality is not determined by the words or the assumptions used to describe it. Reality has its own independent set of characteristics and causes and may bear little resemblance to what the familiar words urge us to believe. If we are diverted from objective perception by loaded words and symbols, we may never come to know reality as it is.

Standards of Evaluation

Analysis—explaining how and why governmental policies take the form they do and what difference that makes to people and problems in the society—is an interesting and important task. However, it is only a preliminary for the person who wants to be more than a passive consumer of the products generated by the power and activity of others. One must decide whether a particular policy is good or bad, whether the political system is working well or not, and whether and how to seek improvements. To do this on a sound basis may seem to require more knowledge and greater wisdom than any person can really expect to develop, but this problem can be rendered manageable.

Several simplifying approaches can make it possible for a person to judge and act in politics in a responsible and still timely manner. One does not need to be intimidated by specialized scholars. Often, there is some solid evidence pertaining to the performance of government, especially with respect to problems with which one is familiar. People can specialize in certain areas of the greatest interest to them, and they can avoid being diverted by rhetoric, ideology, or elaborate explanations about how the procedures of government operated to prevent success.

Perhaps the most important act in preparing oneself for sound evaluation in politics is the clarification of the standards to be used in making judgments. Often the standard applied contains the judgment within itself. For example, a standard that emphasizes maintaining established procedures and policies is likely to lead to a status quo supporting judgment, and so is a standard that emphasizes what is "practical," "pragmatic," or "realistic." Today's procedures and policies, of course, promote the interests and preferences of those who hold the balance of power now; what is "realistic" is what they can permit to take place without serious danger to their own predominance. The use of such standards inevitably directs judgment toward minimal changes that support the basic outlines of today's power distribution.

The key to all evaluation, therefore, is a personal political philosophy, which each of us must construct and apply. This is easier said than done, of course. Developing a view of *what should be* is even more difficult and frustrating than understanding *what is* in politics. Most people can acquire facts about their political system, but too often they do it as passive memorizers in the classroom rather than as analytical, purposeful, and independent persons. Relatively few make the effort to survey, self-consciously and comprehensively, alternative ends and means in politics and to arrive at their own set of standards and goals for political action. But not to do so is to commit oneself in advance to a passive role in the processes that determine the shape of the future. It means acquiescence in the decisions of those now in power about what is best for themselves and for others. The person without an independent basis for analysis and evaluation in politics must be somebody's pawn. The only remaining question is *whose* pawn.

Some Fundamental Questions

Although constructing one's own political philosophy is difficult, it is not impossible. We have centuries of reflection and writing by the great political theorists to guide us. Even though there is little agreement among them or their respective followers, analysis of their work reveals remarkable consensus about the questions they found it essential to face. Because these problems also agree with our view of the intellectual issues involved, we shall use some classic categories to indicate the central questions that must be faced by a student of politics seeking to establish an independent judgmental framework.

1. *What Is the Nature of People and Their Relationship to Their Society and Environment?* To some extent these are factual questions, but for the most part we must simply assume answers for them. Our answers are more or less frank expressions of our value preferences. Some assume that human nature is fundamentally good and that a human being is essentially a cooperative, rational creature; if so, governing processes should be designed to maximize openness and participation. The more open the processes, the more likely it is that right decisions will be made. Others assume that ordinary people are selfish, emotional, likely to pursue short-range interests, and subject to demagogues, while a few people possess superior talents. According to these assumptions, a strong government that is run by the talented few is necessary to maintain order and justice in the society. In other words, a whole series of political conclusions and preferences are built on initial assumptions about human nature.

Assumptions must also be made about the character of society and the way in which both people and their society respond to change. For some, "society" is a term with real meaning; it is an independent entity with a life of its own, distinct from the people comprising it at any given time. Therefore, the "needs of the society" must be placed above any particular member's preferences. Some device for ascertaining societal needs must be found. The net result is likely to be a form of government that is dominated by the relatively few people in the society who are capable of divining those needs. A less mystical use of the term "society" is as a synonym for the individuals who happen to be present at any moment within certain geographical confines. In this case, the needs of society and majority preference are one and the same. Therefore, an entirely different decision-making process is suggested.

Another set of assumptions concerns the extent to which people are irretrievably the product of something innate within their nature, or alternatively, are the product of their environment. If people are products of their environment, they can be changed by manipulation of that environment. There are, of course, some problems in matching characteristic traits with environmental causes, but the basic assumption is still valid. On the other hand, if personal problems such as poverty are based in genetic codes, efforts to change human nature are both hopeless and potentially very dangerous.

Which of these sets of alternative assumptions is better or more soundly based? At the moment, there seems to be no way in which a case for one or the other can be conclusively established or "proved." Indeed, the very assertion that this can happen reflects certain assumptions about human beings. People therefore are forced to adopt what seems to them to be the most reasonable set of assumptions. Such position-taking tells the listener or reader little about human nature but a great deal about the speaker's or author's political values.

2. What Are the Proper Goals of Social and Political Life, and in What Order of Priorities and at What Cost Should They Be Sought? This is the area in which evidence is of least assistance. People must answer these questions in response to their own values. Such questions are rarely put so bluntly, of course. They arise in the context of familiar concepts for the establishment of priorities among familiar and generally shared goals. For example, the concept of "freedom" carries several meanings. To some it means freedom from governmental interference and it leads them to seek severe limitations on the activities of government. To others, it means freedom to develop as one could if the handicaps of poverty and ignorance were removed; this stance leads people to seek broad expansion of the social welfare activities of government.

The concept of "equality" is equally pliable. It may mean the right to use one's talents, whatever they may be, in the pursuit of one's goals. It can be expanded slightly to include the right to at least a minimal education and standard of living. Or it can be broadened still further to signify that all persons are entitled to full social and economic parity with one another.

Economic equality is a much more ambitious goal than mere political equality. But even within the concept of political equality there is room for considerable difference of viewpoint. Most people strongly subscribe to the goal of political equality, or the right to vote. However, those same people can have strong disagreements about whether or not to print ballots in Spanish, lessen residency requirements, or change voting hours or days. There is wide room for disagreement even when the basic goal is shared "in principle." Thus, it is critical to determine the specific content of familiar terms when one is building one's own independent framework. No one definition is necessarily preferable or "correct" because no person is the ultimate arbiter of the meanings of words. But one can be careful about knowing not only what one means, but what others mean, when a central concept is discussed.

These differences in meaning become most apparent when an issue arises that requires the concept to be put into practice (or "operationalized"). At other times, generalized agreements on the undefined concepts of "freedom," "equality," or "democracy" may create the illusion of consensus. A similar illusion may be fostered by the widespread acknowledgment of these goals, despite sharply differing views as to which should be given priority. Once again, the illusion is dispelled when people seek to actually *do* one or the other. That is why there is bound to be disagreement in politics.

When neither specific meanings nor priority ranking have been established, these concepts are not much more than glittering generalities. As such, they are aspects of ideology. We tend to believe that because all right-thinking people share the same views, all that needs to be done to resolve conflicts is to sit down and "reason together." Or we may believe that our leaders' views are the same as ours because they use these words in their explanations, but clearly these concepts offer us nothing but symbolic satisfactions and complacency until we undertake to define their specific content and relative valuations.

3. What Means—Institutions and Processes—Offer the Best Prospects of Reaching the Goals We Establish, Given Our Assumptions About Human Nature? In other words, how can we get from specific assumptions about human nature to the characteristics of the good life? What logically consistent and empirically practicable means are there for reaching the desired goals? This is the area where we should be able to get the most assistance from factual knowledge about the workings of political institutions and processes. In seeking to establish some coherent connection between the nature of human beings and the realization of their goals in life, we have considerable evidence about how particular institutions work and why. We know, for example, that all members of the House of Representatives are not equally influential in determining the provisions of new statutes, and we certainly would not rest our hopes for goal attainment on the illusion that they are. Thus, one of the first necessities in this area is to become familiar with the basic facts and processes that determine how the political system presently works. We can use this understanding to establish certain landmarks around which value preferences are to be exercised.

A second requirement in this area, as we suggested earlier, is logical consistency. If human beings are irrational and selfish, for example, one can hardly expect to achieve equality for all through political mechanisms that are highly responsive to individual preferences. The nature of each set of institutions and processes depends on the characteristics of the people who design and operate them. In turn, this shapes the kinds of goals that can be attained through them. This is a crucial point: *the nature of people, the character of institutions and processes, and the goals that can be realized are interdependent in politics.* When we study institutions and processes, we do so realizing that they have been structured by the values and natures of the people who created and animate them. We also know that their character determines in major ways the nature of the goals that can be achieved through them. Because this is so, we must organize our personal political positions to take this interdependence into account.

This is not to say that we must proceed consecutively from a definition of human nature to a vision of an ideal world, and finally, to the institutional tinkering that is necessary to link the two together. Nor do all the possible questions and problems in these three areas have to be resolved before a personal framework becomes functional. It is enough to be aware of the interdependencies among them and, therefore, to see what is at stake when considering one area in apparent isolation. We must see the implications that findings or assumptions in one area carry for other areas. What *is* important is to begin to build a map in one's mind of what is, can be, and ought to be in politics. This, in turn, will make it possible to respond rationally and selectively to the urgings and pleadings of others and to shape one's own independent course in politics.

SUMMARY AND PREVIEW

We have tried to design an approach that encourages both *scope* and *skepticism* as aids in getting beyond tunnel vision, assumptions, and ideology toward some approximation of reality. We started by stressing the concept of *political economy*—the integration of economy, politics, and society into one coherent order whose nature and dynamics are powerfully affected by the character and needs of the economic system. At this stage, of course, all that was intended was a beginning sketch of an *approach,* and not the full characterization that must await filling in with various kinds of evidence.

Laying out our approach in this way helps to further explain the nature and implications of the two basic questions that will guide our inquiry from this point forward: "Who rules?" and "What difference does it make?" In other words, we tried to emphasize our belief in the necessity for independent, self-consciously critical political actors. We hope to contribute to this process by providing a text that provides the tools of analysis and factual base necessary to become so.

Naturally, this book is biased; every textbook is. There is no such thing as a "neutral" or "objective" textbook. Some books may *appear* to be neutral or objective because they say things that we have heard many times before. They reiterate dominant beliefs and familiar interpretations. However, this only means that we have not *recognized* the biases that are in those orthodox points of view. Such biases reside unconsciously in our minds and shape our responses. The most scrupulously "neutral" authors must select certain facts, present them within a particular conceptual framework, and suggest ways of interpreting them so that they make sense. At every stage, the authors' assumptions and preferences—in short, their biases—will be presented to the reader as truth.

But if all books are thus biased, why read any except those we agree with? What can a serious reader expect to gain from a biased book? This brings us to a vital point. We believe that it is possible, and even necessary, to be both honestly critical and frankly biased without sacrificing intellectual quality, rigor, or utility. The key lies in our conviction that readers can and must become independent thinkers. It is our purpose in this book to provide them with the tools to do so. A critical stance that points out the culture-bound, self-congratulatory, and hence, limiting elements of standard American beliefs is absolutely essential for this purpose. Only then can people begin to analyze where power is located and how and for whose benefit it is and can be used.

Finally, becoming a truly independent person requires that one make repeated value judgments. Change is constant and more drastic change lies ahead. Choices must be made and conscious action must be taken to shape the future. To do these things, people must learn to identify values and preferences, both their own and others, presented as objective answers. They must be able to ask the right questions about both the present and the future so that they can effectively pursue the values they conclude are desirable. Therefore, although we readily acknowledge the biases of this book, we argue that such biases are necessary for the purpose of forcing questions to the surface and equipping the reader to become a truly independent thinker.

Thus, this is not the usual civics book, but it *is* a civics book in the time-honored sense of furthering effective citizen participation in our public life. It is a set of tools and questions, applied to the real world of American politics. It is meant to enable readers to gain a better understanding of the political system, including themselves. In short, it aims to help students decide what they want and how to get it. The purpose of understanding what is happening in politics and why, is to be able to judge and then to act. Of course, all understandings, judgments, and actions are not equally sound. Some are clearly better than others in terms of factual accuracy, human values, or both. Our task is to find ways of understanding, judging, and acting that can lead to a more just and decent society.

In the next four chapters that make up Part II, we will explore the context within which the specifically political institutions and processes must operate, through the perspective of our political economy approach. These chapters in effect describe the four defining components of the American political-economic-social context. Part III concentrates on political institutions and processes without, we hope, losing track of the context within which they operate. Part IV encompasses the variety of ways that American citizens may participate in, and perhaps shape the future of, this political economic order. In that part, we will also return to the notion of transformation politics to discuss the variety of possibilities, problems, and opportunities in the American political future.

PART II

The Context of American Politics

What we are proposing is suggested by both our broad definition of politics and by everyday common sense. We should look at our whole social order together—economics, society, culture, *and* politics—in order to fully understand *politics*. This apparently simple premise carries important implications that will be much clearer by the end of the book. In Part II, we shall look at four leading components of a political economy approach to understanding American politics in a way that will also serve to sketch the *context* of those politics.

There is thus a double purpose involved in this Part:

1. *To fully demonstrate what is implied in our political economy approach.* The only adequate way to do this is through dividing that framework into its four component parts—economy, society, politics, and culture—and describing each in some depth.
2. *To describe the total context in which politics occurs,* so that we will be prepared to undertake more specifically focused analyses later in the book. In Part III, for example, we shall analyze the workings of national government political institutions—Congress, the presidency, the courts, and the bureaucracy—one at a time and in a much narrower fashion. For this reason, it is particularly important now to grasp the full context in which those institutions operate.

CHAPTER 3

Political Economy I: The Economic Context

In this chapter, we shall first characterize the American economy in what amounts to *structural* terms. In other words, we will look at the different elements that make up the economy as well as their size and other important features. Then we will examine the world setting in which the U.S. economy is located and emphasize some of the interconnections that have created a growing interdependence between national economies. Finally, we will quickly sketch some contrasts between the United States and other industrialized capitalist countries, showing how the American economy has declined in recent years.

THE AMERICAN ECONOMY

The most obvious characteristic of the American economy is the sheer size of its major units. A relatively few entities dominate national and international industries and markets, while a multitude of small businesses struggle for the leftovers. The smaller entities' world is often characterized by real competition and the operation of market principles; these are conditions that are not usually confronted by the giants. However, when dealing solely with the major units, a divergence of interest does begin to appear between global or multinational enterprises and those that are more national in character. The needs of each of these sectors (small business, large multinational, and large national) are, of course, different and thus the nature of their relationship to and integration with the government differs. The government itself is an additional sector of the economy, so we will explore its consumption, investment, and other fiscal and monetary activities. Most of the descriptions here will be conceptual and thus oriented toward painting a broad picture of the American political economy today. Many details will be found in the tables, however, and it is essential that the reader move confidently back and forth between the text and the tables.

The Size and Character of United States Business

Table 3.1 summarizes the number and forms of U.S. business enterprises by the size of their receipts. Immediately apparent, and not surprising, is the fact that most of the small businesses (under $25,000 in receipts) are sole proprietorships and partnerships. Only 0.2 percent of the sole proprietorships and 3 percent of the partnerships gross over $1,000,000. On the other hand, of the 2,555 corporations in the United States, 16 percent gross over $1,000,000. Even more impressive is the fact that the 399 corporations at the very top represent 92 percent of the total receipts received by *all* corporations! In other words, 16 percent of the corporations receive 92 percent of the income. On the other hand, 91 percent of the sole proprietorships and 72 percent of the partnerships gross under $100,000. The overall picture is one of a few business entities that are generally corporate in form, which have huge receipts, and a multitude of small firms that are generally owned by one or a few people, which are struggling to make it.

Tables 3.2 and 3.3 attempt to give us some notion of the sheer size of these largest firms. Table 3.2 lists the top ten firms in terms of their assets; each has assets worth over $50 *billion*. The total corporate assets of the *Forbes* 500 sales leaders is almost $4 *trillion* and the annual sales of each firm are over $1 billion. That constitutes 78 percent of the United States' GNP (gross national product). In other words, the difference between the smaller firms and the larger corporations is not merely of degree; it is a quantum leap of immense proportions.

It is difficult to put some reality into billions and trillions of dollars. One way to comprehend that size somewhat better is through comparison. Table 3.3 ranks selected national governments, states, cities, and private corporations by total revenues. Only the eight largest countries in the world exceed the largest corporations. More than 200 U.S. corporations have more revenue than the median of the 50 states (Iowa). Many have more employees than even the largest states. For example, in economic, political, and social terms, Exxon is comparable only to the more important nations of the world. Its annual sales receipts are larger than the *combined* general revenues of ten populous northeastern states: New York, New Jersey, Pennsylvania, Delaware, Massachusetts, plus the other five New England states. Indeed, its annual revenues are more "than the gross national product of Sweden. Exxon operates in 100 countries. It owns 70 refineries and operates 195 ocean-going tankers—more ships than the British navy."[1]

---

[1] Thomas R. Dye, *Who's Running America? The Reagan Years*, 3rd ed. (Englewood Cliffs, N.J.: Prentice-Hall, Inc., 1983), p. 33.

TABLE 3.1
Number and Types of U.S. Businesses, by Size of Receipts, 1979

RECEIPTS	SOLE PROPRIETORS				PARTNERSHIPS				CORPORATIONS			
	No.	Percentage	Receipts ($ billions)	Percentage	No.	Percentage	Receipts ($ billions)	Percentage	No.	Percentage	Receipts ($ billions)	Percentage
Under $25,000	8,788	71	55	11	603	46	5	2	522	20	3	—
$25,000–$99,999	2,446	20	126	26	343	26	18	7	494	19	26	0.5
$100,000–$999,999	1,067	9	243	50	319	25	91	36	1,140	45	387	8
Over $1,000,000	29	0.2	63	13	34	3	139	55	399	16	4,721	92
Totals	12,330	100	487	100	1,299	100	253	100	2,555	100	5,137	100

SOURCE: *U.S. Statistical Abstract, 1983,* Table 876 (recategorized and recalculated).

TABLE
3.2   **Assets of the Ten Leading U.S. Corporations, 1982**

Company	Assets	Percentage of Change Since 1981
American Telephone & Telegraph	$148,186,000,000	7.6
Citicorp	129,997,000,000	9.0
BankAmerica	122,221,000,000	0.9
Chase Manhattan	80,863,000,000	3.9
Federal National Mortgage	73,467,000,000	18.3
Manufacturers Hanover	64,041,000,000	8.3
Exxon	62,289,000,000	− 1.0
J. P. Morgan	58,597,000,000	9.5
Chemical New York	48,275,000,000	7.5
Aetna Life & Casualty	44,211,000,000	11.6

(Total assets of the 500 corporations with the largest sales: $3,829,297,000,000.)

SOURCE: *Forbes* magazine, May 9, 1983, pp. 247–248.

In other words, these larger corporations are equivalent in many ways to medium-sized countries or the largest states of the United States. Only the U.S. federal government is really larger, and it is only bigger than the corporations when they are considered individually, and not as industries. The *Forbes* 500, when considered together, dwarf even the U.S. government on any scale.

The basic character and workings of the American political economy has to be shaped by these few large units. They obviously dominate the American economy in sales, assets, and profitability. In part, this is because two, three, or four giants so dominate key markets that competition is replaced by tacit cooperation. It is estimated that about "half of U.S. goods are manufactured in very concentrated industries."[2] Furthermore, conglomeration has proceeded apace with the largest corporations acquiring others no matter what the product or service. For example, "ITT (the world's eighth-largest corporation) owns Wonder Bread, Sheraton Hotels, Hartford Insurance, Bobbs-Merrill Publishing, and Burpee Lawn and Garden Products."[3] In 1981, a record "$82 billion were spent on acquisitions. Dupont paid . . . $7.5 billion for Conoco; . . . Gulf Oil, $325 million for Kemmerer Coal; and U.S. Steel, $5.9 billion for a controlling interest in Marathon."[4]

---

[2] "Choose Your Poison: Competition or Concentration," *Dollars and Sense*, July/August, 1983, p. 4.

[3] Robert B. Reich, *The Next American Frontier* (New York: Times Books, 1983), p. 146.

[4] Ibid., p. 147.

TABLE   **Selected National Governments, States, Cities, and Corporations,**
3.3   **by Total Revenues and Number of Employees, 1980**

	Total Revenues[1] ($ Billions U.S.)	Number of Employees
Exxon	103	177,000
Canada	86[2]	NA
Mobil	60	213,000
General Motors	58	746,000
Spain	51[2]	NA
Texaco	51	67,000
Ford	37	427,000
California (largest U.S. state)	36	309,000
Norway	27[2]	NA
New York	27	251,000
IBM	26	341,000
General Electric	25	402,000
Texas	13	199,000
Greece	11[2]	NA
Iowa (median of U.S. states)	3.5	54,000
Los Angeles	2.7	41,000
Chicago	1.9	42,000
Detroit	1.4	20,000
Vermont (smallest U.S. state)	0.9	13,000
(U.S.	517	2,200,000)

SOURCES: *U.S. Statistical Abstract, 1983*, Tables 483, 497, 505, 510, 1530. *Fortune* magazine, May 4, 1981, p. 322.

NOTES: 1. Total revenues from all sources for governments, total sales for corporations.
2. For countries other than the United States, the figure includes all taxes raised by subordinate jurisdictions and thus exceeds central government total by a substantial amount. By this method, the U.S. total would be 50 percent higher, or $776 billion. The year 1980 is used throughout for comparative reasons.

The contrast between life in the large corporate sector and the small business sector is sharp. In the lower levels, many businesses are started, and more fail, every year. Production is usually on a small scale, and the markets are local or regional. Typical examples are repair shops, restaurants, independent drug and grocery stores, cleaners, and other service-providing businesses. While the largest corporations dominate markets and thus achieve relative control over supplies, costs, prices, and profits, the situation of the smaller firms is normally the opposite. For them, the market is real; suppliers and purchasers come and go, prices fluctuate widely, and unpredictability reigns. Profit margins are often narrow and highly unstable. Employment is irregular, and many workers are marginal and/or part-time. Wages are substantially lower than in the corporate-banking sector, very few firms are unionized, and incomes are inadequate and constantly in need of supplementation.

The sectors also differ markedly in their respective needs for services and supports from the national government. The size, scope, market domination, and profitability of the largest units make it possible for them to accept unions if need be, survive recessions, and wield massive influence over governmental policy. At the same time, many of them have international interests that require extensive diplomatic and military support. They need an educated workforce and elaborate scientific and technological research and development. Under ordinary circumstances, they can tolerate a network of governmental programs because such programs (unemployment insurance, welfare, social security, and the like) help ensure stability of demand.

For the fragmented and relatively powerless smaller firms, on the other hand, governmental policy is much more often oppressive. Taxes are a greater burden, for example, and demand-assuring spending is of lesser benefit. Unemployment and welfare benefits reduce the number of workers who are willing to work for the lowest wages, and minimum wage laws push pay levels up. Education and other services are of much less value to this sector in which highly skilled workers are largely unnecessary and employment tends to be short-term. A large military is of little direct benefit, and expenditures for research and development are irrelevant.

These differences in the character and interests of the two sectors, and the resulting contrast in their costs and benefits from governmental policies, are not readily recognized. A widely promulgated and almost as widely shared set of beliefs holds that:

1. All business is essentially the same—competitive and dependent on market forces.
2. Government should normally keep "hands off" the activities of the "private economy."
3. Public services and social insurance benefits are aimed exclusively at people in need.

Points 1 and 3 are inaccurate and point 2 is deliberately and regularly violated, because of the character and needs of the larger firms, but this is only the beginning of our reconceptualization of the U.S. political economy.

The Private Economy: Global and National Components

The differences in needs and relationship with the federal government of the major firm and smaller business sectors are fairly obvious. Less obvious but increasingly divergent are the differences in needs and relationship of the members of the major economic units. Those corporations that are primarily national in character require services that are different from, and sometimes opposed to, those firms that are primarily global or multinational in character. We classify a corporation as global or multinational if it receives more than 40 percent of its sales or profits from abroad; conversely, if more than 60 percent of its sales are in the United States, we deem it to be a national firm. It is somewhat arbitrary to classify these economic giants as either global or national because they all have major shares of *both* national and international markets. However, careful perusal of Tables 3.4 and 3.5 reveals the differences in nature between these giants—and, we argue in more detail later, in their needs.

Table 3.4 ranks the twenty largest U.S. (if nationality has any meaning at this level) corporations and banks in terms of foreign sales. Several of them are also among the largest companies in the world. In looking at these top twenty multinationals, notice the very high percentage of their sales, assets, *and* profits that are derived internationally. This "foreign" reliance reflects the growing interdependence of the world economy.

Secondly, the major multinational units are highly concentrated in energy (oil), finance, and exporting manufacturers, especially high technology and communications (newer products). The four largest are oil companies. Of the twenty, six are financial institutions. Over 50 percent, and as high as 70 percent in the case of Chase Manhattan, of these banks' profits are internationally derived. Large banks have potent sources of leverage within the entire system. In the process of making loans (the source of profits), banks make judgments about the management and activities of prospective debtors, both private *and* public. They also gain influence in other ways, such as obtaining positions on boards of directors or imposing certain conditions on loans. The more loans they make, the more their interests are associated with those of the debtors. Obviously, major American banks are closely integrated with the global economy.

In contrast, Table 3.5 lists the "national" sector, those twenty-five of the top forty U.S. corporations that have primarily domestic markets. This list is heavily dominated by manufacturers from the older "smokestack" industries; these are the traditional "heavy" industries, such as steel. The percentages of sales abroad in these corporations are almost insignificant. The smaller oil companies appear there, with wholly domestic markets. Most incredibly, *there are no banks*. Even so, these domestic companies represent large amounts of sales/assets/profits, and, importantly, hundreds of thousands of American jobs.

It is the national companies that are most hurt by imports and, in some ways, in spite of their size, they are subject to the most competitive pressure. In their case, the competition comes from other countries' multinationals, but it does lead to a sometimes uneasy alliance with the smaller business sector. Support for "protectionism" provides one of the most prominent examples of the increasing divergence of interest between the nationals and the multinationals. Domestic manufacturers face competition from abroad. In an attempt to ameliorate that threat, they require "protection" in the form of tariffs or trade agreements enacted and enforced by the federal government.

On the other hand, the multinationals require an open international system that is seriously threatened by the notion of protectionism. The last thing they need from the federal government, or any government, is a variety of trade barriers and tariffs. Thus integration with or control of the

TABLE 3.4
The Global Component: U.S. Corporations and Banks with Major* International Involvement, 1982 (Ranked by Foreign Sales)

RANK		COMPANY	COMPANY TOTALS ($ BILLIONS)			INTERNATIONAL COMPONENT (PERCENTAGE OF COMPANY TOTALS)		
Among Companies in World	Among U.S Companies		Sales	Assets	Profits	Sales	Assets	Profits
1	1	Exxon	97.1	62.3	4.3	71	48	51
5	2	Mobil	61	36.4	1.4	62	52	64
11	3	Texaco	47	27.1	1.3	66	48	65
15	4	Standard (Calif.)	34.4	23.4	1.4	49	38	29
22	5	Phibro-Salomon	26.7	39.7	0.3	62	12	65
12	6	Ford Motor	37.0	21.9	-0.7	45	65	NA
14	7	IBM	34.4	35.4	4.4	45	43	37
19	9	Gulf Oil	28.4	20.4	0.9	41	37	33
33	11	Citicorp	17.8	121.5	0.7	61	60	62
26	12	Int. Tel. & Tel.	21.9	29.2	1.2	45	34	71
54	13	BankAmerica	14.9	119.8	0.4	54	45	65
87	14	Chase Manhattan	10.1	80.8	0.3	61	51	70
84	15	Dow Chemical	10.6	11.8	0.4	52	44	40
31	19	Occidental Petroleum	18.5	15.7	0.5	25	22	63
35	20	Safeway Stores	17.6	3.9	0.2	25	27	53
132	21	J. P. Morgan	6.9	32.9	0.4	62	56	72
119	23	Manufacturers Hanover	7.6	30.3	0.3	51	47	50
105	25	Xerox	8.5	3.5	0.4	43	46	36
50	27	Phillips Petroleum	15.7	2.7	2.3	19	23	52
99	28	Union Carbide	9.0	3.2	0.7	33	30	42

SOURCE: *Forbes* magazine, July 4, 1983 and May 9, 1983. (Recategorized and recalculated from originals.)

* Defined as more than 40 percent of sales *or* profits from abroad.

TABLE 3.5. *The National Component: U.S. Corporations and Banks with Primarily* Domestic Markets, 1982 (Ranked by Sales)*

Rank Among U.S. Companies	Company	Sales (in billions)	Assets (in billions)	Profits (in billions)	Employees (in thousands)	Percentage of Sales Abroad
2	American Telephone and Telegraph	65.0	148.1	6.9	1,015.9	—
3	General Motors	60.0	41.4	0.9	657.0	24
9	E. I. duPont	33.2	24.3	0.9	171.1	33
10	Sears Roebuck	30.0	36.6	0.8	401.8	6
12	Standard Oil of Indiana	28.1	24.2	1.8	58.2	17
14	General Electric	26.5	21.6	1.8	367.0	20
15	Atlantic Richfield	26.5	21.6	1.7	52.9	9
17	Shell Oil	20.0	21.4	1.6	36.9	—
18	U.S. Steel	18.4	19.4	-0.4	120.0	—
22	K Mart	16.7	7.3	0.3	245.0	9
24	Sun Company	15.5	12.0	0.5	43.3	31
25	Tenneco	14.9	17.4	0.8	99.8	17
27	Aetna Life and Casualty	14.1	44.2	0.5	46.7	—
28	United Technologies	13.6	7.9	0.4	186.8	22
29	Standard (Ohio)	13.1	16.0	1.9	53.3	—
30	Getty Oil	12.7	11.4	0.7	19.4	17
31	GTE	12.0	22.3	0.8	200.0	18
32	Procter and Gamble	12.0	7.5	0.8	62.4	31
33	Kroger	11.9	5.2	0.1	129.6	—
34	CIGNA	11.8	31.4	0.5	40.9	—
35	J. C. Penney	11.4	7.9	0.4	176.0	—
36	Travelers	11.4	27.9	0.3	29.1	—
37	R. J. Reynolds Inds.	10.9	10.3	0.9	92.8	23
38	Eastman Kodak	10.8	10.6	1.2	136.5	39
40	Union Oil of California	10.4	8.5	0.8	19.7	14

SOURCE: *Forbes* magazine, May 9, 1983, and July 4, 1933. Reprinted by permission.

* Defined as more than 60 percent of sales in U.S.

governmental apparatus is vitally important to successful operation of the dominant economic units.

The State as a Sector of the Integrated Political Economy

Part of the reason for the larger economic entities' dominance over the small-firm sector is the massive size of the units in the former, which enables them to control markets and withstand bad times. Another reason is the powerful influence they are able to exert over public policy. The State (considering national, state, and local governments as a unit for the moment) might appear to be a potential rival of the largest firms, and in some respects, this is true. The sheer magnitude of revenue and expenditures does place the State squarely on a par with the corporate giants. The federal budget's total receipts for 1982 ($617.8 billion) were larger than the *combined* total sales of the top fifteen industrial corporations, and expenditures equaled about 25 percent of the total Gross National Product.

For two major reasons, however, the State is not an economic *rival*, but an effective *ally* of the dominant private sector. First, "the State" is thoroughly fragmented into independent and sometimes competing units. Each governmental unit is responsive to a particular constituency. This is as true of the federal government as it is of the more obviously independent states, cities, counties, towns, and villages.

Second, the key unit, the federal government, is heavily influenced by the major economic units. Full demonstration of this point requires the detailed analysis that is undertaken in later chapters. Basically, however, many of the crucial decisions that shape governmental taxing, spending, fiscal, and monetary actions, as well as other economy-related policies, are made in one or more of the following ways:

1. By the dominant sector directly through such decisions as whether or not to buy municipal or state bonds, decisions on the part of the World Bank to lend or not lend, and on what terms lending takes place;
2. Jointly by the private sector and governmental officials operating through a public agency such as the Federal Reserve System;
3. By managers from the dominant private units who are temporarily governmental officials;
4. By governmental officials and decisionmakers who, although not actually part of the dominant economic units, recognize that unless its needs are served, there will be serious unemployment or other undesirable consequences; and
5. In response to developments within the economy as a whole that trigger preexisting commitments on the part of the national government, such as unemployment benefits.

In many respects, in other words, *the national government is the major economic units by another name.* We will explore that relationship more fully throughout the text. Here we simply sketch the integration of the State, and more particularly the federal government, with the larger political economy in general conceptual terms. If it is true that money talks, then it should be the starting point. Table 3.6 summarizes the public sector's contribution to the economy in terms of expenditures and employment. We tend to think solely in terms of the national government, but as Table 3.6 shows, it is only one out of 82,688. The large and loosely connected set of enterprises that constitutes the State provides roughly one out of every six jobs in the United States. Over 85 percent of those jobs are with state and local governments.

The amount of money expended by all levels of government in the United States has risen steadily since World War II and now amounts to over $900 billion, or over 40 percent of the Gross National Product. During this period, state and local governments' expenditures have more than doubled, but the federal government still accounts for 61 percent of the total. State and local governments derive their income in large measure from local taxes, but also from substantial transfers by the federal government ($83 billion in 1980), and, of course, borrowing from banks and other investors. Much of this expenditure goes directly to private companies, to build, buy, and perform services. Clearly no treatment of our political economy would be complete without consideration of all of this activity.

One way to grasp the nature of the State's impact on, and its close connection to, the rest of the economy is to consider the national budget. Table 3.7 lists the receipts and outlays of the U.S. government for 1984. On the input side (the first column), careful reading reveals that individual citizens provide most of the revenue. The major source of federal income is the individual income tax, but individuals also contribute to Social Security and other insurance programs.

Of the nearly $848.5 billion in outlays for 1984, less than 1 percent is for maintenance of the government itself, such as upkeep of buildings, and salaries of civilian employees. Close to 30 percent is required for maintenance of the military establishment. Much of this $245.3 billion is designated for purchases of weapons and other supplies that are produced by a significant portion of the major economic units.

Another major component (21 percent) of federal expenditures is Social Security payments to retired or disabled workers. Of course, these workers and their employers pay taxes over an extended period of time to cover a proportion of these costs. Nearly a third of all federal income is derived from such taxes. A similar partially tax-supported expenditure is unemployment compensation. Such payments are not classified separately but are combined with the federal share of welfare and Medicare, military and civil service retirement, and other benefits under the title "other income security." These are often combined in budget language with Social

TABLE 3.6
The Public Sector: Governments in the U.S., 1980

UNIT	NUMBER	TOTAL EMPLOYEES (CIVILIAN ONLY)	TOTAL EXPENDITURES (BUDGET OUTLAYS, IN BILLIONS)	PERCENTAGE OF ALL GOVERNMENTS	LEADING FUNCTIONS (IN BILLIONS)				
					U.S. { Defense / States { —	Education Employment (Education)	Transportation (Highways)	Health (Health)	Income Security Welfare (Welfare)
United States	1	2,150,000	577	61	136	31	21	55	193
States	50	3,726,000	258	27	—	88	25	18	45
Local		9,377,000	110	12	—	45	8	14	1
Counties	3,041								
Municipalities	19,083								
Townships	16,748								
School Districts	15,032								
Special Districts	28,733								
Totals	82,688	15,253,000	945	100	136	164	54	87	239

SOURCES: *U.S. Statistical Abstract, 1983*, Tables 478 and 489.
U.S. Budget in Brief, FY 1984, Tables 3 and 9.

TABLE 3.7
The U.S. Government in the U.S. Economy, 1984

RECEIPTS

Sources	Amounts ($ billions)
Individual income taxes	295.6
Corporate income taxes	51.8
Social insurance taxes and contributions:	
Employment taxes & contributions	213.3
Unemployment insurance	24.1
Other retirement contributions	5.5
Excise taxes	40.4
Estate & gift taxes	5.9
Customs duties	9.1
Miscellaneous receipts	14.0
Total receipts	659.7
Total outlays	848.5
Receipts as percentage of GNP	18.9
Deficit as percentage of GNP	5.8

OUTLAYS

Functions	Amounts ($ billions)	Employees (civilian only)
National defense	245.3	1,018,000
International affairs	13.2	48,000
Science, space, tech.	8.2	22,000
Energy (including TVA)	3.3	59,000
Natural resources	9.8	84,000
Agriculture	12.1	109,000
Commerce & housing	0.4	37,000
Transportation	25.1	62,500
Community development	7.0	12,700
Education, employment	25.3	25,000
Health	90.6	138,000
Social Security	178.2	15,000
Other income security	104.2	—
Veterans	25.7	219,000
General govt. (including legislative & judicial)	6.0	150,000
Administration of justice	5.5	58,200
Fiscal assistance	7.0	
Net interest	103.2	—
Offsetting receipts	(22.8)	—
Totals	848.5	2,056,000

SOURCE: *The U.S. Budget in Brief, FY 1984,* Tables 3, 8, & 9.

Security and listed as either "payments to individuals" or "income security"—at least partly in order to have a category larger than military expenditures. (For an analysis of who actually receives these benefits, see Chapter 13.)

Interest payments to banks and investors who hold U.S. Treasury bonds and other securities represent a different sort of tie to the other sectors of the economy. Roughly 10 percent of the budget is devoted to such interest payments. The U.S. government is the single most secure investment that banks and other investors can find. Its taxing capability, as well as its capacity to print money, represents complete assurance of its ability to repay except in the direst emergencies. This helps explain why banks and investors have been willing to finance and refinance a federal debt now nearing $1 *trillion*. It also suggests that other borrowers will find it difficult to obtain needed loans when the U.S. Treasury is seeking them, as it must whenever there is a deficit in the federal budget. This sum is, in effect, diverted from other potential borrowers, such as cities and corporations, which then have trouble paying their debts or increasing their capabilities.

A final category of government expenditure is devoted to building roads, financing railroads, operating the mail service, supporting agriculture, conducting scientific research and development, and operating and supporting schools. Some of these functions are performed by state and local governments using federal funds. These numerous and diverse direct services are often understood as efforts to help people generally or as the result of pressures from various specific interests, but they may also be understood as providing the underlying but necessary building blocks upon which business can build to become profitable. The fact that the costs are public and the profits private implies that the general public has made vast social investments in order that a few people can enjoy substantial profits.

THE AMERICAN ECONOMY IN THE WORLD ECONOMY

The world emerged from World War II totally dominated by the American economy. No other national economy could come close to matching American wealth or productivity. The power of the U.S. economy to design the framework for world economic activity went unchallenged for approximately two decades. Then, slowly at first but with rapidly increasing speed, the pillars of American dominance were undermined. American economic and military prominence began to wane. By the mid-1970s, the United States was increasingly vulnerable. The process was probably inevitable, and in any event, it represents only the prologue to our present context.

Its first manifestation was Soviet development of nuclear capability, which resulted in a new balance of power. Not long after, the United States appeared to lose its first war; it was simply unable to defeat a small Southeast Asian nation, for whatever reason. Thus, the limits of American military power began to become clear.

The process of U.S. decline continued as Europe and Japan built newly technological and highly productive economies. For awhile, the key status of the dollar enabled American corporations and banks to operate around the world with a cushion of capital and credit, but by the late 1960s, European banks were flooded with dollars. Both European and Japanese products were competing favorably all over the world, and all the industrialized capitalist countries were creeping up on the United States' lead in total output, per capita income, and other key economic indicators.

The Three "Worlds" of the World Economy. The United States clearly faces a different world in the 1980s. Understanding that world and the new limitations it places on American goals and policies is as essential as it is difficult. One way to begin is to distinguish *three* "worlds" and to examine the changing American relations to each. The first is the industrialized, capitalist world. It includes the United States, Western Europe, and Japan. Mutual dependence on closely linked markets and investments does not prevent competition for relative advantage among these "allies." The United States' position with regard to these countries is still clearly that of the biggest and most important economy. But this position is now as "first among equals" rather than totally dominant, as used to be the case.

The second world is made up of the socialist countries. In the case of the Soviet Union and Cuba, the United States' economic relations are clearly subordinate to the renewal of the cold war. Embargoes and boycotts, for example, are used in an effort to turn trade into a weapon. The threat perceived from these countries is used to justify expanded military expenditures, as well as to mobilize Americans to endure sacrifices and reduced standards of living. The situation with respect to Eastern European nations is not as tense, although Poland's debt to Western banks may pose some problems. With regard to China, economic relations may expand as a means of adding a major counterweight to the Soviet Union. All of these relationships are dominated by the renewed confrontation between the United States and the Soviet Union.

The rest of the world is usually imprecisely labeled the *Third World*—a term that blurs many vital distinctions, including wealth, level of development, culture and history, and past or present relationships with developed countries. We use the term to emphasize the contrast with the relatively well-defined and more equal relationship of the United States with countries in the other two arenas. In the Third World, the weight of U.S. economic and political power may be heavy or light, welcome or unwelcome, brutal or subtle, depending on a variety of factors.

The basic relationship between these three economic "worlds" is shown in Table 3.8. Note first the contrasts in size of the various countries' total Gross National Product. GNP, or the total of goods and services produced, is shown in parentheses alongside each country's name. The second largest GNP in the world is that of the Soviet Union, but it is barely half that of the United States. Japan is not far behind, but is only about 40 percent of the U.S. West Germany is next in size. The capitalist world, of which only

TABLE
3.8   **The World Economy: Basic Comparisons**

AREAS AND COUNTRIES (1981 GNP)	PERCENT CHANGE IN GROWTH RATES, REAL GNP, 1960–1983					
	Annual Average, 1960–73	*Annual Average, 1974–81*	*1980*	*1981*	*1982*	*1983*
The Capitalist World						
United States ($2,926)	4.1	2.7	−0.2	2.0	−1.8	4.8
Japan ($1,150)	10.4	4.4	4.2	2.9	2.5	2.0
W. Germany ($687)	4.7	2.2	1.8	−0.3	−1.3	1.2
France ($577)	5.8	2.5	1.6	0.3	1.5	.5
United Kingdom ($502)	3.1	0.9	−1.7	−0.8	0.5	2.5
Developing Countries						
Oil exporting ($540)	—	3.7	2.0	−0.5	1.2	—
Other ($1,425)	—	4.6	5.6	3.1	0.7	—
Socialist World						
U.S.S.R. ($1,587)	5.2	2.3	1.5	1.8	1.6	3.6
Eastern Europe ($671)	4.1	1.8	0.4	−1.0	−0.7	1.0
China ($328)	6.5	5.9	6.9	3.0	5.0	4.0

SOURCE: *Economic Report of the President, 1984,* Table B 107 (reconstructed).

the leading countries appear here, far outstrips the second, or socialist, world in GNP, and the Third World trails both. It may also be of interest that the oil-exporting countries have only about 25 percent of the Third World's total GNP, and that China, despite its population, has a relatively small, though fast-growing, GNP.

Next, notice that while the United States is by far the leader in total GNP, this is the only category in which it has such leadership. Japan has enjoyed much more rapid growth since World War II reconstruction, and to a lesser extent, so have Germany and France. But look at the differences in *all* countries' rates of growth between 1960–73 and 1974–81. In the first period, every country in the capitalist world had substantially higher growth than in the second. And in the early 1980s, all of these countries sank still further; the same recession affected all of them in similar ways, as we shall see in more detail shortly. For the present, the point is that the capitalist world was in decline, and together, in the early 1980s.

Both the socialist world and the Third World show exactly the same pattern. (If comparable data were available, the oil-exporting nations might have shown a spurt after 1973, in the aftermath of the oil price increases, but the entire Third World clearly declines in tandem with the capitalist world in the 1980s.) Obviously, the entire world is so fully integrated that its economies, whatever the kind or level of development, move in similar directions at the same time. Of particular importance to all, of course, is the fact that in the early 1980s, all parts of the world economy appeared to be headed rather steeply downhill. Let us first try to understand the reasons for the apparent integration, and then for the downhill trajectory.

Integration and Mutual Dependence. There are two conditions that effectively define the industrialized, capitalist world of the 1980s: interdependence and transformation. Interdependence means that investment, trade, and other forms of economic activity are so interwoven that each country's prosperity depends on the health of the others. One measure of such interdependence is the extent of investment in other countries. In 1983, U.S. corporations and banks had direct investments or loans of about $619 billion abroad. Most of that was in the industrialized world, but by the late 1970s an increasing proportion was going to the Third World. For the top ten multinational corporations alone, foreign revenue amounted to more than $250 billion in 1982—or about 50 percent of all their revenues. The leading American banks also had about half of all their assets abroad in 1983, some of them in high-risk loans to Third World countries. More than half the major banks' profits was derived from international operations.

In addition, the U.S. government had another $100 billion overseas in loans and foreign currency holdings. Conversely, foreign corporations and individuals had about $557 billion invested in U.S. land, industries, or stocks, bonds, and other securities. Much of this investment came from industrialized capitalist countries in the form of automobile or electronics plants in the United States, or in the investment of cash in the stock market or government securities. But a growing share of the total was in the form of investment by wealthy Third World elites in U.S. farm land, luxury homes, and safe Treasury securities.

These totals include only those sums directly involving American individuals, banks, corporations, or property. They do not touch upon the much larger totals of loans and investments made by other countries, their banks, corporations, and individuals, or by multilateral world organizations like the World Bank or the International Monetary Fund. All these various investments add up to an extensive network of mutual obligation and interest, and help to tie the world together.

Another key to both the interdependence and prosperity generated in the post–World War II world is the new role of international trade. The totals of goods and services exchanged between countries has leaped dramatically, particularly in the last decades. The ability to export means new possibilities for growth, profits, and jobs—and every country has sought to expand its exports. The opportunity to obtain imports, on the other hand, means that a given country will be able to obtain goods that are less expensive, of better quality, or otherwise unavailable locally.

Table 3.9 shows how the volume of international trade contributes to tying the world together. The major trading groups of concern to us are shown in the left column, with the sources of their imports or the destinations of their exports in successive columns across the page. The final column shows the total dollar value of all imports and exports. In the case of the United States, the volume of this merchandise trade has risen to the equivalent of 25 to 30 percent of our GNP. In 1980, exports were at 13

TABLE 3.9
Trade in the World Economy, 1980

	SOURCES OR DESTINATIONS				
	OECD[1]	OPEC[2]	Non-oil Third World	Socialist	TOTAL
United States					
Imports					
Value ($ billions)	121.5	52	62	2.5	241
Source (percentage)	50	22	26	1	100
Exports					
Value ($ billions)	127.7	17.8	64	7.6	221
Destination (percentage)	58	8	29	3	100
European Economic Community					
Imports					
Value ($ billions)	524.7	93.4	71.8	30.8	730.5
Source (percentage)	72	13	10	4	100
Exports					
Value ($ billions)	502	51.5	72.3	26.6	665
Destination (percentage)	76	8	11	4	100
Japan					
Imports					
Value ($ billions)	47.5	56.8	28.3	6.7	141
Source (percentage)	34	40	20	5	100
Exports					
Value ($ billions)	59.7	18.5	40.6	9.0	129.6
Destination (percentage)	46	14	31	7	100

SOURCE: *Statistical Abstract of the U.S., 1983*, Table 1529.
[1] Organization for Economic Cooperation and Development
[2] Organization of Petroleum-Exporting Countries

percent, about double the level of years as recent as the early 1970s. Imports, which traditionally have been higher because the prosperous American market was ever-attractive, still led by a considerable margin.

The U.S. trading pattern is also interesting. Half of our imports come from other developed capitalist countries, and well over half of our exports go to such countries. Very little exchange occurs with the socialist world, even though it is much publicized. There is a considerable imbalance with the oil exporters, of course, as imported oil far exceeds exports to such countries. Indeed, by reading down the OPEC column and recognizing other countries' "imports" as their exports, one can gain some idea of the huge cash surplus that the OPEC nations still had in 1980. Nearly 40 percent of our exports, however, are sold to the Third World, mostly to non-oil-exporting nations. The economic condition of our export customers, therefore, is (or should be) of continuing concern to the United States.

The pattern is somewhat different for the other capitalist countries. The Europeans have a very high volume of trade among themselves, and a better balance with the OPEC countries, despite their heavy dependence on them for oil imports. Their trade volumes with the Third World and the socialist countries are higher than those of the United States, although the proportions that such trade represents are made to seem low by the great volume of their overall trade. Japan has high dependence on OPEC oil, and pays for it by exporting goods aggressively. International trade represents an even higher share of GNP for these countries than it does for the United States, and leads to even greater concern for mutual efforts to maintain steady growth and prosperity.

A final form of mutual dependence in the world economy is that which is brought about by the compelling need that some countries have for raw materials that are available only from other countries. Oil has been the most visible and costly of these in recent years and will remain a vital commodity for decades. Despite reduced use resulting from conservation efforts, the recession of the early 1980s, and the resultant reduced prices, oil will continue to be the most universally vital ingredient for industrial economies. But it is far from the only vital ingredient. In addition, the American economy relies on foreign sources for many of our strategic raw materials. These materials are either not available or are only in very limited supply within the United States. Their sources range from other Western hemisphere countries to nations in all corners of the world, and particularly include Third World countries.

Given this interdependence, countries have two primary concerns. One is to maintain a favorable situation for themselves, with respect to the net balance of payments involved between themselves and all the other countries with which they are exchanging goods and services—and with respect to the growth, profits, and jobs that exist in their own economies. The other concern is to help keep the whole intricate international system working well enough to maintain the general levels of growth, exchange, profits, and jobs on which a prosperous and peaceful social existence depends. Self-interest often appears to conflict with mutual interest, and it can often be much easier politically to urge sacrifices upon others abroad than to undertake them at home.

THE CHANGING CIRCUMSTANCES OF THE AMERICAN ECONOMY

The goals of the American economy are clear enough; we require steady growth with stable prices. Growth is necessary to enable payment of debts, provide profits to owners and investors, and create jobs for a growing population. Growth may be defined and measured in various ways, but these are the bottom-line necessities that make growth essential. Growth must be steady and apparently assured, so that further investments and expansion will be undertaken and thus continued growth will be made more likely. Stable prices are needed to assure that the growth, profits, and income are *real*, and result in increased purchasing power. If prices and other costs do not remain at least relatively stable, what appears to be growth may not be. Most important, steady growth and stable prices mean predictability and opportunity—the essence of a desirable economic context.

By and large, these goals were achieved in the prosperous days of the 1950s and early 1960s, but they have proved to be highly elusive since the late 1960s. The American economy has steadily lost ground to the rapidly expanding European and Japanese economies, and has begun to suffer some significant problems. As the capitalist world grew more integrated, problems also became general. Because they were so unfamiliar and because the United States was still clearly the "first among equals" in the capitalist world, the U.S. economy felt these problems more acutely. The transformation to high technology production and services occupations began in the late 1970s, and the recession of the early 1980s was triggered on top of these underlying structural changes. In response, the problems of the American economy escalated. We will look first at the historical background, then at the problems emerging in the 1970s, and finally at the policies of the early 1980s—all as components of the current U.S. economic context.

The Background

Although our focus now is the U.S. economy, it will help to start with some further comparisons with the capitalist countries that are at once our major trading partners and our closest competitors. Table 3.10 makes some basic comparisons over time and shows current contrasts. As we saw in Table 3.8, the United States still enjoys by far the largest total GNP in the world. When expressed in per capita terms, however, as in the first row of Table 3.10, the gap seems much less great. Indeed, several smaller European countries such as Sweden, Switzerland, Denmark, and the Netherlands currently have GNP per capita ratios that are higher than the United States. This means that their output per person (and in some cases their income per person) is higher than that of Americans. We still hold a lead over our major competitors, but this too is shrinking almost every year.

The next rows of the table give some sense of the relative rates by which the latter countries are overtaking us. The GNP per capita growth rates, for example, indicate that the Japanese have been growing most rapidly. They continued to do so, although at a slower rate, even in the recession of the early 1980s. France and Germany also have been growing rapidly, but suffered more heavily in the recession. Gross Domestic Product is a standard that can shed new light for some countries because international activities of all kinds are eliminated. These ratios are expressed as percentages of the U.S. GDP in order to show in relative terms how far behind these countries started and how far they have come. Once again, it is the Japanese who, starting from very far behind, have come the farthest. The Germans, who were closer to the United States to begin with, have now exceeded the American rate of GDP output per capita. The French have actually caught up more than the Germans, but have yet to reach the

TABLE 3.10
The U.S. and Major Competitors

	U.S.	Japan	W. Germany	France	United Kingdom
Production					
GNP per capita, 1981	$12,783	$9,578	$11,132	$10,619	$8,941
Annual percentage change in GNP per capita					
1975–80	2.6	4.2	3.7	3.0	1.6
1981	0.9	2.1	-0.5	-0.2	-1.9
GDP per capita, as a percentage of U.S. GDP					
1960	100	30	85	69	59
1980	100	68	101	92	56
Inflation					
Average percentage, 1977–81	9.9	5.7	4.4	11.2	13.5
1982 (percentage)	6.2	2.6	5.3	12.0	8.6
Cumulative total, 1967–81 (1967 = 100)	172	196	86	233	374
Unemployment					
Average percentage, 1977–81	6.7	2.1	3.4	6.1	7.4
1982 (percentage)	9.6	2.4	7.7	8.6	12.0
Average percentage, 1959–76	5.4	1.4	1.2	2.4	3.2

SOURCE: *Statistical Abstract of the U.S., 1983,* Tables 1526, 1527. 1532. 1536.

U.S. level. Only Great Britain lags behind the U.S. rates of growth. On both measures, Great Britain actually lost ground to all of these countries.

The next two sets of entries in the table give a time dimension to two major problems that all these countries have experienced with growing severity in the last decades. They also show some interesting differences in national priorities in economic matters, perhaps reflecting historical experience or unique cultural characteristics. Inflation was common to all in the 1970s, partly because of the sharp rise in oil prices and the fact that some countries (particularly Japan) were so dependent on imported oil. In cumulative total since 1967 (the beginning of persistent inflation in the United States), Great Britain and France have suffered the most. Germany, however, perhaps as a result of its ruinous experience in the 1920s, views inflation with great concern and does much better at controlling it. The Japanese, by contrast, put their greatest emphasis on rapid growth, which has meant remarkably low unemployment for decades. The United States is much less concerned about unemployment than any of these countries, it appears, or at least historically experiences rates that are much higher. Only Great Britain even approaches the U.S. rates, and then only in recent times.

The table clearly shows distinctive economic performances over the two decades that it covers. Some countries grew more rapidly or suffered greater inflation or unemployment than others, but the table also shows that in recent years all countries have had more or less the same problems at the same times. In 1977–81, for example, all suffered worse inflation and unemployment than they had in earlier periods. And in 1982 the effects of the recession are equally clear for all. Because the United States is still the leader, all of these countries depend on the United States—its performance and its policies—to help them solve their economic problems. In many respects, the agenda of U.S. economic performance and policies is also the world agenda.

SUMMARY AND PREVIEW

We have seen a vast economy, made up of a few hundred multinational corporations, thousands of small businesses, and thousands of governments, one of which—the U.S. government—is the biggest and most decisive unit of all. This economy is sewn together in many ways; it moves ponderously and as a single unit. However, it is anything but independent; instead, it is delicately intertwined with the world economy. In recent years, the American economy has declined in apparent strength, in contrast to other capitalist countries and its own past experience. But it is still the largest and most powerful in the world, and all other countries depend on it. This economy, its character and its problems, represents the first piece in our ongoing construction project—a political economy view of the world of American politics.

CHAPTER 4

Political Economy II: The Social Pyramid

We have just described the political economic core of the American social order; we have not yet addressed its social and political dimensions:

- How do we conceive of social structure in the United States?
- What values and ideology do we find at various points within it?
- What are the possible causes of such conditions?

Obviously, the social structure is partly a product of the nature and structure of the economy. It is also created by and in turn reflects other factors, including its own historical evolution. In important ways, these are empirical (factual) questions to be pursued throughout the text.

But these are first *conceptual* issues. If we did not conceive of them as important questions to ask, we would never seek factual answers to them. For example, the 1950s and early 1960s were a time when the United States was thought to be an essentially middle-class and affluent society that had reached "the end of ideology." It was generally believed that it was a society in which all conflicting demands had been satisfied and harmony prevailed. The outbreaks of the late 1960s and early 1970s and the economic woes of the late 1970s and early 1980s drastically altered this conception.

In this chapter, we shall first sketch the outlines of the American social pyramid in a kind of snapshot approach. Then we shall search for two additional dimensions of meaning within that snapshot:

1. What do these differentials of wealth, status, and power *mean*—if anything—to the people at various levels within the pyramid? Here we are obliged to take up the notion of social class, and ask what

that often-used but not always well-understood concept might mean in the American context.

2. We shall try to identify how many and what kinds of people are located at the extremes of the American social pyramid. We shall be interested in *why* people are located as they are, and whether they are content with their positions.

Together, these inquiries should give us the beginnings of insight into the social component of the American political economy.

THE AMERICAN SOCIAL PYRAMID: A FIRST APPROXIMATION

A hard look at American society would reveal a highly stratified (unequal, hierarchical, with a few at the top and many at the bottom) system of wealth, income, status, and power. A very few people enjoy the lion's share of the products of the American economy; in fact, most people have trouble making ends meet. Let's examine some basic data regarding income and wealth as a way of sharpening our image of American society. Table 4.1 presents the distribution of family income by each 20 percent or one-fifth of the American population. This is a standard way of assessing changes in the inequality of income distribution over time. If each fifth received the same share of national income, of course, each would end up with an equal 20 percent of all income.

The first column in the table gives some concrete meaning to these ''fifths'' by showing the average family income in each of the five groups of

TABLE 4.1   *Shares of Total U.S. Income Received by Each 20 Percent of U.S. Families, 1981*

	INCOME OF AVERAGE FAMILY, 1981	SHARE OF ALL FAMILY INCOME (IN PERCENTAGES)				
		1981	*1979*	*1970*	*1960*	*1950*
Richest 5 percent	$71,114	15.4	15.7	15.6	15.9	17.3
Richest fifth	$49,020	41.9	41.6	40.9	41.3	42.8
Fourth fifth	$26,680	24.4	24.1	23.8	24.0	23.4
Third fifth	$17,540	17.4	17.5	17.6	17.8	17.4
Second fifth	$10,370	11.3	11.6	12.2	12.2	11.9
Poorest fifth	$ 3,980	5.0	5.2	5.4	4.8	4.5

SOURCES: *U.S. Census Bureau, Current Population Reports–Consumer Income, Series P–60,* 1982.

Average family income estimates are from *National Journal,* Oct. 23, 1982, p. 1792.

NOTES: Poverty level for a family of 4 in 1981 was $9,287. Total number of U.S. families was 61,000,000.

families, and the average for the top 5 percent of all families. The bottom 20 percent of Americans, it indicates, receive less than half the official poverty level of income. The upper 5 percent of families, on the other hand, receive eighteen times that amount annually. The rest of the table compares the shares of all national income received by these categories of families over several decades.

The fact is that the upper fifths regularly receive much larger shares than the lower fifths. The top 5 percent receives as much as the bottom 40 percent combined! The great bulk of the income, more than 65 percent, goes to the upper 40 percent of income-earning families, while the remaining 60 percent of U.S. families share only one-third of the income. Moreover, these patterns are relatively constant. The percentage received by the lower two-fifths increased slightly with the Great Society and its War on Poverty, but is now decreasing to historical levels. By 1981, the poorest fifth was back to the share of national income it received sometime in the early 1960s, and the bottom two-fifths together received just about what they got in 1950.

Table 4.2 renders a more detailed picture of the top and bottom of the social pyramid. What is immediately apparent is the concentration of income and wealth among a very few people at the top, with very little income and no wealth among a great many people at the bottom. Only about 1,000,000 tax returns were filed in 1980 showing income over $75,000 per year; this is roughly 2 percent of all the individual tax returns filed that year. That means that about 2 percent of income-reporting units amassed approximately $100 billion in personal income. A lucky 4,112 of those were over $1 million each.

Income is a relatively small portion of the advantage that accrues to those at the top. When total wealth in the sense of personal assets are compared, the top 1 percent of the population comes out even farther ahead. The most recent data available are for 1972, but the relative permanence of these patterns in the past suggests that these totals remain essentially the same today. The major forms of personal assets, it appears, are tightly concentrated within a very small proportion of the population, which in this case is the top one-half of one percent. This tiny group holds, for example, half of all the corporate stock in the country and almost 20 percent of all the assets of any kind that exist.

In contrast, the bottom 10 percent (29,000,000 people!) lived below the poverty line in 1980, the same year as the previous income data were compiled. (In 1981, that was up 7.4 percent to 31,800,000, or 12 percent of the population.) As usual, poverty was strongly linked to race and national origin. While only 8 percent of white families lived below the poverty line in 1980, 29 percent of black families and 23 percent of families of Spanish origin did. Poverty is also increasingly becoming "feminized." Nearly half of all families in poverty are headed by a woman, and among "unrelated individuals" in poverty, women outnumber men by about two to one. More than 80 percent of the poverty population are women and children.

TABLE 4.2
The Top and Bottom of the Social Pyramid
The Top 1 Percent—Income and Wealth

OVER $75,000 INCOME (1980)

Range	Number of Tax Returns	Percentage in Category
Over $1 million	4,112	0.4
$500,000–$1 million	12,105	1.1
$200,000–$499,999	97,232	9.1
$100,000–$199,999	434,041	40.5
$ 75,000–$ 99,999	524,031	48.9
Totals	1,071,521	100

WEALTH (1972)

Holdings	Share Held by Top 1 Percent	Share Held by Top ½ Percent
Total, all personal assets	24.1%	18.9%
Corporate stock	56.5	49.3
Bonds	60.0	52.2
Debt instruments	52.7	39.1
Trusts	89.9	80.8

The Bottom 10 Percent—Families Below 1980 Poverty Level ($8,414)

NUMBER	FAMILIES (IN PERCENTAGES)			
	All Races	White	Black	Spanish Origin
Families (Persons) 6,217,000 (29,600,000)	10.3%	8.0	28.9	23.2
Female householder, no husband present (2,972,000 families)	47.8	54.1	43.8	—
All other families (3,245,000)	52.2	79.7	16.2	—

SOURCES: Income: Internal Revenue Service reports, as reported in Andrew Hacker, *U/S.*

Wealth: *U.S. Statistical Abstract, 1983,* Table 743. (1972 is most recent year for which data are available, but basic shares have been constant for decades.)

Poverty population: *U.S. Statistical Abstract, 1983,* Table 734.

Taking Tables 4.1 and 4.2 together, we have a beginning sketch of an income/wealth-based social pyramid, with well over half the population providing a solid foundation and a few enjoying vastly disproportionate shares. The income differentials between fifths of the American population suggest in a very gross manner that there are layers or strata within this pyramid that remain relatively constant over time. Income is not the only source of relative position within this pyramid, although it certainly is an important one. Occupations provide another basis for the layering that exists, because they provide consistently different amounts of income to the people that hold them. Professionals and managers, for example, earn far more than laborers or other unskilled workers. These are also occupations that carry with them social status—special respect in the eyes of others—often without regard to the income involved. Social status is thus a partially independent source of the stratification that occurs in the social pyramid.

In turn, levels of education provide opportunities to enter different kinds of occupations. At least some college education, and increasingly advanced degrees as well, are needed for the most prestigious and highest-paying jobs in the U.S. economy. For the most part, the opportunity to obtain a college degree and/or graduate education is related to prior family income and wealth. This relationship results not only from the availability of cash to pay for tuition and other costs but also from the original conviction that it was important to go to college, earlier preparation for it, and the absence of other family obligations that might prevent it. Financial aid available from either colleges or governments never succeeded in removing the income barriers to higher education, and is now declining in any event. These are some of the reasons why the stratification within the American social pyramid is relatively permanent.

Table 4.3 is a composite portrait of this pyramid in which the parts played by education, income, and race are summarized. Occupation may be hypothesized from levels of educational attainment. Social status, although much less tangible than any of the others, is certainly suggested by the clustering of highest educational and income achievements in the upper right corner of the table's entries. We find 21 percent of all white college graduates and only about 9 percent of all black college graduates among the 6.7 percent of all families earning more than $50,000 per year. In the $30,000–$49,999 column just to the left, we find 36 percent of all white college graduates and 28.4 percent of all black college graduates. Keeping in mind that a much smaller proportion of blacks have college experience than whites, we can now look back to the left along the row of college graduates, and down both of these two right-hand columns to see the correlations between education, income, and race—and, probably, social status.

The table shows that education pays off, although more so for whites than for blacks. Education enables people to reach the higher-income categories, but at every educational level among the two highest income categories, there are larger proportions of whites than blacks. Conversely, in

TABLE 4.3
Income, Education, and Race, 1980

HOUSEHOLDER'S EDUCATIONAL ATTAINMENT	FAMILIES BY INCOME LEVELS AND RACE (PERCENTAGES)											
	Under $5,000		$5,000–$9,999		$10,000–$19,999		$20,000–$29,999		$30,000–$49,999		Over $50,000	
	White	Black	White	Black	White	Black	White	Black	White	Black	White	Black
College graduate	1.2	3.9	3.0	8.1	13.9	22.7	24.8	28.1	36.1	28.4	21.0	8.8
1 to 3 years of college	2.7	7.8	6.2	16.2	24.1	31.5	29.1	20.2	30.2	20.2	7.7	4.1
High school graduate	3.7	12.0	9.0	19.5	28.6	31.3	30.8	20.9	23.1	15.2	4.8	1.1
1 to 3 years of high school	7.2	19.4	15.9	26.0	36.2	32.3	24.0	15.3	14.6	6.2	2.2	0.8
8 years of elementary school	7.2	18.2	22.8	35.2	36.7	27.0	20.0	12.7	11.5	6.2	1.8	0.5
Less than 8 years	13.0	21.8	29.7	36.6	35.7	27.5	12.7	10.2	7.9	3.8	1.0	0.2
Total, all 60,309,000 families	6.2		12.7		26.2		24.9		21.3		6.7	

SOURCE: *U.S. Statistical Abstract, 1983*, Table 715 (reclassified).

the lower educational and income levels, there are larger proportions of blacks than whites. What emerges from careful study of the many entries in the table is a sense of the relatively permanent stratification system that is the American social pyramid. Individuals decidedly do vault from the lowest to the highest levels from time to time, but they are spectacular exceptions to the general pattern. What most people experienced in the post–World War II United States was a steady rise in the whole social pyramid's levels of education and income—until about 1973. From that point, as we shall see later, incomes began to drop in terms of purchasing power. Despite apparent educational attainment levels, it became clear in the 1980s that skill levels were actually dropping also. In effect, the pyramid had already begun to shrink toward the bottom before the recession, widespread unemployment, and policy changes of the early 1980s gave it additional impetus in that direction.

FINDING MEANING IN THE SOCIAL PYRAMID

The meanings to be found in this description of basic social patterns depend upon how people feel about their locations, and who these people are. Both questions oblige us to take up the notion of social class and explore the conditions that would give it reality for people. The facts of social stratification are surely important in their own right, but they take on a greater, and more political, importance if they generate a notion of *class*. We must, therefore, face the issues of:

1. A satisfactory definition of the concept of social class, and
2. The existence and political relevance of class and class consciousness in American politics.

Social Class and Its Significance. What do we mean by "class"? Many definitions exist, and some have long and emotional histories. Each definition carries with it a particular set of characteristics and implications. Some refer only to objective characteristics of people, such as their income, education, or occupational status and others define class in subjective terms. Others may include the extent to which people think of themselves as members of a social class, or are "class conscious." A useful definition of class for the purposes of political analysis adds a third dimension—present or potential political power. The concept of class used here includes three conditions.

Obviously numbers of people are affected in similar ways by some fundamental dynamics of the socioeconomic system. In objective terms, they share characteristics such as wealth, income, and education. Secondly, groups of people develop similar values, attitudes, and orientations toward the world that are related to the objective conditions of their lives. Equally as important, these values and attitudes distinguish them from other groups with different patterns of income, wealth, and education. It is not necessary to this definition that members of the group be conscious of how fully they share their particular situation and values with others. In other words, in our definition so far, a class shares both objective and subjective characteristics that distinguish it from another group.

Finally, in order for a class to have real political significance, its members must become aware that they share their situation *and* that the reason for their shared status is that they are similarly affected by the economic system. The realization that their status is systemically rather than personally caused becomes a primary factor in their political orientation; this leads them to define their political goals and mobilize political power to defend or change their relative positions. If a class exists, there is always the possibility of class consciousness. Many forces work against it (which is also, of course, of political relevance), and if these forces are strong enough and sustained enough, class consciousness may never develop, or it may develop in truncated ways. If class consciousness does develop, however, dramatic political consequences may follow; but first we will start with the objective conditions of class in the United States.

The Basic Occupational and Income Structure. We will begin this analysis with the three basic facts that have already been established.

1. The United States is a sharply stratified society. A very few people receive very large proportions of income and wealth. The majority share a relatively modest proportion while a substantial number receive very little indeed.
2. This pattern has persisted for at least the last sixty years, with only negligible change in the War on Poverty years. Indeed, recently the gap has widened rather than closed.
3. Income inequalities are closely related to three major factors—the source of income, sex, and race. Those who gain their income from stocks and dividends and from capital gains are at the top of the income and wealth scale, and wage earners fill the bottom. Men earn more than women and nonwhites earn less than whites, even in comparable jobs with comparable educations. Women and minorities are concentrated in the lowest-paying jobs. Poverty and racism are so closely linked in the United States that it is difficult to talk about them separately. We will do so chiefly for analytical clarity.

The most obvious source of income differentials is the way in which people gain their income. Those who earn their income from wages and salaries are the most numerous and earn a much larger aggregate dollar total than others. However, individually they are concentrated at the lower income levels. At the higher income levels, the source of income is much more likely to be stock dividends and capital gains (increases in the value of property held). Of those receiving more than $100,000 per year in the mid-1970s, for example, 67 percent of all dollars were derived from dividends and capital gains. This ratio held as inflation boosted income totals in the late 1970s. This is another way of saying that the concentration of *wealth* in a few rich people results in sharp *income* differences.

A major cause of income differentials is the occupations of income earners. Professionals, managers, and other white-collar workers earn substantially more than blue-collar, service, and farm workers. Both categories tend to be self-perpetuating, but the former category requires more education. A white-collar family has greater financial resources and the social status that makes college education appear to be not only appropriate but necessary for its children. In other words, white-collar families are likely to produce white-collar children. Conversely, people enter blue-collar occupations in part because their parents held such jobs, were relatively poor, and could offer neither the money nor the social support necessary for further education and occupational mobility.

In Table 4.4, we compare the occupational makeup of the United States in 1972 and 1981 in several ways. First, we show the proportion of workers in each job category in 1972 and 1981. (The actual totals of workers in 1981 are shown in parentheses alongside each descriptive category to give the percentages a bit more meaning.) Note first which job categories are increasing and which are decreasing: managerial and other white-collar jobs are increasing, while blue collar jobs are decreasing. The table also shows the proportion of jobs in each category that are held by women and by blacks. Sex and race remain at least as important as education in determining occupation and income patterns. The largest proportions of women are found in clerical and service occupations, while the greatest concentration of blacks are in service, laborer, and unskilled worker categories.

The contrasts between 1972 and 1981 are worth noting as well. Women have increased in proportion in practically every category, reflecting their larger share of the total work force in addition to a general upgrading of job levels. Most women in the professional category are still elementary school teachers, but there was a substantial improvement in women's share of managerial jobs. On the other hand, there was an even larger proportion of women in clerical jobs in 1981 than in 1972. Blacks, too, appeared to improve their relative job status, but it should be kept in mind that the top row shows 11.6 percent of blacks in the labor force. No higher-paying job category approaches that proportion.

Finally, the table shows which job categories experienced the most unemployment in 1981, comparing the experience of white males, women, and blacks in each job category. The lowest-paying, lowest-status jobs have the highest unemployment, while the higher-status jobs have very little unemployment. We need to translate unemployment figures to find their true meaning; a national average of 7 or 8 percent, for example, really means one-third of that for professionals and managers, but twice that for laborers and unskilled workers.

As suggested in Chapter 1, one of the central facts of life in the American social pyramid in the late 1970s and early 1980s was that the whole pyramid seemed to be sinking onto its base. Inflation and unemployment

TABLE 4.4
Occupational Profile, U.S. Workers, 1972 and 1981

OCCUPATION (TOTAL EMPLOYED, 1981)	1972			1981			Unemployment Rates		
	Percentage of All Workers	Percentage Female	Percentage Black	Percentage of All Workers	Percentage Female	Percentage Black	Male	Female	All
Total (100,397,000)	100	38.0	10.6	100	42.8	11.6	7.4	7.9	7.6
Professional & technical (16,420,000)	14.0	39.3	7.2	16.4	44.6	9.9	2.3	3.4	2.8
Managers & administrators (11,540,000)	9.8	17.6	4.0	11.5	27.5	5.8	2.1	4.1	2.7
Sales (6,425,000)	6.5	41.6	3.6	6.4	45.4	5.4	3.4	5.9	4.6
Clerical (18,564,000)	17.4	75.6	8.7	18.5	80.5	11.6	5.1	5.9	5.7
Skilled crafts (12,662,000)	13.2	3.6	6.9	12.6	6.3	8.5	7.5	6.4	7.5
Operatives, including transportation (14,016,000)	16.6	35.6	13.3	14.0	36.8	16.0	11.0	14.0	12.2
Laborers (4,583,000)	5.2	6.0	20.2	4.6	11.5	16.5	14.8	14.2	14.7
Farmers and farm laborers (2,749,000)	3.7	19.0	9.9	2.7	18.3	7.8	4.6	8.3	5.3
Service workers, excluding domestic (12,391,000)	11.7	57.0	18.5	12.3	59.2	18.4	9.3	8.6	8.9
Private household workers (1,047,000)	1.8	97.6	40.6	1.0	96.5	32.4	—	—	—

SOURCE: *U.S. Statistical Abstract, 1983*, Tables 651 and 655.

Figure 4.1. *Real Wages, 1973–83*

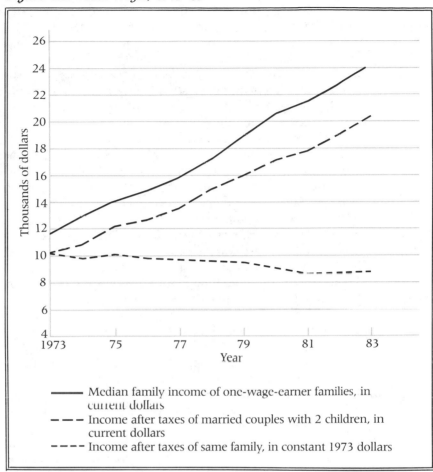

SOURCE: Tax Foundation.

were twin problems throughout that period. One prominent result was that "real" wages, the actual purchasing power of income measured by some constant figure, declined steadily. Figure 4.1 shows graphically the contrast between "current" dollar incomes, which are dollars (of declining value due to inflation) that are actually received in any given year, and "constant" dollars, which in this case are dollars valued as they were in 1973. The contrasts are between median family incomes in the various years. ("Median" means that half of all families received more and half received less than the figure shown.) The median income received rises sharply, and the same family's net income after taxes rises almost as steeply. However, the real income of that family was actually dropping steadily because the rise in prices exceeded even the dramatic increases in dollars received.

No wonder people felt that it was more difficult to make ends meet; it was. The effects of this continuing erosion in peoples' standard of living are hard to measure, but it surely contributed to the general malaise and declining confidence in social institutions and leaders that was widely noted in the late 1970s and early 1980s. The only thing that is worse than continued inflation for people in the lower two-thirds of the social pyramid is high unemployment, which soon followed in the recession of 1982.

Also to be noted is the fact that another major cause of income differences is still sex. Culturally-imposed limitations on educational opportunities and career expectations severely limit the income-producing capabilities of women. Systematic discrimination in both employment and wage or salary levels continues to maintain the gender differences in income levels. The result is that women must fight to open up many jobs to them and, once a job has been attained, a woman must expend as much energy ground-breaking as doing her job. Women are still paid less than men for comparable work, when it is available, and finally, women remain concentrated in the lowest-paying jobs.

The single greatest and most enduring cause of income differentials is racism. It persists across time and despite both individual and collective efforts to fulfill the requirements of mobility within the society. Nonwhite Americans have always been among the last hired and the first fired, and they are systematically excluded from educational and other opportunities. They are paid less for every job than equally-educated or less well-educated whites in the same jobs. The wages of white men are greater than those of nonwhite men. The wages of women trail those of men within races, so that nonwhite women are the lowest paid of all. Race combines with sex to create a self-perpetuating cycle of income limitation.

The Special Problems of Minorities and Women. We have seen repeatedly that race and sex are leading reasons for having a low income. The significance of the effects of multiple disadvantages can be seen most clearly from a close look at the nation's poverty-level population. Table 4.5 gives an overview of this population. In 1981, 14 percent of all Americans lived below the government's official poverty line ($9,287 for an urban family of four). This total included 20 percent of all American children under 18 years old, 34 percent of all black Americans, and 27 percent of all Americans of Hispanic origin.

These proportions are large enough, but they are only the beginning. Poverty in the United States is beginning to be a female phenomenon. This shows up first in the fact that, among individuals living alone, twice as many women as men live in poverty. Among people living in families, only 7 percent of married couples, and 10 percent of male-headed households, live in poverty; but 35 percent of all female-headed households live in poverty. Such households make up almost half of all poverty-level families.

Table 4.6 explores some details about the three leading components of the poverty-level population: the elderly, minorities, and women. Among the elderly in poverty, women and minorities are again prominent. Nearly half of all black women over age 65 live in poverty. Twice as many white

**TABLE
4.5**   *The Poverty Population, 1981*

| | | BELOW OFFICIAL "POVERTY THRESHOLD"* | |
	Totals	*Percentages of U.S. People in Each Category Who Live Below Poverty Line*
All persons	31,822,000	14.0
White	21,553,000	11.1
Black	9,173,000	34.2
Spanish origin	3,713,000	26.5
Under 18 yrs.	12,324,000	19.8
Over 65 yrs.	3,853,000	15.3
All families	6,851,000	11.2
Married couples	3,394,000	6.8
Male householder, no wife present	205,000	10.3
Female householder, no husband present	3,252,000	34.6
Percentage female of all families in poverty	—	47.5
All unrelated individuals	6,490,000	23.4
Male	2,239,000	18.1
Female	4,251,000	27.7

SOURCE: U.S. Bureau of the Census, *Current Population Reports,* Series P-60, No. 138, *Characteristics of the Population Below the Poverty Level: 1981* (U.S. Government Printing Office, Washington, D.C., 1983).

*Definition of poverty varies by family size and location. For urban family of 4, $9,287.

women over age 65 live in poverty as white men over age 65. The comparison between families of white, black, and Spanish origin in 1978 and 1981 shows several important facts, although by now they might be anticipated. The median income of white families averages about two-thirds higher than that of black families, but not quite so much higher than Hispanic families. The median incomes of all dropped by about 10 percent even in this short three-year period. Instead of "catching up," minorities lost ground to whites on the income ladder. Relatively small proportions of white families live in poverty, but a quarter of Hispanic and nearly a third of black families do. As the recession deepened in 1982, these proportions undoubtedly increased. The third section of the table compares the proportion of female-headed households in poverty by race and origin. More than half of all black and Hispanic families headed by a woman live in poverty. Two-thirds of the children in poverty live in such families.

One of the more recent "issue" discoveries has been "the feminization of poverty." In 1981, the National Advisory Council on Economic Opportunity warned:

TABLE
4.6   *Poverty Among Special Populations*

POVERTY AMONG THE ELDERLY, 1981

Percentages of over-65 population by sex and race

	All	*White*	*Black*
Male	10.5	8.5	32.2
Female	18.6	16.2	43.5

POVERTY AMONG MINORITIES, 1978 AND 1981

	White		*Black*		*Spanish Origin*	
	1978	*1981*	*1978*	*1981*	*1978*	*1981*
Median Family Income, 1981, dollars	$25,606	$23,517	$15,166	$13,266	$17,518	$16,401
Percentage of Families below poverty line	6.9	8.8	27.5	30.8	20.4	24.0

POVERTY AMONG FEMALE-HEADED FAMILIES, 1981

	All	*White*	*Black*	*Spanish Origin*
Percentage of families with female head who are in poverty	34.6	27.4	52.9	53.2
Percentage of other families who are in poverty	8.1	7.0	18.0	18.3
Percentage of children under 18 in poverty who are in female-headed families	52.3	42.8	67.7	67.3

SOURCES: Income: Internal Revenue Service reports, as reported in Andrew Hacker, *U/S.* Wealth: *U.S. Statistical Abstract, 1983,* Table 743. (1972 is most recent year for which data are available, but basic shares have been constant for decades.)
Poverty population: *U.S. Statistical Abstract, 1983,* Table 734.

> All other things being equal, if the proportion of the poor in female-householder families were to increase at the same rate as it did from 1967 to 1978, the poverty population would be composed solely of women and their children before the year 2000.[1]

This is also a difficult population to aid simply by requiring work or providing jobs. Many of these women have small children and they need daycare

---

[1] Quoted in Barbara Ehrenreich & Frances Fox Piven, "The Left's Best Hope," *Mother Jones,* September/October, 1983, p. 27.

and other support help if they do find work. Too often the work available to them does not pay enough to cover the cost of childcare needs *and* provide a living (not to mention the difficulty of finding even adequate childcare). However, governmental aid slows or stops if they work, regardless of the wage level, and thus, it is relatively unskilled women and small children (the politically powerless) who are the most dependent on governmental services.

Another dimension of the special problems of women and minorities is found in the population shifts that have been under way in the past decade around the major cities of the United States, Snow Belt and Sun Belt alike. The center cities are declining in population, becoming poverty ghettos with heavy minority populations. Meanwhile, the suburbs are growing rapidly with white populations. The elderly remain disproportionately within the center cities and families with children are equally disproportionately located in the suburbs.

Table 4.7 shows that these trends are nationwide. The center cities of the Snow Belt are actually losing population, but they have large proportions of minorities—in every case vastly more than in their surrounding suburbs. The center cities of the Sun Belt are growing slowly, for the most part, while their suburbs are growing much faster. Sun Belt black proportions are lower, but Hispanic proportions are higher. The total of minorities is much the same as in the Snow Belt. In both cases, incomes are much higher in the suburbs, and the distribution of elderly and couples with children is the same. This raises the prospect that poor people in the cities (particularly minorities and the elderly) will be left to their own devices, without the resources to provide the services that they need. The younger white middle class will raise and educate its children in the suburbs and ultimately, the next generations will be farther apart in skills and income potential than the present ones.

Why are these people poor? Many factors contribute to poverty, but the two major ones are unemployment or subemployment and racial discrimination. Unemployment among the poor usually runs well above the national average. Lacking education and skills, the poor are among the last hired and the first fired as the economy expands and contracts. For blacks, the unemployment rate in 1983 was about 17 percent, as opposed to 10 percent for whites. For young nonwhites, figures over 40 percent are common in most large cities. Low pay and a continuing shortage of jobs reduces the likelihood that the poor can help themselves. Clearly much of the explanation for low income and poverty is structural in character. It has to do with the characteristics of the economic system and the racial biases of the society, rather than with personal failures.

Despite national affluence, the United States as a whole does not enjoy a particularly high level of social welfare.[2] In many Western nations, for

---

[2] For a full comparison of the major industrial democracies on several welfare dimensions, see Kenneth M. Dolbeare, *American Public Policy: A Citizen's Guide* (New York: McGraw-Hill, 1982).

TABLE 4.7
A Tale of Two Kinds of Cities, 1980

SNOW BELT CITIES AND SUBURBS*	PERCENTAGE CHANGE IN POPULATION, 1970–80	RACIAL COMPOSITION (IN PERCENTAGES)			MEDIAN ANNUAL HOUSEHOLD INCOME	PERCENTAGE 65 OR OLDER	PERCENTAGE MARRIED COUPLES WITH CHILDREN
		White	Black	Hispanic			
Chicago	−11	50	40	14	$15,301	11	20
Suburbs	+14	91	6	4	24,811	9	24
Philadelphia	−13	58	38	4	13,169	14	20
Suburbs	+5	90	8	2	20,940	10	33
Detroit	−21	34	63	—	13,981	12	19
Suburbs	+8	94	4	—	24,038	9	35
Baltimore	−13	44	55	1	12,811	13	18
Suburbs	+19	89	9	1	22,272	9	34
SUN BELT CITIES AND SUBURBS*							
Los Angeles	+6	61	17	28	15,746	11	21
Suburbs	+7	72	10	29	19,410	9	33
Houston	+29	61	28	18	18,474	7	26
Suburbs	+71	86	7	11	24,847	5	44
Dallas	+7	61	29	12	16,227	10	22
Suburbs	+48	92	4	5	21,301	7	39
San Francisco	−5	58	13	13	15,867	9	13
Suburbs	+10	81	7	7	22,375	14	27

SOURCE: U.S. Census Bureau.

*Remainder of Standard Metropolitan Statistical Area outside of central cities.

example, family allowances (payments to help support children) are a common means of sharing this financial burden and marginally redistributing income. Most have broad training and re-employment assistance programs, and few either experience or would tolerate the levels of unemployment that are standard in this country.

The general health conditions of Americans are not commensurate with national affluence either, and of course, hardships are concentrated in the lower socioeconomic levels. Americans have lower life expectancies at birth than do the citizens of fifteen other nations of the world; infant mortality rates are higher for the United States than in fourteen other countries; and of course, much higher incidences of infant mortality and death rates from infectious diseases occur in the minority population.

The living conditions of the working and lower classes also differ from those enjoyed by the more affluent. The most drastically substandard housing in the country is found in rural settings inhabited chiefly by the poor—and, again, principally the black poor. Large-city neighborhoods are normally crowded. The cost per square foot of living space is frequently higher than in the suburbs, but blacks, in particular, have little choice over where they will live, as the nation's sharply segregated city ghettos attest.

These conditions might suggest at least some degree of class consciousness among people at the lower strata of the social pyramid. We shall explore this issue in some depth in Chapter 14, in part because the actions of the U.S. government during the Reagan administration seemed to be provoking greater than usual class-based reactions among Americans. The basic fact about the political effects of the American social pyramid is that the class consciousness generated has been relatively modest throughout at least the recent decades. Indeed, although the situation may be changing, Americans seem to be distinguished among industrial countries of the world by the relatively low levels of social class consciousness existing among the lower strata of the population. Why this is so is worth some speculation.

SYMBOLIC POLITICS AND THE PERSISTENCE OF CLASS INEQUALITY

Clearly, the quality of people's lives and their satisfaction with their jobs and with themselves differs sharply with their income level and the status and autonomy they enjoy in their occupations. In our society, people are socialized to attribute such differences in status and "success" to personal merit or personal failings; that view denies that class is a significant issue and implies that both the rich and the poor get pretty much what they deserve. Nonelites who are "class conscious" hold a very different value judgment. They know that "the rich get richer and the poor get poorer." Furthermore, systematic differences in opportunities and obstacles account for the difference. In some degree and in some situations, everyone is likely to accept both of these views. Evidence shows, however, that the prosperous are more inclined to focus on personal qualities as the explanation for success or failure and that the poor, especially the black poor, are much more likely to attribute their low status to systemic economic and social conditions.

It is a striking fact about American society that both disadvantaged groups and privileged groups are willing to accept large inequalities in wealth, income, status, and other basic values. Toleration of persisting inequality and class divisions is all the more impressive in view of the strong emphasis upon the United States as the land of opportunity in which "All men are created equal." Objectively, classes exist and persist; subjectively, many Americans fail to notice them, fail to define their own lives in terms of class, and fail to act politically so as to narrow or end class inequalities. The modern state allocates benefits and burdens unequally, while at the same time inducing people to celebrate the results. How does it do so?

A major part of the answer lies in the power of the government to create an impression of progress toward equality and of governmental sensitivity to the problems of the people. Although fewer people believe that illusion today, the myth that our policies are progressive remains. The policies that are often in the news, and always controversial, are largely those that promise to decrease inequalities, such as civil rights laws, welfare policies, affirmative action, and regulation of monopolies, public utilities, and other powerful business groups. It is precisely these public policies that typically have little or no effect; they normally amount to the use of law as symbolism, tokenism, reassurance, or threat. Governmental action influences mass beliefs and perceptions substantially, but it changes conditions, solves problems, and meets the needs of nonelites only marginally or not at all.

The government encourages us to blame ourselves for misfortune by proclaiming that the interests of the poor, or even working or middle class are protected, and that the state is ensuring the fair operation of the system. It also allows the elite to attribute their good fortune to personal merit and effort. The tendency to see failure and success in terms of individual choice also deters recognition of how the social structure and established inequalities perpetuate themselves.

Study of long-term trends in American wealth distribution reveals substantial inequality since the seventeenth century. It does not show a long-term trend toward greater equality. The colonial era was followed by more than a century of steeply increasing concentration of wealth. By the early twentieth century, wealth concentration in the United States was as great as in France or Prussia. Equality did make significant headway during some periods, such as World War I and between the late 1920s and mid-century. However, since about 1950 there has been no significant change either in wealth or income inequality, even though this thirty-year period includes the years of the War on Poverty and an increase in a great many welfare and social programs.

Some individuals do dramatically improve their class position, of course. Others suffer declines in status and well-being, but such shifts are typically the result of individual good luck or bad luck, illegal or opportunistic actions, or extraordinary talents (acting, or sports) of a kind that brings high monetary rewards. They do not change economic inequality for the population as a whole. Virtually the entire American population enjoys some material and cultural benefits that were unknown in the colonial period or even seventy-five years ago. To some extent, such progress comes from technology and increased productivity and information, but it has not reduced the *gap* in the quality of life between elites and nonelites. In some ways, the gap has increased and shows signs of growing wider.

It is in ambiguous situations that evoke strong fears or hopes that symbolism becomes a powerful influence on what people believe and what they think is happening. To upper middle-class whites, the enactment of civil rights laws is an encouraging signal that the lot of the ghetto black is improving. Their evidence is news stories about the legislative outcome, and not experience of life in the ghetto. For some lower-middle-class whites, the same news stories create a belief that blacks are progressing too quickly and are threatening their jobs; for blacks in the ghetto, it is practically irrelevant.

When hopes or fears are strong and political events cannot be observed directly, governmental acts become especially powerful symbols. Every political belief involves some mix of direct observation and symbolic cuing, although in greatly varying proportions. The hungry food rioter is close to the realistic end of the realism-symbolism scale. Close to the other end of the scale is the German in the 1930s who followed and obeyed Hitler because he believed Hitler's claim that the Nazis would create a glorious empire that would last a thousand years with prosperity for all good Germans.

For most Americans most of the time, the belief that people are rewarded or deprived because of their class position rather than because of personal merit is held intermittently—and when recognized, is blurred. Political symbolism is a major contributor to the blurring. Is responsibility for class status an individual decision, or is it the result of a social structure in which opportunities and advantages are very unequal? That is the critical question. There is no denying the objective fact of a stratified, class based social context; however, its meaning and impact, personally and politically, are more difficult to pin down.

SUMMARY AND PREVIEW

The distribution of wealth, status, and influence in America is highly unequal and has been so for 250 years. Although individuals sometimes rise dramatically in socioeconomic status and others fall, the chances are overwhelming that any person born into the working class or into affluence will stay pretty much at the same level. In short, classes do exist and maintain themselves, and political influence is determined largely by class structure.

But the consciousness of class is blurred in the United States, although less so in the upper class than in the lower classes. Nonelites do not typically think of themselves as a class and do not often try to use political power to further class interests and needs. One reason for the acceptance of inequality is that governmental actions and language reassure people that their needs are being cared for. Progress, we are assured, is being made in removing discriminatory practices. Class consciousness is also blurred by an ideology of individualism that attributes success or deprivations to individual merit or inadequacies rather than to the systematic functioning of economic and social institutions. It creates the belief that both elites and nonelites deserve their lot in life. A rising standard of living for many has also helped dim class differences as a political issue.

Yet for nonelites, working life and home life are often difficult. Discriminatory practices are less acceptable. The hardships and manipulation are increasingly resented. It remains to be seen whether the economic problems of the 1980s will create more awareness among nonelites of common needs and deprivations that are not the fault of individuals. We have suggested that such an awareness may be developing, but it remains to be seen whether such awareness will then lead to a call for common political action.

CHAPTER 5

Political Economy III: Managing the Political Agenda

We have now covered the economic and social contexts within which American politics is embedded. Another vital part of the total context of American government, however, is the way that issues and problems are understood and the way that basic values and beliefs have been drawn upon to shape the agenda for action. Before the specifically political institutions can even consider action, some very important things have happened. A *context of understanding* has somehow arisen in which shared values and assumptions lead to a generally accepted framework for interpreting new events. Some things are taken for granted; memories, fears, and expectations are aroused; and an agreed-upon definition of the situation seems to take shape. Together, these constitute a coherent perspective through which people see and interpret the rising issue or problem. The specific nature and values of that coherent fundamental perspective are covered in the next chapter.

Out of that perspective, a *political agenda* specific to the historical period has been shaped and developed. "New" issues come to the fore, replacing some and changing the priorities of others. Policy solutions that have somehow emerged appear to be the "sensible" way of coping with the most pressing problems. Such policies recommend themselves, in part because they "fit" with today's structures and values, and in part because no other alternatives emerge that seem to so fully respond to the defined problems.

Our first task, therefore, is to try to see how this context of understanding and political agenda has arisen. In particular, we want to know to what extent those who hold power or are advantaged by public policies may have taken part in bringing about the understanding and agenda that created such results. This question boils down to one that has challenged and seriously divided social scientists: Do great wealth and high status translate in some direct way into political power in the United States? If so, how?

THE ROLE OF WEALTH AND STATUS
IN POLITICAL POWER

For those who are ideologically insistent upon seeing the United States as a democracy in which power is equalized, wealth and status do *not* translate directly into political power. Others stand on apparently "objective" grounds, arguing that the role of wealth and status in shaping the public policy product of government has never been empirically demonstrated. What they usually insist upon is proof of a direct relationship between holders of wealth and status and decisionmakers who follow their dictates. Such evidence is, of course, very difficult to find.

We think that the problem is both interesting and complicated, and yet capable of being resolved. This view is supported by two exhaustive studies; undertaken with sharply contrasting ideological perspectives and methods, they nevertheless arrive at nearly identical conclusions. Both G. William Domhoff, a radical sociologist, and Thomas R. Dye, a conservative political scientist, studied the highest strata of American society and how (or *if*) they controlled the government. (We drew upon Dye's work in Chapter 1, when we described the social and economic backgrounds of U.S. leaders.) Both found powerful evidence that they *do*, but not directly in the sense of issuing daily conference call instructions to decisionmakers. Instead, both found systematic shaping of general public understanding and construction of the immediate political agenda as the principal means of managing the government's actions. This combines with powerful influence over decisionmakers, many of whom are members or eager supporters of the same small circle of powerholders. We will first compare these key studies and then examine how both understanding and agenda are actually shaped.

Domhoff is the author of several books analyzing aspects of upper-class life in the United States.[1] His work *The Powers That Be: Processes of Ruling Class Domination in America* summarizes much of his earlier research and applies it squarely to the question we have posed.[2] His method is a combination of social and economic background analysis (wealth, family origins, places of education, types of occupation, intermarriages, etc.) and

---

[1] G. William Domhoff, *Who Rules America?* (Englewood Cliffs, N.J.: Prentice-Hall, 1967). See also *The Bohemian Grove and Other Retreats* (New York: Harper & Row, 1974); *Fat Cats and Democrats* (Englewood Cliffs, N.J.: Prentice-Hall, 1972); and *Who Really Rules?* (San Francisco: Goodyear, 1978).

[2] G. William Domhoff, *The Powers That Be: Processes of Ruling Class Domination in America* (New York: Random House/Vintage Books, 1978).

in-depth biographies and case studies. His premises and conclusions are that a governing class[3] can be identified in this way and that it can be shown to control the government. He concludes that the dominance of such a class is profoundly undemocratic and undesirable.

Domhoff begins by focusing on that 0.5 percent of Americans who hold great wealth, who together control about 25 percent of all the wealth in the country. He shows that these people have continuing school, business, and social relationships, and that they therefore constitute a cohesive class with a high degree of class consciousness (awareness of their values and interests and how distinct they are from the rest of the population). He then identifies "four general processes through which economically and politically active members of the ruling class, working with the aid of highly trained and carefully selected employees, are able to dominate the United States at all levels."[4] These processes are:

1. The special-interest process (the way that individuals and corporations serve their short-term needs).
2. The policy-formulation process (the way that basic policy directions are set in the interest of the ruling class).
3. The candidate-selection process (how the ruling class ensures that the right politicians get elected).
4. The ideology process (the way that the general context of public understanding is shaped, so that ruling-class interests are served).

Domhoff then presents extensive evidence to show how the politically-active arm of the ruling class (the "power elite") operates in each of these processes to see that ruling class interests are served.

Thomas Dye is the author of several books that analyze public policy in the United States and how it came to be that way. He has examined policies produced in the states and in the national government in a variety of ways. His major work, for our purposes, is *Who's Running America? The Reagan Years.*[5] As we saw in Chapter 1, his book focuses on the characteristics and relationships of the elites occupying the key positions of institutional leadership in the United States. His premises and conclusions are that elites are inevitable in any society and that these people *do* constitute a dominant elite controlling the government. On the whole, however, they are a socially responsible group whom the majority of people might well be glad to have managing the country.

Dye starts with recognition of the concentration of economic power in the United States. The presidents and directors of the one hundred largest corporations (0.0002 percent of the population) control approximately

[3] See G. William Domhoff, *The Higher Circles: The Governing Class in America* (New York: Random House/Vintage Books, 1970).

[4] Domhoff, *The Powers That Be*, p. 10.

[5] Thomas R. Dye, *Who's Running America? The Reagan Years*, 3rd ed. (Englewood Cliffs, N.J.: Prentice-Hall, Inc., 1976, 1979, 1983).

one-half of all United States assets. He argues that this control, because of institutional position, is more significant than the holding of great personal wealth. Analysis will yield sounder results throughout if it remains fixed on the levers of institutional control. For our purposes, his most interesting findings are:

1. Most people in these positions come from upper-class or upper middle-class families;
2. Many of them have also held several top positions in their own or other fields; and
3. Major public policy directions are set by elites operating through identifiable "policy-planning groups."

Of special interest to us is the fact that these two leading scholars, with very different political perspectives and methods, identify essentially the same process of elite shaping of the political agenda. Indeed, they both use the same term—"policy-planning groups"—and specify the same organizations as the planners and managers of policy proposals and decisions. Domhoff names the Council on Foreign Relations, the Committee for Economic Development, the Conference Board, and the Business Council as his "Big Four," aided by think tanks such as the Brookings Institution. Dye names the Council on Foreign Relations, the Council on Economic Development, and the Brookings Institution, concurring in the important role of other think tanks also listed by Domhoff. In his updated version, Dye adds the Trilateral Commission and the Business Roundtable. Both authors employ the summary diagram, reproduced here as Figure 5.1, to illustrate the total process of elite consensus-shaping around its preferred policies.[6] We will return to this figure at the close of the chapter.

In the following sections we will draw on these different but concurring sources and other materials to sketch the way in which the context and the agenda for decisionmaking are shaped. Readers should keep in mind that we have not yet begun to analyze government institutions or processes within them. We are still looking at the context; here we are looking at the processes that are *prior to* and perhaps *determinative of* what goes on within the political arena.

SHAPING THE CONTEXT OF PUBLIC UNDERSTANDING

By "context of understanding" we mean:

1. The orthodox American political values and ideology (see Chapter 6) plus the specific beliefs supplementing them.

---

[6] Originally developed by Domhoff, it was modified by Dye, p. 212. Domhoff acknowledges use of Dye's modified diagram, *The Powers That Be*, p. 126.

Figure 5.1. *The Policy Process: The View from the Top*

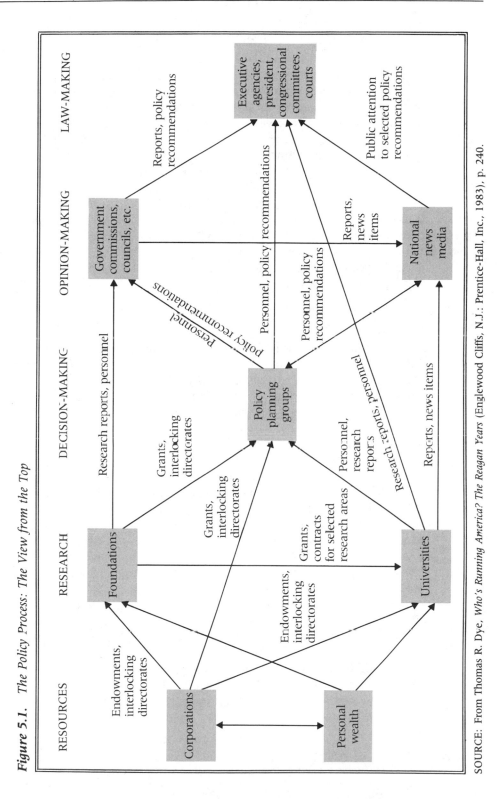

SOURCE: From Thomas R. Dye, *Who's Running America? The Reagan Years* (Englewood Cliffs, N.J.: Prentice-Hall, Inc., 1983), p. 240.

2. The assumptions, perceptions, and expectations about a particular subject area or problem.

If the problem developing, for example, is that of staffing an expanding military presence at minimal costs, the created context of understanding will include a growing threat from perceived enemies and the unworkability and excessive cost of a volunteer army. The particular context of understanding operates to make some actions or policies seem natural or necessary at a particular time, such as the deregulation of oil and gas to encourage exploration. Some alternatives become "far out," or literally unthinkable, such as nationalizing the oil industry.

The context of understanding is shaped by such social institutions as colleges and universities, the foundations, the media (a subcategory of which is the advertising industry), and groups such as higher professionals (doctors, scientists, engineers, and particularly lawyers), and visible intellectuals. We shall touch on what each does and how each is influenced by the highest elite strata.

Social Institutions

Universities. The roughly 2,500 public and private institutions of higher education in the United States range from junior colleges to universities with 50,000 students and several graduate and professional schools. They now enroll nearly 11 million students. These institutions are governed by trustees who are drawn chiefly from the upper classes. They are also linked closely to federal and state governments and perform several vital political functions.

Dye focuses on the trustees of the universities with the largest endowments. He identifies twenty-five institutions, which "together control two-thirds of all private endowment funds."[7] Of these, only *three* are public universities. These prestigious universities are where most of the nation's future leaders receive their education. They also serve as models for the kind of education that will be provided elsewhere in the higher education system. Not surprisingly, the trustees of these institutions include many of the topmost leaders in business and government and, in general, these trustees hold several key positions at the same time.

A more wide-ranging study of trustees and regents of all colleges and universities was conducted in 1967 by the Educational Testing Service.[8] Although not repeated since, the same patterns appear to be holding firm. The researchers compared the trustees of the "selective" (meaning selective in admissions, such as the Ivy League and similar schools) private institutions with those of all U.S. colleges and universities. They found that nearly two-thirds of all college and university trustees in the nation were in

---

[7] Dye, p. 157. For the discussion generally, see pp. 157–160.

[8] Rodney T. Hartnett, *College and University Trustees: Their Backgrounds, Roles, and Educational Attitudes* (Princeton, N.J.: Educational Testing Service, 1969).

the top 1 percent in income level. In the case of the selective private universities, 43 percent earned more than $100,000 per year (roughly equal to $250,000 per year in 1983). Forty-six percent of the trustees overlapped with boards of directors of major corporations, and 18 percent served on three or more such corporate boards. In general, the selective private universities tend to have the wealthiest, highest-status trustees, perhaps partly because board positions are filled chiefly by the boards themselves on a kind of self-perpetuating basis. But state universities are not far behind; in a study focused chiefly on the California system, appointed regents were found to average three major corporate board directorates.

The financing of most institutions of higher education is a major link to the more formal governing structures of both federal and state governments. Public institutions, of course, receive most of their financial support from state (or, in some cases, local) governments. They characteristically charge relatively lower tuitions, with the deficit being made up from public tax revenues. (A provocative and carefully detailed analysis of the sources of revenue and actual recipients points out that overall, this process amounts to working-class financing of low-cost educations for middle-class youth.[9]) The dependence of these institutions on state governments makes them vulnerable to pressures from individual state legislators and the interests dominant in the state in general. There is a strong desire to be "useful," as defined by key businesses and industries and, conversely, to avoid the taint of unorthodox political ideas or behavior that is antagonistic to established powers in the state. Despite these pressures, of course, tension between the better state universities and colleges and their legislatures is frequently high.

Both public and private universities also rely heavily on financial assistance in various forms from the federal government. Prestigious universities receive between 40 percent and 60 percent of their annual budgets from the federal government. Federal assistance takes many forms: loans and grants to students, financing for buildings and equipment, performance of research and teaching functions (ROTC for example) on the campus, and provision of contract services. In the latter case, the university in effect acts as a direct arm of the U.S. government, whether in experimental programs of crime control, poverty amelioration, or in the training of bureaucrats for developing countries.

These funds are valued by universities in every case. A major university must place and keep itself in a position to compete successfully for such grants if it is to retain its status. Not only does the capacity to hire and provide research opportunities for well-reputed faculty depend on funds of this type, but a substantial share of the operating budget of the university is contributed in this way. Some university administrators see this process as

---

[9] Lee Hansen and Burton A. Weisbrod, *Benefits, Costs and Finance of Public Higher Education* (Chicago: Markhan, 1969).

a welcome opportunity to be of service to the society; others are less enthusiastic, and see it as an infringement of academic freedom and detachment. None deny the reality of the pressure.

Three basic purposes of both public and private universities may be identified, although the rankings in terms of priority may be disputed:

1. *To provide social mobility for students and well-trained members within the economy and the society.* These goals are complementary. Students and their parents visualize a college education as a ticket to a good job; the economy and society require alert, aspiring, and adaptable people to perform a multitude of tasks. The result is a vocationally oriented program of instruction whose chief criterion of success is the student's acquisition of a job that offers prospects of income and status. To prepare students for such jobs, the current structure of the economic and social order must be taken as a given, its needs assessed and extended into the future, and students shown how to adapt to and fulfill those needs.

2. *To provide knowledge that will help solve problems facing the society.* To be of assistance, the identification and definitions of such problems must be similar to those of the relevant policymakers. Otherwise, the results of the research will not be used and this purpose will not be served. Much research effort is devoted to finding ways for those who are currently dominant to carry out their policies. In the case of problems perceived by private industry, university efforts often amount to socializing the cost of research and development while benefits accrue chiefly to the user industries.

3. *To transmit the culture and wisdom of the past, adapt it to the needs of the present and the future, and help students develop the capacity to think critically and independently about themselves, their society, and the world.* This intellectual purpose of the university is the most difficult, least accepted, and least accomplished of the university's purposes. To think critically and evaluatively about oneself and one's surroundings requires great effort, self-discipline, and the destruction of a lifetime's complacent assumptions. It is extremely difficult to connect this process to a vocational orientation and explain its worth in "practical" or "dollars and sense" terms. It often provokes sharp reaction from an insecure but financially vital outside world. Lacking all the normal bases of support, it does not often occur, and if it does, it is difficult to sustain.

The faculty must operate within the context defined by these various factors. Let us assume that people who teach seek advancement and security as much as others do in the society. To be well regarded in one's own institution and profession, to get the funds for and do the research that makes for visibility and mobility, and to avoid the controversies that spell an end to advancement, faculty members must accept the basic standards that trustees, financial sources, and accepted university purposes have set for them. This established role is not uncongenial to many of them, because their class origins, identification with a prestigious profession, need for access to people with money and power, and current positions of authority lead them to be perfectly comfortable with the university's requirements. There are, of course, "rebels" who insist on dealing with the third purpose, who point out the status quo implications and support of much of the university's business. They serve an important function—to maintain the idea of the university as an independent and free environment; within the profession and the community, however, they remain just that—isolated "rebels."

What is the impact of these various forces on the students? In general, survey evidence suggests that the more highly "educated" one is, the more likely one is to trust and support the acts of government. College graduates are better informed, take part in politics more, and are more fully imbued with orthodox ideology than are those of comparable age and life experience who do not attend college. Universities serve (and often create) elites by shaping vocational orientations and skills and by instilling the political ideology and broad behavioral cues that will lead to later support.

Foundations. Foundations are tax-exempt organizations that use the income from their invested assets to sponsor research or promote programs in fields of their choice. They are established by wealthy people or corporations that provide the original assets, prescribe the purposes, and establish a governing body that then takes charge. The largest foundations are listed in *The Foundation Directory*. The *very* largest foundations are, of course, the most engaged in deliberate efforts to shape public understanding and public policy. In 1980, 3,138 foundations had either $1,000,000 in assets or $100,000 in annual distributions. The top fifty foundations from which Dye's leaders were drawn controlled more than 40 percent of all foundation assets, or about $13 billion.[10] Most of these were originally established by powerful and wealthy families (Carnegie, Danforth, Ford, Kellogg, Lilly, Mellon, Rockefeller, and so on), and they often still have family members on their boards of directors. These largest foundations' boards of directors are drawn almost exclusively from the highest ranks of the society.

Three of the largest foundations that direct their efforts at shaping national policy in several areas are the Carnegie, Ford, and Rockefeller foundations. Each is governed by a board made up of well-known national leaders, who carefully select the purposes for which the foundation will sponsor research or develop programs. By looking five or more years ahead, giving researchers the necessary cues about foundation goals, and then investing millions of dollars in research, publication, and dissemination of results, such foundations can profoundly shape what is known and what seem to be the alternatives as problems rise to public awareness.

In the eyes of many conservatives, the great foundations define problems and propose solutions from a consistently liberal, internationalist perspective. Accordingly, in the 1970s conservatives sought to develop foundations and "think tanks" of their own to compete for media and public attention. Although they could not equal the bigger foundations in resources, several could and did spend lavishly, establishing solid research and publication reputations. Not to be outdone, the left soon developed still smaller versions of these organizations to try to get their point of view into public debate. For many of these foundations, tax-exempt status as

---

[10] Dye, *Who's Running America?* p. 143.

educational or charitable bodies was essential to their economic survival. Both left and right were on occasion convinced, however, that their tax status was being challenged by the Internal Revenue Service for politically motivated reasons. We shall explore the agenda-shaping activities of many of these foundations and think tanks later in this chapter.

The Media. Much has been written about the impact of mass media, particularly television, on the shaping of public understanding in the United States. Because television emphasizes what is dramatic and because it is far and away the leading source of information for most Americans, it is capable of massive impact in a very short time. With one or two poignant pictures, and three or four descriptive adjectives, television can set the terms within which an issue is to be understood. For the fewer people who read newspapers and/or news magazines, the cues to interpretation are subtler, but no less effective. The media communicate much more than a particular understanding of events; a good part of their impact comes in the form of the values stressed, explicitly and implicitly, by the commercials or advertising that accompany "objective" information. Comedies or dramatic shows on television or the comics in the newspapers often contain not-so-hidden cultural values and political messages.

There is no area of American life in which control over such potential power is so tightly concentrated in a few hands.[11] Only three television networks send news out to nearly all the major television stations in the country. Only two wire services send their version of the news out to thousands of radio stations and newspapers. Four or five "independent" newspapers (and nine chains of newspapers) and their associated news services account for most of what news presentation remains. None of these is subject to government regulation. Only the potential withdrawal of advertising by the businesses that buy time or space operates as a constraint on media policies or interpretations of the news.

Every one of these enterprises is among the largest and most profitable American corporations. Some of them own several different components of the media system. The Washington Post Company, for example, owns not only the newspaper of the same name, but also a radio station, a television station, a news magazine, and a news service. CBS owns, at last count, five television stations, fourteen radio stations, twenty-two magazines, and Columbia Records. The presidents and members of the boards of directors are, of course, drawn from high social origins and have the same backgrounds and relationships with other elites as do other top leadership people.

Professional Groups

Because it is less explicit and less visible than many other activities, the political role of professionals is often ignored or vastly underestimated in analyses of American politics. The status that holding the credentials of

---

[11] Ibid., pp. 120–124.

doctor, scientist, engineer, or lawyer carries with it, however, means that such persons have special credibility, particularly in areas of their expertise. In a society that reveres science, technology, and practical capabilities, professionals with those credentials actually define what is (objectively) scientific, technologically possible, and practical. They prescribe what is "normal," "healthy," "safe," or what is "deviant," "insane," or "impractical." All these terms are value judgments with vast significance for millions of people. This credibility is increased when the profession appears to be united and speaking with one voice, as when, for example, the official governing bodies of the American Medical Association or the American Bar Association take stands on issues. Conversely, it explains the controversial nature and difficulty of acquiring legitimacy that some groups such as Physicians for Social Responsibility, a group of medical doctors fighting nuclear power, have.

Formal action may be quite unnecessary if there appears to be general professional approval for a principle or program. A dramatic example of the latter was the widespread popularity and implementation of the "scientific management" doctrine developed by Frederick W. Taylor, an engineer, in the early decades of the twentieth century.[12] Taylor combined the cultural fascination with science and progress with some very practical measures to control workers and reduce wages; these actions were greatly appreciated by the business community.

Scientific management is a way to reorganize work by eliminating the most skilled workers, breaking down operations into components that can be done by less skilled (and less expensive) personnel, maximizing the speed at which work can be done, and introducing production control into every stage in the process. It is *not* necessarily more efficient, but it has preempted the field and is *presumed* to be the very definition of "efficiency." It often makes the production process cost less for a time, and it certainly makes management of the work force much easier.

Because this form of management is labeled "scientific," it does not appear to be controversial or political, and yet it serves quite well the needs of big corporations or firms to control workers. It is still having an effect; a recent example is its influence in the secretarial and clerical world. The introduction of computerized data and word processing is rapidly breaking down the work into countable, component parts that require only "entry" on the part of the human being. All "creative" work is done by the machine, with the exception of a few highly-paid professionals who program the machines and monitor the keyboard operators. The cultural understanding of "efficiency" is still bound up with the ideas and ideology of scientific management.

This example also suggests some subtler aspects of the political role of

---

[12] For a full description of the nature and effects of scientific management in the United States and in other countries, including the Soviet Union, see Judith Merkle, *Management and Ideology* (Berkeley: University of California Press, 1980).

professionals. The skills or knowledge that make up the expertise of a professional must be skills or knowledge that are useful *to somebody* or *for some purpose*. Both the need for such services and the money to pay for them (mainly from anticipated profits) are found chiefly in the upper reaches of the economy, and the ties between the two are many. Those professionals that are not already linked to the money and status system may be trying by means of actions and rhetoric to connect themselves. Moreover, professional credentials are usually acquired from skilled predecessors or graduate level training programs. In both cases, the new generation of professionals learns skills and ways of thinking that *fit* with the social and economic status quo and that are *useful*—not at all times, places, and circumstances, but here and now—in the values and circumstances of American capitalist society.

Part of being a professional involves asserting the right to control the admission of others to that profession. This control was originally asserted to assure the public of a person's qualifications, but now it often also limits the number of persons who will enjoy the economic opportunities that are available. Sometimes it is the state that officially licenses newcomers, but the judgments in each case are made by professionals. Most professions have an association to which almost all belong in order to manage the instruction and credentialing of newcomers, to advance the profession's image and interests, to speak for the profession as a whole, and sometimes to establish and enforce ethical standards within the profession. The association has a governing body constituted in a more or less representative way. The professionals who have the time and inclination to serve on such bodies tend to be the elite of the elite; they tend to be the wealthier and better connected in a group that is already distinguished by greater education, wealth, and status than the rest of the population. Moreover, this governing body tends to cultivate connections of the same sort as its members enjoy—with the larger and more powerful corporations and banks and the top leadership positions in all areas. Deviants *within* the profession are censured or otherwise constrained so that the status quo supporting role of the profession as a whole is maintained.

Perhaps the most obviously significant profession for politics is the law. More than half of all top government positions and many corporate presidencies and directorships are filled by lawyers. But this is only the beginning; the most prestigious Wall Street and Washington law firms are daily participants in making public policy, serving their large corporate clients, and governing the legal profession through the American Bar Association. Dye identifies twenty top firms in New York City and seven in Washington at the apex of the profession.[13] "The typical path to the top of the legal profession starts with a Harvard or Yale Law School degree, clerkship with a Supreme Court Justice, and then several years as an attorney with the Justice Department or a federal regulatory commission."[14] "Superlaw-

---

[13] See Table 5–1, Dye, *Who's Running America?* p. 137.

[14] Dye, *Who's Running America?* p. 140.

yers''[15] are in and out of governmental positions, serving for a time before returning to "private" practice.

The governing body of the American Bar Association is its House of Delegates. Below it are committees that study problems or proposed legislation and make recommendations. The ABA also asserts the right to screen and make recommendations on all federal judicial appointments. Two recent scholarly studies deserve notice for their persuasive characterizations of the ABA. One study shows that the ABA role is closely supportive of other elites' interests, particularly those of the largest corporations and banks. With or without specific authorization by the membership, ABA officials regularly lobby in the name of the profession for the interests of their client businesses before Congress and federal agencies.[16] The other study shows that, throughout its history, the ABA has systematically sought to prevent the admission of immigrants, minorities, and women to the bar and to inhibit their legal practices, should they be admitted. This was done through changing standards for legal education, managing ethical criteria, and exercising various social exclusions and pressures. At the same time, the ABA was acting on behalf of railroad and banking interests and justifying the various legal steps that were being taken to crush the World War I antiwar movement.[17]

Intellectuals

The political role of intellectuals is similar to, but of course less formally organized than that of the professionals. Intellectuals who wish to be heard by more than academic colleagues usually write articles for relatively small circulation (but highly influential) magazines, or books for somewhat larger audiences. Some are critical of established institutions and practices, and often employ a moderate tone of reform. Not many can sustain themselves for long if they are too critical, for they depend for support on that small slice of the population that is both receptive to such ideas *and* has the money to keep buying books and subscribing to journals. *Most* intellectuals are drawn to thinking and writing in ways that draw approval, support, and money from those who have such things to bestow; by and large, these people are either other intellectuals who have "made it" or powerful business, social, and political leaders.

An interesting fusion of the professional and intellectual functions in maintaining a context of understanding that supports the status quo may be found in the multilevel teaching of economics. Domhoff reports on the activities of the Joint Council on Economic Education, which was started

---

[15] Coined by Joseph C. Goulden, *The Superlawyers* (New York: Dell Publishing Co., 1971). Used by Dye, pp. 135–142.

[16] Albert P. Melone, *Lawyers, Public Policy and Interest Group Politics* (Washington, D.C.: University Press of America, 1979).

[17] Jerold S. Auerbach, *Unequal Justice: Lawyers and Social Change in Modern America* (New York: Oxford University Press, 1976), particularly Chapters 2 and 4.

in 1949 by the Committee for Economic Development. Initially supported by the Committee for Economic Development and the Ford Foundation, the council eventually acquired enough corporate support to publish books and pamphlets, introduce elementary and secondary school courses, provide adult workshops, and shape college teacher training. Related councils were formed in all but three states to press these causes on all fronts.[18]

As in the case of foundations, some intellectuals recently have been funded to counter the "liberal" version of the economic profession. Underwritten by the Business Roundtable and the American Enterprise Institute, "conservative" or "laissez faire" intellectuals have taken a leaf from the old elite's book and mounted a counterattack. Contributing to their own recently begun journals and writing books for more widespread readership, these intellectuals support and justify the economic policies of the "free market" capitalists; they also offer to teach the teachers and provide pamphlets and seminars to instruct beginners.[19]

Another form of the same activity may be seen in the frequently repeated two-week seminars for federal court judges at the corporate-financed Law and Economics Center of the University of Miami Law School. Here free-market economists from the University of Chicago, University of California at Los Angeles, and Harvard educate federal judges on the world as they understand it.[20]

THE PROCESS OF FORMING PUBLIC POLICY

All the activity discussed so far is directed at creating and maintaining a context of public understanding that is favorable to elite interests and priorities. We come now to the process by which the same interests and priorities are translated into public policies to meet specific problems. We shall look at the activities of four policy planning groups named by both Domhoff and Dye as major instruments in this process. These are not the only four; they have recently been challenged in the agenda and public policy—shaping process by groups representing conflicting elite interests. We will discuss these new counterparts in our analysis of the longstanding dominant groups.

It is worth noting immediately that we are not examining some new or previously hidden phenomenon. In an important study of the first two decades of the twentieth century, historian James Weinstein explored the

---

[18] Domhoff, *The Powers That Be*, pp. 179–183.

[19] For example, from The Heritage Foundation, see *Policy Review; Agenda for the 1980s*. From the American Enterprise Institute, see *Public Opinion; Regulation*.

[20] David Dickson and David Noble, "By Force of Reason: The Politics of Science and Technology Policy," in Thomas Ferguson and Joel Rogers, *The Hidden Election: Politics and Economics in the 1980 Presidential Campaign* (New York: Random House/Pantheon, 1981), p. 270.

makeup and activities of the National Civic Federation (NCF), the precursor and model for today's policy-planning groups.[21] The NCF was formed by big business so that different sectors could understand one another's needs, devise solutions that all could accept, and coordinate their strategy to have public policies enacted and implemented. The American Federation of Labor was represented as a means of muting labor opposition, and several prestigious lawyers, academics, politicians, and social notables were also included. But the basic membership included the presidents and directors of the largest corporations and banks. In an era noteworthy for its violent confrontations, the National Civic Federation was eminently successful in appearing to acknowledge and meet the underlying problems caused by an industrializing country. Every major statute of that "reform" period was drafted or approved and ultimately supported by the NCF.

The four policy-planning groups on which we focus are not the only participants in this process. Domhoff includes the Conference Board and the Business Council in his "Big Four" and stresses the effective lobbying role of the Business Roundtable. Both Domhoff and Dye concur on the predominance of the four groups discussed here and other studies support their judgments. We take, therefore, the Council on Foreign Relations (CFR), the Committee for Economic Development (CED), the Brookings Institution, and the recently created Trilateral Commission as examples that are characteristic of the larger process we seek to analyze.

The Council on Foreign Relations.[22] The CFR was founded shortly after World War I by a group of wealthy New York lawyers, bankers, and academics. It was funded initially by personal contributions and later by grants from the Rockefeller, Carnegie, and Ford foundations. Its journal, *Foreign Affairs*, was established in 1922 and soon became the authoritative voice of American opinion on international relations. The CFR is made up of about 1,500 bankers, lawyers, and corporate executives, plus several journalists and subject-area experts from the government and universities. Half of the members are from the New York–Washington area, and half from the rest of the country. It is entirely accurate to say that no major figure in the shaping of American foreign policy over the last half century has *not* been a CFR member; normally these people were members long before they actually engaged in making foreign policy. Henry Kissinger, for example, got his start by performing well on assignments given by the CFR and is reported to have told one of its leaders, "You invented me."[23]

---

[21] James Weinstein, *The Corporate Ideal in the Liberal State, 1900–1918* (Boston: Beacon Press, 1968).

[22] The indispensable resource for the origins, activities, and impact of the Council on Foreign Relations is the meticulously researched volume by Lawrence Shoup and William Minter, *Imperial Brain Trust: The Council on Foreign Relations and United States Foreign Policy* (New York: Monthly Review Press, 1977), from which all data in these paragraphs are drawn, unless otherwise noted.

[23] Ibid., p. 5, citing *Newsweek*, 2 October 1972, p. 40.

The purpose of the Council on Foreign Relations is to bring together the leading people of American finance and industry to discuss world problems and alternative foreign policies; they then attempt to reach a consensus that can be communicated to the government. Studies are commissioned with the aid of foundation support, and their analyses are discussed in small sessions with government and military leaders. Recommendations are then made the basis of discussion for larger sessions until a final consensus is reached. This process takes place entirely off the public record and members do not discuss the sessions. From time to time, books that embody CFR conclusions are published, but more often, CFR decisions are implemented directly as government policy. The Council has been notably successful in this regard. It is generally credited with designing:

1. Every major part of the peace settlement after World War II, including the monetary plan that placed the U.S. dollar in a commanding position.
2. The Marshall Plan for the reconstruction of Europe.
3. The containment policy with respect to the Soviet Union.
4. The subnuclear force strategies that led to the Vietnam War.

As the Vietnam War escalated, President Johnson appointed a fourteen-member Senior Advisory Group to advise him with respect to American strategy; twelve of those fourteen were CFR members. When five of them withdrew their support for the war in March, 1968, Johnson announced his decisions to de-escalate the war and to retire from the presidency.

The Committee for Economic Development.[24] Although the CED is a somewhat less decisive force in domestic policymaking than the CFR is in foreign affairs, it is nonetheless the single most important policy-planning group in domestic affairs. Created in 1942 by executives of the larger corporations, it had two primary purposes: to prevent recurrence of the depression once World War II ended, and to give voice to an enlightened capitalist perspective so that reactionary small business on the right and liberals and socialists on the left would not preempt the field. Many of the initial 200 executives were drawn from the Business Council, which was originally linked to the Department of Commerce. Although it has expanded considerably, it has gone outside of the business world only in the case of some university presidents and economists. Many of its members, however, are also members of the CFR.

The CED operates in much the same way as the CFR, with foundation-financed study groups presenting recommendations on a wide range of problems. Its primary interests, however, lie with policies bearing on gen-

---

[24] There is no source on the Committee for Economic Development equivalent to Shoup and Minter on the Council on Foreign Relations. This account draws on Dye, pp. 244–247; Domhoff, *The Powers That Be*, pp. 67–69 and 109–116; and analysis of Committee for Economic Development reports.

eral levels of profitability, such as fiscal and monetary issues, inflation, unemployment, and trade. CED decisions are issued regularly as pamphlets. Its success in shaping policy has been only slightly less than that of the CFR. The Employment Act of 1946, which created the Council of Economic Advisers, was in effect the CED's reconstruction of an earlier bill that was designed to put the federal government much more decisively into the business of managing the economy. In the 1970s, the Carter energy program closely resembled CED recommendations, as did trade and welfare reform proposals.

The CED has also been successful in placing its members in executive branch positions in both Republican and Democratic administrations. One study reports that of the 150 men (!) who were CED trustees between 1942 and 1957, 38 served in the national government. The practice continued in similar fashion in the Carter administration, as it had previously in the Nixon and Ford administrations.

The Brookings Institution. Dye calls Brookings "the dominant policy-planning group for American domestic policy."[25] It is certainly true that the quality of the research done at Brookings, particularly with respect to taxation, welfare, poverty, defense, and the national budget in general, is the best in the nation. Its personnel move back and forth to the executive branch of the government, although more often *into* Democratic administrations and *out of* Republican administrations and, on the whole, at considerably lower levels than CFR or CED members.

Brookings began in 1916 as the "Institute of Government Research," and was designed to promote economy and efficiency in government. It worked closely with the National Civic Federation. Major Brookings' successes include the development of an integrated federal government budget in 1921, income maintenance and social security reform, and the establishment of a congressional budget office. During the Nixon years, Brookings published a series of counterbudgets, but during the Carter administration, this task was abandoned to the left-wing think tanks.

From the start, Brookings trustees have included people at the pinnacle of the corporate, banking, and academic worlds. They remain so today and have extensive overlapping relationships with corporations, universities, and government. Table 5.1 is a composite sketch of the trustees or directors of Brookings, CFR, CED, and Business Roundtable (discussed later) as of 1980. Note that Brookings' trustees hold even *more* corporate directorships than the leaders of CFR and CED. As a group, these managers of the core policy-planning groups are closely linked to the corporate world and have extensive governmental experience. As Dye notes, *all* the CFR directors (minus one) had government posts at one time or another. The *average* for all these leaders was "over eleven institutional positions each."[26] Until 1971, there were no women or blacks; now "3 percent of

---

[25] Dye, *Who's Running America?* p. 251.

[26] Ibid., p. 256.

TABLE 5.1
The Policy-Planning Directors: A Collective Portrait

	CFR N = 22	CED N = 61	Brookings N = 18	Roundtable N = 44	Total N = 145
Positions Ever Held					
Corporate directorships					
Average number	3.2	4.1	5.0	4.3	4.1
(Percentage with none)	(18.2%)	(4.9%)	(11.1%)	(0%)	(6.2%)
Government offices					
Average number	3.0	1.0	1.2	0.4	1.2
(Percentage with none)	(4.5%)	(65.6%)	(50.0%)	(75.0%)	(51.9%)
University trusteeships					
Average number	1.0	1.2	1.0	1.3	1.2
(Percentage with none)	(31.8%)	(32.8%)	(38.9%)	(27.3%)	(31.7%)
Civic association offices					
Average number	5.2	4.8	5.7	5.3	5.1
(Percentage with none)	(0%)	(1.1%)	(0%)	(6.8%)	(2.7%)
Total institutional affiliations (average)	12.4	11.1	12.4	11.3	11.6
Education					
Percentage with college education	100.0%	100.0%	100.0%	100.0%	100.0%
Percentage that are graduates of a presti- gious university*	81.8%	62.3%	77.7%	52.3%	58.6%
Percentage with law degrees	22.7%	23.0%	11.1%	11.4%	17.9%
Percentage with graduate degrees (including law)	90.9%	52.5%	66.7%	47.7%	58.6%
Social Character					
Percentage female (number)	9.0%(2)	0	11.1%(2)	0	2.7%
Percentage black (number)	4.5%(1)	0	5.5%(1)	0	1.3%
Average age	57.5	62.1	57.7	58.9	59.9
Private club membership					
Average number	2.8	2.8	3.4	3.0	2.9
(Percentage with none)	(36.4%)	(27.8%)	(27.8%)	(34.1%)	(31.0%)

SOURCE: Thomas R. Dye, *Who's Running America? The Reagan Years,* 3rd ed., © 1983, p. 255. Reprinted by permission of Prentice-Hall, Inc., Englewood Cliffs, New Jersey.

* Harvard, Yale, Chicago, Stanford, Columbia, M.I.T., Cornell, Northwestern, Princeton, Johns Hopkins, Pennsylvania, and Dartmouth.

the policy planning directors are women, and 1 percent are black."[27] Dye's table represents the clearest demonstration that perhaps is possible of the integration of the highest echelon sectors with the process of policymaking in the United States.

The Trilateral Commission.[28] In 1972, in response to President Nixon's abrupt shift to nationalistic and protectionist principles, David Rockefeller gathered support and members for an *international* version of the CFR, to be called the Trilateral Commission. "Trilateral" here refers to the three areas of the world in which industrial capitalist societies dominate: Western Europe, North America, and Japan. In the face of increasing economic interdependence and difficulties, the goals of the new organization were:

1. To provide a forum for private international consultation.
2. To come to agreement on basic policies to be followed.
3. To coordinate the influence brought to bear on members' national governments to act in accordance with such international agreement.

Operations formally began in 1973, and several studies with recommendations about world problems have been made the subject of discussion at semiannual plenary sessions or the more frequent executive committee meetings. Recommendations are regularly forwarded (often in person) to the affected governments and international institutions.

The makeup of the commission emphasizes the globally-oriented sectors of contemporary capitalism, particularly multinational banking and export-dependent multinational corporations. There are roughly 260 members, of whom about 60 are from the United States. Many of the American members are also members of the Council on Foreign Relations. Nine of the world's fifteen largest banks are represented, including two of Europe's top three, the five largest in Japan (seven of the largest nine), and two of the three largest in the United States. The leading European and Japanese industrial corporations, nearly all of which are active exporters, are also well represented. But bankers and corporate executives are in every case supplemented by media owners and executives, politicians, prominent academics, and a scattering of trade union leaders.

The commission perceives that the world is undergoing severe crises (of various kinds of resources, including political will) and is in a process of fundamental change. It feels that a new and pervasive integration or rationalization on a world scale must be accomplished, particularly with regard to monetary and trade relations. New international institutions must be developed that are appropriate to this goal. The Third World is and will continue to be a major problem arena, requiring special and coordinated attention, and there must be substantial change in the domestic

---

[27] Ibid., p. 257.

[28] Most of these data rest on our own original research, primarily from the Trilateral Commission's own *Triangle Papers* and its quarterly newsletter, *Trialogue*.

economies and governing practices of the trilateral societies themselves. In every case, of course, the prescription for taking charge of ongoing change is intended to shape the future in a manner that is congenial to the commission's dominant interests—that is, finance capital and multinational and export-oriented enterprises.

The international goals of the Trilateral Commission lead to some clear priorities for foreign policy, such as elimination of military confrontations, stabilization of currencies, control of inflation, expansion of trade, and assurance of Third World debt repayment. To accomplish these ends, certain international institutions are marked for development. The institutions of greatest potential are the International Monetary Fund (IMF) and the Organization for Economic Cooperation and Development (OECD).[29] The IMF is already assuming a policing role in international lending, and is proving to be more successful than private banks or creditor governments at enforcing wage and service cuts and the other conditions that are necessary to ensure repayment from debtor to creditor nations. What is unique and important about this is the TLC's conscious use of the international agenda to manage domestic programs and populations.

It was with Carter's election that the Trilateral connection suddenly became highly visible. Appointment after appointment went to Trilateral members and staff or to Brookings associates. By June 1977, twenty-two present or former Trilateral members or staff and Brookings people closely associated with Trilateral work held positions *at the assistant secretary level or above*. Included were all the top foreign and economic policy-making positions. In addition to the President and Vice-President there were: the secretaries of state, defense, and treasury (plus four high offices in state, two in treasury, and two in defense); the national security adviser; the chairman of the Council of Economic Advisers; deputy director of the CIA; and seven key ambassadors or special representatives (among them the United Nations, Peking, the Panama Canal Treaty, and Nuclear Arrangements). By 1980, the normal turnover in government had resulted in some change of responsibilities, but no less of a Trilateral presence. When the secretary of treasury was replaced by the former head of the Federal Reserve Board (himself only a director of the CED), for example, the appointee to chair the Federal Reserve Board (Paul Volcker) was the Trilateralist president of the New York Reserve Bank.

Contending Groups.[30] As might be expected, such an apparently decisive role by one or a combination of similarly-oriented elite groups could not go unchallenged if other people with power and resources seriously

---

[29] See *Triangle Paper* #11, "The Reform of International Institutions."

[30] Information for this section was drawn from Ronald Brownstein and Nina Easton, *Reagan's Ruling Class: Portraits of the President's Top One Hundred Officials* (New York: Pantheon, 1982); Alan Crawford, *Thunder on the Right: The ''New Right'' and the Politics of Resentment* (New York: Pantheon, 1980); Richard A. Viguerie, *The New Right: We're Ready to Lead* (Falls Church, Va.: The Viguerie Company, 1980).

disagreed with them. More conservative elites, particularly those with strong free-market convictions, less interest in international trade and finance, and greater antipathies to the Soviet Union, began to organize contending groups soon after the Trilateral Commission was formed. One of these, the Hoover Institution on War, Peace, and Revolution had actually been in existence since 1918 in Stanford, California. It began to shift from a respected scholarly library toward a more active support of conservative policy research and recommendation during the Reagan gubernatorial administration in California. Soon it was producing a steady stream of provocative policy-oriented work by a stable of well-funded academics and former practitioners.

The American Enterprise Institute (AEI) of Washington, D.C., which has been in existence since 1943, became more aggressive under new leadership in the early 1970s. It took on the role of defender of the free market and outspoken critic of government regulation, attracting many "neoconservatives" and former Democratic intellectuals to its salaries, fellowships, and publication opportunities. After the defeat of the Ford administration in 1976, it expanded again with personnel who had been displaced from the government and began to compete actively with Brookings for media and policymakers' acceptance. AEI now sponsors studies and publications on a wide range of national and international issues, most of which are very well respected. A similar although less ambitious body is the Institute for Contemporary Studies (ICS) located in San Francisco, which also stresses free market solutions to all problems.

A somewhat more strident body with direct ties to the New Right is the Heritage Foundation, established in 1973 with funds from industrialist Joseph Coors. Heritage has concentrated on immediate policy-oriented work, getting conservative arguments and information into the hands of its friends while bills are under consideration in the Congress. It achieved its greatest success in 1980 with the publication of a comprehensive agenda for the Reagan administration to employ in redirecting the national government; several of the authors ended up as mid-level managers of the new administration's efforts toward that goal.

Perhaps the most visible of this new generation of policy-planning groups, however, was the Committee on the Present Danger (CPD). It was formed in 1976 by a small group of determined "cold warriors" for the purpose of alerting the nation to the need for a massive military buildup to counter growing Soviet power. CPD members included retired admirals and generals, along with a number of leading business and professional people with much government experience. It served as a source of high-level recruits for the Reagan administration in much the same way that the Trilateral Commission did for the Carter administration. Starting with the President himself, CPD claimed fifteen positions at the same high levels of the executive branch as the Trilateralists had in 1977. Still, the CPD has not been entirely satisfied with the speed of the military buildup, and it regularly issues critical comments on the Reagan administration's progress. One of its founding members, however, serves as the chief American negotiator in the arms control negotiations, and another is the head of our Arms Control and Disarmament Agency.

The final recent entrant in the policy-planning arena is the Business Roundtable, which is another organization formed in the mid-1970s. It consists of the chief executives of leading corporations, and is intended to lobby the Congress on behalf of business interests. Its success has been widely recognized, and the group is credited with having effectively turned the Congress toward much greater support for business needs.

These contending groups are not made up of bodies of elites that are totally different than the older ones; there is considerable overlap of membership and leadership between them. In fact, several leading business executives serve as directors of both the CFR or Trilateral Commission *and* AEI or CPD or the Business Roundtable. It is the center of gravity that is different—the mix of their priorities, or the vigor with which they pursue goals that are apparently shared between the two sets of leaders. Much in the way of premises and assumptions *is* shared, and often only the methods by which they should be obtained are at issue.

STYLES OF ELITE AGENDA MANAGEMENT

There are many different ways in which elite definitions of problems and proposed solutions become the generally understood framework for making public choices about them. There is a great distance between the identification of a "problem" and the choice of a particular policy to try to cope with it, and many people can play some role along the way. However, there are certain patterns that regularly appear, and so consistently that they are quite unlikely to be coincidental:

1. New or newly threatening problems are almost always discovered through a process in which either a well-established policy-planning group, or perhaps a leading foundation or university is involved.
2. The prestige and credibility of that source is invested in the particular definition, interpretation, and perhaps solution that is being put forward.
3. The substance of this "context of understanding" is conveyed to government policymakers by informal social, communication, and lobbying networks and to the general public *and* policymakers by the mass media.

In this way, there is a direct link to a plausible elite judgment, and the matter is by definition "news" that the media are almost obliged to report seriously. It may seem that there are a great many problems on the public agenda already, but the fact is that only a small proportion of those that *might* deserve consideration actually reach the point where they get it. There is a complex screen that insulates our decision-making system from most problems, regardless of how hard some people might try to bring them to wide public attention. For the most part, when problems are in their early stages, only those with elite-certified "importance" (and definitions) make it through that screen. In their *late* stages, of course, some problems are so compelling that no screening system could keep them from attention. The task for elites then, is to see that such problems are defined and understood along lines that they find tolerable. At the very least, what is "realistic" and "practical" under the circumstances must be as defined by relevant elites.

In some cases, there may be competing elite definitions and solutions, and much of American politics consists of the struggle for preeminence in defining these intangible mental images. In every case, the effort to attach particular definitions and prescriptions to issues as they work their way to political decisions involves many people and much energy. We shall examine the ways in which elite management people understand and define two categories of issues:

1. The short-term situations in which problems *seem* to have become compelling—sometimes by themselves, but often because of a form of elite selection—and the elite task is to shape a consensus for an immediate policy choice.
2. The long-term situations in which the elite role in selection of the problem and formulation of both definitions and solutions are indisputable.

The task is to create the whole framework within which the problem will be understood for the duration of its existence.

Short-Term Consensus-Shaping. Far and away the most characteristic agenda-managing tactic in American politics is the appointment of an "independent" commission to study the problem and propose a solution. Normally, this occurs when important problems compel public policy choices, but there is no generally agreed on definition of the nature of the problem or the proper solution. The government has been forced to act, in other words, before the policy-planning groups have done all they could to shape the understanding and direction of a probable solution. Conflict is likely, and out of it may come mistakes or unpredictable actions that endanger other interests. The solution is the appointment by the President (sometimes the President and Congress together) of an independent commission to bring forth a legislative proposal within a fixed time limit, which is often from six months to a year.

The commission typically includes representatives of various recognized groups or interests, some business or educational leaders, and former government officials with expertise in the area. Because of the early deadline, there is no time for the commission to develop its own research program. Staff are hurriedly borrowed from other agencies and recognized experts from leading universities and the government are called in. In effect, the commission's job is to provide a forum where established views can make one last effort to say what the problem "really" involves, and suggest what to do about it. Commissions may differ in the extent of their independence. Observers carefully study their makeup in order to draw inferences about the President's real intent with regard to the problem. *Some* degree of presidential purpose is assumed in the selection of just who is to serve on the commission. It is assumed that there will be *some* degree of guidance, however subtle, from the White House as the commission goes about its work.

In the early years of the Reagan administration, referral to commissions was a regular practice. The question of whether or not to produce and deploy the new MX missile was a fundamental issue in the military buildup. It was given to a commission made up of pro-military members and headed by a retired general whose enthusiasm for the MX was well known. The study phase of the commission's work did not take long, but its recommendations nevertheless received wide reporting in the media and came to be cited often in the ensuing debates.

A more truly independent commission, if only because the Congress carries most of the decision-making power in the field, was the commission appointed in 1981 to design a plan for keeping the Social Security System from bankruptcy. In this case, the leaders of the House and Senate each appointed as many members as the President. The President selected as chair a prominent conservative economist who had chaired the Council of Economic Advisers in a previous Republican administration. A compromise was struck after long and hard bargaining among key members, and the resulting legislation was enacted.

But the President's appointment in 1983 of a "National Bipartisan Commission on Central America" is a more characteristic example of the commission method for managing the political agenda. Reagan announced that the commission would "lay the foundation for a long-term unified national approach to the freedom and independence of the countries of Central America."[31] The makeup of the commission was typical: a former Republican governor of Texas, the (Trilateral Commission member) head of the AFL-CIO, a former Justice of the Supreme Court, an eastern businessman who was once a U.S. Senator, the president of a leading business association, a prominent neoconservative, a university president, the president of a liberal organization, the Mayor of San Antonio, and a Cuban exile professor of economics from Yale.

For the chair of the commission, Reagan again turned to a former government official, Henry Kissinger, the Nixon–Ford Secretary of State. Although the appointment drew protests from some conservatives, it seemed to be an effort to reach across the differences among groups of elites. At the time, Kissinger was serving on the Executive Committee of the Trilateral Commission. He promptly brought two former State Department officials that were closely associated with him and the Trilateral Commission to serve as his assistants.

---

[31] *Congressional Quarterly*, July 23, 1983, p. 1493.

The commission was given the task of formulating a long-term policy for the United States and suggesting ways that a national consensus around such a policy could be built. The commission began its work by meeting with Reagan, and then initiated a well-publicized series of hearings at which prestigious people with a lot of experience gave their views on what should be done. The point is not that any of this is necessarily suspicious, but that there are many opportunities in such a process for established elites to powerfully shape how problems are understood and acted upon. From the time that a commission report is issued, its definition of the problem and its proposed solution form the framework of national discussion. Whoever both defines the problem and offers the policy proposal that everybody else must react to has gone a long way toward shaping the eventual outcome.

Long-Term Shaping of the Context of Understanding. Sometimes the moment is right, and a single bold study or idea can catch hold and become the starting point for future discussion. Such was the case, for example, when Murray Weidenbaum, an economist who served in several Republican administrations, produced a study that purported to measure the costs to business of government health and safety regulations.[32] It did not matter that the methods used were crude at best and bizarre at worst; putting a firm total figure on a burden that was strongly felt by business made for instant importance. The paper was aggressively circulated by the American Enterprise Institute. It quickly became a classic bit of conventional wisdom about government excesses, which the Reagan administration committed itself to correct.

The more typical process is one involving years of research, publication, discussion among academics and their elite patrons, and then public dissemination of positions and recommendations for action. One such process with profound consequences for U.S. policy directions surfaced publicly in the early 1980s under the labels "reindustrialization" and "industrial policy." Recognition that the U.S. economic performance was falling behind that of Japan and several European countries led to a vigorous search for explanations. Each explanation, of course, carried its own remedy. If government were the problem, then the remedy would be to change or eliminate the offending activities; if lack of capital investment were the problem, then government should encourage new investment through tax incentives for the wealthy; and if other countries' governments helped them to develop and market new products in various ways, then the U.S. government might have to do the same.

Defining the problem became the focus of vigorous argument. Books and articles were published and conferences were held. Gradually, a consensus began to form around the notion that the problem was "lack of competitiveness" on the part of the United States. This was a definition that justified efforts to increase capital investment, to provide more vigor-

---

[32] Brownstein and Easton, *Reagan's Ruling Class*, pp. 65–66.

ous government aid to business, and to exhort workers to work harder—
perhaps for lower wages. There was no specific moment when a vote was
taken to define the problem; the process was subtler and more complex
than that. But by 1983, quite distinct elite groupings were defining it with
remarkable similarity. The National Commission on Excellence in Education, created by the Secretary of Education in 1981, published a report in
April 1983 entitled "A Nation at Risk." In one of the report's early paragraphs explaining the notion of risk, the Commission declared:

> The risk is not only that the Japanese make automobiles more efficiently
> than Americans and have government subsidies for development and
> export. It is not just that the South Koreans recently built the world's most
> efficient steel mill, or that American machine tools, once the pride of the
> world, are being displaced by German products. It is also that these devel-
> opments signify a redistribution of trained capability throughout the
> globe. Knowledge, learning, information, and skilled intelligence are the
> new raw materials of international commerce and are today spreading
> throughout the world as vigorously as miracle drugs, synthetic fertilizers,
> and blue jeans did earlier. If only to keep and improve on the slim com-
> petitive edge we still retain in world markets, we must dedicate ourselves
> to the reform of our educational system for the benefit of all—old and
> young alike, affluent and poor, majority and minority. Learning is the
> indispensable investment required for success in the "information age"
> we are entering.[33]

In a report requested by the President in 1982 and issued at almost the
same time by an entirely separate organization, the Business–Higher Education Forum, the same theme was articulated. Entitled "America's Competitive Challenge," the report opened with these paragraphs:

> The central objective of the United States for the remainder of the decade
> must be to improve the ability of American industry to compete in mar-
> kets at home and abroad. The new economic realities of global competi-
> tion demand a broadly based national effort to make this possible. . . .
> American society remains confused and divided about both the nature of
> the competitive challenge and the national response it requires. Until
> citizens recognize that industrial competitiveness on an international scale
> is the key to economic growth, and until they appreciate that the overall
> well-being of society itself depends on such economic growth, we fear
> that little progress will be made.[34]

The report then went on to urge a national effort equal to the "crash
program" that enabled the United States to land a man on the moon before
the Russians.

---

[33] "A Nation at Risk: The Imperative for Educational Reform," A Report to the
Nation and the Secretary of Education, U.S. Department of Education, by the
National Commission on Excellence in Education, April, 1983.

[34] "America's Competitive Challenge: The Need for a National Response," The
Report in Brief, A Report to the President of the United States from the Business–
Higher Education Forum, Washington, D.C., April, 1983, p. 1.

The movement toward formulation of a solution to this problem was furthered by the need of the Democratic Party to develop an alternative to the economic renewal policies of the Reagan administration—tax reductions, military buildup, cutbacks in social programs, and reliance on the "free market" for the rest. Efforts were made to bring together representatives of business, labor, and government to discuss possible "industrial policy" alternatives. One such body called itself the "Industrial Policy Study Group"; others went by different versions of the name.[35] There were several Congressional caucuses and study groups that also issued proposals for various kinds of industrial policy. The term usually means the conscious use of government to cushion the decline of older industries, encourage development of newer industries, aid all American producers in selling their products abroad, and perhaps prepare and help relocate workers for the new kinds of jobs available in the future.

The specific policies to be followed remain uncertain, possibly because they are subject to continuing elite conflict. There was little doubt, however, that the public was being prepared for major new efforts on the part of the business community to regain profitability and growth potential in the new world economy. The traditional notion of the free market as the guiding principle for economic policy was being undermined, whether advocates of the new government role wanted to admit it or not. Even those who spoke most strongly in defense of the free-market idea were accepting more and more of a government role on behalf of the particular interests that they represented. At some point, however, the public would have a chance to say in whose interest the government should exert itself. Most of this elite activity occurred in anticipation of that moment and in hopes of shaping it as much as possible.

SUMMARY

We have sketched the manner in which a *context of understanding* is created and the *political agenda* is set before any governmental action occurs. The leading force in both these processes comes from the upper reaches of our social and economic classes. The institutions and groups of people shaping the context of understanding are the universities, the foundations, the media, the higher professions, and the intellectuals. We followed the ways in which upper-class perceptions and priorities are absorbed and passed on to the public.

The actual management of the specific political agenda so that upper-class preferences are implemented as public policy is accomplished by an array of policy-planning groups. We briefly described four that are among

---

[35] See, for example, "With an Eye on '84 Elections, Democrats Lay Foundations for National Industrial Policy," *Congressional Quarterly*, August 20, 1983, p. 1679; Sidney Blumenthal, "Drafting a Democratic Industrial Plan," *New York Times Magazine*, August 28, 1983, p. 31.

the most influential: the Council on Foreign Relations, the Committee for Economic Development, the Brookings Institution, and the Trilateral Commission. We added the recent countering policy-planning groups that reveal the split in perception and priorities at the upper reaches, such as: the Business Roundtable, the Committee on the Present Danger, the Heritage Foundation, and the American Enterprise Institute. Even though there are important differences among and between them, we saw that they are all tightly interlocked at the very top leadership level. They are successful in having their recommendations adopted by the government and serve as a personnel pool from which many government positions are filled.

In other words, we are dealing here with activities *prior* to governmental activity. Whether there are fundamental differences between upper echelon individuals and corporations, the *process of policy shaping* is the same. Corporations and wealthy individuals endow and control foundations and universities, which study coming issues and problems in depth, begin to shape the context of understanding, and then provide specific recommendations. The policy-planning groups occupy the central role in refining studies and recommendations and transforming them into government policies, often by directly staffing the relevant government positions themselves. Public acquiescence is promoted by the news media and the legitimating actions of presidential commissions. Finally, the government makes the policies for which the way has been so carefully prepared. In Part III, we will turn to that stage of the process. In the final chapter of this section, we will describe the fundamental ideological context within which the specific policy recommendations fit.

CHAPTER 6

Ideology and Symbolism

Most Americans appear to be basically satisfied with the political system, despite the troubling nature of the economic and social context. Many others appear to be deeply alienated, but their alienation paralyzes, rather than mobilizes them. Relatively few directly challenge the system, but those challenges generate much of the conflict and change that has characterized our politics. Of course, the American system delivers many things that many people want or think they want, but two other important factors are at work to justify the status quo:

1. People are encouraged to want whatever they get.
2. People are discouraged from challenging, or even participating, in a variety of ways.

Ideology and *symbolism* order and channel the American context at a most fundamental level—in our minds. This chapter will consider these two concepts in some detail.

IDEOLOGY

Ideology is the collection of beliefs that the members of a given society hold about how their government works, or should work, and why. Such beliefs may be fully articulated, but most often, they are simply taken for granted. They may vary somewhat depending upon one's position; they may be held with varying degrees of intensity; and they need not be factually correct or completely expressed. Basically, an ideology serves as a kind of lens through which people see, and provides a set of cues with which they make judgments about their political world. A person's ideology, perceptions, and values are normally acquired very early in life from family and school; they are reaffirmed later in a variety of ways—by the media, the rhetoric of politicians, and the beliefs and actions of other people. Ideology has a life and continuity of its own, and the fact that it fits a reality may be only coincidental. In effect, ideology "shapes" reality by ordering, making sense of, and evaluating the concrete happenings of the world.

In most societies, one particular belief system is predominant, and the United States is no exception. Indeed, the depth and strength of the orthodox American ideology are so great that most citizens do not even recognize it as ideology. Our beliefs about politics and government seem so natural, self-evident, and *right* that other possibilities are unimaginable. This total short-circuiting of independent analysis is the supreme achievement of an ideology.

The Functions of Ideology

Three primary functions of ideology are worth noting here:

1. Ideology affects our perceptions of problems. We are used to thinking in certain ways, and we habitually make certain assumptions. Thus, we tend to "understand" new problems only in a particular limited and narrow context.
2. Ideology both explains why policies take the form they do and justifies or condemns these patterns. It may make judgments on the grounds of the rightness or wrongness of the political system, the structure of power that animates the system, or the basic values underlying it.
3. Ideology serves to organize people and provide them with a coherent sense of the relationship among themselves, their values, and the workings of their government.

The Perception of Problems. What is a "problem"? The first step is merely to define the situation as a problem. For example, for many years, racial discrimination was not regarded as a public problem. Our ideology insisted that it was a purely private matter. Thus, how we understand the character and causes of the "problem" directly leads to what we regard as acceptable "solutions." In other words, our ideological tendency to draw a line between public and private activities meant that the government could only deal with discriminatory policies practiced by public agencies, such as the Jim Crow laws. It could do nothing about private individuals practicing racial discrimination, such as the existence of the Ku Klux Klan, as long as they broke no laws.

In a more current example, is air or water pollution such a threat to life (a legitimate public concern) that measures should be taken to control the industrial (a very private activity) sources of pollution? Or is pollution a necessary price to pay for the continued expansion of the economy and the provision of jobs? One's answer depends only partly on objective facts; many of the "facts," part of the "answer," and certainly much of the "solution" depend on one's ideology.

Our understanding of a problem involves much more than its "objective" characteristics; it is a direct outcome of our values and ideology. The American orthodoxy tends to see each problem in isolation and as a purely technical problem. One merely needs to define the problem, isolate the cause, and the answer appears. Another ideology sees problems as being connected to one another and to the underlying social structures, economic practices, and/or basic values. Such divergent ideologies give rise to very different understandings of the nature of a problem. They "see" different problems, different "facts," and thus different solutions.

Explanation-Justification. Ideology affects not only what we see and understand in the world around us, but also it simultaneously evaluates, implying that what we see conforms to either our hopes or our fears. Things not only *are*, but are also valued as *good* or *bad*, because ideology teaches us to understand in both dimensions at the same time. Newly perceived events fit into long-established and deeply-held convictions; the result is that they are essentially rounded into consistency. Ideology filters all events through a particular perceptual screen. In the view of the dominant ideology, for example, the rightness of the American political system and the propriety of our basic political values mean that the resulting public policies will benefit the society as a whole.

Organization of People. What are the consequences of shaping what people see and whether they see a given phenomenon as good or bad? Clearly, one result is at least the organization of, and potentially the control over, those people. Ideology organizes people by providing a coherent understanding of their world. It molds them into particular relationships with other people, government, and events; and people need not be aware of what is happening to them. This does not mean that they will be marching in lockstep in response to explicit orders from their leaders, but simply that they are organized in the sense that they see and think about similar things at the same time that many others do.

In the case of the dominant ideology, the experiences of most individuals implicitly reinforce and reward acceptance of American orthodoxy. Political leaders often explicitly call for behavior in accordance with American ideology, and it is easier and much more effective if people voluntarily behave in ways that are congenial to this status quo. Thus, an ideology can be a powerful instrument of social control on behalf of those people or interests that are best served by its teachings; in this way, blatant coercion can be held to a minimum. Challenging ideologies may similarly organize people's lives, and serve many of the same functions, because everybody holds *some* ideology, in greater or lesser degrees, and with greater or lesser amounts of self-awareness.

Political Values: The Building Blocks of Ideology

Political values are the most fundamental beliefs that people hold about what is right or wrong in politics. They are the building blocks for thinking about how political systems should be organized and why. This section will discuss five of the values that have had major impact on American political thought and practice.

Individualism. The focal point of political thought in the United States is the individual, and all other relationships and values follow from this base. The individual is the basic unit of politics, and the political system is erected for the individual's benefit. The principal goals of political life have to do with providing a suitable context for the individual's pursuit of satisfaction and happiness. The principles of government are deduced from assumptions about what is required to serve the individual's needs. In the mid-eighteenth century, for example, the chief barrier to individual attainment seemed (with good reason) to be governmental power in the hands of royal or aristocratic authorities. The principal means of ensuring individual opportunity, therefore, was a firm set of limitations on the power of government, which resulted in an equally determined laissez-faire ("hands off") approach to the role of government in the society and economy.

The "Natural Rights" of the Individual. Individuals have certain rights, as part of their entitlement on earth, due solely by virtue of their existence. These rights are:

1. The right to life and liberty. A person cannot be deprived of either without being granted due processes of law, such as a hearing, fair trial, and proper procedures.
2. The right to property is closely related to the first right. Essential to life and liberty is the ability to be secure in the possession of one's goods and land. This also includes the right to dispose of property, control it, and deal with it as one wishes.
3. The right to participate, to some degree at least, in the decisions of government, and the right to equal treatment before the law are also included. The right to equality is generally limited to equality of opportunity or, with even more limitations, simply the right to stand in the same relationship to the government as everyone else. It has no implications beyond that sphere.

Although property rights are only one of several natural rights, they have frequently been elevated to first priority and sometimes to exclusive entitlement. The problem is that property rights often conflict with other natural rights, such as equality. In more recent history, the issue of priority has become crucial. The deep and bitter conflict over slavery may serve to illustrate this point and demonstrate the power of property as an American political value. None of the framers of the Constitution seriously doubted that slaves were property, and should be provided for as such. The early debates over limited slavery versus emancipation foundered on the appropriate compensation for the loss of property; the propriety of compensation was never questioned. The Abolitionists were bitterly resisted by many northerners in part because of the antiproperty implications of their position. When emancipation finally came, it was as a limited expediency in the course of a difficult war. Relatively few voices were raised on behalf of equality, and certainly not at the expense of property rights. It was only the commitment to preserve the Union that finally mobilized the use of force.

This conflict between property and other natural rights is real and recurrent. It arises in debates over the progressive income tax, social security, poverty programs, environmental protection, and the regulation of the economy in general. Such conflict is anticipated and feared by property holders far more than actual inroads on their possessions would seem to justify. The framers of the Constitution and the early Federalists feared attacks on property, because they thought that if majorities were allowed to work their will through the political system, then radical redistribution of wealth would be the result. As a result, they constructed a series of restraints on the power of government, and to justify this principle, they developed and promulgated the idea of "majority rule *and* minority rights." By minority rights, of course, they meant property rights; but the two are logically inconsistent. No political system can provide both majority rule and minority rights in the absolute sense, because an effective limit on majority rule means that real majority rule does not exist. Conversely, if the majority rules in all cases, the system *cannot* always be protecting minority rights. Nevertheless, most Americans subscribe to both principles, acknowledging limitations on the power of majorities, and building in the priority conflict.

Limited Government. As far as eighteenth century thinkers were concerned, a necessary corollary to individualism and natural rights is the principle of limited government. Government is the creation of individuals, who are endowed with natural rights, and its powers have been conferred on it by the collectivity of individuals who originally possess all power. Thus, these conferred powers must be consistent with the protection of the individual's natural rights. Thus, the government's sphere of action is defined by both the limited scope of the powers granted to it and the inviolability of the rights of individuals.

According to this view, government is a marginal and semi-legitimate enterprise. Although the society (or collectivity of individuals) has no other agent that is capable of acting on behalf of the whole, each effort to employ government for particular purposes is viewed with suspicion. Almost every governmental activity is challenged on grounds of its necessity or its propriety. To be sure, this principle is invoked most often to prevent governmental action, and it tends to be forgotten when favorable action is sought.

Materialism and the Business Ethic. Since the earliest days of this nation, observers have repeatedly commented on the special disposition of Americans to seek private economic gain. National celebration of such motivations reached its height at the end of the nineteenth century, in the days of Horatio Alger and the robber barons. Although the situation is somewhat ameliorated today, it is clear that the United States is a business-oriented society. The underlying value system strongly supports such capitalist principles as the value of consumption by individuals; the measurement of the propriety and desirability of new ventures, products, and expenses by their profitability; and the measurement of individual achievement, and often even worth, by the accumulation of wealth.

When these values and motivations are shared by many people, they affect the criteria used to determine governmental programs. Because private profit and consumption are valued so highly, public expenditure is suspect, and government outlays for such public purposes as schools, hospitals, and welfare are seen as "spending," and are therefore undesirable. On the other hand, corporate expenditures for new and often unnecessary consumer products are "investments" and are therefore good. Government action may be judged from a "businessman's" viewpoint, and thus, short-range questions of efficiency and profitability dominate. Will a proposed bridge earn enough income to pay off the cost of building it? Does spending for education result in a good "investment" for our future?

Racism. The assumption of white supremacy is equally as long-lived and pervasive in American society. Originating in Western culture centuries ago, this sense of the superiority of the white race has been an animating feature of Americans and their governmental policies throughout our history. Until very recently, neither the American Indian nor the Afro-American was thought fit for full citizenship. Nearly all the major leaders at the time the Constitution was framed, as well as in subsequent periods, held white-supremacist assumptions. However unconscious such notions may have been, they were instrumental in shaping policies that massacred Indians and oppressed slaves, and built a sometimes unrecognized racist strain into the American value system.

After centuries of action in accordance with these premises, it is not surprising that evidence of the degradation of the nonwhite races can still be found. Efforts to remedy the work of centuries, however, run up against denials of personal responsibility, and the failure to perceive the racist bases of existing policies combines with a normal resistance to change to frustrate progress. Most Americans do not understand the extent to which subtle and not-so-subtle racial barriers have prevented the nonwhite poor from rising by the routes taken by white immigrants. Given such widespread and deep-seated racism, it is not difficult to see why the limited governmental steps that have been taken are highly controversial. One can also understand why the tangible signs of change are so few.

Many important factual questions can be asked about all these values, of course.

- Which groups or strata within the society actually held or hold them?
- How widely shared or intensely felt are they?
- Do the people who assert them actually act on them?

These are questions we shall attempt to answer later.

The Values Applied in Practice

The dominant political belief system holds that the values just described (with the exception of racism) are realized on a day-to-day basis in American politics. In part, this is the natural function of a nation's political ideology, because basically, ideology is a kind of mental map that helps people harmonize what they see with their strongly held convictions about what is good. As stated earlier, because it is simplifying and reassuring, ideology is also seductive and frequently unconscious. Ideology tends to be strongest among those who have had the most formal education, because their economic interests and social positions act to reinforce what they have heard. Those who experience more contrast between the ideology and the realities of their daily existences, have more questions about the goodness of the system. Two major components of the dominant American political ideology will be discussed in the following paragraphs.

1. The ideology holds that the basic political values of the United States are reflected in the structure of the American government and that the resulting political system is democratic in character. Thus, the core political values—individualism, limited government, natural rights (with property rights ascendant), and procedural regularity—are patently manifest within the Constitution and the government it created. Ideology holds that the institutional forms of these principles will operate automatically, and indeed, almost mechanically; they will deliver the results that are considered appropriate by those who subscribe to the core values. The interplay of presidential and congressional power yields a mechanistic (and therefore appropriate) product; the decision of the Supreme Court is seen as representing a higher law's mandate, and not the preferences of five or more judges. In short, ideology suggests that the translation of values into institutions achieves a nonpartisan, depoliticized, neutral apparatus that works to the benefit of all.

Next, the ideology holds that this structure creates a situation that allows full play to the "natural" workings of human capacities and wants, as well as the economic market. Allowing unfettered human activity will result in the greatest good for the greatest number of people. Thus, the established political values are seen as being manifested by a particular set of institutions; these institutions act and interact in a mechanical manner, and the result is the furtherance of a natural order in which talent and effort are rewarded and the incompetent and slothful are carried along by the successful.

The teachings of ideology with respect to the structure and operations of government are that all will benefit equally from the established institutions. But it seems clear that all do not benefit equally, and the results are not merely mechanical operations of the government. Often, the government works to the advantage of those who are situated so as to be able to seize opportunities for gaining power and influence. Separation of powers, distribution of powers between nation and states, and the protection provided for property rights, for example, make it very difficult to enact laws that change the status quo. The principle of laissez-faire means that people with private economic power are free to use that power as they see fit, and it is difficult (and wrong in any event) for others to try to use government to control such activities. If government works mechanically, of course, nobody should be aggrieved by its actions, because they are inherent in the (good) design of the American government itself. Nothing is responsible for the advantages secured by those with economic or social power except their own talents in the free and open struggle for individual achievement.

Perhaps even more important is the way in which our ideology equates the values and institutions of the American government with democracy. Democracy is good; the United States is good; the United States is a democracy; and democracy is what we experience in the United States. Circularity and poor logic are no obstacles to a powerful ideology, and it may be fruitless—and perhaps unpatriotic—to try to unravel the relationships here. Apparently what has happened is that the ideology has adapted to the powerful appeal of democracy and has interpreted American values and institutions in this light. In this way, the commitment to private property and individualism has become a characteristic of democracy. Another example is how the institution of judicial review, which was originally designed to frustrate popular will expressed through elected legislatures, comes to be seen as a vehicle for expression of the democratic values of civil liberties. A statute outlawing political participation by people with a particular viewpoint becomes democratic because it preserves the "freedom" of the "democratic" electoral process. A natural tendency to believe that what we have is good leads to favorable (democratic) interpretations of whatever we have.

We are not arguing that the governmental system of the United States is necessarily undemocratic; we are saying that the acts of *assuming* that American institutions are democratic and of *defining* "democracy" as what exists in the United States are essentially *ideological* in character. In both cases, "American" and "democratic" become synonymous, without any analysis of the facts or values implied in either entity. This is testimony to the power of ideology to suggest conclusions rather than to leave them to critical analysis and judgment.

It is the social-control aspect of American ideology that is so significant to contemporary American politics. Its capacity to disarm analysis and provide benevolent interpretations renders critical understanding difficult. Few, if any, Americans are fully captured by all the characteristics of the dominant ideology, but practically everyone is influenced by at least some of them. In the next section, we will discuss the forms of ideology that are held by many scholars and students of American politics.

2. The ideology holds that the process of political decisionmaking in the United States consists of negotiation and compromise among many factions and groups and that the product is a reasonable approximation of both democracy and the public interest. In the next few paragraphs, we will discuss the generally accepted view of the American political process that is sometimes termed *democratic pluralism,* which is an adaptation of the ideology that has purportedly come to grips with the new, large-scale, and powerful groups that are evident in modern American society.

To begin with, the system is considered to be open to all who wish to take the time and trouble to participate. For the most part, Americans actually do participate through the vehicle of voluntary associations that are organized around the ethnic, religious, occupational, social, economic, political, or other interests that are of concern to them. A single citizen may belong to several such groups. These groups fulfill a variety of functions, and respond to the needs and desires of people at all levels of society. But voluntary organizations play a particularly important role with reference to government.

In organizing support among the population and presenting their claims to the government, groups come into conflict with other groups. Each group's efforts to achieve its goals are likely to call into play another group with different or opposing goals. This is sometimes termed "the principle of countervailing powers." The various interest groups then engage in an elaborate process of negotiation, bargaining, appeals to principle and popular support, pressures on decisionmakers, and finally compromise. Each group is likely to represent a significant segment of opinion, and probably has access to some source of power within the governmental structure. As a result, any one group can usually delay, if not completely frustrate, an extreme demand made by another group. Thus, each group is induced to compromise on a solution that falls short of its full goals; if it does not accept a half-loaf, it may end up with none.

Handling of conflict through compromise is also promoted by the informal rules for group goal seeking. Each group recognizes that the attainment of its goals depends on getting a fair hearing from the others. Thus, a primary commitment of any group is defense of the fairness and openness of the decision-making processes. Parties to the goal-seeking process should be willing to see one another's problems, compromise at a point short of their own goals, and thus avoid absolute disaster for one another.

This is sound strategy, because those who happen to win today may be on the losing side tomorrow, in which case they can expect the same consideration from their new opponents. The informal rules promote compromise, and help to build a shared feeling of mutual approval for the decision-making system itself. One's opponents, after all, are people who play the game by the rules and are entitled to respect for their views and the demands placed on them by their constituencies. Those who do not accept the rules are not playing the right game or are cheating, and are properly censured by all regular players.

When the regular groups do find themselves in disagreement, or at other moments when major decisions must be made, the basic outlines of national policy are determined by popular elections. In this way, the day-to-day activities of group goal seeking are channeled, and groups devote themselves to working out the details of policies decided on by the mass electorate.

Groups perform many functions within the social and political orders. They serve as a major means of representation and provide people with a sense that their voices are heard in the halls of government. A citizen who belongs to the minority political party of any district can nevertheless feel represented in government by the efforts of compatible interest groups. In discharging this representative function, groups also root the citizen more thoroughly in the society, providing a sense of place, status, and fulfillment. In a reciprocal manner, groups give public officials a means of knowing what the people want and need. It is a way of communicating back and forth that makes for more responsive government.

The pattern of group activity in politics has other consequences. People who participate in groups acquire the tolerance for others and respect for fair procedures that help to support a democratic system. They may also belong to two or more groups whose interests are occasionally in conflict. For example, a woman may belong to both the League of Women Voters and the Catholic Church. If the League seeks to take a position contrary to that of the Church, the citizen may be "cross pressured" to take a much less extreme position on the issue than she otherwise would have. At the same time, however, her influence within each organization helps to lead it to a less extreme position.

This "cross pressured" effect, multiplied many times over for many issues, helps to keep the political system on an even keel by reducing the extremity of the pressures on it. This process is both democratic and in the public interest. It is democratic because everybody has a chance to be heard, the procedures for playing the game are known and observed, and a general consensus based on compromise and tolerance emerges before the decision is cast into final form. It is in the public interest chiefly because it *does* represent a consensus that everybody can accept. It is, therefore, very likely to be in harmony with the experience and capacity of the system and responsive to the problem in question.

The foregoing sums up a large body of analysis and interpretation by journalists, academics, and the general public. Most of it, however, is little more than a restatement of the dominant ideology. Taken together, these two major components of the dominant ideology are characterized by a very strong commitment to the established order. In particular, they emphasize over and over again the necessity and propriety of following the rules. Sometimes insistence on procedural regularity is raised to the level of a basic political value and given a label such as "legalism." The importance to Americans of formal written provisions, and of the law in general, has often been noted; indeed, the major role played by lawyers in the governing of this society rests on this procedural legal bias. Beneath the stress on established rules and legalistic procedures, of course, lies a basic conviction that actions taken in the private sphere are the best and should take precedence over, if not be protected against, public policies. The orthodox ideology says, in effect, if policies are developed by the established rules of the political system, then they must be appropriate. Further, if they maximize people's opportunities to gain their ends by private rather than governmental means, they are good. This view makes it almost unnecessary to examine the actual consequences of policies. Their merits are solely determined from the circumstances of their enactment and from the extent to which they leave people free to gain their ends by private means.

The Implications of American Orthodoxy

So far we have analyzed American orthodoxy as a set of specific values and ideological beliefs. We have seen how political images and beliefs are rooted in basic values and have examined the nature of each. The following section will explore how American political beliefs are fused with capitalist values, and what this orthodoxy means for our politics.

How much of our orthodoxy is capitalism by another name? Individualism, materialism, competition, the work ethic and profit motive, property rights, and the primacy of private economic activity are clearly capitalist principles. The concepts of limited government through contractualism and legalism are derived from the application of capitalist principles to the political system. Study Figure 6.1, the advertisement on the Capitalist Liberation Front, to see how it illustrates how capitalism and American values and ideology are deeply-rooted and connected. Some American values have had other origins and independent support, but most have become intertwined with capitalism at some time during our history. Perhaps the best way to conceive of the American orthodoxy is as capitalism with certain modifications, ambiguities, and cultural idiosyncrasies.

What does this orthodoxy mean for our politics? The strength of its influence clearly has several important results. Most Americans are unaware how specific their values and beliefs are, because they consider their values and beliefs to be natural, inevitable, and self-evident. This stance can lead to a failure to understand others' feelings and opinions and to impatience with or intolerance of others' views. Because the orthodoxy exists at such a deep level that it goes unrecognized, those who depart from it may appear to be mentally or morally defective; they can then be imprisoned, hospitalized, or otherwise legally ostracized.

The *shared character* of at least the major elements of the orthodoxy has other implications. All sectors of the population do not hold the orthodox values and beliefs to the same degree. There are levels at which only certain basic elements of it are observed and some where completely other views predominate, but most Americans share the values and beliefs discussed in this chapter to some degree. This means that prominent public officials can draw support for their actions by manipulating revered symbols. They do not have to justify their acts exclusively, or even primarily, in terms of their merits. Instead, they can claim that their acts conform to the values of preservation of private property, or taking government off the backs of business or the "people." In short, the broadly shared character of the orthodoxy facilitates social control, and can cause people to believe in and support their leaders, almost without regard to what those leaders are actually doing.

The *content* of orthodoxy, in conjunction with its strength and shared character, has certain additional implications. Capitalism becomes insulated from critical evaluation because most Americans do not perceive it in ideological terms; they simply believe it to be both good and inevitable.

Figure 6.1.   *The Interrelationship Between Capitalism and American Ideology*

The Capitalist Liberation Front

SOME DAYS, things look bleak. In the worldwide propaganda war our adversaries often seem to steal the headlines. They advance; it seems we decline. They seem to encircle us more tightly.

Except.

Except that the ideas of human liberty and full personal development were never so attractive—or so within the reach of so many human beings—as at present.

Is there a word more exciting to the human race today than "liberation"? Or "do your thing"? Or "individual liberties"? Or "self-determination"? Or "opportunity to be one's self"? Without such conceptions, capitalism would not be possible. These conceptions are the very soul of everything we mean by "free enterprise." These are *our* ideas.

The energy of capitalism is in the human heart. Its name is *liberty*. This is what critics of capitalism have always misunderstood.

In the highest form of flattery, even our enemies embrace our words: in national "liberation" fronts; in "Free" Republics; in "democratic" socialisms. More significant than that, the dreams of the peoples of the world—of billions of individuals—are, at bottom, *our* dreams. Dreams of the fully developed, cooperative, open, free individual.

The critics of capitalism misunderstand. They neglect three features in the human soul.

The number one desire of the human heart is not equality but *liberty*. Equality is an indispensable condition; we are committed to equality. But the further point, the focal point of human aspiration, is *liberty*. No other system, but ours alone, is the system of *liberty:* That deepest human energy of all is ours. Others, as we do, bring equality but we alone deliver *liberty*.

Secondly, the system of free enterprise is *value-giving*. For millenniums, oil lay useless and undesirable beneath the earth. Oil would have no value apart from the industry that capital invented. It was our inventiveness, our exertion, and our creation that in living memory made oil a precious mineral. And so, also, for many other raw materials that today have value. Capitalism is *wealth-creating*—and also *wealth-conferring*. It is true that we "exploited" some nations earlier; but we have also made them wealthy beyond their dreams. Capitalism in its abuses does at times "despoil" the earth. But in its imagination and its practicality it gives humble things values the human race never saw in them before. Capitalism has *enriched* the earth, seeing in it possibilities hidden there by its Creator, evoking marvels and miracles men had never seen before.

Thirdly, capitalism is *transformative*. It has the good of the human race at heart. And so in its unfolding capitalism transforms the world—and in the process transforms itself as well. It has given health to millions who would not have lived before; fed more millions than were ever fed before; built schools and universities for larger proportions of the race than had ever been educated earlier; and distributed higher standards of comfort and amenities, not only for an aristocracy but for ordinary workers and for many of the poor, than the world had ever dreamed of. More precious than all of these, capitalism has taken as its bride—and cherished—political democracy.

If capitalism is surrounded, it is surrounded like the yeast in dough. What capitalism stands for is what is deepest in the human soul. And what eventually, irresistibly, bursts forth: *human liberation*, for the solitary self; for every brother, every sister; and for societies and institutions everywhere.

Rumrill-Hoyt, Inc.

ADVERTISING/PUBLIC RELATIONS · NEW YORK CITY · ROCHESTER · BUFFALO · HOLLYWOOD (FLA.)

SOURCE: *Fortune*, May 1975, p. 90. Used by permission of Rumrill-Hoyt Advertising, Inc.

Nationalism is enhanced because many Americans feel that our system is clearly superior to all others. Some carry their belief to the point that they feel it is our moral mission to bring the blessings of our (democratic and capitalist) system to the rest of the world. Those who willfully oppose or reject our system—for example, Communists or socialists—are seen as evil and inevitable enemies, and those who appear to choose some other system, or who find fault with this one, have obviously been duped or manipulated in some way.

This characterization may seem to be harsh or exaggerated, but we do not believe that it is; it is thoroughly grounded in the interpretations of generations of reputable American scholars. It is more likely that such reactions are the result of—to a greater or lesser degree—a lifetime of uncritical acceptance of orthodox values and beliefs. Ideology is construed as being what the *other* person accepts. The strength and character of American orthodoxy implies that it is very difficult for us to recognize it for what it is—*our* ideology.

SYMBOLISM

Another vital support for the status quo is found in the way that symbolism diverts people, reassures them, creates their wants and needs, and deflects or undermines thrusts toward change. There is no direct relationship between the *fact* or even the *perception* of deprivation and the rationally calculated *action* to change that situation. Even if people accurately understand the causes of problems, they may not consider acting to solve them, because politics is simply not that logical or rational. Indeed, politics is not understandable merely as a series of rational decisions and purposeful actions that are intended to produce certain results. Many actions are unforeseen or unintended and so are many results. What seems logical or likely often simply does not occur, and one of the most powerful reasons why this is true is because of the part played by symbols in politics.

The Scope and Importance of Symbolism

The Nature of Symbolism. Government does not simply reflect the will of some of the people; it also *creates* public wants, beliefs, and demands that have a powerful impact on who gets what in politics. If some of the major demands and beliefs of mass publics are evoked by what the government does and by what public officials say, then talk of responsiveness to the will of the people means less (or more) than meets the eye.

Governmental actions and rhetoric can reassure people and make them apathetic, or it can arouse them to militant action. The messages that reassure or arouse can be either accurate or misleading. Because controversial policies always hurt some people, the temptation is strong for public officials to be reassuring; officials are naturally eager to be reassured themselves and to believe that what they do is in the public interest. Therefore, the fact that political symbols are misleading does not necessarily mean that they are deliberately deceptive. Indeed, the most powerful political symbols are disseminated by people who believe in them themselves.

Public officials can win mass support for actions that would elicit protest and resistance if they were undertaken by private groups. If private gas and electric companies could raise their rates whenever they pleased, without any pretense of governmental supervision, then any company that substantially raised its rates every year or two would certainly evoke massive protests and demands for public ownership or tight regulation. However, few people protest publicly when state public utilities commissions permit precisely the same rate increases. The blessing of a government agency reassures consumers and wins support for actions that would otherwise be resented.

If the wealthy, as private individuals, forced the poor or middle class to give them a substantial part of their earnings, then resistance would be massive and immediate. Yet governmental tax and subsidy policies that have exactly this effect are perceived as being reasonable, even though particular taxes or subsidies are criticized by scattered interests. If private individuals forced millions of young men to leave home, submit to strict discipline, kill others, and be killed themselves, such "slavery" would be regarded as intolerable. But when legitimized by duly enacted draft laws, it is not only tolerated by most, but regarded as highly desirable and even necessary.

The point is that official governmental acts and statements are rarely *simple* in their impacts or their meanings. Their consequences are almost never clear and certain. Economists conclude that public utility laws typically do little to keep gas and electricity rates low, but it still seems likely to most people that the rates would be even higher without governmental regulation. Low tax rates for oil producers force other taxpayers to subsidize an affluent group, but the subsidy is justified on the grounds that oil is a vital natural resource—and it is. In such cases, the financial costs to large numbers of people are high, but they are largely hidden because the method of calculating them is complex and their fairness is difficult for most people to judge. By contrast, the symbolic benefits—protection of the consumer and promotion of national security—are easy to see and understand, even though they often turn out to be trivial, misleading, or nonexistent.

Not all public policy is symbolic or based on deliberate or unintended mystification, of course. The impacts of many governmental acts on people's everyday lives are so clear that there is little question whether they help or hurt. People in a neighborhood who want a playground or a traffic light know when they are getting what they need. The farm corporation that gets several hundred thousand dollars in "price support" subsidies knows precisely how public policy boosts its profits. To the taxpayer, of course, this same public policy may be either invisible or perceived as an aid to the small family farmer and a desirable way of enhancing the nation's food production.

The key question, then, is under what conditions the acts of government become symbolic and help *create* beliefs, wants, and demands in mass publics. Also, under what conditions do the symbolic manipulations become counterproductive? The question is both a highly practical one for the citizen and an intriguing one for the student of government, because public policies have symbolic effects under conditions that we can identify, within rough limits.

Symbol Analysis. Analysis of political symbolism allows us to see some things that are not otherwise obvious and to evaluate or judge them in a new way. People's satisfaction or dissatisfaction with government does not depend only on how much they get; it depends even more on what society, and especially the government itself, cues them to expect, want, and believe they deserve. Corporate farm interests made rich by a price-support program are often dissatisfied if they do not also get tax breaks, such as rapid depreciation allowances. Most of the poor, who are taught by schools, welfare workers, and governmental policies to feel personally inadequate, docilely accept meager welfare benefits. They may feel lucky if their benefits are not cut, and grateful if they are raised ten dollars a month. In both of these cases, it is people's *expectations,* rather than how much they get, that chiefly influences how satisfied or demanding they are. In both examples, and in thousands of others, government helps to shape expectations rather than simply to respond to them.

The study of political symbolism necessarily focuses on *change* and the attitudinal and behavioral conditions of change. Symbols evoke either *change* or *reinforcement* of what people already believe and perceive. It becomes essential to know, for example, how a governmental action or statement may change beliefs or perceptions. A poll may show that virtually all Americans are convinced that the People's Republic of China is their eternal enemy, but these poll results reflect a response to particular stimuli, and not necessarily a stable state of affairs. More important than such a snapshot poll is the way such results change after the President of the United States visits China and the television networks broadcast pictures of beautiful Chinese cities and friendly people. Such changes gain momentum as Chinese leaders visit the United States and businesspeople start to envision profitable trade. Statistics on support or opposition to the President are less important than what kinds of *change* in support will take place if unemployment rises or prices decline. Statistics on attitude, in short, are not "hard data" that are important in themselves, but rather, they are a way of learning something about how governments evoke changes in the direction, intensity, or stability of attitudes. The symbolic perspective is a dynamic one.

Every mode of observing and interpreting the political scene has normative implications. It crudely or subtly suggests that the system, and particular aspects of it, are good or bad, and right or wrong. Here, too, the symbolic perspective makes a difference. The conventional view of the political process sees public policy as reflecting what the people want. The student of symbolism knows that this may be true, but does not avoid the less reassuring aspect of the political process, which is that government can often shape people's wants before it reflects them. It is tempting to take the appearance for the reality. This is true whether the manipulation of public opinion by government officials is deliberate or unintentional. For this reason, the symbolic perspective often raises questions about the legitimacy of political regimes, the obligation to support them, and the desirability of their policies.

Symbolic Politics and Political Quiescence

Legitimacy and Support. Why is there so little resistance to, and such residual support for, a political system that yields such substantial inequalities in wealth, power, status, and sacrifice? Support for the system and belief in its legitimacy are all the more striking in view of the fact that Americans are taught that all people are created equal and that the United States is a land of equal opportunity.

Many governmental processes inculcate both generalized support for the political system and acquiescence to particular policies. Such processes are symbolic in character, because they create meanings and influence states of mind. If they also allocate values, they are both symbolic and instrumental.

The symbols that most powerfully inculcate support for the political system are those that we believe are at the core of the democratic state—the institutions that appear to give the people control over the government. Probably the most reassuring example is the election process. Americans learn early in life to doubt that any state can be democratic without "free" elections, and they are inclined to assume that a country that holds elections must be democratic. Whatever else they accomplish, elections help to create a belief in the reality of popular participation in government and popular control over policy. For the individual voter, elections also create a sense of personal participation and influence in government.

This belief is crucial, regardless of its accuracy. Research raises doubts that belief in popular control through elections is fully warranted. There is evidence that much of the electorate is neither especially interested in issues nor well informed about them. Votes are often cast on the basis of other considerations.[1] But elections powerfully legitimate the political system, regardless of whether they are responsive to people's wants and demands. The realistic political analyst must recognize legitimation as one of

---

[1] See especially Angus Campbell, Philip Converse, Warren Miller, and Donald Stokes, *The American Voter* (New York: Wiley, 1960); Philip Converse, "The Nature of Belief Systems in Mass Publics," in *Ideology and Discontent*, ed. David Apter (New York: Free Press, 1964); Angus Campbell, et al., *Elections and the Political Order* (New York: Wiley, 1966).

the major functions of elections. It also helps to explain the consistent concern over the declining voter participation in the United States. Many observers feel such refusal to participate indicates a growing disbelief in the legitimacy of the political system. On the other hand, we are increasingly encouraged to believe that "if you don't vote, you don't have the right to complain."

Similarly, other institutions that we have been socialized to consider fundamental to democracy help inculcate broad support for the system and acquiescence in policies, even from those who do not like them. The publicized functioning of legislatures promotes widespread confidence that majority will is reflected in the law, and Americans have a fundamental belief that the judicial system will apply that law expertly and impartially. Faith in the symbol of "the rule of law, not men" pervades the American populace. Here again there is evidence that such belief is not warranted. Legislative bodies reflect chiefly the needs of organized interests and strong pressure groups, whereas courts are more sensitive to the interests of certain groups, and are insulated from the "mandate" of the voters of the last election.[2]

Reassurance: Protection Against Threats. Some types of governmental action create the belief that government is providing effective protection against widely feared threats or undesirable developments. One policy area in which this effect is especially dramatic is government regulation of business to protect the consumer. We have antitrust laws to ensure that businesses compete, rather than conspire to concentrate economic power and fix prices. We have many laws to prevent corporations that enjoy monopolies or special licenses in such commodities as telephone, gas, electricity, and radio and TV broadcasting from using their privileged positions to gouge the consumer with high prices or shoddy service. Commissions ensure our safety during air or rail travel, and protect us from impure food and drugs and hazards in our workplace. Antitrust actions are frequently in the news; a recent example is the "breakup" of Ma Bell. Also, public utility commissions hold open hearings. Yet for many decades, studies by economists and political scientists have shown that these laws, and the agencies that administer them, typically offer very little protection; they offer some protection, but they are usually highly sensitive to the economic interests of the businesses they "regulate" and far less so to the interests of consumers. The studies conclude that often the "regulated" become the "regulators."[3]

If the regulatory laws and commissions come close to reversing the economic function they are established to perform, why are they not abolished? They clearly serve political and psychological functions, both for

---

[2] For an exposition of the pertinent evidence and theory, see David B. Truman, *The Governmental Process* (New York: Knopf, 1951), Chapters 11–15.

[3] See, for example, many of Ralph Nader's publications.

politicians and for the mass public; even in the laissez-faire climate of the 1980s, politicians found that supporting and strengthening agencies still brought in votes. Those who fear the concentration of economic power are reassured when the government responds to their anxiety by setting up a regulatory agency. It is rarely clear to consumers just which price ceilings and product standards protect them and which exploit them. In short, the issues are ambiguous and complex. This combination of ambiguity and widespread public anxiety is precisely the climate in which people are eager for reassurance that they are being protected and that publicized governmental actions have the effects they are supposed to have.

The same conditions prevail in many other fields of governmental action. Public policies are partly, and often chiefly, symbolic in character. New civil rights laws reassure liberals that progress is being made, but administrative officials can still ignore the laws or interpret them to permit the very denials of civil liberties that they were intended to prevent. And many among the poor and minorities lack the knowledge and legal counsel to assert their rights. The civil rights laws serve as reassuring symbols for affluent liberals whose own civil rights are fairly well protected, but for the black who is beaten up after being arrested on false charges, there is no ambiguity or symbolic reassurance. For those who are worried about ecological catastrophe, the passage of Clean Air Acts brings reassurance and a sense of victory, but again, it is far from clear that there is any real capacity or intention to act against influential industrial polluters. Tokenism is a classic device for taking advantage of ambiguity and conveying a false sense of reassurance.

Reassurance: The Deprived Deserve Their Fate. Governmental or elitist actions also reassure people about worrisome conditions by instilling a conviction that the deprived deserve their fate, and indeed, some of "those" people are even personally benefitting from it. It is comforting to believe that those who are denied the good things of life suffer from personal pathology, deviance, or delinquency. For elites, this way of defining the behavior of the poor and the unconventional has many advantages. It diverts attention from social and economic problems, and justifies repression of those who deviate from middle-class standards of behavior. Finally, this ideology is accepted by many of the deprived themselves, thus making them docile and submissive. Docility and submission to authority are generously rewarded in schools, prisons, mental hospitals, and welfare agencies; independence, insistence on personal dignity, and imagination are usually penalized, and often severely.

Dissemination of the belief that the deprived are less deserving than others and must be controlled for their own good is a common and potent form of symbolic political action. Such labeling becomes a self-fulfilling prophecy, subtly or coercively requiring people to act as they are defined. This makes it more likely that they will become recidivists—that they will revert to the behavior that got them into trouble in the first place. In a society in which economic and social rewards are very unevenly distributed, such social and psychological control supplements the use of coercive police powers, and is more effective than naked coercion in maintaining quiescence. It minimizes resistance, maximizes support from the general public, and soothes people's consciences.

SPOTTING DANGER AND STANDING FIRM

One of the standard techniques of symbol usage is the discovery or creation of political enemies and danger, followed promptly by exhibitions of reassuring strength and skill by established leaders. We shall illustrate this process at work with respect to a single important foreign-policy problem area at a time prior to actual military engagement. The issue involved was a relatively obscure economic-assistance program begun in 1981 called the "Caribbean Basin Initiative." The Caribbean Basin refers to twenty-four small developing nations in Central America, the Caribbean, and northern South America. The Reagan administration proposed to eliminate most barriers to imports into the United States from those countries, grant certain tax credits to American companies for investing in those areas, and extend a modest amount of additional aid to those nations. Congressional fears about the effects of increased imports on U.S. unemployment kept the first part of the bill from passage for some time, however, and forced the President to stress it more than once in public speeches.

We shall use three brief documents in this illustration: a State Department report issued at the time of President Reagan's first announcement of the program, the President's message transmitting the program to the Congress on March 17, 1982, and the President's State of the Union Address to the Congress of January 25, 1983.[4] The danger was first officially discovered by the State Department, and took three principal forms: "The region forms the third border of the United States, contains vital sea lanes through which three-quarters of our oil imports must flow, is an important market for U.S. exports, and is our second largest source of illegal immigration."[5] The various countries were described as having serious economic problems amounting to an economic crisis that "threatens political and social stability throughout the region which Cuba and others seek to exploit through terrorism and subversion."[6]

By the time the President submitted his proposals to Congress, the dangers had become more active and our goals even more benevolent. He said in part:

> The economic, political, and security challenges in the Caribbean Basin
> are formidable. Our neighbors need time to develop representative and

---

[4] All of the relevant documents may be found in the *Congressional Digest*, March, 1983.

[5] Ibid.

[6] Ibid.

responsive institutions, which are guarantors of the democracy and justice that freedom's foes seek to stamp out. They also need the opportunity to achieve economic progress and . . . the means to defend themselves against attempts by externally-supported minorities to impose an alien, hostile, and unworkable system upon them by force. The alternative is further expansion of political violence from the extreme left and the extreme right, resulting in the imposition of dictatorships and—inevitably— more economic decline, and more human suffering and dislocation.

This is not a crisis we can afford to ignore. The people of the Caribbean Basin are our neighbors. Their well-being and security are in our own vital interest. Events occurring in the Caribbean Basin can affect our lives in profound and dramatic ways. The migrants in our midst are a vivid reminder of the closeness of this problem to all of us.[7]

The enemy involved is not just economic crisis and political instability, but the prospect that somebody will do something about it. The enemy takes a personal form, that of an "outsider" interfering in the normal relationships of "neighbors." The enemy is alternately "Cuba and others," "freedom's foes," and "externally-supported minorities" who apparently believe in an "alien, hostile, and unworkable system." No one trained in the vocabulary of American anticommunism could mistake *that* enemy. Moreover, the enemy is different from us; he or she does not play by the rules. For example, they "exploit" through "terrorism and subversion," "stamp out" freedom, and "impose" their preferences "by force." They are clearly ruthless in their use of others' misery and local "minorities" to gain their ends.

The dangers that we face from this threat are very serious ("formidable") and are of several different kinds. The economic ones are perhaps clearest (exports), the security ones are suggested obliquely (sea lanes for oil imports), and the political ones are left unspecified. The emphasis in the first document on "illegal immigration" and in the second on "dislocation" and "migrants in our midst" may be expressions of concern for displaced Latins and/or displaced American workers, but they may also be not-so-subtle appeals to nationalism or even racism, implying that the United States will be uncontrollably and indigestibly flooded with illegal Hispanic immigrants if we do not stop the march of communism in Central America.

By the start of the 98th Congress in 1983, the proposals had not all been passed. President Reagan now set the need for them in the context of the revived Cold War with the Soviet Union. In consecutive paragraphs of the State of the Union address, our benevolent goals and their evil intentions make a sharp contrast. But we are steadfast, firm, dedicated, unshakeable—and listeners should feel reassured:

---

[7] Ibid.

In Central America and the Caribbean Basin, we are likewise engaged in a partnership for peace, prosperity and democracy. . . . The security and economic assistance policies of this administration, in Latin America and elsewhere, are based on realism and represent a critical investment in the future of the human race . . . the Soviet Union must show, by deeds as well as words, a sincere commitment to respect the rights and sovereignty of the family of nations . . . given the overwhelming evidence of Soviet violations of international treaties concerning chemical and biological weapons, we also insist that any agreement we sign can and will be verifiable. We are prepared to carefully explore serious Soviet proposals. At the same time, let me emphasize that allied steadfastness remains a key to achieving arms reductions.

With firmness and dedication, we will continue to negotiate . . . once they recognize our unshakeable resolve to maintain adequate deterrence, they will have every reason to join us in the search for greater security. When that moment comes . . . we will have taken an important step toward a more peaceful future for all the world's people.[8]

These uses of symbols may seem like ordinary language expressing routine ideas about what is happening in the world, but that is just the point. Symbolic manipulation and reassurance are routine processes, and are all the more effective for being so. Consider the number of times that enemies are portrayed as subhuman, barbaric, or otherwise profoundly different from us. Such characterizations may be necessary to inspire us to levels of sacrifice that we would otherwise be unwilling to make, or to justify actions toward such enemies that we could otherwise not seriously consider or support. And throughout, leaders who stand up to and defend us from such dangers will seem to deserve our greatest appreciation.

SUMMARY

Ideology and symbolism have much in common as ways of justifying and defending the status quo in the face of policies that do not give priority to majority interests. Both are partly in our minds and partly in the actions and rhetoric of leaders; both shape wants and needs in the image of what it is possible or convenient to deliver; and both divert attention and energy away from the actual consequences of public policies and provide layers of legitimacy for government action.

Ideology is grounded in basic political values such as individualism, natural rights, limited government, materialism and the business ethic, and racism. The first four values have a hallowed history and are seen as

---

[8] Ibid.

operative throughout our political institutions and practices today. They help us to understand that whatever our system does is:

1. Based on compromise among all interested groups,
2. Democratic, and
3. The best possible accommodation under all the circumstances.

Racism is unacknowledged and sometimes denied.

Symbolism is the process of creating images in people's minds that call forth approval or revulsion, in part by fulfilling inherent needs in people; it then invokes such reactions to build support or acquiescence for elite action. Much use of symbolism surrounds the legitimacy of government institutions and policies, and converts natural fears or unserved needs into forms of reassurance.

PART III

Institutions and Processes

CHAPTER 7

The Constitution

One of the most concise and tangible expressions of our ideology is the United States Constitution. It materializes the attempt to build a limited government that is based on and protective of individual natural rights. Reasonable men came together, ceded some of their individual freedoms in return for protection of the others, and drew up a contract—the Constitution—sealing the bargain. The Constitution also serves as one, if not *the*, symbol of the United States. Very little public action takes place without reference to it, and policy innovations must maintain links to the past through ties to the Constitution. The U.S. Constitution provides constant legitimacy for some, and reassurance for others; it is the umbrella one *must* be under if one is an American.

The Constitution of the United States is also a political economic document. It is the product of a political/social/economic struggle, and it represents a specific political economy, expresses values, and acts as a powerful symbol in a political economic context. These values and symbols come out of, create, and are part of the larger context, the coherent whole.

This chapter will analyze the Constitution in three steps, keeping in mind its basic character as a manifest expression of values, a very potent symbol, and a political economic document. We will first discuss the principles and purposes underlying its creation and ratification, and then the substance of the document. Exhibit 1 illustrates the Constitution's contribution to a politics of civil disobedience. This is followed by a discussion of its impact on and implications for American politics in more general terms. We will then turn to a discussion of a central question: Who interprets the Constitution? Given the centrality of the Constitution and the notion of constitutionality in our political life, the entity or entities in charge of conferring constitutional legitimacy is a most powerful one.

PURPOSES AND PRINCIPLES UNDERLYING THE CONSTITUTION

Of course, purposes and principles are related. It is very difficult to sort out which comes first, if either does. If one's purpose is to protect property rights against the "tyranny of the majority," then the principle of majority rule/minority rights is very handy. Equally as plausible, one could be committed to maintaining minority rights as a matter of principle, so that the purpose of protecting against majorities follows. For this discussion, we will separate them, discussing first the controversies regarding the purposes of the framers of the Constitution, and then the principles eventually expressed in the document.

Purposes

Generations of historians have battled over the proper interpretation of the Constitutional Convention and the goals and purposes of the men who attended it. To some, it was a conservative counterrevolution following the excessive liberalism of the Declaration of Independence. To others, it was a far-sighted, bold experiment in expanding the frontiers of democracy. People of the era disagreed among themselves from the very moment the veil of secrecy was lifted from the proceedings of the convention. Patrick Henry, for example, declared that he "smelled a rat."

Nineteenth-century historians, who were perhaps sympathetic to Federalist principles, tended to be especially struck by the framers' accomplishments, and some went so far as to imply that they were divinely inspired. In reaction to this school of Constitution-worship, and based on Progressive Movement realism, Charles Beard published his *Economic Interpretation of the Constitution* in 1913.[1] Beard very nearly turned American history upside down by arguing that the framers had a personal economic stake in a new and stronger government. They had acquired vast holdings of the bonds and scrip issued by the Continental Congress during the Revolutionary War. Because the Continental Congress was unable to pay its debts, the framers acquired this paper at very low cost. Beard implied that they then constructed a powerful government that was capable of raising the revenue to pay off the bonds at full value—to their great personal profit.

When other scholars sought to verify Beard's allegations, it appeared that he had, at the very least, overstated his argument.[2] But the controversy had helped others to look at the Constitution as a value-laden document with quite human strengths and weaknesses, and few now deny that there

---

[1] Charles Beard, *An Economic Interpretation of the Constitution* (New York: Macmillan, 1913).

[2] The leading counterargument to Beard is Robert Brown, *Charles Beard and the Constitution* (Princeton, N.J.: Princeton University Press, 1956).

was at least a shared upper-class ethos among the framers and that economic interests played some part in shaping the Constitution.

There were, of course, a wide variety of purposes behind the creation and ratification of the Constitution, and a short historical review will help to bring out some of the major ones. After independence was declared, the American states needed to cooperate in the war against England and the conduct of foreign affairs in general. The Articles of Confederation were drawn up shortly after the Declaration of Independence was issued. They provided the basis of a central government, until they were supplanted by the Constitution of 1787. Under the Articles, the states retained all governing powers within their boundaries. The Congress was the sole institution of the general government, but it had few powers and little capacity to enforce those it had.

The Revolutionary War was followed by a period of economic disruption. Financial and commercial interests with relatively broad markets took the lead in calling for a stronger central government. Alexander Hamilton used a poorly attended meeting called for commercial purposes (the Annapolis Convention) to issue a call to the states to send delegates to a convention in Philadelphia in 1787 to revise the Articles of Confederation. The convention met in June and the delegates immediately decided to violate their instructions by embarking on the consideration of an entirely new plan of government; they also prudently decided to keep the proceedings secret. They finished their work in September—a new United States Constitution for state ratification.

After protracted debate in key states such as Massachusetts, New York, and Virginia, the Constitution was finally accepted by narrow margins. As a price for ratification, supporters agreed to sponsor several amendments, now known as the Bill of Rights, in the first Congress. It is difficult to recapture the bitterness of the opposition to ratification, but it was chiefly from debtors, small farmers, some conservatives in New York, and a great number of people who simply distrusted a potentially strong central government.

From these facts it appears that the major purposes behind the drive for a new Constitution were twofold:

1. The desire for a stronger central government that was capable of protecting merchants and others in the international arena, and presenting a strong and united front; and
2. The desire for a stronger central government that would create and ensure the conditions necessary for the development of a *national* and *commercial* economy.

This does not mean that the framers were out to create a national government for their personal profit (although many profited). It does mean that the framers—and their opponents—were aware of the implications of their actions. The government was created for the purpose of supporting a growing, national, commercial economy, and the Constitution created a specific political economic whole.

Principles

In general, the framers agreed upon the political principles of governmental organization that they considered to be necessary or desirable. Many of these principles arose out of the values discussed in Chapter 6. These principles were widely shared among the population, particularly the principle of adherence to individual natural rights. In other cases, the framers advanced values that were more specific to their class or group interests. We will discuss three major principles, including some developments that have occurred in the two centuries of experience after the ratification of the Constitution.

Limited Government. The U.S. government is a government of limited powers; it has only those powers, express or implied, that are *granted* to it in the Constitution, and it can exercise those powers only in ways that are not *prohibited* by the Constitution. In order to act, the U.S. government must find authorization somewhere in the Constitution *and* act without violating any of the contained limits. This is the reverse of the situation for most governments. They are assumed to have all the powers that are or might conceivably be exercised by any government at any time, *except* as limited by a constitution. But the U.S. Constitution is quite consistent with the basic American political value that governments should be restricted in their scope and activities so that individuals can be as free as possible to seek private goals without interference. It also reflects the American confidence in contracts that spell out in detail each parties' respective powers, limitations, and responsibilities.

Even a limited government can expand its powers, however, as we know from the twentieth-century American experience. The process may be awkward and time-consuming, as well as dependent on the political makeup of the interpreters of the Constitution, but expansion obviously does occur. A major example is the federal government's power "To regulate commerce with foreign nations, and among the several States." Now known as the "interstate commerce" clause, it provides the basis for much congressional activity, but it took many years for the definition of interstate commerce to expand to this point. Originally it was a very limited power. For example, the mere production of goods was not sufficient to define a factory as "in commerce." After the famous "switch in time that saved nine" of the New Deal era, the Supreme Court acquiesced in a gradual enlargement of the definition of "commerce." We have reached the point where Congress can constitutionally require little luncheonettes in the backwoods of Georgia to serve blacks,[3] even though the luncheonette may never see a person traveling in interstate commerce or buy supplies from another state. The supporting argument runs like this: although the luncheonette itself is not "in commerce," it has "an effect" on commerce

---

[3] *Heart of Atlanta Motel* v. *Maddox*, 379 U.S. 241 (1964).

because people who eat in the luncheonette do not go to eat in restaurants that *are* in commerce.[4]

The point is that although powers of the federal government may vastly expand under new historical circumstances, the *principle* of limited government has not been abandoned. Each new exercise of power must be specifically tied to a grant of power in the Constitution. The burden of proof is always on the government.

Separation of Powers: Checks and Balances. Separation of powers argues that governments exercise three distinct powers: executive, legislative, and judicial. These powers need to be placed in the hands of different officials or institutions (separated), because placing all powers in a single entity would result in tyranny. The American Constitution implements this principle by creating separate institutions to exercise each power (Articles I, II, and III respectively). But none of these institutions possesses its power fully; separation of powers can be understood only in connection with the principle of checks and balances, and both are derived from the older idea of "mixed government."

"Checks and balances" applies to the various opportunities that are given to each branch to affirmatively "check" the others. (Under strict separation of powers, the only check would be refusal to cooperate in carrying out a specific policy.) Most of the legislative powers are located in Congress; most of the executive powers are in the Presidency; and most of the judicial powers are in the Supreme Court, but each branch of the American government also has powers that, under strict separation of powers, belong to another branch. The President, for example, has the (legislative) power of veto, and the Senate has the (executive) power of confirming appointments. It has been well said that the American system consists of "separated institutions sharing powers."[5]

"Mixed government" is the concept underlying both separation of powers and checks and balances. This idea was developed in the British constitution and served as a model for Americans; it held that the three major classes of society must each be represented in the government. In the eyes of John Adams, the leading American constitutional theorist, the three classes effectively mixed in the British constitution were the king, the aristocracy, and the commons. Each was dominant in one institution and could, if necessary, prevent the others from acting. According to

---

[4] The original case using this rationale is *Wickard* v. *Filburn,* 317 U.S. 111 (1942) in which a farmer who was growing his full quota of grain under federal crop limitations (an exercise of the power to regulate commerce) decided to grow more, solely for the purpose of feeding his chickens, and not for sale. He was nevertheless held to be in violation of the limitations on growing, because the grain he grew himself he would not buy in commerce. He thereby had an "effect" on commerce and was subject to congressional power.

[5] This apt phrase was coined by Richard Neustadt in his *Presidential Power: The Politics of Leadership* (New York: Wiley, 1960).

Adams, this was the genius of the British system and had led to the highest level of liberty yet known in the world. Unfortunately, in the United States, there was no king and no aristocracy—only an excess of commoners. Tyranny at the hand of the masses seemed inevitable.[6]

The solution to the prospect of commoner tyranny was to separate the powers of government; this would divide the body of commoners against itself. To further promote division, each branch was given powers to check and balance the other branches, which would ensure that governmental power rested in several hands, each with a distinctive constituency with varying values or priorities. An inevitable result is conflict over all but the most innocuous questions.

The framers particularly feared that political parties would be the most likely agents of majority will, and worked hard to prevent parties from becoming accepted or effective. Thus, although many in government belong to the same political party, the fact that they are associated with different institutions and respond to distinctive constituencies leads them to disagree with one another. Separation of powers ensures internal conflict among both majority and minority officeholders in the national government, and encourages attempts at temporary alliances between likeminded elements across party lines. Most of all, it makes concerted action very difficult.

Federalism. The principles of limited government and separation of powers/checks and balances were generally accepted political principles of the day. They arose out of both the British model and the wide acceptance in the United States of the fundamental values of individualism and the protection of individual rights, especially property rights. However, federalism is an organizing political principle that was practically forced upon the Constitution by the circumstances of the time; the framers had little choice, given the independence and power of the states in 1787.

Federalism is the division of sovereignty between constituent units (the states) and a single central unit (the national government); each has defined powers and is supreme in its own allotted sphere. Federalism implies a balance with a certain amount of tension between the two, and it purposefully provides a base of power for local majorities or others that are not dominant in the central government. A *federal* system must be distinguished from a *national* system, in which the central unit has ultimate control over the powers or actions of the states, and a *confederacy* (such as the United States under the Articles of Confederation), in which the states hold the balance of power and thus can frustrate or defy the central government.

In the early decades of the Republic, the states seemed to be the more active and important units of government, but, due partly to Supreme Court decisions favoring national power, the central government increas-

---

[6] For a full discussion, see Bernard Bailyn, *The Ideological Origins of the American Revolution* (Cambridge, Mass.: Harvard University Press, 1967), Chapter 6.

ingly acquired greater leverage. The Civil War and the postwar amendments to the Constitution (Fourteen and Fifteen) confirmed national supremacy. From the 1890s through the early decades of the twentieth century, the Supreme Court revived the idea of inviolable state sovereignty as a rationale for limiting national power. Sometimes known as "dual federalism," this idea held that if a matter were subject to state power, it was therefore *not* subject to national power. The Court reversed itself in 1937, effectively inaugurating a period of "cooperative federalism," in which both the states and the nation may regulate the same activity, provided they do not conflict. If they conflict, of course, the nation is supreme.

Obviously, national power has expanded rapidly and enormously. With grants-in-aid to the states and other revenue-sharing practices, federal involvement in (if not control over) the activities of state and local governments increased. President Reagan's "new federalism" attempted to reshape the balance toward the states, but has been more rhetoric than reality. However, commitment to federalism remains real, and it affects the daily workings of the American political system.

THE CONSTITUTION: THE SUBSTANCE OF THE DOCUMENT

From these purposes and principles emerged the United States Constitution. The Constitution reflects several compromises among divergent interests among the framers against a general background of shared political values. Delegates from small states resisted exclusively population-based representation in the legislature and managed to secure equal status in the Senate, Southerners extracted a prohibition against interference with the importation of slaves for a fixed period of time, and the electoral college was constructed to balance the respective weights of the small and large states in selecting the President. Because of these and other differences among the framers, as well as the need for approval by the country at large, the document is not logically consistent or precisely symmetrical. It has often been called a "bundle of compromises." However, the extent of conflict and the scope and difficulty of compromise at the Constitutional Convention must not obscure the fact that much was shared in the way of political values.

The next section will analyze the document as it might have appeared to the people of the time, emphasizing the scope and implications of the powers granted to the new government. We will do this on an article-by-article basis; this should be read along with the provisions of the Constitution, as set forth in the Appendix. We will then add more general analysis of the substance as a whole, discussing what appears to be an emphasis on protection of property rights and an antimajoritarian bias. We will conclude with an examination of the Bill of Rights, the original amendments designed to allay fears of, and to counteract, the Constitution's enlarged powers.

The Document

The Preamble. The initial phrase ("We the people. . . .") has been taken to indicate that the Constitution, and the government it creates, is the act of the people as a whole. It is not the creation of the states acting in their separate sovereign capacities. The Articles of Confederation, of course, were explicitly a league of such sovereign states. From the very start, however, the nationalists among the framers sought to reduce the part played by the states in forming or controlling the new government. Although it does so without legal standing, the Preamble indicates an intention to have the national government operate directly upon the individual citizen, and vice versa.

Article I. This article creates the legislative branch, which consists of two houses, one based on population and one on equal representation of the states. It replaces the old one-house Congress in which each state had one vote. After providing for the election of each body and the manner of conducting business, the article grants powers (Section 8), sets limits to powers (Section 9), and sets limits on state powers (Section 10). The powers granted are broad in scope, particularly in contrast to the powers of Congress under the Articles. Now, Congress has power to raise revenue, regulate interstate commerce, and maintain national armed forces. Moreover, the final paragraph of Article I grants to Congress an indeterminate power to make all laws "necessary and proper" to carry the others into effect. The limits on granted powers protect the importation of slaves for twenty years, require uniformity in economic legislation, and seek to prevent some of the all-too-familiar excesses of British royalty. The states are excluded from foreign relations and from interfering with the creation of a national market with a single stable currency.

Article II. This article creates the new executive branch. It boldly (in the light of pre-Revolutionary experience with British kings) grants the President broad power to be: commander-in-chief of the armed forces, voice of the nation in foreign affairs, and enforcer of the laws. The scope of powers granted here probably reflects the prospect that George Washington, having chaired the Constitutional Convention, would now accept office as the first President in the new government. Almost the entire nation felt that Washington could be trusted and that conversely, he would be unlikely to accept any merely ceremonial post.

Article III. This article creates a new judicial branch in the form of the Supreme Court. Its justices are to hold office "during good behavior," essentially for life. The jurisdiction of the Court extends to all those "cases or controversies" arising out of the existence of the new government, the Constitution, federal laws, and treaties. It has *no* power over matters of state law or practice, except as such actions might be in conflict with provisions of the Constitution or valid federal laws. Nor is there any mention of the power of judicial review, the power the Court now enjoys of declaring acts of the Congress or the President void because it does not consider them to be authorized by the Constitution.

Article IV. This article prescribes certain relationships among the states. Each state must accept the validity of the governmental actions of other states, such as by enforcing debts for which court judgments have been obtained in other states. States cannot grant haven to persons who have been accused of crimes in another state or do anything for escaped slaves except return them to their owners. States must also permit citizens of other states to do business within their borders on the same basis as their own citizens. Finally, the U.S. government gains power to help maintain existing state governments against the threat of rebellion by their own citizens. The latter provision was aimed at preventing incidents such as the farmers' rebellion against mortgage foreclosures in Massachusetts in 1786–87 ("Shays's Rebellion").

Article V. This article prescribes two ways to amend the Constitution: by two-thirds vote of both houses of Congress or by a convention called by the Congress when requested by the legislatures of two-thirds of the states. In either case, ratification must follow by the legislatures of three-quarters of the states. Amendment was not meant to be a frequent activity.

Article VI. This article accomplishes two things of vital importance to the development of the nation. It assumes the debts of the previous Congress, as Beard emphasized. This was used by Alexander Hamilton to build the credit of the U.S. government and to gain the loyal support of bankers and their creditors who held the bonds and other obligations issued by the Continental Congress. It also asserted the supremacy of the Constitution and laws of the United States over the constitutions, laws, and judicial proceedings of the states. This controversial "supremacy clause" has finally been accepted as putting the laws and actions of the supposedly sovereign states into a secondary status.

Article VII. This article provides for ratification of the Constitution by specially called state conventions, rather than by the existing state legislatures. It hints, as does the Preamble, that the Constitution creates a new and direct relationship between the people as a whole and the U.S. government. This method was probably chosen as the one most likely to secure ratification. Existing state legislatures did not take too kindly to their diminished status.

The Bill of Rights. The first ten amendments, known collectively as the Bill of Rights, were an essential part of the agreement struck by the framers to gain ratification. As such, they are usually considered to be part of the original Constitution. The amendments prohibit Congress specifically or the national government generally from interfering with some of our traditional and hard-won civil liberties. Interference with these rights provided part of the reason for the Revolutionary War. The Bill of Rights helped alleviate fears on the part of many that the newly-created government would repeat some of those tyrannies.

Subsequent amendments are noted at other points in the book, where appropriate.

Protection for Property Rights

Many major business and financial interests were dissatisfied with government under the Articles. They disliked individual states engaging in protectionism of their own products and business. Equally disturbing, if not more so, was the tendency in many states to promote both inflation and the avoidance of debts. These troubles provided much of the motivation for the Annapolis Convention that resulted in the call to revise the Articles of Confederation and the subsequent Constitutional Convention. For the national-minded commercial, financial, and creditor interests, the Constitution was a triumph. They gained:

1. Prohibitions on state import restrictions and taxation.
2. A prohibition on state impairment of the obligations of contracts, which meant that states could not legislate the postponement of debt repayment or prevent the foreclosure of mortgages.
3. A single central agency to coin money and regulate its value.
4. A prohibition on state use of paper money or other legal tender.
5. A system of courts operated by the central government, so that they did not have to take chances with locally run courts in states to which their debtors had fled.
6. A guarantee of full faith and credit in one state to the acts and judgments of another, so that they could pursue their debtors more effectively.
7. A guarantee of a republican form of government for the states as well as provisions for suppressing domestic insurrections so that they need fear no further incidents such as Shays's Rebellion.

In all these provisions, the framers acted consistently to promote the enforcement of contracts, the collection of debts, the maintenance of stable valuation for money, and the promotion of a national economy. Under the conditions of the time, these were undoubtedly economy-building goals, but they were implemented at the expense of many small farmers and artisans.

In this respect, the substance of the Constitution favored the interests of one class over those of another. The desire of some small farmers to promote inflation, avoid debts, or protect their local industries was not merely an ungrateful rejection of contractual obligation; in their eyes, and perhaps objectively, the eastern financiers and businessmen were profiting unconscionably from exorbitant interest rates, as well as taking advantage of unsettled economic conditions to foreclose on land and further exploit hapless and frequently penniless farmers and artisans. To this group of Americans, many of whom fought in the Revolution, the Constitution appeared to be one more means of furthering their exploitation. While they agreed with some of the political *principles* of the Constitution, they felt that the political *economy* reflected in the substance of the Constitution benefited certain classes more than others.

Antimajoritarianism

The framers built into the Constitution layer upon layer of obstacles to simple majority rule. This was consistent with their desire to protect property rights, but drew more specifically on their anticipation of redistribution and regulation of property by the masses. It is instructive to see how almost every one of these restrictions has been moderated (but not erased) in subsequent years. If it had not been possible to find ways around these limitations, the Constitution would probably have aroused even more criticism in recent decades.

The main limitations on majority rule and the means found to circumvent them are as follows:

1. Amendment to the Constitution is very difficult, requiring a vote of two-thirds of both houses of Congress and ratification by three-quarters of the states. Informal means of amendment have been developed, such as the shifting interpretations of the Supreme Court. But as the experience of the Equal Rights Amendment indicates, it takes much more than the support of a majority of the American people to amend the Constitution.
2. The electoral college is a device designed to give discretionary power to the elected delegates and to deny the people direct choice of the President. But delegates to the electoral college run on a pledged basis and very rarely violate their pledges.
3. Separation of powers prevents the people (supposedly represented in the Congress) from working their will in the government as a whole. However, the President, too, claims to represent majority will, and the party system cuts across the separation of powers to induce some degree of cooperation between the branches.
4. Senators were originally elected by the state legislatures. Direct election of senators was accomplished by constitutional amendment in 1917. For decades before that, state legislators had often run for election on the basis of pledges to vote for one or another senatorial candidate.
5. Judicial review is a means of applying restraints to the legislature, supposedly the representatives of the people. But Congress and the President have shown imagination in pressuring the Court or avoiding the implications of its decisions. Ironically, the least accountable institution has come to be seen as a protector of the people, often against the very government that is supposed to be by the people.
6. The division of the legislature into two houses was an attempt to introduce institutional jealousies and constituency rivals into the popular branch and thereby to reduce coherent action. The party system and presidential leadership have promoted some degree of unity between the two houses, but action remains difficult.

This catalog might be expanded, but the point should be clear: The impressive list of conscious efforts to fragment, divide, and neutralize the will of the people cannot be coincidental. It does not mean that the government cannot act at all, but it does mean that simple majority preference will not move it; other conditions must also be present.

The Bill of Rights

The Bill of Rights stands in contrast to the substance of the document. As the body of the Constitution makes clear, a strong central government that was capable of acting directly upon individuals was created. This was not lost upon the citizens of the time and, in order to protect themselves, they insisted upon a Bill of Rights; basic political rights are specifically set forth in the first ten amendments, and particularly in the first six.

The Bill of Rights provides that the U.S. government shall not do certain things. In particular, it "shall make no law . . . abridging the freedom of speech, or of the press; or the right of the people peaceably to assemble, and to petition the Government for a redress of grievances." This sounds absolute, but in a series of decisions from the early days to the present, the Supreme Court has interpreted the First Amendment to guarantee only the limited form of freedom of speech and assembly that was protected by law in 1789 when the amendment was adopted. Thus, the Congress is free to adopt such limitations as it sees fit, provided they meet the Court's standards of *reasonableness*. In practice, only twice in its history has the Court declared a congressional statute void on the grounds that it violated the First Amendment.

Notice that these political rights exist only as limitations on the U.S. government, and do not protect citizens against one another's actions. For example, if someone prevents a person from speaking in a private auditorium, no constitutional rights have been violated. The crimes of assault or trespass may have been committed, but the Constitution provides guarantees only against the acts of government.

As originally written, the Bill of Rights did not apply against state government; in an early case, the Court held that citizens must look to their state constitutions for such protections. In the 1920s, the Supreme Court decided that at least some of the national guarantees *do* apply to the states, and on its own initiative, the Court held that the Fourteenth Amendment's provision that the states not deny their citizens "due process of law" made some of the guarantees of the Bill of Rights applicable to the states. Since that time, in a series of decisions, it has added several of the guarantees of the Bill of Rights to the list of individual rights that are protected against state action. Not all of them are applicable; only those that the Court deems *fundamental* to the concept of due process have been extended to the states.

Overall, the courts' record in defense of the exercise of the political rights that are supposedly guaranteed by the Bill of Rights has not been particularly aggressive or distinguished. Most of the time, courts side with legislative or administrative authorities. Unpopular people, parties, or causes claim protection under the Bill of Rights only to discover that the established authorities were exercising their constitutional powers in imposing limitations on political activity. Political rights are far more firmly established in legal theory than in actual practice, but they are there in the substance of the document, and have an impact on American political activity.

EXHIBIT 1
Civil Disobedience

Civil disobedience has a long and valued history, as Martin Luther King, Jr. points out in the following letter. In general, civil disobedience is the individual's refusal to obey an unjust law, while acknowledging the community's or society's right and necessity to make and enforce laws. There are times when an individual's conscience requires the breaking of a specific civil law in the name of a higher law, be it natural law, God's Law, or Justice.

In the United States, acts of civil disobedience often include a unique slant. The Constitution embodies the higher law, and so, specific civil laws that an individual finds unjust are also perceived to be "unconstitutional." The breaking of an unjust civil law, or committing an act of civil disobedience, can be a prelude to a legal challenge regarding its constitutionality. But the actual legal challenge is a secondary tactic; acting in accordance with the Constitution may mean ending up in jail, which then requires dealing with the courts. However, unlike Exhibit 2 in the following chapter, the major focus of civil disobedience is to seek social change through moral, political action.

During the 1950s and 1960s, a surging civil rights movement challenged longstanding American practices and laws regarding its black citizens. Beginning in the South, American black people demanded an end to segregation, both as embodied in the law and in practice. Arguing for the implementation of their full rights as specified in the United States Constitution, a series of sit-ins, Freedom Rides, and marches brought the issue to the attention of the American public. One of the most brutal testing grounds was Birmingham, Alabama. The following letter, which is now a classic in American political thought, well illustrates the American variety of civil disobedience, as well as the centrality of the Constitution to our most fundamental political problems.

Letter From Birmingham Jail*

April 16, 1963

My Dear Fellow Clergymen:

While confined here in the Birmingham city jail, I came across your recent statement calling my present activities "unwise and untimely." Seldom do I pause to answer criticism of my work and ideas. If I sought to answer all the criticisms that cross my desk, my secretaries would have little time for anything other than such correspondence in the course of the day, and I would have no time for constructive work. But since I feel that you are men of genuine good will and that your criticisms are sincerely set forth, I want to try to answer your statement in what I hope will be patient and reasonable terms. I think I should indicate why I am here in Birmingham, since you have been influenced by the view which argues against "outsiders coming in." I have the honor of serving as president of the Southern Christian Leadership Conference, an organization operating in every southern state, with headquarters in Atlanta, Georgia. We have some eighty-five affiliated organizations across the South, for Human Rights. Frequently we share staff, educational and financial resources with our affiliates. Several months ago the affiliate here in Birmingham asked us to be on call to engage in a nonviolent direct-action program if such were deemed necessary. We readily consented, and when the hour came we lived up to our promise. So I, along with several members of my staff, am here because I was invited here. I am here because I have organizational ties here.

But more basically, I am in Birmingham because injustice is here. Just as the prophets of the eighth century B.C. left their villages and carried their "thus saith the Lord" far beyond the boundaries of their home towns, and just as the Apostle Paul left his village of Tarsus and carried the gospel of Jesus Christ to the far corners of the Greco-Roman world, so am I compelled to carry the gospel of freedom beyond my own home town. Like Paul, I must constantly respond to the Macedonian call for aid.

---

* *Author's Note.* This response to a published statement by eight fellow clergymen from Alabama (Bishop C. C. J. Carpenter, Bishop Joseph A. Durick, Rabbi Hilton L. Grafman, Bishop Paul Hardin, Bishop Holan B. Harmon, the Reverend George M. Murray, the Reverend Edward V. Ramage and the Reverend Earl Stallings) was composed under somewhat constricting circumstances. Begun on the margins of the newspaper in which the statement appeared while I was in jail, the letter was continued on scraps of writing paper supplied by a friendly Negro trusty, and concluded on a pad my attorneys were eventually permitted to leave me. Although the text remains in substance unaltered, I have indulged in the author's prerogative of polishing it for publication.

SOURCE: An abridgement of "Letter from Birmingham Jail, April 16, 1963" from pages 77–92 and 97–100 of *Why We Can't Wait* by Martin Luther King, Jr. Reprinted by permission of Harper & Row, Publishers, Inc.

Moreover, I am cognizant of the interrelatedness of all communities
and states. I cannot sit idly by in Atlanta and not be concerned about
what happens in Birmingham. Injustice anywhere is a threat to justice
everywhere. We are caught in an inescapable network of mutuality,
tied in a single garment of destiny. Whatever affects one directly, affects
all indirectly. Never again can we afford to live with the narrow, provin-
cial "outside agitator" idea. Anyone who lives inside the United States
can never be considered an outsider anywhere within its bounds.

You deplore the demonstrations taking place in Birmingham. But your
statement, I am sorry to say, fails to express a similar concern for the
conditions that brought about the demonstrations. I am sure that none
of you would want to rest content with the superficial kind of social
analysis that deals merely with effects and does not grapple with
underlying causes. It is unfortunate that demonstrations are taking
place in Birmingham, but it is even more unfortunate that the city's
white power structure left the Negro community with no alternative.

In any nonviolent campaign there are four basic steps: collection of the
facts to determine whether injustices exist; negotiation; self-purification; and direct action. We have gone through all these steps in Birmingham. There can be no gainsaying the fact that racial injustice
engulfs this community. Birmingham is probably the most thoroughly
segregated city in the United States. Its ugly record of brutality is widely
known. Negroes have experienced grossly unjust treatment in the
courts. There have been more unsolved bombings of Negro homes
and churches in Birmingham than in any other city in the nation. These
are the hard, brutal facts of the case. On the basis of these conditions,
Negro leaders sought to negotiate with the city fathers. But the latter
consistently refused to engage in good-faith negotiation.

Then, last September, came the opportunity to talk with leaders of
Birmingham's economic community. In the course of the negotiations,
certain promises were made by the merchants—for example, to remove the stores' humiliating racial signs. On the basis of these promises, the Reverend Fred Shuttlesworth and the leaders of the Alabama
Christian Movement for Human Rights agreed to a moratorium on all
demonstrations. As the weeks and months went by, we realized that
we were the victims of a broken promise. A few signs, briefly removed,
returned; the others remained.

As in so many past experiences, our hopes had been blasted, and the
shadow of deep disappointment settled upon us. We had no alternative except to prepare for direct action, whereby we would present our
very bodies as a means of laying our case before the conscience of the
local and the national community. Mindful of the difficulties involved,
we decided to undertake a process of self-purification. We began a
series of workshops on nonviolence, and we repeatedly asked ourselves: "Are you able to accept blows without retaliating?" "Are you
able to endure the ordeal of jail?" We decided to schedule our direct-
action program for the Easter season, realizing that except for Christ-
mas, this is the main shopping period of the year. Knowing that a
strong economic-withdrawal program would be the by-product of

direct action, we felt that this would be the best time to bring pressure to bear on the merchants for the needed change.

Then it occurred to us that Birmingham's mayoralty election was coming up in March, and we speedily decided to postpone action until after election day. When we discovered that the Commissioner of Public Safety, Eugene "Bull" Connor, had piled up enough votes to be in the run-off, we decided again to postpone action until the day after the run-off so that the demonstrations could not be used to cloud the issues. Like many others, we waited to see Mr. Connor defeated, and to this end we endured postponement after postponement. Having aided in this community need, we felt that our direct-action program could be delayed no longer.

You may well ask: "Why direct action? Why sit-ins, marches and so forth? Isn't negotiations a better path?" You are quite right in calling for negotiation. Indeed, this is the very purpose of direct action. Nonviolent direct action seeks to create such a crisis and foster such a tension that a community which has constantly refused to negotiate is forced to confront the issue. It seeks so to dramatize the issue that it can no longer be ignored. My citing the creation of tension as part of the work of the nonviolent-resister may sound rather shocking. But I must confess that I am not afraid of the word "tension." I have earnestly opposed violent tension, but there is a type of constructive, nonviolent tension which is necessary for growth. Just as Socrates felt that it was necessary to create a tension in the mind so that individuals could rise from the bondage of myths and half-truths to the unfettered realm of creative analysis and objective appraisal, so must we see the need for nonviolent gadflies to create the kind of tension in society that will help men rise from the dark depths of prejudice and racism to the majestic heights of understanding and brotherhood.

The purpose of our direct-action program is to create a situation so crisis-packed that it will inevitably open the door to negotiation. I therefore concur with you in your call for negotiation. Too long has our beloved Southland been bogged down in a tragic effort to live in monologue rather than dialogue.

One of the basic points in your statement is that the action that I and my associates have taken in Birmingham is untimely. Some have asked: "Why didn't you give the new city administration time to act?" The only answer that I can give to this query is that the new Birmingham administration must be prodded about as much as the outgoing one, before it will act. We are sadly mistaken if we feel that the election of Albert Boutwell as mayor will bring the millennium to Birmingham. While Mr. Boutwell is a much more gentle person than Mr. Connor, they are both segregationists, dedicated to maintenance of the status quo. I have hope that Mr. Boutwell will be reasonable enough to see the futility of massive resistance to desegregation. But he will not see this without pressure from devotees of civil rights. My friends, I must say to you that we have not made a single gain in civil rights without determined legal and nonviolent pressure. Lamentably, it is an historical fact that privileged groups seldom give up their privileges voluntarily. Individuals may see the moral light and voluntarily give up their unjust posture; but, as Reinhold Niebuhr has reminded us, groups tend to be more immoral than individuals.

We know through painful experience that freedom is never voluntarily given by the oppressor; it must be demanded by the oppressed. Frankly, I have yet to engage in a direct-action campaign that was "well timed" in the view of those who have not suffered unduly from the disease of segregation. For years now I have heard the word "Wait!" It rings in the ear of every Negro with piercing familiarity. This "Wait" has almost always meant "Never." We must come to see, with one of our distinguished jurists, that "justice too long delayed is justice denied."

We have waited for more than 340 years for our constitutional and God-given rights. The nations of Asia and Africa are moving with jetlike speed toward gaining political independence, but we still creep at horse and buggy pace toward gaining a cup of coffee at a lunch counter. Perhaps it is easy for those who have never felt the stinging darts of segregation to say, "Wait." But when you have seen vicious mobs lynch your mothers and fathers at will and drown your sisters and brothers at whim; when you have seen hate-filled policemen curse, kick and even kill your black brothers and sisters; when you see the vast majority of your twenty million Negro brothers smothering in an airtight cage of poverty in the midst of an affluent society; when you suddenly find your tongue twisted and your speech stammering as you seek to explain to your six-year-old daughter why she can't go to the public amusement park that has just been advertised on television, and see tears welling up in her eyes when she is told that Funtown is closed to colored children, and see ominous clouds of inferiority beginning to form in her little mental sky, and see her beginning to distort her personality by developing an unconscious bitterness toward white people; when you have to concoct an answer for a five-year-old son who is asking: "Daddy, why do white people treat colored people so mean?"; when you take a cross-country drive and find it necessary to sleep night after night in the uncomfortable corners of your automobile because no motel will accept you; when you are humiliated day in and day out by nagging signs reading "white" and "colored"; when your first name becomes "nigger," your middle name becomes "boy" (however old you are) and your last name becomes "John," and your wife and mother are never given the respected title "Mrs."; when you are harried by day and haunted by night by the fact that you are a Negro, living constantly at tiptoe stance, never quite knowing what to expect next, and are plagued with inner fears and outer resentments; when you are forever fighting a degenerating sense of "nobodiness"—then you will understand why we find it difficult to wait. There comes a time when the cup of endurance runs over, and men are no longer willing to be plunged into the abyss of despair. I hope, sirs, you can understand our legitimate and unavoidable impatience.

You express a great deal of anxiety over our willingness to break laws. This is certainly a legitimate concern. Since we so diligently urge people to obey the Supreme Court's decision of 1954 outlawing segregation in the public schools, at first glance it may seem rather paradoxical for us consciously to break laws. One may well ask: "How can you advocate breaking some laws and obeying others?" The answer lies in the fact that there are two types of laws: just and unjust. I would be the first to advocate obeying just laws. One has not only a legal but a moral responsibility to obey just laws. Conversely, one has a moral responsibility to disobey unjust laws. I would agree with St. Augustine that "an unjust law is no law at all."

Now, what is the difference between the two? How does one determine whether a law is just or unjust? A just law is a man-made code that squares with the moral law or the law of God. An unjust law is a code that is out of harmony with the moral law. To put it in the terms of St. Thomas Aquinas: An unjust law is a human law that is not rooted in eternal law and natural law. Any law that uplifts human personality is just. Any law that degrades human personality is unjust. All segregation statutes are unjust because segregation distorts the soul and damages the personality. It gives the segregator a false sense of superiority and the segregated a false sense of inferiority. Segregation, to use the terminology of the Jewish philosopher Martin Buber, substitutes an "I-it" relationship for the "I-thou" relationship and ends up relegating persons to the status of things. Hence segregation is not only politically, economically and sociologically unsound, it is morally wrong and sinful. Paul Tillich has said that sin is separation. Is not segregation an existential expression of man's tragic separation, his awful estrangement, his terrible sinfulness? Thus it is that I can urge men to obey the 1954 decision of the Supreme Court, for it is morally right; and I can urge them to disobey segregation ordinances, for they are morally wrong.

Let us consider a more concrete example of just and unjust laws. An unjust law is a code that a numerical or power majority group compels a minority group to obey but does not make binding on itself. This is *difference* made legal. By the same token, a just law is a code that a majority compels a minority to follow and that it is willing to follow itself. This is *sameness* made legal.

Let me give another explanation. A law is unjust if it is inflicted on a minority that, as a result of being denied the right to vote, had no part in enacting or devising the law. Who can say that the legislature of Alabama which set up that state's segregation laws was democratically elected? Throughout Alabama all sorts of devious methods are used to prevent Negroes from becoming registered voters, and there are some counties in which, even though Negroes constitute a majority of the population, not a single Negro is registered. Can any law enacted under such circumstances be considered democratically structured?

Sometimes a law is just on its face and unjust in its application. For instance, I have been arrested on a charge of parading without a permit. Now, there is nothing wrong in having an ordinance which requires a permit for a parade. But such an ordinance becomes unjust when it is used to maintain segregation and to deny citizens the First-Amendment privilege of peaceful assembly and protest.

I hope you are able to see the distinction I am trying to point out. In no sense do I advocate evading or defying the law, as would the rabid segregationist. That would lead to anarchy. One who breaks an unjust law must do so openly, lovingly, and with a willingness to accept the penalty. I submit that an individual who breaks a law that conscience tells him is unjust, and who willingly accepts the penalty of imprisonment in order to arouse the conscience of the community over its injustice, is in reality expressing the highest respect for law.

Of course, there is nothing new about this kind of civil disobedience. It was evidenced sublimely in the refusal of Shadrach, Meshach and Abednego to obey the laws of Nebuchadnezzar, on the ground that a higher moral law was at stake. It was practiced superbly by the early Christians, who were willing to face hungry lions and the excruciating pain of chopping blocks rather than submit to certain unjust laws of the Roman Empire. To a degree, academic freedom is a reality today because Socrates practiced civil disobedience. In our own nation, the Boston Tea Party represented a massive act of civil disobedience.

We should never forget that everything Adolf Hitler did in Germany was "legal" and everything the Hungarian freedom fighters did in Hungary was "illegal." It was "illegal" to aid and comfort a Jew in Hitler's Germany. Even so, I am sure that, had I lived in Germany at the time, I would have aided and comforted my Jewish brothers. If today I lived in a Communist country where certain principles dear to the Christian faith are suppressed, I would openly advocate disobeying that country's antireligious laws.

I must make two honest confessions to you, my Christian and Jewish brothers. First, I must confess that over the past few years I have been gravely disappointed with the white moderate. I have almost reached the regrettable conclusion that the Negro's great stumbling block in his strike toward freedom is not the White Citizen's Counciler or the Ku Klux Klanner, but the white moderate, who is more devoted to "order" than to justice; who prefers a negative peace which is the absence of tension to a positive peace which is the presence of justice; who constantly says: "I agree with you in the goal you seek, but I cannot agree with your methods of direct action"; who paternalistically believes he can set the timetable for another man's freedom; who lives by a mythical concept of time and who constantly advises the Negro to wait for a "more convenient season." Shallow understanding from people of good will is more frustrating than absolute misunderstanding from people of ill will. Lukewarm acceptance is much more bewildering than outright rejection.

I had hoped that the white moderate would understand that law and order exist for the purpose of establishing justice and that when they fail in this purpose they become the dangerously structured dams that block the flow of social progress. I had hoped that the white moderate would understand that the present tension in the South is a necessary phase of the transition from an obnoxious negative peace, in which the Negro passively accepted his unjust plight, to a substantive and positive peace, in which all men will respect the dignity and worth of human personality. Actually, we who engage in nonviolent direct action are not the creators of tension. We merely bring to the surface the hidden tension that is already alive. We bring it out in the open, where it can be seen and dealt with. Like a boil that can never be cured so long as it is covered up but must be opened with all its ugliness to the natural medicines of air and light, injustice must be exposed, with all the tension its exposure creates, to the light of human conscience and the air of national opinion before it can be cured.

In your statement you assert that our actions, even though peaceful, must be condemned because they precipitate violence. But is this a logical assertion? Isn't this like condemning a robbed man because his possession of money precipitated the evil act of robbery? Isn't this like condemning Socrates because his unswerving commitment to truth and his philosophical inquiries precipitated the act by the misguided populace in which they made him drink hemlock? Isn't this like condemning Jesus because his unique God-consciousness and never-ceasing devotion to God's will precipitated the evil act of crucifixion? We must come to see that, as the federal courts have consistently affirmed, it is wrong to urge an individual to cease his efforts to gain his basic constitutional rights because the quest may precipitate violence. Society must protect the robbed and punish the robber.

I had also hoped that the white moderate would reject the myth concerning time in relation to the struggle for freedom. I have just received a letter from a white brother in Texas. He writes: "All Christians know that the colored people will receive equal rights eventually, but it is possible that you are in too great a religious hurry. It has taken Christianity almost two thousand years to accomplish what it has. The teachings of Christ take time to come to earth." Such an attitude stems from a tragic misconception of time, from the strangely irrational notion that there is something in the very flow of time that will inevitably cure all ills. Actually, time itself is neutral; it can be used either destructively or constructively. More and more I feel that the people of ill will have used time much more effectively than have the people of good will. We will have to repent in this generation not merely for the hateful words and actions of the bad people but for the appalling silence of the good people. Human progress never rolls in on wheels of inevitability; it comes through the tireless efforts of men willing to be co-workers with God, and without this hard work, time itself becomes an ally of the forces of social stagnation. We must use time creatively, in the knowledge that the time is always ripe to do right. Now is the time to make real the promise of democracy and transform our pending national elegy into a creative psalm of brotherhood. Now is the time to lift our national policy from the quicksand of racial injustice to the solid rock of human dignity.

You speak of our activity in Birmingham as extreme. At first I was rather disappointed that fellow clergymen would see my nonviolent efforts as those of an extremist. I began thinking about the fact that I stand in the middle of two opposing forces in the Negro community. One is a force of complacency, made up in part of Negroes who, as a result of long years of oppression, are so drained of self-respect and a sense of "somebodiness" that they have adjusted to segregation; and in part of a few middleclass Negroes who, because of a degree of academic and economic security and because in some ways they profit by segregation, have become insensitive to the problems of the masses. The other force is one of bitterness and hatred, and it comes perilously close to advocating violence. It is expressed in the various black nationalist groups that are springing up across the nation, the largest and best-known being Elijah Muhammad's Muslim movement. Nourished by the Negro's frustration over the continued existence of racial discrimination, this movement is made up of people who have lost faith in America, who have absolutely repudiated Christianity, and who have concluded that the white man is an incorrigible "devil."

I have tried to stand between these two forces, saying that we need emulate neither the "do-nothingism" of the complacent nor the hatred and despair of the black nationalist. For there is the more excellent way of love and nonviolent protest. I am grateful to God that, through the influence of the Negro church, the way of nonviolence became an integral part of our struggle.

If this philosophy had not emerged, by now many streets of the South would, I am convinced, be flowing with blood. And I am further convinced that if our white brothers dismiss as "rabble-rousers" and "outside agitators" those of us who employ nonviolent direct action, and if they refuse to support our nonviolent efforts, millions of Negroes will, out of frustration and despair, seek solace and security in black nationalist ideologies—a development that would inevitably lead to a frightening racial nightmare.

Oppressed people cannot remain oppressed forever. The yearning for freedom eventually manifests itself, and that is what has happened to the American Negro. Something within has reminded him of his birth-right of freedom, and something without has reminded him that it can be gained. Consciously, or unconsciously, he has been caught up by the *Zeitgeist,* and with his black brothers of Africa and his brown and yellow brothers of Asia, South America and the Caribbean, the United States Negro is moving with a sense of great urgency toward the promised land of racial justice. If one recognizes this vital urge that has engulfed the Negro community, one should readily understand why public demonstrations are taking place. The Negro has many pent-up resentments and latent frustrations, and he must release them. So let him march; let him make prayer pilgrimages to the city hall; let him go on freedom rides—and try to understand why he must do so. If his repressed emotions are not released in nonviolent ways, they will seek expression through violence; this is not a threat but a fact of history. So I have not said to my people: "Get rid of your discontent." Rather, I have tried to say that this normal and healthy discontent can be channeled into the creative outlet of nonviolent direct action. And now this approach is being termed extremist. . . .

. . . I hope the church as a whole will meet the challenge of this decisive hour. But even if the church does not come to the aid of justice, I have no despair about the future. I have no fear about the outcome of our struggle in Birmingham, even if our motives are at present misunderstood. We will reach the goal of freedom in Birmingham and all over the nation, because the goal of America is freedom. Abused and scorned though we may be, our destiny is tied up with America's destiny. Before the pilgrims landed at Plymouth, we were here. Before the pen of Jefferson etched the majestic words of the Declaration of Independence across the pages of history, we were here. For more than two centuries our forebears labored in this country without wages; they made cotton king; they built the homes of their masters while suffering gross injustice and shameful humiliation—and yet out of a bottomless vitality they continued to thrive and develop. If the inexpressible cruelties of slavery could not stop us, the opposition we now face will surely fail. We will win our freedom because the sacred heritage of our nation and the eternal will of God are embodied in our echoing demands.

Before closing I feel impelled to mention one other point in your statement that has troubled me profoundly. You warmly commended the Birmingham police force for keeping "order" and "preventing violence." I doubt that you would have so warmly commended the police force if you had seen its dogs sinking their teeth into unarmed, nonviolent Negroes. I doubt that you would so quickly commend the policemen if you were to observe their ugly and inhumane treatment of Negroes here in the city jail; if you were to watch them push and curse old Negro women and young Negro girls; if you were to see them slap and kick old Negro men and young boys; if you were to observe them, as they did on two occasions, refuse to give us food because we wanted to sing our grace together. I cannot join you in your praise of the Birmingham police department.

It is true that the police have exercised a degree of discipline in handling the demonstrators. In this sense they have conducted themselves rather "nonviolently" in public. But for what purpose? To preserve the evil system of segregation. Over the past few years I have consistently preached that nonviolence demands that the means we use must be as pure as the ends we seek. I have tried to make clear that it is wrong to use immoral means to attain moral ends. But now I must affirm that it is just as wrong, or perhaps even more so, to use moral means to preserve immoral ends. Perhaps Mr. Connor and his policemen have been rather nonviolent in public, as was Chief Pritchett in Albany, Georgia, but they have used the moral means of nonviolence to maintain the immoral end of racial injustice. As T. S. Eliot has said: "The last temptation is the greatest treason: To do the right deed for the wrong reason."

I wish you had commended the Negro sit-inners and demonstrators of Birmingham for their sublime courage, their willingness to suffer and their amazing discipline in the midst of great provocation. One day the South will recognize its real heroes. They will be the James Merediths, with the noble sense of purpose that enables them to face jeering and hostile mobs, and with the agonizing loneliness that characterizes the life of the pioneer. They will be old, oppressed, battered Negro women, symbolized in a seventy-two-year-old woman in Montgomery, Alabama, who rose up with a sense of dignity and with her people decided not to ride segregated buses, and who responded with ungrammatical profundity to one who inquired about her weariness: "My feets is tired, but my soul is at rest." They will be the young high school and college students, the young ministers of the gospel and a host of their elders, courageously and nonviolently sitting in at lunch counters and willingly going to jail for conscience' sake. One day the South will know that when these disinherited children of God sat down at lunch counters, they were in reality standing up for what is best in the American dream and for the most sacred values in our Judaeo-Christian heritage, thereby bringing our nation back to those great wells of democracy which were dug deep by the founding fathers in their formulation of the Constitution and the Declaration of Independence.

Never before have I written so long a letter. I'm afraid it is much too long to take your precious time. I can assure you that it would have been much shorter if I had been writing from a comfortable desk, but what else can one do when he is alone in a narrow jail cell, other than write long letters, think long thoughts and pray long prayers?

If I have said anything in this letter that overstates the truth and indicates an unreasonable impatience, I beg you to forgive me. If I have said anything that understates the truth and indicates my having a patience that allows me to settle for anything less than brotherhood, I beg God to forgive me.

I hope this letter finds you strong in the faith. I also hope that circumstances will soon make it possible for me to meet each of you, not as an integrationist or a civil-rights leader but as fellow clergyman and a Christian brother. Let us all hope that the dark clouds of racial prejudice will soon pass away and the deep fog of misunderstanding will be lifted from our fear-drenched communities, and in some not too distant tomorrow the radiant stars of love and brotherhood will shine over our great nation with all their scintillating beauty.

Yours for the cause of Peace and Brotherhood,

Martin Luther King, Jr.

THE IMPACT AND IMPLICATIONS OF THE CONSTITUTION

The original provisions of the Constitution are only the beginning. Although they reflect the framers' values, assumptions, principles, and purposes, the Constitution has responded to a growing political economy. Much of its substance has been implemented in practice, and much has been adapted or changed through the years. Throughout our history, many, if not most, of our ongoing political struggles have revolved around the Constitution. The Constitution has contributed to the development of the American political economy, and provides the framework within which political activity takes place. More specifically, three very significant implications follow:

1. It leaves an impression of continuity and stability,
2. The constitutional framework encourages a certain political style, and
3. Law and lawyers become central to the functioning of the American system.

The three are, of course, closely related and mutually supporting, although we separate them for purposes of discussion.

Stability

The Constitution both conditions political behavior and legitimizes acts in the eyes of the general public. People generally revere the Constitution, because it radiates a sense of continuity and propriety; thus it is important for any political activity or policy to be consistent with its provisions and spirit. Political officeholders compete with one another for the constitutional interpretation that favors their own positions in political controversies. With the Constitution on your side, acquiescence by those less involved is almost automatic (but only almost, as the case study on abortion following Chapter 8 makes clear). Thus, there is potential payoff in promoting and sustaining the idea that the Constitution contains all the necessary answers to public problems—if only we adhere to its principles.

In one important respect, the Constitution itself promotes this continuity-symbolizing role. Some of its provisions are eminently precise, leaving little to chance, but in other respects, it is almost unconscionably vague and indeterminate ("the President shall take care that the laws be faithfully executed. . . ."). Careful analysis indicates that the precise provisions have to do principally with the manner in which elections are to be conducted and the question of who is to hold office. The vague and ambiguous provisions, for the most part, have to do with the powers of officeholders. We can, therefore, have confidence that officials are duly elected, but the direction in which officeholders may lead the nation is marginally circumscribed. With the exception of a few specific prohibitions, whatever can be justified by the political mandate and circumstances can be done, provided the institutional obstacles can be overcome.

However, overcoming those obstacles is no small task. The Constitution, as we have seen, scatters official power across a wide spectrum of positions within the governments of the United States. Subsequent developments have extended this fragmentation well beyond the framers' intentions. This means that significant portions of the capacity to govern are located in, for example, the committees of the Congress, the Joint Chiefs of

Staff, department and cabinet officials, and the middle ranges of the executive bureaucracy. This pattern of power distribution creates a multitude of pressure points (which are sometimes less neutrally characterized as veto points) across the map of American government. What results is a political system that is highly sensitive to the status quo. It takes a wide-ranging and determined effort to neutralize all these veto points, but some form of accommodation must be reached with them if even a broadly supported new policy is to be instituted.

There is nothing casual about the status quo-enforcing consequences of the Constitution's dispersal of power. It is entirely consistent with the framers' antigovernment biases, and conforms to their (and their successors') views on the need for private freedom of action. The Constitution is meant to make action difficult, because it is purposefully designed to make stability the norm.

Continuity and symbolic reassurance are also furthered by the fact that contention over the meaning of particular phrases in the Constitution translates political controversies into the less heated arena of legal debate. It also simultaneously reminds both participants and the public of what they share—acceptance of the same Constitution and the accumulated political association it represents. Reducing tensions by translating them into legalistic and constitutional debates has probably contributed to the tradition of non-fundamental political debates that have been part of the American political style.

Political Style: The Rules of the Game

American politicians and officeholders tend to assume the posture of referees. As referees, they play by and uphold "the rules of the game"—the specified ways in which people or groups are supposed to go about gaining their ends. Theoretically, at least, fairness, open hearings, due process, elections, and tolerance of opposing positions are part of these rules of the game.

Concentrating on the rules of the game, as the Constitution encourages us to do, obscures two crucial aspects of the process of politics. The nature of the rules is to allow certain kinds of competition among certain established players; this forecloses and renders illegitimate other types of conflict. Bargaining, negotiation, compromise—the leading characteristics of the American political style—are possible only when the antagonists share assumptions about what the game is and how it should be played. Management and labor can agree to submit issues to arbitration only when the issues at stake are sufficiently confined within shared value premises that compromise solutions do not deprive either side of its essential holdings. Wages or specific assembly line grievances have this potential, but nationalization of the factory or the workers' right to hire the company president do not. Similarly, the rules of the game of politics allow only those disagreements that acknowledge shared value premises, and these are disagreements within the basic framework of the status quo. In other words, to play by these rules is to acknowledge the premises and continuity of the basic economic and political structure of the American social order.

The rules also shape the results that can be obtained. Behind the rules lies a *particular* status quo, a *particular* political economy, and not an ideal form of political order. When the rules limit the scope of challenge, they eliminate much of the possible range of alternatives, and specify that the status quo can be changed only to a certain degree. If only limited changes are possible, then the rules become part of the means of maintaining the status quo. To defend the rules as if they were neutral is really to defend the substance of the status quo. This is another way of describing the American penchant for concentration on procedure—how things are done—rather than on substance; it is as if it were more important that all the established procedures were followed than that the right thing were done.

The inducements to engage in politics under the essentially pluralistic rules of the game are very strong. The Constitution's structure, intentions, and current political style all militate in this direction. Actions that are at odds with the rules—in short, provoking serious conflicts of values or challenging behavioral norms—are deplored as violating the "American way," but there is nothing inherently immoral or socially reprehensible about conflict as such. Conflict of a fundamental kind (that is, conflict over ends and not just over means) may sometimes be essential to release constructive forces in a society and remove restraints that simply will not remove themselves, as was illustrated in Exhibit 1.

The distinction between nonviolent and violent conflict is not sufficient grounds to dismiss an action. To take a very obvious example, slavery would not have been eliminated in the United States without violent conflict. Conflict, in short, must be judged not on the basis of its existence, and not on the basis of its nonviolent or violent nature, but in light of the entire context in which it takes place. Too often, disapproval of conflict is essentially a vote on behalf of one's private interest in maintaining the status quo. The American style of not facing issues, and insisting instead on following the rules and letting the results fall where they may, has the merit of reducing conflict. On the other hand, avoiding issues may lead to explosive and self-destructive conflict. The crucial variable is the nature of the context. Neither conflict nor consensus has meaning except in terms of goals and existing conditions. What is useful and desirable in one setting may be disastrous in another. The point is that a concentration on playing by the rules of the game may lead us to ignore the game itself, not to mention the players.

Legalistic Politics

As mentioned earlier, the Constitution reflects an American confidence in contracts. In many ways, the Constitution is perceived to be a contract and is reacted to as such. Thus, interpretation of the contract becomes vital to the day-to-day operation of government. Interpretation is itself the focus of political struggle, and this means that lawyers, the skill group with the greatest claim to interpreting contracts, rise to a special governing role in the society. In addition, political issues must be translated into legal terms that will fit into the existing contractual framework.

The powerful symbolic appeal of the Constitution as the fundamental law of the land has meant that the United States developed a style of politics that often revolves around the *constitutionality* of an issue or action. As de Tocqueville noted some time ago, "scarcely a political question arises that does not become a *judicial* question." In order to challenge public policies on a fundamental level, as Exhibit 1 illustrated, one often needs to break a statutory law, which can then be challenged in the courts as to whether it conforms to the more fundamental law, the Constitution. Newly passed innovative statutes must also be passed by the judiciary before implementation. Arguing that the Constitution embodies the "Law," and that we are a government of laws, not of men, means that our disagreements about policies must be fought out in the courts, and adds a crucial dimension to any political strategy. Issues must be framed in constitutional, or legal terms, such that they have a chance to be successfully resolved in a judicial arena.

The emphasis on constitutionality and appeals to fundamental or higher law means that lawyers carry a special role in the American political system. As both guardians of the law and specialists trained in its development and application, lawyers are essential to the functioning of our politics. The ability of the common folk to make policy becomes suspect, and people who are not lawyers lack the expertise necessary to translate ideas into statutes. All Americans can be voters and their support is needed in the campaign to get new or innovative ideas accepted, but the final strategy and development should be, and often is, done by the lawyer, in the courtroom and in the halls of government.

There has, of course, been much change in the *meaning* of the Constitution over the years, but that change has been consistent with the original intent and purpose of the document. Putting politics into "legalese" contributes to the concentration on procedure, rather than substance. The numerous lawyers also contribute to the emphasis on bargaining and negotiation that are carried on by professionals, not the general public. Stability and style are closely connected with the emphasis on the legal, which prides itself on slow and measured growth through the orderly process of the Law.

INTERPRETING THE CONSTITUTION

We are not saying that the provisions and substance of the Constitution are merely the province of lawyers and forever cast in stone. There are traditions and expectations surrounding many specific provisions. These provisions take on an independent status and meaning, which, *in the absence of compelling reasons to the contrary,* will probably control the outcome in any given case. However, when determined and powerful people or groups seek particular goals, constitutional words are not likely to prevent them from attaining their ends. In time, their preferences will become the new and accepted interpretation of the Constitution's meaning, and new generations will begin their political goal-seeking starting from this new point of departure.

The most vital single point to be made is that there is simply no mechanical inevitability about American politics inherent in the Constitution. Nothing *necessarily* follows because of the wording of the document. This realization lends crucial significance to the process by which the Constitution is interpreted and applied to contemporary politics. Whoever manages to interpret the Constitution acquires the aura of legitimacy and traditionalism that the Constitution evokes from others; for example, it is not a matter of indifference to most people whether the Constitution is interpreted to permit abortion, busing, or sex discrimination.

Who *interprets* the Constitution is therefore a more important issue than *what the document says*. It is not clear in any given instance which institution or other participant will win the battle to establish the authoritative constitutional interpretation. There are many participants in the grim and sometimes invisible struggle within the national government for power to determine what the Constitution requires on any particular issue. However, most Americans, if pressed, would probably say that the Supreme Court is the proper vehicle for interpretation of the Constitution, and it would be difficult for them to imagine a basis for challenging the right and power of the Court to do so. Such is the triumph of Alexander Hamilton's argument, which was written into constitutional doctrine by Chief Justice John Marshall.

The complete acceptance of Hamilton's argument today, however, should not obscure the bitter clash of values and competing philosophies over the question of who was to interpret the Constitution. Hamilton's victory brought with it mixed costs and benefits, and has had fundamental consequences for the nature of the American system of government. To more fully understand these consequences, we will review the battle between Hamilton and Jefferson over the proper interpreter of the Constitution and then examine the effects of Hamilton's victory.

The Positions of Hamilton and Jefferson

Alexander Hamilton was one of the strongest supporters of the Constitution. For the most part, Hamilton stressed the utility of union and the need for a strong central government as reasons for accepting the document. However, he saved his special enthusiasm for two innovations in the Constitution: a strong and vigorous executive to administer the laws with force where necessary, and an independent judiciary with the power of judicial review (the power to declare acts of Congress unconstitutional).

In arguing for judicial power to declare acts of the other branches unconstitutional and therefore void, Hamilton argued that the people had granted the national government certain powers and not others, and therefore, any act in excess of those granted powers must be void. But how does anybody know when an act of a legislature is in excess of the powers granted to it? Certainly the legislators would have decided that the act *was* within their powers, or they would have chosen another means. Hamilton argued that these determinations were questions of *law* (the Constitution conveniently declares that it is the law of the land), and as such, they ought to be decided by the Supreme Court.

Jefferson, by contrast, insisted that the question of whether the people had delegated a particular power to the government ought to be decided by the people, and not an institution of that government. In other words, he wanted the people to determine whether the act of the legislature was authorized. The Constitution itself does not specify by what means its provisions are to be interpreted. Thus, the issue evolved into a test of logic, persuasiveness, and power between the two positions. Two major disagreements divided the parties, and both of these disagreements are rooted in the same conflict of values.

First, Hamilton and Jefferson had quite different views on the nature of a constitution. Jefferson believed that it was a fundamental allocation of the people's powers and superior to the ongoing acts of government. It was not law in the ordinary sense of a statute or code, but the people's instructions to their government about the goals and purposes it should pursue. These goals and purposes might change over time, of course, as circumstances changed. Therefore, Jefferson insisted on the right of the people to change the Constitution regularly.

Hamilton, on the other hand, saw the Constitution as a technical legal document with more or less fixed meaning, thus requiring legal expertise for interpretation. He argued that the Court was more likely than people to possess the expertise and wisdom necessary to divine the meaning of the document's words. Acknowledging that the Constitution flowed from the people, he still insisted that their ratification had carried with it authorization of the Court as interpreter.

Secondly, the two men disagreed over the nature of the *act* of interpretation. Jefferson believed that interpretation required a value-based choice, and that choice should be made by the people themselves. If that was not feasible, it should be made by the institution closest to the people—their elected representatives in either state or national legislatures. Jefferson was particularly opposed to being subjected to the value choices of judges who were appointed (for life terms) by members of the very national government whose exercise of powers was being questioned.

Hamilton blandly declared that there was no act of choice involved in interpretation of the Constitution. It was simply a matter of comparing the statute with the words of the Constitution, and registering the mechanical judgment that would be apparent from the comparison. He argued that the independence and life terms of judges enabled them to rise above the petty strifes of the day and render decisions in this neutrally mechanical way.

What really divides Hamilton and Jefferson is their respective value premises and priorities. Jefferson feared the self-serving tendencies of the financiers and businessmen represented by Hamilton and the Federalist party. His trust in the people was by no means complete, but he preferred their judgments to those of any self-selected elite. Hamilton feared the property-redistributing tendencies of the masses, and thus sought to keep control over the scope of legislative powers in the hands of a trustworthy body that was sympathetic to property rights. Lawyers, accustomed to reverence for the traditions and practices of the past, would be another bulwark in defense of the Constitution's protections for the established order.

In principle, Jefferson's position appears the more logical and democratic. If, as seems evident, the act of interpretation involves value choices, who chooses? Choice by the people or their recently elected representatives is more democratic than choice by an appointed body that is not accountable to the people in any way. But Hamilton's view was made into authoritative doctrine by Chief Justice John Marshall in the case of *Marbury* v. *Madison*[7] in 1803. Despite some wavering in the face of Jefferson's pressure, Marshall stuck to the principle of the Court's power of judicial review throughout his term on the Court. He had the political sophistication not to exercise it again, however. It was not until 1857 that the second test of judicial review occurred in the *Dred Scott*[8] case. This case, too, met with strong political reaction, and the principle of judicial review did not become firmly established in practice until after the Civil War. By then, the Court had proved to be an effective defense against state experiments with social legislation. In spite of recurring political outcries against specific Court decisions, the Hamiltonian position on judicial review as a principle has become widespread.

The Hamilton Victory

Why did Hamilton win the argument so fully that it is now difficult to convey the significance of the choice that was made? Surely the American penchant for legalism and the law is both cause and effect here. Americans were a receptive audience for Hamilton's legalistic approach to political problems. Further, the group to which Hamilton first appealed was made up chiefly of the upper and upper-middle classes of propertied people. They may have perceived the same advantages in the prospective role of the Court as he did. Business and wealthier interests consistently supported the Court's power of judicial review right up through the Court-packing conflicts of the New Deal.

The (in)famous "switch in time that saved nine" suggests another reason why Hamilton's argument may have succeeded in the long run. There is nothing inevitable about the Court's decision in any given situa-

---

[7] *Marbury* v. *Madison*, 1 Branch 137 (1803).

[8] *Dred Scott* v. *Sanford*, 19 Howard 393 (1857).

tion, because the real determinant of a decision is less the power of the Court than the preferences of the judges who happen to be on it at the time. This realization may lead to acceptance of the Court's power of judicial review by *all* political activists, each of whom hopes to control the presidency and thus appointments to the Court. Careful choice of appointees to the Court—and longevity on their part—may permit greater impact on the direction of public policy than some Presidents generate in limited terms in the White House.

This is little doubt, however, that the power of judicial review by the Supreme Court adds an important dimension to the character of American politics. It contributes to the tendency to depoliticize issues and convert them into a form in which only some people—lawyers and, minimally, their clients—become the relevant decisionmakers. Taking some of the great value conflicts of the society to the Supreme Court for resolution probably siphons off some tensions and bitterness from our politics, thus contributing to its stability. But this can be a mixed blessing, because people probably *ought* to become engaged in vital questions affecting their futures.

The Supreme Court is not the final authority on any question about which a large number of people care strongly. There are many ways to combat or circumvent a decision. Nevertheless, it is able to structure public understanding of many issues and to resolve many others without much public attention. The desirability of this situation depends on one's attitude toward popular participation, but we cannot escape the fact that the Supreme Court, and the judiciary in general, are important parts of our political system. In the next chapter we will turn to an examination of the Supreme Court and the judicial branch as political institutions.

CHAPTER 8

The Judicial Branch

Law comes in many forms, from constitutional and statutory provisions through regulations and ordinances to court decisions. Law originates in a variety of institutions: legislatures, administrative bodies, executives, the people, courts, and accumulated social practices. It serves a variety of functions, from resolution of the most fundamental (or *constitutional*) questions to day-to-day disputes, and is engaged in managing thousands of routine economic and political transactions between individuals, corporations, and governments. However, we generally associate law with the judicial branch, and it is the judicial system that is the subject of this chapter.

As one author noted while discussing state trial courts, "enormous sums of money are transferred through court actions and out-of-court settlements."[1] Another author said: "The [federal] courts of appeals still play active policy-making roles in economic disputes in the private sector."[2] Of course, the U.S. Supreme Court obviously plays a major policy-making role in the American political economy. No matter which way you turn, courts at one level or another are engaged in the political process of determining who gets what, when, and how.

This chapter discusses the judicial system from its lowest levels, such as traffic court, to the rarefied atmosphere of the U.S. Supreme Court. Often,

---

[1] Herbert Jacob, "Trial Courts in the United States: The Travails of Exploration," *Law and Society Review,* Vol. 17, No. 3 (1983), p. 412.

[2] Laurence Baum, Sheldon Goldman, and Austin Sarat, "Research Note: The Evolution of Litigation in the Federal Courts of Appeals, 1895–1975," *Law and Society Review,* Vol. 16, No. 2 (1981–82), p. 306.

when we speak of the judicial branch, we mean simply the Supreme Court, so we will begin with it, the major and most visible judicial institution in the American system. Then we will describe the less well-known, but equally important policymakers, the federal and state judicial systems. A major function of the judiciary is dispute resolution in the American context, and so the resolution process, the participants, and some alternative methods are examined next. We will conclude with an analysis of another major role of the state and federal judicial systems, the administration of criminal justice.

THE SUPREME COURT AS A POLITICAL INSTITUTION

The Supreme Court obviously has a major impact on a wide range of public issues; segregation, political freedoms, defendants' rights, and environmental regulation provide only a few examples. Although it can make decisions only on cases brought before it, most significant political issues reach the Court one way or another. In this sense, the Court contributes to the distribution of values and resources in the American system.

The Supreme Court is also a political institution in its internal makeup and workings. Although there is a tendency to think of courts as being removed from, or somehow above, politics, judges make choices. Judges have been trained in legal reasoning and precedent, but their choices inevitably are based, at least in part, on their personal values, preferences, and goals. Judicial decisions are also the product of a process of accommodation among the actors internal to the system. The Court differs from the other branches in form, but not in political character or impact on the society.

The Supreme Court consists of only nine persons, and each has a vote of equal weight. The Court has no committees and, with rare exceptions, all the justices personally hear arguments, discuss, and vote on every case that is accepted for full argument. Nevertheless, influence can and does become concentrated within the Court. Not all justices are equally determinative of the Court's policy positions. Official status, the division of labor among the justices, reputations, personalities, and style are major reasons for sometimes sharp differences in real power.

The Chief Justice

The position of chief justice offers the principal opportunity within the Court to affect the nature of its decisionmaking. In nearly two centuries under the Constitution, there have been only fifteen chief justices. A politically astute person who becomes chief justice at a relatively young age may leave a more lasting imprint on the public policies of the nation than some presidents. Chief Justice John Marshall (1801–35), for example, had con-

TABLE   Cases on Supreme Court Docket Disposed of
8.1   and Remaining on Docket, 1981

Cases on docket	5,311
Cases disposed of	4,433
Remaining on docket	878
October Term, 1981	
Cases argued	184
Disposed with full opinion	169
Disposed per curiam opinion	10
Set for reargument	4
Granted review	210
Reviewed and decided without argument	134
Total available for argument at outset of next term	126

SOURCE: "Reports of the Proceedings of the Judicial Conference of the United States: Held in Washington, D.C., March 16 and 17, 1982, and September 22 and 23, 1982; Annual Report of the Director of the Administrative Office of the United States Courts, 1982," (Washington, D.C.: U.S. Government Printing Office, 1982), Table A-1.

siderably more effect on the development of the United States than did several of the presidents who held office at the same time. Not all chief justices leave the mark of a Marshall, a Hughes, or a Warren. (Note: Up to the time of this writing, all Chief Justices have been male so we will use the male pronoun in describing the position. However, we certainly do not mean to imply that all future Chief Justices will be, or should be, males.) To be effective, a chief justice must employ the political skills of bargaining and accommodation, and must develop and use the formal powers of the office in harmony with the more personal techniques of small-group leadership in order to bring a majority of the justices into agreement with his positions.

The formal powers of the chief justice are few in actuality, but tradition and practice, combined with an increasing caseload, have made them important sources of leverage within the Court. Many thousands of cases are appealed to the Court every year. In 1981, there were 5,311 cases on the Supreme Court docket, as shown in Table 8.1; of those, only 184 were argued and even fewer disposed of by a full written opinion by the Court. Obviously, the Court must decline the vast majority of cases in order to allocate its time to the 150 to 200 cases that the justices feel present the most important issues.

Figure 8.1 presents the usual caseload flow chart for the Supreme Court. As shown, approximately 95 percent of the petitions never make it past the preliminary conference, and 75 percent of those were "deadlisted" even earlier. Although each justice has the right to review all the potential cases, the chief justice has the largest staff and he generally takes responsibility for seeing that all the appeals are reviewed. He also presides over the conference at which the justices select the cases they will hear, and suggests the cases that should be selected for further hearings and those that

Figure 8.1. *Judicial Decisional Flow Chart for the Supreme Court*

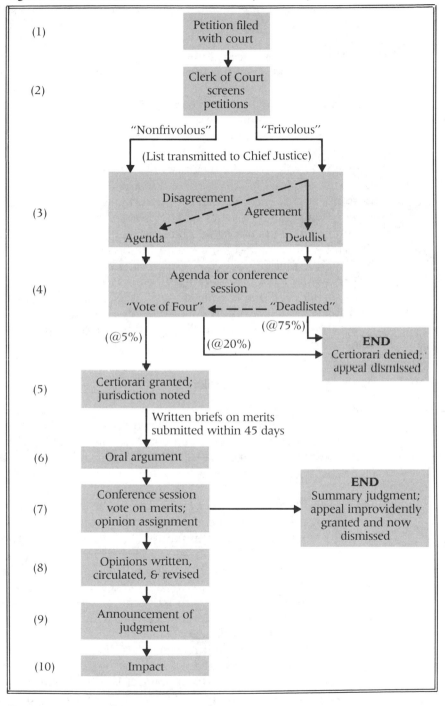

SOURCE: Howard Ball, *Courts and Politics: The Federal Judicial System*, © 1980, p. 251. Reprinted by permission of Prentice-Hall, Inc., Englewood Cliffs, N.J.

should be rejected. Discussion at these conferences thus proceeds according to an agenda and a preliminary selection set by the chief justice. If the work has been done carefully, his original list will closely resemble the cases that are actually chosen for the Court's subsequent calendars.

The Court's practice is to hear oral arguments on accepted cases for a two-week period. Then they devote the next two weeks to research, decisions, and opinion writing. Decisions on the cases are made at regular conferences of all justices, which again are presided over by the chief justice. At these conferences, the chief justice normally articulates the issues for resolution in each case and then opens the floor for discussion among the justices. When in the majority, the chief justice assigns the justice who will write the majority opinion. A chief justice may choose to write the opinion himself or assign it to another justice of similar views for reasons such as expertise in the subject matter, political patronage, or attempts to maintain a majority. The abortion case study that follows illustrates the politics that are often underlying the choice of the author of the majority opinion. Speculation about the reasons Burger chose Blackmun to write the majority opinion varies. Some believe it was because Blackmun was the most medically informed, having served as counsel to the Mayo Clinic, and others suspect that Burger wanted to delay the opinion and knew that Blackmun was a cautious and slow draftsman. In any event, the chief justice controls the writing of the opinion and thus, to some extent, its content.

Writing the Majority Opinion

The writing of the majority opinion is a crucial stage in the Court's work. Other political activists and the public are advised of the Court's position and reasoning through this document. Most important is the fact that the opinion adds a new bit of substance to the body of law and precedent that supposedly guides the nation thereafter. The scope and nature of the rule asserted by the Court is often of greater interest than who wins or loses the case itself. The opinion exercises the justices' broad discretion as to whether the decision will be grounded in a new, perhaps drastic, interpretation of the Constitution or in narrow, technical grounds. The author of the opinion can write it in such a way that the reasoning appears to apply to many similar situations, or the opinion can be confined so strictly that no other cases or behavior appear to be affected.

The justice who is chosen to write the majority opinion in a crucial case can acquire substantial influence within the Court, at least in that subject area. Such justices also achieve public and professional visibility and some stroking of the judicial ego, a fact that gives the politically astute chief justice a kind of patronage to bestow on favored associate justices. There are limits to this power, of course. If the opinion writer seriously misrepresents the views of the other justices who voted with the majority, one or more may decline to join in the opinion, and this can mean loss of the vote(s) necessary to make up a majority.

The only other institutional position of importance derives from seniority relationships among the associate justices. Should the chief justice vote with the minority, the senior associate justice in the majority chooses the writer of the opinion. The senior justice in the minority either writes that opinion, or assigns it to someone else in the minority. Minority opinions can also be important to the decision, because they may point out weaknesses or loopholes in the majority opinion that will allow a new statute to be rewritten in such a way as to pass judicial scrutiny. Strong minority positions sometimes become majority opinions over the passage of time. Justice O'Connor's dissent in the *City of Akron* case, which is cited in the following case study, illustrates all these possibilities.

Opinion drafts are circulated for comments by the other justices. The process of negotiation and compromise over precise wording may take weeks. In some instances, the uniting solution is an opinion in which conflicting or ambiguous positions are taken; in effect, this postpones precise formulation of new rules of law to some future time or passes them on to another institution.

The chief justice has other powers of a generally housekeeping nature, such as assigning tasks and making clerks and secretaries available. These powers also have patronage-type possibilities, as they are the amenities that make the daily routines of the other justices more or less pleasant. The chief justice is also the administrative head of the lower federal courts, and as such, he may influence the opinions of lower federal court judges in a number of issue areas. Within the Supreme Court, however, the chief justice must mainly rely for further influence on the personal support and regard of the other justices.

Influence of the Justices

Power within the Supreme Court is very much the product of individual reputation, effort, personality, and style. Justices can maximize their influence in many ways. Some may have an expertise in or familiarity with a difficult subject area, such as Justice Blackmun's familiarity with medical issues from his long representation of the Mayo Clinic. Justice Douglas had been a tax lawyer before his tenure on the Court, and thus many of the complicated tax cases were assigned to him. By earning a reputation for hard and effective work on the Court, justices may end up writing more than their share of opinions. Also, justices may form coalitions that establish Court policy positions of great significance by joining with other justices through preconference "caucuses" or simple trading of votes. For example, four votes are needed to select a case to be heard on appeal (see Figure 8.1, Step 4), and justices who are convinced that particular aspects of existing law should be changed may simply vote to hear *any* cases raising such issues.

Extra-Court prestige, such as intimacy with the President, may contribute to a justice's capacity to exercise influence with the Court. More often, real power depends on the persuasiveness with which a justice argues cases. A justice who is almost always accurate, incisive, and un-abrasive in intellectual discourse; tolerant of the views and mistakes of others; able to combine disagreement over policy with personal friendship; understanding of what is practical for the Court; and does not seek decisions that are inconsistent with the underlying nature of the system may become highly influential. In short, the Court places a premium on an accepted political style and in following the rules of the game, in much the same way as do the two houses of Congress. The style here just happens to be much more influenced by the language and techniques of legal scholarship. Mavericks who challenge the long-established operating procedures of the Court, fail to do their share of the work, or advocate actions that are extreme, are not likely to be effective.

Because of the relatively small number of people who have served as chief justice, or even as justices of the Supreme Court, it is difficult to make generalizations about them. Table 8.2 summarizes the makeup of the present Court. As noted, all the justices have had legal training, and most have been prominent in the law or in political life. The President consistently nominates those who are likely to share his policy preferences, and senators just as consistently resist confirmation when a nominee holds views that are contrary to *their* preferences. Republican presidents tend to nominate from the ranks of the federal and state judiciary or from large private law firms, and Democrats are more likely to nominate someone from political life, such as the Congress or the cabinet.

Presidents occasionally have guessed incorrectly about a nominee's probable actions on the Court. The example most often cited is Eisenhower's nomination of former Chief Justice Earl Warren. At the time of his appointment, Warren came from a prominent, somewhat conservative, Republican political career in California. No one, least of all President Eisenhower, suspected he would come to be viewed as an almost "flaming" liberal, steering the Court through a highly activist period. By and large, however, the best cues to the political preferences of the chief justice and the associate justices are the goals of the president who appointed them.

From 1941, when Roosevelt appointees gained full control of the Court, until 1971, the members had been generally liberal. The character of four Nixon administration appointees moved the Court toward a more conservative stance. President Carter made no appointments, but President Reagan appointed the first woman, Justice Sandra Day O'Connor, whose appointment was expected to solidify the conservative turn. However, as of 1983, although the Court was more conservative, it was not fully accepting the Reagan administration's attempts to reverse much of the earlier liberal rulings.

Return to Table 8.2 now, and note that several justices are over 70; three are over 75. These three senior justices are those who are perceived to be more liberal. This raises the possibility of a more fundamental change in the makeup of the Court as these justices leave the Court. The replacement of Supreme Court members sometimes can be controlled by the justices

TABLE 8.2
Supreme Court Justices, 1984 (in order of seniority)

Name	Year of Birth	Home State	Law School	Prior Experience	Appointed by	Year of Appointment
Warren Burger	1907	Minnesota	St. Paul College of Law	Assistant Attorney General, Federal Judge	Nixon	1969
William Brennan	1906	New Jersey	Harvard	State Judge	Eisenhower	1956
Byron White	1918	Colorado	Yale	Deputy Attorney General	Kennedy	1962
Thurgood Marshall	1908	Maryland	Howard	Counsel to NAACP, Federal Judge	Johnson	1967
Harry Blackmun	1908	Minnesota	Harvard	Federal Judge	Nixon	1970
Lewis Powell	1907	Virginia	Washington & Lee	President, ABA, Federal Judge	Nixon	1972
William Rehnquist	1924	Arizona	Stanford	Assistant Attorney General	Nixon	1972
John P. Stevens	1916	Illinois	Chicago	Federal Judge	Ford	1975
Sandra Day O'Connor	1930	Arizona	Stanford	State Court of Appeals Judge	Reagan	1981

themselves; they can, for example, time a retirement decision to coincide with a likeminded presidential administration. In other words, more liberal justices would retire when their replacement would be nominated by a more liberal president, and vice versa. There was speculation that some retirement decisions were awaiting the outcome of the 1984 presidential election—as the justices waited to see who would do the nominating of their replacements.

THE FEDERAL AND STATE COURT SYSTEMS

One of the most conspicuous illustrations of American federalism is the dual court system. The national and state governments each maintain distinct and complete court systems with separate jurisdictions and powers. Each set of courts has both civil and criminal jurisdictions. Both courts are hierarchically organized—that is, the highest court in each system is the nominal administrative and legal head of the system. Intermediate appellate courts, if any, must follow the precedents set by the higher court, as well as its determinations as to rules and procedure. In turn, trial courts are bound by the rules, procedures, and precedents established by the appellate courts. However, each court has control of its own internal institutional setting and, of course, the sitting judge has the final word in his or her courtroom.

A crucial distinction exists between trial and appellate courts in each system. Trial courts are those institutions that hear the entire case; they hear witnesses, scrutinize evidence of all admissible types, rule on procedural, technical, and substantive motions, and listen to and referee the legal battle between opposing attorneys. At the conclusion of a case, the facts are determined and the law applied. Trial courts are the workhorses of the system.

In contrast, appellate courts deal only with issues of law. The facts that are determined at the trial court level (with a few carefully prescribed exceptions) remain the facts. Because an appellate court's only concern is legal issues, it hears only from attorneys. If the issue is deemed substantial enough, an appellate court may hear oral arguments from the opposing attorneys, as well as read the written brief each attorney submits in support of his or her version of the legal issue. But oral argument is just that; the opposing attorneys have a chance to present their case to the court and answer any questions the justices may have. Compared to a full court trial, which may last from days to years, an appellate appearance is usually relatively brief. Furthermore, the attorneys must stick to the single issue framed by the court.

The Federal System

Figure 8.2 outlines the basic federal court system. In 1983, it rested on a base of eighty-nine district courts, with at least one in each state. Washington, D.C. also has a district court, as do Guam, Puerto Rico, and the Virgin

Figure 8.2. *Federal Court System*

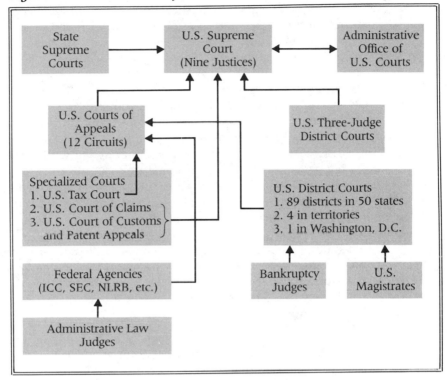

Islands. District courts are the major trial courts in the federal system, and hear both civil and criminal cases. The civil cases involve federal laws, such as antitrust issues, civil rights, and social security problems. The criminal cases must involve violation of a federal statute, such as income tax fraud or transporting narcotics across state lines. A single judge presides at most district court trials, although each district employs many judges in order to keep up with the volume of business. In an attempt to alleviate some of the caseload pressure, Congress authorized the addition of federal magistrates. Magistrates hear certain minor matters, such as bail proceedings and petty offenses, thus freeing judges to deal with more serious matters.

The federal government also has specialized trial courts to hear income tax questions, claims against the federal government, and customs or patent cases. Three judges are convened to form a special district court for certain constitutional issues involving state or federal statutes. This procedure is designed to speed the hearing of important constitutional questions. After their decision has been made, as shown in Figure 8.2, direct routes of appeal to the U.S. Supreme Court are open.

The circuit courts of appeal are above the district and specialized courts in the federal system. Twelve such courts exist in the country, with one for each geographic circuit. Losing litigants may appeal trial court cases to the circuit courts of appeal, but not all issues are reexamined at the appellate level. Only matters of *law* that have been specifically raised at the trial court level may be raised on appeal. This means that once a question of *fact* (such as whether the defendant performed a particular act), has been decided by the trial court judge or jury, it is forever concluded and no new evidence may be presented on appeal—except under very special circumstances. The appellate court limits itself solely to the problem of the disputed points of law.

The highest federal court, of course, is the U.S. Supreme Court. It exercises supervisory and administrative authority over all federal courts, and is responsible for standardizing actions and procedures across the country. It does possess original jurisdiction (meaning trial court capability) in a few limited instances that are set out in Article III of the Constitution, but generally, it only hears appellate cases. It can hear a case from losing litigants in the courts of appeal, especially if there is a conflict between two or more circuits, and it may accept appeals from state supreme courts if a substantial federal constitutional question is involved. As noted earlier, on certain significant issues, it hears appeals from a specially constituted three-judge district court. Obviously, although it is nominally the administrative and supervisory body for the federal system, the Supreme Court's major business is serving as the American court of last resort.

A battery of screening procedures make it unlikely that any given case will reach the Supreme Court.

1. Only losing litigants may appeal, and then only on points of law that have been explicitly raised at the trial court level.
2. The appellate process is very expensive. Skilled attorneys must be retained and briefs must be prepared and printed, often several times, as the case wends its way through the long and costly process.
3. The Supreme Court does not have to hear every case appealed to it. As we saw in Table 8.1, it selects approximately 5 percent of the petitions it receives. Generally, the case must involve serious constitutional questions, interpretations of key sections of federal statutes or of powers and procedures of administrative bodies, or present an issue in which two federal courts of appeal have ruled differently.

The State Systems

Each state's court system has certain distinctive features; very few state court systems are exactly alike. In general, however, they parallel the federal system. At the trial-court level, states maintain a great variety of courts, but they are generally of two levels. In many states, minor matters, such as traffic offenses, are handled by local magistrates, justice of the peace courts, small claims courts, or similar, more informal institutions. Every state has a set of trial courts that hear more serious matters, such as felony cases and tort or contract actions involving more substantial sums of money. In some states, civil and criminal courts are combined, as in the federal system, but in others, civil and criminal jurisdiction is separated. Many states have also created specialized courts for such matters as domestic relations or juvenile offenders.

Thirty-one states have intermediate appellate courts that are similar to the federal courts of appeal. In the other cases, appeals from the major trial courts go directly to the state's highest court. Generally, the criteria for the right to appeal are the same as in the federal court system—only losing litigants can appeal and only on matters of law raised at the trial-court level. Similarly, each state's highest court is responsible for maintaining consistency in state law, and consistency between state law and the state constitution, just as the U.S. Supreme Court does in the federal system. All matters of state law are determined solely within the legal system of that state, and as a result, the laws and practices of the fifty states may greatly vary.

If a question of federal law or a constitutional issue is raised in a state case, however, ultimate appeal to the U.S. Supreme Court is possible. In these areas, only the U.S. Supreme Court is superior to the highest courts of the states. The U.S. Supreme Court's power rests on the argument that there must be a single authority to interpret the meaning of federal laws and the Constitution. Once again, however, the Supreme Court decides whether the constitutional or other federal question raised is important enough for it to hear. If it does decide to hear the case, it considers only the federal questions. Of course, state statutes or practices are often alleged to be contrary to the U.S. Constitution; if the Supreme Court agrees and declares them void, then there is considerable opportunity for conflict between the Court and the state or states involved.

DISPUTE RESOLUTION

The U.S. Supreme Court is only the most visible court among many hundreds of judicial institutions, and at that, much of its work goes unheralded. It is the few highly visible issues, such as abortion or the legislative veto, that keep us tuned in for the latest developments. But these highly visible and controversial cases often serve mainly symbolic purposes. Although many women may eventually be aided directly by the Supreme Court's decision on abortion, the ruling has only an indirect effect centering on what it symbolizes rather than what it does for the vast majority of us. This is particularly true in areas such as civil rights, prisoner rights, and the rights and duties of the branches of government, which are the cases that occupy the news media. However, the impact on the majority of citizens takes the form of reassurance that the individual's rights are being protected in this day of overwhelming national power.

But the legal system as a whole operates daily and directly affects all of us at one time or another in a variety of ways. Most of us have encountered a court of one kind or another—from traffic court to domestic cases to probate to consumer disputes to automobile accidents. As the Council of State Governments found:

> The volume of litigation in the state courts has been rising out of all proportion to increases in both population and court resources. According to the most recent national statistics available, state courts process annually some 90 million cases; 25 million of these are non-traffic and include approximately 130,000 appeals, 12 million civil cases, 11 million criminal cases and 1.2 million juvenile proceedings.[3]

Even if we have not been physically within a courtroom, we try to arrange our affairs with an eye to their legality so that we *don't* wind up in court. We simply cannot escape it; our entire public life and much of our private existence, for example, is based on one or another type of *contract*. And whenever a dispute arises with regard to one of our many contracts, the forum that immediately comes to mind for resolution of the dispute is some type of court.

This section will discuss the American form of dispute resolution, the lower court, or trial court, system and some alternative dispute-resolution mechanisms. We will concentrate here on the civil side, leaving the criminal justice system to the next section. We will start with the question of what is a case and what resolution means in this context. Then, we will look at the actors and participants that make up the system, and finally, we will examine the questions surrounding various reform proposals for alternative dispute-resolution mechanisms.

What's a Case?

Courts are *reactive* mechanisms. They cannot initiate action; a problem must come to them. First, a case must arise out of a dispute. Real people or institutions must have a real disagreement with each other. Disputes may be fabricated as part of a strategy to get them into the legal process so that the issue can come before the Supreme Court, but the general rule is that the dispute must be genuine. In the American system, courts are meant to be a neutral arena for the adjudication of disputes, and their role is not to give advice to other policymakers *prior* to their resolution of an issue.

This derives from the fact that our system is adversarial; it is based on the notion that there are at least two sides to every dispute. The court provides an arena where the two, or more, can present their case before a neutral party, the judge, and possibly a jury. It has been described as the modern version of trial by combat, with the best person winning and thus establishing the truth. Blame or guilt is affixed, someone wins and someone loses, and the dispute is resolved.

There are matters, such as adoption or probate, where there appears to

---

[3] *The Book of the States* (Lexington, Ky.: The Council of State Governments, 1982–83), Vol. 24, p. 247.

be no adversarial party. In these cases, the state intervenes in order to protect the interests of the infant, or missing heirs, just in case. Many of the everyday issues, especially those of a domestic nature, have begun to be seen as non-adversarial, and some even argue that the adversarial process inhibits or makes impossible successful resolution of the dispute. One proposal for reform came through the passage of no-fault laws. In many states it is now possible to obtain a divorce without affixing blame on one or the other spouse; this is a no-fault divorce. Many also argue for a no-fault law in auto accident cases. There appear to be many accidents that are truly accidents, and attempts to fix blame and thus payment become counterproductive and unfair. However, no-fault laws leave the form of the adversary process intact, because one still goes through a court case, with attorneys. Other reform proposals suggest removing many types of disputes to alternative forums; we will discuss this subject later.

Another major shaping factor is that the dispute must be based on a "right for which there is a remedy." In other words, the case must be soluble by a court. You cannot, for example, sue God for damaging your crops with a hailstorm. You probably cannot even sue your insurance company because they rarely insure you for acts of God. A case must have a tangible wrong done by someone or something, for which the Court can provide a remedy. For example, if a family member is injured by a negligent driver, you can sue to collect money damages for hospital bills, pain and suffering, and loss of income. But you cannot sue if there was no tangible damage and you are simply angry and want the other driver to repent. *Resolution* of disputes must fit within the adversarial process. Someone must *win* something, and that something must be a tangible act, completion of the contract, or a monetary award for damages or to pay someone else to complete the contract.

Dispute resolution in the United States thus takes a special form. Based on the American belief in contracts, it attempts to spell out everyone's rights and responsibilities in very tangible ways. Either one has followed the contract, or not. Disputes over the interpretation of the contract and one's rights and responsibilities go to the courts. An individual is either right or wrong, or innocent or guilty, and once blame or fault or guilt is affixed, then the individual pays the appropriate price. Thus, American dispute resolution is adversarial and tangible.

Actors and Participants

Obviously, the major participants in this process are lawyers and judges, who are also lawyers. Although lawyers are found everywhere in the American political system, the legal system is their special province. Trained to "think like lawyers," they see disputes in the terms we have just discussed. Their job is to turn a messy real-life problem into a case that is resolvable by a court. (Preferably, a lawyer has already organized a person's affairs in such a way that court intervention is minimal or unnecessary or, if necessary, eminently winnable.) The litigious nature of the

American public is a subject that is often discussed; expanding, some say exploding, caseloads testify to the alacrity with which Americans turn to the courts for dispute resolution.[4]

More specific to the institutional setting are the judges, and those persons necessary to the administration of the court such as clerks, bailiffs, and secretaries. The major actors here, however, are the judges. There are over 8,000 judges in the states alone, counting all tiers of the state court system.[5] Depending upon the historical development of the state, the numbers range from 14 or 15 lower-court judges in states like Maine or Vermont to over 600 in California. With the sole exception of a very few minor courts (some justices of the peace may still be non-lawyers), judges are lawyers who have been elevated to the bench. The bench was predominantly white male until recently, because judges came from the bar, and the bar was predominantly white male, especially at the levels from which judges are chosen. That is changing very slowly. President Carter, for example, had the opportunity of appointing 262 judges in federal district and circuit courts. Among his appointments were 29 black persons, 14 Hispanics, and 29 women (of which 6 were black and 1 Hispanic).[6] Although this is still a small percentage, it is larger than before.

Judges become judges either through election or appointment, or a combination of the two. All federal judges are appointed by the President, although such appointments are subject to confirmation by the Senate. Supreme Court appointments are the most visible, but others follow essentially the same process. These are, of course, *political* appointments. Democrats tend to appoint Democrats and Republicans appoint Republicans. Although incompetent or overly partisan judges sometimes slip through, there is generally enough prestige in the judicial office to encourage executives to appoint qualified people. "[President] Carter set up his own citizen panels to select appellate court judges and encouraged Democratic senators to use the same system to compile their lists for district court slots. Reagan is returning to the traditional method of letting Republican senators submit lists for all vacancies in their jurisdictions."[7] In the case of Supreme Court Justices, the participation of the American Bar Association in investigating and rating candidates has become so traditional as to be almost institutionalized.

State judicial offices are filled in a greater variety of ways: some states elect all their judges, including the state's highest appellate justices, on a partisan ballot; some elect all their judges, but with a non-partisan ballot; and many use a combination of appointment and election, often with an investigation and rating service performed by the state bar. For example, in Vermont:

---

[4] Jethro K. Lieberman, *The Litigious Society* (New York: Basic Books, 1981).

[5] Derived from Table 2, pp. 254–255, *The Book of the States.*

[6] "How Reagan Is Shaping His New Judiciary," *Business Week,* July 20, 1981, p. 80.

[7] Ibid.

Supreme court justices, superior court judges (presiding judges of superior courts) and district court judges appointed by governor, with consent of senate from list of persons designated as qualified by the Judicial Nominating Board. Supreme, superior and district court judges retained in office by vote of legislature. Assistant judges of superior courts and probate judges elected on partisan ballot in the territorial area of their jurisdiction.[8]

On the other hand, Arkansas, Louisiana, Georgia, Illinois, Kentucky, Michigan, Minnesota, Mississippi, Montana, Nevada, New Mexico, New York, North Carolina, North Dakota, Ohio, Oregon, Pennsylvania, Texas, Washington, West Virginia, and Wisconsin rely mainly on election. There is little evidence, however, that the quality or makeup of the judiciary varies as widely as the method of selection. Elected judges are as competent as appointed ones, and partisan ballots produce approximately the same type of judges as non-partisan ballots. In other words, judges do not appear to be more or less competent, more or less liberal, or any other defining variable depending upon their route to the bench.

Although one could argue that judicial selection is an opportunity for citizen participation, citizen involvement in the judicial branch mainly takes the form of jury duty. Originally, juries were meant to inject a democratic element into an essentially conservative institution. Juries decided both questions of fact *and* issues of law. This gave juries a great deal of latitude in deciding a dispute, and thus a great deal of power. Through the years, however, their role has been progressively narrowed, and juries are now limited to deciding the *facts*. The law is the province of the judge, and, as a further safety measure, the judge gives detailed instructions to the jury to help them to stay within proper legal bounds. Despite these restrictions, if a case reaches the trial stage, juries are still a frequent participant. In federal district courts, for example, juries are used in about 32 percent of the civil cases, and in criminal cases that go to trial, over half (54 percent) request a jury.[9]

But all these actors must be put into motion by a case—and a case requires a plaintiff and defendant. In 1975, an important study by Marc Galanter found that two general types of participants used the lower courts. He characterized them as "one shot only" and "repeat players."[10] In examining this process as a political question of who gets what, Galanter found that the ongoing participants, such as insurance companies, collec-

---

[8] Derived from Table 5, pp. 260–261, *The Book of the States.*

[9] "Reports of the Proceedings of the Judicial Conference of the United States: Held in Washington, D.C., March 16 and 17, 1982, and September 22 and 23, 1982; Annual Report of the Director of the Administrative Office of the United States Courts, 1982," (Washington, D.C.: U.S. Government Printing Office, 1982), Table 42, p. 141.

[10] Marc Galanter, "Why the 'Haves' Come Out Ahead: Speculations on the Limits of Legal Change," *Law and Society Review*, Vol. 9, No. 1, Fall, 1974, pp. 95–160.

tion agencies, and governmental agencies have an important advantage. The great bulk of the litigation in the lower courts find these repeat players as plaintiffs and one-shot players as defendants. We would expect repeat players to have a high win ratio, but other researchers found that it often exceeds 90 to 95 percent.[11] Figure 8.3 is Galanter's summation of the problem. Others have noted the same pattern, especially with regard to small claims courts:

> In practice, despite the suspension of technical rules of evidence and the elimination of attorneys, small-claims courts have generally not measured up to the task. On the contrary, many of these courts have become collection mills where merchants obtain default judgments against consumers. Dramatic evidence of the problem was provided by one California study that found that business and government initiated some 60 percent of all small-claims actions and that individuals rather than businesses were defendants about 80 percent of the time.[12]

The policymaking role of the Supreme Court is relatively obvious. However, circuit courts of appeals and district courts also reflect public policy choices as well as the relationships in the current political economy. As noted in a 1982 *Law and Society Review* article:

> The impact of federal government policy and activity on the business of the federal courts of appeal cannot be ignored. These courts continue to serve as arbiters of essentially private disputes, but increasingly this function has been overtaken by the task of arbitrating disputes arising from government decisions. Politics of the federal government and the problems associated with them now provide the basis for most federal appellate activity.[13]

Careful perusal of Table 8.3, which lists the civil cases commenced in U.S. District Courts by nature of suit, reveals some significant policy shifts from year to year. Note, for example, the huge increase in debt-collection cases by the federal government. "The largest single increase in filings was in cases for recovery of overpayments and enforcement of judgments, which rose 65.5 percent . . . in 1982."[14] Another major increase was in social security disability insurance cases, which rose 44.5 percent from 1981 to 1982. These are cases pursuing student loans, and military and disability

---

[11] Lawrence M. Friedman and Robert V. Percival, "A Tale of Two Courts: Litigation in Alameda and San Benito Counties," in Sheldon Goldman and Austin Sarat, eds., *American Court Systems: Readings in Judicial Process and Behavior* (San Francisco, Cal.: W. H. Freeman and Company, 1978), p. 75.

[12] Benedict S. Alper and Laurence T. Nichols, *Beyond the Courtroom: Programs in Community Justice and Conflict Resolution* (Lexington, Mass.: D.C. Heath and Company, 1981), p. 116.

[13] Baum, Goldman, and Sarat, p. 308.

[14] "Report of the Judicial Conference," p. 98.

Figure 8.3.   *Types of Litigants*

I. One-Shotter vs. One-Shotter	**II. Repeat Player vs. One-Shotter**
Parent v. Parent (Custody)	Prosecutor v. Accused
Spouse v. Spouse (Divorce)	Finance Co. v. Debtor
Family v. Family Member	Landlord v. Tenant
(Insanity Commitment)	I.R.S. v. Taxpayer
Family v. Family (Inheritance)	Condemnor v. Property Owner
Neighbor v. Neighbor	
Partner v. Partner	
III. One-Shotter vs. Repeat Player	**IV. Repeat Player vs. Repeat Player**
Welfare Client v. Agency	Union v. Company
Auto Dealer v. Manufacturer	Movie Distributor v. Censorship
Injury Victim v. Insurance	Board
Company	Developer v. Suburban
Tenant v. Landlord	Municipality
Bankrupt Consumer v. Creditors	Purchaser v. Supplier
Defamed v. Publisher	Regulatory Agency v. Firms of
	Regulated Industry

ELEMENT	ADVANTAGES	ENJOYED BY
Parties	—ability to structure transaction	
	—specialized expertise, economies	
	of scale	—repeat players
	—long-term strategy	large,
	—ability to play for rules	professional
	—bargaining credibility	
	—ability to invest in penetration	
Legal Services	—skill, specialization, continuity	—organized, professional,
		wealthy
Institutional	—passivity	—wealthy, experienced,
Facilities	—cost and delay barriers	organized
		—holders, possessors
		—beneficiaries of existing
		rules
	—favorable priorities	—organized, attentive
Rules	—favorable rules	—Older, culturally dominant
	—due process barriers	—holders, possessors

SOURCE: Marc Galanter, "Why the 'Haves' Come Out Ahead: Speculations on the Limits of Legal Change," *Law and Society Review*, vol. no. 1, Fall, 1974, pp. 107 and 125.

TABLE 8.3
U.S. District Courts Civil Cases by Nature of Suit

Nature of Suit	1978	1979	1980	1981	1982	Percentage of Change 1982/1981
Total	138,770	154,666	168,789	180,576	206,193	14.2
Contracts	25,728	36,898	49,052	51,159	67,276	31.5
Insurance	3,265	3,343	3,733	4,234	5,324	25.7
Marine	4,013	4,681	4,762	5,143	5,552	8.0
Miller Act	971	886	799	754	866	14.9
Negotiable Instruments	2,139	2,266	4,072	3,332	3,987	19.7
Recovery of Overpayments and Enforcement of Judgments	1,856	9,254	15,588	18,161	30,048	65.5
Other	13,484	16,468	20,098	19,535	21,499	10.1
Real Property Actions	12,781	11,876	11,067	8,887	8,812	-0.8
Mortgage Foreclosure	4,159	4,711	4,674	4,725	5,754	21.8
Land Condemnation	7,021	5,599	4,763	2,179	1,055	-51.6
Other	1,601	1,566	1,630	1,983	2,003	1.0
Tort Actions	26,375	28,901	32,539	33,767	34,218	1.3
Employers' Liability Act	1,494	1,540	1,990	1,876	2,017	7.5
Airplane	975	1,231	943	801	963	20.2
Marine	4,843	4,905	5,006	5,235	5,394	3.0
Motor Vehicle	5,839	5,991	6,321	6,199	6,651	7.3
Other Personal Injury	5,921	6,255	7,288	7,997	8,253	3.2
Personal Injury Product Liability	2,874	4,034	5,969	7,212	6,856	-4.9
Property Damage	4,429	4,945	5,022	4,447	4,084	-8.2
Actions Under Statutes	73,034	76,067	75,574	86,172	95,294	10.6
Antitrust	1,477	1,284	1,496	1,352	1,066	-21.2
Bankruptcy Suits	1,712	1,731	1,688	1,985	2,340	17.9

Civil Rights:					
Accommodations	497	434	342	336	237	-29.5
Employment	5,504	5,477	5,017	6,245	7,689	23.1
Voting	139	145	160	152	170	11.8
Welfare	214	195	212	253	215	-15.0
Other Civil Rights	6,475	6,917	7,213	8,433	8,727	3.5
Commerce (ICC rates, etc.)	2,365	1,395	1,105	1,080	1,057	-2.1
Deportations	163	141	139	113	134	18.6
Economic Stabilization Act	40	50	35	47	27	-42.6
Energy Allocation Act	79	121	153	104	47	-54.8
Environmental Matters	519	559	557	582	394	-32.3
Forfeiture and Penalty Suits	2,988	2,779	3,019	2,963	3,340	12.7
Freedom of Information Act	532	627	627	507	381	-24.9
Labor Laws	7,461	8,404	8,640	9,300	10,227	10.0
Patent, Copyright, Trademark	3,265	3,374	3,783	4,027	4,592	14.0
Prisoner Petitions:					
Federal	4,955	4,499	3,713	4,104	4,328	5.5
State	16,969	18,502	19,574	23,607	24,975	5.8
Securities, Commodities and Exchange	1,703	1,589	1,694	1,768	2,376	34.4
Social Security Laws	9,950	9,942	9,043	9,780	12,812	31.0
Tax Suits	2,669	3,527	3,271	3,930	4,234	7.7
Other	3,358	4,375	4,093	5,504	5,926	7.7
Other Actions	852	924	557	591	593	0.3
Domestic Relations (Local Jurisdiction)	304	269	94	12	5	-58.3
Insanity (Local Jurisdiction)	101	115	123	135	113	-16.3
Other	447	539	340	444	475	7.0

SOURCE: Table 17, "U.S. District Courts Civil Cases Commenced by Nature of Suit During the 12 Month Period Ended June 30, 1978–1982," in "Reports of the Proceedings of the Judicial Conference of the United States: Held in Washington, D.C., March 16 and 17, 1982, and September 22 and 23, 1982; Annual Report of the Director of the Administrative Office of the United States Courts, 1982," (Washington, D.C.: U.S. Government Printing Office, 1982).

payments, reflecting the Reagan administration's policy of "cracking down" and "tightening up" social welfare standards.

The important point to be made here is the *political* nature of the dispute resolution process and its participants. Lawyers and judges have a natural bias toward maintenance of the status quo, because their training and experience incline them to look to precedent (the past) for present solutions. The structure of the institution gives an advantage to those who would use the courts to pursue their own interests. But, as previously noted, regardless of policy outcomes, the courts reaffirm basic American values such as the belief in contracts and individualism. This is symbolically reassuring, regardless of the outcome of individual cases. However, analysis of the type of cases and consistent outcomes does tell us much about who gets what, when, and how, and thus the place of the judiciary in the American political economy.

Alternative Dispute Resolution

Criticism of the consistent policy outcomes of the courts has given rise to renewed interest in alternative methods of resolving disputes. Since the early 1900s, the judicial system has received calls for two major types of reform. The first has centered on the problem of serving the poor and working-class, even middle-class, citizens. The expense, lack of legal representation, and inability or unwillingness to use the courts, gave rise to reforms such as public defenders, small claims courts where attorneys were barred, volunteer time by private attorneys, and federally provided Legal Aid.

Since the 1970s, the second major critique of the judicial system has begun to be heard with more frequency. This complaint focuses on the *nature* of the adversarial system and its effectiveness as a means of resolving disputes. In 1976, the Department of Justice summarized these two major problems in its introduction to a proposal for federal legislation supporting alternative dispute resolution mechanisms:

> Throughout the United States persons with grievances involving relatively small amounts of money or consisting of altercations with neighbors or relatives often are unable to find a satisfactory forum where they can seek redress. For disputes of relatively minor dimensions, the traditional legal procedures of the courts are generally slow and costly.
>
> Moreover, the adversary process is not always the best mechanism for resolving such disputes. Many of the more informal mechanisms for resolution of these grievances, such as the justice of the peace, the responsive ward committeeman or precinct captain, the policeman on the beat, have faded from the American scene. Furthermore, many people are unaware of the formal mechanisms that have been created such as small claims courts, and of other small dispute resolution services that may be available, such as consumer protection offices or family counselling services.[15]

[15] Office for Improvements in the Administration of Justice, *Neighborhood Justice Center Program* (Washington, D.C.: Department of Justice, July 11, 1977), p. 1.

Often the two critiques are lumped together, as in the quotation. The first reform proposals for less expensive but adequate legal representation are directed specifically at a social grouping. However, the second critique, the need for an alternative method, covers more territory, and extends to many different *types* of disputes rather than to the ability to deal with dispute resolution at all. It is the minor, neighborhood disputes that seem to require alternative dispute-resolution mechanisms, for both reasons.

This section discusses alternative dispute-resolution mechanisms in more general terms. Arbitration and mediation are methods that have been used for some time in the United States, but are finding more and more applications as the caseload of the United States judicial system increases. Neighborhood Justice Centers are a relatively new phenomenon that were given public visibility in the Dispute Resolution Act of 1980, which sought to "assist the States and other interested parties in providing to all persons convenient access to dispute resolution mechanisms which are effective, fair, inexpensive, and expeditious."[16]

Arbitration and Mediation. Many contract disputes are better served by a process of bargaining rather than by forcing them into a win-or-lose situation. Arbitration and mediation arose as long ago as 1913 with the creation of the Department of Labor and federal provision of arbitrators or mediators to aid in the settlement of labor disputes. The American Arbitration Association is an institutional expression of the need for skilled and trustworthy arbitrators. Table 8.4 compares mediation and arbitration as methods of dispute resolution. As you can see, as concepts they are not far removed from the judicial system, but they do provide a less formal and less *adversarial* forum where competing claims can be offset and compromised.

Arbitration and mediation originally were used in labor/management disputes, and were adopted later by many trades or businesses that felt the need for a subject expertise in their adjudicators. Now the same idea has been extended to other types of disputes. For example, in many jurisdictions domestic disputes may be submitted to a mediator, who helps to alleviate some of the residual anger that is only exacerbated by a court battle. "In California, Pennsylvania and a few other states, commercial lawsuits up to a certain dollar amount must be referred first to arbitration; the statistics suggest that few thereafter are appealed to judges."[17] The mediator or arbitrator attempts to reach a mutually-satisfactory resolution rather than have one party win and then enforce that judgment.

Neighborhood Justice Centers. Neighborhood justice centers are a conscious attempt to combine the two major types of reform. The belief is that many disputes, even though minor, are very important to ordinary people. Consumer complaints, landlord-tenant disputes, and family matters can be

---

[16] Dispute Resolution Act of 1980, 94 Stat. 17; P.L. 96–568.

[17] Jethro K. Lieberman, reviewing Jerold S. Auerbach, *Justice Without Law?* (New York: Oxford University Press, 1982), *New York Times Book Review*, June 5, 1983, p. 13.

**TABLE
8.4**   ***Comparison of Mediation and Arbitration***

Dimension	Arbitration	Mediation
Relation to official system	Closer to adversary process; involves adjudication	Further from adversary process; does not involve adjudication
Relation between disputants	May have equal or unequal power	Should have roughly equal power
Underlying process	Compromise and adjudication	Compromise
Degree of formality	More formal	Less formal
Role of facts	Establishing facts more important	Establishing facts less important
Role of sanctions	Authoritative; enforcement more important	Not authoritative; enforcement less important
Model of justice	Reconciliation and affirmation of rights	Reconciliation

SOURCE: Reprinted by permission of the publisher, from *Beyond the Courtroom: Programs in Community Justice and Conflict Resolution,* by Benedict S. Alper and Lawrence T. Nichols (Lexington, Mass.: Lexington Books, D.C. Heath and Company, Copyright 1981, D.C. Heath and Company).

much too costly and time-consuming for the ordinary person to pursue. Small claims courts were one answer to this problem, but, as noted earlier, they quickly became collection agencies for repeat-player plaintiffs. One solution was to take the original idea behind small claims *courts* and create neighborhood forums, or centers, using mediation or arbitration as the dispute-resolution mechanism. These would be easily accessible, relatively cheap, and respond promptly. They would be staffed by mediators who came from or were familiar with the neighborhood, and had been given some mediation training.

Neighborhood justice centers accept all types of disputes, from landlord-tenant to family to those that would normally go to the criminal justice system. The line between criminal and civil is purposefully blurred because the purpose is to resolve the problem rather than affix guilt and penalize an offender. Since 1970, several states have attempted versions of the neighborhood justice centers, and often very successfully. Although the Dispute Resolution Act of 1970 passed, federal funding has been slow in coming. A few pilot projects have been funded and have operated successfully, but, as of 1983, most projects were still considered experimental and were under review, although alternative dispute resolution itself remains an important movement.

On the other hand, alternative dispute resolution is not without its critics. As Jerold Auerbach argues:

EXHIBIT 2
Legal Services Corporation

There is an American tendency, especially among lawyers, to believe that the law and legal institutions are fine mechanisms for social change. Social change achieved through litigation is orderly, rational, slow-paced, and probably just. In the 1960s, this became a widespread belief as the civil rights movement gained legal victories and class action suits on behalf of the less powerful became frequent. The courts appeared to be the one place where the politically unrepresented and powerless could get a hearing—and sometimes even win. Whether it was illusion or reality, or some of both, there was an *appearance* of success. This exhibit discusses the Legal Services Corporation, the entity that some credit and others blame for much of this apparent success.

In 1919, a man named Reginald Heber Smith wrote a book entitled *Justice and the Poor.*[1] In it he pointed out that many of our nation's citizens were too poor to afford a lawyer, and that their encounters with the law were almost all unpleasant. Therefore, they distrusted, if not actually hated, the law and the legal profession. Smith argued that if we were to truly offer equal justice before the law, then all people, and not just those who could afford it, must have access to the services of a lawyer. This would change poor peoples' views of the legal system as well as tangibly benefit them. It would also benefit the legal profession and the United States by removing a possible source of discontent and instability.

Needless to say, Smith's book was very controversial. Eventually the logic of his position swayed the legal profession, and the National Legal Aid and Defender Association, an offshoot of the American Bar Association, was begun in 1923. It provided a national organization for those agencies and persons interested in providing legal aid to poor people.[2] At this point, the underlying philosophy was simply to provide representation to those who were too poor to pay for it. It was preferred that funding come from private sources, such as the bar itself or charitable community organizations. Municipal funding eventually came to be accepted as well. Legal aid services grew, in fits and starts, until the 1950s. However, in 1949, England passed the Legal Aid and Advice Act that

---

[1] Reginald Heber Smith, *Justice and the Poor* (New York: Carnegie Foundation, 1919).

[2] Earl Johnson, Jr., *Justice and Reform: The Formative Years of the OEO Legal Services Program* (New York: Russell Sage Foundation, 1974), p. 7. The original name was the National Association of Legal Aid Organizations. Much of this history is based upon Johnson's work.

effectively provides, through government funding, legal services for all who cannot afford them. In this country, lawyers saw it as "socialized law," and thus a major threat. Combined with the anti-communist/ socialist hysteria of the 1950s, it effectively forestalled federal funding for legal services for years and scared many municipalities into getting out of the legal aid business.

Although the National Legal Aid and Defender Association (NLADA) and its lawyers continued to provide legal services, it was extremely difficult to expand without federal or governmental support, because funding was a constant problem. However, the Legal Services Corporation (LSC) did not arise from this tradition. Legal Services and the NLADA were eventually to learn to coexist, but the LSC had its origins elsewhere.

In the 1960s a "War on Poverty" was declared. As part of that war, community services of all kinds were to be provided to the poor. One of the needed services appeared to be legal help, but the legal services were to be only part of an entire package, and not even a major part. The impetus to include legal services in the War on Poverty came from the social workers and not from the bar itself. As a matter of fact, at first the organized bar was leery of the entire idea, and the NLADA was out-and-out opposed to it.

As the various factions committed to curing poverty struggled to draft the Organization for Economic Opportunity (OEO) legislation, several things became clear. First, even the lawyers involved from the beginning had come to feel that the legal services needed to be separate or independent from the community agencies. Lawyers did not want to be part of a "package," especially if it meant subservience to social worker bureaucrats. They wanted control over their actions and the ability to challenge even the OEO bureaucracy or agencies if the client's needs required it. There was a certain tension between the social worker's vision of what was needed to "cure" poverty and the poverty lawyer's vision.

Secondly, the poverty lawyers realized that they would need the support of the organized bar if they were to succeed. After all, they would be doing legal work within the legal community. So the proposals for a legal service agency moved closer and closer to legal argument and away from social analysis. At the same time, the organized bar began to realize that some sort of federal funding of a legal services agency was coming. They saw Medicare ("socialized medicine") pass in spite of a long and costly fight by the AMA. The ABA, and eventually the NLADA, realized that it might be better to recognize the inevitable and move in early enough to help shape the legislation, and so they did.

In 1964 the OEO passed, including a provision for awarding federal funds to provide legal services to the poor. From January 1, 1966 to June 30, 1967, 300 Legal Service organizations were given OEO grants out of a $42 million annual budget. Furthermore:

> 800 new law offices and almost 2,000 new lawyers were funded. By
> the conclusion of this burst of activity, OEO had constructed a system

of law offices and lawyers about the size of the United States Department of Justice and all its U.S. Attorneys' offices.[3]

Through the late 1960s and 1970s, legal services continued to grow slowly. In 1974, Legal Services Corporation was made an independent corporation, with a board of eleven members appointed by the President and confirmed by the Senate. It now submits its budget directly to Congress.

However, this marriage of the organized bar and the community-oriented poverty lawyers produced a conflict in the original goals of LSC, because it combined two different visions of social change through law. It is generally agreed that equal justice before the law requires legal representation. (It is constitutionally mandated in criminal cases, but there is no similar constitutional requirement for civil cases.) However, what that "representation" means is subject to debate. Does equal justice merely require that a lawyer be provided? What does that lawyer do? Many lawyers believed that simply providing legal representation was sufficient; on the other hand, many poverty lawyers believed that proper representation of the poor would result in the necessity of changing the legal structure through legal casework, class action suits, and test cases. They argued that LSC should do for poor people what lawyers do for the rich, and that meant challenging the status quo if necessary.

It is this "social change" aspect of their work that has kept the LSC controversy alive. In spite of the fact that such legal activity is a very small proportion of their work, it is the most highly visible. "Most staff time is spent on routine litigation: 35 percent on divorce and family law, 15 percent on landlord-tenant and housing cases, 13 percent on unemployment and social security eligibility problems and 12 percent on bankruptcy and consumer finance matters."[4] Less than 1 percent of its cases are class action suits, but these "offer lawyers a potent weapon against the two institutions most capable of injuring classes of people—government and big business."[5]

In spite of the controversy, until the administration of Ronald Reagan there was no concerted effort to undo the LSC. In March of 1981, President Reagan requested no funds for the LSC and that legal services be provided for the poor through the mechanism of block grants to the states. This would, of course, remove the independence of the poverty lawyers. Congress continued to fund LSC, but cut its budget by 25 percent. In fiscal year 1981, the LSC's budget was $321 million. In fiscal years 1982 and 1983, the budget was $241 million. The drop to $241 million forced LSC to cut its services:

---

[3] Ibid., p. 71.

[4] "Legal Services Corp. Supporters Fear It May Be 'Block Granted' to Death," *National Journal*, February 28, 1981, pp. 358–60.

[5] Jo Ann Boyd, "Despite Setbacks, Reagan's Assault on Legal Services Corp. Bears Fruit," *National Journal*, March 12, 1983, p. 563.

[LSC] estimates that seven million poor persons have legal problems that make them eligible for Legal Services assistance, but the corporation was able to pursue only 1.1 million cases in 1982, down from 1.2 million in 1981.

Last year, Legal Services closed nearly 300 of its 1,475 local storefront offices and lost almost a third of its national staff. California alone closed 35 offices and lost 187 attorneys.[6]

In fiscal year 1984, the LSC requested $275 million and received it. The LSC again does not appear in the President's proposed budget for fiscal year 1985.

Defeated in the attempt to dismantle LSC through budgeting and the block grant proposal, President Reagan used his power to appoint members to the LSC board who were personally opposed to it. Generally, these board members must be confirmed by the Senate, but President Reagan has consistently made them as "recess" appointments, which means they are made while Congress is away. The appointments are good for a year before Congress must confirm them. From 1980 until November 5, 1983:

[The LSC board] has operated with non-confirmed members appointed during congressional recesses. At present, the board has only four members, enough to do business under LSC rules.[7]

The President of the Legal Services Corporation in 1983 was Donald Bogard. He was previously chief counsel in the Indiana attorney general's office and the director of litigation for Stokely-Van Camp, Inc; he has no poverty law experience. In August of 1983, he ordered a raid of his own local offices' files in an attempt to find evidence of "lobbying" on the part of the local LSC lawyers; very little evidence was uncovered. It is believed that he would be in favor of dismantling the LSC (as Reagan wishes). However, in response to that question in an interview, he said:

Presently, there is no other mechanism in place to do what we are doing. If some alternate way were proposed to continue our work more effectively and efficiently, then I would review it.[8]

Meanwhile he and President Reagan are busy trying to find ways to put more of this work in private attorneys' hands. Ten percent of the present budget must be spent in encouraging participation in legal-services work by the private bar.

President Reagan and other conservative critics of LSC believe that LSC represents "leftists" and extremists, who are usually against the

[6] Ibid., p. 562.

[7] "Hearings Open on Legal Services Nominees," *Congressional Quarterly Weekly Report,* November 5, 1983, p. 2320.

[8] "Reforming an 'Incredibly Political' Agency," *U.S. News and World Report,* October 31, 1983, p. 67.

government that funds them. They say that they are not against legal services for the poor per se. But would it matter if President Reagan and the conservative members of Congress were able to succeed in dismantling the Legal Services Corporation? The "American Bar Association and many other legal service advocates have stressed that the private bar, while vital in helping meet the needs of the poor, is no substitute for federally supported legal services."[9] This returns us to the fundamental question: What are the legal needs of the poor? If they are simple representation—"a lawyer for every poor person with a legal problem"[10]—LSC is doing the best job it can with limited funding and resources.

On the other hand, the nagging problem of law as a mechanism for social change remains. Originally:

> The architects of the neighborhood lawyer programs on the other hand, for all their differences over ends and means, were united in their commitment to a basic objective, the reduction of poverty.[11]

Reduction of poverty does not necessarily come about through representation during divorces, bankruptcy hearings, and landlord-tenant disputes. It means bringing and developing test cases that more fundamentally challenge the law and legal structures. Instead of a single individual benefit, such cases would provide the maximum economic and social dividends for an entire class of people. Obviously, the conservative critics feel LSC has been much too successful in this area. On the other hand, it is difficult to find much tangible evidence of a reduction in poverty in the United States.

What does the Legal Services Corporation provide? What kind of social change can be accomplished through the mechanism of the law, the lawyers, and the courts?

---

[9] Jo Ann Boyd, "Despite Setbacks, Reagan's Assault on Legal Services Corp. Bears Fruit," p. 563.

[10] Johnson, *Justice and Reform*, p. 187.

[11] Ibid.

> Until the Civil War alternative dispute settlement expressed an ideology of community justice. Thereafter, as it collapsed into an argument for judicial efficiency, it became an external instrument of social control. That momentous shift still pervades the use of alternative dispute settlement more than a century later.[18]

Justice centers, and other reforms designed to bring justice to the people, rest on a mistaken assumption that poor people's problems are *minor* matters.[19] To reserve the court for major matters is simply a new version of discrimination. Those citizens who are "disadvantaged in American society by race, class, age, or national origin—those who most need legal rights and remedies—face the prospect of reduced possibilities for legal redress, in the name of increased access to justice and judicial efficiency."[20]

The American public and American lawyers are generally reluctant to give up the centrality of the courts to dispute resolution. This means that most reforms are still directed either at the courts themselves or at the provision of adequate legal services. The symbolic reassurance provided by having "one's day in court" persists; Americans believe courts provide, or should provide, justice. As Auerbach argues, in today's conditions, it may be true. Even though courts consistently show a bias toward conservation of the status quo and support for the business interests who clog the courts, where else would one go?

CRIME AND PUNISHMENT

Alternative dispute resolution maintains its biggest claim to funding because of its applicability to the criminal justice system. Concern over crime in the streets translates into support for suggestions of ways to alleviate that condition. "Crime" has been a political issue in the United States since the 1960s and shows no signs of abating. Crime statistics are routinely reported; the local evening news sometimes seems to consist solely of stories of one violent crime or another. However, even though the alternative forums have often proved successful, most controversy and visibility still centers on the judicial system itself, particularly as it works to control crime and maintain order.

"Today more than one out of every 600 Americans is in prison—not jail or reform school, but prison."[21] If all offenders "locked up or under some form of parole" are counted, in one recent year the figure was over two million persons, "or 1 in every 110 Americans."[22] Prisons are so overcrowded that many states have been forced to begin early-release programs in order to make room for incoming inmates. These facts help to make the political issue more visible as the struggle rages over obtaining the funds necessary to maintain those prisons and build extra facilities.

---

[18] Jerold S. Auerbach, *Justice Without Law?* (New York: Oxford University Press, 1982), p. 57.

[19] Barbara Yngvesson and Patricia Hennessey, "Small Claims, Complex Disputes: A Review of the Small Claims Literature," *Law and Society Review*, Vol. 9, No. 2, Winter 1975, pp. 219–74.

[20] Auerbach, *Justice Without Law?* p. 124.

[21] Kurt Anderson, "What Are Prisons For?" *Time*, September 13, 1982, pp. 38–41.

[22] Thomas E. Cronin, Tania Z. Cronin, and Michael E. Milakovich, *U.S. v. Crime in the Streets* (Bloomington, Ind.: Indiana University Press, 1981), p. 164.

The problem is complicated by the fact that there is a reality to the high crime figures, and many Americans are truly frightened. Statistics such as: "In four or five years, some experts predict, every household will be victimized!"[23] feed such fears. On the other hand, statistics tend to hide the fact that the poor and the minority populations are the most likely to be both victim and perpetrator. Over 50 percent of our prison population is comprised of blacks, Hispanics, or Native Americans; they populate our prisons and criminal justice system out of all proportion to their proportion in the population. This also means that the minority populations are highly overrepresented in the victim category.[24] In both cases, these are the populations that are the least likely to be adequately represented in the other branches of the government.

The criminal justice system is also obviously political because it is the state that is responsible for maintaining order, and some governmental entity is always the plaintiff in a criminal case. However, there are major differences over how best to maintain that order. We will first look at the criminal justice system as it stands, and then at crime and punishment as a political problem. Later, we will take a look at "political" crimes, or those arguments where the *nature* of the order being maintained is the issue.

The Criminal Justice System

Most of the criminal justice process is completed long before the issue reaches the court. The minute a police investigation focuses on a suspect or an arrest is made, the suspect must be informed of his or her constitutional rights.[25] Following arrest, the defendant must be formally charged within approximately forty-eight hours. The police give their information to the district attorney or prosecuting attorney (the official who represents the state as the plaintiff in the case) and that person makes a decision on whether to proceed and on what charge. Following formal arraignment by the court, at which time bail, if available, is set, the defendant and the state prepare for trial. The defendant can change his or her plea at any time and avoid full trial, and also has the right to choose a jury or non-jury trial. The defendant may then be found innocent (and released) or guilty. A guilty verdict can come in a variety of ways depending on the charge, but in most cases, sentencing is then up to the judge. A separate hearing is often held to determine the sentence.

We have just reviewed the general and theoretical criminal-justice process. Notice at how many points decisions can be made—on everyone's part. Police have discretion on investigations and arrest; prosecutors and

---

[23] Cronin, et al., *U.S. v. Crime in the Streets*, p. 163.

[24] "Crime and Its Victims: An Official Look," *U.S. News & World Report*, September 12, 1983, p. 72.

[25] *Miranda* v. *Arizona*, 384 U.S. 436 (1966).

Levy's Law, ® by James Schumeister

SOURCE: Reprinted by permission. © 1983 NEA, Inc.

district attorneys have discretion in pursuit of the case; and defendants have a variety of decisions to face. This capability to make choices, combined with the case overload of all members of this system, has led to a process called *plea bargaining*. Plea bargaining is mediation applied to the criminal justice system; the defendant may plead guilty to a lesser charge in order to avoid the hazards of a trial and receive a lighter sentence. Prosecutors can lighten their and the courts' workload and also avoid the hazards of a trial.

Table 8.5 summarizes the action taken on the total number of defendants encountering the federal district courts in 1982. (State court numbers, of course, are much higher because the major responsibility for crime control still rests with the individual states.) As illustrated, only 15 percent

TABLE 8.5	Criminal Defendants Convicted and Not Convicted, 1982		
Total Defendants			40,466
(U.S. District Courts)			
Dismissed		7,051	
Acquitted by court		225	
Acquitted by jury		938	
Not convicted			8,214
Pled guilty		26,355	
Pled nolo contendre		1,037	
Found guilty by court		1,205	
Found guilty by jury		3,655	
Convicted			32,252

SOURCE: Derived from Table 42, "U.S. District Courts, Summary of Criminal Defendants Convicted and Not Convicted During the Twelve Month Periods Ended June 30, 1981 and 1982," in the "Reports of the Proceedings of the Judicial Conference of the United States: Held in Washington, D.C., March 16 and 17, 1982, and September 22, and 23, 1982; Annual Report of the Director of the Administrative Office of the United States Courts, 1982," (Washington, D.C.: U.S. Government Printing Office, 1982), p. 141.

of the total defendants had a trial for resolution of guilt or innocence. Sixty-five percent of these defendants pleaded guilty—this is the famous plea bargain process. In this case, the court's job is merely to ratify the deal that has been made between the state and the defendant. The court also pronounces the sentence, but the sentence is often what has been recommended by the state and has been part of the original bargain.

Crime and Punishment as a Political Problem

This quick stroll through the criminal justice system reveals a conflict at its heart. Respect for constitutional law and protections and due process often conflicts with the efficient administration of justice. If every criminal defendant who pleaded "not guilty," was presumed to be innocent until proven guilty, and offered all the constitutional protections of an attorney, full and open trial by a jury of one's peers, chance to confront the accusers, the criminal justice system would grind to a halt. The conflict that greeted the *Miranda* decision is a good example of the controversy.[26]

The Supreme Court ruled in *Miranda* that every defendant has a right to have an attorney present, that they must be apprised of that right, and that an attorney would be provided should they be unable to afford one. These rights come into play as soon as investigation focuses on a suspect. The police felt that this decision tied their hands, making it infinitely more difficult to get a conviction, but actually, conviction records have changed very little since *Miranda*. However, the controversy is indicative of the split between wanting to maintain due process while making sure that no guilty people go free. Administrative efficiency keeps bumping up against individual rights; it is an obvious value choice that keeps being made over and over again—and shows no signs of going away.

Often underlying this political argument is the argument over how best to maintain order. What are the causes of crime and how do you cure it? Sometimes this argument is summed up in the phrase "nature versus nurture." Do environmental conditions cause crime, or are crimes solely the individual's responsibility? The criminal justice system at present responds to both of these choices at once. The individual crime may be the individual's responsibility, but mitigating factors are often taken into account, both in the placing of responsibility and in the sentencing of the offender. These same value choices inform the arguments over whether or not to maintain or extend the "innocent by reason of insanity" plea, which was brought into public prominence by the trial of John Hinckley, the person who shot President Reagan. Similarly, efforts are consistently made in state legislatures to restrict or take away the judge's discretion in sentencing by defining determinate sentences that are mandatory upon conviction of the crime. The problem is how much to treat individuals in

---

[26] Ibid.

exactly the same manner, while focusing on the nature of the crime, or how much to recognize individuality, while focusing on those factors that make this individual and thus the specific crime unique. Both are basic values in the American context—equality before the law and the uniqueness of each individual.

"Political" Crimes

There are cases in which the *nature* of American order is being challenged. During the 1960s, there was an argument, for example, that all black prisoners were political prisoners. The rationale for this was that the American political order was so racist that black people had few choices to exercise. Furthermore, the criminal justice system was purposefully out to oppress black people; their rights were fundamentally denied by every portion of the system, from the cop on the beat to the judge in the courtroom. The order being maintained by the state, and thus the criminal justice system, was a political definition to which black people did not adhere nor belong. Therefore, their incarcerations for defiance of that order were political decisions and actions. Although this argument never won wide acceptance, it did point to the political nature of the definition of the order that is maintained by the state, and revealed some systematic biases in the criminal justice system that prompted efforts at reform.

More common than the general denunciation is the idea that courts provide protection for those people who challenge the nature of the status quo. Even though the police and the criminal justice system may attempt to silence protesters or other unpopular ideas or persons, the courts will insist that the constitutional guarantees of free speech, assembly, and petition, be honored. It is somehow the Court's peculiar province to keep the political process open. Although there is some truth in the argument that courts must provide that political protection, their record is not particularly encouraging. Most of the time, courts side with legislative or administrative authorities, and they typically consider claims made by unpopular people, parties, or causes only to conclude that the established authorities were exercising their constitutional powers of maintaining order in imposing limitations on political activity. Rights to dissent and assembly are far more firmly established in legal theory than in actual practice.

The strategy of deliberately breaking a law in order to raise constitutional issues, as illustrated by Exhibit 1 is most widely used. Many of these cases begin in the criminal courts. During the 1960s, Jim Crow laws were initially challenged by the use of sit-ins; black people were arrested for crimes such as "trespassing" and "disturbing the peace," as they purposefully entered business establishments and sat at lunch counters marked "Whites Only." Recently, nuclear war protesters were arrested for "trespassing" as they attempted to stand on railroad tracks in front of a train carrying nuclear warheads. All of these criminal cases are meant to raise constitutional issues, as the state attempts to maintain order. No one argues that the state should not maintain the peace, but it is permissible, and sometimes even one's duty, to break that peace if it is maintaining an unjust or unconstitutional situation. Under these conditions, the state maintains that it is merely enforcing the law, and the defendants maintain it is a political trial. These criminal cases often wind up in the Supreme Court as part of the American political policymaking process.

CONCLUSION

The Supreme Court does not perform the task of constitutional interpretation all by itself, and the judicial system as a whole does not exist in a vacuum. Many other institutions and political participants take part in shaping any particular situation. Courts are, after all, essentially passive institutions that require several prior decisions by a variety of interested parties before a case even reaches them. Litigation is not the most direct and sure way of gaining one's political ends, but it is often utilized because other routes appear blocked or unpromising. The courts can become a kind of supplementary political level—a means of impelling other institutions to action or occasionally a route to limited, specific ends.

The many participants in the legal process are not allowed to decide important questions through internal interaction alone. Neither the Congress nor the President has been submissive to the Supreme Court in American history. Both have reacted strongly to decisions that they considered to be inappropriate or undesirable. Congress can pass a new statute that is only marginally different from one ruled unconstitutional, and can initiate constitutional amendments to overrule decisions. And it can and does express its displeasure by modifying the Court's jurisdiction or by severely challenging and perhaps rejecting confirmation of newly-appointed justices.

Because the President's cooperation is usually necessary to enforce Court decisions, he is often in an even stronger immediate position to prevent the Court's interpretation of the Constitution from becoming definitive or final. Presidents have ignored the Court, flatly refused to obey its decisions, or simply nominated judges with totally different views from those that previously prevailed. Thus, even when the Court does receive and decide a case in such a way as to assert a particular interpretation of the Constitution, the other institutions may reverse, modify, or ignore its determination.

The history of interactions among the many participants in American politics suggests that interpretation of the Constitution is considered to be too important an act to be left to the Supreme Court. Even if it were capable in practice of hearing cases on all the disputed aspects of the Constitution, the other political participants are too vitally concerned about gaining their ends to defer to the preferences of the judges. The contest over whose preferences shall be asserted as the established meaning of the Constitution involves great stakes—and so is on occasion bitterly fought. The final, authoritative meaning of the Constitution (assuming one ever finally emerges) is thus more a product of relative political power than of legalistic analysis alone.

The judicial branch as a whole is a very important part of our political process, but it is just that, a part. It is generally reactive, a supporter of the status quo. The Supreme Court plays a hugely symbolic role, reassuring us of the protective vision of the Law and the Constitution. The lower courts generally implement and maintain the order and values that arise out of the other parts of the American political system. The following case study on the abortion issue illustrates many of these points. It then leads us into the remaining institutional chapters on the other participants in the policy-making process.

Case Study—Legal Politics: The Abortion Case

Although this case study focuses on the politics of the legal system, and specifically the Supreme Court of the United States, we cannot ignore the surrounding political institutions and practices. We will see how cases arise out of a historical, social, and political context, how they are presented to the Court, and how the justices decide them. We will look at an edited version of the text of the majority opinion in the famous (or infamous) case of *Roe* v. *Wade,*[1] in which the Court held certain state laws prohibiting abortions to be unconstitutional. Then we will survey some of the reactions, effects, and continuing controversy that followed the announcement of the Court's decision, including some of the later cases. Although *Roe* and its subsequent decisions were and are highly controversial, they are entirely typical of the Supreme Court's decision making and role in the larger system.

The case study illustrates two separate but connected aspects of the legal system—the Supreme Court and constitutional politics. There is a politics *internal* to the system and one *external* to the system. For example, the question of which Justice will write the opinion of the Court is an internal political decision. The members of the legal system confront the question of who gets what, when, and how as part of their daily workings. Appointments of new Justices have both internal and external political ramifications. A change in the composition of the Court creates different relationships within the institution and changes expectations from actors outside the system.

Similarly, the legal system and the Supreme Court are part of the entire policy-making process. The external environment and its activities impact upon the Court and it, in turn, impacts upon them. This relationship is a political one, albeit unique. Legal politics is often politics for the less powerful, and usually involves an attempt to bring in the Constitution as a resource in the dispute rather than numbers of people. In other words, legal politics generally focuses on individual *rights* in conflict with policies coming from the legislative or executive branches of government, which supposedly represent majority preferences.

The abortion case study aptly illustrates all these facets. Obviously, the right to choose to have an abortion is an issue that confronts more than the judicial branch, but the latest round in this continuing controversy grew essentially out of the *Roe* decision. All subsequent activity, internal and external to the legal system, occurs within the context created by *Roe*, and similarly, the Court must deal with a changing

---

[1] *Roe* v. *Wade,* 410 U.S. 113; 93 S.Ct. 705; 35 L.Ed.2d 147 (1973). Its companion case was *Doe* v. *Bolton,* 410 U.S. 179; 93 S.Ct. 739; 35 L.Ed.2d 201 (1973), but they are familiarly and generally considered together as the *Roe* case.

internal environment while it faces the challenges posed by the external reactions to its original decision.

THE CASE COMES TO THE COURT

Statutes prohibiting abortions were part of the criminal law in most states during the first half of this century. Previous to that time, abortion appears to have been an accepted practice, at least until the time of *quickening* (the moment when the woman felt the fetus move, around twenty to twenty-four weeks). With the increase in medical knowledge and professionalization in the mid-to-late 1800s came (at least a professed) concern for the woman's health.[2] Looking at the issue from a medical perspective, it made sense to make the act of performing an abortion the crime. Assuming or accepting the fact that women were often desperate, and also assuming that women were less competent to make such decisions, the criminal intent was placed on the abortionist. On the other hand, it made it difficult for women to get standing to challenge the laws as they could show no direct harm.

By the 1960s, however, there was a strong movement for repeal of these statutes. Birth control procedures had become widely accepted, medical capabilities had improved greatly, and general social attitudes and particularly the growing feminist movement had helped raise the issue to the level of public controversy. In 1970 the American Medical Association passed resolutions endorsing abortion when it was in accordance with the best interests of the patient and sound medical judgment. The American Law Institute had developed a model statute for possible adoption by state legislatures that provided for abortions under certain medical circumstances. About a fourth of the states had enacted laws of this sort by 1973. Some states had gone even further in the way of liberalizing opportunities for abortions.

---

[2] There is considerable controversy regarding the rationale for criminalizing abortion. Barbara Hayler, in her review of "Abortion" in *Signs,* Winter 1979, pp. 307–23, summarizes two major works, as follows:

> . . . Mohr (James C. Mohr, *Abortion in America: The Origins and Evolution of National Policy, 1800–1900* (New York: Oxford University Press, 1978) argues that the change in attitudes toward abortion was brought about by a move among "regular" (AMA-affiliated) physicians to professionalize the practice of medicine, combined with nativist distrust of new immigrants by both physicians and state legislators. . . . Barker-Benfield (G.J. Barker-Benfield, *The Horrors of the Half-Known Life: Male Attitudes Toward Women and Sexuality in Nineteenth-Century America* (New York: Harper & Row, 1976) points out that the criminalization of abortion coincided with "the gynecological crescendo" which replaced midwives—who were relatively sympathetic to women's desires to end unwanted pregnancies—with male physicians and enabled men to take control of the procreative function.

This process was agonizingly slow, however, and not very productive. State legislatures were, to say the least, reluctant to deal with the abortion issue, which had the potential to alienate a lot of voters and not many clear advantages. Women were not a generally recognized, politically powerful, special-interest group. The notion of women's *rights* as a general principle was struggling for acceptance and the particular right to control one's own reproduction was far from generally accepted.

A legal strategy to challenge the abortion laws on a nationwide basis was developing simultaneously through the Supreme Court avenue. Feminists of varying persuasions believed that criminal abortion laws were an unconstitutional invasion of their individual rights. However, rarely does a case arise out of the blue, just as the litigants desire, and travel blithely to the Supreme Court for review. It is very difficult and time-consuming to get a case to the Supreme Court. To begin with, one needs lawyers who are willing to take the case, as well as litigants who are willing to spend the time, money, and energy to pursue it. The system itself poses technical obstacles such as standing, justiciability, and jurisdiction, as discussed in Chapter 8. All of these hurdles must be cleared before the substantive merits of the issue can even be addressed.

In one sense, the most important development was the increase in the number of women graduating from law schools in the 1960s and early 1970s. Many of these women were willing and eager to take on cases with respect to women's rights and specifically the abortion laws.[3] Thus, the first hurdle, that of a lawyer who was willing to handle the case, was taken care of, but the others remained. In the abortion case, finding clients presented a real problem. Doctors had to break a criminal law in order to challenge it, and risked their professional lives as well as jail and fines; nevertheless, several doctors in well-publicized cases did. Also, women were often reluctant to come forward in those circumstances. By the time the case could come to some sort of court, the pregnancy would have ended, through one means or another and, therefore, the case was moot (there was no issue to decide since there was no longer a pregnancy). The mere technical details of standing to sue, justiciability of the issue, and jurisdiction consumed many hours of legal work—and many cases.[4]

The lawyers slowly widened their areas of expertise and built a series of precedents that overcame the technical problems. A network developed that provided information and assistance, and other organiza-

---

[3] Two excellent works that include a history of the development of the litigation strategy are Barbara Milbauer, in collaboration with Bert N. Obrentz, *The Law Giveth: Legal Aspects of the Abortion Controversy* (New York: Atheneum, 1983) and Eva R. Rubin, *Abortion, Politics, and the Courts: Roe v. Wade and Its Aftermath* (Greenwood, Conn.: Greenwood Press, 1982).

[4] For an exhaustive legal history, see Milbauer, *The Law Giveth*; Rubin, *Abortion, Politics, and the Courts,* Chapter 2, is a concise summary.

tions, such as the American Civil Liberties Union, began to contribute time and money. Several cases had made it into the federal system, with widely varying substantive results. The Supreme Court was faced with increasing pressure to take on the merits of the issue, both by the volume and seriousness of the cases and the increasing chaos that was created by conflicting opinions in the lower federal courts.

The Supreme Court had decided in 1965, in the case of *Griswold* v. *Connecticut*[5] that the Constitution included a right to privacy, at least such that a Connecticut law preventing a married couple from access to birth control information and devices was unconstitutional. Later, in another opinion, the Court intimated that the vagueness of some abortion statutes might make them unconstitutional. Two cases soon presented the abortion question directly to the Court.

Early in 1970 a single woman (given the pseudonym "Jane Roe" to protect her identity) began a challenge to the criminal abortion law of Texas. The Texas statute had been enacted in 1854 and was typical of the "old style" laws prohibiting abortion at any time and without exceptions. Joining Roe were a Texas doctor who had been arrested for violating the statute, a married couple, and "all others similarly situated," which is the way that a litigant seeks to argue as representative of a class of persons. The case was brought against the district attorney of Dallas County, Texas, in the federal district court, on the grounds that Roe's constitutional rights had been denied by the Texas prohibition of a safe, medically performed abortion.

At about the same time, a similar challenge was raised by a woman and her doctor to a Georgia statute that was based on the American Law Institute's model version. Georgia's modern statute required that abortions be performed only when necessary to preserve the life of the woman and then only in certain approved hospitals when a hospital abortion committee approved and the judgment of two physicians confirmed the attending physician's diagnosis. As in *Roe*, the *Doe* (equally pseudonymous) case was brought directly to the federal district court. Because the Court ultimately resolved the major abortion issues in its opinion in *Roe*, the *Doe* case is relegated to a secondary status. The Court's opinion in *Doe* follows immediately after the opinions in *Roe* and merely applies the reasoning in *Roe* to the different nature of the Georgia statute. We shall concentrate on *Roe*, as did the Court.

The way in which the suit was initiated reveals the relationship between the federal and state court systems, which contributed to the Supreme Court's decision to hear the case. In both cases, the litigants went directly to a federal court to challenge a state law on constitutional grounds. The federal district courts in Texas and Georgia upheld their respective state statutes. Both cases were carried to the Supreme Court on a writ of *certiorari*, a procedure under which the Court itself has

---

[5] *Griswold* v. *Connecticut*, 381 U.S. 479 (1965).

discretion to decide whether to hear the case. Apparently these cases were accepted by the necessary four justices because of the jurisdictional issue they presented: Should federal courts accept all or most cases challenging state laws as violating the U.S. Constitution before those laws had been actually applied to the people challenging them?[6] If the Court were to rule against such openness on the part of the lower federal courts, it would both lighten the federal court's workload and strike a blow for states' rights. Apparently the intent of the four justices who originally accepted was to prevent the federal courts from taking such cases except in the most extreme circumstances. Roe's attorney in the Supreme Court was Sarah Weddington. Her 145-page brief argued that:

1. The right to seek and receive medical care is a fundamental personal liberty secured by the Ninth and Fourteenth amendments;
2. The Texas law violated the right to privacy included as a personal right in the due process clause of the Fourteenth Amendment as well as via the Ninth Amendment;
3. The Texas law was unconstitutionally vague; and
4. There was no compelling state interest sufficient to justify such a burden on either Roe or her doctor.

Included with the brief were almost 500 pages of medical, social-scientific, and other evidence in support of her claim. A number of other parties and organized groups filed *amicus curiae* ("friend of the court") briefs to urge the Court to strike down the statutes.

The cases were argued before the Court in the fall of 1971. Justices Powell and Rehnquist had been nominated, but not yet confirmed, so only seven justices were involved. Justices Douglas, Brennan, and Marshall were favorable to the rights of women to have abortions; Chief Justice Burger and Justice White were opposed. Justices Blackmun and Stewart were generally known to be conservative supporters of state legislative prerogatives, but each was also aware of women's issues and, most importantly, were responsive to the informed opinion of the medical profession. Blackmun had been counsel for the famous Mayo Clinic in his home state of Minnesota, and as such, he had become sensitive to the burdens placed on doctors by the statutes.

At the mid-December conference, a prior case presenting the same

---

[6] Characterizations of the justices' attitudes and actions in this and the next several paragraphs are drawn from Bob Woodward and Scott Armstrong, *The Brethren: Inside the Supreme Court* (New York: Simon & Schuster, 1979), pp. 165–77, 182–89, 229–40, and 413–16. Readers should keep in mind that investigative reporting in such a sensitive, complex, and unverifiable area may include serious errors of fact and interpretation. We have tried to avoid the more sensational and doubtful assertions by the authors and have employed only those that fit with other evidence.

jurisdictional issue as the abortion cases was decided in favor of allowing the federal courts to hear constitutional challenges to state laws.
Justice Stewart unexpectedly joined Justices Douglas, Brennan, and
Marshall to make a 4-to-3 majority. In effect, this vote also resolved the
jurisdictional question in the abortion cases. Thus, the justices now had
to take up the merits of the women's claims in each case.

Justices Douglas, Brennan, and Marshall took broad constitutional
ground, and were joined by Stewart and Blackmun on much narrower
grounds. This made five votes against the statutes, with White voting in
support of the state laws. Chief Justice Burger's practice was to argue his
position, in this case in favor of the statutes, but to reserve his vote until
the other justices had voted. In this way he could join a majority he did
not necessarily agree with in order to exercise his privilege as senior
justice to assign the writing of the Court's opinion. This enabled him to
exercise some control over the legal principles enunciated by the Court, if
necessary by assigning the opinion to himself. But this also violated
traditional procedures and created tensions on the Court; Justice Douglas, as the most senior associate justice, would otherwise have made
many of the assignments and thus felt particularly aggrieved.

In these cases Burger, despite arguing for the state statutes, voted
with the majority and assigned the opinion to Justice Blackmun, who
was known to be the slowest draftsman of the justices. Some of the
justices believed that Burger was stalling, hoping to delay the decision so
that it did not come down during the 1972 election year and/or so that it
would be reargued after the two new Nixon appointees had joined the
Court. Blackmun realized the importance of the case and wanted to
write an opinion that would withstand all the criticism that was likely to
be directed at it. The grounds he sought particularly to master were the
medical ones, consistent with his earlier experience. If Burger had voted
with the minority, the chances are that Douglas, as the senior justice in
the majority, would have assigned the opinion to himself. It is quite likely
that he would have written a broad opinion based on the woman's right
to privacy and control of her own body, as he did in his concurrence. It is
suspected that Burger also wanted to avoid this possibility. For all these
reasons, Blackmun's progress on the opinion was even slower than
usual.

In January 1972, with Justices Powell and Rehnquist now present,
Chief Justice Burger suggested that all cases with a vote of 4-to-3 be
reargued the next year before the full Court. He included on the list both
the earlier case that had settled the jurisdictional question and the abortion cases. He argued further that the new justices should also vote on
whether the cases should be reargued, but the new justices refused to
vote on the question. The antiabortion majority held on both the jurisdictional issue and the need to hand down opinions on decided cases.
Blackmun was still working on his first draft of the opinion, however, and
did not circulate it until mid-May. Even then, it was an unfinished version
that drew criticism from the majority and a vigorous dissent from White.

Finally, after an extended conference with Burger, Blackmun suggested that his draft be withdrawn and the case put over to the next session (fall, 1972), and reluctantly, the majority justices agreed.

Blackmun worked on his draft over the summer, developing the medical rationale carefully. It was circulated early in the fall and a number of suggestions from justices in the majority (particularly Brennan) were incorporated. One issue of concern to Douglas and Stewart was whether the grounds of the decision were the (new) right to privacy (Douglas) or just one dimension of the substantive meaning of the due process clause (Stewart). Reargument changed no positions, but allowed Powell to join the majority and Rehnquist the minority.

The majority and two concurring opinions and the two dissents were all ready by early December 1972, but nothing came from Chief Justice Burger. By early January 1973, the other justices were growing impatient about these and other cases that all seemed to be unnecessarily delayed. Burger resisted their suggestions that the decision be announced on Monday, January 15, and/or that he let the announcement be made without his vote. Instead, he said that he would vote with the majority, but needed time to add his own concurrence. The other justices concluded that Burger was insisting on one final bit of delay; he meant to put off the historic and inevitably controversial decision until after he had sworn in antiabortion President Richard Nixon on January 20, 1973. In any event, Burger finally wrote a three paragraph "concurrence," in which he denied much of what the majority opinion held.

THE TEXT OF THE SUPREME COURT OPINION IN *ROE*[7]

MR. JUSTICE BLACKMUN delivered the opinion of the Court [in *Roe*]: . . .

We forthwith acknowledge our awareness of the sensitive and emotional nature of the abortion controversy, of the vigorous opposing views, even among physicians, and of the deep and seemingly absolute convictions that the subject inspires. One's philosophy, one's experiences, one's exposure to the raw edges of human existence, one's religious training, one's attitudes toward life and family and their values, and the moral standards one establishes and seeks to observe, are all likely to influence and to color one's thinking and conclusions about abortion. In addition, population growth, pollution, poverty, and racial overtones tend to complicate and not to simplify the problem.

Our task, of course, is to resolve the issue by constitutional measurement free of emotion and of predilection. We seek earnestly to do this, and, because we do, we have inquired into, and in this opinion place some emphasis upon, medical and medical-legal history and what that

---

[7] *Roe* v. *Wade, supra.*

history reveals about man's attitudes toward the abortive procedure over the centuries. We bear in mind, too, Mr. Justice Holmes' admonition in his now vindicated dissent in *Lochner v. New York,* 198 U.S. 45, 76 (1905):

"It [the Constitution] is made for people of fundamentally differing views, and the accident of our finding certain opinions natural and familiar or novel and even shocking ought not to conclude our judgment upon the question whether statutes embodying them conflict with the Constitution of the United States." . . .

The principal thrust of appellant's attack on the Texas statutes is that they improperly invade a right, said to be possessed by the pregnant woman, to choose to terminate her pregnancy. . . . Before addressing this claim, we feel it desirable briefly to survey, in several aspects, the history of abortion, for such insight as that history may afford us. . . .

The Constitution does not explicitly mention any right of privacy. . . . the Court has recognized that a right of personal privacy, or a guarantee of certain areas or zones of privacy, does exist under the Constitution. In varying contexts the Court or individual Justices have indeed found at least the roots of that right in the First Amendment [*Stanley* v. *Georgia*]; in the Fourth and Fifth Amendments [e.g., *Terry* v. *Ohio*]; in the penumbras of the Bill of Rights [*Griswold* v. *Connecticut*]; in the Ninth Amendment [id.]; or in the concept of liberty guaranteed by the first section of the Fourteenth Amendment, see [*Meyer* v. *Nebraska*]. These decisions make it clear that only personal rights that can be deemed "fundamental" or "implicit in the concept of ordered liberty" [*Palko* v. *Connecticut*] are included in this guarantee of personal privacy. They also make it clear that the right has some extension to activities relating to marriage [*Loving* v. *Virginia*], procreation [*Skinner* v. *Oklahoma*], contraception [*Eisenstadt* v. *Baird*], family relationships [*Prince* v. *Massachusetts*], and child rearing and education [*Pierce* v. *Society of Sisters; Meyer* v. *Nebraska*].

The right of privacy, whether it be founded in the Fourteenth Amendment's concept of personal liberty and restrictions upon state action, as we feel it is, or, as the District Court determined, in the Ninth Amendment's reservation of rights to the people, is broad enough to encompass a woman's decision whether or not to terminate her pregnancy. The detriment that the State would impose upon the pregnant woman by denying this choice altogether is apparent. Specific and direct harm medically diagnosable even in early pregnancy may be involved. Maternity, or additional offspring, may force upon the woman a distressful life and future. Psychological harm may be imminent. Mental and physical health may be taxed by child care. There is also the distress, for all concerned, associated with the unwanted child, and there is the problem of bringing a child into a family already unable, psychologically and otherwise, to care for it. In other cases, as in this one, the additional difficulties and continuing stigma of unwed motherhood may be involved. All these factors the woman and her responsible physician necessarily will consider in consultation.

On the basis of elements such as these, appellants and some *amici* argue that the woman's right is absolute and that she is entitled to terminate her pregnancy at whatever time, in whatever way, and for whatever reason she alone chooses. With this we do not agree. . . . The Court's decisions recognizing a right of privacy also acknowledge that some state regulation in areas protected by that right is appropriate. [A] state may properly assert important interests in safeguarding health, in maintaining medical standards, and in protecting potential life. At some point in pregnancy, these respective interests become sufficiently compelling to sustain regulation of the factors that govern the abortion decision. . . . In fact, it is not clear to us that the claim asserted by some *amici* that one has an unlimited right to do with one's body as one pleases bears a close relationship to the right of privacy previously articulated in the Court's decisions. The Court has refused to recognize an unlimited right of this kind in the past. [*Jacobson* v. *Massachusetts*] (vaccination); [*Buck* v. *Bell*] (sterilization).

We therefore conclude that the right of personal privacy includes the abortion decision, but that this right is not unqualified and must be considered against important state interests in regulation. . . .

Where certain "fundamental rights" are involved, the Court has held that regulation limiting these rights may be justified only by a "compelling state interest" . . . and that legislative enactments must be narrowly drawn to express only the legitimate state interests at stake. . . .

A.

The appellee and certain *amici* argue that the fetus is a "person" within the language and meaning of the Fourteenth Amendment. In support of this they outline at length and in detail the well-known facts of fetal development. If this suggestion of personhood is established, the appellant's case of course, collapses, for the fetus' right to life is then guaranteed specifically by the Amendment. . . . On the other hand, the appellee conceded on reargument that no case could be cited that holds that a fetus is a person within the meaning of the Fourteenth Amendment.

The Constitution does not define "person" in so many words. . . . In nearly all these instances, [in which the Constitution employs the word] the use of the word is such that it has application only postnatally. None indicates, with any assurance, that it has any possible prenatal application.

All this, together with our observation . . . that throughout the major portion of the nineteenth century prevailing legal abortion practices were far freer than they are today, persuades us that the word *person*, as used in the Fourteenth Amendment, does not include the unborn. . . . This conclusion, however, does not of itself fully answer the contentions raised by Texas, and we pass on to other considerations.

B.

. . . Texas urges that, apart from the Fourteenth Amendment, life begins at conception and is present throughout pregnancy, and that, therefore, the State has a compelling interest in protecting that life from and after conception. We need not resolve the difficult question of when

life begins. When those trained in the respective disciplines of medicine, philosophy, and theology are unable to arrive at any consensus,
the judiciary, at this point in the development of man's knowledge, is
not in a position to speculate as to the answer. It should be sufficient to
note briefly the wide divergence of thinking on this most sensitive and
difficult question. . . .

In areas other than criminal abortion the law has been reluctant to
endorse any theory that life, as we recognize it, begins before live birth
or to accord legal rights to the unborn except in narrowly defined
situations and except when the rights are contingent upon live birth.
. . . In short, the unborn have never been recognized in the law as
persons in the whole sense. In view of all this, we do not agree that, by
adopting one theory of life, Texas may override the rights of the pregnant woman that are at stake. We repeat, however, that the State does
have an important and legitimate interest in preserving and protecting
the health of the pregnant woman, whether she be a resident of the
State or a nonresident who seeks medical consultation and treatment
there, and that it has still *another* important and legitimate interest in
protecting the potentiality of human life. These interests are separate
and distinct. Each grows in substantiality as the woman approaches
term and, at a point during pregnancy, each becomes "compelling."

With respect to the State's important and legitimate interest in the
health of the mother, the "compelling" point, in the light of present
medical knowledge, is at approximately the end of the first trimester.
This is so because of the now established medical fact . . . that until the
end of the first trimester mortality in abortion is less than mortality in
normal childbirth. It follows that, from and after this point, a State may
regulate the abortion procedure to the extent that the regulation reasonably relates to the preservation and protection of maternal health.
Examples of permissible state regulation in this area are requirements
as to the qualifications of the person who is to perform the abortion; as
to the licensure of that person; as to the facility in which the procedure
is to be performed, that is, whether it must be a hospital or may be a
clinic or some other place of less-than-hospital status; as to the licens-
ing of the facility; and the like.

This means, on the other hand, that, for the period of pregnancy prior
to this "compelling" point, the attending physician, in consultation
with his patient, is free to determine, without regulation by the State,
that in his medical judgment the patient's pregnancy should be ter-
minated. If that decision is reached, the judgment may be effectuated
by an abortion free of interference by the State.

With respect to the State's important and legitimate interest in potential
life, the "compelling" point is at viability. This is so because the fetus
then presumably has the capability of meaningful life outside the
mother's womb. State regulation protective of fetal life after viability
thus has both logical and biological justifications. If the State is interested in protecting fetal life after viability, it may go so far as to proscribe abortion during that period except when it is necessary to preserve the life or health of the mother.

Measured against these standards, [the law] sweeps too broadly. The statute makes no distinction between abortions performed early in pregnancy and those performed later, and it limits to a single reason, "saving" the mother's life, the legal justification for the procedure. . . .

To summarize and to repeat:

1. A state criminal statute of the current Texas type, that excepts from criminality only a *life-saving* procedure on behalf of the mother, without regard to pregnancy stage and without recognition of the other interests involved, is violative of the Due Process Clause of the Fourteenth Amendment.
   a. For the stage prior to approximately the end of the first trimester, the abortion decision and its effectuation must be left to the medical judgment of the pregnant woman's attending physician.
   b. For the stage subsequent to approximately the end of the first trimester, the State, in promoting its interest in the health of the mother, may, if it chooses, regulate the abortion procedure in ways that are reasonably related to maternal health.
   c. For the stage subsequent to viability the State, in promoting its interest in the potentiality of human life, may, if it chooses, regulate, and even proscribe abortion except where it is necessary in appropriate medical judgment, for the preservation of the life or health of the mother.
2. The State may define the term *physician* . . . to mean only a physician currently licensed by the State, and may proscribe any abortion by a person who is not a physician as so defined.

In *Doe* v. *Bolton,* post-procedural requirements contained in one of the modern abortion statutes are considered. That opinion and this one, of course, are to be read together.

This holding, we feel, is consistent with the relative weights of the respective interests involved, with the lessons and example of medical and legal history, with the lenity of the common law, and with the demands of the profound problems of the present day. The decision leaves the State free to place increasing restrictions on abortion as the period of pregnancy lengthens, so long as those restrictions are tailored to the recognized state interests. The decision vindicates the right of the physician to administer medical treatment according to his professional judgment up to the points where important state interests provide compelling justifications for intervention. Up to those points the abortion decision in all its aspects is inherently, and primarily, a medical decision, and basic responsibility for it must rest with the physician. If an individual practitioner abuses the privilege of exercising proper medical judgment, the usual remedies, judicial and intra-professional, are available. . . .

It is so ordered.

MR. JUSTICE STEWART, concurring: . . .

Several decisions of this Court make clear that freedom of personal choice in matters of marriage and family life is one of the liberties

protected by the Due Process Clause of the Fourteenth Amendment.
. . . As recently as last Term, in [*Eisenstadt* v. *Baird*], we recognized "the
right of the *individual,* married or single, to be free from unwarranted
governmental intrusion into matters so fundamentally affecting a person as the decision whether to bear or beget a child." That right
necessarily includes the right of a woman to decide whether or not to
terminate her pregnancy. . . .

It is evident that the Texas abortion statute infringes that right directly.
. . . The question then becomes whether the state interests advanced to
justify this abridgment can survive the "particularly careful scrutiny" that
the Fourteenth Amendment here requires.

The asserted state interests . . . are legitimate objectives, amply sufficient to permit a State to regulate abortions as it does other surgical
procedures, and perhaps sufficient to permit a State to regulate abortions more stringently or even to prohibit them in the late stages of
pregnancy. But such legislation is not before us, and I think the Court
today has thoroughly demonstrated that these state interests cannot
constitutionally support the broad abridgment of personal liberty
worked by the existing Texas law. Accordingly, I join the Court's opinion holding that that law is invalid under the Due Process Clause of the
Fourteenth Amendment.

MR. JUSTICE DOUGLAS, concurring [in *Doe* v. *Bolton* as well as in *Roe* v.
Wade]:

While I join the opinion of the Court [except as to the dismissal of Dr.
Hallford's complaint in the *Roe case*], I add a few words.

The questions presented [in these cases] involve the right of privacy,
one aspect of which we considered in [*Griswold* v. *Connecticut*], when
we held that various guarantees in the Bill of Rights create zones of
privacy. . . .

The Ninth Amendment obviously does not create federally enforceable
rights. It merely says, "The enumeration in the Constitution of certain
rights shall not be construed to deny or disparage others retained by
the people." But a catalogue of these rights includes customary, traditional, and time-honored rights, amenities, privileges, and immunities
that come within the sweep of "the Blessings of Liberty" mentioned in
the preamble to the Constitution. Many of them in my view come
within the meaning of the term "liberty" as used in the Fourteenth
Amendment.

*First is the autonomous control over the development and expression
of one's intellect, interests, tastes, and personality.*

These are rights protected by the First Amendment and in my view they
are absolute, permitting of no exception: . . .

*Second is freedom of choice in the basic decisions of one's life respect-
ing marriage, divorce, procreation, contraception, and the education
and upbringing of children.*

These ["fundamental"] rights, unlike those protected by the First Amendment, are subject to some control by the police power. . . .

Third is the freedom to care for one's health and person, freedom from bodily restraint or compulsion, freedom to walk, stroll, or loaf.

These rights, though fundamental, are likewise subject to regulation on a showing of "compelling state interest." . . .

[A] woman is free to make the basic decision whether to bear an unwanted child. Elaborate argument is hardly necessary to demonstrate that childbirth may deprive a woman of her preferred life style and force upon her a radically different and undesired future. Such a holding is, however, only the beginning of the problem. The State has interests to protect. . . . While childbirth endangers the lives of some women, voluntary abortion at any time and place regardless of medical standards would impinge on a rightful concern of society. The woman's health is part of that concern; as is the life of the fetus after quickening. These concerns justify the State in treating the procedure as a medical one. . . .

MR. JUSTICE WHITE, with whom MR. JUSTICE REHNQUIST joins, dissenting [in *Doe* v. *Bolton* as well as in *Roe* v. *Wade*]:

At the heart of the controversy in these cases are those recurring pregnancies that pose no danger whatsoever to the life or health of the mother but are nevertheless unwanted for any one or more of a variety of reasons—convenience, family planning, economics, dislike of children, the embarrassment of illegitimacy, etc. The common claim before us is that for any one of such reasons, or for no reason at all, and without asserting or claiming any threat to life or health, any woman is entitled to an abortion at her request if she is able to find a medical advisor willing to undertake the procedure.

The Court for the most part sustains this position. During the period prior to the time the fetus becomes viable, the Constitution of the United States values the convenience, whim or caprice of the putative mother more than the life or potential life of the fetus; the Constitution, therefore, guarantees the right to an abortion as against any state law or policy seeking to protect the fetus from an abortion not prompted by more compelling reasons of the mother.

With all due respect, I dissent. I find nothing in the language or history of the Constitution to support the Court's judgment. The Court simply fashions and announces a new constitutional right for pregnant mothers and, with scarcely any reason or authority for its action, invests that right with sufficient substance to override most existing state abortion statutes. The upshot is that the people and the legislatures of the fifty States are constitutionally disentitled to weigh the relative importance of the continued existence and development of the fetus on the one hand against a spectrum of possible impacts on the mother on the other hand. As an exercise of raw judicial power, the Court perhaps has authority to do what it does today; but in my view its judgment is an improvident and extravagant exercise of the power of judicial review which the Constitution extends to this Court.

The Court apparently values the convenience of the pregnant mother more than the continued existence and development of the life or potential life which she carries. Whether or not I might agree with that marshalling of values, I can in no event join the Court's judgment because I find no constitutional warrant for imposing such an order of priorities on the people and legislatures of the States. In a sensitive area such as this, involving as it does issues over which reasonable men may easily and heatedly differ, I cannot accept the Court's exercise of its clear power of choice by interposing a constitutional barrier to state efforts to protect human life and by investing mothers and doctors with the constitutionally protected right to exterminate it. This issue, for the most part, should be left with the people and to the political processes the people have devised to govern their affairs.

It is my view, therefore, that the Texas statute is not constitutionally infirm because it denies abortions to those who seek to serve only their convenience rather than to protect their life or health. . . .

[Mr. Justice Rehnquist's dissent, as well as Mr. Justice Blackmun's opinion for the Court in *Doe* v. *Bolton*, are omitted. In the latter, the Georgia statute's requirement that abortions be performed only under strictly limited circumstances was voided.]

MR. CHIEF JUSTICE BURGER concurring in both cases:

I agree that, under the Fourteenth Amendment to the Constitution, the abortion statutes of Georgia and Texas impermissibly limit the performance of abortions necessary to protect the health of pregnant women, using the term health in its broadest medical context. . . . I am somewhat troubled that the Court has taken notice of various scientific and medical data in reaching its conclusion; however, I do not believe that the Court has exceeded the scope of judicial notice accepted in other contexts.

In oral argument, counsel for the State of Texas informed the Court that early abortive procedures were routinely permitted in certain exceptional cases, such as nonconsensual pregnancies resulting from rape and incest. In the face of a rigid and narrow statute, such as that of Texas, no one in these circumstances should be placed in a posture of dependence on a prosecutorial policy or prosecutorial discretion. Of course, States must have broad power, within the limits indicated in the opinions, to regulate the subject of abortions, but where the consequences of state intervention are so severe, uncertainty must be avoided as much as possible. For my part, I would be inclined to allow a State to require the certification of two physicians to support an abortion, but the Court holds otherwise. I do not believe that such a procedure is unduly burdensome, as are the complex steps of the Georgia statute, which require as many as six doctors and the use of a hospital certified by the JCAH.

I do not read the Court holding today as having the sweeping consequences attributed to it by the dissenting Justices; the dissenting views
discount the reality that the vast majority of physicians observe the
standards of their profession, and act only on the basis of carefully
deliberated medical judgments relating to life and health. Plainly, the
Court today rejects any claim that the Constitution requires abortion on
demand.

AFTER THE DECISION: REACTIONS, EFFECTS, CONTINUING CONTROVERSY

As expected, the *Roe* decision was greeted with both delight and denunciation. However, contrary to Blackmun's hopes that his guidelines
would put the matter to rest, *Roe* was the catalyst around which political
forces would swirl. Right to Life and other antiabortion groups mobilized
and sought to have the decision reversed by means of a constitutional
amendment and/or new restrictions on abortions enacted by Congress
and the state legislatures. Right to Choose groups originally assumed
that the decision was a victory and then were forced to play catch-up as
the Right to Life groups gained more and more restrictions.

The Supreme Court's opinions in *Roe* and *Doe* distinguished between trimesters of pregnancy, allowing the state a successively greater
interest in controlling abortions within each three-month period. With
the exception of Justice Douglas, the Court was unwilling to grant a
woman an uncontrolled right to privacy with regard to the abortion
decision or an unrestricted substantive due-process right to control over
her own body. Blackmun's decision:

> balanced the interests of the fetus, the interests of the state in regulat-
> ing health and medical practice, and the rights of the woman. Justice
> Blackmun appears to have worked out the basis for such a compromise
> in terms of the "viability" of the fetus.[8]

However, by balancing and defining separate interests, the door was left
open for regulations that did not "unduly burden" the woman's right to
privacy to make the decision. After all, "what the Court specifically upheld in *Roe* is the right to decide in private about abortion, not the right
to *have* an abortion."[9]

From 1973 on, antiabortion forces introduced restrictive legislation at
all levels: city, county, state, and federal. "In the twenty-four months
immediately following the Supreme Court's decision, sixty-two laws directly related to abortion were adopted by thirty-two states."[10] These

[8] Rubin, *Abortion, Politics, and the Courts*, pp. 68–9.

[9] Milbauer, *The Law Giveth*, p. 164.

[10] Rubin, *Abortion, Politics, and the Courts*, p. 126.

revolved around the loopholes Blackmun had left open, particularly the state's interest in health through regulating where, when, and by whom abortions would be performed. Originally, especially with respect to first trimester abortions, the lower courts consistently held these restrictions unconstitutional.

However, abortion increased in strength as a political issue, and the Right to Lifers appeared to grow.

> More abortion laws were enacted in 1977 than in any other year since 1973. Reflecting the increased power and presence of antiabortion forces in state politics, the tone of the statutes became increasingly restrictive. The Right-to-Life groups seemed to be better organized and better motivated and to work harder than the pro-Choice forces.[11]

What had led to this apparent strength was a coalition of the Right to Lifers with the New Right, the fundamentalists captured in the phrase Moral Majority or the Christian Voice, and the Republican Party. Although abortion was not originally an issue for the conservative political right, they recognized the Right-to-Lifers as "a potentially valuable ally in a six-year strategy of the 'winning coalition' to capture as many congressional seats as possible for conservatives."[12]

Abortion thus became part of an overall conservative strategy. Its power lay in its symbolism, and the right to choose to have an abortion represented a host of other political issues revolving around the notion of the family. To the conservative coalition, the women's movement, which was symbolized by the ERA and the right to abortion, was bringing about the destruction of the family—and thus the United States. As one major feminist author concluded, "antiabortion forces 'are reacting not merely to a "loosening of morals" but to the whole feminist struggle of the last century; they are fighting for male supremacy.' "[13]

The abortion issue is a good illustration of symbolic and value-laden politics. Some Right-to-Lifers genuinely believe that life begins at conception and, therefore, an absolute prohibition on abortion is necessary. The *political* usage of abortion as an issue, however, became tied to the package of conservative issues. The public furor over the right to have an abortion found one side labeling themselves pro-*choice* and the other side pro-*life*. The Supreme Court, as we noted earlier, ruled that women had a right *to choose* relatively privately, and not necessarily a right to an abortion. They also ruled that the state's interest in protecting life became more compelling as that life became viable. In other words, the decision supports both labels. However, abortion as a *political* issue came to

[11] Ibid., p. 136.

[12] Connie Paige, *The Right to Lifers: Who They Are, How They Operate, Where They Get Their Money* (New York: Summit Books, 1983), p. 182.

[13] Linda Gordon, *Woman's Body, Woman's Right: A Social History of Birth Control in America* (New York: Grossman Publishers, 1976), p. 415.

embody a more fundamental political argument; it grew out of an entirely different vision of a woman's role and purpose, and ultimately the relationship between people and the government.

On the other hand, for that very reason, as the conservatives gained legislative—and eventually presidential—victories, the abortion issue became less necessary. Economic and other social issues were more pressing, and the Right-to-Lifers' original victories turned out to be "something of an illusion."[14] As Ms. Paige explains:

> In short, it looks as if abortion is losing its usefulness to the Republicans, the President and the New Right, and, by association, the fundamentalists. . . . This does not mean that the "winning coalition" might not regroup at some point, but only that the prospects do not look good.[15]

They have failed in their attempts to get a constitutional amendment overturning the *Roe* decision and in the effort to pass a federal statute attempting to do the same thing. Although abortion has not disappeared from the political arena, other issues have come to the forefront.

Antiabortionists have been the most successful in their efforts to cut off public funding for abortions. This raises another continuing issue in American politics. Eva Rubin writes:

> Stated simply, the question was: does government have any obligation to equalize access to constitutional rights when poverty creates the conditions that prevent their exercise? . . . the abortion-funding cases opened up again to debate questions of the nature of the constitutional guarantees in our governmental system; are these guarantees primarily negative, are they constitutional *limitations* only, or are there more positive duties that the government owes to its citizens.[16]

The Supreme Court has ruled that poverty cannot deny the exercise of some fundamental rights; thus, the state must provide a lawyer for an indigent defendant. However, it has been very wary of establishing *rights* to health, income, or other welfare measures. Although the fact that the refusal to fund an abortion is in many cases an effective denial, the Court denied "any responsibility for removing conditions that make the exercise of constitutional rights impossible."[17]

From 1973 to 1983, the Court heard dozens of abortion cases. In general, the Court struck down those that unduly burdened the exercise of the fundamental right to privacy announced in *Roe*, especially if there were no compelling or legitimate state interest in the regulation. On the other hand, it upheld all of the regulations that, although they were

---

[14] Paige, *The Right to Lifers*, p. 217.

[15] Ibid., p. 239.

[16] Rubin, *Abortion, Politics, and the Courts*, pp. 158–59; the full discussion runs from pp. 157–61; also see Chapter V, pp. 85–110 in Milbauer.

[17] Ibid., p. 159.

making the exercise of the right more difficult, were an exercise of legitimate state concern. Actually, the regulations had gotten more and more
restrictive while being consistently upheld. In 1978, the Akron City Council passed an ordinance consisting of seventeen provisions regulating the
performance of abortions. Several other jurisdictions adopted it as a
model. There was very little doubt that it was meant to discourage
abortions, to say the least. The Akron ordinance went to the Supreme
Court.

In 1981, President Reagan nominated Sandra Day O'Connor to be a
justice of the Supreme Court. It was one of the decisions that began to
crack the alliance between the Right-to-Lifers and their more multi-issue
allies. Antiabortion forces maintained that she had cast a pro-abortion
vote while she was a member of the Arizona State Legislature. Others
countered that it had been a purely procedural matter and that her
sympathies were basically antiabortion. It was generally agreed, however, that she would add to the more conservative votes on the Court.
O'Connor herself maintained a discreet silence, arguing that it was her
capabilities as a jurist that should be the issue. She was confirmed by the
Senate and assumed her duties in the Fall of 1981. The Akron Ordinance
case presented her with the opportunity to make her views known.

With a 6-to-3 majority, the Court struck down several provisions of
the Akron Ordinance as unconstitutional infringements upon a woman's
right to choose an abortion. Justice Powell, writing for the majority,
stated:

> These cases come to us a decade after we held in *Roe* v. *Wade,* 410
> U.S. 113 (1973), that the right of privacy, grounded in the concept of
> personal liberty guaranteed by the Constitution, encompasses a wom-
> an's right to decide whether to terminate her pregnancy. Legislative
> responses to the Court's decision have required us on several occa-
> sions, and again today, to define the limits of a State's authority to
> regulate the performance of abortions. And arguments continue to be
> made, in these cases as well, that we erred in interpreting the Constitu-
> tion. Nonetheless, the doctrine of *stare decisis,* while perhaps never
> entirely persuasive on a constitutional question, is a doctrine that de-
> mands respect in a society governed by the rule of law. We respect it
> today, and reaffirm *Roe* v. *Wade.*[18]

The dissenters included Justice O'Connor. As a matter of fact, she
wrote the dissenting opinion that White and Rehnquist joined. Her opinion makes very clear that "she feels *Roe* v. *Wade* should be drastically
modified, if not reversed altogether."[19] Her fundamental argument rested
on the problem of medical knowledge:

---

[18] Slip Opinion, *City of Akron* v. *Akron Center for Reproductive Health, Inc., et al.,*
No. 81–746. Argued November 30, 1982; decided June 15, 1983, pp. 1–2.

[19] "Supreme Court Reaffirms Abortion Rights," *Current American Government,
Fall 1983 Guide* (Washington, D.C.: Congressional Quarterly Inc., 1983), p. 107.

The *Roe* framework, then, is clearly on a collision course with itself. As the medical risks of various abortion procedures decrease, the point at which the state may regulate for reasons of maternal health is moved further forward to actual childbirth. As medical science becomes better able to provide for the separate existence of the fetus, the point of viability is moved further back toward conception. Moreover, it is clear that the trimester approach violates the fundamental aspiration of judicial decision-making through the application of neutral principles "sufficiently absolute to give them roots throughout the community and continuity over significant periods of time."[20]

Justice Powell was sufficiently disturbed by the dissent to add a long footnote countering it, as follows:

There are especially compelling reasons for adhering to *stare decisis* in applying the principles of *Roe* v. *Wade*. That case was considered with special care. It was first argued during the 1971 Term, and reargued—with extensive briefing—the following Term. The decision was joined by the Chief Justice and six other Justices. Since *Roe* was decided in February 1973, the Court repeatedly and consistently has accepted and applied the basic principle that a woman has a fundamental right to make the highly personal choice whether or not to terminate her pregnancy. See *Connecticut* v. *Menillo*, 423 U. S. 9 (1975); *Planned Parenthood of Central Mo.* v. *Danforth*, 428 U. S. 52 (1976); *Bellotti* v. *Baird*, 428 U. S. 132 (1976); *Beal* v. *Doe*, 432 U. S. 438 (1977); *Maher* v. *Roe*, 432 U. S. 464 (1977); *Colautti* v. *Franklin*, 439 U. S. 379 (1979); *Bellotti* v. *Baird*, 443 U. S. 622 (1979); *Harris* v. *McRae*, 448 U. S. 297 (1980); *H.L.* v. *Matheson*, 450 U. S. 398 (1981).

Today, however, the dissenting opinion rejects the basic premise of *Roe* and its progeny. The dissent stops short of arguing flatly that *Roe* should be overruled. Rather, it adopts reasoning that, for all practical purposes, would accomplish precisely that result. The dissent states that "[e]ven assuming that there is a fundamental right to terminate pregnancy in some situations," the State's compelling interests in maternal health and potential human life "are present *throughout* pregnancy." *Post*, at 8 (emphasis in original). The existence of these compelling interests turns out to be largely unnecessary, however, for the dissent does not think that even one of the numerous abortion regulations at issue imposes a sufficient burden on the "limited" fundamental right, *post*, at 15, n. 10, to require heightened scrutiny. Indeed, the dissent asserts that, regardless of cost, "[a] health regulation, such as the hospitalization requirement, simply does not rise to the level of 'official interference' with the abortion decision." *Post*, at 16 (quoting *Harris* v. *McRae*, 448 U. S. 297, 328 (1980) (WHITE, J., concurring)). The dissent therefore would hold that a requirement that all abortions be performed in an acute-care, general hospital does not impose an unacceptable burden on the abortion decision. It requires no great familiarity with the cost and limited availability of such hospitals to appreciate

---

[20] *City of Akron, supra,* dissenting opinion.

that the effect of the dissent's views would be to drive the performance of many abortions back underground free of effective regulation and often without the attendance of a physician.

In sum, it appears that the dissent would uphold virtually any abortion regulation under a rational-basis test. It also appears that even where heightened scrutiny is deemed appropriate, the dissent would uphold virtually any abortion-inhibiting regulation because of the State's interest in preserving potential human life. See *post*, at 23 (arguing that a 24-hour waiting period is justified in part because the abortion decision "has grave consequences for the fetus"). This analysis is wholly incompatible with the existence of the fundamental right recognized in *Roe* v. *Wade*.[21]

Women's rights groups celebrated the decision as an attempt to finally put the abortion issue to rest. "Lawyers at the American Civil Liberties Union . . . hailed the Supreme Court ruling on the Akron, Ohio law and said they expected it to lead to nullification of laws limiting women's choices in many other states."[22] On the other hand, even though they acknowledged the setback, antiabortion groups vowed to keep on fighting for a constitutional amendment. Although it would seem that, for the moment, *Roe* v. *Wade* was the uncontested law of the land, Congressional Quarterly pointed out:

> The three dissenters—O'Connor, Byron R. White and William H. Rehnquist—are among the youngest justices on the court. The possibility that President Reagan, should he serve a second term, would have an opportunity to appoint more justices led some to speculate that the court itself could yet overrule *Roe* v. *Wade*.[23]

It is assumed, of course, that should President Reagan have such an opportunity, he would appoint a conservative, and most likely antiabortion, justice.

Thus the legal politics of abortion continue at all the levels, internally on the Court itself, in consideration of the appointment process, in both state and federal legislative halls, and in the electoral process itself. An action in one place, such as the *Akron* case, results in the reintroduction of a constitutional amendment in the U.S. Senate and increased concern for the composition of the U.S. Supreme Court, and it all revolves around definitions and interpretations of the meaning of "life" and "person" and those "rights" granted them under the U.S. Constitution.

---

[21] *City of Akron, supra,* footnote 1, pp. 2–3.

[22] Joseph B. Treaster, "Civil Liberties Lawyers See Women's Rights Victory, *The New York Times,* June 16, 1983, p. 12.

[23] "Supreme Court Reaffirms Abortion Rights," p. 107.

CHAPTER 9

The Congress

The Constitution appears to envision the Congress as the nation's chief policymaking body. Article I, which creates and empowers the Congress, is nearly three times longer than the next longest article, which defines the presidency. It alone accounts for more than half of the U.S. Constitution. All the legislative powers of the government are given to the Congress, including the powers to tax and spend, to regulate commerce, to declare war and maintain the armed forces, and to "make all laws which shall be necessary and proper" to exercise the various powers granted to the national government. This is a sweeping grant of power and authority, and, on this basis, one might expect the Congress to be the decisive source of policymaking within the government.

However, when Congress is looked at as a whole, and placed within its political, social, and economic context, it appears to be much less powerful, and certainly not decisive. From its inception, Congress was divided into two chambers, the House of Representatives and the Senate, which share the lawmaking powers. The two chambers' makeup is purposefully different and is based on different constituencies so that they operate to check each other. In addition, the presidency and the judiciary each possess a veto over congressional action; this is consistent with our conception of separation of powers and checks and balances. In other words, the Founding Fathers' fear of the tyranny of the majority led them to ensure that the "people's" branch, the House of Representatives, was very well contained. Although the Constitution gives Congress great powers, the structure of the legislative branch makes action in pursuit of these powers very difficult.

The present structure, organization, and makeup of the Congress operate to give special interest groups many points of entry into the lawmaking process. Although these are often referred to as veto points (which is true), they are also often opportunities to change a phrase or add an amendment to gain a private advantage or ameliorate what might be disadvantageous. On the other hand, the present structure, organization, and makeup render both achieving and holding a majority very difficult. The overall effect is to maintain the fundamental status quo, and that means to maintain the present distribution of power, status, and wealth—the present political economy.

This chapter will begin with the lawmaking process itself. It will describe the rules of procedure of how a bill becomes a law. These procedures are part of institutions that are structured and organized in ways that also impact upon the legislative process. Congress is made up of 100 Senators and 435 voting Representatives, for a total of 535 individuals, plus a huge supporting staff; the second section will describe the structure, organization, and makeup of the present Congress. Finally, we will discuss the reforms of the 1970s that were meant to *re*-assert congressional authority and capability. Changes were made in the rules, structure, and organization in an attempt to make Congress more responsive to the majority. Two major acts were also passed in an attempt to regain congressional control and initiative in substantive policymaking: the Budget and Impoundment Control Act and the War Powers Resolution. Their impact has yet to be solidified, because old patterns may reassert themselves—but may not. Let's look at the general process first.

THE LEGISLATIVE PROCESS

Any proposed legislation must be introduced into the House or the Senate by a member of that body. Any measure can originate in either chamber, with one exception; all bills for raising revenue must originate in the House of Representatives as stated in Article I, Section 7 of the U.S. Constitution. This provision meant to give the House a major power, the "power of the purse." The people's branch was to have control of the money that the national government required in order to function. Although in practice this power is now shared (the tax cut measures of 1981 originated with the President), constitutionally the House alone retains the initiative to introduce revenue-raising bills.

Thousands of measures are introduced during any one session. In the 96th Congress, for example, 12,583 measures were introduced, of which 11,722 were proposed bills and 862 joint resolutions. Of those, 736 were enacted, 613 public bills and 123 private ones.[1] Obviously, the major portion of this workload passes relatively easily through the process. Many are of a housekeeping nature or of interest to only a few, such as bills authoriz-

[1] Roger H. Davidson and Walter J. Oleszek, *Congress and Its Members* (Washington, D.C.: Congressional Quarterly Press, 1981), Table 2.2, p. 32.

ing small federal projects or changing the printing of the Congressional Record. Although all measures go through approximately the same process, those that are most likely to receive careful, stringent, and media attention have been proposed by the President and/or deal with highly visible national issues such as the economy, foreign policy, or the budget. However, they all start by being dropped "in the hopper" by a member of Congress. Figure 9.1, and the following paragraphs illustrate how a bill becomes law.

The first stage of the legislative procedure is referral to the appropriate standing committee or committees. Each chamber has a number of standing committees that are divided according to subject area, such as agriculture or armed services. (Table 9.1, pp. 226–27, lists all the committees of the 98th Congress.) In the House, the Speaker refers bills to committees, and in the Senate, the majority leader performs this function.

In most cases, it is evident which committee should deal with a particular bill. However, very complicated or controversial measures could conceivably fall under any number of categories: many environmental issues could go to House committees on Energy and Commerce, Public Works, Science and Technology, or Interior, depending upon how one perceives the intent of the bill. Similarly, a bill may meet with a more or less warm reception by one committee than another. Some bills may be referred to multiple committees, or various sections may be referred to separate committees in order to either avoid or take advantage of jurisdictional disagreements between standing committees. In any event, each measure is referred to (at least one) committee for consideration before any other action is taken.

The committee chair then refers the measure to the appropriate subcommittee, thus narrowing the subject area expertise even more closely. The same jurisdictional considerations are present for the chair when choosing the appropriate subcommittee; they may be even more crucial because the subcommittee will be the first body to *consider* the measure, and for practical purposes, this first consideration is the most crucial. The rest of the process depends in large measure upon what the subcommittee does with the measure.

If a measure is to go any further, it must be reported out of the subcommittee to the committee and then out of the committee to the floor. The work is generally done in the subcommittee, however, and the measure goes through three steps:

1. Hearings
2. Markup
3. Report

Hearings involve publicly examining the bill, including its intent and the problem it's meant to solve or prevent; building a record for or against the bill as a general idea; and offering suggestions for improvement. The subcommittee chair schedules hearings and their participants and may use that power to shape the record in ways that promote a certain outcome on

Figure 9.1.   *How a Bill Becomes a Law*

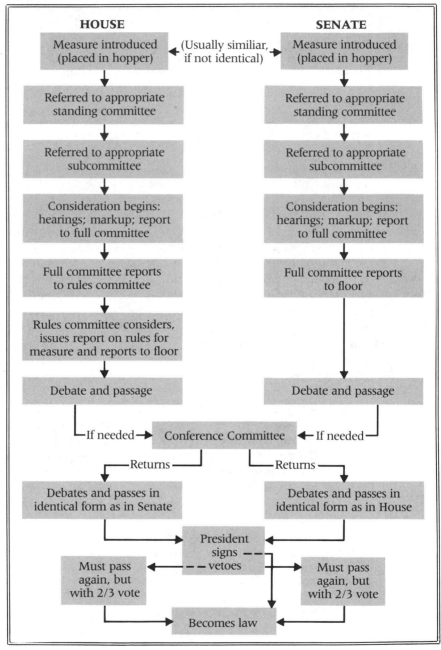

the bill as a whole. However, hearings do offer an opportunity for *public* input and debate on the issue.

Markup sessions go through the proposal section by section, word by word, and approve specific language to turn the proposal into the law; these are the working meetings for the committee members. Formerly, markup sessions were closed to the public so that the necessary bargaining and compromise could take place. In the 1970s, however, as part of the congressional reforms, they were opened so that the public could watch its lawmakers at work. Opinion is now mixed as to whether open sessions are a help or a hindrance. Some say it has curbed the power of lobbyists; others say that it has merely made compromise more difficult and moved the negotiations into the back rooms. In any event, the crucial shaping of a bill—its actual drafting—now takes place in a public forum.

Finally, following hearings and the markup, the subcommittee issues its report to the full committee. The report may or may not recommend passage, may suggest rules for debate, and may carry a minority report arguing against the bill as a whole or against certain passages of it. Although the full committee could go through the entire process again, generally the subcommittee's report is accepted as the definitive word on the measure. As Mark Green reported:

> According to R.D. Markley, Jr., for twenty years a major auto industry lobbyist, "The way Congress has been restructured, if a measure you don't like gets to full committee, forget it, you've had it. It's down here in the subcommittees where you've really got to do your work."[2]

In other words, the real legislative work goes on in the subcommittees. The full committee most often adopts the subcommittee's report as its own and reports the bill with the accompanying report.

Up to this point, the procedure is approximately the same in both chambers. However, in the House the measure must go through one more committee, the powerful Rules Committee. The Rules Committee acts as a "traffic cop" for the House's business. It decides under what rules the bill will come to the floor of the House, as well as the timing and the personnel for the debate. It can allow unlimited amendment, limited amendment, or no amendment. In other words, the Rules Committee can make passage easier or tougher, depending upon *its* feelings about the bill. Reforms of the 1970s curbed some of the Rules Committee's power by increasing its membership, changing the method of selection of its members, and adding some procedures by which measures can be released from the Committee by other members of Congress, but it is still a powerful and important hurdle on the road to enactment of legislation.

The Senate, with fewer members and a tradition of courtesy, directly receives legislation from its substantive policy committees. One anthropologist studying Congress has argued that floor consideration of a

---

[2] Mark Green, *Who Runs Congress?*, 3rd ed. (New York: Bantam, 1979), p. 63.

TABLE 9.1
House and Senate Standing Committees 98th Congress

SENATE

Committee	Number of Subcommittees	Number of Members	Partisan Ratio Republicans to Democrats
Appropriations	13	29	15/14
Banking, Housing, and Urban Affairs	9	18	10/8
Finance	9	20	11/9
Judiciary	9	18	10/8
Small Business	9	19	10/9
Commerce, Science, and Transportation	8	17	9/8
Agriculture, Nutrition, and Forestry	7	18	10/8
Foreign Relations	7	17	9/8
Governmental Affairs	7	18	10/8
Labor and Human Resources	7	18	10/8
Armed Services	6	18	10/8
Energy and Natural Resources	6	20	11/9
Environment and Public Works	6	16	9/7
Budget	0	22	12/10
Rules and Administration	0	12	7/5
Veterans	0	12	7/5
(16 Standing Committees) Total	103		
Plus:			
Select Committee on Ethics	0	6	3/3
Select Committee on Indian Affairs	0	7	4/3
Select Committee on Intelligence	4	15	8/7
Special Committee on Aging	0	15	8/7
Joint Committee on Economics			
Joint Committee on the Library			
Joint Committee on Printing			
Joint Committee on Taxation			

measure is now "pure ritual."[3] However, floor consideration does offer opponents (or supporters of a bill going down to defeat) another chance, which is often taken. The strategic usage of amendments or timing of votes may give a legislator who is skilled in the rules a victory that would be otherwise unattainable. And, of course, the Senate still has the filibuster. This is a procedure whereby a Senator can literally talk a bill to death. Originally used by conservative Southern Senators to kill or gut civil rights legislation, it has grown in use in the late 1970s and 1980s by all members of the ideological spectrum. Its use, or the threat of its use, which effectively brings the entire Senate to a halt, has forced many a compromise

---

[3] J. McIver Weatherford, *Tribes on the Hill* (New York: Rawson, Wade, 1981), pp. 176–77.

TABLE 9.1 (cont.)
House and Senate Standing Committees 98th Congress

HOUSE OF REPRESENTATIVES

Committee	Number of Subcommittees	Number of Members	Partisan Ratio Democrats to Republicans
Appropriations	13	57	36/21
Budget	9 (Task Forces)	31	20/11
Agriculture	8	41	26/15
Education and Labor	8	32	21/11
Armed Services	7	45	29/16
Banking, Finance, and Urban Affairs	7	47	30/17
Foreign Affairs	7	37	24/13
Government Operations	7	39	25/14
Judiciary	7	31	20/11
Post Office and Civil Service	7	25	16/9
Science and Technology	7	41	26/15
Energy and Commerce	6	42	27/15
Interior and Insular Affairs	6	42	28/14
Public Works and Transportation	6	50	32/18
Small Business	6	41	26/15
Ways and Means	6	35	23/12
House Administration	5	19	12/7
Merchant Marine and Fisheries	5	40	26/14
Veterans Affairs	5	33	21/12
Washington, D.C.	3	12	8/4
Rules	2	13	9/4
Standards of Official Conduct	0	12	6/6
(22 Standing Committees) Total	137		

Plus:

Select Committee on Aging	4	60	38/22
Select Committee on Children, Youth and Families	0	25	16/9
Select Committee on Intelligence	3	14	9/5
Select Committee on Narcotics Abuse and Control	0	25	16/9

through the years. In 1975, the Senate changed the number of votes needed for cloture (cutting off debate) from 2/3 to 3/5 of the full Senate, or 60 Senators. However, cloture is much rarer than the filibuster, which continues to be used as an effective legislative strategy.

Once the measure is passed on the floor, it must go to the other chamber, where it goes through the same process once again. Unless the same bill is passed by both chambers, it must go to a Conference Committee. Actually, many identical measures are simultaneously introduced in both chambers, and go through the process approximately together. On minor measures, congressional staff from each chamber attempt to ensure that the measures *emerge* in identical form as well. The vast majority of the legislation is at least close enough that the differences can be settled by the staff and the bills can be brought into alignment without the necessity of a Conference Committee meeting.

On the major and controversial measures, however, congruence is rare and Conference Committee sessions are the rule rather than the exception. Conference Committees are composed of equal numbers of members from each chamber. Most often, the conferees include those legislators who are most directly involved with the bill, such as members of the committees that originally considered it. "Increasingly, members of the subcommittee that reported the bill are being appointed to conference committees, as they are most directly acquainted with the legislation in question."[4]

The Conference Committee hammers out the compromises it believes can pass *both* chambers. In some cases, influential members wait until this point to shape a bill to their liking. Knowledgeable members usually know when a bill is going to eventually require a Conference Committee. In order to gain floor passage, and keeping in mind the Conference negotiation process, a bill can be passed full of "bargaining chips." The bill that finally emerges from the Conference Committee may resemble the earlier version only vaguely. It is this version that goes back to both floors with a recommendation that it be passed—intact—which usually happens.

One final hurdle remains—the President. The President must sign the bill before it becomes law, and he also has the power to veto legislation. Should that happen, the bill would come back to the Congress and each chamber must repass the measure by a 2/3 vote. In other words, 1/3 plus one of either chamber can undo months and even years of work. Any compromise or change in the bill means that the legislative process starts all over again from the beginning. Thus, the veto is a powerful weapon, and the threat of a veto is often used by the President to force changes in a bill before final passage.

Lest we think this process too easy, never fear—appropriation's here. All legislation that requires funds for implementation faces a two-step legislative process—authorization and appropriation. We have just described only the authorization stage, which provides passage of a bill proposing a new policy or activity for the national government. It now becomes in effect a commitment by the government to execute that policy. However, if new funding is required to launch such a program, as is generally the case, all costs must be inserted in the budget proposed to the Congress the next year. (The budgetary process is specifically considered in Chapter 12.) In other words, money must be *appropriated* to implement the *authorization*.

The appropriations process, in effect, subjects the issue to a second consideration. It must now face an entirely different set of subcommittees,

[4] Walter J. Oleszek, *Congressional Procedures and the Policy Process* (Washington, D.C.: Congressional Quarterly Press, 1978), p. 186.

but the entire process once again. Now the arena is not the policy area standing committees, but the respective Appropriations Committees. The Appropriations Committees are divided into subject-area subcommittees. These subcommittees then hold hearings, markup sessions, and issue a report—as previously described. Authorizations may be essentially defeated by refusal to appropriate sufficient funds; alternatively, unpopular or controversial programs may be encouraged or enhanced. And, similarly, when a budget has been passed by each chamber, differences are settled by an Appropriations Conference Committee.

Obviously there are many points at which any legislative proposal may die, but the first and most important obstacles are the subcommittees. The legislative body as a whole has a limited opportunity to consider an issue. Most of the work is done in the subcommittees, out of the public eye and certainly with relatively little public debate. These are the points at which lobbyists, lawyers, and the special interest groups are able to keep tabs on the process, and most importantly, it gives them the capacity to shape the final piece of legislation that does emerge.

A serious question is whether this can be considered the "people's" government. We need to consider the problem of how the subcommittees fit within the overall institution.

- How is the Congress structured and organized?
- How does it operate?
- How do those committees and subcommittees come into being and how are they staffed?

These are the issues of the next section.

EXHIBIT 3
The Flight of the MX

The MX Missile, termed the "Peacekeeper" by President Reagan, has been a controversial weapon since the early 1970s. Nevertheless, as of January 1983, approximately $5 billion had already been spent on research and development of the MX. In the immediate past (1981–82), the major issue was its "survivability." Various methods of basing the missile had been proposed in an effort to better insure that Soviet missiles could not destroy it. Because it is a multiple-warhead missile, losing an MX poses greater problems than losing a single warhead at a time. Basing suggestions had ranged from underground tunnels in Colorado or Nevada to moving the MX from Minuteman to Minuteman silo in a deadly version of the old shell game. We will pick up the story at the start of 1983.

JANUARY

The fiscal year 1983 defense budget did not include the $988 million Reagan had requested to begin procurement (purchasing) of the MX, but it did include $2.5 billion to continue development. A continuing resolution had also been passed directing the President to make a basing recommendation to Congress in the spring. Upon acceptance of a basing plan, within forty-five days of receiving the report, the FY 1983 funds reserved for basing the MX would be released.

The Scowcroft Commission was formed in response to that congressional resolution. Composed of ten members, it was chaired by Brent Scowcroft, a former national security adviser, and included four former members of the Carter Administration.

APRIL

In April, 1983, the Commission issued its report. A crucial summarizing paragraph reads:

> The Commission has concluded that the preferred approach for modernizing our ICBM force seems to have three components: initiating engineering design of a single-warhead small ICBM, to reduce target value and permit flexibility in basing for long-term survivability; seeking arms control agreements designed to enhance strategic stability; and deploying MX missiles in existing silos now to satisfy the immediate needs of our ICBM force and to aid that transition.

House and Senate Armed Services Committees begin hearings on the proposed plan. There are essentially two decisions being considered. The first is whether to release the FY 1983 funds and the second is the authorization and appropriation for FY 1984.

MAY

The Senate Appropriations Committee begins hearings on MX. The House Defense Appropriations Subcommittee holds hearings as well.

Several House and Senate members will only support the MX if the President makes a commitment to adhere to *all* the Scowcroft Commission recommendations, specifically development of a small, single warhead weapon ("Midgetman") and to greater flexibility in arms control talks. President Reagan issues a letter assuring that he will do so.

The House Defense Appropriations Subcommittee votes to release the FY 1983 funds reserved for MX basing as does the full committee and the Senate Appropriations Committee. The House Armed Services Committee approves ("authorizes") $4.9 billion for FY 1984 for the MX, which includes procurement of 27 missiles.

The House and Senate consider the resolutions releasing the FY 1983 funds for development of a basing method and lifting the ban on flight testing the MX. The House passes it May 24 on a vote of 239 to 186; the Senate passes it at 59 to 39; and finally the House passes the Senate version 223 to 167.

JUNE

The House considers its Armed Services Committee report for FY 1984 defense authorization (HR2969). The report included a stipulation that none of the MX funds could be spent until the Pentagon submitted a detailed schedule for development and deployment of the Midgetman. Vote postponed until July.

JULY

The House authorizes production and procurement, but by 13 votes, with the appropriations battle yet to come. Senator Hart delays the Senate authorization vote and moves to delete funds entirely, but loses 41 to 58. The Senate then passes the entire authorization bill, including the funds for MX production and procurement.

AUGUST

The Conference report on the defense authorization bill agrees to fund 21 ($2.1 billion) rather than 27 ($2.4 billion) missiles and also conditions the MX on continued development of the Midgetman.

SEPTEMBER

The House and Senate adopt the conference report on the defense authorization bill, but appropriations, it is felt, still hinge on whether several congressional moderates feel there has been a significant change in the President's stance on arms control, as promised in the May letter.

The House and Senate Appropriations Committee consider the defense budget. Support for the MX again hinges on the President's arms control proposals scheduled to be released in October. Negotiations continue between the administration and these key members of both the House and Senate.

(A Korean airliner is shot down by the Soviets in September and START talks resume in October with new U.S. proposals.)

NOVEMBER

The House and Senate consider the defense appropriations bills for FY 1984. The House rejects an amendment, 208–217, that would have blocked initial production of the MX. Both House and Senate pass defense appropriations that include funds for procurement of 21 MX missiles.

But the battle is not yet over. As the FY 1985 budget battle arises, many of the congressional moderates who voted for the MX on the basis of the President's letter now feel that the President has not lived up to the commitments with regard to arms control that they felt they had won. The administration's request for funds to procure 40 more MX missiles appears to again be in jeopardy. The Democratic presidential candidates all opposed any further monies for the MX. The flight of the MX was far from over.

STRUCTURE, ORGANIZATION, AND MAKEUP

The structure, organization, and makeup of Congress also influence the legislative process. In order to understand more fully how a bill becomes a law, we also need to know how the Congress is structured, how it is organized to transact its business, and who actually populates it. The concepts of structure and organization overlap each other. In this case, by structure we mean the formal organization of Congress. The Constitution only says that the House "shall chuse their Speaker and other Officers" and "The Senate shall chuse their other Officers, and also a President pro tempore, in the Absence of the Vice President." Structure thus includes those other officers and the official and unofficial bodies that are developed by both chambers to expedite their lawmaking duties, such as the committee, subcommittee, and caucus structures.

This structure results in certain members gaining positions of greater influence than others, by means of filling those positions of leadership and chairing committees and subcommittees. By organization, we mean how the Congress goes about determining who shall fill those positions. How does it organize itself to fill out that structure and make it work? We will deal here with both the formal rules of selection and those informal folkways that can have as much to do with election as the formal rules.

Finally, we will look at the results, the actual makeup of the leadership positions, congressional committee and subcommittee chairs, and then at Congress as a whole. This raises the question of "representativeness." Does "the people's branch" represent the people? Do the leadership and other positions of power reflect Congress as a whole? Of course, it is possible to have a predominantly white male Congress and argue that it *represents* the people, as many do. On the other hand, many argue that major portions of the population, such as women and minorities, need spokespeople from that population in order to be adequately represented. In any event, it is necessary to understand how Congress works in order to know *who* Congress is.

This section then begins with the congressional structure, the institutional leadership and working bodies that Congress has set up in order to expedite its business. We will next discuss the ways in which those institutional positions are filled; how Congress organizes itself. Finally, we will examine the makeup of Congress as a whole and its leadership positions.

Structure

The major congressional leadership positions are the Speaker of the House, and the Senate and House majority and minority leaders. These leaders are generally responsible for organizing and scheduling the flow of legislative business. They have greater visibility, which is a major asset for a person in public life; in addition, they nominally head their respective political parties in the Congress and represent the party position, while trying to influence their colleagues as well as the public. As Davidson and Oleszek point out:

> By custom, rule, and law, party leaders have a number of useful prerogatives and perquisites that augment their influence. They are accorded priority in recognition on the floor, they receive higher salaries and more office space than other members, and they receive added staff. They attract national media attention that they can use to influence public and member attitudes on issues.[5]

In the House, the key position is that of Speaker; this is the only position that is constitutionally recognized. The Speaker presides over the House, which means that he has the power to decide points of order as well as to recognize speakers from the floor. The Speaker shapes the House agenda, and decides which bills have priority and the calendar on which they will appear. He refers measures to their appropriate committees and designates the members of joint and conference committees. He can make the public visibility fellow members need for continued re-election possible—or he can ignore them. In addition, the Speaker is privy to the President's preferences and intentions regarding the administration's legislative program. He can, if he desires, work in harmony with the President to schedule and obtain passage of desired legislation, or he can make passage more difficult, if not impossible, by forcing concessions and compromise, should he and the House differ from the President.

The majority and minority leaders of the House are also crucial. The majority leader comes from the political party that holds a majority in the House and the minority leader from the minority political party. After any given election, the majority and minority leaders may change places, so there is mutual acknowledgment of each by the other. The Speaker of the House has often previously served as majority or minority leader. "In practice, the majority leader's job has been to formulate the party's legislative program in cooperation with the Speaker and other party leaders, steer the program through the House, ensure that committee chairmen report

[5] Davidson and Oleszek, *Congress and Its Members*, p. 183.

bills deemed of importance to the party, and help to establish the legislative schedule."[6]

The minority leader may or may not be consulted regarding legislative scheduling and priorities, depending on the minority party's strength and general position in the other portions of the government. But in any event, he does for the minority party what the majority leader does for the majority party, appointing whips and committee members, and trying to influence colleagues to vote with their party position.

The majority and minority leaders are assisted by whips and a series of assistant whips. The whip's major duty is to mobilize party members behind the legislative positions that the leadership has decided are in the party's interest. They attempt to keep an accurate count of the votes on any measure at any one time, and are supposed to know the leanings of each member. They issue weekly reports to keep the leadership abreast of the state of the membership so that the leadership can make informed decisions regarding scheduling and timing of legislation.

Members of the House are often under pressure to support the position of the President when he is a member of their party. Conversely, they are pressured to join with other members of their party in opposition to a President of the other party. Many measures before the House, of course, are not partisan matters, and in such cases, members are free of all pressures to vote with the leadership.

Although the position of President Pro Tem of the Senate corresponds in form to that of Speaker of the House, in practice it is no more than an honorific title. The actual managerial functions performed by the Speaker in the House are in the hands of the Senate majority leader. The Senate majority and minority leaders serve informing, scheduling, and unifying functions for their respective parties, and in effect, they combine the duties of Speaker, party leader, and Rules Committee in the House. The majority leader:

1. Coordinates the activities of Senate committees and seeks to bring bills to the floor in accordance with his or her view of the proper priorities for that session.
2. Selects members of the conference committees.
3. Is the chief source of information for other senators, as well as the dispenser of public visibility, additional institutional responsibilities, and improved committee status.
4. Consults regularly with the minority leader so that most of the Senate's business can proceed with the support of a broad consensus. Both leaders are normally consulted and kept informed of major developments by the President. However, matters of party strategy or program are reserved for the leader of the President's party.

Leadership positions are derived from the entire membership of both chambers and attempt to impose coherence on the entire body. On the

---

[6] Oleszek, *Congressional Procedures and the Policy Process,* p. 31.

other hand, both congressional chambers are divided into a series of committees and subcommittees, and sometimes even subcommittees of subcommittees. In 1983, there were 22 standing committees in the House and 16 in the Senate. Table 9.1 lists them, together with their subcommittee number and their partisan ratio makeup. Most House committees have 30 to 40 members, although Appropriations has 50 members. Senate committees are, of course, smaller, being drawn from a much smaller total membership; committee members are appointed from each party roughly according to the partisan ratio in the respective chambers.

Each representative usually serves on two committees. Representatives naturally seek assignment on committees whose work will be of importance to their home districts or will help keep them visible for re-election purposes. However, exact matchups between positions and applicants is not always possible. The two most sought-after policy committees are those dealing with money matters—Ways and Means (taxation, social security, and Medicare, for example) and Appropriations (all expenditures). Raising and spending money is absolutely crucial to the operation of the government, and is, therefore, the route by which Congress has the greatest chance to influence the conduct of the rest of the government.

This subdivision into a multiplicity of committees and subcommittees adds a layer of influential positions, committee and subcommittee chairs, and ranking members. The chair is usually the senior member of the committee from the majority party and the ranking member is the senior minority party member. Committee and subcommittee chairs, of course, have the power to call meetings, establish the agenda, and chair the sessions. They control the committee funds and are responsible for hiring and firing staff. They also follow the legislation, designating the floor manager as well as the conference committee members. Ranking members assist in setting the agenda and taking responsibility for their measures on the floor, and have the capacity to hire and fire staff for the minority members. They are, in other words, influential members of the Congress.[7]

Because of the proliferation of subcommittees and the reforms that reduced the committee chairs' powers, subcommittee chairs have added to the number of people with special bailiwicks. It has become increasingly difficult for one or a few members of Congress to control it. J. McIver Weatherford, an anthropologist who studied the Congress, suggests:

> The big struggles now are within committees rather than among them. Subcommittee chairmen struggle against each other and against the whole committee chairman, while committees fight less against each other. In this Congress of rapidly changing jurisdictions, . . . how is it possible to tell where power is actually located. . . . Behind this ever-changing facade, however, is a simple arrangement that clarifies the location of power. Power is where the staff is.[8]

---

[7] Davidson and Oleszek, *Congress and Its Members*, p. 215.

[8] Weatherford, *Tribes on the Hill*, p. 61.

What is suggested here is a complicated assessment of power based on an ability to get things done. This includes not only institutional position, chair or ranking minority member, but also control of vital information and work production. Some committee chairs and subcommittee chairs are more equal than others.

Completing the structure are the caucuses, which are more informal bodies. A congressional caucus exists to represent almost every imaginable subject area. For example, one of the newest is the Senate Wine Caucus. In the words of California Sen. Pete Wilson, one of its sponsors, "The new wine caucus is an idea whose time has come." As with other subject area caucuses, the prime purpose is "to focus attention on the problems of American winemakers."[9] Other, more well-known, and one suspects more powerful, industries and special interests, such as oil, steel, and banks, have their caucuses of congressional representatives as well.

There are also caucuses with a political or representational point of view. For example, the Congressional Black Caucus (obviously composed of the members of Congress who are black) toured Grenada on its own factfinding mission, which was separate from and followed the formal congressional delegation. "The Congressional Caucus for Women's Issues was at the hub of most congressional activity involving women, serving as the clearinghouse for information and strategy on legislation."[10] The Conservative Democratic Forum operated as the caucus for the Southern Democrats in the House who supported Reagan's proposals in conflict with their party's leadership.

The political party caucuses of each chamber are separate from the bewildering array of special interest caucuses, and are crucial to the structure and organization of Congress. These caucuses are composed of the entire membership of the party in the chamber; all Democrats are members of the Democratic Party Caucus and vice versa. Members who are elected as Independents or who are from some other political party choose which caucus to attend. As these are the essential bodies in the organization of Congress, all members belong to and attend one or the other, which brings us to the problem of the organization of Congress.

Organization

The fundamental principle underlying congressional organization is the party principle. Figures 9.2 and 9.3 detail the lines of communication and organization for the 97th Congress in the House and Senate, respectively. In both cases, the fundamental base is the members in their respective

---

[9] Ross Anderson, "D.C. Scrapbook," *The Seattle Times/Seattle Post-Intelligencer*, December 11, 1983, p. C3.

[10] "Women Shift Focus on Hill to Economic Equity Issues," *Fall 1983 Guide, Current American Government* (Washington, D.C.: Congressional Quarterly, Inc., 1983), p. 78.

Figure 9.2.   Organization of the House of Representatives (97th Congress, 1981–82)

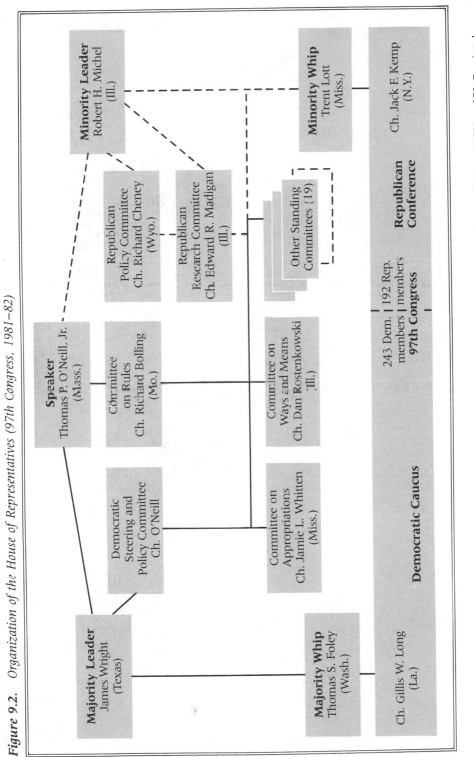

SOURCE: Roger H. Davidson and Walter J. Oleszek, *Congress and Its Members* (Washington, D.C.: Congressional Quarterly Press, 1981), p. 173. Reprinted by permission of Congressional Quarterly, Inc.

Figure 9.3.   Organization of the Senate (97th Congress, 1981–82)

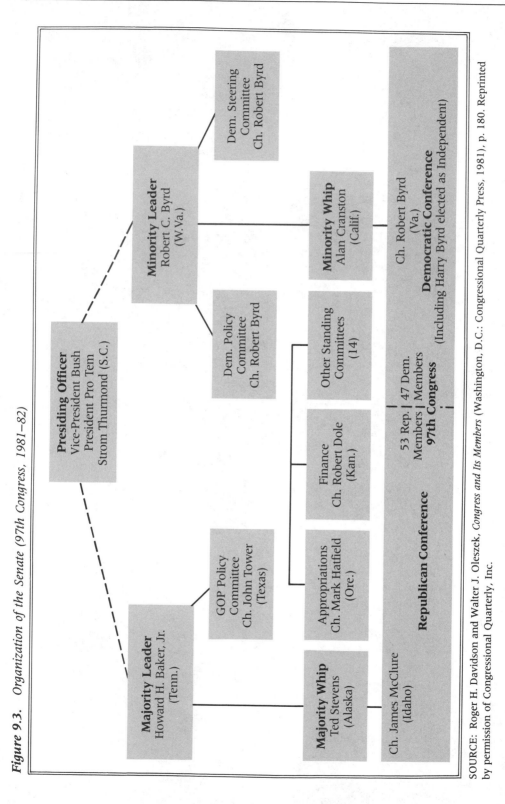

SOURCE: Roger H. Davidson and Walter J. Oleszek, *Congress and Its Members* (Washington, D.C.: Congressional Quarterly Press, 1981), p. 180. Reprinted by permission of Congressional Quarterly, Inc.

political parties. Actually, in 1981, Representative Michel, who is listed in Figure 9.2 as Minority Leader, changed his designation to House *Republican* Leader. It was not long before the rest followed suit, and each previous majority and minority leader is now referred to with his or her political party designation. This appears to reflect an increase in partisanship, an emphasis upon the fact that these leaders are *party* leaders.

Although the Speaker of the House is formally elected by the chamber as a whole, it is confirmation of a decision previously made in the majority party caucus. Theoretically, any member of the House could be Speaker, but to date the Speaker has been the majority party's choice, with voting in the full chamber following strict party lines. The other leadership positions of majority and minority leader are party caucus decisions, with the full membership of each party electing its leader. House Republicans also elect their whip, while House Democratic whips are appointed by the majority leader after consultation with the Speaker. Similarly, Senate leaders are elected by their respective party caucuses on a biennial basis, prior to the beginning of the legislative session in January.

The size and party ratio of standing committees is negotiated between the majority and minority leaders. Staffing and leadership of those committees then becomes a partisan matter. All committee chairs and chairs of the Appropriations subcommittees are elected by the majority party caucus, and other subcommittee chairs are selected by their party members on the full committee. In the Senate, the Democratic Steering Committee makes committee assignments, while the Committee on Committees does so for the Republicans. Committee assignments in the House are made by the Democratic Steering and Policy Committee and the Republican Committee on Committees. The lists are approved by the caucus as a whole and then by the respective chambers (a pro forma approval).

There are few formal rules for election to any of these posts. As noted, for example, the Speaker theoretically does not even need to be a member of the House. The only formal restrictions pertain to the number of chairs that any one member may hold. Each member may hold only one chair of a major standing committee, and each standing committee chair may chair only one of its subcommittees. In the House, any one member may hold a total of five committee and subcommittee chairs. These restrictions grew out of the reforms of the late 1970s and were meant to disperse power among junior members.

However, many informal traditions that almost have the force of rules have grown up around the selection of leaders and committee chairs and assignments. The most consistent has been that of seniority. For many years, those members who had been in the chamber the longest were automatically granted their choice of committee chairs and assignments. The House Committee on Ways and Means, which was in the hands of longstanding members, was responsible for committee assignments. Those members with the longest record of service tended to come from the South (in the case of the Democrats) and the Midwest (in the case of Republicans), and they tended to be conservative in their political outlook and actions. Similarly, the House Rules Committee, which was also in the hands of senior—and more conservative—members, consistently blocked major pieces of legislation, especially civil rights bills. Younger, more liberal, and often more urban members were becoming increasingly frustrated.

The reforms of the 1970s followed Watergate and the increase in the number of Democratic members in the House. In 1974, committee assignments were transferred to the Democratic Steering and Policy Committee. The Rules Committee was increased in size and its members were appointed by the Speaker in consultation with the caucus as a whole. But most importantly, seniority as an automatic guarantor of position was removed. What had had the force of law now became a courtesy, which was withdrawable for cause, as all committee chairs became elected (by secret ballot) positions. In the first rush of reforms, three major committee chairs were removed and replaced with more junior members. Several subcommittee chairs have been successfully challenged and subcommittee chair elections are more frequently real contests. But, since the reforms:

> No senior member of a major committee in either chamber has been denied the chairmanship though a handful of subcommittee chairs have not gone to the longest sitting member. At the same time, no chairman can easily indulge in old-fashioned arrogance without to some extent looking over his shoulder.[11]

Seniority still holds sway as a general rule; however, it appears that the power that used to accompany it has been somewhat moderated.

Assignment to committees is much more fluid. Members request assignments to committees that will aid them back home, and/or seats on the major and most influential committees, such as Appropriations and Ways and Means. Obviously, not everyone can get their first choice. Some are easy—members from seacoast states may request Merchant Marine and Fisheries, whereas those from the Great Plains prefer Agriculture. Although in general, assignments are made, again, on the basis of seniority, mini-campaigns may be waged by members attempting an assignment. Major assignments have been more spread out since the reforms, because each member gets a first assignment before any member gets a second choice. However, seniority stacks the major committee assignments with the longest sitting members.

A more subtle tradition also influences the selection and promotion of congressional members. Walter Oleszek describes "folkways" as follows:

> Folkways . . . are unwritten norms of behavior that members are expected to observe. . . . Several of the more important are "legislative work" (members should concentrate on congressional duties and not be publicity seekers), "courtesy" (members should be solicitous toward their col-

---

[11] Green, *Who Runs Congress?* p. 91.

leagues and avoid personal attacks on them), and "specialization" (members should master a few policy areas and not try to be a "jack of all trades"). Those who abide by these and other norms are often rewarded with increased influence in the policy process, for example, by being appointed to prestigious committees.[12]

In other words, folkways encourage collegiality and loyalty to the institution and each other. Rocking the boat can get one permanently assigned to the Washington, D.C. Committee (where Ron Dellums has now been long enough to be the chair). Positively viewed, such folkways are designed to enable members to work together. Negatively viewed, they encourage and reinforce the status quo, making passage of controversial or innovative legislation extremely difficult. Protection of each other and the institution may be to the detriment of the public interest.

All of these factors work together in the selection of the leadership. It is beginning to be a tradition in the House for leaders to move up the ladder, from whip to majority leader to Speaker. This at least has held true for the Democrats for the last twenty-six years, the period in which they have been the majority party. Seniority has not been a controlling factor, though, because both Senate and House have seen hotly contested elections for majority and minority leadership in recent years. Factors such as personality, experience and expertise on the floor, and geographical and ideological distribution, have appeared to play at least as large, if not a larger, part as length of service. It may be a little early to celebrate the possibility of leadership and chair selection on the basis of merit, but it does appear, however, that simply outlasting everyone else is no longer the major criterion for selection.

So who does get selected? Do the leaders that emerge reflect the body as a whole? Do they reflect the American population as a whole? We have reached the point where we need to know the makeup of Congress. The process, the structure, and the organization reveal much about the legislative branch, but equally, if not more important, are the living bodies that work in and with it.

Makeup

Before we describe the makeup of the leadership, we will examine the characteristics of the general population. Not surprisingly, Congress is heavily populated with white males. The 98th Congress had more minorities than ever before, but that meant 21 blacks (including the Washington, D.C. representative, who has no vote) and 11 Hispanics. Although blacks comprise almost 12 percent of our population, they barely reach 4 percent of the Congress. Even more impressively, women, who comprise over 50 percent of our population, made up a grand total of 4 percent of

---

[12] Oleszek, *Congressional Procedures and the Policy Process*, p. 12.

**TABLE
9.2**   *Beliefs and Trades of Congress Members*

BELIEFS (Religion of Congress Members)		TRADES (Occupations of Congress Members)	
AME Zion	2	Aeronautics	5
Apostolic Christian	1	Agriculture	38
Baptist	48	Business/banking	174
Christian Church	3	Clergy	3
Church of Christ	6	Education	54
Christian Science	2	Engineering	5
Disciples of Christ	1	Journalism	28
Episcopal	62	Organized labor	2
Greek Orthodox	7	Lawyers	261
Jewish	37	Law enforcement	5
Lutheran	24	Medicine	7
Methodist	75	Military	2
Mormon	12	Politics	51
Presbyterian	59	Sports	4
Roman Catholic	141		
Seventh-Day Adventist	1		
Society of Friends	2		
Unitarian	10		
United Church of Christ/ Congregationalist	11		
Unspecified Christian	1		
Unspecified Protestant	25		
Unspecified	2		

SOURCE: Reprinted by permission of Congressional Quarterly, Inc., Washington, D.C.

the 98th Congress.[13] There are four black committee chairs: Washington, D.C., Small Business, Standards of Official Conduct, and the Select Committee on Narcotics Abuse and Control. There are no female committee chairs, and women hold only four subcommittee chairs. These figures may go up and down with each new Congress, but not by very much. Consistently, around 90 percent of the members and all of the leadership will be white males.

For the past several years, Congress has been getting younger. The average age for a member of the 98th Congress was 47. Senators are slightly older than members of the House, with an average age of 53 as compared to 46. Table 9.2 lists the religious affiliation and occupations of the members of the 98th Congress. By far, the major occupation of congressional members is, and consistently has been, the law. Almost 50 percent were attorneys, while business and banking careers ran a close

---

[13] *Seattle Post-Intelligencer*, November 27, 1983, p. B5.

second. Together, law, business, or banking accounted for 80 percent of the professions of members of the 98th Congress.

Tables 9.3 and 9.4 profile the leadership, chairs, and ranking members of the major committees of the House and Senate. Careful perusal of these charts reveal that the leadership fairly accurately reflects the makeup of the Congress. The leaders are all white males, nineteen of them are attorneys, and many of them came to Congress from a background of previous public service.

Two more observations can be made about the profiles in Tables 9.3 and 9.4. One difference between the leadership and the members is their average age. In both the House and Senate of the 98th Congress, the average age of the leadership positions listed was 64. Secondly, most of them have served for many years; they are not newcomers to the legislative process. Given what we know about seniority requirements for advancement, that is not surprising. On the other hand, over half of the House was elected since 1974. In 1980, the Senate came under Republican control with the addition of twelve new members. Pressure for reforms and the ability to enact them came with the addition of many new members, but those reformers apparently have been content to let leadership remain with the "old salts."

On the other hand, careful perusal of the tables reveals that leadership may be in the process of shifting from the New Deal generation to a younger one. In the House, Claude Pepper of Rules was 84 in 1984; Clement Zablocki in the House and Henry Jackson in the Senate have died since the table was compiled; and Senators Baker and Tower announced they would not run for re-election at the expiration of their terms.

One final note regarding the makeup of congressional leadership remains. Included in the tables are the liberal ratings of each person compiled by the *National Journal*.[14] Granting that members of Congress probably represent a rather narrow range of the liberal/conservative spectrum, one immediately notices a sharp divergence between Democratic and Republican members of Congress, at least on the National Journal ratings. It is particularly marked in the Senate, but also appears in the House leadership. Several committee chairs and ranking members appear to be almost poles apart. This indicates that control of the chamber, and thus the leadership and chair positions, may have impact on legislation content.

In terms of representing the membership, the Senate Republicans averaged 28 percent liberal on economic issues, 30 percent foreign, and 36

---

[14] These percentages were taken from Michael Barone and Grant Ujifusa, *The Almanac of American Politics: 1984* (Washington, D.C.: The National Journal, 1984). They were compiled as follows:

> In the second session of the 97th Congress (1982), 49 key Senate votes and 42 key House votes were chosen to illustrate the voting behavior of all members on economic, foreign and cultural policy issues. . . . Members of Congress were rank ordered according to relative liberalism or conservatism (and) assigned percentiles showing their rank relative to others in their chamber. (p. 1325)

TABLE 9.3
Senate Leadership, 98th Congress

	YEAR BORN	YEAR ELECTED	OCCUPATION	RELIGION AND EDUCATION	NATIONAL JOURNAL RATINGS— PERCENTAGE LIBERAL		
					Economic Issues	*Foreign Issues*	*Cultural Issues*
Majority Leader: Howard Baker (R)	1925	1966*	Attorney	Presbyterian Tulane Univ. U. of the South U. of Tennessee	10	16	42
Minority Leader: Robert Byrd (D)	1917	1958	West Virginia House West Virginia Senate U.S. House	Baptist 4 small colleges American U.	68	33	56
Chairs (1) and Ranking Members (2):							
Appropriations: (1) Mark Hatfield (R)	1922	1966*	Political Science Professor Oregon House Oregon Senate Oregon Sec'y of State Oregon Governor	Baptist Willamette U. Stanford U.	50	84	66
(2) John Stennis (D)	1901	1947	Mississippi House Prosecutor Judge	Presbyterian Mississippi State U. U. of Virginia	61	42	14

	Born	Elected	Occupation	Religion / Education			
Finance:							
(1) Robert Dole (R)	1923	1968	Kansas House / City Attorney / U.S. House	Methodist / U. of Kansas / Washburn Municipal U.	2	44	31
(2) Russell Long (D)	1918	1948	Attorney	United Methodist / Louisiana State U.	53	33	26
Judiciary:							
(1) Strom Thurmond (R)	1902	1956*	Teacher / Attorney / Public Service	Baptist / Clemson College	9	16	10
(2) Joseph R. Biden, Jr. (D)	1942	1972*	Attorney	Roman Catholic / U. of Delaware / Syracuse U.	86	72	68
Armed Services:							
(1) John G. Tower (R)	1925	1961*	Gov't Prof.	United Methodist / Southwestern U. / U. of London	23	16	20
(2) Henry Jackson (D)	1912	1952	Attorney / U.S. House	Presbyterian / U. of Wash.	93	54	78
Foreign Relations:							
(1) Charles H. Percy (R)	1919	1966*	Business	Christian Science / U. of Chicago	24	58	70
(2) Claiborne Pell (D)	1918	1960*	Public Service	Episcopal / Princeton U. / Columbia U.	73	90	79
Budget:							
(1) Pete Domenici (R)	1932	1972*	Attorney	Roman Catholic / U. of New Mexico / Denver U.	21	16	23
(2) Lawton Chiles (D)	1930	1970	Attorney / Florida House / Florida Senate	Presbyterian / U. of Fla.	55	48	50

*Up for re-election in 1984.

TABLE 9.4
House Leadership, 98th Congress

	YEAR BORN	YEAR ELECTED	OCCUPATION	RELIGION AND EDUCATION	NATIONAL JOURNAL RATINGS— PERCENTAGE LIBERAL		
					Economic Issues	*Foreign Issues*	*Cultural Issues*
Speaker: Tip O'Neill (D)	1912	1952	Insurance Massachusetts House	Roman Catholic Boston College	does not vote		
Majority Leader: James Wright (D)	1922	1954	Veteran Business Texas House	Presbyterian U. of Texas	72	45	33
Majority Whip: Thomas Foley (D)	1929	1964	Attorney Chief Clerk and Special Counsel to House Interior Committee	Roman Catholic U. of Washington Gonzaga School of Law	63	66	62
Minority Leader: Robert Michel (R)	1923	1956	Veteran Administrative Assistant to Rep.	Apostolic Christian Bradley U.	32	28	4
Minority Whip: Trent Lott (R)	1941	1972	Attorney Administrative Assistant to Representative	Baptist U. of Mississippi	25	25	34
Chairs (1) and Ranking Members (2):							
Appropriations: (1) Jamie L. Whitten (D)	1910	1941	Attorney Mississippi House Dist. Prosecuting Atty.	Presbyterian U. of Mississippi	57	49	37

Member	Born	Elected	Occupation / Prior Office	Religion / University			
(2) Silvio Conte (R)	1921	1958	Attorney; Massachusetts Senate	Roman Catholic; Boston College; B.C. School of Law	54	79	81
Armed Services:							
(1) Melvin Price (D)	1905	1944	Journalist; Secretary to Representative	Roman Catholic; St. Louis U.	73	10	62
(2) William Dickinson (R)	1925	1964	Attorney; Judge	United Methodist; U. of Alabama	4	15	22
Foreign Affairs:							
(1) Clement Zablocki (D)	1912	1948	Organist, choir director; High school teacher; Wisconsin Senate	Roman Catholic; Marquette	83	57	58
(2) William Broomfield (R)	1922	1956	Michigan House	Presbyterian; Michigan State U.	30	37	18
Ways and Means:							
(1) Dan Rostenkowski (D)	1928	1958	Illinois House; Illinois Senate	Roman Catholic; Loyola U.	62	64	73
(2) Barber B. Conable Jr. (R)	1922	1964	Attorney; New York Senate	Methodist; Cornell U.	38	47	61
Rules:							
(1) Claude Pepper (D)	1900	1962	Attorney; Public Service	Baptist; U. of Alabama	96	57	83
(2) James H. Quillen (R)	1916	1962	Business; Tennessee House	Methodist; Harvard	21	12	4
Budget:							
(1) James Jones (D)	1939	1972	Attorney; Legal Assistant; White House Ass't	Roman Catholic; U. of Oklahoma; Georgetown	54	59	46
(2) Delbert Lotta (R)	1920	1958	Attorney; Ohio Senate	Church of Christ; Ohio Northern U.	25	12	4

percent social. The majority leader ranked 10 percent, 16 percent, and 42 percent respectively. With one exception (Mark Hatfield, R., Ore.), none of the major chairs reached 28 percent on economic issues. With regard to foreign policy, with the exception of Budget and Armed Services, all the chairs ranked well above the average. The averages for the House Democrats (majority party and thus in control) were 69 percent economic, 63 percent foreign, and 63 percent social. In economic issues, the leadership generally leads, but in foreign affairs it generally follows. This may reflect the assumed expertise on either side; the House is the major domestic entity and the Senate has a primary role in foreign policy. In any event, the leadership differs markedly from each other in partisan terms, but does not get too far from its base in general terms.

The makeup of congressional leadership generally reflects its institutional base. However, just as the makeup of the institution does not conform to the makeup of the population as a whole, neither does the leadership. The major actors in Congress, and Congress as a whole, tend to be white, male, at least middle-aged, and from an occupation that is generally classified as white-collar professional, although many have made public service their actual occupation.

CONGRESSIONAL POWER

Congressional procedures, structure, and organization purposefully make passage of legislation a difficult and time-consuming process. With 535 members, who are mostly strong personalities in their own right, concerted action is very rare. Prior to the 1970s, Congress was well-organized on a seniority principle that meant that most committees were in the hands of the more conservative members. Any measure had only to gain the assent of the few crucially placed members to stand a good chance of passage. It also appeared however, that this Congress was unable, or unwilling, to deal with the pressing issues that were raised by the turmoil of the 1960s and Watergate.

In order to deal substantively with the issues of the 1970s, Congress reorganized itself to break what appeared to be the logjams. In other words, it (with the addition of newer, younger, and more liberal members) tried to democratize its internal workings. Reforms were instituted to make the body as a whole more responsive to the majority of its members and make power and position more widely shared. Furthermore, Congress has made a determined effort to regain the policymaking initiative and to reassert its power, both as the representative of the people and as the predominant branch of the national government.

This section will discuss three major areas and efforts by Congress to regain or enhance its role in the operation of the federal government.

1. We will discuss the continuing impact and debate regarding the reforms of the 1970s in the rules, procedure, and organization.

2. We will more specifically address those portions of the reforms that were meant to reassert the congressional role in oversight of the executive. After several years of executive dominance and what was perceived to be growth in executive power, post-Watergate concerns led to a concerted effort on Congress's part to regain its role as administrative watchdog.

3. We will address the two major acts of this era that were designed to reassert congressional power in the fundamental policy areas that Congress once believed were its peculiar province—the budget and the commitment of American military power.

1970s Reforms

Many of the reforms of the 1970s were meant to enable Congress to act more effectively as well as more democratically. In a way, their very success has raised new problems. The democratic reforms, such as dispersing power and making markup sessions and conference committee sessions public, tend to make efficient action more difficult. Reforms that are meant to make lawmaking more effective, such as subcommittee specialization or increasing powers in the Speaker, work against democracy. The major changes can be summarized as follows:

1. No House member can chair more than one legislative subcommittee. Adopted in 1971, this rule resulted in the rise to subcommittee chairmanships of several younger Democrats. Changes in 1979 reduced the number of subcommittee positions members could hold and set up procedures whereby junior members could get better assignments.

2. Subcommittee members have a kind of "bill of rights" that assures them of real influence and consideration throughout the committee process. The power of committee chairman has been reduced and is now more broadly shared with members of subcommittees. In the larger committees, the formation of subcommittees was mandated, and subcommittees were authorized to hire their own staffs.

3. Committees were required to have written rules, again reducing the capacity of chairmen for arbitrary action.

4. In late 1974, the Democratic caucus limited senior Democrats to two subcommittee positions and effectively diminished conservatives' power on the Appropriations Committee. It also required that the chairmen of such subcommittees be elected by the caucus; it subsequently unseated the chairmen of three key committees and replaced them with younger and presumably more active members.

5. Committee meetings, including actual bill-drafting sessions, were required to be open to the public (and thus to reporters and lobbyists) except under limited circumstances. Even joint House-Senate conference committee sessions, the most sensitive of all such meetings, were included.

6. A series of changes culminating in 1979 reduced opportunities for members to block floor debate or otherwise tie up the entire House to prevent or delay votes on bills. Many of these placed additional powers in the hands of the House leadership.

The Senate began the change process somewhat more slowly than did the House, in part because its smaller size and more open floor procedures already enabled members to have more committee opportunities and floor impact. But by 1980, several important changes had been made:

1. The celebrated filibuster rule, which made it possible for a small number of senators to prevent legislation from being enacted at times, was loosened. Instead of requiring the votes of two-thirds of senators present and voting to shut off debate and bring a bill to a vote, the rule now requires only three-fifths of the full Senate, or sixty votes when there are no vacancies. In 1979, new limits were set on postcloture delaying tactics.
2. Committee meetings, including bill-drafting sessions, were required to be open to the public (and reporters and lobbyists) except under limited circumstances.
3. Committee chairmen were to be elected by secret ballot in the Democratic caucus whenever one-fifth of the caucus requested.
4. A number of committees and subcommittees were eliminated, and the number of such positions that senators could hold was reduced proportionately. The resulting streamlined committee system had fifteen standing committees and eleven special, select, joint, or temporary committees. The number of chairmanships that any senator could hold was also reduced.

It appears that there has been a substantial dispersal of power in Congresses of the 1980s. The enormous increase in staff allows more members to become specialists and well-informed on at least some issues. On the other hand, this means that even more access points, or veto points, have become available. In a series of postelection articles in November, 1978, for example, the *New York Times* stressed the new emphasis among members of Congress on "service to the District" and the increasingly powerful role of special interest groups.[15] The Spring 1983 Congressional Quarterly *Guide to Current American Government* entitled one of its major feature articles "In the Senate of the '80s, Team Spirit Has Given Way to the Rule of Individuals."[16]

In May, 1983, the Senate Committee on Rules and Administration began hearings on a report recommending another series of reforms. In an

---

[15] *New York Times*, November 13, 1978, p. B9.

[16] "In the Senate of the '80s, Team Spirit Has Given Way to the Rule of Individuals," *Spring 1983 Guide, Current American Government* (Washington, D.C.: Congressional Quarterly, Inc., 1983), pp. 6–13.

attempt to become a more "deliberative" body, they considered a report that recommended:

> limits on debate, rules to ensure attendance, election of a permanent presiding officer, elimination of several committees and all staffed subcommittees, and changes in the congressional budget process . . .

> The report recommended greatly contracting the committee system, and thus shrinking or eliminating the power base of many senators . . .

> Traditionally, the primary power base for many senators had been the chairmanship of subcommittees and the staff that went with those panels. The report said this had resulted in extreme specialization. To avoid that, it recommended prohibiting all staffed subcommittees.[17]

In other words, dispersal of power, or democracy, may have resulted not in majority rule but in lots of little power bases that acted just like the previous fewer-in-number power bases.

The new Congress does represent more *interests* than the old Congress. The problem may be that Congress operates in a total context where some interests remain more equal than other interests; it also may lie in adherence to the value of representing *interests*. This raises the question of an apparent conflict between efficiency and democracy, which also must be addressed at the level of value choices. Thus, structural and procedural reform of Congress is not a technical problem, but a very political one.

At present, Congress has not shown much capacity to provide steady or sustained direction for the basic course of American public policy. It has, on occasion, blocked important presidential or other policy initiatives, but it reserves its most systematic attention to the needs of local interests, or at least those interests that are represented by members of Congress with power in their respective houses. Reform has certainly enhanced this capability, but further capacities remain interesting possibilities.

Legislative Oversight

Another reason lurking behind the proliferation of subcommittees was enhancing the capability of the Congress to monitor the executive branch agencies. Congress increasingly fell behind in the ability to gather sufficient information to counter executive assertions regarding its performance. Executive agencies specialized, and Congress did not; indeed, Congress was dependent upon the information supplied to it by the very agencies it was supposed to be monitoring. The development of subcommittees, and especially the growth of subcommittee staff, gave Congress the capacity to develop its own specialization and information base. (The Congressional

---

[17] "Report Urges Major Changes in Senate Structure, Rules," *Fall 1983 Guide, Current American Government* (Washington, D.C.: Congressional Quarterly, Inc., 1983), pp. 26–27.

Budget Office and legislative oversight through the budget mechanism is more fully covered in Chapter 12.)

The major mechanism developed by Congress to deal with an increasingly powerful executive was the "legislative veto." First used in 1932, a legislative veto provision in a statute delays an executive agency decision for a certain period, during which time one or both houses of Congress (and sometimes even committees of one or the other) can veto the proposed executive action. "By 1980 there were 200 laws containing more than 250 legislative veto provisions, one-third of them enacted since 1975."[18] Some of the major acts with legislative veto provisions are the War Powers Resolution and the Congressional Budget and Impoundment Control Act of 1974, which are discussed in the next section. Others include the Military Appropriation Authorization Act of 1975, the Nuclear Nonproliferation Act of 1978, the Federal Trade Commission Improvements Act of 1980, and the Federal Land Policy and Management Act of 1976.[19]

In June, 1983, the Supreme Court ruled that the legislative veto is an unconstitutional violation of the principle of separation of powers. Although Congress can delegate power to the executive, it cannot unilaterally make policy. The Court stated:

> Disagreement with the Attorney General's decision to deport Chadha— no less than Congress' original choice to delegate to the Attorney General the authority to make that decision, involves determinations of policy that Congress can implement in only one way; bicameral passage followed by presentment to the President. Congress must abide by its delegation of authority until that delegation is legislatively altered or revoked . . .

> The veto . . . doubtless has been in many respects a convenient shortcut; the "sharing" with the executive by Congress of its authority . . . is, on its face, an appealing compromise. In purely practical terms, it is obviously easier for action to be taken by one House without submission to the President; but it is crystal clear from the records of the Convention, contemporaneous writings and debates, that the Framers ranked other values higher than efficiency.[20]

In other words, one of Congress's major means of exercising legislative oversight appears to be no longer practical. As Justice White pointed out in his dissent:

> Without the legislative veto, Congress is faced with a Hobson's choice: either to refrain from delegating the necessary authority, leaving itself with a hopeless task of writing laws with the requisite specificity to cover

[18] Davidson and Oleszek, *Congress and Its Members*, p. 336.

[19] *Immigration and Naturalization Service* v. *Chadha, et al.*, Slip Opinion, No. 80–1832. Argued February 22, 1982; reargued December 7, 1982; decided June 23, 1983. See the Appendix.

[20] *INS* v. *Chadha*, Majority Opinion, p. 38.

endless special circumstances across the entire policy landscape, or in the alternative, to abdicate its lawmaking function to the executive branch and independent agencies. To choose the former leaves major national problems unresolved; to opt for the latter risks unaccountable policymaking by those not elected to fill that role.[21]

What remains to be seen is what action Congress will now take to maintain its control over executive action. Some suggest that Congress will simply give up and delegate its authority to the executive, subject only to the regular process of annual review. Others suggest that the new Congress is less amenable to diminution of its power and will take back many of the powers that it previously delegated. Instead of broad grants of authority to the executive, Congress will be much more specific in its policymaking. It all remains to be worked out between future Congresses, Presidents, and the Supreme Court.

Major Acts

The Budget Control and Impoundment Act and the War Powers Resolution of 1974 signaled Congress's intent to reassert its policymaking power in major ways. The Budget Act created an entirely new budgetary process. Although the President still submits a budget, Congress created mechanisms by which it would be the major actor in the process, and not just a re-actor. This process is fully described in Chapter 12, "Working Together: The Budgetary Process."

The War Powers Resolution of 1974 attempts to check what appeared to be unrestrained power in the executive branch with regard to the usage of the American military as part of our foreign policy. Secret wars, such as Cambodia and Laos, and the deployment of American troops without the consultation of Congress, increasingly put Congress in the position of funding a military presence and a foreign policy for which it had no say. Arguing that only Congress had the power to declare war, the War Powers Resolution passed, and then repassed over President Nixon's veto.

Figure 9.4 lists the major provisions of the Act. Secs. 1542 and 1543 are the crucial passages. They require executive consultation with and reporting to the Congress with regard to the commitment of American troops. Presidents have always insisted that their power as Commander-in-Chief left them in sole charge of this function. Furthermore, according to the executive, movement of American troops often cannot wait upon congressional action. On the other hand, Congress claims that it has the sole and exclusive power to declare war and to raise and support armies. In a democracy, a decision to engage in hostilities with another nation has such far-reaching implications that it must come from the "people's" branch, according to Congress. Acknowledging the necessity of swift action at

---

[21] *INS* v. *Chadha*, Justice White's Dissent, p. 2.

Figure 9.4. *Major Provisions of the War Powers Resolution*

§ 1541. Purpose and policy

(a) Congressional declaration

It is the purpose of this chapter to fulfill the intent of the framers of the Constitution of the United States and insure that the collective judgment of both the Congress and the President will apply to the introduction of United States Armed Forces into hostilities, or into situations where imminent involvement in hostilities is clearly indicated by the circumstances, and to the continued use of such forces in hostilities or in such situations.

(b) Congressional legislative power under necessary and proper clause

Under article I, section 8, of the Constitution, it is specifically provided that the Congress shall have the power to make all laws necessary and proper for carrying into execution, not only its own powers but also all other powers vested by the Constitution in the Government of the United States, or in any department or officer hereof.

(c) Presidential executive power as Commander-in-Chief; limitation

The constitutional powers of the President as Commander-in-Chief to introduce United States Armed Forces into hostilities, or into situations where imminent involvement in hostilities is clearly indicated by the circumstances, are exercised only pursuant to (1) a declaration of war, (2) specific statutory authorization, or (3) a national emergency created by attack upon the United States, its territories or possessions, or its armed forces.

(Pub. L. 93–148, § 2, Nov. 7, 1973, 87 Stat. 555.)

§ 1542. Consultation; initial and regular consultations

The President in every possible instance shall consult with Congress before introducing United States Armed Forces into hostilities or into situations where imminent involvement in hostilities is clearly indicated by the circumstances, and after every such introduction shall consult regularly with the Congress until United States Armed Forces are no longer engaged in hostilities or have been removed from such situations.

(Pub. L. 93–148, § 3, Nov. 7, 1973, 87 Stat. 555.)

§ 1543. Reporting requirement

(a) Written report; time of submission; circumstances necessitating submission; information reported

In the absence of a declaration of war, in any case in which United States Armed Forces are introduced—

(1) into hostilities or into situations where imminent involvement in hostilities is clearly indicated by the circumstances;

(2) into the territory, airspace or waters of a foreign nation, while equipped for combat, except for deployments which relate solely to supply, replacement, repair, or training of such forces; or

(3) in numbers which substantially enlarge United States Armed Forces equipped for combat already located in a foreign nation;

the President shall submit within 48 hours to the Speaker of the House of Representatives and to the President pro tempore of the Senate a report, in writing, setting forth—

(A) the circumstances necessitating the introduction of United States Armed Forces;

(B) the constitutional and legislative authority under which such introduction took place; and

(C) the estimated scope and duration of the hostilities or involvement.

254

(b) Other information reported

The President shall provide such other information as the Congress may request in the fulfillment of its constitutional responsibilities with respect to committing the Nation to war and to the use of United States Armed Forces abroad.

(c) Periodic reports; semiannual requirement

Whenever United States Armed Forces are introduced into hostilities or into any situation described in subsection (a) of this section, the President shall, so long as such armed forces continue to be engaged in such hostilities or situation, report to the Congress periodically on the status of such hostilities or situation as well as on the scope and duration of such hostilities or situation, but in no event shall he report to the Congress less often than once every six months.

(Pub. L. 93–148, § 4, Nov. 7, 1973, 87 Stat. 555.)

§ 1544. Congressional action

(a) Transmittal of report and referral to Congressional Committees; joint request for convening Congress

Each report submitted pursuant to section 1543(a)(1) of this title shall be transmitted to the Speaker of the House of Representatives and to the President pro tempore of the Senate on the same calendar day. Each report so transmitted shall be referred to the Committee on International Relations of the House of Representatives and to the Committee on Foreign Relations of the Senate for appropriate action. If, when the report is transmitted, the Congress has adjourned sine die or has adjourned for any period in excess of three calendar days, the Speaker of the House of Representatives and the President pro tempore of the Senate, if they deem it advisable (or if petitioned by at least 30 percent of the membership of their respective Houses) shall jointly request the President to convene Congress in order that it may consider the report and take appropriate action pursuant to this section.

(b) Termination of use of United States Armed Forces; exceptions; extension period

Within sixty calendar days after a report is submitted or is required to be submitted pursuant to section 1543(a)(1) of this title, whichever is earlier, the President shall terminate any use of United States Armed Forces with respect to which such support was submitted (or required to be submitted), unless the Congress (1) has declared war or has enacted a specific authorization for such use of United States Armed Forces, (2) has extended by law such sixty-day period, or (3) is physically unable to meet as a result of an armed attack upon the United States. Such sixty-day period shall be extended for not more than an additional thirty days if the President determines and certifies to the Congress in writing that unavoidable military necessity respecting the safety of United States Armed Forces requires the continued use of such armed forces in the course of bringing about a prompt removal of such forces.

(c) Concurrent resolution for removal by President of United States Armed Forces

Notwithstanding subsection (b) of this section, at any time that United States Armed Forces are engaged in hostilities outside the territory of the United States, its possessions and territories without a declaration of war or specific statutory authorization, such forces shall be removed by the President if the Congress so directs by concurrent resolution.

(Pub. L. 93–148, § 5, Nov. 7, 1973, 87 Stat. 556; H. Res. 163, Mar. 19, 1975.)

times, Congress nevertheless insists upon full consultation and reporting once an action has been taken.

The War Powers Act has not resolved these questions. There is not much history to inform us as to how it will affect, if at all, presidential initiative and control of foreign policy by military means. Presidents Ford, Carter, and Reagan all were involved in military ventures during their administrations. Although each did report to Congress, none were willing to fully acknowledge the constitutionality of the War Powers Resolution. In each case, the evacuation of Americans from Cambodia and Vietnam, the *Mayaguez* incident, and the abortive Iranian hostage rescue attempt, troops were only involved for a matter of days.

The situation of the Marines in Lebanon during President Reagan's administration posed more troubling questions. When are troops in situations where "imminent involvement in hostilities is clearly indicated by the circumstances"? The President maintained that the Marines were there in a "peacekeeping" capacity alone. Although he regularly made reports to Congress, such reports never specifically cited or acknowledged the War Powers Resolution provisions. As Congress became increasingly concerned about the U.S. presence, and as casualties mounted, a constitutional crisis loomed. In November, 1983, a compromise was reached whereby Congress essentially gave the President eighteen months to find a solution. However, the President "made it clear that he does not regard the compromise as an agreement inhibiting Presidential powers. This is consistent with the positions taken by previous Presidents."[22] But by February 1984, Congress was considering new resolutions regarding the Lebanese situation under their War Powers Resolution functions. The controversy over the War Powers Act was far from over.

Interpretations of many of the Act's provisions remain to be solidified. When does the clock begin to run? What are "hostilities"? Questions arise over almost each phrase. When President Carter attempted to rescue the hostages in Iran with a very secret operation (which stalled in the desert), he explained his prior nonconsultation with Congress as a necessity for the success of the operation. Congress granted that a "rescue" mission did not fall under the provisions of the Act. Acting on this precedent, President Reagan's secret and sudden invasion of Grenada was consistently termed a "rescue" of American students, and thus, this presidential action did not come under the terms of the War Powers Act. Similarly, American support of the counterrevolutionaries in Nicaragua involves the CIA, and not "troops." Movements may be described as "training exercises," such as those in Honduras and Guatemala, so that they do not come under the reporting requirements of Sec. 1543(a)(2). The struggle continues.

In other words, as of now, the War Powers Act stands as a signal of congressional intent; Congress has not yet successfully intervened or op-

---

[22] "The War Powers Act Controversy," *Congressional Digest*, November, 1983, p. 259.

posed a president in this area. It does, however, stand as a possibility or opportunity for congressional assertion of policymaking power.

SUMMARY

Congress holds the potential to be the nation's lawmaking body, the "people's" branch. In recent years, it has attempted to move closer to and regain its predominance. However, it works in a total context that includes both an external environment of a myriad of special interests to which it must respond and an institutional environment wherein the executive branch has become the major policymaker and initiator. An old adage asserts that "the President proposes, Congress disposes." In spite of repeated efforts to ameliorate that problem, the President does appear to be the major actor in the policymaking process. This leads us, of course, to the next chapter— the presidency.

CHAPTER 10

The Presidency

In the early 1960s, Americans accorded the presidency "great respect," and most children regarded the President as a "benevolent leader."[1] In the next twenty years, no American president served two entire terms. President John F. Kennedy was assassinated in his first term. His successor, President Lyndon Johnson, who had won a landslide victory in 1964, was forced to withdraw from a reelection bid in 1968, because the public deeply distrusted him and his Vietnam War policies. Six years later, President Richard Nixon was forced to resign under threat of impeachment for abuses of power and serious violations of the law. In 1976 and 1980, incumbent Presidents Ford and Carter were defeated in their respective reelection bids. Americans had obviously lost much of their earlier confidence in the presidency.

Was it just personal defects that led Presidents Johnson and Nixon into serious trouble? Did their media images defeat Presidents Carter and Ford? Personal characteristics are a part of the story, of course, but only a small part. The President stands at the head of an executive branch that employs more than 2 million people and affects the lives of Americans and other people all over the world. As the powers of the office increase, opportunities for mistakes and abuse grow. Simultaneously, the advent of television and radio networks and instantaneous worldwide communications have made *any* presidential action the focus of the news.

The modern presidency is a very different institution from what it was before World War II and the Great Depression. In 1932, there were three

---

[1] Fred I. Greenstein, "What the President Means to Americans," in *Choosing the President*, ed. James David Barber (Englewood Cliffs, N.J.: Prentice-Hall, 1974), p. 125.

258

people on the White House staff; in 1984, there were over 400, plus those staff members that the President has borrowed from the staffs of other departments. The White House Office is part of a larger, ever-changing Executive Office of the President. In 1930, 601,319 people administered all the functions of the federal government; in 1984 the number was over 2,000,000. Throughout most of American history, including the first third of the twentieth century, Congress dominated the government. Occasionally, a "strong" President, such as Theodore Roosevelt, was able to have his way for a short time, but now every President is "strong"; this suggests that the office has changed more than the personalities of the men who have occupied it.

It is very difficult not to personalize the presidency. In our entire history up to 1984, only forty individuals have occupied the office. (They have, so far, all been male, so we will use the masculine pronoun throughout this chapter; this is not to imply that all future presidents will be males.) The President's power is of a kind that no other government official has at his disposal. He is the executive head of the nation *and* the symbol of the United States both to Americans and citizens of other countries. Most countries have a head of state (like the Queen of England or the President of Israel) who symbolizes the nation, and a prime minister who is the executive in charge of day-to-day affairs. American presidents are in a unique position because they combine both roles. They are holders of particular powers conferred by the Constitution, the laws, and court decisions, but they also shape their own powers by creating and guiding the very public opinion to which they respond.

Although the powers of and checks on the President that are specified by the Constitution have hardly changed, practice has changed enormously. In order to understand the place of the President in American government today, we must look not only at the person who lives in the White House, but also at power centers and tensions in the society as a whole, what a President can do to shape them, and what they can do to shape a President. In a sense, therefore, this entire book describes the forces that make the presidency what it is.

In this chapter, however, we will focus directly on what the President can do and how he does it. We will begin with the formal and informal institutional powers that are derived from the Constitution. We will then discuss the structure and organization of the presidency as a whole, especially as it impacts on the ability to exercise those powers. However, we cannot escape the fact that it is *a* president with which we deal, so it is also important that we know how one becomes *the* president; this subject will be covered in the last section.

POWERS

The Constitution and the hundreds of laws Congress has enacted over the years confer formal powers on the President. The full meaning of these provisions is never fully apparent from the legal language in which they are stated; rather, their meaning resides in the actions of particular presidents and the court decisions interpreting them. This is another way of saying that these meanings change continuously—and usually in the direction of wider presidential powers.

On the other hand, the Constitution and our traditions created a government of limited powers that operates under a principle of separation of powers and checks and balances. Because they were extremely fearful of an absolute monarch, the Founding Fathers tried to balance a felt need for an "energetic" executive with an equally felt need for curbs on his powers. These checks worked well for about a century and a half. Some historians believe that they worked too well, because they often created impasses among the three branches of the government that prevented effective governmental action—as they were designed to do. These restraints appear to be far less effective now. The predominant criticism of the 1970s was that the presidency had grown too powerful, "imperial," and capable of the kind of abuse of executive power that the delegates to the Constitutional Convention of 1787 tried to prevent.[2] As was described in the previous chapter, Congress has attempted to redress that balance, and the developments in the next several decades will reveal just how effective the checks still are.

In addition to the legal and constitutional restrictions on the President, there are more informal restraints, such as the President's need to maintain broad political support. Although the President may act contrary to popular opinion, it increases his difficulties should he choose to do so, because it gives the other actors in the situation ammunition and support. Similarly, he must maintain some kind of support from the members of Congress if any of the presidential program is to actually pass. As the previous administrations of Reagan, Carter, and Ford will testify, this is no longer an easy task.

Furthermore, although it is supposed to be subject to presidential orders, the federal bureaucracy is a tough, although not insurmountable, obstacle for every President. The bureaucracy, which will be considered in Chapter 11, restricts the President simply because agencies develop their own ways of doing things, beliefs about what is or is not desirable, and devices for ignoring or sabotaging directives from the executive that they do not like. The prevailing attitude is that presidents, cabinet secretaries, and assistant secretaries come and go, while the real work is done by experts. For this reason, political scientist Richard Neustadt has argued that the only way for presidents to be influential is to persuade others to go along.[3] Otherwise, a president may issue orders only to realize later that little or nothing has happened.

On the other hand, we are all aware that the power of the presidency

---

[2] Arthur M. Schlesinger, *The Imperial Presidency* (Boston: Houghton Mifflin, 1973).

[3] Richard E. Neustadt, *Presidential Power* (New York: New American Library, 1960), pp. 42–63.

appears to have grown tremendously. In addition to the powers derived from specific provisions of the Constitution, the President has the capacity to directly influence and shape public opinion. No citizen can have direct knowledge of more than a tiny fraction of the thousands of issues on which the government acts every day. It is chiefly what the President and White House staff say publicly that causes the average citizen to worry about a military threat from Russia or Grenada or to believe that the high cost of American goods is due to overregulation by government. The President can usually do a great deal to influence what people support and what they oppose by shaping their hopes and fears.

It is extremely difficult to pin down the powers and restraints on the President. Defining the *institution* becomes doubly difficult because we are hampered by the almost irresistible tendency to speak of *a* president in a specific administration. Scholars disagree on a definition; their views range from those who speak of the imperial presidency and presidential government to those who see the "twilight" of the president and the "illusion of presidential government."[4] It is agreed that the presidency can be powerful, but it is highly unlikely that it is, or can be, all-powerful. The mix and the emphasis depend on a large number of factors—the person in the presidency, the institutional traditions, and the internal and external environment in political economic terms.

In this section, we will survey the President's powers, both informal and formal, in domestic and foreign policy. Again, let us emphasize that it is somewhat artificial to separate domestic and foreign, and formal and informal, powers. They really are intertwined, different sides of the same object. However, for purposes of discussion, we divide them into administrative and legislative domestic policy, and diplomatic and military foreign policy.

The Domestic Arena

"The executive Power shall be vested in a President of the United States of America"

". . . he shall take care that the Laws be faithfully executed,"

". . . he shall nominate, and by and with the Advice and Consent of the Senate, shall appoint Ambassadors, and other public Ministers and Consuls, Judges of the supreme Court, and all other Officers of the United

---

[4] Hugh Heclo and Lester M. Salamon, eds. *The Illusion of Presidential Government* (Boulder, Colo.: Westview Press, 1981); George E. Reedy, *The Twilight of the Presidency: An Examination of Power and Isolation in the White House* (New York: World Publishing Co., 1970); and Louis Koenig believes the presidency "has . . . become a diminished office of declining power [which needs to be placed] on a secure upward course in the ever-working cycle of presidential history." Louis W. Koenig, *The Chief Executive* 4th ed. (New York: Harcourt Brace Jovanovich, 1981), pp. iii and 420.

States, whose Appointments are not herein otherwise provided for, and which shall be established by Law; but the Congress may by Law vest the Appointment of such inferior Officers, as they think proper, in the President alone,"

As part of the "executive Power," the President manages the administrative branch of the government. Legislators make law, judges interpret law, and executives enforce the law. In one sense, the executive power is a neutral activity; the President simply carries out the dictates of the legislative bodies. But it has, at least recently, become quite clear that the administration and execution of the law carries policymaking capability. The President has consistently, for example, withheld or "impounded" funds appropriated by Congress for specific purposes if he felt the activity either did not require the funds or was being handled inappropriately. This was considered part of his responsibility. However, President Richard Nixon impounded hundreds of thousands of dollars in order to frustrate projects or activities with which he personally disagreed. This eventually led to the Budget Control and Impoundment Act of 1974, whereby Congress tried to stop the practice.

The executive power vested in the President by the Constitution appears to be a most general grant of power. This provision depends upon what presidents actually *do* as well as on occasional reviews of their authority by the courts. After America's entry into World War II, President Franklin Roosevelt imposed far-reaching economic controls by "executive order." This is a procedure whereby the President essentially makes law without waiting for Congress. Roosevelt's measures included nationwide price, wage, and rent ceilings, limits on the use and export of raw materials, and curbs on employment practices that discriminated against blacks. President Truman integrated the armed forces via executive order. Thus, the executive order can be and has been used in a variety of ways.

A great many laws also confer powers on the President. Over the years, Congress has delegated many rulemaking capabilities to executive agencies. The underlying argument is that Congress simply cannot attend to the day-to-day details such as setting rates and devising environmental guidelines. Thus, it delegates its authority to make the specific laws under a general law that grants that authority to the executive, within the general guidelines Congress enacts. On the other hand, Congress tried to restrain the executive in the pursuit of this power by the legislative veto device, as we noted in Chapter 9.

Finally, the President has a major means of exerting influence on the executive and judicial branches through the power of appointment. At the top levels of government, such as federal judges and high officials in the executive branch, Senate confirmation is necessary. The occasional rejection of a nominee makes presidents think twice about ignoring popular values. President Kennedy's nomination of Francis X. Morrissey to a district judgeship and President Nixon's nomination of Clement F. Haynsworth and G. Harrold Carswell to the Supreme Court were rejected because the nominees' competence or fairness were in serious doubt.

In all but the rare case, however, presidential appointments win routine approval. Occasionally presidents use the power of appointment for ends that would be politically harmful if they avowed them openly or asked for legislation to accomplish them. Senator John Kennedy, for example, won wide support from liberals for his strong stand on civil rights. However, as President, he appointed a large number of district judges in the South whose decisions crippled much of the civil rights legislation that he had initiated or publicly supported. In this way the President paid debts to powerful Democrats in the South who were less than enthusiastic about his rhetorical stance on civil rights. Richard Nixon appointed a director of the Office of Economic Opportunity, Howard Phillips, who disapproved of that agency's programs to help the poor. Phillips succeeded in virtually killing the agency by dismantling its programs and replacing or firing many members of the staff who tried to take their duties seriously.

The notion that administration of the laws is a neutral activity has been undergoing erosion for some time. As the power of the presidency grew, it became more and more obvious that "faithfully executing the laws" left wide latitude for policymaking. President Reagan's appointments to the Scientific Advisory Commission, Environmental Protection Agency, and Civil Rights Commission brought the argument before the public. In the first case, what could be more objective and neutral than "scientists"? However, it was discovered that nominations for these appointments were only being made *after* checking out the names with the Republican Party. The administration admitted quite frankly that a Republican scientist of the right persuasion was infinitely preferable to a Democratic one. It was argued that even scientists come to different scientific conclusions, depending upon their political values. The appointments were confirmed.

In the second case, in spite of the rhetoric of adherence to the Commission's avowed purpose, President Reagan's appointees were clearly opposed to the previous work of the Civil Rights Commission. The new commissioners were intended to redirect it in ways that were more politically acceptable to the administration. After a lengthy standoff with Congress, the Commission was enlarged and its tenure extended, but the new appointments were made. Walter Mondale, a Democratic candidate for President, made the issue one of his campaign promises—"he would fire the new members and rehire the previous ones."

Although the President attempts to maintain the myth of simply "administering the laws," it is increasingly clear that the executive power is a highly political one, even in simply "faithfully executing the laws."

> "He shall from time to time give to the Congress Information of the State
> of the Union, and recommend to their Consideration such Measures as he
> shall judge necessary and expedient; he may, on extraordinary occasions,
> convene both Houses, or either of them, and in Case of Disagreement
> between them, with Respect to the Time of Adjournment, he may adjourn
> them to such Time as he shall think proper; . . ."

It is this constitutional provision that underlies the President's annual State of the Union address, but it is only in the last century that the message has become the vehicle for the President's program. Televised nationwide and reported internationally, the State of the Union address now serves as the administration's intentions for the coming year. It is the President's opportunity to shape the agenda, essentially defining the issues that will be addressed by the rest of us. Recognizing the crucial character of the ability to define the problems in need of solution, and to suggest the solutions, the President came to be called "the Great Legislator."

As the presidency increased, so did its legislative responsibilities. Several pieces of legislation now require annual reports from the President; the Employment Act of 1946 laid the basis for the annual economic report, and the budgetary process depends upon submission of the budget and its report by the President. All of these messages carry with them proposed legislation to implement their recommended solutions to the problems that are posed and discussed. Vast portions of the measures introduced into the Congress come from the executive, either the President or one of the executive agencies. As noted in the previous chapter, sometimes it seems as if "the President proposes, Congress disposes."

In other words, there seems to be a reversal of the process originally envisioned by the Founding Fathers. At least some, such as James Madison and Thomas Jefferson, expected Congress to be the active branch. The President's legislative participation was limited to the reactive process of either accepting (and signing) or rejecting (and vetoing) congressional work. While both of those possibilities still lie with the President, the executive now plays a much more active role in initiating legislation as well, which puts Congress in the reactive role.

On the other hand, the President's power to shape even the agenda is not absolute. Furthermore, although the presidential package is the one that is most likely to maintain media attention, it must still go through the congressional process. Although determined presidents have found ways to circumvent some of the most important congressional powers, Congress has recently moved to reassert its prerogatives. Even though the power of Congress to act as the chief legislative branch is no longer clear-cut, congressional prerogatives remain important. Presidents are subjected to criticism for bypassing them and are forced to justify actions that are seen as exceeding executive powers. Once the initial honeymoon period of a new administration is over, very little presidential legislation makes it through the Congress without substantial modification.

Foreign Policy

". . . he shall receive Ambassadors and other public Ministers"

"He shall have Power, by and with the Advice and Consent of the Senate, to make Treaties, provided two thirds of the Senators present concur; and he shall nominate, and by and with the Advice and Consent of the Senate, shall appoint Ambassadors, and other public Ministers and Consuls,"

The President is our Chief of State as well as our chief executive officer. This means that he represents the United States in our relationships with all other nations, both symbolically and substantively. Although the President often designates a representative, such as the Vice-President, for purely ceremonial affairs, such as attending funerals and coronations, they are still a presidential function. More importantly, the President is the Chief Diplomat. The power to receive ambassadors and other public ministers gives him the sole responsibility of recognizing and establishing full diplomatic relations with other nations. This is often more than a mere gesture, as it lends legitimacy to a new government. For example, the United States was very quick to recognize Israel in 1948, signaling to the world its intention to help Israel maintain its existence as a separate state. Similarly, President Roosevelt's delayed recognition of the Bolshevik government of Russia in 1933 ended a period of formal opposition to its assumption of state power.

The more fundamental power is the substantive one of conducting negotiations and making agreements with other nations. The Constitution authorizes the President to make treaties, but he must then secure the consent of a two-thirds vote in the Senate before they are officially ratified. Recent presidents have increasingly evaded the requirement of Senate approval by entering into "executive agreements" with other nations. These agreements effectively make treaties without regard for the advice-and-consent role of the Senate that is provided for in the Constitution. Many of these agreements revolve around trade, both between countries and between the private citizens of our country and those of another country.

> "The President shall be Commander in Chief of the Army and Navy of the United States,"

According to the Constitution, the President is commander in chief of the armed forces, while Congress has the power to declare war and to raise and support armies. However, many presidents have waged wars without congressional approval, and they have also created situations that left Congress little choice. During the first twenty-five years of American history, presidents waged three undeclared naval wars. In 1846, President James Polk ordered troops into territory claimed by Mexico, provoking a war that Congress then had to declare. Presidents Johnson and Nixon later waged wars in foreign countries without formal declarations by Congress.

Issues of foreign policy, internal and external security, and other matters that have a deep impact on our lives depend on actions over which most of us have little control. When President Lyndon Johnson told the country in August 1964 that the North Vietnamese had fired on two American ships in the Tonkin Gulf, he immediately created overwhelming public and congressional support for sending troops into Vietnam. No one was in a position to question his claim. The President himself may not have known that he was distorting the facts, although it later became clear that he had. Johnson had been planning for at least several months to ask the Senate for a resolution that could be used to authorize military intervention, and his administration helped to create an incident that would arouse public opinion in support of such intervention.

The President benefits in personal popularity from any development

Figure 10.1.   *Approval of Carter's Handling of the Presidency*

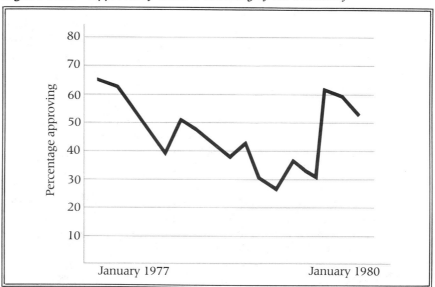

SOURCE: *New York Times,* 16 January 1980, p. A18. Copyright © 1980 by The New York Times Company. Reprinted by permission.

that increases patriotic or nationalistic feeling. Threatening events abroad have this effect, whether the President had any role in them. Figure 10.1 shows that President Carter's popularity shot up sharply after the takeover of the American embassy in Iran in 1979 and the holding of its staff as hostages. This steep rise in popularity ran counter to the usual trend. The same has been true of previous presidents, as is illustrated by Table 10.1. Virtually every President loses popularity in the first several years of his term, as Figure 10.2 indicates. Even when a President's foreign actions have been unsuccessful, they increased his popularity if they were dramatic. In 1962, for example, President John Kennedy's unsuccessful effort to invade Cuba at the Bay of Pigs brought an increase in his popular support. Foreign policy decisions are undertaken with at least one eye on domestic politics, a factor that sometimes tempts presidents into dramatic or bold actions.

It is precisely this ability of the active presidency to create situations with the use of American troops, leaving Congress little room to react, much less act, that led to the War Powers Resolution of 1974. As previously discussed, this is far from a settled issue. Certainly, the usage of U.S. troops as an arm of our foreign policy has not lessened. In 1984, in addition to our longstanding troops in South Korea and other areas, there were Marines in Beirut, advisors in El Salvador, training exercises in Honduras and Guatemala paving the way for a permanent presence, and CIA sponsored counterrevolutionaries in Nicaragua, not to mention the invasion and occupation of Grenada. Figure 10.3 illustrates the U.S. military presence in the world. All of these actions were justified under the President's

TABLE 10.1
War and Military Crises and Popularity, 1945–75

			PERCENTAGE POPULARITY		DURATION
DATE	PRESIDENT	WAR OR CRISIS	*Pre*	*Post*	(MONTHS)
4/48	Truman	Berlin blockade	36%	39%	1
6/50	Truman	North Korea invades South Korea	37	46	5
7/58	Ike	Troops to Lebanon	52	58	3
7/61	JFK	Berlin crisis	71	79	12
10/62	JFK	Cuban missile crisis	61	73	8
2/65	LBJ	Bombing North Vietnam	68	69	1
4/65	LBJ	Troops to Dominican	64	70	3
6/66	LBJ	Extends bombing of Hanoi, North Vietnam	48	56	2
6/67	LBJ	Mideast war	44	52	1
4/70	Nixon	Troops to Cambodia	56	59	2
1/71	Nixon	Expand war to Laos	56	49	14
5/75	Ford	*Mayaguez* incident	40	51	8

SOURCE: Adapted from Jong R. Lee, "Rally Around the Flag: Foreign Policy Events and Presidential Popularity," *Presidential Studies Quarterly*, (Fall 1977), 254. Lee used the Gallup poll for his data. Reprinted by permission of The Center for the Study of the Presidency.

power as commander-in-chief, but not all were uncritically accepted as Congress struggled to find a way to become a part of the foreign policy-making process without appearing to be unsupportive of our "boys at war."

STRUCTURE AND ORGANIZATION OF THE PRESIDENCY

The presidency is really a group of organizations rather than an individual person. The thousands of agencies, bureaus, and other subunits of the federal government represent the interests of many different and often conflicting groups. Some wield enormous economic and social power, while others have very little. Because presidents must try to prevent open and serious conflict among the complex set of interests in American society, they cannot rely only on the established departments of the government for information. Increasingly, presidents have had to create organizations under their own control that often duplicate the functions of many of the regular administrative agencies. As is so often true in politics, the same conflict expresses itself in several forms and can be interpreted in alternative ways. The competing interests of unions and employers, for example, may take the form of conflicting policy recommendations from the Labor

Figure 10.2.   *Presidential Popularity*
a. President Carter's Job Rating

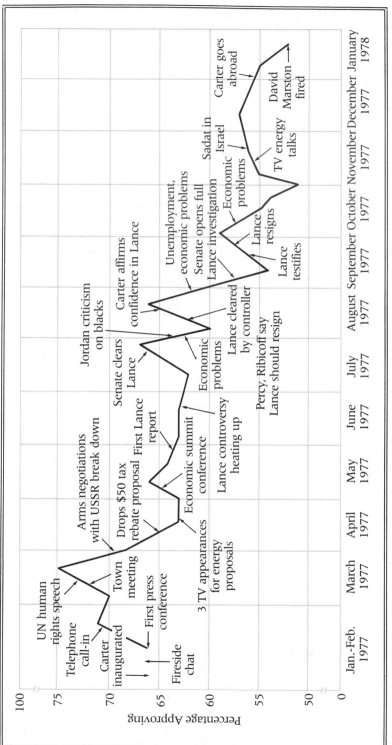

SOURCE: *Gallup Opinion Index*, January 1978, p. 17. Reprinted by permission of The Gallup Poll.

Figure 10.2 (cont.)
b. Approval Ratings of Reagan, Carter, and Nixon

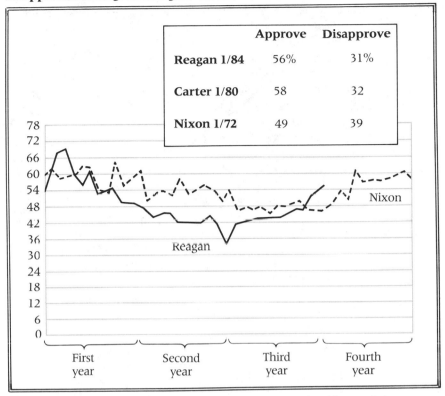

	Approve	Disapprove
Reagan 1/84	56%	31%
Carter 1/80	58	32
Nixon 1/72	49	39

SOURCE: *The National Journal,* January 28, 1984, p. 190. Reprinted by permission.

and Commerce Departments. The same conflict may also be reflected in personal infighting between the secretaries of those departments or between other officials who are responsive to the two interests. The student who is interested in personal sparring for position will find it, and the student who is interested in conflicts over value allocations will also find it; typically, they each will be seeing different aspects of the same battle.

Although the federal government consists of over 3 million employees, we are dealing here with those that the President appoints, who can rightly be called a part of *this* administration. The others remain from administration to administration. Obviously, the President individually does not handpick each of the appointments, but the major ones occupy his attention. Many of the other appointments are staff that come with the major appointment. For example, cabinet members or members of the Council of Economic Advisers often have assistants and a supporting staff with which they prefer to work. The lesser appointments are often handled by a presidential team for which it is the primary function. In President Reagan's case, E. Pendleton James headed the Personnel Commission that filled over 2,000 positions as the Republican administration moved in.

The problem is to find the right combination of administrative and substantive capability with political support and acumen. Obviously, these appointments have patronage aspects, and the President is expected to fill them with people who are sympathetic to administration aims. Similarly, there are political debts and promises to be repaid. An appointment also can be used to gain support, sometimes grudgingly, from an interest group, such as labor. Recently, presidents have tried to ensure that minorities and women received some positions. On the other hand, there is constant pressure to find the "right" person for the job, the person that has the expertise and experience to competently perform the necessary work. These forces are often in conflict, and this results in a relatively high turnover in these positions. Very few cabinets or White House staffs are composed of the same members at the beginning and at the end of a presidential term. It does not, however, lessen the number of people who are more than willing to serve in the presidency in some capacity.

Figure 10.4 depicts the structure and organization of the working presidency. We have already discussed the President, the administrative head of this organization. In a sense, we are now dealing with middle management, or, in another metaphor, the general's lieutenants. There are three levels, starting with those closest to the President, the White House Office. Next is the Executive Office of the President, which is a more inclusive group. Finally, we will discuss the cabinet, the working heads of the vast federal bureaucracy.

The White House Office

The White House Office consists of 400 to 500 people. These are the President's *personal* staff, and include trusted and loyal assistants, many of whom were previously friends or employees of the President. The organization of the White House Office is as individualized as the President. Some functions remain consistent, such as secretaries, clerks, and housekeeping, but the more responsible positions are incredibly fluid. Only a few, such as the "Assistant to the President—Press Secretary," have attained some kind of institutional permanence. The other "Assistants to the President—Fill in the Blank" tend to be defined in terms of both the person filling them and the needs or perceived needs of the President. Usually it becomes clear after two or three months of operation which members of the White House Office are the President's closest advisers and which members will be handling particular functions, but this is more a matter of learning by operation than by an organizational flow chart.

Modern presidents need to collect reliable information as well as exercise control, and in theory, the White House staff performs this function. Trusted assistants channel information to the Oval Office. The crucial nature of this function is a subject of some concern:

> People with experience in government soon come to realize likewise that the power to "define" options is the power to choose some and eliminate

Figure 10.3. United States Military Personnel Around the World

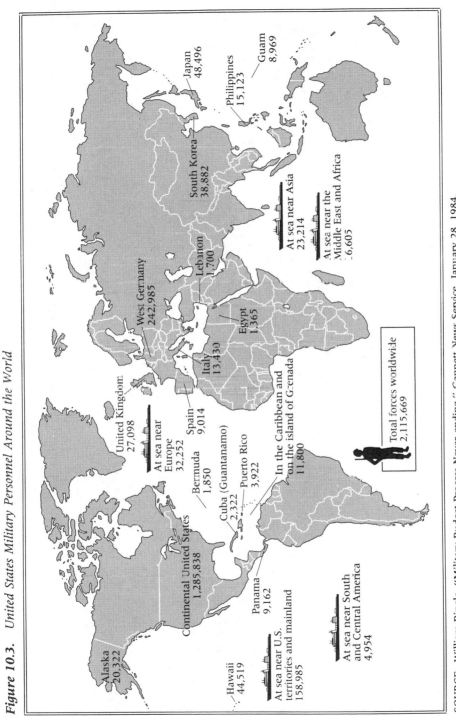

Japan
48,496

Guam
8,969

Philippines
15,123

South Korea
38,882

At sea near Asia
23,214

At sea near the
Middle East and Africa
6,605

West Germany
242,985

Lebanon
1,700

Egypt
1,365

Italy
13,430

United Kingdom
27,098

At sea near
Europe
32,252

Spain
9,014

Bermuda
1,850

Cuba (Guantanamo)
2,322

Puerto Rico
3,922

In the Caribbean and
on the island of Grenada
11,800

Total forces worldwide
2,115,669

Continental United States
1,285,838

Panama
9,162

Alaska
20,322

Hawaii
44,519

At sea near U.S.
territories and mainland
158,985

At sea near South
and Central America
4,954

SOURCE: William Ringle, "Military Budget Process Never-ending," Gannett News Service, January 28, 1984.

Figure 10.4. Organization of the Presidency

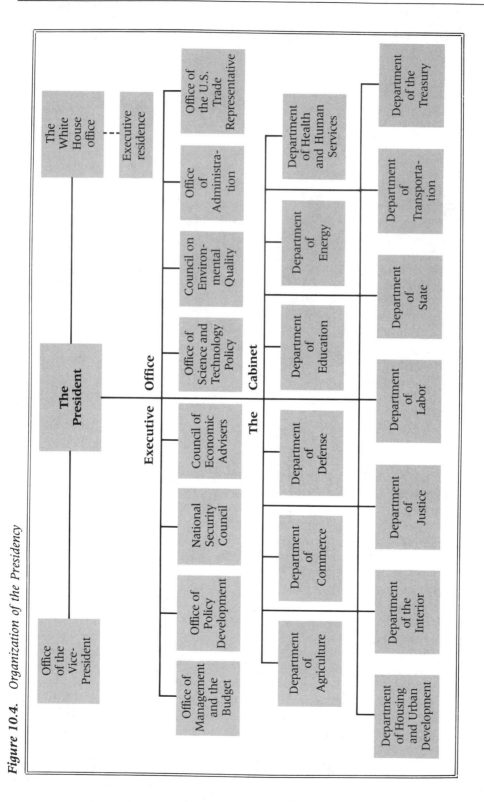

others. That is often the power in the hands of the White House staff. . . .
Most staffers are generalists, are substantially younger than their boss, and
tend to be subject to pressures to be a good team player. Too often, staffers
believe that, because they have access to the president, they are intelligent
enough to define options for him.[5]

Presidents have tried to alleviate this problem in a variety of ways. Franklin
Roosevelt liked to know about serious conflicts, was relatively open to
reports from the various agencies, and appointed trusted people to subordinate positions in key departments as sources of information and advice.
President Eisenhower preferred his staff to screen all information in a (not
surprisingly) military-type hierarchy so that only the most pressing problems reached him, and when those problems did reach the Oval Office, the
options had been narrowed to one or two.

Most presidents come into office determined to adopt a Franklin
Roosevelt-type approach to the organization of their White House staff.
They fully intend to be open, with information coming in to the center
from a variety of sources. This is termed the "spokes and wheel" approach,
with the President as the hub of the wheel and the various assistants as the
spokes. There is a constant tendency, however, under the pressures of time
and necessity, to rely more and more upon one or two most trusted advisors. A commitment to openness may remain while the institutional
realities leave many members of the White House staff jockeying for the
President's ear and others in increasingly informally powerful positions.

The growth and fluidity of the White House Office arouses another
major concern. The number of assistants surrounding the President tend to
isolate and insulate him. George E. Reedy, a former Special Assistant to the
President under Johnson, writes:

A president's most persistent problem in staying in touch with reality lies
in his staff. It is the aspect of White House life that bears the most striking
resemblance to a court. . . . [The staff] is the creature of the president, a
group of men who have one purpose in life and one purpose only—to
perform personal services for the man in charge.[6]

Reedy also argues that, as part of losing touch with reality, constant personal subservience on the part of all those surrounding the President
makes it very difficult for him to resist feelings of increasing, if not absolute,
power. Whether one accepts Mr. Reedy's entire argument, one can acknowledge the natural reaction of loyal employees to shield the President
from unwelcome information and advice. Screening is obviously necessary, but the temptation every White House staff feels to minimize criticism
reaching the Oval Office and to tell the President what he wants to hear
can hurt the President and the country, as was the case with both Lyndon
Johnson and Richard Nixon.

---

[5] Frank Kessler, *The Dilemmas of Presidential Leadership: Of Caretakers and Kings*
(Englewood Cliffs, N.J.: Prentice-Hall, 1982), p. 74.

[6] Reedy, *The Twilight of the Presidency*, p. 84.

The Executive Office

The White House Office is part of the Executive Office of the President. The Executive Office's composition varies depending upon prevailing national problems and presidential character. It is composed of approximately eight agencies that are directly answerable to the President. Some of the groups, such as the Office of Management and Budget, the Council of Economic Advisers, and the National Security Council, are obviously of much greater consequence than others. Although the approximately 2,000 personnel change with administrations, the Executive Office is much more a policy staff than a personal staff.

One of the key units in the Executive Office is the Office of Management and Budget (OMB), which carries out the responsibility of the President to prepare the federal budget. The Director carries such weight that his or her appointment must be confirmed by the Senate. The OMB's staff of more than 600 people reviews the annual budget requests of all executive departments and agencies, in addition to reviewing all the legislation these agencies would like to recommend to Congress. This is a critical form of presidential control, because an agency's effectiveness depends on its appropriation and the statutes that pertain to its policy area. Some agencies have enough private backing and influence in Congress to push legislation through even if the OMB refuses to make it part of the President's program. Such occasional "end runs" around the OMB in effect tell the President that the current strength of the interest group that accomplishes them has been underestimated.

Other agencies in the Executive Office—notably the Council of Economic Advisers, the United States Trade Representative, and the Council on Environmental Quality—help presidents keep abreast of economic trends. The CEA has sufficient impact that its three members also must face confirmation hearings and agreement. In conjunction with the budgetary and legislative powers of the OMB, these agencies contribute to a trend toward White House coordination of the entire executive branch in pursuit of a cohesive economic policy. It is important to remember, however, that an organizational structure that permits presidents to coordinate the policies of other agencies does not free them from the need to be sensitive to politically powerful groups. It also does not allow presidents to do whatever they please on behalf of the poor, consumers, or other groups with little political power of their own.

Another major agency is the National Security Council, which is composed of the Joint Chiefs of Staff, Secretaries of Defense and State, and the President's National Security Adviser. Its purpose is to coordinate and hopefully keep coherent the nation's foreign policy. There are often conflicts between the military and the state departments over proper handling of foreign policy issues. The NSC supposedly provides a forum whereby these differences can be worked out in-house. Although the President appoints the Secretaries of Defense and State, as well as the National Security Adviser, the Secretaries are not as likely to be as close to the

President as the Adviser; they must answer to other masters as well as the President. Generally, therefore, a working group emerges that is particularly close to the President—and the President's views—which consistently is able to promote its view.

The leading Executive Office agency positions, and particularly the CEA, are the most likely to be filled by members from the elite, as discussed in Chapter 5. The major policy shaping decisions are made at this level. Although there may be conflict among the politically powerful, it is not the same as the battle between special interest groups that occupy the Congress. It is here that the broad contours of the nation's fundamental domestic and foreign policies are worked out before being turned into specific legislative proposals to be funneled to the Congress. Furthermore, much that is done at this level can be accomplished without legislation through the use of executive agreements, executive orders, and various federal regulations from the appropriate agencies.

The Cabinet

The term *cabinet* has been used since George Washington's administration to refer to the heads of the large executive departments. The term implies that these officials collectively plan broad national policy, but the cabinet has never done so regularly. As George Reedy explained:

> The cabinet is one of those institutions in which the whole is less than the sum of the parts. As individual officers, the members bear heavy responsibilities in administering the affairs of the government. As a collective body, they are about as useful as the vermiform appendix—though far more honored.[7]

Actually, the cabinet has engaged in less and less joint policymaking through the last several years. The perceived need for presidential coordination and control made the Executive Office agencies under direct White House control a more logical arena for that purpose.

There are 13 cabinet posts (see Figure 10.4) and approximately 187 key sub-cabinet posts.[8] All of these appointments are subject to Senate confirmation, but usually only the major cabinet secretaries or outlandish appointments occasion any controversy. They can be removed by the President at any time, but it does require a presidential decision. Members of Congress, for example, consistently and regularly called for the resignation of the controversial Secretary of the Interior James Watt, but it was not until after he committed a particularly egregious social gaffe that he re-

---

[7] Ibid., p. 73.

[8] Dick Kirschten, "You Say You Want a Sub-Cabinet Post? Clear It With Marty, Dick, Lyn and Fred," *The National Journal*, April 4, 1981, p. 564.

signed from the office.[9] At that, President Reagan did not fire him nor ask for his resignation; Mr. Watt voluntarily decided it was time to move on to other things. It is the rare cabinet member who is out and out fired; they all, at least publicly, part amicably from the cabinet, still in full support of their President and with the President's full support.

Cabinet members can be useful to the President in a variety of ways. Some are appointed because of their political appeal to a wing of the President's party or a segment of the public. Some cabinet members have reputations as experts on the matters for which their departments are responsible, some have done political favors for the President, and others have followings in regions of the country where the administration is politically weak. Several recent presidents have appointed women to cabinet posts, with at least one eye on the fact that more than half of all eligible voters are women.

The same qualities that make cabinet members valuable politically give them some independence from the President, and tend to incline them to represent particular interests rather than to work together. They may feel a sense of obligation to the groups whose departments they head, whether farm organizations, defense contractors, or advertisers interested in low postal rates for junk mail. Conflicts among cabinet members, or among cabinet members and Executive Office officials, are not unusual. President Carter's National Security Adviser Brzezinski and his Secretary of State Vance developed an open feud. Similarly, President Reagan's Secretary of the Treasury Regan and his Council of Economic Advisers chair, Martin Feldstein, consistently contradicted one another, often publicly.

One student of the presidency makes a useful distinction between the "inner" cabinet—the heads of the Defense, State, Justice, and Treasury departments and a few other high-level White House staff members—and the "outer" cabinet—the heads of the departments dealing with domestic affairs: Interior, Agriculture, Commerce, Labor, Education, HUD (Urban Development), Transportation, and Health and Human Services.[10] Members of the inner cabinet, as individuals if not collectively, enjoy close ties to modern presidents. Their departments deal with matters that enable presidents to appeal powerfully to broad public opinion by invoking national and internal security.

Increasingly, presidents pay little personal attention to the outer cabinet members, and delegate this function to White House aides and to the director of the OMB. The outer cabinet departments deal primarily

---

[9] Secretary of the Interior James Watt had been a controversial figure in the Reagan Administration from his first days—to the last. The final blow came after he joked, in a public address, about his adherence to affirmative action by appointing to a government commission "a black, a woman, two Jews and a cripple." He managed to offend just about everyone.

[10] Thomas E. Cronin, *The State of the Presidency* (Boston: Little, Brown, 1975), pp. 190–91.

with the problems of groups possessing few political resources (welfare recipients, students, and Indians) or with the interests of organized groups whose well-established influence presidents could not change substantially even if they wanted to (large manufacturers, corporate farmers, organized labor, and cattle grazers). Because these circumstances leave little room for maneuvering, the problems addressed by these departments tend to involve relatively small changes in existing policies and conflicting demands that are often politically embarrassing. Understandably, tension is constant between cabinet secretaries who are under pressure to make concessions to one group or another and White House aides who are eager to minimize domestic spending and avoid politically harmful publicity. Such conflict transcends personalities because it involves basically incompatible roles. The White House is subject to a wider range of political pressures than the secretary of a cabinet department, so it must resist his or her demands and recommendations much of the time while expecting that he or she will run the department in a way that will reflect well on the administration *all* of the time.

HOW TO BECOME PRESIDENT

The framers of the Constitution devised a method of presidential election that they felt would ensure the selection of the most qualified person. They did not intend that election of the President would be by popular vote. On the other hand, they did not want the President to be the creature of the states. Their solution was the Electoral College, whereby each state's legislature would devise a means of choosing "electors" who are equal in number to the state's representation in Congress. These electors would then meet as the "Electoral College" and choose a president, with the person receiving the second highest number of votes becoming vice-president. Each elector voted for two people, one of whom could not be from the elector's home state. The theory was that only a nationally known statesman of high reputation could garner the necessary votes from such a body. It was a deliberate attempt to remove as much politics as possible from the presidential selection process.

It was not long before many of the framers' assumptions and hopes were dashed. The presidential election became a political party matter, and people actually began to campaign specifically for the office. At first, legislative caucuses chose a candidate upon which they could unite. Then, with the development of political parties came national political party conventions, which, among other things, chose presidential and vice-presidential candidates. By the twentieth century, the Electoral College had become a mere formality with the actual choice being made elsewhere.

This section will examine the process by which presidents are now selected, keeping in mind the question of the impact of the method of selection upon the final product. The nomination process has become a crucial part of presidential selection; this is the point at which a variety of people are actually running for president. A presidential election usually offers a choice of only two candidates. Many others may be running, but the strength of the two-party tradition and the structural constraints in the United States means that it is only the Democratic or Republican nominee who has a real chance. The election of 1984 provides the most recent illustration. The problem of presidential succession during a term leads us to a consideration of that process, as well as the vice-presidency.

Nomination

The choice of presidential nominees by the two major political parties is more critical than the general election because it eliminates all but two people from any chance of becoming President. Millions of people meet the constitutional requirements for serving as President—native born citizens who are at least thirty-five years old. However, only a very small number are ever seriously considered as nominees. The narrowing-down process is neither a lottery in which everyone starts with an equal chance nor a rigorous screening to find the best or most popular candidate. Only aspirants whom newspapers and television news programs have mentioned frequently are regarded as serious contenders; and publicity as a serious contender in turn gives an aspirant a public following.

In one sense, a kind of self-fulfilling prophecy seems to pervade the nominating process. An aspirant who makes a good early showing in the polls and the primaries finds it much easier to raise the millions of dollars that are necessary to continue to pursue the nomination. Even the "fat cats" and corporations that make large contributions, directly or indirectly, want a winner as well as a candidate who will support their interests. Names that are familiar from previous contests or political arenas are most often mentioned in conjecture about future ones. Those who are known can afford to hire the direct-mail professionals who can raise the funds from small contributors that are necessary to receive federal matching funds, and federal matching funds also enable one to keep going. The longer a person stays in the race, the more seriously the campaign is taken so money can be raised, and so on ad nauseam.

There are other barriers, in addition to the financial-publicity squeeze, that serve to screen out all but a select few. Rather rigid informal taboos confront women, blacks, Jews, and people whose ancestors emigrated from any part of the world other than Northern and Western Europe, because it is assumed that large numbers of voters are prejudiced against these groups.[11] A serious assault on those barriers was launched by the campaign of the Reverend Jesse Jackson for the Democratic presidential nomination and the determined efforts of women's groups to gain the vice-presidential nomination for a woman. But, at least through 1984, presi-

---

[11] Donald R. Matthews, "Presidential Nominations," in *Choosing the President,* ed. James David Barber (Englewood Cliffs, N.J.: Prentice-Hall, 1974), pp. 39–40.

dents have virtually all been male, white, Protestant (with the exception of John F. Kennedy), Anglo-Saxon, public officeholders, fairly old, and, importantly, fairly wealthy.

First-term presidents can normally have their party's nomination for a second term if they want it, and they usually do. President Ford came close to losing his quest for nomination to Ronald Reagan in 1976, but he had come to the presidency through the resignation of Richard Nixon and had not been previously nominated by the Republican Party. Victorious generals are the chief exception to the practice of nominating only individuals who have held elective office before, often as vice-president or senator. An impressive military record has helped nominate and elect seven presidents, although it is hardly likely that the same qualities make for success in both jobs. The last two presidents, Jimmy Carter and Ronald Reagan, were previously state governors. There is some concern that the nomination process has become so long, now beginning two years before the presidential election, that anyone seeking the nomination must make campaigning their fulltime job. This means that the informal barrier of finances has become even more compelling.

The actual nominating process is a creature of the political parties. The candidate must win the nomination of his or her party at the national presidential convention. That means the majority of the delegates at that convention must vote for the aspiring candidate. How those delegates are selected is obviously the crucial factor. It is the political party that decides the number of delegates each state will receive and the state party decides, within certain national guidelines, how the delegates will be selected.

Delegates may be selected in one of two ways: by presidential preference primaries or by party caucus and conventions. Table 10.2 lists the delegate selection processes for both parties in all the states for the 1984 election. In the caucus and convention system, delegates who are chosen at the neighborhood level go to a county or legislative district convention where they choose delegates to a state convention, who then in turn select delegates to attend the national convention. Twenty-four states conduct presidential primaries in which voters may express a preference for one of the aspirants, and they actually select delegates to their party's nominating convention. But primaries come in a variety of forms. Table 10.3 computes the results of a presidential primary under three different sets of rules. As illustrated, the number of delegates each candidate receives is quite a bit different depending upon the type of primary system employed; the same is true of the caucus and convention system.

Following the tumultuous Democratic convention of 1968 in which Hubert Humphrey was nominated without entering a single primary, the delegate-selection process was reformed. The Democratic Party led, but the Republican Party also instituted some reforms. The reforms were intended to encourage participation by minorities and women and to make the process more responsive to the people. They were, at least rhetorically, attempting to be more "democratic." For awhile, the Democrats even had a 50 percent quota on female delegates, or male delegates, depending upon

TABLE 10.2
The Long, Long Road to Nomination

The House and Senate Democratic caucuses will meet, probably in January, to select 164 House Members and 27 Senators to serve as unpledged delegates to the national convention next July. The number of unpledged delegates allocated to each state will then be reduced by the number of Members of Congress chosen from those states.

	DEMOCRATS				REPUBLICANS		
	Delegates	Caucuses	Primary	Unpledged	Delegates	Caucuses	Primary
Alabama	62		March 13	March 31	38		March 13
Alaska	14	March 14		May 5	18	April 6, April 20–21, May 18–19	
Arizona	39	April 14		May 26	32	May*	
Arkansas	42	March 17, March 31		May 5	29	Jan.	
California	345		June 5	June 16	176	Feb. 4, Feb. 18	June 5
Colorado	51	May 7, May 17–June 6, May 27–June 17		June 9	35	May 7, May 17–June 6, June 16–July 18	
Connecticut	60		March 27	May 8	35		March 27
Delaware	18	March 14		May 24	19	Two weeks before state convention, Late May–early June	
D.C.	19		May 1	June 14	14		May 1
Florida	143		March 13	May 5	82	Jan. 24	March 13
Georgia	84		March 13	May 26	37		March 13
Hawaii	27	March 13		May 27	14	Jan.–April 20, April 20–May 1, May 13	March 13

State							
Idaho	22	May 24		June 14–16	21		May 22
Illinois	194		March 20	May 8	93		March 20
Indiana	88		May 8	June 5	52		May 8
Iowa	58	Feb. 27* April 7 May 5		June 9	37	Feb. 27* March 24 April 28 June 15–16	
Kansas	44	March 24 April 14		May 12	32	May–June	
Kentucky	63	March 17 March 31		April 14	37	March 10 March 17 May 11–12	
Louisiana	68		April 7	May 5	41	Jan.–March 15	April 7
Maine	27	March 4*		May 4–6	20	April 27–28	
Maryland	74		May 8	June 12	31	Jan. 11	May 8
Massachusetts	116		March 13	June 9	52	Jan. 27–28	March 13
Michigan	155	March 17 April 14		April 28	77		
Minnesota	86	March 20 April 7–15 May 4–6		June 15–17	32	March 20 April 2–21 May 5–19 June 14–16	
Mississippi	43	March 17 March 31 April 14		May 4	30	June 5*	June 5*

TABLE 10.2 (cont.)
. . . And the Caucus and Primary Stops Along the Way

	DEMOCRATS				REPUBLICANS		
	Delegates	Caucuses	Primary	Unpledged	Delegates	Caucuses	Primary
Missouri	86	April 17 May 1 May 22		June 2	47	March 31–April 7 May 5–12 June 8–9	
Montana	25	March 25		After May 1	20		June 5*
Nebraska	30		May 15	June 16	24		May 15
Nevada	20	March 13 April 13		May 4–6	22	Before April 5 Before April 10	
New Hampshire	22		March 6*	April 15	22	May 3–5	March 6*
New Jersey	122		June 5	June 16	64		June 5
New Mexico	28		June 5	June 9	24		June 5
New York	285		April 3	Date not set	136		April 3
North Carolina	88		May 8	June 16	53		May 8
North Dakota	18	March 14–28		April 13	18	Jan. 15–March 15 Feb. 1–March 15 April 5	
Ohio	175		May 8	Jan. 26*	89		May 8
Oklahoma	53	March 13 March 31 April 14		May 5–6	35	March 5 March 24 April 7 April 28	
Oregon	50		May 15	June 16	32		May 15
Pennsylvania	195		April 24	June 2	98		April 24
Rhode Island	27		March 13	June 11	14		March 13

State							
South Carolina	48	March 17 / March 26		April 14	35	Feb. / March / April 14	June 5 / May 1 / May 5
South Dakota	19		June 5	June 23	19	April 16	
Tennessee	76		May 1	May 19	46	May–June	
Texas	200	May 5 / May 19		June 15	109	June 30	
Utah	27	April 16 / April 26–May 31 / June 14		June 15	26	April 24 / May 19	
Vermont	17	April 24		May 26	19		
Virginia	78	March 24 or 26 / April 27–May 18		May 18–19	50	Jan.–March / March–May / June 2	
Washington	70	March 13 / April 21 or 28 / June 2		June 10	43	March 6 / April–May / July 14	
West Virginia	44		June 5	June 15	19		June 5
Wisconsin	89	March 31 / May 5		May 26	46		April 3
Wyoming	15	March 10* / March 13		Date not set	18	Feb. 4–March 5	
American Samoa	6						
Democrats Abroad	5		March 13				
Guam	7	mid-April			4	March or April	
Lat. Amer. Dems.	5	March 17					
Puerto Rico	53		March 18	April 29	14	Feb. 19*	
Virgin Islands	6	June 5			4	May 3*	

SOURCE: *The National Journal*, October 24, 1983, pp. 2218–2219. Reprinted by permission of National Journal, Inc.

*tentative

**TABLE
10.3**   *Different Primary Rules Yield Different Results*

	Winner Takes All	Proportional	Districted
Pennsylvania:			
Humphrey	182	66	93
Wallace	—	40	16
Muskie	—	38	34
McGovern	—	38	39
Ohio:			
Humphrey	153	78	96
McGovern	—	75	57
Indiana:			
Humphrey	76	40	49
Wallace	—	36	27

SOURCE: Adapted from "Primary Rules: Political Power and Social Change," by James I. Lengle and Byron E. Shafer, in *American Political Science Review*, Vol. 70 (March 1976), pp. 25–40. Reprinted by permission of the American Political Science Association.

how you look at it. It has since been removed, but minority and female participation is strongly encouraged. The automatic seating of party officeholders was greatly reduced, thus reducing their power to determine the nominee. Convention delegates were required to vote for their declared candidate, at least on the first ballot.

The upshot of these series of reforms did appear to be a more open and democratic convention. As a matter of fact, it appears that it got a little too democratic and much less controllable. More recent reforms have tried to reintroduce political party leadership control. For example, the Democrats set aside 566 uncommitted delegate slots for party officials and removed the binding rule for all delegates. They added a rule by which any nominee must receive at least 20 percent of the voting population in order to receive a delegate. The Reverend Jackson attempted to challenge this rule, but dropped it when it was clear it would not be changed. He realized that the rule works to the disadvantage of less well-known candidates. The point is that the rules help to shape the outcome, and the party leaders tend to make the rules.

The presidential primaries receive a lot of publicity as a progressive reform in the presidential selection process. However, their chief consequences are to encourage intraparty competition and divisiveness, to increase the cost of the election process substantially, and to create the often illusory impression that "the people" have a major voice in the selection of nominees. Again, it is the distribution of delegates that determine the selection, and the rules for distribution come from the party leadership.

Although occasionally the outcome may be uncertain, generally the decision has been made long before the national convention meets. It is in the delegate-selection process, and the rules for that selection and distribution, that the key to the presidential nominating procedure lies. Presidential nominating conventions now serve mainly as occasions for hoopla, party propaganda, and the *legitimization* of choices made earlier, as opposed to being key decisionmaking events.

Election

Let us consider some features of election campaigns that are distinctive to presidential elections. (The general account of electoral politics in Chapters 15 and 16 will elaborate on this.) It used to be standard wisdom that incumbent presidents enjoyed an advantage. For one thing, they could use press releases and other reports by the entire executive branch to create an impression of accomplishment, and recent presidents have increasingly done so. During the Nixon administration, approximately 60 people in the White House and 6,144 people in the executive branch worked on public relations, at a cost of $161,000,000 a year.[12] Figure 10.5 lists the public affairs employees at the time of the Carter administration.

Incumbent presidents may also spend federal funds to help them win renomination and election. In an effort to meet a challenge to his renomination, President Carter allocated $24.8 million in discretionary funds to Chicago in 1979. This was $7.8 million more than a presidential candidate is allowed to spend for the entire primary campaign.

The needs of news reporters make it all the easier for the incumbent regime to tout its activities. A sitting President also finds it easier to manage the news; public affairs are so wide ranging that even the wealthiest and most conscientious newspaper, television network, or wire service must rely on official releases for most of its information. Although pools of reporters follow all "serious" presidential candidates, the White House Press Corps is an ongoing institution. The President is *always* news, which means he receives a great deal of free air time. Non-incumbent candidates have more difficulty breaking the newsworthy barrier, but it can be done. The Reverend Jackson's trip to Syria and the subsequent release of the captured pilot gave him desperately needed free news coverage, and boosted his legitimacy as a "serious" presidential contender. Of course, he had to share that coverage with the incumbent in a carefully managed news conference in the majesty of the White House.

On the other hand, in the elections of 1976 and 1980, incumbent Presidents went down to defeat. This could have been due to a previously erected image built by the media over the administration's term. Asked in one study what they looked for in a President, people seemed concerned

---

[12] David Wise, *The Politics of Lying* (New York: Random House, 1973), pp. 188–213.

Figure 10.5. *An Overview of the Public Affairs Operations*

Trying to determine the budgetary and personnel figures of the department public affairs operations is something of an esoteric science, which so far has defied bureaucracy-wise analysts at the Office of Management and Budget (OMB). The following are the best available numbers at several of the major departments and agencies, compared with the first year of the Carter Administration.

Commerce—The department reports 240 public affairs employees, a sizable jump from the 170 of four years ago.

Defense—The current public affairs budget for the office of assistant secretary Henry E. Catto Jr. is $28 million, $4 million more than in 1977. This does not include the public affairs budgets for individual military services. Catto's immediate staff is listed at 304, a sharp reduction from four years ago.

Education—Its fiscal 1981 budget for the office of public affairs is set at $2.3 million, and its staff is listed at 55.

Energy—The current budget for the office of Robert C. Odle Jr., assistant secretary for congressional, intergovernmental and public affairs, is set at $20 million. Of that amount, $15 million is earmarked for community impact programs, Odle reports. He presides over a staff of about 250 but has been directed by OMB to cut it to 153. "That will take a lot of creativity," Odle conceded.

Health and Human Services—Its 1981 budget is $37.3 million, compared with $22.9 million in 1977. Personnel figures show 360 assigned to public affairs and another 340 in information and education programs. Assistant secretary Pamela Needham Bailey has a staff of 40, a few more than her predecessor in 1977.

Housing and Urban Development—Spokesmen maintain it has one of the smallest public affairs operations among the Cabinet departments. They report 36 people on the public affairs staff and operating costs of $1.7 million, about the same as last year.

Interior—Officials estimate the number of public affairs professionals in the department at 200, half of whom are in the field. The Secretary's public affairs budget is pegged at $800,000. But the department's total budget is reported to be about $6 million.

Labor—Its 1982 public affairs budget is placed at about $9.3 million, an increase from $7 million in 1977. The staff has remained level at an estimated 200.

State—Its public affairs budget is fixed at $5.5 million, almost $1 million more than in 1977. The department's manpower level has remained stable over the past several years, with 125 authorized positions in the public affairs office and 12 in the press section. In addition, there are more than 50 public affairs officers assigned to geographic and functional bureaus at the department.

Treasury—Assistant secretary Ann Dore McLaughlin has 19 people on her personal staff but expects to expand it to 24 with the addition of some writers, researchers and a press aide. In 1977, the office had 18 people. McLaughlin has a budget of $800,000, up only slightly in recent years.

Central Intelligence Agency—The agency admits to having 16 staff members in its public affairs office at its Langley (Va.) headquarters outside Washington. That is four more than in 1977. A spokesman reported that the office was expanded under former director Stansfield Turner at the very same time he was purging the ranks of the rest of the agency.

SOURCE: Dom Bonafede, "The Selling of the Executive Branch—Public Information or Promotion?" *National Journal*, June 27, 1981, p. 1156. Reprinted by permission of National Journal, Inc.

primarily with strength and toughness. Compassion was hardly mentioned.[13] Every landslide victory since Roosevelt's in 1936 was won by an incumbent who had coped or seemed to cope resolutely with a major crisis: Roosevelt with the Great Depression; Eisenhower with the ending of the Korean War; Johnson in 1964 with the War on Poverty and the aftermath of the Kennedy assassination; and Nixon in 1972 with the ending of the Vietnam War and detente with Russia and China. Their opponents, by contrast, were reputed to be indecisive or inconsistent (Landon, Stevenson, McGovern) or wild, trigger-happy, and therefore unreliable (Goldwater). The incumbents Gerald Ford and Jimmy Carter, however, appeared to be bumbling and somewhat incompetent (Ford) and indecisive and incompetent, especially with regard to the Iranian hostage situation (Carter).

Although the results of the 1980 presidential election campaign appeared dramatic—the defeat of an incumbent president and a landslide victory for Ronald Reagan, the deeper meaning of the campaign lay in other factors: its showing that a large part of the public is alienated from the electoral process; its encouragement of groups favoring conservative causes; and its discouragement of people advocating policy changes to help the disadvantaged and minorities and to reduce the burdens and the dangers of large military expenditures.

From the start of the 1980 campaign, it was clear that a great many voters were unhappy with the electoral choices available to them. Their indecisiveness was not due to apathy; there was deep popular discontent with high prices, high unemployment levels, and ineffectiveness in foreign policy. There were widespread doubts about the competence of Jimmy Carter and fears that Ronald Reagan might act rashly, become embroiled in nuclear war, and remain indifferent to the country's social problems. Until two days before the election, the polls showed the two candidates very close, with Reagan holding a lead smaller than the margin of error. At the last minute, the undecided vote went heavily to Reagan, some Carter supporters switched, and many people did not vote at all.

The wholesale last-minute switching, the large number of undecided people, and especially the upturn in nonvoting may in the long run be a more significant political development than the Republican victory. Only 52 percent of the eligible voters voted. Of that number, Reagan received 51 percent, meaning approximately 27 percent of those eligible voted for President Reagan. An exit poll conducted by the *New York Times* revealed that of that 27 percent, 10–15 percent were voting *against* Carter. This means that Reagan's "mandate" rested upon a positive vote of 17 percent of the American voting public. These are probably signs of voter alienation, and call into question the effectiveness of voting as a legitimizer of the regime for a great many Americans. They suggest that many people now doubt that presidential elections give them a significant voice. From one

---

[13] Doris A. Graber, ''Personal Qualities in Presidential Images: The Contribution of the Press,'' *Midwest Journal of Political Science* 16 (February 1972), pp. 54–55.

perspective, the 1980 election was a mandate for conservative policy directions; from another perspective, it was a signal of popular discouragement and anger.

The 1984 Presidential Election

The 1984 presidential election resulted in a massive personal triumph for President Ronald Reagan. The Republican candidate swept all but the state of Minnesota and the District of Columbia, producing a record total of electoral ballots and one of the most lopsided electoral ballot ratios in American history: 525–13. (See Table 10.4 for a state-by-state breakdown of the electoral and popular votes and a comparison with the 1980 electoral vote.) Reagan won 59 percent of the national popular vote. This total, though clearly decisive, fell below that of Richard Nixon in 1972 and Lyndon Johnson in 1964 (60.7 and 61 percent, respectively). The President's "coattails"—his ability to pull Republican candidates for the Senate, House, and state positions into office with him—did not reach very far. The Democrats actually gained two seats in the Senate, and emerged with a net loss of only 14 in the House, fewer than expected and half the number needed for a working Republican majority. As we will analyze in detail in Chapter 16, the election amounted to a broad-based show of support for Reagan, but not necessarily for his party or even his policies. Whether it could be used accurately as a "mandate" in the future would remain uncertain and controverted.

There was never any doubt about who the Republican nominee for the presidency in 1984 would be; rarely does an incumbent president face opposition for renomination, and certainly not the popular Reagan. In the Democratic Party, however, the situation was just the opposite. Walter Mondale, Vice-President in the Carter administration from 1977 to 1981, announced early that he would be a candidate. Many party officials and officeholders, and particularly the leadership of organized labor, made commitments to his nomination before the primaries even started. But Democratic primary voters were restive and volatile in their support of other candidates, with many in the so-called "baby-boom generation" supporting Senator Gary Hart of Colorado and some younger people and minorities behind the Reverend Jesse Jackson. With more financial support and more of the party regulars in his camp, however, Mondale won enough delegates in primaries and state conventions to lay claim to the nomination before the Democratic nominating convention even began.

In retrospect, it appears that the primary campaigns may have contributed to the later impressions of Mondale as a candidate who was not as strong, decisive, and competent as President Reagan. Both Hart and Jackson criticized Mondale as being weak, a captive of special interests, and a representative of the "old politics." Despite their later endorsement and support, some of their earlier characterizations seemed to linger on in (or were shared by) the public mind. An interesting sidelight on the primaries was the fact, reported in *The New York Times*–CBS News post-election poll

(*The New York Times*, Nov. 8, 1984, p. 11) that, although primary supporters of Mondale and Jackson continued their support for the Democratic
candidate in the final election by margins of more than 93%, more than
one-third of Senator Hart's supporters voted for Reagan. (See Table 10.5.)

Mondale's boldest and most decisive act was the selection of U.S.
Representative Geraldine Ferraro of New York as his vice-presidential running mate. When this choice was announced, and throughout the Democratic convention, emotional reactions among women ran high and there
appeared to be a chance that the Democratic ticket would draw significant
new support from women across the country. Soon after the convention,
however, the press and the media began to focus on Ferraro's finances
rather than on her positions on issues. Both the ways that she had financed
her earlier Congressional campaigns and her husband's income tax obligations came under the most intense scrutiny, costing her nearly a month of
precious campaign time and energy. When this issue receded, Ferraro
became the special target of anti-abortion hecklers at nearly every campaign appearance. Despite these problems, Ferraro showed herself a vigorous and effective campaigner, and was widely believed to have a promising
political future, even though the Mondale-Ferraro ticket ultimately lost the
election.

In the end, Mondale's gamble in selecting Ferraro did not appear to
make much difference to the outcome. A majority of women still preferred
President Reagan, although to a lesser extent than did men; the differences
that various polls showed in proportions of male and female support for
Reagan, moreover, remained at about the same levels as they had been
throughout Reagan's first term.

Another Mondale gamble seemed to backfire, even though most people concerned about the size of the federal deficit believed he might be
right. Mondale flatly declared that he would raise taxes to help cover the
deficit, and that Reagan would have to do the same. This charge drew
repeated denials from the President, who insisted not only that he would
not allow taxes to be raised but also that he would not allow Social Security benefits to the elderly to be cut in any way. The Republicans soon went
on the offensive, charging that Mondale was for higher taxes and bigger
government, the "old politics." Judging from the election results, those
allegations apparently stuck in many people's minds.

The presidential campaign of 1984 set new records for expenditures, as
television and other media were used to a greater extent than ever before.
Estimates of campaign expenditures varied, but $350 million is the level
most widely accepted, a $75 million increase over 1980. Most of it went to
the Republican Party, as always far more successful in fund raising than the
Democrats. Both parties made special efforts to register new voters and
bring them to the polls. Republicans seemed to do a bit better than Democrats in this respect, despite the many more nonvoters who prefer Democratic policies and programs. But the total of voters who actually turned
out to vote on November 6, 1984, was not much different than the bare
majorities of past years. Although a four- or even five-percentage-point

TABLE 10.4 Breakdown of the 1984 Presidential Election

STATE	1980 ELECTORAL VOTES Reagan	1980 ELECTORAL VOTES Carter	1984 ELECTORAL VOTES Reagan	1984 ELECTORAL VOTES Mondale	1984 POPULAR VOTE Reagan	1984 POPULAR VOTE Mondale
Alabama	8		9		851,978	546,070
Alaska	3		3		116,662	51,737
Arizona	6		7		676,715	331,548
Arkansas	6		6		532,950	337,783
California	45		47		5,305,434	3,815,992
Colorado	7		8		768,711	434,560
Connecticut	8		8		885,159	567,078
Delaware	3		3		151,494	100,632
D. of Columbia		3		3	26,805	172,459
Florida	17		21		2,582,980	1,397,097
Georgia		12	12		1,063,579	704,945
Hawaii		4	4		185,050	146,654
Idaho	4		4		296,687	108,447
Illinois	26		24		2,686,974	2,065,776
Indiana	13		12		1,332,681	814,659
Iowa	8		8		700,779	603,810
Kansas	7		7		675,366	332,476
Kentucky	9		9		819,045	536,888
Louisiana	10		10		1,030,091	648,040
Maine	4		4		336,113	212,190
Maryland		10	10		836,395	759,205
Massachusetts	14		13		1,297,737	1,226,490
Michigan	21		20		2,247,058	1,528,558
Minnesota		10		10	1,024,631	1,039,904
Mississippi	7		7		585,052	351,677
Missouri	12		11		1,268,408	838,599
Montana	4		4		214,382	135,172
Nebraska	5		5		447,810	184,058
Nevada	3		4		188,794	91,654
New Hampshire	4		4		262,191	118,941
New Jersey	17		16		1,914,942	1,255,115
New Mexico	4		5		305,425	200,958
New York	41		36		3,557,822	3,023,726
North Carolina	13		13		1,340,274	821,364
North Dakota	3		3		199,606	104,063
Ohio	25		23		2,655,395	1,805,845
Oklahoma	8		8		861,757	384,918
Oregon	6		7		645,308	512,080
Pennsylvania	27		25		2,572,472	2,213,429
Rhode Island		4	4		204,450	191,914
South Carolina	8		8		559,078	314,639
South Dakota	4		3		200,162	116,089
Tennessee	10		11		1,002,722	705,820
Texas	26		29		3,395,417	1,923,329
Utah	4		5		467,214	155,098
Vermont	3		3		134,252	94,518
Virginia	12		12		1,338,585	798,507
Washington	9		10		945,052	736,260
West Virginia		6	6		400,261	324,073
Wisconsin	11		11		1,198,379	992,807
Wyoming	3		3		132,073	53,272
TOTALS	489	49	525	13	53,428,357	36,930,923

TABLE
10.5   **The Makeup of the 1984 Vote**

CATEGORIES (PERCENTAGES OF THE 1984 TOTAL)	PERCENTAGE VOTING FOR	
	Reagan	Mondale
Men (47%)	61%	37%
Women (53%)	57%	42%
White (86%)	66%	34%
Black (10%)	9%	90%
Hispanic (3%)	33%	65%
18–29 years of age (24%)	58%	41%
30–44 years of age (34%)	58%	42%
45–59 years of age (23%)	60%	39%
60 and older (19%)	63%	36%
White Protestant (51%)	73%	26%
Catholic (26%)	55%	44%
Jewish (3%)	32%	66%
White born-again Christian (15%)	80%	20%
Union household (26%)	45%	53%
Under $12,500 in income (15%)	46%	53%
$12,500–24,999 (27%)	57%	42%
$25,000–34,999 (21%)	59%	40%
$35,000–$50,000 (18%)	67%	32%
Over $50,000 (13%)	68%	31%
Professional or manager (30%)	62%	37%
White-collar worker (13%)	59%	40%
Blue-collar worker (14%)	53%	46%
Full-time student (5%)	51%	48%
Teacher (6%)	55%	45%
Unemployed (3%)	31%	68%
Homemaker (14%)	63%	36%
Retired (11%)	62%	37%
Republican (35%)	92%	7%
Democrat (38%)	26%	73%
Independent (26%)	63%	35%
Liberal (17%)	29%	70%
Moderate (44%)	54%	46%
Conservative (35%)	81%	18%
1980 Presidential vote:		
Reagan (50%)	88%	11%
Carter (31%)	19%	80%
Anderson (5%)	29%	67%

SOURCE: *The New York Times*–CBS News Poll, as reported in *The New York Times*, November 8, 1984, p. 11.

increase had been predicted, the actual increase was only three-tenths of 1 percent, for a total turnout of 52.9 percent of the voting-age population. A total of 81 million people of voting age did *not* vote—a new record.

The Vice-President and Succession

The vice-presidency is a key office in the federal government, but only because there is a very good chance that he or she may become president, either because of the death of the President or by election at a later time. Nine vice-presidents have assumed the presidency upon the death of the President. In the twentieth century, four of the five who ran succeeded to the presidency by winning the office following their tenure as vice-president.

The Vice-President is formally the presiding officer of the Senate and may vote only on the rare occasions when there is a tie vote. This may, however, constitute an important power. In the 98th Congress, with the Republicans holding a slim majority in the Senate, Vice-President George Bush cast several key votes in aid of President Reagan's program. Vice-presidents have traditionally not been given important functions, although most presidents make some pretense of doing so. President Eisenhower, when asked near the end of his term to name a key administration policy in which Vice-President Richard Nixon had played an important role, replied, "Give me a week and maybe I'll think of one." A recent defender of the position, however, points out:

> Traditionally the Vice President was seen only in the Senate and heard nowhere. Since the New Deal, the political fortunes of the Vice President have become more closely tied to those of the Chief Executive. Consequently, Presidents have assigned him necessary political chores. Vice Presidents have become lobbyists for selected legislation, energetic party workers, frequent administration spokesmen, and presidential surrogates in primary campaigns. . . . in performing these functions he relieves the Chief Executive of time-consuming, and often undignified, responsibilities.[14]

The last two vice-presidents, Walter Mondale and George Bush, were given offices in the White House rather than the Executive Office Building, signaling an increase in vice-presidential importance. As one Reagan aide remarked: "In Washington, the EOB is Siberia."[15] However, even with increased status, the vice-presidency remains somewhat of a white elephant.

The Twenty-fifth Amendment, which was ratified in 1967, ensures

[14] Joel K. Goldstein, *The Modern American Vice Presidency: The Transformation of a Political Institution* (Princeton, N.J.: Princeton University Press, 1982).

[15] Sara Fritz and Robert A. Kittle, "The Power Brokers Around the President," *U.S. News and World Report,* February 9, 1981, pp. 19–22.

that there will be no lengthy period without a vice-president. The President responds to a vacancy in the vice-presidency by nominating a candidate who then takes office if confirmed by majority vote of both houses of Congress. Vice-President Spiro Agnew's resignation in 1973 brought this provision into play and President Nixon appointed Gerald Ford. Ford became President upon Nixon's resignation in August 1974 and in turn invoked the Twenty-fifth Amendment to appoint Nelson Rockefeller Vice-President. This exceptional sequence of events meant that for several years neither the President nor the Vice-President had been elected to their offices. This extraordinary state of affairs led to some criticism of the Twenty-fifth Amendment.

The major difficulty arises from the provision that the Vice-President is to serve as Acting President if the President is *unable* to perform the presidential duties. In case of the death of the President, succession is clear; the Vice-President assumes the office. From the Vice-President, the line of succession is as follows: Speaker of the House of Representatives, President Pro Tem of the Senate, and then by the members of the cabinet in the order in which their departments were established historically.

But the question of inability to serve is much less clear. Who determines "inability"? What does inability mean? The issue was most recently raised when President Reagan was shot in March, 1981. The President publicly attempted to show that he was "able" as soon as possible, by signing some letters and seeing his top aides the very next morning. But at the time when President Reagan's condition was uncertain, it took awhile to find Vice-President Bush, who was in Texas on a speaking tour. There was a period of several hours (which easily could have been days) when the President was clearly unable to perform his duties. During those hours, there was considerable confusion at the uppermost levels of the executive branch, which was compounded by a press conference where Secretary of State Haig announced that he was "in charge," contrary to any constitutional interpretation. These problems have not been resolved.

SUMMARY

The executive branch of the government is the place where broad national policy begins. The uppermost levels of our social and economic system find their most willing listeners in the presidency. The conflicts we discussed in Part II find their way onto the agenda, if not in presidential campaigns, then through Executive Office policy proposals. Members of the Executive Office and the cabinet often come from the policy-planning groups discussed in Part II, pp. 96–104. Members of the "establishment" personally occupy executive branch positions, moving back and forth between the public and private sectors. One of the executive branch's major powers is the power to set the agenda, define the problem, and then offer the appropriate solution.

It is, however, the President upon which most attention focuses. The President is an enormously powerful figure, because of his symbolic importance; his ability to define issues, problems, and crises; and his discretionary spending powers. Both constitutionally and traditionally, the executive power vested in the Chief Executive has expanded to the point where some scholars believe it has become "imperial."

On the other hand, there are other political, economic, and social power centers that even the President cannot flout arbitrarily. More often, the President responds to them by coordinating governmental, corporate, and military activities and by maintaining public support for the policies that further what have been defined as national objectives. Sometimes this means concessions to public groups that can bring political and economic pressure, sometimes it means explaining problems, and sometimes it means compromising and negotiating with the Congress.

In other words, it seems that the presidency, both in the personal form of the President and the institutional executive branch, is at its best in formulating and initiating broad national policy goals. The public and other political branches then respond. The next question is, what happens to a policy when it reaches the implementation stage? And so we go on to the bureaucracy.

CHAPTER 11

The Bureaucracy

Although the President, representatives, senators, cabinet members, and Supreme Court justices often appear in the headlines, what they do rarely has a direct effect on people's everyday lives. It is police officers, income tax auditors, welfare department caseworkers, field examiners for the National Labor Relations Board, customs officers, FBI agents, army sergeants, wheat inspectors for the Department of Agriculture, and thousands of other public employees, often in relatively lowly positions, who decide whether individuals and groups of individuals will be helped or hurt by the statutes, court decisions, and executive orders they apply and interpret.

THE NATURE, GROWTH, AND INFLUENCE OF THE BUREAUCRACY

Bureaucrats Make Public Policies

It is not true, as primary school textbooks sometimes assert, that administrators only "carry out" decisions made at the higher levels of the government. It is seldom possible for a President, legislature, or high court to make policies that take effect automatically and do not need to be interpreted in the course of application to a specific case. For example, Congress has directed the Federal Communications Commission (FCC) to grant and renew radio and television licenses so as to promote "the public interest, convenience, or necessity," but this legal phrase hardly specifies who gets licenses or what types of applicants are favored in grants of a scarce, influential, and very lucrative public resource. The real policymakers include FCC accountants who decide whether applicants have adequate financial resources, FCC engineers who decide whether a proposed station will interfere excessively with other stations, and FCC lawyers and other employees who decide whether proposed programs meet standards of fairness and balance.

A 55-mile-per-hour speed limit posted on a highway does not mean what it says if the highway police never issue tickets to anyone traveling less than 60 miles per hour, as is often the case; it means whatever the police officer chooses to do about it. An applicant for welfare benefits who is turned away by a caseworker at the welfare office does not benefit from the words in the law, even though a different caseworker might have interpreted those words in the applicant's favor.

Public administration, in short, involves discretion, and it involves politics as well, for administrators have a great deal to do with determining who gets what, when, and how. Administrators' decisions reflect the conflicts of interest that divide people. Should TV and radio licenses be awarded to applicants with ample financial resources to ensure the use of good equipment, or should they be awarded to applicants who represent diverse economic and social groups and diverse ideologies? In deciding thousands of such matters, administrators are making critical choices on politically divisive issues.

Bureaucrats are embroiled in politics in another way as well: their actions and the language in which they describe their policies *create* public opinion at least as much as they reflect what the public already thinks. Citizens are typically unaware of an issue until the news media bring it to their attention. It is often news about administrative actions that shapes what large numbers of people recognize as a problem and what they then think about it. A welfare administrator who was quoted as declaring it necessary to clear the chiselers off the welfare rolls is obviously creating the belief in many people's minds that many welfare recipients have no legal or ethical right to their benefits. He or she is intensifying conflict between resentful taxpayers and those who need or favor the current level, or higher levels, of welfare payments. Nor is the public's attention directed to related public issues such as whether people who are legally entitled to benefits are being denied them or whether welfare payments amount to a significant or a minimal drain on the public treasury relative to other politically controversial costs, such as armaments or space research. What the public statement implies may be accurate or inaccurate, but few who hear and react to it have access to any source of information other than the statement of a supposed authority on the subject.

Administrative *actions* often create public beliefs even more effectively than language, because their effect is more subtle. The sudden mobilization of troops or a military alert awakens fears that a hostile country is about to attack and so musters support for a larger armaments budget and greater influence on the part of military experts in foreign policy decisions. When the Department of Labor undertakes retraining programs to help the unemployed, its action encourages the belief that unemployment is due largely to the failure to match vacant jobs with those who have the skills to perform them. Although this belief is partly valid, it points to a relatively minor cause of unemployment and so may awaken false hopes in many trainees and false beliefs in the public in general.

Still another reason that administrative actions are a form of politics is that they are closely linked to outside pressure groups and to the opinions and demands of influential people. In favoring radio and TV license applicants with large financial resources, the FCC is taking a position that pleases the National Association of Broadcasters. When a state public utilities commission allows gas and electric companies to raise their rates several times in a single year, as many have in recent years, it is responding to pressure from the utilities and recognizing that the people who must pay the higher bills are neither organized to protect their interests nor able to refuse to pay. Decisions on controversial matters made inside a public administrative agency reflect the political clout of groups outside the agency that are helped or hurt by what it does; in turn, the agency's policies often *contribute* to the political power or weakness of outside groups.

The result is that administrative agencies are bound to reflect and also to *strengthen* the interests of groups that are already powerful. Although public bureaucracies maintain public support by claiming impartiality and expert knowledge, they use that support—with few exceptions—to further the goals of elites. That is the common theme of analyses of bureaucratic growth, structure, decisionmaking, and impact. Administrative agencies' claims that they simply "carry out" policies made by representatives of the people can be understood largely as a way of legitimizing administrative actions that further the goals of the economically and politically powerful. It will be clear from our analysis that many of the actions of the most controversial administrative agencies are taken without the knowledge or direction of legislative or executive superiors, and in some cases, they *violate* the law. To understand and predict such actions, a realistic analysis must focus on the groups with the power to influence the thinking, careers, and budgets of the agencies.

The Growth of the Bureaucracy

Throughout most of the nineteenth century, American federal, state, and local governments dealt chiefly with foreign relations and national defense, the prevention of crime, delivery of the mail, public schooling (especially in the primary grades), and the use and disposal of public lands. Governmental functions were few and simple relative to today, costs were relatively low, and the number of people needed to administer the laws was small.

The big increases in the number of people employed in government occurred in the second third of the twentieth century, when all levels of government acquired new functions that were made necessary by the development of an extremely complex industrialized economy, sharp increases in population, and a large shift of population from rural to urban areas. These changes brought about pressures on government to help both those who were benefiting from such changes and those who were suffering from the social problems that had become serious and chronic in the twentieth century: poverty, health problems, emotional disturbance, bad housing, and monotonous and unsatisfying work.

As a result, public employees today perform just about every kind of work found in private industry as well as some types that only governments undertake. Every professional, scientific, and managerial skill is represented, as is every form of unskilled labor. Public administrative activities include regulating and aiding industries, fighting wars, performing scientific research, running hospitals, prisons, and schools, and building roads.

Employees of the federal government account for only a small fraction of the number who perform these diverse governmental functions; there are close to 2.7 million civilian federal employees (counting the U.S. Postal Service) and well over 11 million employees of state and local governments. At least 7 million more work for private firms that are hired by governmental agencies to build highways and public buildings, manufacture equipment for the armed forces and space exploration, undertake research, and execute other public contracts (see Table 11.1).

TABLE 11.1   ***Paid Civilian Employment in the Federal Government, 1816–1983***

Year	Total	Executive Branch	Legislative Branch	Judicial Branch
1816	4,837	4,479	243	115
1851	26,274	25,713	384	177
1881	100,020	94,679	2,579	2,762
1901	239,476	231,056	5,690	2,730
1921[a]	561,142	550,020	9,202	1,920
1930	601,319	588,951	10,620	1,748
1940	1,042,420	1,022,853	17,099	2,468
1945	3,816,310	3,786,645	26,959	2,706
1950	1,960,708	1,934,040	22,896	3,772
1955	2,397,309	2,371,462	21,711	4,136
1960	2,398,704	2,370,826	22,886	4,996
1965[b]	2,527,915	2,496,064	25,947	5,904
1970	2,921,909	2,884,307	30,715	6,887
1975[c]	2,850,448	2,803,678	36,851	9,919
1978	2,838,806	2,786,873	39,148	12,785

SOURCE: U.S. Bureau of the Census, *Historical Statistics of the United States: Colonial Times to 1957* (Washington, D.C.: U.S. Government Printing Office, 1957), p. 710; *Statistical Abstract of U.S., 1975*, p. 243; and *1978*, p. 278.

[a] As of July 31.

[b] Includes 33,480 appointments under Youth Opportunity Company.

[c] As of January 31.

The Structure of the Federal Bureaucracy

Organizational charts, like Figure 11.1, call attention to the many different kinds of organizations in the executive branch and also depict legal and formal lines of authority; they tell us who can give orders to whom. Such charts are useful as long as the reader remembers that formal legal authority sometimes has very little bearing on real influence in the day-to-day operations of a governmental bureaucracy. As we have already noticed, an outside pressure group is often the key influence on a particular administrative agency, even though it does not appear on the organizational chart at all. And, as we will see in more detail later, subordinates often wield more real power than their superiors.

Organizational charts also oversimplify by making it look as though each governmental function is neatly assigned to a particular agency or subunit within an agency. In practice, governmental organizations' functions often overlap. Consider, for example, responsibility for monitoring of the activities of labor unions in foreign countries. Although the labor attaché assigned to each major American embassy is formally under the authority of the State Department, he or she is chosen largely by the Department of Labor, with the understanding that the AFL-CIO can veto choices it does not like. The attachés have frequently been CIA agents as well, and their reports and activities are often influenced by the concerns of the Department of Commerce, the Department of Labor, the Department of Defense, or the Council on International Economic Policy in the Executive Office of the President. When the British Labour party won an election in 1946 and unexpectedly came into power, the labor attaché in our London embassy was for a time the most influential member of its staff; he had already developed close ties with key people in the new Clement Atlee government, many of whom had trade union backgrounds, while senior embassy officials hardly knew them. Organizations must have formal and legal structures, but it is necessary to examine each situation to learn who calls the shots and how often.

Links to the President and Congress

Administrative agencies have various sorts of formal ties to the President and Congress. The President can remove heads of the cabinet departments at will, but members of independent regulatory agencies, like the Interstate Commerce Commission, can be dismissed only for specific causes, such as misuse of their official positions. The Federal Bureau of Investigation is a subdivision of the Justice Department, but its popularity and strong support on Capitol Hill have rendered it quite independent of its nominal superior, the attorney general, and to some extent even of the President. The Army Corps of Engineers, although officially subject to the Defense Department, enjoys similar independence because of the strong support of localities in which it can create jobs by building bridges, dredging rivers, and granting other favors that also win it independent congressional backing.

Some executive branch agencies are corporations owned by the gov-

Figure 11.1.   *The Government of the United States*

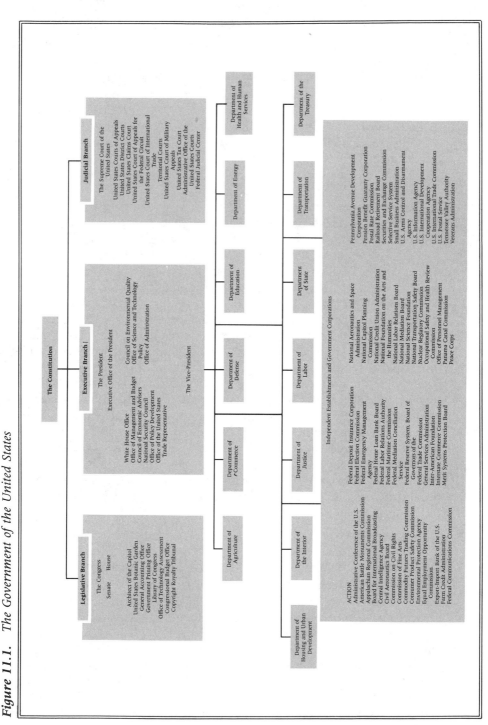

SOURCE: *U.S. Government Manual, 1983–84,* p. 808.

NOTE: This chart shows only the more important agencies of the government; many others exist.

ernment; one such is the Tennessee Valley Authority, which generates and sells electric power, guards against flooding by means of an intricate system of dams in seven southeastern states, manufactures fertilizers, and demonstrates good farming practices. Some are service organizations, like the General Services Administration, which performs housekeeping jobs (purchasing, building, storage of equipment) for other agencies. There are also research organizations, like the National Institutes of Health.

The Civil Service System

Government jobs can be dispensed to serve a number of different purposes. Until late in the nineteenth century, federal jobs were awarded to people who had actively supported victorious political parties and candidates. Jobs were part of the spoils of office, but the spoils system also encouraged people to work for political parties, which play an important part in any government. In 1883, Congress passed the Pendleton Act, which was intended to make ability rather than party or personal loyalty the criterion for choosing federal workers. The act established a Civil Service Commission to draw up detailed rules and regulations, and Congress gradually extended the merit system to cover more employees. By 1938, 80 percent of all federal employees were covered; in 1940, 95 percent were covered.

The top officials in each agency and those on whom the President relies for general policy advice are not part of the civil service. They are ordinarily chosen because the President likes their political beliefs or because their appointment to high posts is politically advantageous for the administration—not necessarily because of skill or expertise and certainly not because they score high on a competitive examination. Cabinet secretaries and assistant secretaries, commissioners in the regulatory agencies, top White House aides, ambassadors, and some other leading figures in the executive branch fall into this group.

There have been exceptions to the merit principle. Veterans, for example, receive preference for federal employment, as a result of lobbying by the American Legion. Some agencies, such as the CIA, are exempt from hiring by civil service criteria because they claim to have special requirements. The National Labor Relations Board, established in the 1930s to prevent employers from interfering with labor unions, was allowed in its early years to discriminate in hiring in favor of people who believed in the principle of union organization. A trend toward more comprehensive application of the merit principle has been apparent, however, even in many state and city governments.

DECISIONMAKING IN BUREAUCRATIC ORGANIZATIONS

Each administrative agency is formally charged with achieving some goal that the legislature has decided the people want: regulating public utility rates, ensuring that food and drugs are not contaminated, defending the nation, protecting citizens against crime, protecting lakes and air against pollution, helping cities build airports, ensuring fair incomes for farmers, protecting the interests of Indians, and thousands of comparable objectives. Most of the tasks that public administrative organizations undertake involve assembling complicated facts and deciding among the claims of people with diverse personal interests and conflicting values.

Such agencies, organized in a pattern we call "bureaucratic," are basically similar regardless of their field of operation. For one thing, they are hierarchical, which means that staff positions are ranked so that occupants of lower positions are formally subject to the authority of those in higher positions. The army, which is characterized by ranks running from commander in chief to private, is an especially clear example of a hierarchy.

The subunits into which a bureaucratic organization is divided are grouped so that each can devote its attention to a given topic and employ a staff that is qualified to deal with that topic. The Federal Communications Commission, for example, maintains a law department and an engineering department because every application for a broadcasting, telephone, or other communications license involves both legal and engineering questions. Sometimes an agency's organization reflects the variety of people or clients with whom it deals; thus, a welfare department may have separate subunits for the elderly, children, the handicapped, and so on. Specialization makes it possible to bring together staff members who supposedly have the skills to find the necessary facts and to interpret them.

But administrative decisions depend on more than facts. Values—judgments about what is good or bad, desirable or undesirable—also shape choices. It is commonly assumed that the laws an agency administers give it its values and that officials make judgments that will achieve those values in the particular policy areas for which they are responsible.

As an example, consider a typical National Labor Relations Board case in which an employer is charged with having fired a worker for taking an active role in a labor union. The law prohibits such a dismissal as an unfair labor practice. The employer admits to firing the worker, but says that the person was a poor worker and that union activities had no part in the firing. A relatively low-level NLRB employee, called a field examiner, is sent out to find the facts. The field examiner probably interviews the employer, the discharged employee, and other workers; examines the past history of labor relations within the company; compares the work record of the fired employee with those of other workers; and looks into any other evidence he or she can turn up. The field examiner then files a report containing the "findings of fact." Other NLRB offices review the report and add their own comments. If the case is not settled by informal agreement, as are more than 80 percent of unfair labor practice charges, another NLRB official presides over a hearing at which all interested parties testify and are cross-examined. He or she then files a report, including a decision on the legality of the firing. This report is reviewed by the five-member board, which may uphold it or overturn it. Finally, the board issues a legally binding finding and order. It may, for example, find that the employer did indeed commit an unfair labor practice and order the employee reinstated, with or without retroactive pay, or it may find that the firing was for incompetence and therefore did not violate the law.

Decision-making procedures vary in other kinds of NLRB cases and in other agencies. Some administrative decisions result not in judgments on the rights of particular individuals, but in general rules, such as a Department of Agriculture regulation specifying the proportion of adulterated matter allowed in grain intended for export. Both forms of administrative policymaking are based on the interpretation of facts in light of the values of those who make the decisions.

A realistic student of bureaucratic decisionmaking must realize that the values of an agency's staff members influence its policies no matter how high or low they rank in an organization. This is true even when administrators are supposed to limit themselves to finding facts. In the case just discussed, it is impossible for an NLRB field examiner to cast aside his or her own beliefs about unionism when deciding whether a complex set of acts in a plant amounts to antiunion discrimination; his or her conclusions are presented as facts and are bound to influence higher NLRB officials, who cannot reexamine every complaint themselves. Similarly, decisions by relatively low-level officials in American embassies are usually decisive in determining whether aliens wishing to come to the United States may do so. In making such decisions, the officials are supposed to consider the moral character of the applicant and any prior political activity that could be potentially harmful to the United States. Obviously, no one can make such decisions except in the light of his or her own value judgments; the precedents of many such judgments influence general State Department rules about which aliens may be admitted to America and which must be kept out.

Facts are never completely objective; the values of the people who perceive them shape their meanings. Thus, administrative decisionmaking is never the wholly impersonal, expert, professional process that bureaucrats often claim it is. The claim itself, however, is a way of mobilizing public opinion to support administrative policies. For example, people dislike paying higher rates for telephone service, but a public utility commission that lets the phone company increase its charges can assume that few citizens will seriously challenge its "findings of fact" about the company's need for higher earnings to cover higher production costs or future investments in equipment.

Although administrative agencies are therefore relatively free from strong pressures by consumers and unorganized clients, they must be responsive to pressures from interest groups whose resources give them political influence. Bureaucrats are in constant contact with the organized groups that have a stake in their policies. Many agency employees either begin their careers in such industries or are later employed by them. Studies regularly document the "circulation" of officials from industry to government and back again, and military officers with procurement responsibilities are often employed by defense suppliers and producers at a later date.

The typical result is that agency staff members come to see issues from the point of view of the groups they are supposed to regulate. It is never clear exactly how much such "regulation" is benefiting consumers and how much it simply authorizes industries to do what they would do anyway, legitimizing their actions with a governmental stamp of approval. Many studies of administrative regulation of business conclude that the second result is more common than the first.

Some bureaucratic organizations are established to help large groups of people who are politically and economically weak, rather than to regulate relatively small groups of people who are politically and economically strong. Welfare departments are set up to help the poor, public hospitals to help the sick, education departments to help people get educations, and the Bureau of Indian Affairs is supposed to protect the Indian population. These agencies do help, but they also *control* the politically powerless, making sure that they will not offend the economic interests, morals, and norms of the middle class.

Welfare agencies, for example, provide money to some who need it, offer counseling services that may assist people, and help clients find other governmental and private services that might be able to alleviate their problems. Yet the helping agencies regulate their clients as well. Welfare agencies are under constant pressure from conservatives and groups purporting to represent taxpayers to *limit* the money they give welfare recipients and to pressure them to take jobs, often on terms that other workers will not accept. Welfare counseling consists largely of pressure on the poor to adopt middle-class patterns of living, raising children, keeping house, and working industriously. Most children acquire a basic education in school, and some schools provide liberating education, but virtually all schools indoctrinate their students to play the social roles that employers, the government, armed forces, and/or the middle class expect of them: to work hard, to be loyal to superiors, and if necessary to sacrifice for the benefit of the state or the corporation. Hospitals and health departments help cure sick people, but when dealing with what they call "mental illness," they also regulate unconventional behavior, especially on the part of poor people, and drug or lock up nonconformists who resist efforts to make them conform.

This is, at least, the view of many critics. That supporters and critics of organizations to help the powerless see them so differently is itself an important political phenomenon; these agencies respond both to the groups they are established to help and to more powerful groups that want to be sure that such help is limited and accompanied by controls on unconventional and uncooperative behavior and rebelliousness. An agency head who is not sufficiently sensitive to such pressures becomes a target of public criticism and budgetary cuts, and is charged with coddling lazy people who refuse to work or failing to train students for practical work. Here again, the political analyst must be sensitive to the actual effects of

Capitol Games

SOURCE: © by James Stevenson.

administrative actions on people's lives, regardless of the formal goal of the agency in question.

Organizational Effectiveness

Every organization must adjust to the pressure groups that are concerned about its policies. This fact raises some important questions about administrative agencies' "effectiveness," suggesting that such judgments depend as much on the values of the student or observer of such organizations as on the agencies' acts. The Civil Aeronautics Board, for example, seems to be fairly effective in protecting the interests of the scheduled airlines through deregulation and otherwise, but how much protection it offers the airplane passenger and shipper is disputed. Whether it is judged a useful agency depends, therefore, on which of these goals is more important to the observer. In the same way, evaluations of a typical welfare agency depend on the relative importance to the observer of the various policies such an agency enforces. Administrative organizations reflect the values of the more powerful groups in the community and cannot survive for long if they try to do otherwise.

Bureaucratic organizations fall short of total effectiveness for another reason: they can almost never acquire enough information to make the best possible decision, regardless of whose interpretation of "best" is applied. Consider the problem facing the Secret Service, which is charged with protecting the President. Such an objective is much more specific and more widely supported by public opinion than are those of most other governmental organizations; thus, it ought to be relatively easy to make the necessary policy decisions. But is it? The only way to give the President virtually complete protection from an assassination attempt is to prevent *all* public appearances. But all presidents resist such an edict and so does much of the public, so the Secret Service must adopt other strategies, all of which involve far more guessing than knowledge.

- How can people who are likely to try to shoot the President be identified in advance?

SOURCE: From *Herblock on All Fronts*, New American Library, 1980.

- How much public support and opposition will there be for detaining such people as a preventive measure when they have not committed any crime?
- In what cities and situations are assassination attempts most likely?
- What qualities are most desirable in Secret Service agents?
- In choosing among strategies, none of which is foolproof, which will minimize public criticism of the agency if it fails?

These questions are a sample of those that Secret Service policymakers must ask themselves; moreover, they must make policies without ever having definite answers. When dealing with complex issues involving economics, military planning, and social policy, the uncertainty is far greater.

A Crackdown on Effectiveness: The Case of the Federal Trade Commission. Administrative agencies that can help or hurt groups of people financially are naturally subjected to pressures that reflect the political clout of those groups. Such pressures explain administrative actions and inactions better than do the laws that create the agencies and give them their formal goals.

Congress established the Federal Trade Commission (FTC) in 1914 to protect consumers by encouraging business competition and by preventing misleading advertising. Throughout most of its history, the commission was known as a timid agency, and contented itself with token actions and wrist slaps against offending companies. But in 1975, Congress dramatically increased the commission's power. The Magnuson-Moss Act empowered the FTC to set standards for an entire industry rather than having to take on one firm at a time. At about the same time, some new appointments to the commission, especially that of Chairman Michael Pertschuk, infused the FTC with the willingness to enforce the laws effectively. During the next several years, it issued regulations that required funeral home operators to disclose burial costs to grieving relatives; investigated suspected price fixing by some billion-dollar-a-year agricultural cooperatives; found some insurance companies guilty of selling millions of dollars worth of virtually worthless policies, especially to the poor and the elderly; proposed a rule that would give consumers information about major mechanical and safety defects in used cars; and proposed rules for other powerful industries as well.

The corporations affected by these actions charged that the FTC was engaging in "overregulation"; they brought pressure on Congress, which responded by considering a number of measures that would gut or kill the Commission. By a variety of means, Congress made clear its determination that the FTC should "back off" from such aggressiveness. Thus, legislative threats, and also presidential disapproval, send clear messages to regulatory agencies that they should be wary about offending powerful interest groups by actually enforcing the laws they are supposed to enforce.

Conflicts Among Powerful Interests

Agencies sometimes clash with one another over policy. The Department of Labor, for example, is traditionally sensitive to the concerns of unions and of the AFL-CIO leadership; the Department of Commerce, which maintains close ties with the National Association of Manufacturers, the U.S. Chamber of Commerce, and the Business Roundtable, can be counted on to reflect the concerns of businesspeople. When the President is considering measures to curb inflation, therefore, it can be taken for granted that the secretary of commerce will favor effective controls on wages, while the secretary of labor will be more sensitive to the political problems arising from the unions' distaste for tight wage controls. But the latter will be more willing than Commerce Department officials to support controls on industrial prices.

The Labor Department can do little to promote unions' interests with regard to many issues of grave concern to workers, because it has no jurisdiction over these issues. In a time of high unemployment, for example, the department has no power to expand the credit and money supply or otherwise encourage an upturn in business activity that would mean more jobs for the unemployed; the Federal Reserve Board, which does have such powers, includes no representatives of unions, although the law specifies that industry, banking, and agriculture must be represented on the board. The Federal Reserve Board is therefore bound to be more sensitive to businesses' and banks' concerns about inflation and decline in the value of the dollar than to workers' concerns about unemployment, especially because the policies that cut unemployment sometimes promote inflation.

An especially dramatic example of infighting among administrative agencies responsive to conflicting interests was the War on Poverty in the 1960s. The Office of Economic Opportunity, which was established in 1964 to help the poor, was staffed largely by people who were dedicated to pursuing that goal with considerable zeal. In many cities, agencies established by OEO aroused the opposition of local welfare departments, mayors, and other units of city and county government by bringing legal actions to force the latter to put more people on the welfare rolls and to end long-established policies that allegedly discriminated against the poor. Opponents of OEO eventually succeeded in dismantling some of its programs and in transferring others to different agencies.

Bureaucratic Budgets and Policy Choices: Routines or Reassessments

Officials of any given administrative agency typically take it for granted that in the coming year the agency will continue to do as it has been doing, with minor changes that justify a somewhat higher budget. The previous year's appropriation is almost always the benchmark for deciding how much money the government will spend on the agency's programs. Reassessment of an established program seldom takes place to determine whether it ought to be drastically expanded, reduced in size, or eliminated entirely; to do so would require time and effort that are seldom available. Furthermore, administrators do not want to challenge the policies that give them their roles, jobs, and sense of accomplishment; also, they know that there is rarely any chance of winning executive and legislative support for drastic expansion. At best they can make a case for more funds to handle an increased workload, rising costs, or other relatively small additions—a budgeting strategy known as *incrementalism*.

The interest groups concerned with an agency's field of operations are a known political force with which the agency has established a more or less stable relationship; some of these groups, however, can be counted on to resist reductions in its program, while others are just as certain to resist expansion of its program. A proposal to halve the budget of the Food and

Drug Administration, for example, might be welcomed by drug and food manufacturers, but would quickly elicit charges of a sellout from consumers and the opposition political party. Interest-group concern is therefore another reason why major changes in the scope of an ongoing program are rare. The expedient course for everybody concerned is to treat most budgetary decisions as routine.

That strategy is safe, easy, and almost always adopted, but it is by no means neutral with regard to who gets what. Supporters of incrementalism make the following kind of case for it:

1. It is an efficient way of making most decisions, because it builds on past decisions; it would be wasteful—in fact, impossible—to reassess past decisions about the importance of each program every year or two.
2. It minimizes conflict. To accept last year's appropriation as generally appropriate means that conflicts over the basic worth of the program are not raised or fought repeatedly. Political argument is limited to marginal issues, such as whether the Federal Aviation Agency should be allowed to increase its spending for the improvement of electronic landing devices at commercial airports. Whether the government *should* be subsidizing commercial airlines by providing them with electronic landing devices is not raised as an issue.

Decisions, in short, are made relatively easily and usually without divisive, bitter, or ideological disputes.

The opponents of incrementalism use the same observations to criticize it. It is, they say, a strategy for ignoring critical political issues while focusing on the relatively trivial ones with which incremental change is concerned. For this reason, it is undemocratic and conservative in its consequences, while pretending to be democratic and liberal in its procedures and forms. Incrementalism also makes it likely that ineffective programs will continue and even expand as long as no powerful group has reason to attack them, and budget drafters' systematic focus on minor changes rather than basic programs makes it unlikely that administrators will evaluate their effectiveness either.

Regardless of the opposing arguments, incrementalism continues to be the characteristic strategy of the great majority of programs. The exceptions are chiefly emergency policies, such as those adopted in response to wartime needs, steep inflationary surges, or major depressions.

Even deliberate efforts to abandon the incremental strategy seem to have a way of flickering out. In the mid-1960s, for example, President Johnson ordered that a system of evaluating administrative programs called Planning, Programming and Budgeting (PPB) be adopted in all federal agencies. PPB emphasizes evaluation of the contribution of every expenditure to the achievement of specific objectives. It is designed, in short, to force administrative staffs to consider in a systematic way everything they do, rather than to rely on routine incremental increases. But within a few years PPB was judged a failure and largely abandoned. It did require agencies to present their budgets in a new form, but the language used to present and justify such budgets changed more than did the agencies' acts or the care with which they assessed their goals and achievements. Here is added evidence that political pressures and values continue to influence administrative policies despite commands from on high. From all this experience, there developed some well-established lore about the inevitability of bureaucratic independence and intransigence. But much of that was suddenly challenged by the advent of the Reagan administration.

THE REAGAN REVOLUTION

When President Reagan took office in January, 1981, he was committed to several goals that had been themes of his campaign: to reduce the size and cost of the national government, to sharply increase military expenditures, and to deregulate business. To most observers, these goals seemed contradictory and quite unlikely to be realized. Much of the national government budget was legally obligated in the form of "entitlements," which meant that the government was already legally committed to providing levels and kinds of financial support that would in the nature of things steadily rise year after year. The bureaucracy was famous for defeating presidents' efforts to gain control over it and manage its activities to suit their priorities and goals. Besides, the Congress seemed certain to prevent any major changes in the usual patterns of allocation of federal funds. In short, there were too many ways in which inertia and political opposition could block change, and too many well-established groups and interests with experience in defending their gains to believe that this President would fare any better than his predecessors.

But President Reagan proved remarkably successful in reshaping the government toward his goals. Whether one approves or disapproves of those goals, Reagan must be recognized as having achieved more in the way of changing the priorities and practices of the standing bureaucracy than any president since Franklin Roosevelt. The government in Washington is very different than it was when Reagan came to office, and it literally may never be the same again. Many long-lived "principles" of bureaucratic imperviousness seem to be much less certain than they were before, and other widely-shared assumptions have simply been discarded.

In this section, we shall look primarily at some readily visible and tangible measures of the changes that have been accomplished, and particularly at spending and employment figures. Qualitative measures—those addressed to less tangible factors such as the attitudes, job priorities, and actual behavior of appointed officials and their lower-echelon employees—would probably show significant additional dimensions of change. In addition, it should be recognized that all this has been achieved in a single term, and in the midst of the worst recession since the Great Depression of the 1930s.

**TABLE
11.2**   *National Government Finances Compared with GNP, 1979–87*

Fiscal Years	GNP ($ Current)	Revenues	Deficit	Total Debt
			(as Percentage of GNP)	
1979	2,357.7	19.7	1.7	35.4
1980	2,575.8	20.1	2.9	35.5
1981	2,882.0	20.8	2.7	34.8
1982	3,057.3	20.2	4.2	37.5
1983	3,228.8	18.6	6.4	42.8
1984	3,558.7	18.8	5.6	44.7
1985	3,890.1	19.2	5.0	47.0
1986	4,231.3	19.3	4.4	48.9
1987	4,589.3	19.3	4.1	50.5

SOURCE: *The Budget in Brief, FY 1985*, Table 8, p. 82.

The Size and Cost of the National Government. The size of the national government is often measured simply in terms of how much it costs to conduct the business of the government. Many conservative economists focus on the amount of revenues that the national government requires to be withdrawn from the private economy in the form of taxes each year. They see this as the burden that government imposes on the economy, and argue that this is the key figure that should be forced down as low as possible. They also believe in balancing the revenues and spending of the government, and in reducing the national debt (the accumulated borrowing made necessary by "deficits," or excesses of spending over revenue in previous years).

In these areas, President Reagan has traded unbalanced budgets and increased national debt for lower levels of revenue withdrawn from the economy in taxes. In part, this is a result of his "supply-side" approach, which is described in Chapter 13, but it means that the "burden" of the national government on the economy is lower in one sense, because its revenue needs are lower *when computed as a proportion of the total Gross National Product of the economy.* In other words, although the total dollar amount of the national budget and the revenues associated with it are increasing every year, the GNP is increasing at a faster rate and the ratio of revenues withdrawn is below that of the Carter administration.

Table 11.2 shows these trends. In each case, the revenue, deficit, and total debt figures are shown as proportions of the nation's GNP, which is the only meaningful way to compare these totals over time. The later years shown are estimates only, of course, and may be optimistic (as presidents' budgets normally are) in setting relatively high total GNP and relatively low deficit figures. What the table demonstrates is that federal revenues have been held below the levels of the late 1970s and early 1980s, and remain roughly stable. The federal deficit, however, is rising sharply, and as a result the total debt is also. The size of the federal government, therefore, as measured by *total* costs imposed on the economy, is thus higher than in the 1970s and shows little sign of decreasing. In this category, the Reagan achievement is an ambiguous one.

There is no doubt, however, about the President's success in reducing the size of the government when it is measured in terms of civilian employees.[1] By October, 1982, at the close of the first full fiscal year after taking office, the Reagan administration had reduced the federal work force by a total of nearly 5 percent. Some agencies were down quite sharply, while others were up. Big losers were Education (down 25 percent), Transportation (down 14 percent), Commerce (down 26 percent), Labor (down 21 percent), Energy (down 19 percent), and Health and Human Services (down 9 percent). In contrast, Defense was up 4 percent and the Selective Service System was up 65 percent.

Table 11.3 shows civilian employment totals as they were projected into the future by the President's proposed 1985 budget. For almost every agency, the trend continues down, and for those out of favor, the decline is steep. The Defense Department and Veterans' Administration, and agencies having to do with international affairs, gain in employees. The net result, however, if the estimates prove to be accurate, would be a total reduction in federal civilian employees of more than 6 percent between January 1981 and October 1986.

Reallocation and Military Expansion. In both of the measures just employed—dollar costs and number of employees—there is much more going on than mere reduction in totals. The more powerful factor at work is *reallocation* of funds and personnel between departments and agencies. Dramatic changes in the size and character of particular units of the executive branch are concealed within the net totals. The latter are important enough, but still far from indicative of the changes that are occurring. The story of the Reagan administration's impact lies in the reallocations that have been accomplished in order to achieve the expansion of the military that was such a paramount goal of the President's 1980 campaign.

Table 11.4 illustrates these reallocations by comparing the shares of the federal budget allocated to various functions over the fiscal years from 1977 to 1985. Energy expenditures, for example, which once rose as a share of the national budget total, are now declining sharply and by 1985 will be less than a quarter of what they were at the end of the Carter administration. In 1985, both education and natural resources and the environment will have shares that are less than half of what they were in 1979. (Some of the social consequences of these cuts in domestic spending will be examined in Chapters 13 and 14.) Social Security and Medicare, on the other hand, are much harder to cut back. A combination of increasing numbers of elderly people and their political power has meant that the Reagan administration has succeeded only in slowing the rise of the share of national expenditures that goes to such purposes.

The most significant increases, however, are in the share of the budget

---

[1] All data in this paragraph are drawn from *The U.S. Budget*, Fiscal Year, 1984.

that goes to national defense uses. A steady increase involving tens of billions of dollars annually has been implemented in the midst of a deep recession and all the political support that the competing domestic programs could mobilize. The share of the budget going to the military has risen about 25 percent since 1980, and has surpassed Social Security and Medicare as the leading object of national expenditure. The proportion committed to the military will continue to rise in the future; estimates are that it will reach 31.3 percent in 1986 and 32.6 percent in 1987. In dollar amounts, this means budget authority of more than $313 billion in 1985 and nearly $400 billion in 1987.[2]

Figure 11.2 shows how this rising share and dollar investment will be employed through 1987. The largest increase is in conventional forces, particularly rising pay and benefits for military personnel and procurement of new aircraft and other equipment. The increases in strategic forces are chiefly the planned investment in the MX missile system.

These vast sums and the increasing priority that is given to them suggest that the Defense Department is a unique bureaucratic entity within the U.S. government, one that justifies a brief digression. For most of American history, the military was very small and organized in separate war and navy departments. After the vast expansion of World War II, however, the Congress created the integrated Department of Defense with army, navy, and air force components. This organizational change occurred at a time when domestic shifts were also taking place in the nature and frequency of American involvement in wars and in the importance to the American economy of the production of goods for military use. Fear of attack from abroad and preparation for war are, of course, the justification for having a Department of Defense and the basis of popular support for the department and the armed forces. Since World War II, American involvement in wars has been more frequent, and these wars have lasted longer. Equally important, the definition of Russia, China, and other foreign countries as ideological threats to the United States has accustomed the American public to the idea of "cold war"—to the belief, that is, that very high levels of armament, tough military postures, resistance to diplomatic concessions, and readiness to go to war at any moment are necessary to prevent a Communist takeover of the free world. The cold war, interrupted by frequent shooting wars and American intervention in wars in various parts of the world, keeps the public anxious and supportive of the large defense budget and gives military considerations a dominant place in the formulation of all governmental policies. The department constantly publicizes foreign threats; critics charge that it helps create them by frightening potential adversaries into increasing their own military budgets so they will not fall too far behind the United States.

The Department of Defense spends about 30 percent of the total U.S. government budget and almost two-thirds of the executive branch budget. It employs about 1 million civilians, well beyond the work force of General

---

[2] *The Budget in Brief,* FY 1985, p. 31.

TABLE 11.3
Full-Time Equivalent of Total Federal Civilian Employment in the Executive Branch[1]
(Excluding the Postal Service)

	FISCAL YEAR				
	1982 Revised Budget Estimate[2]	1983 Actual[3]	1984 Estimate	1985 Estimate	1986 Estimate
Agriculture	121,000	109,773	108,900	107,400	107,400
Commerce	36,300	32,715	33,505	32,507	33,095
Defense—civil functions	32,100	30,973	29,088	29,034	29,034
Education	6,600	5,360	5,189	4,979	4,749
Energy	18,700	16,984	16,757	16,042	15,711
Health and Human Services	154,000	141,715	137,321	130,445	127,184
Housing and Urban Development	15,700	13,779	12,878	12,442	12,073
Interior	81,700	73,451	73,232	72,826	72,826
Justice	54,400	55,686	58,748	60,473	61,488
Labor	21,600	18,968	19,246	18,634	18,697
State	22,900	23,786	24,759	25,442	25,744
Transportation	68,100	61,752	62,000	61,369	60,468
Treasury	124,300	118,507	125,526	122,522	122,400
Environmental Protection Agency	12,900	10,883	11,598	12,298	12,298
National Aeronautics and Space Administration	22,700	22,246	22,000	22,000	22,000
Veterans Administration	209,600	216,848	219,347	221,555	222,677

Other:

Agency for International Development	5,600	5,169	5,201	5,108	4,983
General Services Administration	32,800	28,591	29,128	28,812	28,209
Nuclear Regulatory Commission	3,400	3,403	3,416	3,491	3,491
Office of Personnel Management	6,600	5,601	5,837	5,822	5,822
Panama Canal Commission	9,100	8,636	8,578	8,490	8,525
Small Business Administration	4,700	4,231	4,200	4,100	3,900
Tennessee Valley Authority	44,700	35,646	35,500	36,000	36,000
United States Information Agency	7,600	7,906	8,356	8,810	8,897
Miscellaneous	45,000	39,625	39,853	39,578	39,199
Contingencies	1,000				
Estimated nondefense lapse			−13,752	−8,176	−5,434
Subtotal	1,163,100	1,092,034	1,086,411	1,082,003	1,081,436
Defense—military functions[4]	937,700	984,806	995,499	1,002,823	1,003,000
Total	2,100,800	2,076,840	2,081,910	2,084,826	2,084,436

SOURCE: Reprinted from *U.S. Budget in Brief, FY 1985*, Table 9, p. 82.

[1] Excludes developmental positions under the Worker-Trainee Opportunity Program (WTOP) as well as certain statutory exemptions.

[2] As contained in the revised 1982 Budget, transmitted to the Congress in March 1981.

[3] Data are estimated for portions of Defense—civil functions as well as for the Federal Reserve System, Board of Governors and the International Trade Commission.

[4] Section 904 of the 1982 Defense Authorization Act (Public Law 97–86) exempts the Department of Defense from full-time equivalent employment controls. Data shown are estimated.

TABLE 11.4
Internal Reallocation of Federal Spending, FY 1977–85

FISCAL YEAR	TOTAL BUDGET ($ CURRENT)	PERCENT OF BUDGET ALLOCATED TO:				
		National Defense	*Energy*	*Natural Resources & Environment*	*Education*	*Social Security & Medicare*
1977	400.5	24.3	1.0	2.4	5.2	26.0
1978	448.4	23.4	1.3	2.5	5.9	26.0
1979	491.0	24.0	1.4	2.5	6.0	26.6
1980	576.7	23.6	1.1	2.4	5.3	26.1
1981	657.2	24.3	1.6	2.1	4.8	27.2
1982	728.4	25.7	0.6	1.8	3.6	27.8
1983	796.0	26.4	0.5	1.6	3.3	28.0
1984	853.8	27.8	0.4	1.4	3.4	28.1
1985	925.5	29.4	0.3	1.2	3.0	28.1

SOURCE: *The Budget in Brief, FY 1985*, Table 3, p. 71. (Calculations by authors.)

Motors, the largest private employer, and about half of all the civilians employed by the U.S. government. In addition, the armed forces account for roughly another 2 million employees. The impact of this huge civilian-military apparatus on the government and the society is genuinely hard to grasp. It has major social and economic consequences, only some of which can be effectively described in concrete terms.

In combined past-present terms, the total expenditure is a massive burden. Literally trillions of dollars have been invested in direct military spending over the past decades, and the investment is now running at the rate of more than $300 billion per year, or a trillion dollars every three years. The words of a 1970 critic are still applicable today:

> Each year the federal government spends more than 70 cents of every budget dollar on past, present, and future wars. The American people are devoting more resources to the war machine than is spent by all federal, state, and local governments on health and hospitals, education, old-age and retirement benefits, public assistance and relief, unemployment and social security, housing and community development, and the support of agriculture.[3]

One obvious current consequence is the impact of military spending on the economy. For one thing, an entire new industry has been created since the end of World War I. New companies, some of which do all or nearly all of their business with the government, have been created to supply military needs. Fewer than thirty companies regularly receive about half of all defense procurement dollars, and the hundred largest contractors average about three-quarters of all procurement spending. But thousands of smaller firms depend heavily on subcontracts for military production,

---

[3] Richard Barnet, *The Economy of Death*, (New York: Atheneum, 1970), p. 5.

Figure 11.2. *National Defense Budget Authority, FY 1977–87*

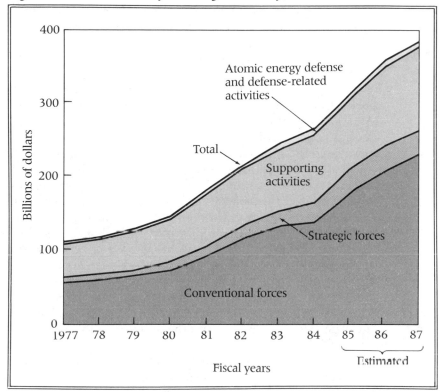

Atomic energy defense
and defense-related
activities

Total

Supporting
activities

Strategic forces

Conventional forces

Billions of dollars

400

300

200

100

0

1977 78   79   80   81   82   83   84   85   86   87

Fiscal years

Estimated

SOURCE: Reprinted from *U.S. Budget in Brief, FY 1985*, p. 31.

NOTE: Military retired pay is included in supporting activities through 1984. In 1985 and later years, military retirement costs are calculated on an accrual basis and are distributed to all categories.

and perhaps 20,000 do some kind of work for the Defense Department.

This suggests that defense spending represents a major government prop for the economy, and one that puts an important sector of the economy into a very dependent relationship with the government. This relationship is what the outgoing President Dwight Eisenhower once referred to as the danger of a "military-industrial complex" whose interests might combine to force increasing militarization upon the country. It also implies that some sections of the United States benefit much more from military expenditures than others. Bases and manufacturing plants tend to be located in the South and Southwest; Florida, Texas, and California alone account for about one-third of all military spending. Such areas may well become dependent on the government's military spending for their economic well-being.

The sale of American weapons abroad is also a major factor in the American political economic situation. Providing American arms helps to make another country more dependent upon the United States, and leads to close relationships between their armed forces and ours. It also provides a market for American producers, such as aircraft manufacturers. Arms sales currently make up about one-tenth of all exports, and help to improve our precarious balance of trade with other countries.

Military spending also represents decisions *not* to spend the same money for other purposes. The difference between $1 billion spent in the standard pattern of military expenditure and the same amount left for consumers to spend in their usual pattern would mean a net loss of 12,000 jobs, according to economists working for the International Association of Machinists.[4] For the economy as a whole, the purposeful expenditure of federal dollars could create many more jobs in other industries than is possible in the capital-intensive military manufacturing industries.

The overall pattern of job loss and gain in the economy because of military spending is shown in Table 11.5. The assumptions and methods used to produce the table's estimates are given in the notes to the table, and are important to understanding it. What this analysis indicates is that the Defense Department's allocation of $154 billion in 1981 cost the U.S. economy a net loss of 1,520,000 jobs, with the principal losses and gains in the major industries shown. This finding stands in sharp contrast to the often-argued point that military spending *creates* jobs. It does, but the tradeoffs involved apparently eliminate many more jobs than are created. This is because military spending involves more technology and less labor, and creates fewer jobs as it reverberates through the economy, than does the equivalent consumer spending.

Other economic consequences from increased military spending include reduced civilian investment, and ultimately a lower level of competitive advantage in the world economy. Civilian producers must compete for engineering talent and for investment dollars with a heavily-funded government program. Research and development dollars and personnel are diverted away from non-military applications. In the period 1980–85, for example, the ratio of dollars devoted to military versus all other research and development shifted from about equal to more than two-to-one in favor of military research. If some major share of the current military investment were made available for rebuilding the nation's roads, bridges, and water and sewer systems, for example, the result in jobs, economic activity, and long-term advantages might be substantial, but the choice made was to expand the military and the Defense Department, in order to counter the perceived Soviet threat.

Deregulation of Business. One of President Reagan's first actions was to appoint a task force on deregulation, which was headed by the Vice-President. Every agency was asked at the same time to eliminate all unnecessary regulations, and to review existing regulations to see where they could be made less onerous. Over time, new personnel appointments began to infuse the independent agencies as well as the executive branch departments with attitudes that were more responsive to business.

---

[4] Employment Research Associates, "The Price of the Pentagon," (Lansing, Mi.: Employment Research Associates, 1982), p. 1.

TABLE   *Impact (Net Job Loss or Gain) of 1981 Defense Budget*
11.5   *on Major U.S. Industries*

	Net Job Loss or Gain
Net Loss Industries	
Agricultural products and processed foods	− 85,000
New residential construction	− 116,000
Lumber & wood products	− 70,000
Textiles & clothing manufacturing	− 260,000
Newpapers & publishing	− 31,000
Motor vehicles	− 206,000
Primary metals	− 35,000
Fabricated metals	− 45,000
Transportation	− 15,000
Retail Trade	− 585,000
Wholesale Trade	− 66,000
Services	− 76,000
Banking, insurance, and real estate	− 184,000
Net Gain Industries	
Ordnance & guided missiles	+ 132,000
Aircraft	+ 189,000
Shipbuilding	+ 39,700
Radio & communications & electronic eqpt.	+ 159,000
Net loss of jobs:	−1,520,000

SOURCE: Derived from "The Price of the Pentagon," (Lansing, Mi.: Employment Research Associates, 1982), pp. 3–6.

METHOD OF COMPILATION: The authors of the cited publication first used Bureau of Labor Statistics data on how consumers respond to incremental changes in their income to determine how consumer expenditures would decrease as money was transferred to the federal government's defense spending. The Bureau's "input-output" model of how consumer demand affects output in various industries was then used to determine how many jobs would be created or displaced in those industries. For example, a demand for cars has an impact on steel, rubber, and other sectors of the economy, and a particular amount of new demand for cars creates a specific number of jobs in those industries. The same model was then used to determine how many jobs would result from military expenditures, and the two totals were compared to reach the judgments indicated. See pp. 1–2 and 12 of "The Price of the Pentagon."

Table 11.6 compares the budgets and operating personnel of some of the major regulatory agencies in 1981, the year in which President Reagan came to office, and 1983. It should be remembered in interpreting this table that each one of these agencies had experienced a steady rise in both budget and personnel over the previous decade. This growth *averaged* more than a *tenfold* increase in dollars and almost a *doubling* of personnel employed. The impact of the Reagan changes is thus even more dramatic than might appear from the reductions evident in almost every case.

Once again, it is easier to measure the tangible changes in a systematic way than it is to assess such qualitative changes as the vigor with which inspections are conducted, the imagination with which affirmative action

TABLE
11.6   Regulatory Agency Changes, FY 1981 to FY 1983

	CHANGE, FY 1981 TO FY 1983 (IN PERCENTAGES)	
AGENCY	Spending	Personnel
Civil Aeronautics Board	−45	−24
Equal Employment Opportunity Commission	+ 9	− 6
Environmental Protection Agency	−15	− 6
Federal Communications Commission	+ 3	− 6
Food & Drug Administration	+ 7	+ 1
Federal Trade Commission	− 5	− 9
Interstate Commerce Commission	−25	−24
Occupational Safety and Health Administration	+ 6	− 8
Securities and Exchange Commission	+15	− 0.3
Total	−13	− 6

SOURCE: U.S. Budget, 1984.

guidelines are pursued, or the extent of follow-up on prior violations. An entire generation of federal government priorities and steady expansion has been arrested and reversed. One can only guess at the scope of confusion, demoralization, and frustration among lower-level bureaucrats. They came to federal employment in part because they believed that one way to serve the public interest was through government regulation of the economy, but that was no longer an important government function, or at least it had a much lower priority than before.

Higher-level managers had similar problems. Reagan appointees were often openly opposed to the established functions of the departments or agencies that they were responsible for administering, as in the case of Secretary James Watt of the Department of the Interior. Or they held views that were at odds with the trends of the thirty-year past in which many higher civil service personnel had risen to stature in government. The result in many cases was the resignation or early retirement of personnel, and/or effective dismantling of capabilities in government that had taken years to develop.

One implication of all these changes appears to be that it may take several years to restore the national government bureaucracy's ability to implement social policies. Even if elections, resources, and revived political will seemed to lead in that direction, the government might simply lack the personnel and the spirit to try to change the society for the better. For the foreseeable future, innovation and service to social needs may have to come from the states, and not the federal government. That may be the single greatest acknowledgement of the success of the Reagan administration's efforts to redirect American public policy. The lesson should be a profound one for all students of bureaucracy and public policy.

CHAPTER 12

The Budgetary Process:
Working Together

The federal budget has become a major arena for governmental battle in recent years. The executive, the Congress, and the bureaucracy all play a part in putting together the final product; each, of course, has the power to check and balance, and therefore frustrate, the other. However, if the federal government is to continue to operate, a budget *must* be passed, and the major institutions must reach an agreement. If one or the other falters, the possibility for governmental stalemate becomes very real.

The budget's significance is twofold:

1. It is an economy-managing tool.
2. It is a policy-making and priority-setting instrument.

From 1946 on, the government accepted responsibility for fine-tuning the economy; and the budget is assumed to be a major vehicle for accomplishing that task. The size of the federal budget, where funds are allocated, and the deficit and debt ceiling obviously have an impact on the private economy. Economists differ as to the nature of that impact, and the relationship between various facets of the budget and the private economy. However, there is no doubt that the federal budget reflects assumptions about what the government should be doing with regard to the private economy. For example, in the 1980s, a major concern was the deficit. Many economists felt that the size of the deficit would undermine the recovery; others argued that the deficit was of little consequence. Ultimately, the federal budget is a reflection of certain economic assumptions, value choices, and, of course, political power.

Even if everyone agreed that the deficit would have undesirable consequences for the national economy, the question of how to reduce it has an almost infinite number of answers. The constant question of guns versus butter, or military versus domestic spending, is only one of the priority-setting questions captured in the budget-making process. Should the military budget be cut? What about Social Security? By how much? Trade-offs between raising revenue or cutting spending must be confronted, because each budgetary item carries policy-making implications. In other words, the basic political questions of who gets what and who pays are played out in the federal budget.

This chapter will address the budgetary process, acknowledging its centrality to American politics. The first section will recount the history that led to the Budget Control and Impoundment Act of 1974. The next two sections will discuss the current budgetary process and institutions created by that Act. First, we will look more closely at the major institutions and actors engaged in budgetmaking; we will next examine the process by which a budget is produced; and then, we will look at the final product, the federal budget. In the last sections, we will return to the problem of the major institutions working together to confront the central political questions raised by the budget and its process.

INTRODUCTION

As noted in Chapter 9, Congress was intended to have the "power of the purse." The Constitution gives Congress the "power to lay and collect taxes, duties, imposts and excises, to pay the debts and provide for the common defense and general welfare of the United States" and "to borrow money." (Article I, Section 8) "All bills for raising revenue shall originate in the House of Representatives." (Article I, Section 7) Very little, if any, governmental activity can be maintained without money, and all funds for governmental purposes must be authorized and appropriated by the Congress. Congress holds the purse strings, and the original assumption was that this power would mean congressional dominance.

For approximately 150 years, the need for a budgetary process was minimal; indeed, Congress had to deal with a surplus of funds rather than the necessity of making policy choices based on the availability of money. Federal spending, with the exception of military adventures, was relatively low. However, beginning with World War I, the federal budget began to grow. In addition to the wartime buildup, the federal government began to assume new responsibilities domestically. These activities, such as business regulation, continued and increased, following the war. All that time, the responsibility for authorizing, appropriating, and raising funds was scattered among a wide variety of congressional committees, and each revenue-raising bill and appropriation was dealt with as a separate legislative measure.

In response to an increasing need for some coherence in the raising and spending of money, Congress passed the Budget and Accounting Act of 1921, which created an independent executive agency called the Bureau of the Budget that was housed in the Department of the Treasury. The

Bureau's responsibility was to present one coherent budget that included all the previously separate items. Congress could then address items individually, but the Bureau would keep track of and advise Congress as to their impact on the budget as a whole.

Federal government activity mushroomed with the Depression, and World War II. In 1939, President Franklin Roosevelt submitted, and Congress approved, a reorganization plan that "tightened presidential control over the budgetary process."[1] As part of that reorganization, the Bureau of the Budget was moved into the new Executive Office. Roosevelt used the presentation of the annual budget to chart his program, a device subsequent presidents adopted. He also "broadened the bureau's clearance function by giving it responsibility for coordinating executive branch views on all legislation, not just appropriations bills."[2] The budget increasingly became an executive tool, a document to which Congress reacted.

In 1970, President Nixon submitted an executive reorganization plan to the Congress that it subsequently approved. As part of that reorganization, the Bureau of the Budget became the Office of Management and the Budget (OMB). The OMB not only has responsibility for preparing and presenting the budget, but also it has become a major liaison between the President and the Congress, as well as between the President and the executive agencies. It also became an active proponent of the President's program as reflected in the budget. The director appears before congressional committees to explain and defend the budget as presented. In 1974, in recognition of the growing importance of the OMB, the appointment of its director and deputy director became subject to confirmation by the Senate.

Although Congress chafed under what appeared to be executive control of the power of the purse for many years, the straw that broke the camel's back was President Nixon's use of impoundment. Impoundment is a procedure whereby the President refuses to spend money that has been authorized and appropriated by the Congress. The basic argument is that because the executive spends the money, he therefore has the power *not* to spend the money. Impoundment had been used by many presidents, but usually for administrative reasons, such as the fact that conditions may change between the time Congress appropriates the money and the time it is to be spent. The funds may no longer be needed, because employment has risen, the weather has warmed, or emergency fuel aid is no longer appropriate.

However, President Nixon aggressively used impoundment in explicitly policy-making ways. He refused to spend funds for programs of which he disapproved, usually on the grounds that it would be inflationary. He even impounded funds "despite explicit expressions of intent by Congress

---

[1] Congressional Quarterly, Inc. *Budgeting for America: The Politics and Process of Federal Spending* (Washington, D.C.: Congressional Quarterly, Inc., 1982), p. 36.

[2] Ibid.

that the funds be spent."[3] In response, Congress passed the Budget Control and Impoundment Act, and then repassed it over President Nixon's veto.

Although impoundment provided the final impetus, efforts at budgetary reform had been attempted throughout the previous fifty years. One of the reasons, of course, was the continuing tension and struggle between the executive and legislative branches. As the budget increased in importance as an economy-managing tool, it also centered in the executive branch. Similarly, Congress was losing its legislative responsibility for policymaking, as the President's budget increasingly became the place where policies and priorities were set. Congress, of course, had the power to pass or not pass the budget and to change budgetary priorities and policies, but it was forced to respond to the President's agenda. Even more importantly, the President had the OMB, and thus the tools, staff, and information upon which Congress was forced to rely.

In addition to the institutional rivalry, both the more conservative and the more liberal members of Congress had an interest in budget reform. The more conservative members felt that reform would enable them to put the brakes on uncontrollable spending by Congress, believing that a coordinated budgetary process would force Congress to be responsible. Of course, what conservatives meant by acting responsibly and controlling spending was to end domestic social programs. They argued that a single cohesive budget would match revenues and expenditures instead of having piecemeal appropriations add up and up; this would hopefully lead to a more businesslike attitude toward governmental activity.

On the other hand, the more liberal members of Congress wanted a greater say in the policy-making arena. They thought that too many decisions were being made by a few major committees and the executive, and felt that a budgetary process would give Congress a chance to publicly debate and set priorities. The same forces that led to other congressional reforms pushed for budgetary reform. Recognizing that the major committees, such as Ways and Means, Finance, and Appropriations were controlled by more conservative members, the liberals needed a means by which they could get into the budgetary process.

Thus, the conservative and liberal congressional members, as well as the institution as a whole, had a reason to accept budgetary reform. Everyone, of course, expected something different from the final product: conservatives expected balanced budgets; liberals expected great debates on national priorities; and the Congress as a whole expected to regain its power of the purse. On the other hand, there were power centers, such as the major congressional committees, that stood to lose and had to be taken into account. The result was the Budget Control and Impoundment Act of 1974, which created a new budgetary process, three new institutions (the House and Senate Budget Committees and the Congressional Budget

---

[3] James P. Pfiffner, *The President, the Budget, and Congress: Impoundment and the 1974 Budget Act* (Boulder, Colo.: Westview Press, 1979), p. 42.

Office), and set new rules for executive impoundment of funds. The next two sections will more fully describe that budgetary process and its major institutions and relevant actors.

MAJOR INSTITUTIONS AND ACTORS

Although everyone gets a crack at the budget at one time or another, a relative few can be identified as the major actors in the process. This section will discuss the institutions that are directly involved in the making and passage of the federal budget. On the executive side, there is, of course, the President and the bureaucracy; the Office of Management and the Budget provides the executive branch with a continuing research and policy arm, especially with respect to the budget. On the legislative side, the major actors are the House and Senate Budget Committees and their respective staffs, but we cannot omit the House Ways and Means and Appropriations Committees and the Senate Finance and Appropriations Committees. Finally, there is the newly created Congressional Budget Office, Congress's counterpart to the OMB.

The President and Executive Agencies

Chapter 10 covered the presidency, remarking on its size and delineating its various offices and agencies, and Chapter 11 discussed the bureaucracy. These two parts of the executive branch account for the vast majority of the budget. However, the fact that an entity is located within the executive branch does not necessarily mean that the President will champion its cause. On the contrary, often an agency's greatest ally is its substantive congressional committee. For example, the National Institute for the Humanities is more likely to get a friendly hearing for its request to fund summer seminars for college professors from the House Education Committee than from the director of the OMB.

In any event, each agency or program puts together a budget; program budgets add up to an agency budget; and agency budgets are combined into departmental budgets under the appropriate cabinet member. These are presented to the OMB and are also funneled to appropriate congressional committees. Agency directors and deputy directors, program directors, and cabinet secretaries, assistant secretaries, and program secretaries then defend their figures to the OMB (and thus indirectly to the President) as well as to congressional appropriations committees.

Executive departments very rarely bypass the OMB. However, the Department of Defense reports directly to the President, and the President consults with the Joint Chiefs and the National Security Council to decide what the national security requires. (As was fully explored in Chapter 11, President Reagan felt that national security required a boost in military spending.) The details are worked out between the President and the Defense Department, but the OMB gets a general figure and a certain set of priorities; other agencies must compete within those parameters.

The major actor in the budgetary process is the President. The OMB may prepare the budget, but it is the President's priorities and program that shape the final product. The President's economic advisers set the economic assumptions underlying the proposed budget and the parameters within which the others must maneuver. Recent candidates have campaigned on budgetary issues, with some promising to cut the defense budget while adding to education or Social Security, but it is the President and his or her budget message that sets the political stage.

Office of Management and the Budget

The OMB is one of the agencies in the Executive Office of the President. The Director and Deputy Director are nominated by the President, but their appointments must be confirmed by the Senate. In 1984, the OMB had 574 full-time employees and a budget of $40 million. As was noted in Chapter 10, in addition to its budgetary duties, the OMB bears responsibility for legislative liaison, "clearing and coordinating departmental advice on proposed legislation."[4] Its legislative division is also engaged in budget-making, but from the policy side rather than from the technical maintenance aspect.

The budgetary functions of the OMB are equally important, if not more important. The OMB began as the Bureau of the Budget, and although its responsibilities have greatly expanded, its major task is "to assist the President in the preparation of the budget and the formulation of the fiscal program of the Government," and "to supervise and control the administration of the budget."[5] Its director, who was David Stockman in 1984, carries the President's budget to Capitol Hill. The director is the major witness in House and Senate Budget Committee hearings on the President's budget. He or she defends the budget, tries to persuade others to support it, and argues both for the budget's specific figures and for acceptance of the economic assumptions upon which it is based. The director represents the President at Congress during the budgetary process.

The OMB also acts as the President's "front person" with regard to other executive agencies and the bureaucracy. In this case, the term "hatchet person" may be more accurate. The OMB has the reputation of holding the line on budget requests; it tends to resist new programs, unless they come from the President, and is impatient with budgetary increases or changes that may interfere with the President's program.

The OMB performs less as an economic adviser or policymaker than the Congressional Budget Office often does. The President, as was noted in

---

[4] *United States Government Organization Manual* (Washington, D.C.: U.S. Government Printing Office, 1984), p. 84.

[5] Ibid.

Chapter 10, has other sources of economic and policymaking advice. The OMB's job is to translate the President's desires, preferences, and economic theories into budget figures; it acts as presidential staff, taking its cue from the President and the relevant policy groups, such as the National Security Council and the Council of Economic Advisers. That does not mean, however, that it is not a powerful entity; within the guidelines set by the President, the OMB holds the line and attempts to enforce the budget. It operates as a very effective screen and is an agency that must be reckoned with by all other actors in the process.

House and Senate Budget Committees

The House and Senate Budget Committees were created by the 1974 Budget Act. The House committee is composed of 31 members, with a partisan ratio that is approximately that of the full House; in 1984, that meant 20 Democrats and 11 Republicans. Members of the committee are selected by their respective party caucuses, and the leadership, the Rules Committee, the Ways and Means Committee, and Appropriations must be represented in some way. Members of the House committee may only serve six years out of any one ten-year period, and the chair of the committee is chosen by the majority party caucus. James Jones, who was the chair in 1984, actively campaigned for the position and, even though he was not the first choice of the Democratic Party leadership, attained the chair.

The Senate Committee is, of course, smaller, and consisted of 22 members in 1984. Again, the partisan ratio approximates that of the chamber, with 12 Republicans and 10 Democrats. The Senate members are chosen at large, serve indefinite terms, and are less closely tied to the partisan leadership and other major committees. Both committees work with task forces rather than subcommittees, and both committees have full-time staff that work continuously on the budget, providing information, continuity, and expertise to the committee members.

Table 12.1 lists the members of each committee, with their other committee affiliations and pertinent data. Notice that 8 of the 12 Republicans and 6 of the 10 Democrats on the Senate Budget Committee also serve on either Appropriations, Finance, or Armed Services. In the House, 9 of the 20 Democrats also serve on Ways and Means, Appropriations, Armed Services, or Rules; the same is true for 5 of the 11 Republicans. The House Budget Committee members voted on President Reagan's 1981 budget on a strictly partisan basis; every Democrat voted against the budget, while every Republican voted for it. The same was not true for the Senate; only 4 members (all Democrats) of the Senate Budget Committee voted against the 1981 budget.

Because of the different nature of each chamber and their slightly different makeup, the respective Budget Committees have tended to develop different emphases. The Senate Committee appears to see its role in broader policy terms, and it emphasizes the overall philosophy of the

TABLE 12.1
House and Senate Budget Committees, 1984

HOUSE BUDGET COMMITTEE

MEMBERS	OTHER COMMITTEES	PERCENTAGE LIBERAL ON ECONOMIC ISSUES	VOTES ON		
			Reagan's 1981 Budget	Reagan's Tax Cut	Balanced Budget Amendment
Democratic Members:					
Jones (OK) Chairman	Ways and Means	54	no	no	no
Wright (TX)	Majority Leader	72	no	no	no
Solarz (NY)	Foreign Affairs	83	no	no	no
Wirth (CO)	Energy and Commerce	71	no	no	no
Panetta (CA)	Agriculture	65	no	no	no
Gephardt (MO)	Ways and Means	57	no	no	no
Nelson (FL)	Science and Technology	46	no	yes	yes
Aspin (WI)	Armed Services	68	no	no	no
Hefner (NC)	Appropriations	44	no	no	yes
Downey (NY)	Ways and Means	98	no	no	no
Donnelly (MA)	Merchant Marines and Fisheries	75	no	no	no
Lowry (WA)	Banking, Finance, and Urban Affairs	87	no	no	no
Derrick (SC)	Rules	52	no	no	yes
Miller (CA)	Education and Labor	82	no	no	no
Gray (PA)	Appropriations	94	no	no	no
Williams (MT)	Education and Labor	78	no	no	no
Ferraro (NY)	Public Works and Transportation	80	no	no	no
Wolpe (MI)	Foreign Affairs	96	no	no	no
Frost (TX)	Rules	96	no	no	no
Fazio (CA)	Appropriations Standards of Official Conduct	83	no	no	no

Republican Members:

Member	Other Committees	Percentage Liberal on Economic Issues	Reagan's 1981 Budget	Reagan's Tax Cut	Balanced Budget Amendment
Latta (OH)	Rules	25	yes	yes	yes
Shuster (PA)	Public Works and Transportation	27	yes	yes	yes
Frenzel (MN)	House Administration; Ways and Means	11	yes	yes	yes
Kemp (NY)	Appropriations	36	yes	yes	no
Bethune (AR)	Banking, Finance, and Urban Affairs	13	yes	yes	no
Gramm (TX)	Veterans Affairs	5	yes	yes	yes
Martin (IL)	House Administration	37	yes	yes	yes
Fiedler (CA)	—	21	yes	yes	yes
Gradison (OH)	Ways and Means	25	yes	yes	yes
Loeffler (TX)	Appropriations	25	yes	yes	yes
Mack (FL)	Post Office and Civil Service	0	newly elected		

SENATE BUDGET COMMITTEE

MEMBERS	OTHER COMMITTEES	PERCENTAGE LIBERAL ON ECONOMIC ISSUES	Reagan's 1981 Budget	Reagan's Tax Cut	Balanced Budget Amendment
			VOTES ON		

Republican Members:

MEMBERS	OTHER COMMITTEES	PERCENTAGE LIBERAL ON ECONOMIC ISSUES	Reagan's 1981 Budget	Reagan's Tax Cut	Balanced Budget Amendment
Domenici (NM)	Appropriations; Energy and Natural Resources; Environment and Public Works	21	yes	yes	yes
Armstrong (CO)	Finance; Banking, Housing, and Urban Affairs; Governmental Affairs	4	yes	yes	yes
Kassebaum (KS)	Commerce, Science, and Transportation; Foreign Relations	14	yes	yes	no

TABLE 12.1 *(cont.)*

Boschwitz (MN)	Agriculture, Nutrition, and Forestry Foreign Relations Small Business Veterans Affairs	11	yes	yes	yes
Hatch (UT)	Agriculture, Nutrition, and Forestry Judiciary Labor and Human Resources Small Business	6	yes	yes	yes
Tower (TX)	Armed Services Banking, Housing, and Urban Affairs	23	yes	yes	yes
Andrews (ND)	Appropriations Agriculture, Nutrition, and Forestry	42	yes	yes	yes
Symms (ID)	Finance Environment and Public Works Joint Economic Committee	12	yes	yes	yes
Grassley (IA)	Finance Judiciary Labor and Human Resources	29	yes	yes	yes
Kasten (WI)	Appropriations Commerce, Science, and Transportation Small Business	39	yes	yes	yes
Quayle (IN)	Armed Services Labor and Human Resources	25	yes	yes	yes
Gorton (WA)	Banking, Housing, and Urban Affairs Commerce, Science, and Transportation Small Business	36	yes	yes	no

Democratic Members:

Member	Committees				
Chiles (FL)	Appropriations	yes	yes	yes	55
	Governmental Affairs				
Hollings (SC)	Appropriations	yes	yes	no	64
	Commerce, Science, and Transportation				
Biden (DE)	Foreign Relations	no	no	yes	86
	Judiciary				
Johnston (LA)	Appropriations	yes	yes	yes	53
	Energy and Natural Resources				
Sasser (TN)	Appropriations	yes	yes	yes	75
	Banking, Housing, and Urban Affairs				
	Governmental Affairs				
	Small Business				
Hart (CO)	Armed Services	no	no	no	78
	Environment and Public Works				
Metzenbaum (OH)	Energy and Natural Resources	—	yes	no	77
	Judiciary				
	Labor and Human Resources				
Riegle (MI)	Banking, Housing, and Urban Affairs	no	yes	no	91
	Commerce, Science, and Transportation				
	Labor and Human Resources				
Moynihan (NY)	Finance	no	yes	no	99
	Environment and Public Works				
Exon (NE)	Armed Services	yes	yes	yes	59
	Commerce, Science, and Transportation				

SOURCE: Derived from Michael Barone and Grant Ujifusa, *The Almanac of American Politics 1984* (Washington, D.C.: National Journal, Inc., 1983).

budget, dealing with aggregates and economic assumptions. This reflects its view of itself as the more statesmanlike body.

On the other hand, the House Committee is seen as a more partisan institution. It concerns itself with budgetary details rather than hewing solely to the aggregate figures and letting the committees deal with the specifics. It has even been known to direct other committees in rather specific ways as to how to meet the aggregate figures; it also tends to put forward its own budget. However, this may be a function of the fact that from 1980 to 1984 a Democratic House was dealing with a Republican President and Senate, and the budget was a good way to make political differences known.

In institutional terms, the longevity and standing of the Budget Committees was in some doubt. The Budget Committees were created to deal with a subject matter that was already occupied by powerful major committees in each chamber. In the House, the rotation of members meant that it would be difficult to build up seniority, and thus power, by serving on the Budget Committee. Fixed terms made it a less attractive option for individual members, and other committees also would have less incentive to deal with it.

However, in their short existence in both the Senate and the House, the Budget Committees' centrality to the issues of the day became clear. Prominent members began to seek seats, and the Budget Committees' ability to reinsert Congress into the budgetary process appears to have earned them some permanence. Efforts to reform the process, or to do away with the Budget Committees altogether, have so far failed.

House Ways and Means and Appropriations Committees and Senate Finance and Appropriations Committees

The major toes that were stepped on by the creation of the Budget Committees belong to these four committees. Previously, the House and Senate Appropriations Committees had sole power to appropriate money, making them the spending side of the budget, while the Senate Finance Committee and the House Ways and Means Committee were the sole revenue raisers. The finance committees also have within their jurisdiction the major entitlement programs of Social Security, Medicare, and Medicaid. In their case, at least in the spending-cuts climate of the 1980s, not much power has been lost. Revenue totals have so far left choice of method in the hands of the congressional finance committees, because tax bills are extremely complicated and congressional committee expertise is vital.

Appropriations, however, is another story, because most efforts at gutting the budgetary process have come from this quarter. Approximately one-quarter of the federal budget comes out of appropriation measures handled by the Appropriations Committees. Since the reform, a great deal of the emphasis has been on cost cutting (a subject we will take up more fully in the last section). Much of those cuts have come from programs in the jurisdiction of the Appropriations Committees, and thus, it is their territory that has been the most invaded. The House Budget Committee has even suggested ways that appropriations may be cut in order to reconcile them with the budget. Not surprisingly, the Appropriations Committee feels that this is presumptuous on the part of the Budget Committee.

Many Appropriations subcommittees have developed special relationships with the client groups. The same agencies or programs whose funds were cut at the OMB often got renewed at the Appropriations subcommittee level. Those pushing budget reform complained that Appropriations "could not provide a comprehensive view of federal spending. You wanted someone to think in macro terms and the Appropriations Committee had a tradition of thinking in micro terms."[6] How far Congress has actually strayed from this process is a matter of dispute, but the Appropriations Committees obviously feel that it is no longer so, and that the new process has been instituted at their expense.

At this point, the Budget and Appropriations Committees are still struggling to develop a working relationship. The proposals to change the new budgetary system often come from members of Appropriations. A recently proposed bill would "radically overhaul the system, securing a larger role for Appropriations."[7] A 1984 appointee to the Budget Committee, Vic Fazio of California, came there from Appropriations. He hoped to "ease some of this tension." He said:

> We've got to make the [budget] system work. I'm not offering to be the compromiser. But I know members on the Appropriations Committee. I understand their problems and their frustrations with the Budget Committee. So I believe I can play a coordinating or conciliatory role. I think this is something those on the Budget Committee wanted too.[8]

Congressional Budget Office

The Congressional Budget Office was created by the 1974 Budget Act to function as Congress's counterpart to the OMB. In 1983, the CBO had 222 full-time employees and a budget of $16.3 million. Its major task is to issue a budget in counterpoint to the President's, as well as to develop its own economic projections and forecasts. Congress thus has its own source of information and analysis upon which to base budgetary decisions. It is, of

---

[6] Diane Granat, "Special Report: House Appropriations Committees: House Appropriations Panel Doles Out Cold Federal Cash, Chafes at Budget Procedures," *Congressional Quarterly Weekly Report*, June 18, 1983, p. 1215, quoting "Richard F. Fenno Jr., a political science professor at the University of Rochester who spent five years studying the Appropriations panel in the early 1960s."

[7] Ibid.

[8] "Pragmatism Is the Watchword as House Budget Committee Heads Into 1984 Fiscal Storms," *Fall 1983 Guide, Current American Government* (Washington, D.C.: Congressional Quarterly, Inc., 1982), p. 7.

course, supposed to be a nonpartisan agency that is capable of providing objective data and analysis to the Congressional Budget Committees.

Figure 12.1 is an organizational chart of the CBO with the number of positions per functional division as of 1980. As can be seen, the CBO has two major functions: budget analysis (the budget, fiscal, and tax analysis divisions) and policy analysis (represented by the remaining three). There is somewhat of a tension between the two major functions, but so far coexistence has been possible. In its short history, the House has tended to emphasize utilization of the budget analysis functions while the Senate leans more heavily toward CBO's policy analyses.

Budget analysis includes several tasks:

1. Bill costing. CBO estimates the amount an authorization will cost over extended periods of time. It is an attempt to make the full cost of a program clear by projecting the entire life of the program and all the possible variables.
2. Inflation impact. This task was added in the latter 1970s as more and more measures were assessed in terms of their impact on the economy, and specifically as to whether they would contribute to inflation.
3. Scorekeeping. The CBO keeps a running record of outlays and revenues so Congress can know where it stands in terms of the budget at any time. It may also warn Congress if an expenditure is threatening to go way over—or under.
4. Multiyear projections. For some time, budget experts have argued for budgets that extend into the future, rather than an annual, one-shot effort. It is assumed this will force Congress to confront issues rather than to continually put them off, to be paid for "next year." The federal budget is still done annually; however, the CBO does prepare multiyear projections each year.
5. Budget estimates. The CBO also prepares a budget, but with a variety of alternatives and estimates, that are based on differing forecasts or priority choices.

The policy analysis functions of the CBO can be divided into two major areas: fiscal policy strategies and program analysis. Fiscal policy is the package of revenues and expenditures that are devised to influence the direction and growth of the private economy. It is the overarching term used to describe the economic theory behind the budget *as an entirety*. The CBO develops a budget that reflects varying fiscal policy strategies. When President Reagan argues for "supply-side" policies, they show up in the tax cuts and cuts in domestic spending in the budget. When Congress wishes to encourage employment, it shows up in tax policy and domestic programs in the budget. The CBO makes clear what budgetary policies would follow from which economic assumptions and theories.

Program analysis is meant to be an ongoing congressional oversight capability. Obviously the OMB performs this function by reviewing agency requests before placing them in the President's budget. Substantive com-

Figure 12.1. The Congressional Budget Office

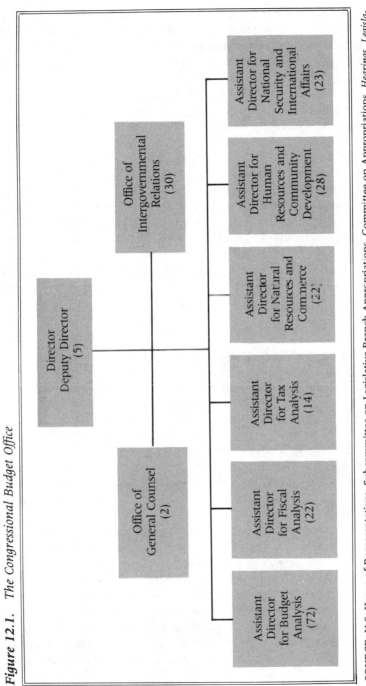

SOURCE: U.S. House of Representatives, Subcommittee on Legislative Branch Appropriations, Committee on Appropriations, *Hearings. Legislative Branch Appropriations for 1981* (Washington, D.C.: Government Printing Office, 1980), pp. 144, 160.

mittees of Congress supposedly performed this function for those programs that they had created, but in many cases, the committee and the program developed a symbiotic relationship where oversight by the committee was less than objective. The CBO took on this function in order to aid Congress in its oversight responsibilities.

The Director and Deputy Director of the CBO are appointed jointly by the Speaker of the House and the President Pro Tem of the Senate. In practice, leadership of both chambers and the relevant committees must also agree. The first director, Alice Rivlin, came from the Brookings Institution and was quite a controversial appointment. She was, however, reappointed for a second four-year term. Although she was often outspoken, and decidedly liberal personally, the CBO's reputation flourished under her guidance, and gained everyone's respect for its objectivity, its professionalism, and its very good work. The new director, Rudolph Penner, comes from the American Enterprise Institute. His "affiliations are as Republican as Rivlin's are Democratic,"[9] but he was recommended for the job by Ms. Rivlin. The tradition of CBO neutrality, although short-lived, appears to be strong. The CBO has earned a solid place in the governmental structure, even though it is a "young" institution.

THE BUDGETARY PROCESS

The Budget Act changed the fiscal year to October 1 through September 30. This gives the Congress almost a full year to work on the President's January proposals before the fiscal year begins. Figure 12.2 is an overview of the budgetary process created by the Act. Obviously, there is really no beginning or end to the budgetary process. As one set of proposals is wending its way through the process, executive agencies and congressional authorization committees are busy preparing for the next one. However, we will enter the circle a few months prior to the President's Budget Message.

In November, the Office of Management and Budget submits a "current services budget (CSB)" to Congress. This is a budget that assumes that the next year will be like the last one and is intended to give Congress a base from which to work. But, because the real proposed budget will be the President's proposed budget, very little attention is given to the CSB. At the same time, or in the meantime, all executive agencies must submit their requests for the coming fiscal year to the OMB. With the exception of the Department of Defense, most agencies have great difficulty defending their individual budgets. The OMB tends to cut budgets; very seldom does it encourage expansive spending.

On the congressional side, all authorizing legislation must be passed a

---

[9] Dale Tate, "CBO Under Penner: Maintaining Neutrality," *Congressional Quarterly Weekly Report,* August 20, 1983, p. 1700.

Figure 12.2.   The Budgetary Process*

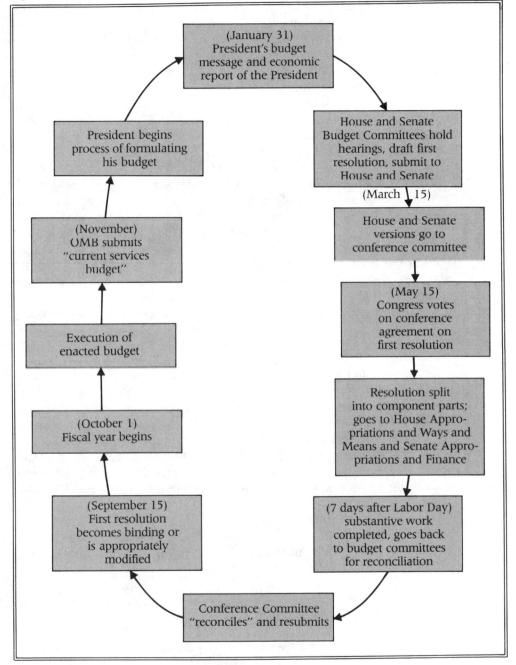

* Approximate dates.

full year before the fiscal year in which it will be funded. As was discussed in Chapter 9, any governmental activity must go through two processes: authorization and appropriations. In order to be considered for appropriations, any new activity must be authorized prior to the beginning of the budgetary process. New activities must also be submitted to the Budget and Appropriations Committees with the President's Budget, in order to be included in the First Budget Resolution.

Once the OMB has collected all the agency requests, hammered out compromises, and reconciled the bureaucracy's needs with the President's policy, it prepares a budget. The budget reflects the President's economic theories and his policymaking priorities, and is usually previewed in the President's State of the Union message in January. Normally, it is presented to the Congress with the President's Budget Message and the Economic Report of the President by February 1, or shortly thereafter. It includes the economic assumptions upon which the budget is based, such as forecasted growth in Gross National Product (GNP) as well as inflation and unemployment projections. These forecasts, of course, have an impact on estimated revenues and outlays, and thus on the size of the deficit. All aspects of the report, from the fundamental assumptions to the most detailed portions of the budget, are subject to challenge.

The official Congressional First Budget Resolution that sets spending and revenue targets is due May 15. In order to reach that target, the House and Senate Budget Committees should submit their proposed resolutions to the full chamber by March 15. The House and Senate Budget Committees divide into task forces, have a supporting staff of approximately 130,[10] and can draw on the services of the Congressional Budget Office (CBO). Both Budget Committees receive the President's budget, upon which they hold hearings. The CBO also analyzes the President's proposals, which it provides to Congress. The CBO also analyzes proposed congressional versions of the budget and includes its own economic forecasts. The Budget Committees report a resolution that includes economic forecasts, aggregate spending and revenue targets, and the deficit and proposed debt ceiling from this information.

As with any legislation, the House and Senate versions must agree. If the versions differ (which they usually do), a conference committee attempts to reconcile them; this is where the real work takes place. Both

---

[10] Aaron Wildavsky, *The Politics of the Budgetary Process*, 3rd ed. (Boston, Mass.: Little, Brown and Company, 1979), p. 228.

> The staff of the Senate Budget Committee has fifty-five professionals and thirty support personnel in total. Thirty-four professionals and fifteen support personnel, who act as the core staff of the Senate Committee, are appointed by the Committee Chairman. The rest of the staff are hired by Committee members. The House Budget Committee has a smaller staff of forty professionals and twenty-five support personnel. The House Committee determined that the rotating nature of its membership required expertise in programmatic and budgetary areas. The Senate staff, on the other hand, are more experienced politically than technically.

TABLE
12.2   *Date of Adoption of First Budget Resolution*

Fiscal Year	Date of Adoption
1977	May 13, 1976
1978	May 17, 1977
1979	May 15, 1978
1980	May 23, 1980
1981	June 11, 1980
1982	May 21, 1981
1983	June 23, 1982

SOURCE: Statement of Les Aspin, Wisconsin Representative, "Budget Process Review," Hearing Before the Committee on the Budget, 97th Congress, 2nd Session, September 14, 1982, p. 101.

Budget Committees, House and Senate leadership, and the President are well represented in the Conference Committee, which helps to insure that any compromise reached will hold. The Conference Committee report becomes the First Congressional Budget Resolution, and is supposed to be adopted by May 15. Table 12.2 lists the dates of adoption of the first resolution from 1977 through 1983. As shown, the first few years met the schedule, but for fiscal year 1980, it was an entire year late! However, the other resolutions have been only two to four weeks late.

The first budget resolution sets targets and ceilings in aggregate totals in functional categories (see Table 12.9, pp. 360–61). It is now up to the House and Senate Appropriations and the Senate Finance and House Ways and Means Committees to draw up the detailed legislation necessary to meet those figures. *No* appropriations bills may be considered before the passage of the first resolution, and action on all appropriations measures should be completed by seven days after Labor Day. If the May 15 resolution is late, then the appropriation and revenue-raising committees are left with less time to do their work. It is difficult enough to complete the detail work in the full time allotted, and so delay in adoption of the first resolution delays the entire process.

The budget is broken into its component parts, following adoption of the first resolution. There is a great deal of controversy and tension about how specific the budget resolution can or should be. The House and Senate Appropriations and Senate Finance and House Ways and Means Committees, of course, do not want to be told what they can do. The budget resolution sets an estimated aggregate revenue figure, but cannot detail how the money is to be raised, because that is the job of the Senate Finance and House Ways and Means Committees. The aggregate totals for spending pose a similar problem, because even the functional categories the resolution now covers are resisted by the Appropriations Committees. Through 1984, the aggregate figures were taken more or less seriously depending upon the politics and personnel of the moment.

TABLE
12.3   **Appropriations Reports and Enactments**

	1977	1978	1979	1980	1981	1982
Average days between adoption of first budget resolution and House Appropriations Committee reports	30.8	27.8	25.5	28.7	29.8	75.5
Average days between House Appropriations Committee reports and final enactment of appropriation bills	62.8	93.5	113.8	134.8	125.8	129.6
Number of appropriation bills enacted	13	12	12	11	9	10
Number of appropriation bills enacted at beginning of fiscal year	13	10	5	3	2	1

SOURCE: Statement of Les Aspin, Wisconsin Representative, "Budget Process Review," Hearing Before the Committee on the Budget, 97th Congress, 2nd Session, September 14, 1982, p. 101.

The necessary implementing legislation now goes through the regular process, as was detailed in Chapter 9. The major difference is that we are dealing only with the House and Senate Appropriations and House Ways and Means and Senate Finance Committees. Budget components are referred first to the appropriate committee and then to the appropriate subcommittee. The subcommittee holds hearings, markups, and makes its report to the full committee. By the end of the process, there are generally a series of appropriations bills and revenue-raising measures to be passed. Once both the House and Senate have passed their various appropriations and revenue bills, they too go to a conference committee. Table 12.3 lists the time taken and the number of appropriations bills passed for the years 1977 through 1982. Notice that each year Congress managed to enact fewer of the bills by the beginning of the fiscal year. This means that separate appropriations and revenue measures were combined into what is known as an "omnibus" bill in order to meet the budgetary deadline.

After both House and Senate agree on separate appropriation and expenditure measures, the problem of staying within, or changing, the budget resolution remains. The separate measures are returned to the House and Senate Budget Committees for the reconciliation process. The deadline for the second budget resolution, which supposedly sets binding expenditure and revenue aggregate figures, is September 15. However, in recent years, for the sake of efficiency, the second resolution is actually the adoption of the revised and reconciled first budget resolution. When the first resolution is passed, it includes a caveat that makes it binding after a certain time. This helps make the October 1 fiscal year deadline a reality. If the parties cannot agree, the original figures will hold, and thus the entire budgetary process is actually a working out of the first resolution, which eventually becomes *the* budget.

If the individual appropriation and revenue measures do not fit within the first budget resolution, which is the usual case, the Budget Committees must reconcile them. The House and Senate Budget Committee versions generally differ, and so a budget conference committee attempts to work it out. The reconciliation process is also a source of controversy and friction. The Budget Committee is, of course, redoing other committees' work. The budget resolution itself is nonbinding and nonimplementing, and the problem is to get legislation that stays within the budget-resolution guidelines.

By this time, the beginning of the fiscal year is rapidly approaching. The usual result is "omnibus" bills, which combine several appropriations and/or expenditure measures into a single package. These reconciliation measures come to the chambers from the Budget Committees, to be voted on as a whole. As many members complain:

> The often truncated omnibus approach rarely makes time for committee hearings, markups and detailed floor consideration with the opportunity for amendments.[11]

The reconciliation measures are usually considered very close to, if not after, the fiscal year deadline of October 1. Once all the measures are passed, the total becomes the federal budget for the following fiscal year.

---

[11] "Use of Omnibus Bills Burgeons Despite Members' Misgivings: Long-Term Impact Is Disputed," *Spring 1983 Guide, Current American Government* (Washington, D.C.: Congressional Quarterly, Inc., 1982), p. 17.

EXHIBIT 4
The Balanced Budget Amendment

Text of the Amendment

ARTICLE

Resolved by the Senate and House of Representatives of the United States of America in Congress assembled (two-thirds of each House concurring therein), That the following article is proposed as an amendment to the Constitution of the United States, which shall be valid to all intents and purposes as part of the Constitution if ratified by the legislatures of three-fourths of the several states within seven years after its submission to the states for ratification:

SECTION 1. Prior to each fiscal year, the Congress shall adopt a statement of receipts and outlays for that year in which total outlays are no greater than total receipts. The Congress may amend such statement provided revised outlays are no greater than revised receipts. Whenever three-fifths of the whole number of both Houses shall deem it necessary, Congress in such statement may provide for a specific excess of outlays over receipts by a vote directed solely to that subject. The Congress and the President shall, pursuant to legislation or through the exercise of their powers under the first and second articles, ensure that actual outlays do not exceed the outlays set forth in such statement.

SECTION 2. Total receipts for any fiscal year set forth in the statement adopted pursuant to this article shall not increase by a rate greater than the rate of increase in national income in the year or years ending not less than six months nor more than twelve months before such fiscal year, unless a majority of the whole number of both Houses of Congress shall have passed a bill directed solely to approving specific additional receipts and such bill has become law.

SECTION 3. The Congress may waive the provisions of this article for any fiscal year in which a declaration of war is in effect.

SECTION 4. Total receipts shall include all receipts of the United States except those derived from borrowing and total outlays shall include all outlays of the United States except those for repayment of debt principal.

SECTION 5. The Congress shall enforce and implement this article by appropriate legislation.

SECTION 6. On and after the date this article takes effect, the amount of federal public limit as of such date shall become permanent and there shall be no increase in such amount unless three-fifths of the whole number of both Houses of Congress shall have passed a bill approving such increase and such bill has become law.

SECTION 7. This article shall take effect for the second fiscal year beginning after its ratification.

The unprecedented budget deficits have given new life to the Balanced Budget Amendment. The National Taxpayers Union, a right-wing conservative organization, began a drive to get the Amendment passed more than seven years ago. After an initial flurry of activity, the effort seemed to be defeated. Table 12.4 lists the states that have called for a constitutional convention on a balanced federal budget. Notice that only Alaska and Missouri did so after 1982, but the other states did so in or previous to 1979. However, with the recent addition of Alaska and Missouri, only two more states are required to attain the 34 necessary to call a constitutional convention.

The possibility of a constitutional convention encouraged Congress to consider the Amendment. Another method for amending the Constitution is for a two-thirds majority of each chamber of the Congress to propose to do so. In August 1982, the Senate passed the Amendment by the necessary majority. However, the House fell 46 votes short of the required two-thirds. It is expected that the renewed interest in the Amendment will continue.

Critics point out that calling a constitutional convention would be extremely risky. There has not been one since the original convention in 1787. Although the proponents argue that such a convention would be limited to a consideration of a balanced budget amendment, the only precedent, the Constitutional Convention of 1787, immediately violated the instructions included in its call. Just as that convention scrapped its entire document (the Articles of Confederation) and started over, so might a present-day convention. Many other legal issues have been raised by the possibility. For example, is there a time period within which 34 states must agree to the call? Does each state's call need to be identical? How would delegates be selected? The whole idea is giving constitutional scholars legal nightmares!

Another major critique comes from those who believe that such an amendment is impractical, unenforceable, and thus useless, except to contribute to disrespect for the Constitution. They point to the example of Prohibition as an example of an unenforceable law under which practically the entire nation became lawbreakers. A Balanced Budget Amendment is not as likely to force the desired congressional behavior as it is to encourage evasion and thus lawbreaking by our highest officials. To write such a provision into the Constitution would deface the document, and would draw away from the exalted status and stability that the Constitution now provides.

In spite of this barrage of opposition from constitutional scholars, and respected experts, it is very difficult for an elected official to vote *against* a balanced budget. The Balanced Budget Amendment is one of the most striking illustrations of symbolic politics in action. Many of those who vote for the amendment admit that it is unenforceable, but, they argue, maybe the symbolism of a *commitment* to a balanced budget would help *reduce* the deficit, and, of course, it would look very good to constituents. Very few elected officials (President Reagan and company excepted) appear to want a Balanced Budget Amendment *as a binding constitutional requirement.* On the other hand, very few have the courage to oppose it. As the King of Siam in *The King and I* said, "It's a puzzlement!"

THE PRODUCT

Perhaps the most important part of the budgetary process is the product—the federal budget. As one representative stated, "The process is not worth more than the product."[12] It is the one piece of legislation that is absolutely necessary to the functioning of the United States government. The govern-

---

[12] Dale Tate, "Congress Rebuffs President, Clears '84 Budget Resolution," *Congressional Quarterly Weekly Report,* June 25, 1983, p. 1270.

TABLE
12.4   *States Call for a Balanced Budget*

The legislatures of these 32 states have passed resolutions calling for a constitutional convention on a balanced federal budget. It takes action by 34 states to force Congress to convene such a convention.

State	Year Approved	State	Year Approved
Alabama	1976	Nebraska	1976
Alaska	1982	Nevada	1977, 1979
Arizona	1977, 1979	New Hampshire	1979
Arkansas	1979	New Mexico	1976
Colorado	1978	North Carolina	1979
Delaware	1975	North Dakota	1975
Florida	1976	Oklahoma	1976
Georgia	1976	Oregon	1977
Idaho	1979	Pennsylvania	1976
Indiana	1979	South Carolina	1976, 1978
Iowa	1979	South Dakota	1979
Kansas	1978	Tennessee	1977
Louisiana	1975, 1978, 1979	Texas	1977, 1978
Maryland	1975	Utah	1979
Mississippi	1975	Virginia	1976
Missouri	1983	Wyoming	1977

SOURCE: Tom Raum, "High Deficit Revives Drive for Balanced Budget Amendment," *Seattle Post-Intelligencer*, February 16, 1984, p. B6.

ment can continue to operate under continuing resolutions, but essentially it is stalled, and the possibility exists for real stalemate. In other words, while the various branches may negotiate for years over a single piece of legislation such as Medicare, the budget imposes an absolute necessity for working together within a time limit.

This section will look at the final product, the composition of the federal budget. Careful perusal of the budget reveals who gets what, as well as who pays in the American political economy. We will then examine the major controversies surrounding the budget's composition. The "problem" of the deficit rests on varying assumptions about its impact, but the attempt to reduce the deficit comes back to the question of who gets what, and who pays. The final discussion will return to the problem of working together to decide these issues, the politics of the budgetary process and the final product.

The Budget Composition

Figure 12.3 is a broad overview of the budget, which illustrates where the budget dollar comes from and where it goes. On the revenue side, as illustrated, the largest percentage comes from individuals' payment of in-

Figure 12.3.   *The Budget Dollar—Fiscal Year 1985 Estimate*

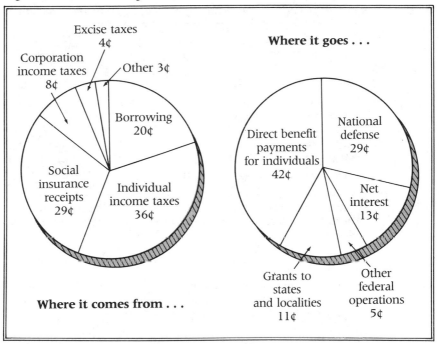

Excise taxes 4¢

Corporation income taxes 8¢

Other 3¢

Borrowing 20¢

Social insurance receipts 29¢

Individual income taxes 36¢

Where it comes from . . .

Where it goes . . .

Direct benefit payments for individuals 42¢

National defense 29¢

Net interest 13¢

Grants to states and localities 11¢

Other federal operations 5¢

SOURCE: *Budget in Brief* (Washington, D.C.: USGPO, 1984), frontispiece.

come taxes. Social insurance payments (from both individuals and businesses) provide the second largest revenue, but many of these are earmarked for entitlement programs. For example, the Social Security taxes you pay go into the Social Security program, which is represented in the diagram in the direct benefit payments for individuals category. Table 12.5 and the charts provided in Figure 12.4 illustrate revenue raising from 1940 through 1987. As illustrated, the proportion paid by individuals has steadily risen while the proportion provided by corporations declined. John McDermott translates the graphs into concrete numbers:

> In 1946, individual taxpayers paid 50.1 percent of all the taxes Washington took in; 45.9 percent of this amount was paid in income taxes and 4.2 percent in payroll assessments. Corporate taxes made up 30.7 percent of the total, with virtually the entire amount coming from taxes on profits. For every $5 in Federal revenues paid by individuals, corporations paid $3.

> By 1976, the picture had altered dramatically. Personal income taxes made up 52.6 percent of Washington's take, and payroll taxes (which are notoriously regressive) had climbed to 24.5 percent. But business's share of the tax load, meanwhile, had fallen to 15.5 percent. In other words, the Internal Revenue Service was drawing 77 percent of its collections from personal income taxes. For every $5 in Federal revenues paid by individuals, big business paid $1. By 1980, the corporations' share was 13.9

TABLE
12.5   **Sources of Federal Government Revenue, 1940–80 (percentages)**

| | YEAR | | | | |
SOURCE	*1940*	*1950*	*1960*	*1970*	*1980*
Individual income taxes	17.5	39.9	44.0	46.7	46.9
Corporation income taxes	15.4	26.5	23.2	16.9	12.4
Social insurance (payroll) taxes	27.0	11.1	15.9	23.4	30.9
Excise taxes	29.0	19.1	12.6	8.1	4.7
All other receipts	11.2	3.4	4.2	4.9	5.1
Total receipts	100.0	100.0	100.0	100.0	100.0

SOURCES: U.S. Office of Management and Budget, "Federal Government Finances," Jan. 1979, p. 7; U.S. Office of Management and Budget, *The Budget of the United States Government,* fiscal year 1982 (Washington, D.C.: U.S. Government Printing Office, 1981), pp. 560–62.

percent, and this should drop another percentage point or two once all the tax breaks written into the Reagan Administration's "economic recovery program" have taken hold.[13]

In other words, individuals pay the lion's share into the federal coffers.

Figure 12.3 covers 1985 estimates in broad categories. Table 12.6 breaks down the payment of the fiscal year 1983 budget dollar into more detailed functional categories. Notice that the interest percentage has risen from 11 to 13 percent. This is, of course, occasioned by the increasing national debt. National defense, as was fully covered in the previous chapter, has risen from 26 to 29 percent of the dollar. "Other" federal operations have declined 1 percent. The remaining categories must share the declining remainder.

The expenditure figures are "outlays," or the actual amounts of money paid out by the government. (See Figure 12.5.) In the 1980s environment of budget-cutting, one controversy centered on "entitlements." Entitlements are those payments that have been previously authorized, such as Social Security, Medicare and Medicaid, and veteran's pensions and benefits, for which annual appropriations are no longer necessary. The original legislation was written in such a way that people who meet the criteria receive the benefits automatically. They are "entitled" to payment and the federal government must respond. Detailed estimates vary on the amount of the budget that is covered by entitlements. Dennis Ippolito, a congressional budget expert, states that "by 1980, entitlement spending was 60 percent of total outlays and almost 80 percent of all uncontrollable

[13] John McDermott, "The Secret History of the Deficit," *The Nation,* August 21–28, 1982, p. 1, cont'd 144.

Figure 12.4. The Changing Sources of Federal Revenue

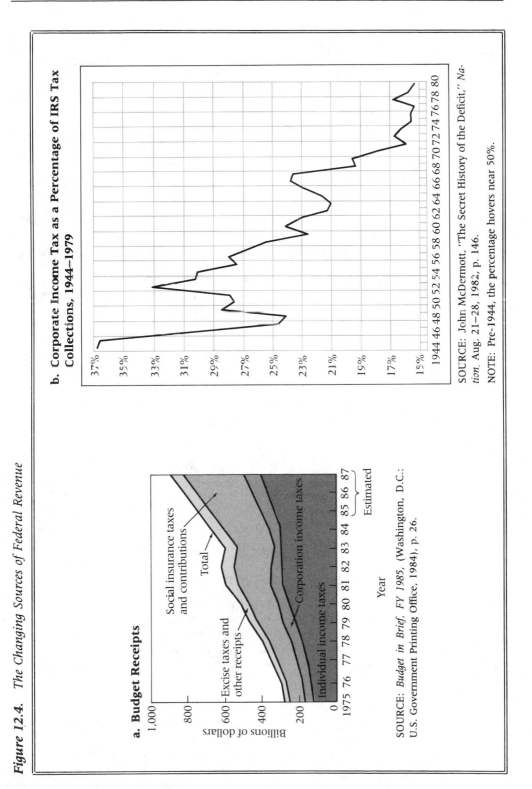

a. Budget Receipts

SOURCE: *Budget in Brief, FY 1985,* (Washington, D.C.: U.S. Government Printing Office, 1984), p. 26.

b. Corporate Income Tax as a Percentage of IRS Tax Collections, 1944–1979

SOURCE: John McDermott, "The Secret History of the Deficit," *Nation.* Aug. 21–28, 1982; p. 146.

NOTE: Pre-1944, the percentage hovers near 50%.

TABLE
12.6   ## Where Our Tax Dollars Go

A one-earner family of four, making $25,000 a year, will pay about $6,323 in taxes this year. Here's how the federal government will spend that money in fiscal year 1983.

Item	Amount	Percentage of Total
Income security[1]	$2,163	34%
Defense	1,645	26%
Interest	681	11%
Health	631	10%
Social services	204	3%
Veterans' benefits	187	3%
Transportation	168	3%
Agriculture	161	3%
Environment	93	1%
International affairs	91	1%
Science and space	59	1%
Other	240	4%
Total	$6,323	100%

SOURCE: The Tax Foundation Inc., based on official federal budget estimates.
[1] Includes Social Security, federal employee retirement and disability, unemployment compensation, housing assistance, food and nutrition assistance and other programs.

spending."[14] However, President Reagan's budgetary inroads into entitlements make the term "uncontrollable" somewhat suspect.

As Congress and the President struggle to match outlays and revenues, another target is "tax expenditures." These are provisions in the tax laws that provide tax breaks or loopholes for special-interest groups. They are not meant to raise revenue, even though they appear in the tax codes. As a matter of fact, many argue that they should be considered as outlays because they cost the government money. Dennis Ippolito summarizes the controversy:

> Those who argue that tax expenditures are the equivalent of direct spending want to see tax expenditures treated like regular spending programs and incorporated in the debate on budget priorities. They believe this procedure would make it easier to attack specific tax expenditures and would eventually cause them to be replaced by direct expenditures, a

---

[14] Dennis Ippolito, *Congressional Spending* (Ithaca, N.Y.: Cornell University Press, 1981), p. 213. Other "uncontrollable" spending is "spending required by contracts made in past years, borrowing authority, guaranteed loans, and other obligations," p. 214.

change they advocate on grounds of equity and efficiency. Tax expenditures, such critics claim, disproportionately benefit higher income groups, and the government could achieve the same policy goals at lower cost by direct expenditure. For opponents of tax expenditures, revenues forgone are the same as money spent, but spending is the preferred means to achieve policy goals; tax reform therefore means the closing of loopholes.[15]

Tax expenditures have been unofficially compiled each year since the late 1960s. The Budget Act of 1974 finally included them as an official category in the budgetary process. Table 12.7 is a sample of the tax breaks included within the category. The number of tax expenditures grew from 50 in 1967 to 104 in 1982. President Reagan's 1981 tax law "added eight new categories of tax expenditures and expanded 21 others, while reducing only two."[16]

Another major, and often controversial, portion of the budget is the economic forecasts and the assumptions that underlie them. Representative Les Aspin (D., Wisc.), in a hearing on the budget process, stated:

> So a second reason why spending goes over the budget ceilings is that the economic predictions turn out not to be correct, and in fact turn out to be rosier than the real world.[17]

Economic forecasts and assumptions are an integral part of the budget. First, they inform how the budget will be structured. For example, with supply-side assumptions, the administration cut taxes, especially with regard to corporations, and added tax advantages for investment purposes. This, of course, meant a reduction in revenues that were offset by cuts in domestic spending. It was *assumed* that the economic recovery that these tax incentives would produce would eventually increase revenues. More conventional Keynesianism (some argued, as represented by the CBO) would increase domestic spending in order to increase consumer demand. These theories are then translated into projections of revenue and outlay— which becomes the budget. This also explains why the adopted and projected budget rarely matches the year's end figures.

The Deficit and Conflicting Priorities

Until recently, it was assumed that a budget deficit was not a desirable thing, except, of course, under certain circumstances. Under Keynesian theory, if the economy is in a recession, a short-term deficit may be neces-

---

[15] Ibid., pp. 189–90.

[16] Karen W. Arenson, "The 25% of 'Expenditures' Washington Never Sees," *The New York Times*, February 7, 1982, p. 4E.

[17] Statement of Les Aspin, Wisconsin Representative, "Budget Process Review," Hearing Before the Committee on the Budget, 97th Congress, 2nd Session, September 14, 1982, p. 97.

Figure 12.5.   *Glossary of Budget Terms*

AUTHORIZING LEGISLATION—Legislation enacted by the Congress to set up or continue the operation of a Federal program or agency. Authorizing legislation is normally a prerequisite for subsequent appropriations, but does not usually provide budget authority (see below).

BUDGET—A plan of proposed receipts and spending for the coming fiscal year. By law the President's budget for the Federal Government must be transmitted to Congress within fifteen days after Congress convenes, which is usually in early January.

BUDGET AMENDMENT—A proposal that the President transmits to the Congress to revise his budget request after he formally transmits the budget but before the Congress has completed appropriations action.

BUDGET AUTHORITY (BA)—Authority provided by law to enter into obligations that will result in immediate or future outlays. It may be classified by the period of availability, by the timing of congressional action, or by the manner of determining the amount available. The basic forms of budget authority are:

Appropriations—Authority that permits Federal agencies to incur obligations and to make payments.

Authority to borrow—Authority that permits Federal agencies to incur obligations and to borrow money to make payments.

Contract authority—Authority that permits Federal agencies to enter into contracts or incur other obligations in advance of an appropriation.

BUDGET RECEIPTS—Money, net of refunds, collected from the public by the Federal Government through the exercise of its governmental or sovereign powers. Budget receipts also include gifts and contributions. Excluded are amounts received from strictly business-type transactions (such as sales, interest, or loan repayments) and payments between Government accounts. (See offsetting receipts.)

BUDGET SURPLUS OR DEFICIT—Difference between budget receipts and outlays.

CONCURRENT RESOLUTION ON THE BUDGET—A resolution passed by both Houses of the Congress, but not requiring the signature of the President, setting targets or binding Federal budget totals for the Congress.

CONTINUING RESOLUTION—Legislation enacted by the Congress to provide budget authority for specific ongoing activities when a regular appropriation for those activities has not been enacted by the beginning of the fiscal year.

CREDIT BUDGET—A plan of proposed direct loan obligations and guaranteed loan commitments. Budget authority and outlays associated with the credit budget are included in the Federal on- and off-budget totals.

CURRENT SERVICES ESTIMATES—Estimates of receipts, outlays and budget authority for coming fiscal years that assume no policy changes from the year in progress. The estimates include the effects of anticipated changes in economic conditions (such as unemployment or inflation); beneficiary levels, pay increases, and changes required under existing law.

DEFERRAL—Executive branch action that temporarily delays the obligation of budget authority. Deferrals may be overturned at any time by an act of the Congress.

FEDERAL FUNDS—Amounts collected and used by the Federal Government for the general purposes of the Government. There are four types of Federal fund accounts: the general fund, special funds, public enterprise revolving funds, and intragovernmental funds. The major Federal fund is the general fund, which is derived from general taxes and borrowing. The other form of Federal funds involves earmarked collections, such as those generated by and used to finance a continuing cycle of business-type operations.

FISCAL YEAR—The Federal Government's yearly accounting period, which begins on October 1 and ends on the following September 30. The fiscal year is designated by the calendar year in which it ends; e.g., fiscal year 1985 begins on October 1, 1984, and ends on September 30, 1985. (From 1844 to 1976 the fiscal year began on July 1 and ended on the following June 30.)

IMPOUNDMENT—Any action or inaction by an officer or employee of the Federal Government that precludes the obligation or expenditure of budget authority provided by the Congress (see deferral and rescission).

OBLIGATIONS—Amounts of orders placed, contracts awarded, services received, or similar legally binding commitments made by Federal agencies during a given period that will require outlays during the same or some future period.

OFF-BUDGET FEDERAL ENTITIES—Federal organizations or programs that belong in the budget under current budget accounting concepts but that have been excluded from the budget totals under provisions of law.

OFFSETTING RECEIPTS—Collections deposited in receipt accounts that are offset against budget authority and outlays rather than being counted as budget receipts. These collections are derived from Government accounts (intragovernmental transactions) or from the public (proprietary receipts) through activities that are of a business-type or market-oriented nature.

OUTLAYS—Payments, normally in the form of checks issued or cash disbursed. Outlays include interest accrued on the public debt, or other forms of payment, net of refunds, reimbursements and offsetting collections.

RECONCILIATION—A reconciliation directive is a provision in the concurrent resolution on the budget that calls on various committees of the Congress to recommend legislative changes that reduce outlays or increase receipts by specified amounts. A reconciliation bill contains these changes.

RESCISSION—A legislative action canceling budget authority previously provided by the Congress.

SUPPLEMENTAL APPROPRIATION—An appropriation enacted subsequent to a regular annual appropriation act. Supplemental appropriation acts provide additional budget authority for programs or activities (including new programs authorized after the date of the original appropriation act) for which the need for funds is too urgent to be postponed until the next regular appropriation.

TAX EXPENDITURES—Provisions of the Federal income tax laws that allow a special exclusion, exemption, or deduction from gross income or provide a special credit, preferential rate of tax, or deferral of tax liability. Tax expenditures frequently have results similar to spending programs, loan guarantees, or regulations.

TRUST FUNDS—Amounts collected and used by the Federal Government for carrying out specific purposes and programs according to a statute or trust agreement, such as the social security and unemployment trust funds. Trust funds are not available for the general purposes of the Government. Trust fund receipts that are not needed immediately are generally invested in Government securities and earn interest for the trust fund.

SOURCE: *U.S. Budget in Brief, FY 1985* (Washington, D.C.: U.S. Government Printing Office, 1985), pp. 85–86.

sary in order to increase government and consumer spending and stimulate demand. In periods of inflation, a surplus would be better because that would draw money from the economy and slow it down, but generally these were assumed to be short-term, relatively small amounts. Under the economic conditions of the 1970s and 1980s, with inflation and unemployment occurring simultaneously (stagflation), many of the previous arguments about the deficit lost force. With the staggering deficits of the 1980s, the argument took on added urgency.

Figure 12.6 summarizes the deficit problem in a variety of ways. The deficit is the yearly discrepancy between revenues and expenditures. As

TABLE
12.7   **A Sampling of Tax Breaks**

Revenue losses due to various special benefits (in billions of dollars)

	1977	1981	1984*
Deductibility of mortgage interest on owner-occupied homes	5.435	19.805	37.960
Deductibility of property tax on owner-occupied homes	4.500	7.740	15.160
Deductibility of charitable contributions, other than education and health	4.255	7.520	13.055
Investment credit (other than for employee stock ownership plans, rehabilitation of structures, and energy)	10.610	19.525	25.445
Net exclusion of pension contributions and earnings			
Employer plans	8.715	23.605	38.855
Plans for self-employed and others	1.305	2.105	2.770
Residential energy conservation credits	0	0.425	0.435
Deferral of income of domestic international sales corporations	1.030	1.600	1.870
Oil and gas percentage depletion allowances	1.310	2.130	2.285
Exclusion of interest on state and local industrial development bonds	0.285	1.230	2.410
Exclusion of interest on state and local government pollution control bonds	0.245	0.720	0.860
Exclusion of scholarship and fellowship income	0.250	0.410	0.655
Capital outlays under farm income stabilization program	0.450	0.530	0.610

SOURCE: Adapted from artwork in Karen W. Arenson, "The 25% of 'Expenditures' Washington Never Sees," *The New York Times*, February 7, 1982, p. 4E. Copyright © 1982 by The New York Times Company. Reprinted by permission. (Figures originally taken from Congressional Budget Office publications.)

* Projection; does not reflect changes in 1981 tax act.

shown, by 1985, the projected deficit ranges from $250 to $300 billion, but the annual deficit adds up each year. In other words, the government does not start the year with a clean slate; last year's *deficit* becomes part of the *debt*, upon which the government pays interest (thus, the increasing interest amount in Figure 12.3 and Table 12.6). Analysts estimate that in 1985 the federal government's debt will be $1.8 trillion!

The vast majority of economists and governmental officials express great concern about the increasing deficit and mounting governmental debt. However, a growing minority are beginning to argue that deficits do not really matter. The following quotations are from the two viewpoints on the question "Do federal deficits really matter?" The first is from Rudolph

G. Penner, formerly the Director, Tax Policy Studies, American Enterprise Institute, and now CBO Director. The second is from Norman Ture, Economic Consultant and Chairman of the Board, Institute for Research on the Economics of Taxation. Both men can be considered "conservative" economists.

> *Penner:* Yes, they do, for a variety of reasons. Most important, deficits put upward pressure on interest rates. That inhibits investment by business, which is vital for long-term economic growth.
>
> *Ture:* Not very much. The notion that deficits crowd out the private sector's use of the nation's productive capability is simply wrong. It isn't deficits that do that. It is government spending and taxing that does that.
>
> The deficits are only the accounting result of comparing expenditures against revenues. They have no active role in the economy.[18]

Although the argument that the deficit may not matter is becoming more prominent, it has not yet penetrated the governmental process very far, and it has had no impact on the budgetary process. The major concern is still finding some way to reduce the deficit.

Reducing the deficit is a major political battle cry in the budgetary process. The first part of the problem is affixing blame. President Reagan insists that it lies with the Democratically controlled Congress and previous Democratic administrations. They are responsible for enacting uncontrollable entitlement spending and a proliferation of domestic programs. These programs not only cost too much, but are probably unnecessary if not actually harmful to the economy as a whole. Congress, and the Democrats, point out that the deficits have ballooned since the advent of Ronald Reagan. They argue that increased military spending, combined with tax cuts and expenditures (mainly for the wealthy), are the reason for the unequalled deficits. They argue that such programs benefit the rich at the expense of the poor, and that the military increases are not only unnecessary but positively harmful both to the economy and to our security.

Obviously, affixing the blame also points to conflicting priorities for solving the problem. Each position not only has conflicting economic theories and assumptions but also conflicting ideas regarding who is to get what, and who is to pay. Much of the budget terminology is designed to win a point of view. (See Figure 12.7.) For example, those who wish to cut domestic spending often refer to it as "uncontrollable" spending. The main problem is to "get control" of those programs. It is not often noted that this has only become a "problem" since Congress began to respond to the needs of the less powerful as well as the powerful. Almost all of the "uncontrolled" spending is purposefully protected because it is directed at the constituencies who are least able to defend themselves.

---

[18] "Do Federal Deficits Really Matter?" *U.S. News and World Report*, March 7, 1983, p. 85.

Working Together?

In one sense, the budgetary process works like any other legislation. The President proposes, the committees consider, Congress disposes, and the President signs or vetoes the resulting product. On the other hand, there are significant differences. The first is that there must be a product; the

Figure 12.6.   *The National Debt*

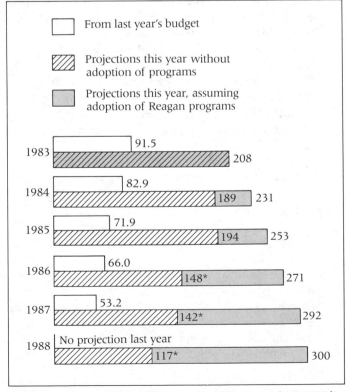

a. Deficit Projections

In billions of dollars, for fiscal years. This chart illustrates the degree to which the size of the Federal deficit was underestimated in the budget the President submitted to Congress last year, as well as his current projections of the deficit with and without the enactment of his proposals for tax increases and spending reductions. The deficit estimates in Presidential budgets over the years have often proved to be unrealistic. Congress generally does not approve all of a President's recommendations, and changing economic conditions affecting revenue and expenditures cannot be anticipated.

From last year's budget

Projections this year without adoption of programs

Projections this year, assuming adoption of Reagan programs

Year	From last year's budget	Without programs	With Reagan programs
1983	91.5	208	
1984	82.9	189	231
1985	71.9	194	253
1986	66.0	148*	271
1987	53.2	142*	292
1988	No projection last year	117*	300

SOURCE: *The New York Times*, January 29, 1983. Copyright © 1983 by The New York Times Company. Reprinted by permission.

* Includes adoption of contingency tax increases.

b. Government's Share of the National Wealth

This chart shows the ups and downs of government spending and revenue.

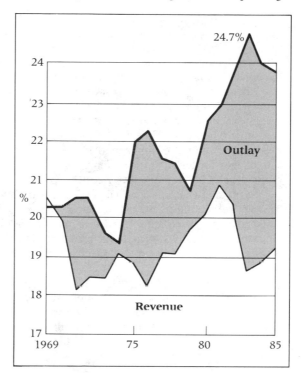

SOURCE: *Seattle Times, P.I.*, February 5, 1984, p. A3. Reprinted by permission.

* Estimated

c. Increase in the Debt

A look at statistics that shape the nation

The national debt has increased nearly a thousandfold since 1900. The biggest increase, $537.6 billion, or 245 percent, occurred between 1970 and 1980. The debt has decreased only twice since the century began.

	Debt	*Per Capita*
1900	$1.3 billion	$17
1910	$1.1 billion	$12
1920	$24.3 billion	$228
1930	$16.2 billion	$132
1940	$43 billion	$325
1950	$256.1 billion	$1,688
1960	$284.1 billion	$1,572
1970	$370.1 billion	$1,807
1980	$907.7 billion	$4,063
1982	$1.1 trillion*	$4,741*

SOURCE: Statistical Abstract of the U.S., 1981. U.S. Dept. of the Treasury.

* Estimated

Figure 12.7.   *The Budgetary Bafflegab*

All federal budgets are filled with arcane jargon and euphemisms. But in the fiscal 1984 budget, the administration has coined some new phrases.

Tax increases, known last year as "revenue enhancers," have become a "deficit insurance policy." Budget cuts to reduce the deficit are now "long-term structural reforms" and "spending freeze measures." The exception is when discussing the military. In that case, the United States needs a "restoration of our national defense," but in keeping with this lean budget, the level of funding must strive to provide the "maintenance of the defense buildup at a lower cost."

Most of the sacrifice called for by the budget could have been avoided, President Reagan says, if he hadn't been stuck with an "inherited budgetary imbalance" and "structural disequilibrium" when he took office in 1981. And despite both the president's and Congress' efforts, one of the unfortunate results was a "corrective interlude," in other words, the recession.

But the president is confident that Congress will not falter. "I believe that the revitalized congressional budget process signifies a refreshing willingness on the part of the Congress to work with my administration to address squarely the many crucial, complex, and politically difficult budgetary dilemmas before us." This is the same budget process that the president last year called "Mickey Mouse."

SOURCE: *Congressional Quarterly* Weekly Report, February 5, 1983, p. 306. Reprinted by permission.

government comes to a standstill without a budget. This strongly encourages negotiation and compromise that are not usually achieved within such a short timetable.

Technically, although the President proposes the initial budget, Congress also submits a budget. Tables 12.8 and 12.9 compare the budget totals and more detailed targets for the fiscal year 1984 that have been proposed by the various institutions. As noted, in standard fashion, there is a presidential version, a House version, a Senate version, and finally a conference committee version, and, again, it is the conference committee version that will most likely become the adopted budget. Although the various figures do not seem that far apart, remember that these numbers are in *billions* of dollars. For example, the difference between Reagan's revised April request of $245.4 billion dollars and the conference agreement of $240.0 billion is $5.4 *billion* dollars. Generally, the House targets are the highest, but the Senate targets also tend to be larger than the President's. The conference agreement, unsurprisingly, falls somewhere in between.

Because the Congressional Budget Resolution is a resolution and not legislation, it is not subject to presidential veto. However, the President can veto the appropriations and revenue bills that are passed in order to implement the resolution, and, of course, presidents have threatened to veto implementing legislation in order to influence the budget set forth by the resolution.

For the first ten years of the new process, the institutions appeared to be working together, although not without a good deal of friction. At least they have produced a budget for each fiscal year. Although the timetables may have been missed now and then, and the government run by continuing resolution for a period of time, the budget imposes enough pressure to force resolution. It is not, however, a smooth and administratively objective process. The budgetary process is as fraught with politics as any other legislation. As Dennis Ippolito points out:

> The federal budget has no doubt always been a political document, but its widening economic and social impact over recent decades has magnified its political importance.[19]

Although other issues may be more glamorous or symbolic, and thus more newsworthy than "number crunching," the budget sets the frame for all the others. If there are no funds, there is no governmental activity.

One of the purposes behind the new budgetary process was to look at the budget as a whole. Previously, last year's budget became essentially this year's budget, a process called *incrementalism*. Each agency redid its old budget, and added a little bit more for inflation and increased activity and some for the OMB to cut. It was safe, relatively easy, and generally accepted. Although agencies may still operate this way when drawing up their budgets, the necessity of addressing the budget as a whole has resulted in trade-offs and conscious choosing of priorities. As was described in the last chapter and will be discussed in the next, deliberate cutting and pasting has become the norm. The automatic incremental adjustments of the 1950s and 1960s appear to be a thing of the past. Bureaucratic agencies have much less clout than they previously appeared to possess.

Has the budgetary process been as successful in controlling runaway spending? The answer here, of course, depends upon what one means by "runaway" spending. Social programs have been deeply cut, as will be more fully discussed in the next chapter. Programs that were previously considered "uncontrollable," or "entitlements," have had their budgets lowered. On the other hand, spending on the military has drastically climbed. Aggregate spending has not declined; it has simply shifted categories. On the other hand, the call to "control runaway spending" has consistently been a stand-in for the call to reduce domestic programs.

---

[19] Ippolito, *Congressional Spending*, p. 23.

TABLE 12.8
The Federal Budget

a. Budget Totals Compared
(Fiscal years, in billions of dollars)

	1983	1984	1985	1986
Budget Authority				
Revised Reagan budget	$867.9	$906.4	$997.6	$1,082.5
House resolution	886.2	936.55	998.65	1,058.4
Senate resolution	875.93	914.7	986.37	1,050.2
Conference agreement, excluding reserve fund items	877.2	919.5	990.5	1,054.6
Conference agreement, including reserve fund items	883.36	928.725	996.75	1,059.3
Outlays				
Revised Reagan budget	808.5	843.9	917.0	988.4
House resolution	814.7	863.55	912.6	967.55
Senate resolution	807.33	849.7	910.77	966.0
Conference agreement, excluding reserve fund items	807.4	849.5	906.75	962.95
Conference agreement, including reserve fund items	812.85	858.925	911.6	966.635
Revenues				
Revised Reagan budget	598.3	653.7	732.4	843.8
House resolution	606.2	689.1	765.9	831.5
Senate resolution	603.3	671.1	743.1	835.9
Conference agreement	604.3	679.6	750.5	835.8
Deficit				
Revised Reagan budget	−210.2	−190.2	−184.6	−144.6
House resolution	−208.5	−174.45	−146.7	−136.05
Senate resolution	−204.0	−178.6	−167.7	−130.1
Conference agreement, excluding reserve fund items	203.1	169.9	156.25	127.15
Conference agreement, including reserve fund items	208.55	179.325	161.1	130.835

SOURCE: *Congressional Quarterly*, June 25, 1983, p. 1270. Reprinted by permission of Congressional Quarterly Inc.

b. The Budget-Approval Process

President's Budget

Proposed for the fiscal year 1984, in billions of dollars. Economic assumptions, in percentages, are for calendar 1983.

OUTLAYS	$848.5
RECEIPTS	659.7
DEFICIT	−188.8
MILITARY SPENDING	$245.3
NONMILITARY SPENDING	603.2

Economic Assumptions

REAL G.N.P. GROWTH	3.1%
INFLATION (G.N.P. deflator)	5.6
UNEMPLOYMENT	10.4

(To Congress) →

House and Senate Versions

Proposed for the fiscal year 1984, in billions of dollars. Economic assumptions, in percentages, are for calendar 1983.

	House 3/23	Senate 5/19
OUTLAYS	$863.6	$849.7
RECEIPTS	689.1	671.1
DEFICIT	−174.5	−178.6
MILITARY SPENDING	$235.4	$241.6
NONMILITARY SPENDING	628.2	608.1

Economic Assumptions

REAL G.N.P. GROWTH	3.9%	3.9%
INFLATION (G.N.P. deflator)	4.8	4.8
UNEMPLOYMENT	10.2	10.2

→

Conference Version

Proposed for the fiscal year 1984, in billions of dollars. Economic assumptions, in percentages, are for calendar 1983.

OUTLAYS	$849.5
RECEIPTS	679.6
DEFICIT	−169.9
MILITARY SPENDING	$240.0
NONMILITARY SPENDING	609.5

Economic Assumptions

REAL G.N.P. GROWTH	4.8%
INFLATION (C.P.I.)	3.9
UNEMPLOYMENT	9.9

The conference agreement earmarked in a "reserve fund," a new budget category, $8.5 billion of tentative 1984 outlays for several types of proposed recession relief sponsored by House Democrats. The conferees agreed that these outlays would be added to the budget spending total and the deficit only if Congress authorized the proposed programs.

SOURCE: *The New York Times*, June 22, 1983. Copyright © 1983 by The New York Times Company. Reprinted by permission.

TABLE 12.9 Detailed Comparison of FY '84 Budget Targets *(in billions of dollars, excluding reserved funds)*

Category	Reagan Revised April Request	House Target	Senate Target	Conference Agreement
National Defense				
Budget Authority	$280.5	$263.85	$270.65	$268.60
Outlays	245.4	235.40	241.60	240.00
International Affairs				
Budget Authority	16.7	18.85	18.20	18.70
Outlays	13.4	13.20	12.70	12.95
Science Space & Technology				
Budget Authority	8.5	8.85	8.50	8.70
Outlays	8.2	8.85	8.20	8.30
Energy				
Budget Authority	2.9	4.40	3.90	4.20
Outlays	3.6	4.30	4.10	4.30
Natural Resources & Environment				
Budget Authority	9.0	12.10	12.00	12.05
Outlays	10.3	12.50	12.50	12.50
Agriculture				
Budget Authority	13.5	14.85	11.60	13.00
Outlays	9.7	14.65	11.40	11.50
Commerce & Housing Credit				
Budget Authority	7.6	6.10	5.90	6.00
Outlays	0.9	2.30	1.80	2.25
Transportation				
Budget Authority	27.8	28.30	27.70	28.00
Outlays	25.9	26.15	25.90	26.00
Community & Regional Development				
Budget Authority	6.0	8.25	6.60	6.85
Outlays	7.7	8.55	8.10	8.10
Education, Employment & Social Services				
Budget Authority	25.5	39.15	31.80	33.95
Outlays	25.3	32.70	27.25	28.35

Health				
Budget Authority	94.3	96.25	32.75	32.10
Outlays	90.6	90.60	32.75	32.00
Medical Insurance				
Budget Authority	—	—	61.40	62.50
Outlays	—	—	60.30	60.60
Income Security				
Budget Authority	287.2	310.60	25.90	124.80
Outlays	276.5	284.70	104.00	102.35
Social Security				
Budget Authority	—	—	174.90	176.00
Outlays	—	—	176.40	176.40
Veterans Benefits & Services				
Budget Authority	26.0	26.00	25.70	25.55
Outlays	25.6	25.55	25.60	25.45
Administration of Justice				
Budget Authority	5.5	5.60	6.00	5.85
Outlays	5.5	5.50	6.00	5.85
General Government				
Budget Authority	6.0	5.80	5.70	5.60
Outlays	6.0	6.05	5.70	5.60
General Fiscal Assistance				
Budget Authority	6.8	7.60	7.10	7.25
Outlays	6.8	7.60	7.00	7.15
Net Interest				
Budget Authority	102.3	96.15	95.90	97.10
Outlays	102.3	96.15	95.90	97.10
Allowances				
Budget Authority	0.9	1.20	0.60	.75
Outlays	0.9	1.25	0.60	.80
Offsetting Receipts				
Budget Authority	-20.8	-17.35	-18.10	-18.05
Outlays	-20.8	-17.35	-18.10	-18.05

SOURCE: *Congressional Quarterly Inc.*, June 25, 1983, p. 1274. Reprinted by permission.

The budgetary process does appear to have given Congress a greater role to play in the fundamental political battle over fiscal policy. At least the potential is there, and, in recent years it has begun to be realized. It is probably too early to tell where the balance of political power will fall. That balance probably depends upon factors outside the governmental arena, in the economic and social structures, and in the political participation of others, as we will see in Part IV.

PART IV

Political Participation

CHAPTER 13

The Impact of Economic and Social Problems

For some people, political participation is a routine civic duty that is performed in regular ways like any other daily practice. But for most people, it is a highly variable impulse, one that must be sparked by events, government actions, felt needs, or momentary outrage at some person or thing. Dramatic events and silent environmental pressures combine with what governments have done or might do to generate a stream of forces that impel people into action of some kind. Exactly *which* people are induced to take *what* kinds of action will be the main focus of later chapters. In this chapter, we will focus on the way that major problems and public policies affect people and lead them toward political participation.

Our premise is that economic and social problems, and what government has done or might do about them, are a powerful impetus to political participation. Economic issues generate such important social impacts because they have to do with the most fundamental aspects of daily existence—first the presence or absence of food, clothing, and shelter, and then the level of well-being that a person experiences. The fact and/or prospect of inflation or unemployment, or of recession or depression, carries such vital significance that it can shatter long-held beliefs and practices and send people off toward wholly new forms and directions of political participation.

There are other sources of participation generation, of course, such as crises in foreign policy, energy shortages, or social issues like the right to abortion or the right to carry guns, but these are usually either secondary to basic questions of economic conditions and prospects, or only briefly displace them under special circumstances. For most people, political participation is shaped by issues such as jobs, prices, and the prospects for economic security. These are, quite literally, the "bread and butter" issues of politics.

In this chapter, we shall look first at world and national economic problems of the 1980s and the government policies that are deployed to cope with them. We want to understand both problems and policies as they appear likely to translate themselves into threats or promises of inflation, stable prosperity, or unemployment. Our emphasis will be on how such problems and policies affect people, which next requires us to see those people in their social context, and as they see themselves. This will lead us to the exploration of how attitudes and opinions change, which is the subject of the following chapter.

THE WORLD AND NATIONAL ECONOMIC CONTEXT

We saw earlier that the United States is fully integrated into the capitalist world economy as a kind of "first among equals"—the largest economy, but one that cannot help but rise and fall in concert with the rest of the world. It has some advantages, but some vulnerabilities as well, in that our level of economic prosperity is not totally subject to control by either American government or private economic action. Let us identify and illustrate how we can be affected by what is happening elsewhere before we focus specifically on U.S. problems and policies. We shall start with international-trade and balance-of-payments issues.

The "balance of payments" issue has to do with the relative volumes of merchandise—imports and exports—that are being exchanged, and also with the payments that are exchanged for services provided overseas and/ or the principal or interest on outstanding loans. If the net result of all these transactions is a substantial outflow of capital from a given country, its economy will be weakened. Such weakness will show up as inflation, or reduced value of its currency, or both. Disadvantages in further transactions with other countries will accumulate until the weaker country becomes, in effect, an economic colony of stronger countries. Consequently, all major countries try to keep their international transactions at least roughly in balance.

For the United States, balance of payments problems arise because the volume of imports nearly always exceeds the volume of exports, and sometimes by a wide margin. In recent years, only the export of services and the growing volume of loan payments has maintained an approximate balance in total payments. In the early 1980s, for example, merchandise trade balances were negative (imports exceeded exports) by about $30 billion per year, but payments for services and loans more than made up for this imbalance.

This problem took a new twist in the mid-1980s. Because of high interest rates in the United States, which were brought about by deliberate U.S. policies in the early 1980s, the U.S. dollar rose sharply in value as compared to other currencies. This meant that it was harder to sell the (now more expensive) U.S. exports in foreign countries, and easier to sell (newly less expensive) foreign imports in the United States. The United States experienced an unprecedented imbalance of merchandise trade of $60 billion in 1983. Moreover, reduced exports meant lower growth, fewer profits, and lost jobs in the United States. *Business Week* estimated in 1983 that the high-value dollar would cost $100 billion in lost GNP and 1,600,000 jobs in that year alone.[1]

Self-interest resulting from the need to keep payments roughly in balance can encourage countries to limit imports into their jurisdictions, and make them act contrary to the general interest in expanding international trade. This situation has been rendered more acute by some governments' practices of subsidizing exports to make them more competitive in foreign markets. Both workers and industry often seek help from their national governments to protect them from foreign goods entering their domestic market. All the major capitalist countries pledge repeatedly not to impose restrictions, but all were under pressure from local businesses to help save them from foreign competition that appeared to be hurting sales and profitability.

Import restrictions can take several forms, including tariffs, quotas, prohibitions, and conditions pertaining to the sending country's acceptance of exports in exchange. If one country imposes such limits, others are tempted to do so, either in retaliation or because of their own domestic pressures. However, retaliation by other governments could then set off a ruinous trade war. On the other hand, certain advantages might be gained by some industries in more powerful countries by insisting on complete elimination of all restrictions, and so what seems to be clearly in the common interest is not readily achieved when opportunities arise for serving the needs of powerful domestic industries.

A related danger is the instability of the international monetary system. This is the set of arrangements between banks and governments whereby the exchange values of various currencies are maintained. Stable exchange rates are vital to carrying on all international transactions and particularly to the level of trade. If sellers cannot be sure of the value of the currency in which they will be paid, they are much less likely to sell. The results, of course, are lower profits and growth, and greater unemployment. When one nation's economy seems to be very strong, its currency may serve as the international standard, as did the U.S. dollar for a long time. Exchange rates may be *fixed* in relation to such a standard; all countries' currencies are set at a specific ratio to the dollar by their governments. In a time of economic instability, however, when no standard is generally accepted, exchange rates are permitted to *float,* or vary. The rates then depend on the actual trading between buyers and sellers in the currency markets.

---

[1] *Business Week*, August 23, 1983, p. 41.

It might appear that the capitalist world has everything to gain from close cooperation, but neither avoidance of all import restrictions nor stable exchange rates can automatically be anticipated, even though they are in the long-run best interest of the entire capitalist world. The crux of the question is what national governments actually do; each country's attempt to deal with inflation, unemployment, interest rates, domestic economies, or balance of payments problems impacts on the others in crucial ways. Also, some sectors of world capitalism stand to gain from every restriction or fluctuation—and some stand to lose. The struggle for comparative advantage is reflected in the behavior of national governments, some of which profit from endangering the whole. That danger, of course, is not only the threat of economic collapse, but also the social and political unrest that accompanies severe dislocations.

The World Financial Crisis of the Mid-1980s. A prime example of mutual dependence *and* risk is provided by the debt crisis that developed in the early 1980s and seemed likely to continue for some time. Capitalist world banks, including all the major American banks, had made more and more (and larger and larger) loans to developing Third World countries throughout the late 1960s and 1970s. There were several reasons behind this expanding investment activity. One was simply that the banks wanted to get in on the high-profit opportunities provided by overseas investments in the late 1960s that were caused by the success of American multinational corporations. Another was that the oil crisis of the post–1973 period seemed to call for "recycling" of OPEC oil deposits into loans to non-oil Third World nations so that they could pay for the oil they needed for continued development. Finally, the pressure to expand export trade led to a number of loans and credits to Third World countries for the purchase of capitalist world products.

In the expanding, inflationary world of the late 1960s and 1970s, these loans looked safe enough. The substantial share of loans that went into marginal energy-development projects seemed sound, given the prospect of continuing oil shortages and price increases that appeared certain in those years. But then came the energy-conservation response to the sustained price rises of the 1970s, followed by the reduced usage stemming from the recession of 1980–82. In the transformation toward high-technology production and services and away from heavy industry, further drops in energy usage occurred. The recession reduced demand for Third World products and raw materials, and in some cases reduced prices as well, leaving many of these countries with greatly reduced sources of export income. The high value of the U.S. dollar also made it difficult for the Third World countries to repay the loans—most of which were due for payment in dollars.

Suddenly, many formerly solid Third World countries were not only suffering the same or higher inflation as the industrialized countries, but were also in danger of defaulting on their loan obligations. Their problems quickly translated into great danger for capitalist world banks, particularly the biggest American banks. In several cases, the banks had loaned major shares of their assets, and depended on repayment for much of their annual profit. (See Table 13.1 for an indication of how much the major U.S. banks are involved in the world economy as a whole and the Third World in particular.) Failure of repayment by Third World countries could mean bankruptcy to the banks and vast losses to their stockholders.

The most important goal for capitalist world bankers, therefore, is to assure continued payments by the Third World governments who are involved. Most of all, outright repudiation must be avoided. If one government should refuse further payments, others might follow and the whole structure of assets and prospective earnings could come tumbling down— and with it the world financial system. Panic and depression would be likely, unless national governments stepped in and took over the banking system on a completely unprecedented scale.

There are repudiation movements in many Third World countries that are based among those who believe that the industrialized world has done far too little to help the Third World toward development. Instead, they see the capitalist world banks and corporations as being engaged in continuing exploitation of the Third World for their own profit. Unless there is more no-strings aid offered, they argue, the Third World should simply repudiate its debts and accomplish a massive transfer of wealth in one decisive act. They urge at least the formation of a "debtors' cartel" that is equivalent to the OPEC alliance. Such a collective organization could extract better terms from the capitalist countries than individual nations now do from the IMF.

For a considerable period of time, there are likely to be problems associated with Third World debt repayment. The roots of these problems lie in the basic relationship between the industrial, wealthy nations and the poorer, developing ones, and in the level of international activity and prosperity that exists at any given time. Immediate and recurring crises are likely, however, to have specific grounding in a particular government's political perspective and situation. A nationalist government that is coming to power in a debt-ridden Third World country might seek domestic support and some economic gain by repudiating loans to capitalist world banks.

The question then would be whether the other banks and governments of the capitalist world could put enough economic (or military) pressure on such a government to force it to pay or cause its collapse (as was done in Chile in 1973). If not, then the question would become how long it would take before enough other countries repudiated or delayed their payments to bring about the collapse of the international financial system. There is no question about the seriousness of this problem for the long-term future.

This mutual dependence extends well beyond the mere repayment of loans, however vital to the capitalist world banks that may be. The capitalist countries need economic recovery and prosperity in the Third World in order to be able to sell their exports in those markets. The large dollar amounts and shares of all exports represented by Third World markets are very important to growth, profits, and jobs in the developed countries. At

TABLE 13.1
Third World Debts: The Lenders' Problems, 1982

TOP TEN U.S. BANKS (RANKED BY TOTAL ASSETS)	FOREIGN LENDING IN GENERAL				LOAN EXPOSURE IN THIRD WORLD		
	Foreign Assets ($ Billions)	Foreign Assets Percentage of Total	Foreign Revenue Percentage of Total	Foreign Profits Percentage of Total	Loans ($ Billions)	Percentage of Total Loans	Percentage of Total Equity
Citicorp	73.3	60	61	62	9.8	11.4	203
Bank America	54.8	46	54	65	6.8	9.2	148
Chase Manhattan	41.4	51	61	70	6.1	11.0	220
Manufacturers' Hanover	30.3	47	51	49	6.8	16.0	245
Morgan Guaranty	32.9	56	62	72	4.1	12.8	150
Chemical N.Y.	18.6	39	44	39	3.5	11.5	182
Continental Illinois	14.8	34	36	65	2.0	6.2	119
First Interstate	8.1	20	18	9	1.2	4.7	64
Bankers Trust	21.1	52	55	51	2.2	10.6	143
Security Pacific	9.2	25	25	32	1.2	4.8	80
Totals, Top Ten Banks					43.7	10.3	169

SOURCE: *Forbes*, July 4, 1983; *The American Banker*, as reported in *The New York Times*, March 18, 1983.

the same time, Third World countries need economic recovery and prosperity in the capitalist world in order to be able to sell their products at prices that will earn them enough to cover both imports and loan payments.

U.S. Economic Problems. We shall take up only four leading problems, which will be enough to show the complexity of the difficulties that the United States faces in the 1980s. These are inflation, unemployment, low growth, and (probably a leading cause of all the others) low productivity and lack of competitiveness.

Inflation is a general rise in the prices of goods and services such that the *real* value, or purchasing power, of money is reduced. Three dollars are necessary today to buy what one dollar bought yesterday. More specifically, what cost $1.00 in 1967 cost $3.05 in 1984. The blame for inflation is variously attributed to, depending on one's ideology, government spending and regulations, lack of investment in new plants, OPEC oil price rises, wage pressures, the power of large corporations to keep their prices going up, and the "inflation psychology" that leads people to buy now in fear of future inflation. Each, and all, have been promoted as being major causes.

What are the consequences of inflation? The first and most damaging impact is on the standards of living of millions of ordinary people. Every dollar previously saved or currently earned can buy less than half of what it did only a few years before. Both middle-class and working-class people find that they must fundamentally alter their styles of living. With the greatest price rises coming in such necessities as housing, energy, food, and health care, many families can manage only by cutting down or eliminating "basics" that they have taken for granted for years. While nearly everybody suffers from inflation, people do not suffer equally. Some workers, usually those in the unionized fields, *may* be able to stay ahead of inflation. Those whose incomes are derived from ownership of real estate or corporate stock stand the best chance of staying ahead, because profits and stock value often rise in value faster than the rate of inflation.

Individual businesses may benefit from inflation or for brief periods of time, but inflation eventually threatens them also. Major corporations and banks, for example, need predictability and stability, in order to be able to plan ahead. If profits are to be ensured, then return on investment must exceed the rate of inflation. If loans and other investments made this year are repaid ten years from now in money that is of substantially lower value, then they will return insufficient real profits to investors, and soon there will be no willing investors. Similarly, businesses must be confident that their investments in plant and equipment today will lead to sales at prices that will mean real profits tomorrow. The problem is not so much the prospect of inflation itself, because that can be planned for; it is the uneven or unpredictable rate of inflation that most troubles business and financial interests.

Finally, inflation, if prolonged, is likely to have an unsettling effect on broad segments of the population. Those who have fallen behind economically, and even those who by dint of special efforts have managed to stay even, begin to feel the pressure. Expressions of resentment at the economic and political system that has permitted such conditions begin to be heard. Over a prolonged period of time, such resentment could give rise to rejection of the system and eventually action to fundamentally change it.

Unemployment—people without jobs—is for many an even more serious problem than inflation. A lively argument rages over which of the two should receive primary government attention; of course, much depends on how one is affected. The low-skilled workers and minorities who make up the bulk of the unemployed often suffer hardships far beyond those imposed by inflation, but their destitution and hunger may not be as visible to the politically more powerful middle-class white-collar workers whose primary difficulty is with inflation. Economists, bankers, and others, whose focus is primarily on aggregate statistics and the behavior of the economy as a whole, tend to be concerned first with inflation.

It is not easy to measure unemployment accurately. There is good evidence that the official rates considerably understate the actual amount of unemployment in the country. The government's rates are based on its data on people who are receiving unemployment benefits and/or currently looking for work. However, such figures do not include people who have given up looking for work, who are working part-time when they want and need full-time jobs, who are in school because they couldn't find work, or who are working at jobs that are well below their skill capacities. Moreover, many more people actually experience unemployment during a year than show up in the unemployment statistics at any given time. In 1982, about one-third of all households in the United States had at least one member who was unemployed for some part of the year. For every worker who actually suffers involuntary unemployment, two or three others live in continuing fear of losing their jobs.

In a variety of ways, unemployment is costly to the economy as a whole as well as to the individuals who are out of work. Lost production is one component, but so is the reduced level of health that results when people no longer have health insurance that enables them to obtain medical care. The impact on the federal budget is more tangible. It is estimated that each percentage point of unemployment represents about $30 billion in costs to the government—$20 billion in taxes not received, and $10 billion in unemployment insurance and welfare costs that must be paid out to people denied their usual source of income.

It is now as difficult to sort out the causes of unemployment as it is the causes of inflation. The combination of low skills on the part of some people and a generally slack economy have kept unemployment rates in the United States relatively high ever since the Vietnam War. The transformation toward high technology production, the use of lighter materials, and the multiplication of data-processing services has displaced many workers on a more or less permanent basis. The recession of the early 1980s produced even greater numbers of unemployed people, however. Together, these various causes made for a problem that seemed likely to continue well into the future. Like inflation, sustained unemployment can lead to social upheaval, and for that reason it will command prominent attention in the next decade.

Low economic growth means simply that the U.S. economy has not grown at rates that are equal to its major competitors or even to its own previous performance; the level of growth has been consistently low. Although not a sustained recession (negative growth), it has been so low that inflation and unemployment occurred *together*—an unprecedented combination. Usually a capitalist economy experiences a cycle of high growth (with very low unemployment), then inflation, and subsequently declining growth to the point of recession, and then depression and high unemployment, but in the 1970s, inflation, unemployment, and low growth occurred together, leading to the term "stagflation."

The consequences of low growth are not only persistent unemployment and the continuing problem of inflation, but low profits for most major businesses. Better investment opportunities elsewhere lead to the shift of capital, and ultimately to the loss of more growth, profits, and jobs in the domestic U.S. economy. American corporations end up manufacturing products overseas for sale in the American market, and American banks make most of their loans to foreign countries and projects; then the domestic U.S. economy starts on a long-term decline. This is pretty much the story of the period from the mid-1960s to the present.

Productivity refers to the rate at which hours or days of labor input result in tangible output—products or services that can be sold to somebody else. When productivity rates increase, more products are made in a given number of hours of labor, and businesses that sell such products can make more profits without raising prices. Some of those profits can be given to workers, so that wages can rise but not prices; so *real* wages can rise. On a base of high and steadily increasing productivity, the U.S. economy prospered for years, with U.S. workers enjoying higher wage levels than workers in other countries.

But productivity in the United States began to decline in the late 1960s and 1970s. Both U.S. corporations and other investors were building new plants with modern technological capabilities in Europe and the Third World. Fewer plants were built in the United States, where growth and profits were low, and many existing plants were closed. Investment capital was used to finance mergers, in speculative ventures, or in other ways that did not result in increased productive capability in the United States. Because of a lack of newer tools of production, and with increasing ratios of managers and administrative employees to support, U.S. workers could not increase productivity at past rates.

Along with slowing growth in productivity came increased competition from goods produced abroad. Newer plants, streamlined production arrangements, and quick and inexpensive transportation meant that foreign manufacturers could produce high-quality goods for sale at lower prices than American-made products—and in American markets. Competition from imports became heavy within the United States, and American exports met stiff foreign competition in every market around the world. In

TABLE
13.2   *U.S. Economic Performance, 1960–83 (in percents)*

	AVERAGES					
INDICATOR	*1960–67*	*1968–72*	*1973–80*	*1981*	*1982*	*1983 (est.)*
Inflation	1.6	4.6	8.9	10.4	6.2	4.5
Unemployment	5.1	4.7	6.6	7.6	9.6	9.6
Rate of Growth in GNP	4.3	3.3	2.8	2.0	− 1.8	5.5
Rate of Growth in Productivity	3.8	2.3	1.1	1.8	0.4	2.5

SOURCE: *Economic Report of the President, 1983,* Table B–41 (calculations by the authors).

the industrialized countries that were our major competitors, wage levels rose to equal or exceed those of American workers. The advantage that these foreign producers enjoyed was not due to lower wages, but to higher productivity. In the Third World, where many American corporations shifted their production, workers' wages were indeed much lower, and American jobs were lost for both productivity *and* wage reasons. The problem of productivity and competitiveness thus has several parts, and it also seems likely to continue for some time into the future.

Table 13.2 summarizes the U.S. experience with these key problems from 1960 to the present. This table is best read by columns. The four problems are listed in the column at the left, and time periods range consecutively in columns across the page. In the first period, 1960–67, growth and productivity were relatively high, and (partly as a result) inflation was very low, but unemployment was well above the 3 percent considered "normal" at the time.

In the second period, the height of the Vietnam War economic speedup of 1968–72, productivity and growth slowed substantially and inflation picked up sharply—but the war effort temporarily employed more people. In the period after the first "oil shock," growth and productivity dropped almost as much as in the prior period, inflation almost doubled, and unemployment increased by about 40 percent, exceeding earlier levels by large margins.

The final years of the table show the impact of the recession of the early 1980s. Growth was negative, productivity was lower until the "recovery" began, and unemployment was very high. As might be expected, once the recession took hold, inflation was down sharply. The problem that remained for American policymakers was that of trying to return to the steady growth, low inflation and unemployment, high productivity years of the bygone era—or to come as close to those halcyon days as current conditions would permit.

The Policies of the Early 1980s. Just as current problems form part of the

political economic context at any given time, so do the policies that have
been implemented in the past. What the government (or other major
forces) actually *does* enters and becomes part of the larger context that
shapes what people do. The U.S. government has operated on the assumption that it should control the excesses of the business cycle since the
Employment Act of 1946. When inflation threatens, the government
should spend less, take in more revenues than it spends, and generally
"dampen" the economy. When recession and unemployment threaten,
the government should spend more, take in less revenue than it spends,
and generally "pump up" the economy.

In the 1960s, through a set of happy circumstances, this seemed to
work, and it was assumed that we had solved all problems. We were
committed to full employment; everyone could share in an ever-
expanding pie. This euphoria lasted about five years; after that, the problems we have just reviewed set in and began to redefine the American
economic and political context. Moreover, each effort to solve one problem
seemed to exacerbate the others. No national administration of the 1970s
was successful in coping with the economic difficulties. As we have seen,
they worsened throughout the 1970s, until the 1980 election produced a
president who promised a drastic change of direction. In the next paragraphs, we will describe the essence of the policies actually pursued.

1. *Fiscal policy: the "supply-side" tax cuts.* Fiscal policy refers to the
taxing and spending practices of the government itself, and to the ratio
between them (either surplus or deficit). Since the New Deal, national
government fiscal policy had been based on "Keynesian" principles,
named after the British economist John Maynard Keynes. Keynes's thesis
was that the key to economic growth was the maintenance of consumer
demand. Further, that government could and should manage demand
through its own fiscal policies. Taxing the unproductive excess income of
the wealthy and transferring funds to the poor, who would spend it for
immediate needs, were part of this design. However, the major component
was management of the annual budget by running deficits in years when
the economy needed speeding up, and surpluses when it should be slowed
down.

As noted, Keynesianism seemed to work—for a while. However, these
principles came under heavy criticism in the late 1970s. It was argued that
they applied only to the "demand side." They neglected the need to encourage the investment in plants and facilities that would make U.S. industry productive and competitive again. Too much money was being transferred from the investment resources of the rich to the consumption desires
of the poor, with resulting inflation and lack of investment. Government
was great at running deficits and pumping up the economy, particularly in
election years, but was politically unable to achieve the budget constraints
that were needed to control inflation.

Thus, the "supply-side" theory that dominated the early years of the
Reagan administration came into existence. Supply-side thinking focused
squarely on the need for capital investment to produce new goods and

services, which was the reverse of Keynesian concern for maintaining demand. The way to achieve such investment was to see to it that the wealthy had more money to invest; one way was to cut taxes sharply, particularly those of people who had the greater incomes and were most likely to invest it. It would also be desirable to cut government transfers to the poor, who used such funds for consumption instead of investment. Even more important would be the reduction or elimination of government regulations that added costs to the production process, such as safety or environmental requirements.

In 1981, the Reagan administration moved to implement all of these principles. The largest tax cut in American history was enacted, with the greatest reductions for corporations and the rich. Scheduled increases in many social programs and individual "entitlements" (previous government commitments) were reduced, and some programs were eliminated entirely. Regulations were relaxed, both officially and informally, by reduced enforcement efforts.

At the same time, however, the Reagan administration was committed to a military buildup that was equally unprecedented in American peacetime history. Fears that the Soviet Union was achieving military strength that was well in excess of that of the United States had begun to surface in the mid-1970s. The Carter administration decided in 1978 to expand the military share of the national budget steadily in future years. But, both as a candidate and as President, Reagan far outdistanced any of his predecessors in his determination to expand American military spending. The rate of expansion, and the levels sought, were equalled only in wartime emergency years.

This combination of priorities had a dramatic effect on national fiscal policy, as we saw in detail in Chapter 11. In this chapter, we are concerned particularly with the size of the national budget deficit in future years, and its implications. Table 13.3 shows how the Reagan tax cuts and military buildup combine to make for record-breaking deficits for several years to come. The first three rows show the expansion in military spending, both in dollars and as proportions of the federal budget and the country's GNP. The increases are steady and substantial, leading even some supportive members of Congress to wonder whether the military are capable of spending so much money in such a short time.

The size of the federal deficits are shown in different versions in the next several rows of the table. Notice first the contrasts between the deficits as they are first estimated and as they actually occur; the estimates are always much lower than the final reality. The actual deficit for 1983 was the highest in history, although both the military outlay and the budget deficit were lower as a proportion of total GNP than during the World War II years of greatest spending for military purposes. The projected deficits for the rest of the 1980s are huge, however. If, as seems likely, they are well below what will actually occur, the United States is in for vast new deficits and additions to the national debt.

The irony in this is that Ronald Reagan is by far the most conservative

TABLE 13.3
The Military Buildup and the Federal Deficit, 1981–86

	FISCAL YEARS					
	1981	*1982*	*1983*	*1984*	*1985*	*1986*
Military outlay in 1983 $ billions	159.8	187.4	214.8	245.3	285.3	323.0
Military outlay as percentage of total budget	24.3	25.7	26.7	28.9	31.0	32.6
Military outlay as percentage of GNP	5.6	6.2	6.7	7.0	7.5	7.8
Budget deficit, 1983 estimate	16.0*	27.5*	91.5*	82.9	71.9	66.0
Budget deficit, 1984 estimate	57.9**	110.7**	208.0**	189.0	194.0	148.0
Budget deficit, 1984 estimate without proposed social cuts or contingency taxes	—	—	—	231	253	271
Budget deficits as percentage of GNP	23.6**	24.6**	25.7**	24.7	24.4	24.1

SOURCE: Calculated from Office of Management and Budget, *The U.S. Budget in Brief, 1984.*
* First estimates.
** Actual year-end deficits, and percentage of GNP.

president of recent decades, and has been strongly committed to the principle of balanced budgets throughout his political career. With these deficits already estimated in his budget, he nevertheless endorsed in 1983 the proposal for a constitutional amendment to require that the national budget be balanced each year. Traditional fiscal conservatives of both political parties, however, were predictably aghast at the size of these deficits. They appealed to the President to slow the rise in military spending and/or raise taxes so as to reduce the deficits and avoid what was otherwise assumed to be massive inflationary consequences; they prevailed briefly in 1982, so that the largest tax cut in history was followed by the largest tax increase in history. The budget deficits shown in the table were those that remained after such actions, and, as the next to last row of the table shows, the deficits will be much higher without further cuts in social programs and/or tax increases.

2. *Monetary policy: from inflation to recession.* Monetary policy refers to the way that the supply of money in the economy is managed, and particularly affects the level of interest rates. Some people believe that there is a level of growth in the money supply that is appropriate for steady economic growth with stable prices; this is roughly 4 percent per year. If inflation threatens, the government should contract the money supply below this level, which will make money scarce and credit more expensive. Interest rates will rise, discouraging investment and expansion of the economy, and economic activity in general will be slowed. When expansion is

desired, on the other hand, the money supply can be increased, interest rates will drop, and general economic activity will pick up again.

In the United States, power over the money supply lies primarily with the Federal Reserve System, the independent agency governed by the Federal Reserve Board (the "Fed") that we used as an illustration at the outset of Chapter 2. The Chairman of the Fed is often referred to as the second most powerful person in American economic affairs. We will now focus on what the Fed *did* in the early 1980s; it took responsibility for controlling inflation once and for all by firmly contracting the money supply.

When this happened, interest rates were forced up sharply and economic activity slowed almost immediately. Growth, which formerly was sluggish, turned into actual decline. In this way, the country was pushed into recession before the end of 1981. (Two consecutive quarters of "negative growth" is officially recognized as a recession.) The Fed kept the money supply low throughout early 1982 despite rapidly increasing unemployment and business bankruptcies—both of which were at levels that had not been reached since the Great Depression of the 1930s. With these conditions, in which some major industries were virtually at a standstill, it was little wonder that inflation dropped rapidly to its lowest level in a decade. Only later in the year, when the Fed was satisfied that inflation had been controlled, and the elections were approaching, was the money supply allowed to increase.

Not surprisingly, these policies were highly controversial. Some argued that inflation was being controlled at the cost of unemployment and suffering on the part of working people. It could have been managed more effectively through wage and price controls in which all would share the burden roughly equally. Even some of those who were most concerned about inflation's damage to the economy felt that interest rates had been pushed too high for too long. Too many businesses were being forced into bankruptcy, and the economy was being damaged in new and unnecessary ways. The federal budget deficit was thrown into further imbalance by the lack of tax revenues from the depressed economy and the expanding costs of unemployment compensation and welfare. State governments were forced by the lack of revenues to cut back on services just at the time that the federal government was also cutting back.

When the Fed eased up on the money supply and interest rates moderated, a recovery began—a much-heralded recovery for which both supply-siders and monetarists claimed credit. But the character and prospects of the recovery remained in doubt. The continuing and apparently unavoidable prospect of historically-unprecedented deficits made it seem likely that inflation could return at any time. The expectation of high deficits and inflation led to continuing high interest rates in the United States and a high value for the American dollar. The consequences of these conditions would be to reduce American export sales (and the growth, profits, and jobs that accompany them). Perhaps more important, capital was being drawn out of foreign countries, which impeded their recoveries and development. Most important of all, however, was the prospect that

U.S. unemployment would remain high because of the transformation to high technology production and service occupations.

PROBLEMS AND POLICIES AS THEY AFFECT PEOPLE

What we have seen so far is a delicate and uncertain world and national economic context, in which the possibility of inflation and/or unemployment remains a reality in the future of many Americans. National government policies—particularly the approaches that are taken to control inflation, achieve economic recovery, and accomplish the military buildup—are very important factors in shaping the economic conditions of peoples' lives. How they affect people, particularly the people who depend on government social programs for assistance, will play a powerful role in shaping future political participation.

The lowest income levels of the American social pyramid are the people who are most affected by government social programs. As we have seen, the ranks of the poor are quite disproportionately made up of minorities and the elderly, with female-headed households in these categories being particularly likely to be included. Women generally suffer significant disparities in income, even when they hold jobs similar to those held by men, and have also been dependent on government "affirmative action" and anti-wage discrimination programs in recent years. In this section, we shall look closely at how government policies have affected income distribution, and at the changes of the Reagan administration years on such policies and their effects on lower-income groups.

Before doing so, however, it may be useful to set the context for such analysis a bit more deeply. Our contention is that, at least in the case of minorities, it has been government policies that have contributed to low-income status in the first place. Government action is one of the major reasons these people are poor today, and the history of such actions forms an important part of the context in which they see government and decide whether or not to take part in politics. We shall review this background briefly, and then move to the changing roles of the government in income distribution.

U.S. Minorities and Government Policies

What have governments done with respect to nonwhite races on the American continent—and why? And what have their acts meant for not only the affected minorities, but also the dominant society? For each minority, we will touch only on certain basic policies to illustrate generalized and long-established practices.

Native Americans. When Columbus "discovered" America, there were probably about 1 million persons living on the North American continent.

Believing that he had reached India, Columbus mislabeled those he met "Indians"; this was to be the first of many instances of Europeans' failure to understand native Americans except on their own terms. The "Indians" of the time were highly diverse people, but they shared the beliefs that land is a resource for all to share and that human beings should live in harmony with nature, appropriating only those animals needed for food and clothing. As waves of land-hungry white settlers arrived, the Indian was introduced to the concepts of private ownership of land and the use of nature for commercial purposes such as fur-trapping. Indian lands were "bought," acquired by means of governmental decrees or soon violated treaties, or despoiled by the hunting and trapping of commercially-oriented whites.

By 1840, Indians had been displaced from practically all their lands east of the Mississippi. In some cases, broken treaties were accompanied by forced marches (or "removals"), in which thousands of Indians were resettled farther west by whites who wanted their remaining lands. In a series of "Indian Wars," thousands of Indians were killed, injured, or rendered homeless to make first the South and then the West available for commercial and homesteading opportunities. On the Great Plains, millions of buffalo were slaughtered by white hunters for commercial purposes, depriving the Indians of their major source of food and hides. Indians were confined to reservations on then unwanted lands and caught between the Army's urge to exterminate them completely and the Bureau of Indian Affairs' preference for simply managing their affairs and making "good Americans" out of them.

By 1900, displacement, removals, wars, and disease had reduced the Indian population to one-sixteenth its original size. Reservation schools enforced the dominant society's customs and religions, thus preventing Indians from knowing their own heritage. Not until 1924 was the right to vote extended to Indians, and other forms of political redress have been unavailable or ineffective. Many treaties that had been made over the years were broken to serve the needs or desires of governments and private economic interests.

Blacks. The first blacks arrived on the American continent in 1619 and were sold as slaves in Virginia. Slavery was incorporated into the legal structure of the southern colonies somewhat later in the seventeenth century. Jefferson's proposal to abolish slavery found no place in the Declaration of Independence's glowing language about the rights of men, and the Constitution specifically provided for representation based on slave-holding and for protection of the slave traffic for a period of years. Slavery was too important to the economic and social structure of the South, and too fully in accordance with general beliefs in the North as well, to be seen as inconsistent with the assumptions and goals of either document.

The abolition of slavery that was accomplished during the Civil War, did little to change the practical effects of previous policies. The war was justified as a means of preventing the spread of slavery to the new western states—that is, of keeping the territories free for the wage-earning white working man. The Emancipation Proclamation was thus a tactical act of warfare as well as a principled policy. The Fourteenth and Fifteenth Amendments to the Constitution were intended as much to build the political strength of the struggling Republican Party as to ensure freedom for blacks. The swift passage of Jim Crow segregation laws, whose constitutionality was confirmed by the Supreme Court in the famous case *Plessy* v. *Ferguson* (1896), officially and legitimately subjected black people to a condition only abstractly better than slavery.

Official segregation continued to be the law of the land until 1954, when a well-orchestrated legal campaign by blacks finally led the Supreme Court to rule segregated education unconstitutional. The federal government practiced segregation in the armed forces until after World War II. Aside from these official policies, governments at all levels condoned or practiced systematic discrimination against blacks. Educational systems not only were segregated and unequal, but also actually taught that blacks were inferior; other agencies and activities of governments were almost equally "white only."

Hispanics: (a) Chicanos. Spanish explorers, settlers, and missionaries were the first whites to enter New Mexico, Texas, and California in the late sixteenth, seventeenth, and eighteenth centuries, respectively. Contacts with the surrounding Indians of the Southwest and with Mexico, where the Spanish had intermarried with Aztecs and other Indians, led eventually to a mixed Spanish-Indian-Mexican population in these areas. In some cases, vast landholdings existed in relative isolation.

Then came the Anglos, or English-speaking North Americans. The influx of Americans into Texas was followed by the acquisition of the entire Southwest in the Mexican War. The people now known as Chicanos, or Mexican-Americans, owe their status as Americans chiefly to this conquest, particularly to the Treaty of Guadalupe Hidalgo in 1848. The treaty confirmed all existing land titles as it granted the ostensible subjects of Mexico living in those areas American citizenship; however, in the words of one historian, "Mexicans quickly became the Negroes of the Southwest."[2] Although they were not officially slaves, they were not far from slavery, living in conditions of peonage and officially condoned discrimination. Land was taken from them, stock stolen, voting rights denied, and physical violence employed to intimidate and prevent efforts at redress.

The discovery of gold in California led to the rapid Anglicization of that territory, and once again the population of Mexican origin was displaced and reduced to near-peonage. In both law and practice, the Republic and then the State of California aided the rapid private exploitation of a captive population while denying them effective redress. Not until the advent of mass farming techniques and the resulting need for cheap labor

[2] Paul Jacobs, Saul Landau, and Eve Pell, *To Serve the Devil: Volume 1, Natives and Slaves* (New York: Random House, 1971), p. 237.

were Mexican-origin people in demand, and then only as the lowest form of laborers. Whenever they were not needed, Mexicans and Mexican-origin people were uprooted from their homes and deported.

The Mexican-origin population of New Mexico and Arizona was incorporated into the American system somewhat later. Lack of resources or of opportunities for development kept rural areas essentially unchanged until the end of the nineteenth century, and in some cases later. At that time, a somewhat modernized version of the familiar process began. In time, family land titles were completely replaced by Anglo ownership, and Anglo forms of organization were imposed on whole communities.

(b) Puerto Ricans. The Puerto Rican population, which is concentrated principally in major East Coast cities, is the other major, although smaller, group of Spanish-speaking Americans. The island of Puerto Rico was also acquired by conquest, in the Spanish-American War of 1898. Although legally American citizens since 1917, Puerto Ricans have suffered from the same officially condoned and systematic peonage and discrimination as have Chicanos. The lack of economic opportunities on their native island has led many to seek jobs in New York, Philadelphia, and Boston, where until quite recently they were ignored by governments at all levels.

Asians. Asians have been subject to governmental policies that, although inconsistent, have always condoned private discrimination and exploitation. In the nineteenth century, for example, thousands of Chinese were imported as cheap labor to build railroads; when no longer needed (and when white workers' demands that they be prevented from undercutting wage levels led to riots and lynchings), they were excluded by law in 1882. The same exclusion applied to Japanese after 1907. California's land laws prevented Asians from acquiring title to property for many years, and during World War II, the federal government uprooted American citizens of Japanese descent from their homes and businesses to relocate them to camps in Utah and Nevada, fearing that they might be disloyal.

Conclusion

Why has there been a consistent pattern of discriminatory public policies toward racial minorities? Neither economic necessity nor racism is a sufficient answer in itself, although both are major factors—independent but mutually reinforcing. It is not necessary to speculate on which is more important or whether economic interests lead to an increase of racism. It is enough to see that neither could function without the other. A recent history sums up four centuries of American policy as follows:

> The colonizers came to the New World believing that colored people were inferior, and used that ideology to justify the enslavement of blacks, the killing of Indians and Mexicans, and the importation of Oriental labor for work considered unfit for whites. The identification of colored skin with evil, with the devil, with inferiority, infused the entire culture of the Anglo-Saxons during the first centuries of colonization.

In each case, the racism coincided with economic need for slave labor and for land. At the same time, racist attitudes were institutionalized as laws, religion, and everyday practice. Each school child learned, along with the principles of republicanism and democracy, about the inferiority of colored people. Ministers explained to their flocks that slavery was God's will.

Racist law and racist behavior became an integral part of American culture. . . . Racist attitudes not only made whites feel superior by virtue of their skin color; it also made all colored, colonized people feel inferior because of their skin color.[3]

As this passage implies, it is not only minorities who experience the consequences of racially discriminatory public policies. Dominant groups are also deeply affected, both in the circumstances of their individual and social lives and in the ideology and mythology they accept. Belief in the superiority of whites and the "natural" inferiority of other races can come to serve as an underlying principle of social order. No discriminatory public policy can long persist without a myth of this kind, and the institutionalization of the myth in such policies serves in turn to sustain it. If today most whites concede that they are not biologically superior to other races, they still tend to believe that they are socially, economically, and/or culturally superior. Some members of racial minorities have also come to believe in the supremacy of whites and white culture. Once established, this myth penetrates all levels of society and serves to justify subordination as well as supremacy. Many in the dominant society do not even realize that their actions reflect such assumptions. They may believe that they are merely "following the rules" or being "realistic" or "practical," but their actions are essentially racist because they cannot escape assumptions.

However, the effects of racial myths are the least visible consequences of American policies toward minorities. More readily apparent are the actual social and economic conditions of such minorities today. Because we have already analyzed the situation of blacks and Hispanics to some extent, we shall focus briefly here on the situation of Native Americans.

Policy Consequences and Native Americans

Lack of agreement about who qualifies as an Indian and the absence of concern for the question until very recently have made it impossible to say precisely how many Indians now live in the United States. Estimates range from 600,000 to 1 million. The best estimate is probably that of the Bureau of Indian Affairs (BIA), which puts the number of Indians on reservations at about 450,000, with at least another 200,000 or so living in cities. In recent years, there has been substantial migration from reservations to the cities, partly as a result of federal programs aimed at reducing the reserva-

---

[3] Ibid., p. xxi.

tion population (and its landholdings). More than 112,000 Indians, or from one-tenth to one-sixth of the total Indian population, migrated to the cities in the period 1952–70, when such programs were in effect. Los Angeles is thought to have the largest number of urban Indians (about 60,000), followed by San Francisco–Oakland, Dallas–Fort Worth, Oklahoma City, Minneapolis–St. Paul, Phoenix, Cleveland, Chicago, and New York.

The economic and social conditions of Indians are probably the worst of all American minorities. The average annual income per Indian *family* is about $1,500 per year; unemployment is very high, reaching ten times the national average in some areas. U.S. Census reports show that about 60 percent of families living on Indian reservations were below the poverty line in 1973. The life expectancy of Indians is one-third less than the national average, incidence of tuberculosis among Indians is eight times the national average, infant mortality rates are twice the national average, and the suicide rate is double that of the general population. According to Senator Edward Kennedy, 50,000 Indian families (that is, nearly half of all Indian families) live in unsanitary, dilapidated dwellings; many live in huts, shanties, or abandoned automobiles. Those who migrate to the cities often find that they are untrained for employment and unable to adapt to urban life. The average educational level for all federally educated Indians is under five years, and dropout rates are twice the national average in both federal and local public schools.

A recent Senate subcommittee study examined the history of, and current policies toward, Indian education and issued a scathing indictment of such policies and their underlying purposes.[4] It not only found failures of education to lie at the root of current Indian conditions, but also—far more important—declared that the whole approach to education exemplifies what is wrong with American policy toward Indians. In a sense, this report is applicable to the dilemma facing all racial minorities; a brief review of it may highlight the problem to be dealt with in the next section.

The subcommittee report declares in its opening sentences: "A careful review of the historical literature reveals that the dominant policy of the Federal Government toward the American Indian has been one of forced assimilation which has vacillated between the two extremes of coercion and persuasion. At the root of the assimilation policy has been a desire to divest the Indian of his land and resources."[5] Referring to the federal statute dividing reservations into 160-acre parcels so that Indian families would learn about property ownership and become successful farmers—which resulted in the sale or abandonment of much of the acreage because such principles were totally inconsistent with Indian culture—the subcommittee states:

---

[4] U.S. Senate, Subcommittee on Indian Education, *Indian Education: A National Tragedy—A National Challenge* 91st Congress, 1st Session.

[5] Ibid., p. 9.

During the 46-year period it was in effect it succeeded in reducing the Indian landbase from 140 million acres to approximately 50 million acres of the least desirable land. Greed for Indian land and intolerance for Indian cultures combined in one act to drive the American Indian into the depths of poverty from which he has never fully recovered.

From the first contact with the Indian, the school and the classroom have been a primary tool of assimilation. Education was the means whereby we emancipated the Indian child from his home, his parents, his extended family, and his cultural heritage. It was in effect an attempt to wash the "savage habits" and "tribal ethic" out of a child's mind and substitute a white middle-class value system in its place.[6]

The subcommittee's basic points are that racism and economic interests have combined to place Indians at the very bottom of the socioeconomic pyramid and that the only route by which they are allowed to rise out of poverty and degradation—education—has required that they abandon everything that is unique to their culture. In other words, the purpose of education has been to remake the Indian into a person whose attitudes and goals are consistent with white capitalist American society. Naturally, Indians resisted such "education" and instead fought a continuing battle to maintain their cultural heritage and integrity.

Probably the most serious attack on Indian integrity and culture has been the practice of removing large numbers of Indian children from their families. A recent study found that twenty times as many Indian as non-Indian children are placed in foster care or put up for adoption, often only because the Indian family is poor and also, the study found, because Indian children are "marketable": there are long waiting lists of whites who want to adopt them. In 1978, Congress tried to remedy this situation by passing an Indian Child Welfare Act that will let Indian tribal courts decide child-custody cases.[7]

The situation is not very different for most other minorities, although the process is somewhat less visible. "Progress," in the sense of the increasing capacity to earn income and gain status in the dominant society, has been available only for certain individuals among minorities and only at the cost of abandoning the distinctive features of their cultures. Unless they give up those values and habits of thought that are inconsistent with competitive individualism and materialistic self-seeking, they will not succeed in American economic life. How much of a cost does this represent? Clearly, some minority-group members would gladly pay the price in order to gain the material and other benefits of full participation in American society, but for others the cost is too high. Either the gap between the values and habits of mind of their cultures and those of the dominant society is too great, or they prize their own values and cultures too highly to give them up.

---

[6] Ibid.

[7] *New York Times*, December 25, 1978, p. 1.

TABLE 13.4
Income Before and After Taxes, 1981

INCOME SOURCES AND PAYMENTS	U.S. FAMILIES BY SHARES OF TOTAL INCOME				
	Poorest Fifth (up to $7,168)	Next Poorest Fifth (up to $13,709)	Middle Fifth (up to $21,573)	Next Highest Fifth (up to $32,730)	Highest Fifth (over $32,730)
Income from non-federal sources (average per fifth)	$1,740	$7,660	$15,350	$25,100	$47,340
Non-federal income distribution (percentage of total non-federal income)	1.8	7.9	15.8	25.8	48.7
Tax payments (average per fifth)	$160	$940	$2,450	$4,650	$11,850
Tax payments as percentage of all taxes	0.8	4.7	12.2	23.2	59.1
Net income* (average per fifth)	$3,820	$9,430	$15,090	$22,030	$37,170
Net income as percentage of all income	4.4	10.8	17.2	25.2	42.5

SOURCE: U.S. Census Bureau, Joint Committee on Taxation, Congressional Budget Office estimates, supplemented and reported by *National Journal*, Oct. 23, 1982, pp. 1788–95.

* Includes cash transfers from federal government; see Table 13.5 for detailed analysis.

The Role of the Government in Income Distribution. What we saw in our analysis of the poor population in Chapter 4 suggested strongly that, for whatever combination of reasons—limited education or skills on the part of workers, or limited job availability and low wages on the part of the economy—many people do not have much income. Minorities, women, and the elderly were particularly prominent among this population.

This is the point at which the government has been called in. Over the years, and particularly since the 1930s, government programs have made up some of the lack in resources for the poorer levels of the social pyramid. But government has also done things that help people at other income levels. In this section, we will sort out the role of the government in income distribution in a comprehensive manner, using the now-familiar distribution by income-fifths of families as the basis for analysis.

Let us start with the basic pattern of income distribution as it is accomplished by the private economy, and then add in the various activities of government. Table 13.4 will start us off. The five income-fifths are ranged across the table. We show the thresholds between them as of 1981 (the relationship remains the same, even if the numbers change over time). It is worth noting that in each fifth, the *average* income per family (shown in the row below) is very much lower than the uppermost income of the category. This indicates that most families in the category are at the lower edge, which brings the average down.

When the private economy's distribution is considered by itself, the highest fifth gets nearly half of all income; the poorest fifth barely receives any income. When tax payments are added in, the highest group pays a much larger share; the poorer groups pay lower shares in taxes than they receive in proportion of national income. The next to last row shows the average family income of families in each fifth again, this time *after* taxes have been paid *and* cash transfers (benefits, entitlements, etc., as are detailed in Table 13.6) from the federal government have been received. These income levels should be compared with those in the first row of the table. The poorer fifths have improved their relative position sharply, while the higher fifths have declined in their shares of total income.

However, the distribution accomplished by all these taxes and cash transfers is still highly skewed toward the upper fifths. For the highest fifth, the difference between what it received from the private economy and what it had after taxes and cash transfers was 6.2 percent of national income (48.7 percent minus 42.5 percent). This represents billions of dollars, but not exactly massive equalization. For the lowest fifth, the lower tax rates and cash transfers make the difference between destitution and bare survival. What would have been less than 10 percent of national income for the bottom 40 percent of American families is instead half again higher. The bottom 40 percent gets a grand total of 15.2 percent of the national income.

Table 13.5 helps us to examine these cash transfers more closely. The major cash transfer programs are listed at the left, with the number of beneficiaries, total benefits paid, and distribution between income-fifths ranged across the table. (Again, although the figures are for 1981, which is the latest year available, and totals have increased since then, the relative proportions remain essentially the same.) Social Security is by far the largest in terms of both number of beneficiaries and dollars dispensed. More than half goes to the two poorest fifths, but the rest is spread across the income levels. Military and civil service retirement, however, go more to the upper 20 percent than to any other level. Veterans' and unemployment compensation go least to the bottom 20 percent; the two final welfare categories go primarily to that group.

When all of this distribution has been accomplished, two critical sets of figures stand out. First is the comparison between income fifths as to who receives how much from the federal government. The poorest fifth not only does *not* receive the biggest share of federal transfers; with 21.5 percent, it actually receives less than one-third more than the highest fifth! These data hardly support images of massive redistribution by means of federal cash transfers. Even so, they are absolutely essential to the cash income of the poorest fifth; they are 56.2 percent of the total cash income of that 20 percent of Americans. On the other hand, they are only 3.4 percent of the total cash income of the highest fifth, and thus far less important at that level.

Cash transfers are not the only way the government aids people; much assistance is rendered by "in-kind" transfers or benefits. These are valuable

TABLE 13.5
Federal Cash Transfers, and Share of Total Income, 1981

TYPE OF FEDERAL CASH TRANSFER PROGRAM	BENEFICIARIES (MILLIONS)	TOTAL BENEFITS ($ BILLIONS)	PERCENTAGE DISTRIBUTION OF EACH BY INCOME FIFTHS				
			Poorest	Next Poorest	Middle	Next Highest	Highest
Social Security	22.5	$118.3	23	31	22	13	11
Railroad Retirement	0.7	3.7	22	31	22	14	11
Civil Service Retirement	1.4	14.3	3	14	28	24	32
Military Retirement	1.2	11.9	2	4	10	23	61
Veterans Compensation	3.4	9.2	17	18	23	22	21
Unemployment Compensation	8.4	11.9	10	22	25	25	19
Supplementary Security Income	3.0	6.3	56	24	9	6	4
Aid to Families with Dependent Children	4.1	9.2	55	30	9	4	1
Total from federal sources		$184.8	21.5%	26.0%	21.1%	15.1%	16.1%
Total* $ income from all sources (average per family)		—	$3,980	$10,370	$17,540	$26,680	$49,020
Federal share of total cash income		100	56.2%	26.2%	12.5%	5.9%	3.4%

SOURCE: U.S. Census Bureau, Joint Committee on Taxation, Congressional Budget Office estimates, supplemented and reported by *National Journal*, Oct. 23, 1982, pp. 1788–95.

* Includes nonfederal sources; see Table 13.4 for distributions.

**TABLE
13.6**   ***Federal In-Kind Benefits by Income Fifths, 1981***

IN-KIND BENEFIT CATEGORIES (MAJOR ONES ONLY)	ANNUAL DISTRIBUTION TO AVERAGE FAMILY IN $				
	Poorest	*Next Poorest*	*Middle*	*Next Highest*	*Highest*
Means-tested benefits:					
Food stamps	220	90	30	10	—
School lunch	30	30	20	10	—
Subsidized housing	190	90	30	10	—
Medicaid	500	230	110	70	40
Non-means-tested benefits:					
Medicare	760	700	430	300	200
Tax deductions for housing*	10	30	130	320	1100
Medical insurance tax deductions**	40	170	300	400	450
Total all benefits	$1750	$1340	$1050	$1120	$1790

SOURCE: U.S. Census Bureau, Joint Committee on Taxation, Congressional Budget Office estimates, supplemented and reported by *National Journal,* Oct. 23, 1982, pp. 1788–95.

EXPLANATION: * Tax deductions for housing include property taxes and mortgage interest.
** Tax "deductions" are actually tax-free medical, hospital, and other insurance paid by employers *or* as deductions by self-employed.

Not included: all other business deductions available primarily to upper fifths.

commodities or services that people would otherwise have to pay for, such as food stamps, school lunches, or medical care. Table 13.6 summarizes the distribution of major in-kind benefits by income fifths. The in-kind benefits have been divided according to whether people have to prove that they have incomes that are low enough to qualify for such assistance ("means tested").

We have added two advantages that are enjoyed primarily by the wealthier levels: the opportunity to take tax deductions for payment of property taxes and mortgage interest on homes and to have tax-free medical and other insurance paid by employers. These are normally called "tax subsidies," in that they represent money that the government is not receiving from people. We have treated them as being equivalent to other in-kind transfers for this purpose.

It is often argued that the poor get the lion's share of the federal government's in-kind transfers. Therefore, these should be included in any calculation of total income and poverty levels. It is clearly true that the means-tested benefits go primarily to the lower income fifths, and the health-related ones are of substantial value. But when tax subsidies of the sort described are included in the comparison, they more than equal the in-kind transfers to the poor. We are not arguing that in-kind transfers are not substantial and vital to the poor. Indeed, they are crucial. We are raising the question of whether they show distinctive favoritism by the government toward the poor.

The role of government in income distribution is thus to spread its cash and in-kind transfers across the entire population. There may be some heavier emphasis on the sorts of things that poor people need most. Cash transfers make up more than half of all cash income that the poorest income fifth receives. In-kind transfers might be equivalent to another third to half of the income of such families. These patterns should be kept in mind while examining the changes in government policies that were undertaken by the Reagan administration in the early 1980s.

The "New Class War" of the 1980s. In 1982, two well-known social scientists published a book entitled *The New Class War: Reagan's Attack on the Welfare State and Its Consequences.*[8] The notion of "class war" seems out of place in the United States in the 1980s, given our history and the lack of the kind of workers' consciousness that we noted earlier. The authors meant a class war by the upper class, with President Reagan's policy redirections being the principal weapon leveled against the unorganized lower classes. This is certainly a provocative idea, and one for which there are some substantial bits of supportive evidence. We shall survey some of the impacts of the policy changes accomplished by the Reagan administration in terms of their probable effects on political participation, and leave it to the reader to decide whether they add up to such a characterization.

We showed earlier in this chapter that real wages or actual purchasing power had been dropping for eight years when the Reagan administration came to office in 1981. Within six months, because of the strict monetarist policies followed by the Fed, the recession of 1981–82 began in earnest. While the President did not (and could not) order such policies, the Fed was certainly encouraged in the severity of its actions by the President's expressed determination to control inflation once and for all. In any event, unemployment totals spurted in the second half of 1981.

The year 1982 set records as the year of the worst unemployment experienced in the United States since the Great Depression of the 1930s. More than 22 percent of all workers were out of work at some time in 1982. Four million people were unable to find any work at all during the year, and a record low 62 percent of male workers had full-time jobs all year.[9] These losses of income for most workers were not covered by unemployment benefits. The Department of Labor reported in July 1983 that only 38.6 percent of jobless workers received such benefits. In states where coverage was low to start with, such as Texas and Florida, the proportion of jobless receiving benefits was 27 percent and 24 percent respectively.[10]

---

[8] Frances Fox Piven and Richard A. Cloward, *The New Class War: Reagan's Attack on the Welfare State and Its Consequences* (New York: Pantheon Books, 1982.)

[9] *National Journal,* August 20, 1983, p. 1754.

[10] *USA Today,* August 17, 1983, p. 1.

Added to this steady drop in real wages and high unemployment was the situation of the nation's labor unions. The weakening economy made it difficult for the unions to achieve gains, and many of their members were unemployed. Job-hungry workers were reluctant to join unions in many areas, and in some cases they undercut wage levels of existing unions. In this context, it was easy for employers to blame union wages for part of their economic troubles, resist expansion of unions, and even obtain concessions or "give-backs" of gains made earlier in the way of wages or working conditions. Unions are not generally popular in the United States, and without such support, it was possible for employers to defeat pro-labor legislation in Congress and the states and begin to mount a counteroffensive of their own.

The legal status of a union with respect to a given employer depends on the union's winning an election as the collective bargaining agent for that company's employees. Employers seized upon these "certification" elections and actively resisted unionization, often with the help of "Right to Work" laws, particularly in the Sun Belt states, which limited the unions' power in various ways. Unions began to lose certification elections, and to be forced to undergo and often lose decertification elections, as employers used a variety of "carrot and stick" techniques to persuade their workers that the union was undesirable.

The general economic situation and the stiffening resistance of employers combined to bring about a sharp decline in the ranks of organized labor in the late 1970s and early 1980s. Between 1970 and 1983, the auto workers' union lost almost one-third of its membership, the steelworkers' union dropped almost half of its membership, and the carpenters and machinists lost about 25 percent of their membership. Retail and service employee unions were up slightly, as were the teacher unions and other public employee unions, but it was very hard to organize the newer high-technology industries, and public employees were often limited as to their collective bargaining rights. The net result was that union membership, which was once up around 35 percent of the labor force, dropped below 20 percent for the first time since the 1930s.

Thus, union weakness was added to declining real wages and unemployment as being key parts of the economic context in which the Reagan program was enacted. This program (excluding the military buildup for these purposes) had three major components. By far the largest and most important was the sequence of tax cuts that was enacted in 1981 to take effect over the three years from 1982–84. After a partially compensating tax increase, the total returned to taxpayers over that period is estimated at $280 billion.[11] There were also two major areas of spending cuts—in the cash transfer programs and in the in-kind transfer programs. The total in the former was $30 billion, and in the latter $35 billion. These are large sums, and the programs are of vital importance to the lowest income fifths,

---

[11] All data in this paragraph are drawn from *National Journal*, October 23, 1982, p. 1791.

TABLE 13.7

Net Impact of Federal Program Reductions and Tax Reductions, on 1981 Income

	U.S. FAMILIES GROUPED BY FIFTHS OF TOTAL U.S. INCOME RECEIVED (12,000,000 FAMILIES PER FIFTH)				
	Poorest Fifth	Next Poorest Fifth	Middle Fifth	Next Highest Fifth	Highest Fifth
Threshold between fifths	7,168	13,709	21,573	32,730	
Reductions in cash transfers, in $	80	90	50	40	50
Reductions in in-kind federal benefits and tax subsidies, in $	178	106	67	40	12
Additions to income from tax reductions, in $	10	110	330	690	2,080
Total net impact, average family	− $248	− $86	+ $213	+ $610	+ $2,018
Total cash income of average family after all changes	$3,760	$9,450	$15,370	$22,680	$39,200
Share of that income derived from cash transfers from federal government (in percentages)	56	26	13	6	3
Resulting shares of total U.S. income (in percentages)	4.2	10.4	17.0	25.1	43.3

SOURCE: Calculated by author from data reported in *National Journal*, Oct. 23, 1982, pp. 1788–95. Original sources include U.S. Census Bureau, Congressional Budget Office, and the Joint Committee on Taxation.

ASSUMPTIONS: Spending and tax reductions enacted for 1983 applied to actual 1981 income. Tax subsidies (property tax and mortgage interest payments, value of tax-free health-related insurance) estimated by various sources.

as we saw in the previous section, but the total amounts of tax reductions dwarf these changes.

The impact of the Reagan program therefore must be examined in terms of the net effects of all three of these components together. Table 13.7 does this, once again with respect to the way that the federal government actions affect each of the five income fifths. The three major reductions—in cash transfers, in-kind benefits, and taxes—are shown separately in the first three rows. Cash transfer reductions affect all income-fifths, but hit the poorest hardest. In-kind transfer reductions hit the poorest fifths very hard, and barely touch the highest fifth. However, tax reductions almost literally pour money onto the highest fifths, and do not help the lowest ones for the simple reason that they do not pay taxes in the first place.

This brings us to the climactic line of the table, the next row entitled "Total net impact." The various reductions are added up and compared here. The poorest fifth *loses* an average per family of $248 per year; the highest fifth *gains* an average of $2,018 per year; and the intermediate fifths lose or gain in proportion. This is a sharp bias indeed, but one that the Reagan economists insist is necessary to free up capital in the hands of the only people who are able to invest it. It raises the question of a "new class war" to the point of serious consideration. Part of the validity of such a characterization lies in the reactions of the people who are most powerfully affected—those who have actually suffered the losses of income and in-kind transfers that are involved. We shall start on that analysis by looking in general terms at the ways in which attitudes and opinions are formed and changed in the next chapter.

CHAPTER 14

Public Opinion and Attitude Change

Much of this book explores the relationship between what the people want and what the government does. One of its major premises is that what the government does, and what other visible leaders do, play a major role in shaping what people think, feel, and want. In this chapter, we will focus particularly on the dynamics of opinion formation. We will look first at some general characteristics of public opinion. Then we will confront the prospect that a relatively few people—the nation's leaders, and the top editors and reporters of the mass media—can play a dominant role in managing public understanding of events and issues. Finally, we will examine the results—the basic goals people seem to want and the expectations they have, and how people actually do respond to changing conditions and efforts to shape their views. We shall pay special attention to changes in popular attitudes in the 1980s, so that we can begin to see what lies ahead in American politics.

KEY CHARACTERISTICS OF PUBLIC OPINION

Every government, even the most dictatorial or totalitarian one, must take account of public opinion, because people who feel strongly and act together can block public programs, give them the support they need to survive, or bring about the downfall of regimes. But governments take public opinion into account in many different ways. They may respond to it, as pluralists assume they do in democratic countries, or they may create it, as our analyses of symbolic politics show all branches of government do on some occasions. They may respond to the opinions of people who feel strongly about an issue even if they are a small minority, assuming that most of the general public, chiefly nonelites, will be uninformed, apathetic, unorganized, and therefore unable to act effectively in their own interests. Whatever else "democracy" means, the term suggests that government should be responsive to the interests and concerns of the people. But that idea is not as simple as it might first seem to be.

"Public opinion" is commonly spoken of as a force to which governments respond, which is an idea that is as misleading as it is reassuring. Politics involves controversy. On virtually every public issue, there is a range of opinions and a range of interests among people rather than a common point of view. On the issue of whether to build the very expensive MX missile, for example, some people think that it is too costly, some doubt that it will work effectively, some maintain that it is a necessary deterrent to Soviet aggression, and some favor it because it will help win Senate support for an arms limitation treaty even if they doubt that it is needed. In addition, many other people have not heard of it, are not interested in it, or have no opinion. A news report of a Soviet buildup or a cut in the Soviet arms budget or a scientist's testimony about the MX missile's workability is likely, moreover, to shift many opinions. For every controversial issue, there are many opinions, often a substantial group with no opinion, and changes in opinion over time.

Dimensions of Public Opinion. An observer must consider a set of dimensions of opinion to get a useful picture of where people stand on an issue. One of these is *direction*, or whether people favor or oppose a particular policy proposal. A second dimension is *stability*, or how much or how little change there is in people's positions with the passage of time and with change in conditions. A third dimension is *intensity*, or how strongly people feel about their positions.

However, the direction, stability, and intensity of a person's opinions about public issues are not embedded in his or her mind and personality; rather, they are created and changed by the people, events, and pressures that he or she encounters in his or her daily activities. Some of these conditions remain largely unchanged for long periods or even for a person's lifetime. The great majority who are born into poverty, the working class, or affluence, respectively, will remain in the same social class; that condition, in turn, will probably go far toward shaping their opinions on a wide range of public issues, such as attitudes toward labor unions, welfare policy, and regulation of corporate products and prices. Some opinions are linked fairly closely to specific occupations, regional locations, and other conditions that change more often than social class does but are still fairly stable. News reporters are more likely than FBI agents, for example, to rank freedom of the press high on their scale of values. People who live in the arid western states are more likely to favor federal programs to improve irrigation than are easterners who are not aware of such programs. A high proportion of hunters are likely to oppose gun control, but their ardor on that issue may cool if they give up hunting for skiing and bird watching. Social situations encourage opinions that may change in direction or in intensity as the situations change.

Effect of Information. Opinions also depend on what information people have about public issues, and the amount and the nature of their information usually change faster than their social class or their occupations, regional location, or personal interests. As Table 14.1 dramatically shows, many people are poorly informed about political matters, but they may nonetheless hold opinions. Some who favor capital punishment may change their views after learning that being poor or black strongly increases a convicted criminal's chances of execution and that evidence of the innocence of an executed person occasionally comes to light too late. People may also misperceive facts in order to be able to retain opinions they cherish. As an extreme example, Nazi sympathizers today sometimes deny that there was any holocaust or genocide against Jews in Hitler's Germany. Or those who favor nuclear power plants are likely to interpret news about them, such as the Three Mile Island accident, as demonstrating that they are safe, while those who oppose them interpret the same news as proving that they are dangerous.

The popularity of political leaders is relatively unstable and is usually closely related to news developments that give them a chance to appear to be coping well or, by contrast, make them look ineffective. After the seizure of hostages in the American embassy in Iran in 1979, for example, the percentage of people who approved of President Carter's performance in office jumped from 32 percent to 61 percent in about three weeks.[1] Similar, although less dramatic increases occurred during President Kennedy's "Cuban missile crisis" of 1962 and President Reagan's invasion of Grenada in 1983.

Conflict and Consistency. Still another key characteristic of a great deal of political opinion is ambivalence, which is the presence of two or more conflicting beliefs in a person's mind. This kind of internal conflict is a natural result of the fact that people respond to a range of other people and authorities who are often in disagreement. A great many people see reports of crime in the streets as proving the need for enlarged police authority in order to maintain law and order, yet many of these same people are disturbed at reports of violations of the law and of people's civil rights by the FBI and local police departments. Whether they support one or the other of these divergent goals is likely to depend on the sympathies of those around them at the time, what news they have heard lately, or other passing cues. Reports of the results of opinion polls typically leave the impression that each human mind holds an opinion on each issue, so that supporters and opponents of a particular policy or candidate can be neatly counted as opposing forces. While that model helps to justify the results of elections and the actions of regimes, it grossly oversimplifies the human mind and its capacity for change, subtlety, complexity, and contradictory beliefs and actions.

An individual's continuing concerns often conflict with one another,

[1] *New York Times,* 10 December 1979, p. A22.

TABLE 14.1

The Level of Political Information Among the Adult Public

		Year	Source
94%	Know the capital city of United States	1945	[AIPO]
94%	Know the president's term is four years	1951	[AIPO]
93%	Recognize photograph of the current president	1948	[AIPO]
89%	Can name governor of their home state	1973	[Harris]
80%	Know meaning of term "veto"	1947	[AIPO]
79%	Can name the current vice-president	1978	[NORC]
78%	Know what initials "FBI" stand for	1949	[AIPO]
74%	Know meaning of the term "wiretapping"	1969	[AIPO]
70%	Can name their mayor	1967	[AIPO]
69%	Know which party has most members in U.S. House of Representatives	1978	[NORC]
68%	Know president limited to two terms	1970	[CPS]
63%	Know China to be Communist	1972	[CPS]
63%	Have some understanding of term "conservative"	1960	[SRC]
58%	Know meaning of term "open housing"	1967	[AIPO]
52%	Know that there are two U.S. senators from their state	1978	[NORC]
46%	Can name their congressman	1973	[Harris]
39%	Can name both U.S. senators from their state	1973	[Harris]
38%	Know Russia is not a NATO member	1964	[AIPO]
34%	Can name the current secretary of state	1978	[NORC]
30%	Know term of U.S. House member is two years	1978	[NORC]
31%	Know meaning of "no fault" insurance	1977	[AIPO]
28%	Can name their state senator	1967	[AIPO]
23%	Know which two nations involved in SALT	1979	[CBS/NYT]

SOURCE: Robert S. Erikson, Norman R. Luttbeg, and Kent L. Tedin, *American Public Opinion: Its Origins, Content, and Impact*, 2d ed. (New York: Wiley, 1980), p. 19. The data is taken from American Institute of Public Opinion (Gallup); Center for Political Studies; Lou Harris and Associates; National Opinion Research Center; CBS/NYT.

producing what are sometimes called "overlapping interests" or "cross-pressures." A member of the United Automobile Workers who is prejudiced against blacks, for example, may be "cross-pressured" about the union's official stand in favor of fair employment practices. In an influential book, David Truman has argued that such overlapping interests moderate social conflict and promote stability; people who are opponents on some issues are allies on others, and such crisscrossing divisions of opinion help to cement the society together.[2] If people who disagreed on foreign policy also disagreed on economic policy, educational policy, civil rights, and everything else, the society would be divided into two hostile camps,

---

[2] David Truman, *The Governmental Process* (New York: Knopf, 1951).

and civil war would probably be inevitable; however, because disagreements are moderated by cross-cutting agreements, we have moderation and stability.

This view is a reassuring one, and overlapping interests often do have that result, but the United States is in fact characterized by frequent outbreaks of violence, deep polarization of opinion, and occasional instances of riot and civil war. Critics of Truman's argument make several important points. First, it is not justifiable simply to assume that a person who holds membership in two groups with conflicting goals is in fact cross-pressured and therefore inhibited from taking a strong position. Cross-pressuring is a *subjective* condition and can be shown to exist only by empirical examination of people's actual behavior when pressured to act in inconsistent ways. Often they simply ignore one of the pressures.

Furthermore, it is argued, people do not necessarily try to reduce tension in their lives; they often *seek out* tension-producing situations, including those produced by conflicting political pressures. There is evidence, for example, that voters often seek out conflicting opinions rather than selectively exposing themselves only to congenial views.[3] The implication of this finding is that cross-pressuring is not necessarily a moderating influence on pressure groups or on political conflict; it is also compatible with intense feelings, social tension, and the outbreak of political violence.

The apparent lack of consistency of many individual opinions is so striking and important and can be explained in so many different ways that it provides a useful example of the dependence of political analysis on the values and assumptions of the observer or analyst. One political scientist, Philip Converse, concluded from a study of successive opinions of the same individuals over time that "a mass public contains significant proportions of people who, for lack of information about a particular dimension of controversy, offer meaningless opinions that vary randomly in direction during repeated trials over time."[4] Converse found that the opinions of elites are more consistent because issues are more meaningful to them; thus, his theory can be interpreted as a putdown of the logic or the seriousness of nonelites.

But other studies challenge that conclusion. Norman Luttbeg analyzed the attitudes of "citizens" and of "community leaders" toward various local issues and found that *both* groups' opinions were organized in a logical way, although the leaders and the mass of citizens used different organizing principles.[5] How consistent a person's opinions seem to be, whether that person is an ordinary citizen or a member of an elite group,

---

[3] Peter W. Sperlich, *Conflict and Harmony in Human Affairs: A Study of Crosspressures and Political Behavior* (Chicago: Rand McNally, 1971).

[4] Philip E. Converse, "The Nature of Belief Systems in Mass Publics," in David E. Apter, ed., *Ideology and Discontent* (New York: The Free Press, 1964), p. 243.

[5] Norman R. Luttbeg, "The Structure of Beliefs Among Leaders and the Public," *Public Opinion Quarterly* 32 (Fall 1968), pp. 398–409.

very likely depends on the reasons the issue is important or unimportant to him or her. Another political scientist, Lance Bennett, has contributed to this debate by suggesting that it is the range of social influences and pressures to which a person is subjected that determines how consistent or contradictory his or her opinions are. If Bennett is right, then it does not make much sense to expect an outside observer's view of what is logical to fit people whose social situation is different from that of the observer.[6]

The Bennett view recognizes that people's opinions do not emerge from thinking machines that are isolated from the world, but rather from human beings who are in a particular class and social condition and that they are bound to reflect that condition. Opinions often serve to justify or rationalize people's high or low social status or the political actions they have supported in the past.

If opinions are responses to the past and current situations in which people find themselves, they do not necessarily tell us how people will act under circumstances that are different from the one in which they voiced their opinions, even though it is often assumed that responses to an opinion poll predict future behavior. Because opinions help people accept the lives they can usually do little to change, expressions of satisfaction with political conditions are more likely to predict future behavior than are expressions of discontent. When large proportions of the American people voiced the suspicion in 1973, and again in 1979, that the very large oil price increases of those years were unnecessary and unjustified, it did not mean that there would be serious resistance to paying them, or widespread demands to nationalize the oil companies or roll back the prices. People will usually accept a rationalization, such as allegations of an oil shortage, even if they feel strong ambivalence about it, rather than disrupt their lives to devote time to political action or resistance. Talk and action often serve different purposes in politics, so that the political opinions people express may not be a clue to how they will act. For this reason, as well as the fact that opinions are often ambivalent, the results of polls must always be interpreted in the light of other information about people's social conditions and concerns.

Intensity versus Numbers. Another characteristic of public opinion is especially important to take into account in assessing the impact of opinion upon public policy. On most issues, most of the public has no opinion or none that is strong enough to matter to a government agency charged with formulating policy. Farmers whose land and crops may be damaged by the path of a power line are likely to try to block the line by bringing pressure on the state public utility commission; in considering the question, however, the commission can take it for granted that most people in the state will have little interest in the question. The very nature of a great many

[6] Lance Bennett, "Public Opinion: Problems of Description and Inference," in Susan Welch and John Comer, eds., *Public Opinion* (Palo Alto: Mayfield, 1975), pp. 117–31.

policy proposals predetermines which groups will have strong opinions and in what direction, which will have weak opinions, and which will feel no concern. People in the first of these classes often comprise only a small minority, but if they have the incentive and the resources to act on their opinions, they are likely to be the most influential group. On issue after issue, organized and powerful elite groups therefore exert the key influence on policy, regardless of their small numbers.

On some political issues it is ideology rather than economic interest that makes the intense opinions of a small group more influential than the contrary opinions of most of the population. For a long time, some 85 percent of the population has favored some form of gun control, but has had little success in achieving that goal because the small minority opposing gun control can be counted on to vote only on the basis of an official's record on that one issue, while the proponents are likely to forget that issue on election day in their concern with other matters. Intensity is often far more important than numbers as far as influence on policy is concerned.

The fact that people respond to different social pressures that are not necessarily logically consistent has still another important implication for policy formation. The responses that come from fears of external or internal threats can often be deliberately aroused by political leaders or interest groups and are likely to overshadow other opinions, even if the latter are more logical or more realistic. When the Johnson administration announced, misleadingly, in 1964 that American ships had been attacked while on a routine maneuver in the Tonkin Gulf, it was predictable that most Americans would respond by supporting military action against North Vietnam. Often, the mobilization of intense opinions in a large part of the public depends less on deliberate lying than on the particular *interpretation* of a political development that comes to be widely accepted.

THE POTENTIAL FOR MANAGING PUBLIC OPINION

These reflections suggest that people's attitudes and opinions can be manipulated in at least two important ways. One is through symbolic means, which either can be employed deliberately by leaders or occur in "natural" ways. The other is through the activities of the leading editors and reporters of the mass media—again sometimes purposeful and sometimes unintended, but inherent in the nature of the media themselves. We shall look at each kind of opinion-managing potential in turn.

Symbolic Politics and Public Opinion

Political Metaphors. Some of the most powerful influences on public opinion are more subtle than deliberate propaganda or dramatic news developments. The metaphors we use, usually unconsciously, to describe political events and issues also shape political thought. A metaphor describes the unknown by comparing it to something that is well known, and in doing so it highlights some features and conceals others. "A crusade for freedom" and "legalized murder" are two metaphoric descriptions of war that place it in quite different perspectives. A wage-control program can be viewed either as "a battle against inflation" or as "a subsidy to employers." Every controversial political development is described and perceived by the use of conflicting metaphors, not necessarily because of a deliberate effort to influence or to mislead (although that, of course, happens too), but because we cannot speak or think about any complex matter without resorting to metaphor.

The particular metaphor that describes a political issue for a person reinforces the other symbolic processes. A person who works in a defense industry and fears Soviet aggression is likely to adopt the political role of defender against a foreign enemy and to see the cold war as a crusade for freedom; those who call war "legalized murder" will look like dupes or traitors. His or her beliefs, self-concept, and language reinforce one another and are, in fact, components of a single pattern of thought and behavior. They can be fully understood only as aspects of one another, and this is the important function of political language; it is always a vital part of a larger pattern of thought and action.

Political metaphors help shape both what we see as fact and how we *evaluate* political developments. Some think of abortion as a form of murder, and some think of it as a form of freedom. Whichever metaphor is in a person's mind influences what he or she imagines when reading a news story about an abortion clinic or about the legalization of abortion. And, obviously, it influences whether he or she favors or opposes legal abortion.

The metaphoric mode in which people perceive complex political issues and events is an obstacle to complete understanding and to changes in perception and belief as new information becomes available. New information is ordinarily screened to conform to the metaphor, rather than to change it. Two people with opposing views can read the same news about abortion clinics, and both will find that it confirms their earlier opinions. Metaphors become self-perpetuating in this way, because they are the patterns into which we fit our observations of the world. If, for example, army communiqués describe the bombing of "structures" in Southeast Asian villages, people feel better than they would if they were told that our bombs were destroying people's houses or huts; the word *structures* evokes an image of military installations rather than homes.

Political Arousal

The symbols that promote quiescence create the widespread conviction that people are being protected from the threats they fear or that those who behave unconventionally need to be restrained or punished both for their own good and that of society. Protection of the public is the key symbolic theme in either case. The symbols that arouse mass publics to protest or to become violent evoke the opposite expectation—that a widely feared threat to their interests is growing more ominous, that those who pose that threat are malevolent, and that these enemies must be resisted or, sometimes, exterminated. In the face of such a threat, people are generally likely to set aside the lesser conflicts that ordinarily divide them and to fight together against what they perceive as a more serious hazard to their common interests.

Political protest and militance are often based upon realistic recognition that some other group is threatening or oppressive. However, mass arousal can be based upon symbolic cues when the facts are unclear, as they often are in politics. Nothing helps American "hawks" win support for larger military budgets and incursions into foreign countries as much as allegations that hawkish sentiment and action are growing in foreign countries that are commonly believed to be hostile. It is therefore hardly surprising that hawks in rival countries are careful to observe, publicize, and exaggerate the militaristic actions and rhetoric of their adversaries. As they observe and exaggerate their enemies' alleged escalations, rival hawks serve each others' interests; they win added public support for their opponents as well as for themselves. Nothing so powerfully contributes to anti-police sentiment and behavior in American cities as allegations or evidence that police are arbitrarily harassing, beating, or arresting the poor, black, or ideologically unconventional. Political conflicts of these kinds engage more people and greater passions on both sides as each adversary group comes to see the other as the enemy who is bent on its repression or extermination. A new and sudden step-up in harassment typically arouses widespread fear and support for escalation on the other side. This is the general pattern for escalating political conflict on any issue that arises.

A central feature of this process is the personification of adversaries. Hostile or potentially hostile groups or nations are not seen as internally divided, although this is bound to be true of every formal organization or nation. Instead, the enemy is seen as monolithic and resolute; they are loyal followers of the alien leader or oligarchy, who symbolizes evil. This view simplifies the situation, and substitutes a vision of malevolence for the more realistic recognition that there is a large measure of drift in policymaking, that people change their positions from time to time, and that political leaders must respond to contending groups within their own countries in order to retain their positions. Simplification promotes solidarity against, and eagerness to escalate attacks on, the enemy.

The Uses of Enemies

The choice or creation of political enemies is often a symbolic way of widening political support. Some political enemies are real enough. Migrant fruitpickers, whose employer houses them and their families in shanties without sanitary facilities, underpays them, and overcharges them for necessities, have a real adversary. So do prisoners who are arbitrarily thrown into solitary confinement because they displeased a guard. Jews in Nazi Germany had little doubt about who their enemies were. Those who have real enemies benefit from their elimination or loss of power.

There is another kind of political enemy, however, who *helps* his or her adversary politically by providing a purpose, a cherished self-concept, and political support. For the Nazis, the Jews served as a politically useful enemy. Hitler portrayed the Jews to the German people as the satanic force he had to fight to preserve the country. Without this enemy to arouse their passions, minimize their internal differences, and unite them behind him, Hitler could hardly have achieved power or maintained it as long as he did. The Americans, the Russians, and the Chinese served similar functions for one another during the cold war years. Without native radical movements, the FBI would win far less public support and far lower budgetary appropriations. In cases like these, the enemy is partly or entirely symbolic. The symbolic enemy looks the same to adversaries as real enemies do, but it helps them as much as or more than it hurts them. It is in the interest of such enemies not to eliminate one another, but to perpetuate one another—and to create a popular belief in the strength and aggressive plans, and not the vulnerability, of the enemy.

Belief in real enemies is based on empirical evidence and is relatively noncontroversial. Belief in symbolic enemies is based on rumor and social suggestion and is often highly controversial. Such beliefs tell us more about the believers than about the ostensible enemies, because they bring political and social benefits for those who hold them, and for this reason, they are not easily challenged by facts that are incompatible with them. A group that is eager to marshal political support for its cause is likely to define as the enemy whatever adversary will most potently create and mobilize allies. A foreign country that has been long regarded as hostile, heretics among true believers, anarchists in the early decades of the twentieth century, Communists after the Russian revolution, capitalists in the Soviet Union, the yellow peril, blacks—all have served such a political purpose.

Groups perceived as the enemy are consistently defined in ways that dehumanize them. They are seen as alien, strange, or subhuman; often a single feature or alleged mode of behavior is emphasized, such as their color, alleged lack of intelligence (or uncanny shrewdness), clannishness, and so on. This is politically effective because people can deliberately hurt or kill only those whom they do not acknowledge as sharing their own human qualities.

Political symbolism is a major influence upon public opinion because people look to politics not only for realistic understanding and control over their lives, but also for reassurance that their fears are unfounded and that their own political roles are not only justified but also noble. The language we speak and the process by which our minds accept or screen out information lend themselves both to remarkable creative accomplishments and to illusion and misperception. To recognize these dangers is not to grow cynical or to despair; it is a necessary step toward the realistic assessment of politics and an attempt to avoid its pitfalls and realize its promise. No analysis of the prospects for political change can fail to take these processes into account.

THE MEDIA: REPORTERS OR MANUFACTURERS OF THE NEWS?

One image of the communications process is that the media keep citizens informed and enable them to exercise influence over public policy. Another is that the media are a means by which elites derive support for their actions. There are ways in which the first image is correct, of course. Without information from newspapers, magazines, radio, and television, most people would have little chance of exercising influence on government at all or even of knowing when an issue of concern to them arises.

At the same time, studies of opinion formation and opinion change point unmistakably to a number of mechanisms through which mass publics are placed at a disadvantage and are subjected to both deliberate and unconscious influence by elites.[7] A substantial proportion of the people have relatively little interest in news of public affairs and do not especially try to expose themselves to it. One study, which questioned people about their knowledge and opinions on eight different public issues, found that from 22 to 55 percent of the population, depending on the issue, either had no opinion or had one but did not know what the government was doing.[8] Also relevant is the finding that much political information is "retailed" by opinion leaders to large audiences. Such a two-step flow of messages in the media gives elites, who are somewhat better educated and have somewhat higher status than the recipients of the messages, a disproportionate influence.[9]

People get most of their political information from television and radio stations that rely chiefly on a few networks to supply their news programs and from newspapers that rely heavily on a few wire services. Understandably, there is concern both about the possibility of mass manipulation and about the concentration of influence. As the late A. J. Liebling, a critic of American journalism, once remarked, "To have freedom of the press, you have to own one."

On this issue, as on others we discuss, different levels of analysis yield somewhat different conclusions. Many of the major studies of mass communications conclude that the media can have only limited effect on opin-

---

[7] Converse, "The Nature of Belief Systems in Mass Publics," pp. 206–61; see also Robert E. Lane and David O. Sears, *Public Opinion* (Englewood Cliffs, N.J.: Prentice-Hall, 1964), pp. 57–71.

[8] Lane and Sears, *Public Opinion,* pp. 59–60.

[9] Elihu Katz and Paul Lazarsfeld, *Personal Influence* (New York: Free Press, 1955).

ions regarding political issues.[10] The human mind is not a blank slate on which those who control the media can write whatever they like. Female secretaries who are demeaned in the office will not be impressed by a television program proclaiming that the feminist movement has dramatically improved the status of women. A dedicated Republican is unlikely to change his vote even if he repeatedly sees a Democratic spot commercial. People's loyalties to their fellow workers, professions, ideologies, political parties, religions, and other beliefs are often stronger than the persuasive power of political rhetoric or drama. Studies of election campaigns typically find that they change the voting intentions of a relatively small proportion of the electorate (although that may be enough to change the result).

At another level, however, the mass media do have substantial effects by publicizing and legitimizing established institutions, including the major political parties; justifying inequalities in power; and predetermining the political issues that people will regard as important. In other words, the very stability in opinion that some studies see as *limiting* the effects of the media is itself a significant result of media influence.

Those who want to influence the public go to great lengths to win media coverage for their points of view. The kidnapping of political figures and other violent actions of political dissenters are a dramatic way of ensuring media attention to their grievances. Opposition groups see desperate measures of this sort as being necessary at times to win public notice, largely because the media so consistently reflect the positions of officials and other elites.[11]

Media attention is similarly prized in election campaigns, and it is won increasingly by the efforts of professional campaign management firms that contrive impressions, events, and the candidates' personalities when they can. Most people, especially those with relatively low incomes and limited education, get most of their news from television. A recent study concluded that television news teaches viewers little about the issues and has no effect on voters' images of the candidates, but the same study found that viewers do learn about the issues from television commercials, including spot commercials, which therefore encourage rational voting.[12] The next sections will provide a more systematic discussion of the part played by the media in opinion formation.

The Media System: Owners and Audiences. The principal mass media that are of direct relevance to politics are newspapers and newsmagazines,

---

[10] Some studies that emphasize this conclusion are: David O. Sears and Richard E. Whitney, *Political Persuasion* (Morristown, N.J.: General Learning Press, 1973); Lee Becker et al., "The Development of Political Cognitions," in Steven H. Chaffee, ed., *Political Communication* (Beverly Hills: Sage Publications, 1975), pp. 21–64; Joseph T. Klapper, *The Effects of Mass Communication* (New York: Free Press, 1960).

[11] This point is discussed on p. 92.

[12] Thomas E. Patterson and Robert D. McClure, *The Unseeing Eye* (New York: Putnam, 1976).

radio, and television. Books, other magazines, and motion pictures all carry political messages, some of which are dramatic and quite powerful, but their authors and actors are not day-to-day participants in politics like those of the first group.

Nearly 50 percent of the nation's roughly 1,800 daily newspapers are owned by the ten leading newspaper chains. With the exception of the major independent papers and a few others, their national news is supplied by one of two wire services, the Associated Press or United Press International. The *Los Angeles Times* reaches about 1 million people per day, the *New York Times* about 850,000, and next come the *Chicago Tribune* and the *Washington Post* at around 800,000 and 600,000, respectively, in daily circulation.[13]

The leading weekly newsmagazines in terms of circulation are *Time, Newsweek,* and *U.S. News and World Report. Time* sells well over 4 million copies per week, but does not come near the top ten of American magazines (the leaders, *TV Guide* and *Readers Digest,* sell about 20 million copies per week). *U.S. News and World Report* sells about half as many copies as *Time,* and *Newsweek*'s circulation is between the two. More than three-quarters of all Americans *read* one or more newspapers or newsmagazines each week, and spend an average of about 4 hours with them.

There are nearly 7,500 radio stations in the United States (AM and FM). Together, they reach 98 percent of all households and nearly every car. The average American is exposed to radios about eighteen hours per week, although this figure may overstate "real" listening.

Television is the most widely used medium of communication. There are about 700 stations, but 90 percent of their programming is provided by the three major networks (ABC, CBS, and NBC). Local television stations depend on the networks because the cost of producing programs—or of collecting, editing, and broadcasting the news—would be prohibitive. The networks each own and operate five local stations (the maximum allowed) in the nation's leading market cities, and reach almost 40 percent of American households by themselves.

There is at least one television set in 98 percent of all American households, and two or more in almost half of all households. The average American watches television about three hours per day, and the average family watches television about forty hours per week; the usual audience for the network evening news is more than 10 million people. Television regularly is reported to be the leading source of news for most people (it passed newspapers in the early 1960s), as well as the most believable (by large margins).

It would be hard to exaggerate the impact of the relatively recent rise of mass media, particularly television, on American politics. In later chapters,

---

[13] Data in this section are drawn from Doris A. Graber, *Mass Media and American Politics* (Washington, D.C.: Congressional Quarterly Press, 1980) and Elie Abel, ed., *What's News* (San Francisco: Institute for Contemporary Studies, 1981).

we shall weigh the extent to which the media are responsible for the decline of our political parties, the shrinking proportions of people who vote, and the elimination of issues from political dialogue. Here, we shall explore the implications of the single most important characteristic that shapes the gathering and dissemination of news in the United States, which is the fact that the news media are themselves big businesses, and they must therefore show a satisfactory level of profit. In other words, *news must be entertaining*, or people will not read, listen, or watch—and there will be no justification for such costly investment. Advertising slots will not bring the same sums, and people will not "stay tuned" for the prime time shows with their even higher advertising revenues that immediately follow these news programs.

The need to produce entertainment in the guise of the news means that violence—disasters, crime, wars—is emphasized, preferably with some kind of local connection. What is reported should be "new" rather than important, linked to an event rather than deeper trends, and something that people can relate to their personal lives in an emotional way such as accidents, grief, and scandals. Personalities of leaders and celebrities dominate presentations, and the world seems to be exciting, dangerous, and compelling. Similarly, the personalities of newscasters attain great significance in the continuing competition for audiences.

The Media Managers: Editors and Reporters. In addition to the overriding necessity of presenting the news in a manner that makes it a form of entertainment, two other factors help to make media reporting an independent force in shaping public opinion. (The media cannot simply *mirror* events in a neutral way; they inevitably introduce a systematic bias of their own.) One is the imperative need to plan ahead, to be able to line up background information, camera crews, and scripts, based on a commitment to air a particular bit of news at a scheduled date and time. Without such planning, news programs would be utterly chaotic; editors and producers must know at least some part of the content of their programming in advance. A day of fast-breaking "hot news" may mean a change of plans, but there will always be a portion of taped segments or essentially staged "events" to fill in around the more spontaneous coverage.

What this leads to is a special role for those who stage such events in a way that captures media attention. Producers and editors naturally prefer some bizarre or unusual action, or perhaps a dramatic confrontation—but one that has been carefully planned days or weeks in advance so that the camera crews and lighting are arranged in order for the incident to be well photographed. The need for active entertainment means that editors and producers cannot allow any single event to be on the air for more than a minute or so; another activity must supplant it, because people may tire or be uninterested in the first event. Editors must select from all the materials they have available to capture the most dramatic or exciting shots and words used, and then quickly move on to the next item. Not much depth can be provided under such circumstances, and the values of editors are necessarily reflected in the choices made.

The second factor is the conscious or unconscious bias of the people who report, interpret, select, and rewrite the news to be shown or reported. Both editors and reporters, and sometimes publishers, are involved in this unavoidable means of introducing biases. Despite the most ethical intent to be scrupulously fair (an intent that is not always present), choices have to be made about what is most newsworthy, what actually happened, and how it should be presented. These choices are affected by some predictable factors, such as the social class makeup of the media professionals, the governmental focus of their reporting, and their concern not to miss out on something that might be important.

Most media personnel are better educated and more liberal than most Americans, and as journalists they are inclined to take roles as investigators or at least questioners who want to be sure their sources are revealing all that is newsworthy. Editors and publishers, however, may be more concerned about what advertisers think, or about the perspective of the giant corporation that employs them all. In search of entertaining stories, however, reporters are impelled to look for what is dramatic and wrong or bad, and even scandalous if possible.

The focus of most reporting is on government, partly because it is important to everybody but also because it is *there* and available for planned news items. Government officials have a vital interest in obtaining favorable news reporting of their activities, and maintain large public relations staffs for this purpose. These staffs (and indeed anybody who is seeking to reach the public through the media), generate a vast amount of press releases and other predigested handouts that describe their work in a favorable light. Some reporters faithfully embody such handouts in their reporting, and nearly all give some credence to the official interpretation of events that is promulgated by government officials. The aura of legitimacy that naturally surrounds government actions, particularly in times of crisis, helps to slant interpretation toward the government position.

However, some correction is provided by the liberal bias of reporters and their tendency toward investigative efforts to expose some kind of wrong-doing. What emerges is often the appearance of tension between the press and the leading officials of government. Sometimes viewers resent the media's apparent criticism of the government, or blame the media for bringing to light facts that are troubling. Media personnel live in some isolation, with a shared focus on the government in Washington and a shared liberal perspective, and can be a group that is socially and ideologically quite at odds with the center of gravity of the American population as a whole.

Journalists tend to make similar judgments and see the news from the same perspective perhaps partly for this reason, but also to avoid making mistakes. Most network news programs, for example, cover the same stories in essentially the same way. Presidential campaigns and candidates' chances are evaluated in roughly similar terms by many reporters and newscasters, partly because they have been living together for weeks on the chartered press aircraft. When events intervene to change evaluations, of course, they all change to the new "conventional" interpretation at the same time. When this phenomenon is added to the concentration of ownership of networks, wire services, and newspapers in the hands of a relatively few great corporations, the chances seem slim that the American people will receive information that is truly independent and accurate.

And yet, Americans seem to trust the press. Public opinion studies repeatedly show that, despite some (usually, but not exclusively, conservative) antipathy to the press, people have more confidence in the press than they do in the government itself. Questions are regularly asked in national surveys about the extent of confidence that respondents have in a wide number of societal leaders. Throughout the post-Watergate period, and again in the later years of the Carter administration, respondents declared much greater confidence in the press than in the executive branch. Only during the Reagan years has the executive branch held a slight edge over the press in the people's confidence.[14]

WHAT DO PEOPLE THINK IN THE 1980s?

This question is obviously unanswerable in any comprehensive way. However, we can suggest a method for searching out the beginnings of understanding that is based on the general characteristics of opinion and the potential role of the media that we have just reviewed. We will begin with the enduring, historically-validated patterns of basic ideology and felt needs that Americans exhibit, and temper these with some reflections about diversions that are equally long-lived in American experience. Then we will look briefly at opinion polls and how to employ them. Finally, we will explore some of the forces that seem to be making changes in American public attitudes in the 1980s.

Some Fundamental Wants and Needs

Some wants and needs are so fundamental that they barely change over time. For example, in nearly three decades of polling, the two dominant personal hopes have been for good health for oneself and a better standard of living; the two dominant fears have been of ill health and a lower standard of living. War and peace usually rank next in each sequence. When the question is phrased in terms of hopes and fears for the country as a whole, war and peace far outdistance all others, and only economic stability ever challenges these responses.

These basic concerns seem to underlie broad support for governmental action in the social welfare field. Since responsible public opinion surveying began in the 1930s, large majorities have favored the basic social security and social assistance programs that were ultimately enacted.

---

[14] *National Journal,* February 4, 1984, p. 238.

Public support often preceded enactment by several years or even decades, as in the case of medical care. The federal social welfare programs of the 1960s enjoyed no less support, with two-thirds of the population favoring most aspects of the poverty program, aid to education, housing, the reduction of unemployment, and so forth. There can be little doubt about the strength of public demand and support for these "welfare state" policies.

However, this desire for government to be of service in coping with the problems of daily living in an industrial society does not transcend some basic practical and ideological limits. Nearly equal majorities say that taxes are too high, and the lower income levels are usually most resistant to taxation. The latter fact is sometimes cited as an inconsistency on the part of those who are the probable beneficiaries of much of the social legislation to be funded by such taxes, but it may represent an insistence that those who can better afford the burden of taxation should carry a larger share.

The Basic Ideology. One interesting illustration of the tension between felt needs and received ideology is provided by Lloyd Free and Hadley Cantril, who are professional students of American opinion.[15] Using the responses of a national cross section to a series of questions in 1964, they constructed two "spectra" of opinion. The "operational" spectrum was composed of answers to questions regarding specific governmental actions or proposals in the areas of Medicare, poverty, housing, and aid to education. The "ideological" spectrum was made up of answers to more abstract, less tangible questions about how problems ought to be solved and whether the government interferes too much in private and economic affairs. Those who consistently favored governmental assistance in the specific issue areas were labeled either strong liberals or predominantly liberal, depending on the number of affirmative responses they gave. Opposition to governmental assistance led to classification as predominantly conservative or strongly conservative. The same approach was applied to the ideological spectrum, with endorsement of governmental solutions and denial that the government interferes too much characterizing the liberal category.

When the two spectrums were compared, some very interesting and revealing findings emerged. In *operational* terms, 65 percent of respondents were completely or predominantly liberal. But in *ideological* terms, only 16 percent were. Fully 50 percent of respondents were *ideologically* conservative, as compared to only 14 percent who were *operationally* conservative. This suggests that when it comes to a question of what government should do in a specific situation, people want action to solve problems, but when issues are cast in the form of abstract philosophies or basic values, people endorse the conservative and more traditional assumptions. In other words, the grip of ideology remains strong even in the face of specific needs

---

[15] Lloyd A. Free and Hadley Cantril, *The Political Beliefs of Americans* (New York: Simon & Schuster, 1968). The analysis in the following paragraphs is drawn from Chapter 3.

and desires to the contrary. The questions that gained such support for the conservative side of the ideological spectrum involved standard American nostrums: the federal government is interfering too much—it is regulating business and interfering with the free-enterprise system; social problems could be solved if government would keep hands off and let people handle them themselves; anybody who wants work can find it; and we should rely more on individual initiative and not so much on welfare programs. No doubt some people can cheerfully voice such beliefs and then endorse governmental action to solve problems; 46 percent of ideological conservatives were operational liberals. However, people of conservative ideology gave only half as much support to liberal measures as did those of liberal ideology, and those who were conservative ideologically accounted for almost all those who were conservative operationally. Thus, the conservative nature of the ideology and its continuing strength appear to contribute in an important way to resistance, even among the general public, to governmental social legislation.

Implications of the Findings. What are the implications of these findings? For one thing, they suggest a gap between rhetoric and performance. For another, they suggest that the ways in which people focus on politics and what they see as important may coincide with those differing dimensions. Those who think and perceive in ideological terms may care most about the abstract principles and rhetoric surrounding government. Those who are operationally oriented may be more concerned with solutions to concrete problems. This conjecture is confirmed by Free and Cantril's analysis of their respondents' ranking of public concerns. Ideological conservatives ranked such intangibles as preserving economic liberties and states' rights at the top of their list of concerns, while liberals gave first place to specific actions such as aid to education and ending unemployment. Thus, in addition to the familiar divisions among people along class, racial, religious, and other such lines, we must distinguish among them on the basis of perceptual orientation. The phenomenon is related to class status, but is not identical with it.

Diversions by Means of Racial Conflict and Scapegoating

Several kinds of diversions operate to deflect nonelites from making efforts to fulfill their wants and needs through coherent political action. War, which causes people to forget their differences and to unite in patriotic support for their government, is the classic example. Even if the war is unpopular, it serves as a focus for conflict that aligns people in ways other than the class-based contests that could bring fulfillment of nonelite wants and needs. Space programs, races to the moon, and other forms of international competition—particularly against communism—serve many of the same functions.

Other diversions divide groups of nonelites. Ethnic and religious conflicts and sex discrimination are examples, but the single most important diversion for all Americans is racism. Outbursts of racist violence have served to vent nonelite resentments throughout American history. Continuous systematic denigration of minority groups has provided satisfactions for those who are just above such minorities on the social ladder. In part, such continuing tensions are kept alive by the natural tendency of employers to seek the lowest possible labor costs. Historically, this has meant the use of minorities as cheap labor and as strikebreakers, to the detriment of white working-class wage levels. Aid to the poor has also been interpreted as aid to minorities, particularly blacks; as a result, whites have been less supportive than they might have been had they understood the potential recipients to be people like themselves.

Racism and racial tensions remain prominent focuses of nonelite attention today. Whites blame blacks for wanting too much too quickly and for not working hard enough to get it. Blacks see whites as being unresponsive and racist. The more blacks seek equality, the more whites resent it, and the less either group sees its problems as being caused by anything but the other. How rapidly white resistance stiffened in the 1960s is apparent in the shift in whites' opinions about whether blacks "have tried to move too fast."

Other forms of scapegoating also frequently occur in American politics. Youth, protesters, and unorthodox or dissenting people have served from time to time as objects of such scapegoating. Hostility to protestors and to black demands tends to be highest among the lower echelons of nonelites. In 1971, one study found that twice as many blue-collar people expressed high hostility toward student demonstrators and black demands as did professional white-collar persons.[16]

Intolerance of dissent or unorthodoxy is a familiar feature of nonelite attitudes. It is sometimes argued that this finding means that nonelites are "undemocratic" or that elites' support for free speech and due process is the main pillar of democracy in the United States. We think it is better understood as evidence of a tendency toward scapegoating that is brought about by the unfulfilled wants and needs and other ambivalences we have explored.

Opinion Polls and Surveys

In the last forty years, the taking and reporting of opinion polls has become a major influence in election campaigns and in governmental policymaking. Aspirants to public office win or lose financial backing according to how well they do in the polls, and some abandon their candidacies if they make a poor showing. Officials and candidates often shape their rhetoric and policies to conform to what the polls say the public wants. Political spectators learn from the polls whether they are in the mainstream or are

---

[16] H. Edward Ransford, "Blue Collar Anger: Reactions to Student and Black Protest," *American Sociological Review* 37 (June 1972), p. 339.

deviant. The effects of all this on who gets what from government and on the concentration or dispersal of power are substantial. Let us first examine how poll takers reach the conclusions they do and then consider their influence in contemporary politics.

Polls are based on interviews with only a small number of people. Presidential preference poll takers, for example, typically interview only 1,200 to 1,500 people, although they are usually fairly accurate in learning the preferences of the approximately 50 million people who vote in presidential elections. This rather remarkable result is predictable if the respondents in the poll are so chosen that each person in the population has an equal chance to become part of the interviewed sample—that is, if the respondents are chosen in a truly random way. A sample of 1,500 respondents will produce responses that, 95 percent of the time, vary by no more than three percentage points from what the results would be if the entire population were interviewed. In a close election, a 3 percent error may be enough to yield the wrong result, of course, but that outcome is not common in election polling.

The number of respondents, as well as the cost, can be reduced still further by "quota sampling"—that is, by choosing a sample that accurately reflects the various groups of the population that differ with respect to the questions asked. If it is believed that views on a controversial issue differ by religious preferences, age, and gender, for example, a sample representing the proper proportions of each of these groupings could be chosen, but there is no way to be certain which groups should be represented or to calculate the margin of error if quota sampling is used.

If we think of each citizen as a self-contained generator of opinions about candidates, issues, and causes, opinion polls are a valuable technique for making government more democratic. They might be thought of as supplementing elections by giving public officials and candidates a reading of public opinion regarding specific issues. This reassuring view of polling is in fact the view that is usually taken for granted when poll results are reported. It is assumed by the polling organizations and reinforced by the candidates and interest groups whose positions are supported by current poll results. There is an important sense in which polls do tell us what the people think when we might otherwise have no idea or a mistaken idea. If poll results are kept in the proper perspective and are considered in the light of everything else we know about opinion formation and change, they are certainly useful.

The proper interpretation of polls, however, is not always simple, and they easily yield misleading conclusions if they are accepted as the last word on what the public wants. The major reason is that individuals are not independent generators of their own opinions. Instead, we are all influenced by what we perceive to be happening around us and thus by the opinions of other people who are important to us.

Another, and more general, reason that the opinions individuals express cannot be taken as the only evidence of what the people want from government is that opinion polls not only reflect opinions, but also help to shape them. It is not so much that they give people cues as to how to respond to specific questions, although they sometimes have that effect too. Rather, the more important function of the polls is to define for people who read them what *range* of views on public issues is realistic and respectable. What others are reported as thinking is shaped, as we have just seen, by existing conditions, and the polls in turn reinforce the same opinions by defining as extreme or as deviant views that are not in accordance with them. As a result, the public usually supports only marginal policy changes on issue after issue.

There may be heated controversy over whether the arms budget should increase 5 percent or 15 percent, but the polls make it clear to the general public that an opinion in favor of substantially reducing the arms budget, or of tripling it, is wild and defines its holder as not to be taken seriously. In time of inflation, people favor different degrees of tightness in monetary policy, but the polls constantly remind everyone that an opinion favoring the abolition of the Federal Reserve Board or a change in the board to make it reflect the interests of nonelites is deviant and not to be taken seriously. As a result, few opinions that are based on a vision of a different social order or political institutions that are different from those in existence ever appear. Polls intrigue people because they tell them what others are thinking; in doing so they exert some democratic influence, but they are unquestionably a conservative influence as well.

The form of the question in a poll is important, for it may shape answers in several ways. A long checklist of possible answers may result in the impression that people have many strong opinions, even though the checklist itself may have suggested them to the respondent. A "free-answer" question that requires the respondent to come up with his or her own reply may come closer to revealing real knowledge and concerns. A word or phrase in the question often taps associations that influence the response or distort it. Industrial psychologist Robert Kahn has suggested, for example, that a direct question about workers' satisfaction with their jobs strikes too close to the worker's self-esteem to be answered simply, and most workers do answer that kind of question by saying that they are moderately satisfied. According to Kahn, a worker

> tells us more only if the questions become more searching. Then we learn that he can order jobs clearly in terms of their status or desirability, wants his son to be employed differently from himself, and, if given a choice, would seek a different occupation.[17]

Rather than asking a national sample a standardized set of questions, attitudes are sometimes probed by interviewing a group of people in depth regarding their views about issues of concern to them; this method provides a far more complete picture of opinion, but is more costly and calls for greater interviewing skill. In a subtle and revealing study of eighty-two

---

[17] Quoted in *Work in America: Report of a Special Task Force to the Secretary of Health, Education, and Welfare* (Cambridge, Mass.: MIT Press, 1972), p. 15.

poor men in a southern city, for example, Lewis Lipsitz sought to learn their opinions about priorities in government spending. He found that of those who thought that the government spent too much money, 79 percent identified the space program, military expenditures, or foreign aid as projects for which too much was spent; *none* named domestic welfare programs. Conversely, of those who thought that government was not spending enough money, only 5 percent said that more should be spent for space exploration, the military, or foreign aid, while 95 percent thought that domestic welfare programs should receive more funds. Summarizing his analysis, Lipsitz concludes:

> The dominant theme is the sense of being cheated: one's government is not concerned enough with one's well-being; one's government is willing to spend money on what appear to many of these men as frivolous or illegitimate enterprises while it fails to meet their own deeply felt day-to-day needs.

> In keeping with this sense of deprivation, we also found a desire among the poor for some sort of assistance from the government, and a series of dissatisfactions with the kind of work the government was engaged in. . . . We should acknowledge that poor people have many grievances concerning both what the government does and does not do.[18]

Lipsitz adds that in his view, one of the reasons such grievances are not expressed more forcefully in politics is that political activists do not always take them up—that is, the elites who frame grievances into issues have not been concerned with these matters. He argues that poor people with grievances do not necessarily know how to carry them into the political arena by themselves.

Conventional polls sometimes create the impression that the public has opinions, when it is doubtful that many people have thought about the issue or have crystallized their views except to the extent that the polls themselves have encouraged them to do so. One authority with long experience in conducting polls has cogently summarized several of our observations:

> We think of public opinion as polarized on great issues; we think of it as intense. . . . Because of the identification of public opinion with the measurements of surveys, the illusion is easily conveyed of a public which is "opinionated." . . . The public of opinion poll results no doubt acts as a reinforcing agent in support of the public's consciousness of its own collective opinions as a definable, describable force. These published poll data may become reference points by which the individual formulates and expresses his opinions.[19]

---

[18] Lewis Lipsitz, "On Political Belief: The Grievances of the Poor," in *Power and Community: Dissenting Essays in Political Science,* ed. Philip Green and Sanford Levinson (New York: Random House, 1970), pp. 165–67.

[19] Leo Bogart, "No Opinion, Don't Know, and Maybe No Answer," *Public Opinion Quarterly* 31(Fall 1967), p. 336.

A public that is apathetic or unsure can be made to seem "opinionated" because respondents feel some social pressure to have an answer when an interviewer for a polling organization asks a question. Nonetheless, public opinion and the polls that help us learn what it is are an important part of politics, for they influence what we know, what government does, and even what people think.

CHANGING ATTITUDES IN THE 1980s

Before we conclude that American ideology has locked people's beliefs in place for all time, we should consider some strong evidence from the early 1980s that some key parts of that ideology are seriously eroding. The changes include both a sharp general decline in confidence in the government and some quite specific feelings that the Reagan administration is "unfair." The biggest drop in trust in government, and indeed in all social institutions, seems to have occurred in the late 1960s. This distrust appears to be generalized among all sectors of the population; feelings of class bias on the part of the government, however, are a distinctive reaction to the Reagan administration. They are felt by all, but most strongly by those who are most severely affected by policy changes. When considered with the surrounding economic and social upheavals of our times, these attitudinal changes suggest that the range of future public policy alternatives may be much wider than observers have previously assumed.

So profound and sustained was the loss of confidence in both leaders and social institutions between the 1960s and the 1980s that many pollsters and other professional observers regularly referred to a "confidence gap" or a "crisis of legitimacy." The social science authors of a book entitled *The Confidence Gap: Business, Labor, and Government in the Public Mind* collected and re-analyzed national surveys for more than a twenty-year period. Their conclusion in 1983 was that:

> The United States enters the 1980s . . . with a lower reserve of confidence in the ability of its institutional leaders to deal with the problems of the polity, the society, and the economy than at any time in this century. . . . Serious setbacks in the economy or in foreign policy, accompanied by a failure of leadership, would raise greater risks of a loss of legitimacy now than at any time in this century.[20]

Such conclusions rest in part on answers given by representative samples of the U.S. population to essentially the same question. Over this period, various polling organizations asked: "As far as the people running (various institutions) are concerned, would you say that you have a great

---

[20] Seymour Martin Lipset and William Schneider, *The Confidence Gap: Business, Labor and Government in the Public Mind* (New York: The Free Press, 1983), pp. 411–12.

deal of confidence, only some confidence, or hardly any confidence at all in them?'' The reports are always cast in terms of the proportion of respondents that have a great deal of confidence in the institutions named. Medicine, for example, enjoyed the highest average ranking in the twenty-four such polls conducted between 1966 and 1981; 50 percent of respondents reported a great deal of confidence in its leaders. Medicine's highest rating was 72 percent in 1966, but it dropped into the 40 percent level by the mid-1970s. In the 1980s, confidence was down to the mid-30 percent level.

Education and the military were next with 39 percent averages; organized religion and the Supreme Court followed with 32 percent averages; major companies and the press then followed with 25 and 24 percent respectively. Confidence in the executive branch averaged 21 percent, but since the Watergate scandal, it has been almost continuously below 20 percent. Congress shared the same experience, and occasionally threatened to fall below 10 percent. It managed to average 19 percent only on the basis of the scores of the 1960s. Only organized labor trailed the two major political institutions, compiling a dismal 15 percent average.

Nearly all of these ten major institutions achieved their highest ratings in the 1960s and their lowest in the late 1970s and early 1980s. The combination of Watergate and the mid-1970s recession, followed by the Carter administration's failures, seems to have been the principal cause of the erosion of trust in social institutions, particularly government institutions. However, the decline continued in the early years of the Reagan administration, indicating that these might be only obvious correlates rather than the real underlying causes. In 1982, the average scores of all these institutions combined was the lowest in the history of this kind of polling.

What do all these data mean? No observers really *know,* but almost all display concern equivalent to that of the authors quoted earlier. At worst, the findings could indicate a volatile and dangerous situation in which the general public might support anti-establishment appeals or "extremist" measures against existing institutions. At the least, the findings seem to suggest widespread alienation and cynicism about social institutions and purposes. Under such conditions, people are not likely to accept claims made in the public interest by established leaders. Concerted public action involving sacrifice for the common good is hard to imagine. These general attitudes are more likely to create a context where many people are responsive to new ways of thinking about or understanding both public affairs and their own interests.

It seems likely, in fact, that this "confidence gap" helped to pave the way for the quite unusual reactions to the Reagan administration in the early 1980s. What emerged in this period looked very much like *class-conscious* thinking—an uncharacteristic expression on the part of the lower strata of the U.S. population. Table 14.2 is a composite of the responses to two questions, producing class-related images of the U.S. government under President Reagan. The first question, which was asked at several

**TABLE
14.2**   *Class-Biased "Unfairness" in Reagan Administration, 1981–83*

Q. Would you say Reagan cares more about serving low-income people, middle-income people, or upper-income people, or does he
care equally about serving all people?

	Feb. 1981	April 1981	Nov. 1981	Aug. 1982	June 1983
Low	3	1	1	2	1
Middle	6	6	7	8	7
Upper	23	29	54	56	58
All equal	64	58	35	29	32

SOURCE: ABC–Washington Post poll, reported in *National Journal*, July 2, 1983, p. 1410.

Q. Would you say that each of these groups is being treated fairly or
unfairly by the Reagan administration?

	Fairly	Unfairly	No Opinion
Wealthy	90	3	7
Business executives	78	5	17
People like you	42	51	7
Middle-income people	41	49	10
The average citizen	40	50	10
Poor people	30	62	8
Small-business people	29	54	17
Elderly	27	66	7
Farmers	26	58	16

SOURCE: Gallup Organization, Inc., reported in *National Journal*, Aug. 20, 1983, p. 1757.

different times in the early 1980s, required respondents to say which group
(low-, middle-, or upper-income—or all equally) Reagan "cares more
about serving." Although practically nobody ever thought of Reagan as
favoring either the low- or middle-income groups, nearly two-thirds at first
expected him to "care equally" about all. Over time, however, the ratio
between treating all equally and favoring the upper-income group steadily
shifted, and by late 1982 it was essentially reversed. Well into 1983, the
proportion seeing the President as favoring the upper-income group was
still increasing.

Confirmation that this series was accurately tapping an important
public judgment came from a different question asked by another polling
organization. This judgment, like that just shown, also had to do with
fairness in regard to economic matters. It is documented in the second part
of Table 14.2. The Gallup Poll asked a national sample in August 1983 to
state their feelings as to whether various groups were "being treated fairly
or unfairly by the Reagan administration." Almost unanimously, respon-

dents said that the wealthy and business executives were being treated fairly, but a variety of ordinary people—particularly those most economically vulnerable—were not. The American public has not seen their government in such clearly class-related terms since 1936.

Indicators from the 1982 elections, such as the unusually high turnout of the unemployed and minorities, and the anti-Reagan voting attitudes and voting of women, minorities, and single people, provide some confirmation of these new attitudes. We shall take up these specific electoral manifestations in the next chapter. For the moment, it is enough to see how they help confirm changes in the basic attitudes and beliefs constituting an ideology underlying government itself. If people begin to see their government as unfairly serving other already-advantaged people, then the United States may be on its way to a fundamental change in the ideology that has helped to maintain the status quo for so long.

The fact that a level of change has also occurred in public attitudes toward the government's proper role in the economy adds another fragment of evidence in the same direction. Americans have traditionally been strong supporters of the free enterprise principle. They believed that government should keep hands off the economic "free market" as much as possible. However, an early-1980s study compared the attitudes of the general public with those of business executives on several economic matters.[21] The general public was far more favorable to a government role that was connected to the idea of an "industrial policy." It may be that the public is simply more ready than business executives to take on a changed basic ideology, or it may be that the would-be managers of opinion have reached the public more effectively than they have the more firmly-convinced business community. In any event, the general public was almost four times as ready as business executives to have the government provide retraining and relocation for workers who were displaced from older industries. It was twelve times readier to have the government develop a "national industrial plan" to determine where and how our resources are used.

These fragments do not prove that American ideology has lost its grip, but they do suggest that cracks in some hitherto solid foundations may be appearing. If the underlying ideology is undergoing change in important dimensions, almost anything might be possible; the less we take for granted, the better.

Perhaps the two most important issues of the early 1980s were the state of the economy and the question of how much to increase military spending. On these vital questions, the public showed utterly contrasting attitude-change patterns. With regard to the economy, opinion was highly volatile, changing in accordance with monthly changes in GNP and the inflation/unemployment ratio. It also was intimately connected to Democratic–Republican voting intentions in 1984. As the GNP sank and unem-

---

[21] Ibid., pp. 278–79.

TABLE
14.3   **Economic Expectations, 1982–83**

A. Inflation.	Q: "By this time next year, what do you think the inflation rate will be?"		
	June 1982	*November 1982*	*December 1983*
8 percent or higher	50%	40%	25%
7 percent	16%	9%	15%
6 percent	10%	17%	12%
5 percent or less	12%	18%	38%
No opinion	12%	16%	10%

B. Unemployment.	Q: "By this time next year, what do you think the unemployment rate will be?"		
	June 1982	*November 1982*	*December 1983*
9 percent or higher	75%	70%	26%
8 percent	9%	10%	21%
7 percent	5%	4%	16%
6 percent or lower	2%	3%	28%
No opinion	9%	13%	9%

SOURCE: *National Journal,* Feb. 18, 1984, p. 346, citing Gallup Organization, Inc., polling data.

ployment rose in the recession of 1981–82, about half the population felt that the economy was getting worse and less than a quarter felt it was improving. A massive switch began in late 1982, however, and by March, 1983, the proportion that felt that the economy was getting worse was below 20 percent while those that thought that it was getting better comprised over 40 percent.[22]

Table 14.3 also shows the dramatic volatility in popular attitudes toward the economy. In the period of a year and a half between June, 1982, and December, 1983, popular expectations shifted rapidly from pessimistic to optimistic. Here is a clear example of the impact of media reporting about economic conditions. It is certainly true that a good number of people had personal experience with the hardships of unemployment and inflation, and that they could tell from their own circumstances how the

---

[22] *National Journal,* Feb. 18, 1984, p. 346, citing ABC News–*The Washington Post* polling data.

**TABLE
14.4**   *Cuts in Military Budget vs. Other Programs, 1982–84*

Q: "President Reagan has said he wants no cuts in his defense budget, which calls for an increase over last year. Instead, he wants more cuts in domestic social programs. If you had to choose, would you prefer to see more cuts in _____ or in the increased defense budget?"

Alternative programs to be cut:	February 1982	November 1982	January 1984
1. Cut aid to cities	42%	36%	34%
Cut defense	52%	57%	54%
2. Cut health programs	27%	21%	21%
Cut defense	66%	73%	67%
3. Cut education aid	29%	22%	19%
Cut defense	65%	71%	71%

SOURCE: *National Journal*, Feb. 18, 1984, p. 346, citing Louis Harris and Associates, Inc., polling data.

economy was doing, but most people had to rely on government statistics and the declarations of elected officials, and apparently were convinced by them. Notice how sharply expectations about future inflation and unemployment changed in that relatively short period. To be so affected with regard to overall national prospects, a respondent *had* to be listening carefully and taking cues from what the news media reported government officials were saying about present and future economic conditions!

The fact that this may be true, and connected to political attitudes as well, is suggested by the breakdown of attitudes toward the economic "recovery" of 1983 and voting intentions in 1984. Those who saw the economy embarked on a long-term growth period (30 percent of all respondents) were ready to vote for Reagan by almost a four-to-one ratio. Those who saw no real recovery at all (24 percent) were inclined to vote for Mondale by well over three-to-one. A plurality of respondents (42 percent) viewed the economy as showing only "temporary improvement," and these were for the Democratic candidate by a small but solid majority.[23]

In the area of military spending, however, almost the reverse is true. In this field, there was steady official and media appeal for increased military spending. The survey question was asked alternatively, in terms of the areas in which the respondent would prefer to see spending cuts, and was prefaced with a statement that said that President Reagan was opposed to cuts in the defense budget. Nevertheless, as Table 14.4 shows in detail, the

---

[23] *National Journal*, Jan. 7, 1984, p. 37, citing *Los Angeles Times* polling data.

public opted for cuts in defense spending by very steady majorities over a period of nearly two years. There was little or no change in the proportions by which people preferred to cut the military, despite heavy government and media efforts to make the case for greater spending.

What explains the volatility and apparent susceptibility to media reporting in one case, and the opposite response in the other? Each area seems important, and laden with emotional overtones. But for some reason, perhaps even a quite rational one, people were more convinced of the economy's improvement than of the necessity for greater military spending at the cost of various social programs. If there is a continuing thread here, it seems to be that economic prosperity takes precedence over practically everything else. Even the military, when their fiscal needs become excessive, must take second place to restoring economic stability in the country.

These hints at changing patterns of attitude and opinion in the United States are only a tiny tip of a massive submerged iceberg. Much more data collection and interpretation would be required to get under the surface and really grasp all the changes that seem to be taking place in American thinking in the 1980s. One major manifestation of how people are changing in attitudes, however, occurs in November of every year—in our voting patterns. Let us turn to that most significant of all expressed opinions.

CHAPTER 15

Political Parties in the 1980s

Political parties are usually expected to play a crucial role in democratic political systems. They are supposed to be the principal organizational means by which people come together, work out programs, and then jointly compete in elections for the right to carry out their programs through government action. They are the linkage between people and government that makes democracy real in any society that is larger than one in which all the members can sit in face-to-face dialogue with each other.

The American political parties do not perform such functions today, however. The story of our political parties in the 1980s is one of at least two decades of steep decline in their capacity to discharge any of their supposed responsibilities. Much of this chapter will be invested in trying to understand the reasons for this decline. We shall also look at the special-interest groups and other forms of political organization that have risen to fill the vacuum left by the degeneration of the parties. Our concern shifts in closing to the question of what the parties' current state means for American democracy and whether the parties can and/or should be restored.

PARTIES AS ORGANIZATIONS

Political parties help spectators of the political scene make sense of the complexities of government by reducing them to a small number of key choices and by dramatizing the differences among party candidates and policies. Party organizations nominate candidates for public offices, draw up "platforms" to appeal for voter support, and so try to mobilize public

423

opinion in order to elect their own candidates. In countries such as Italy and France, where fairly stable blocs of voters are divided on ideological grounds, usually five to eight parties regularly elect candidates to the national legislative bodies and to local offices; the various parties compete on the basis of differences in ideologies and specific issues as well as on the basis of candidates' personalities.

In the United States and in other countries with a two-party system, party competition is far less ideological, although there are sometimes differences on particular issues. The existence in any country of a two-party system has always been taken as evidence of a basic consensus in most of the population on central policy directions; thus, most public opinion lies in what is usually perceived as the center of the political spectrum, so that the major parties either have to appeal to that body of opinion or else keep their statements on controversial issues so fuzzy that voters will be able to read whatever they want into them. The Republicans and Democrats have usually followed that strategy, for it is the way to win votes.

Such a system has little need for policy consistency or clarity among the supporters or candidates of either party, and these qualities have seldom been conspicuous in the American major parties. Each party typically includes within its ranks a range of people from conservatives to liberals, with the center of gravity in the Democratic Party usually being somewhat more liberal than that in the Republican Party in the last half-century, except in the Deep South.

The relative unimportance of coherent policy stands in American parties is underlined by the slackness of party discipline. Only rarely and in the most flagrant cases have legislators been disciplined for opposing the positions the party has taken in its campaign platforms or in legislative caucuses, which means that the voters can have little confidence that the promises party leaders or organizations make in election campaigns will be carried out by candidates who win elections. At the same time, individual legislators are free under this party system to respond to the opinions of their constituents when they are strong or to follow their personal policy or ideological inclinations when those are strong. In the South, for example, Democratic candidates for Congress ignored the pro–civil rights positions of party platforms with impunity for many years because voter turnout was low on election day, and relatively few blacks or civil libertarians voted. With the increase in black voting and the influx of industry into the South in recent years, this situation has begun to change, resulting both in the election of Republicans from the once solidly Democratic South and in the beginning of greater Democratic responsiveness to these new constituents, at least in some districts.

Third Parties

The United States has maintained the same basic two-party system for more than 150 years. This means that with rare and temporary exceptions, only two parties have had any serious chance of winning the presidency or even a substantial minority in the Congress. A great many "third parties" have existed over the course of American history, and one of these, the Republican Party, even managed to become a major party. Most American third parties (Know-Nothing, Prohibition, Populist, Greenback, Socialist, Communist, Progressive, Liberal, American Labor, Peace and Freedom, and others) have had relatively short lives. Third parties have occasionally elected candidates to public offices at every level of government except the presidency. They have chiefly espoused policy positions that were regarded in their times as being more or less deviant or "extreme," although many of these positions gained broad popular support and eventually began to look quite conventional. The chief function of these parties has been to introduce policy innovations into the political system; they have made it clear that a course of action that was earlier thought to be deviant was in fact widely supported and thus induced one or both major parties to espouse that position. Universal compulsory education for children, the progressive income tax, prohibition of the sale or use of intoxicating beverages, the Tennessee Valley Authority, governmental guarantees of the right of workers to organize labor unions, and many other policies first became live options because a third party made them campaign issues.

An idea that wins enough public support becomes attractive to the major parties. The Socialist Party, for example, had favored unemployment insurance and federally financed old-age benefits long before the Democrats concluded in the middle 1930s that these programs would win more votes than they would lose. And today, the Republican Party, which opposed the Social Security Act of 1935, accepts it as necessary and desirable, partly because experience with the law has demonstrated that it benefits industry by providing pensions for workers that are financed so that the costs can be shifted to consumers and to the workers themselves. A policy innovation that appeals to a wide range of groups, even though it is for different reasons, is sure to be embraced in time by the major parties. In taking over such programs, the major parties keep third parties from benefiting from their own political proposals.

Party Organizations

The two major American parties do not have a base of dues-paying party members, as do most political parties in foreign countries with multiparty systems. Instead, they consist of a large number of voters with strong or weak loyalties to the Republicans or the Democrats and a relatively small cadre of activists who serve in the party organizations and work in political campaigns.

The organizations of such "cadre parties" are weak and perform only a limited set of functions. Laws of each of the fifty states provide for party committees, usually at the precinct, county, congressional district, and state-wide levels, as is illustrated in Figure 15.1. The committees usually play a role in finding candidates for elective offices at these various levels and in choosing delegates to the quadrennial national conventions, but in

Figure 15.1. *Units of Party Organization and Their Primary Electoral Responsibilities*

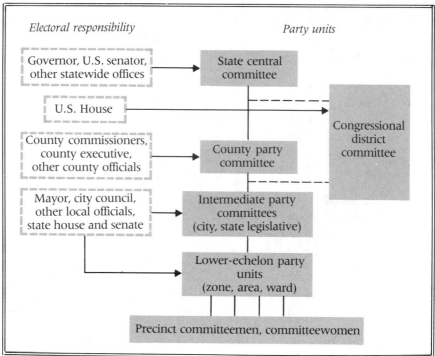

SOURCE: Dennis S. Ippolito and Thomas G. Walker, *Political Parties, Interest Groups, and Public Policy: Group Influence in American Politics,* © 1980, p. 77. Reprinted by permission of Prentice-Hall, Inc., Englewood Cliffs, New Jersey.

some states, the party organization of one or the other major party does little or nothing, usually because it has little chance of winning elections.

Each party also has a national committee, with representatives from every state. Its chief function is to arrange for the national nominating convention in presidential election years. Party committees also function in Congress and in the state legislatures to try to muster votes for or against measures favored by the President or governor. The congressional party committees also have a role in distributing campaign funds from the party coffers.

Why Parties Are Important. Democratic political systems involve participation by millions of people. Most of these people have little more than their vote with which to influence which candidates will be elected or what they will do while in office. Only a relative few have the special talent, institutional position, or private financial resources that assure them of a greater role in shaping who will be elected and how they will carry out their responsibilities. In other words, the many are at a disadvantage— unless they can join together behind agreed-upon programs and candidates who will implement their preferences.

The only vehicle for bringing people together, providing an arena for them to negotiate compromises and reach agreement, and helping them to unite behind candidates and programs, is what we know as a "political party." Without an organization that is devoted to trying to build a coalition of voters large enough to elect candidates who will work for them, most people have little or no way of seeing their preferences carried out in government. Parties are desirable for almost everybody, and essential to the democratic qualities of a political system, but they are absolutely indispensable to those who have nothing but their votes with which to gain their ends.

Without political parties, candidates and voters have no continuing relationship. Candidates can make a bewildering variety of promises and voters may try to assert their equally various wants and needs, but there is no effective way of achieving order in this all-persons-for-themselves chaos. Candidates run because they are ambitious and because they have somehow raised the money that is necessary to fund their campaigns. Voters may or may not locate a candidate they find acceptable. Their many different preferences may effectively cancel each other out—leaving officeholders free to do as they must to please powerful special interest groups.

Thus, there is no capability in the voters to hold newly-elected officials responsible for carrying out their promises, or even accountable for their actions while in office, and the vote becomes meaningless as a means of influencing policy directions. Voting is reduced to a symbolic pledge of allegiance to the political system. Democracy, in the sense of popular control over government actions, is not to be found. "Democracy" can mean only formal participation (voting), and not the prospect that one's vote will have any effect.

In other words, parties are a crucial link in making democracy workable in a large-scale society. This is by no means to say that they always or even usually perform this function adequately; there are many instances of self-serving actions, corruption, or abdication in American political party history. We *do* mean to emphasize, however, that without viable political parties—social organizations with a continuing membership and sustained purposefulness—people who depend chiefly on their vote for political influence are at an enormous disadvantage. Other people with money, status, or institutional position will exercise much greater leverage, and effectively control what happens.

Most Americans probably do not recognize the validity of this point. Instead, they see political parties as ways in which they lose their independence to a group; often they see themselves as falling under the influence of a hierarchy of leaders in a group whose interests may be at odds with their own. They pride themselves on "voting for the candidate and not for the party," and disparage those who are "party regulars." In doing so, of course, they are acting against their own interests as people who *must*, to be effective, join with others in a coherent aggregation that is sufficiently large to be able to get what they want. In effect, they voluntarily abandon their capacity to affect outcomes by means of the ballot and leave the business of deciding what is to be done to those with money, status, or other sources of political leverage.

It is not just the opportunity for a working democracy that is lost by this sort of anti-party action. Effective political parties provide means whereby relatively large numbers of people (if not majorities) are more or less directly involved in politics, even if their activities are in practice something short of democratic ideals. These people play at least some part in choosing and electing candidates, who are in turn aware of their responsibility to such constituents. Moreover, these same people feel that they have a stake in the system, or a role of sorts in the overall governing process, and officeholders can feel that they have some basis in popular consent for the actions that they believe they must take in the national interest.

Parties thus can be very important components of a political process that depends even to a limited extent on popular engagement and support. Why are the American political parties in such a low and declining state today? What, if anything, could be done to restore them in the future? These are the questions that will shape the rest of this chapter.

THE DECLINE OF THE PARTIES

Two events of the late 1960s and early 1970s, and responses to them, vastly accelerated a process of degeneration of the American political parties that was already well under way. These events were the Democratic National Convention of 1968 and the "Watergate" scandal, which culminated in the resignation of President Nixon and the passage of amendments to the Federal Election Campaign Act in 1974.

The Democratic Convention

The Democratic nominating campaign of 1968 was a period of high drama—mostly tragedy—unequaled in the history of American political parties. The year began with considerable opposition among Democrats to the way in which President Lyndon Johnson was conducting the Vietnam War. Opposition focused on the early primaries, and sought to make them a referendum against the war. Senator Eugene McCarthy offered himself as the vehicle for this effort, and when an apparently successful offensive by the North Vietnamese helped to escalate opposition to the war in February, 1968, McCarthy appeared likely to do quite well in the first primary in New Hampshire. A special campaign for Johnson was hastily organized and managed to win the primary, but so narrowly that the media reported the results as a victory for McCarthy and the anti-war movement.

The first consequence of the McCarthy "victory" was that Senator Robert Kennedy quickly joined the race, entered the next available primaries, and declared, however late in the game, that he represented the real anti-war opposition to President Johnson. Next, Johnson startled the country at the end of March by declaring that he would not be a candidate for reelection. This led directly to an announcement by Vice-President Hubert Humphrey that he would run for president. But Humphrey was by that time too late to qualify for most of the primaries, and besides he had much greater strength among the legions of party loyalists who had known him favorably for so many years. Humphrey therefore directed his campaign almost entirely at the party regulars—congressional, state, and local party leaders, big-city mayors, Southern delegates, and organized labor.

The biggest prize in the primaries at that time was the winner-take-all California primary, with a large group of delegates at stake. At the time, Humphrey had a sizable lead in delegates and a larger lead in the preferences of both party officials and rank-and-file Democrats. Without contesting any of the primaries, Humphrey appeared to be on his way to the nomination. When the California primary results came in, however, Robert Kennedy had won, and the whole question of who would be nominated seemed to be in doubt. But at that time, Kennedy was assassinated, and everything changed.

What changed the most was the atmosphere among Democrats. Bitterness and conflict among all factions that had been muted by efforts to elect candidates suddenly surfaced in uncontrollable ways, and frustrations took extreme forms. Humphrey, who had suspended campaigning in the immediate aftermath of the Kennedy assassination, was obliged to pick up the reins left to him by the Johnson administration. For those reasons, he was deeply resented by both McCarthy and Kennedy supporters. Their opposition focused not only on his alleged support of the war, but also on the fact that he had entered no primaries.

Complaints took the form of a challenge by McCarthy and anti-war groups to the delegate-selection process. They argued that they had won primaries but not delegates, because delegates were appointed by party officials as the latter saw fit. A variety of cases were cited in which McCarthy supporters were denied delegates to which the primaries or their overall strength in the state apparently would have entitled them. The basic issue seemed to be between the "new politics" of openness and democratic participation, and the "old politics" of closed-door decisionmaking by party regulars. The convention, which was held in Chicago under the dominance of the old-style machine of Mayor Richard Daley and heavy security forces, was itself an example of old politics in the ruthlessness with which the majority worked their will. Outside the convention, a virtual police riot ran on unchecked for days—or until the various forms of opposition had been effectively suppressed, with what turned out to be very high cost to the Humphrey candidacy.

For our purposes, however, the important result of all this was the passage of (Humphrey-supported) resolutions to assure that:

1. State convention delegations in the future would be selected with wide public participation, and
2. State convention delegations would not be required to vote as a

unit, but in accordance with some other division of preferences within the state.

Not long after the election, the Party created a Commission on Party Structure and Delegate Selection (later known by the names of its co-chairs as the McGovern–Fraser Commission) to report on better ways of selecting delegates. Taking its guidance from the experience of 1968 and the resolutions passed at that convention, the Commission issued a "Mandate for Reform" that required participatory selection of delegates and set standards for the inclusion of women and minorities among those delegates. These recommendations helped initiate a momentous process of change in American political party structures and practices.

The Watergate Scandal

The second event of these years was the involvement of President Richard Nixon in the break-in at the Watergate headquarters of the Democratic National Committee in 1972. After a series of investigations, revelations, and conflicts between Congress and the President, Nixon finally resigned. One of the peripheral issues in the case was the fact that the original break-in was conducted by employees of the Committee for the Re-Election of the President (CREEP). The Committee or other members of the administration also were alleged to have acted illegally in seeking campaign contributions from corporations in exchange for governmental favors. Thus, the financing of campaigns seemed to be involved in the problems summarized by the scandal-word "Watergate."

Faced with such an apparent moral blot on our political system, Congress was in a position and a mood where it had to do something. That something turned out to be new legislation with respect to election financing that has had powerful and far-reaching effects on the political parties, the presidential selection process, and American electoral politics in general. For the first time in American history, the funding and conduct of federal elections was regulated in a way that could actually be enforced—and was clearly intended to be. The first set of rules was partially invalidated by the Supreme Court and new amendments enacted by Congress in 1976 that remain in effect today—in many ways creating a whole new "game" of national politics.

The rules themselves are rather complicated, but the principles behind them are fairly simple:

1. The Congress granted the Federal Election Commission powers to oversee national elections.
2. Federal subsidies were provided for primary elections, nominating conventions, and presidential elections, with strict reporting and other requirements.
3. Extensive requirements were laid down for reporting by candidates of the contributions to and expenditures of their campaigns. Those candidates who accepted federal subsidies also had to accept the

placement of strict limits on their total spending in both primaries and general elections.

4. Limits were placed on the amount of money that individuals could give to or spend in coordination with the candidates they wished to support. Money that was spent independently of candidates' knowledge or plans, however, was *not* limited.

One effect of these rules was the development of a variety of new organizations and ways of spending money. Reporting requirements have generally been followed where they apply, but ways around the limits have also been found. For example, a political action committee (PAC) was limited in the amount that it could contribute to a party or directly to a candidate in any one year. This led to two developments: the multiplication of such committees, and vast expenditures "independently" of candidates but clearly in favor of that candidate's position or against the opposing candidate. How these reforms articulate with other changes will be seen repeatedly in the analysis that follows, and then we shall focus exclusively on the booming field of political action committee proliferation and spending.

These two major changes in the rules and practices of elections—the "opening up" of the delegate selection process in the Democratic Party (which affected the Republican Party too, although in a much milder form), and the campaign financing legislation of 1974 and 1976—greatly speeded up the ongoing process of deterioration in the two political parties. It is clear that the process was already under way as a result of other, independent factors, but these two sets of changes helped generate new momentum behind what now looks like the disintegration of the parties. We shall look briefly at four important factors that contributed to the decline of the parties, as a way of characterizing their current state.

DECLINING VOTER IDENTIFICATION WITH THE TWO MAJOR PARTIES

There are several ways of measuring voter identification with the political parties:

1. To ask people in opinion surveys, and include measures of the strength of their attachment.
2. To look at the extent to which they actually vote for most or all candidates of "their" party in a given election, and at patterns of such voting over time.
3. To explore the links between voters' issue preferences and what the parties seem to stand for. If the parties have a clear image in voters' eyes that is consistent with their issue positions, "party identification" is likely to be stronger than "candidate orientation" for such voters.

Figure 15.2.   *Party Identification, 1920–83*

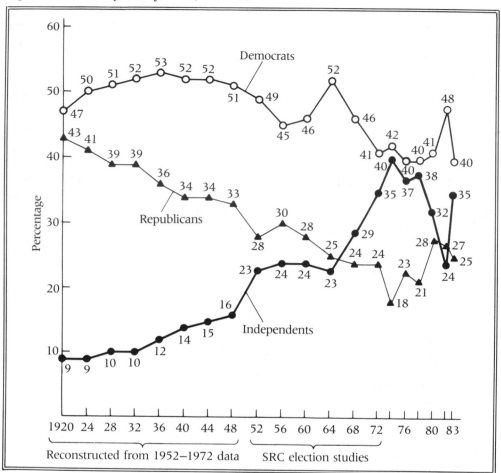

SOURCE: Derived from Norman H. Nie, Sidney Verba, and John R. Petrocik, *The Changing American Voter* (Cambridge, Mass.: Harvard University Press, 1976), p. 83. Updated by the authors from data reported in *National Journal*, October 29, 1983, p. 2231.

By any of these indicators, however, voters' identification with the political parties has been declining for decades. But there are some indications that this process may have reached its end, possibly because it simply could not go much further.

Party identification as reconstructed from and revealed in surveys over the last three decades is shown in Figure 15.2. The figure demonstrates a very strong attachment to parties felt by most voters at the outset, in the 1920s, and a very small proportion of "independents." In the 1930s, however, the Democrats gain party identifiers, while the Republicans lose, apparently because many of their supporters think of themselves as independents. After the war, both parties began to lose identifiers. After 1964, the process picks up speed, with the ranks of independents climbing sharply. This is probably caused by the lowering of the voting age to 18 in 1971; young people are less likely than older voters to have strong party loyalties. But obviously there are other factors at work, because these trends are so long-lived (as are the trends toward independent *voting*).

In recent years, each election seems to have drawn voters out of the ranks of independents and toward identification with the winning party (Republicans in 1980, Democrats in 1982). The ranks of each group appear to have roughly stabilized. At least these facts permit speculation that the shift to independent status may have peaked, and that either polarization toward the parties or even realignment between the parties is possible in the future.

The tendency of voters to vote a straight party ticket has dropped in even more striking fashion than their survey-reported identification with the parties. The measure most often used is a comparison of votes for president with votes for congressional candidates of the same party. From 1920 through 1946, less than 20 percent of all voters actually voted a "split-ticket," but after that the proportion voting for a president of one party and a representative of the other party began to climb steadily. In 1964, split-ticket voting reached 35 percent, by 1976 it was over 65 percent, and in subsequent elections it has remained at that or even higher levels.[1] What shows up clearly is a preference for Republican presidents and Democratic representatives. Party ties seem less important than characteristics of the candidates, at least with respect to the highly visible office of president.

It is much more difficult to sort out the extent to which voters identify with a party because of shared issue preferences. This requires that a voter have issue preferences, see a party position clearly, and then make a connection between the two that is not derailed by orientation to particular characteristics of the candidates.

What is the relative influence of party affiliation, the candidates' personalities, and the issues? Studies of this question necessarily rely on surveys of voters' beliefs and behavior. They find that in the 1950s, the issues were less important than either candidate images or party identification, which was by far the most important influence. But in the 1960s and 1970s, issues grew in significance as parties declined. That was especially true in two elections in which a major-party presidential candidate was widely perceived as "extreme" on the issues: Goldwater as a conservative in 1964 and McGovern as a liberal in 1972. The most thorough recent survey of voting behavior concludes: "If the public is faced with candidates distinguished from each other on the basis of the issues, it will vote on the issues. If the public is offered a more centrist choice, the vote will depend much more heavily on partisan identification."[2] The same study finds that

[1] Richard W. Boyd, "Electoral Trends in Postwar Politics," in James D. Barber, ed., *Choosing the President* (Englewood Cliffs, N.J.: Prentice-Hall, 1974), p. 185.

[2] Norman H. Nie, Sidney Verba, and John R. Petrocik, *The Changing American Voter* (Cambridge, Mass.: Harvard University Press, 1976), p. 318.

Figure 15.3. *Frequency of Evaluations of Candidates in Terms of Party Ties, Personal Attributes, and Issue Positions, 1952–72*

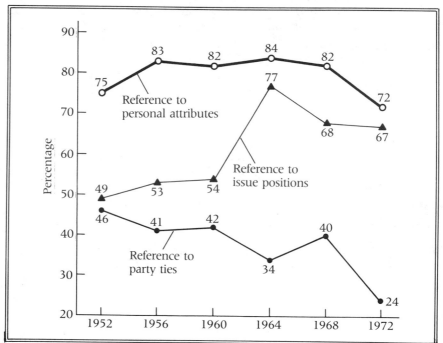

SOURCE: Reprinted by permission of the publishers from *The Changing American Voter* by Norman H. Nie, Sidney Verba, and John R. Petrocik, p. 167. Cambridge, Mass.: Harvard University Press © 1976, 1979 by the Twentieth Century Fund.

most voters prefer a candidate with a centrist position when the opponent takes an extreme position (see Figure 15.3).

At another level of analysis, these statements may look a little less like a law of human nature and more like a statement about symbolic politics. The labeling of some political positions as "centrist" and others as "extreme" is not an objective judgment, but a reflection of mainstream opinion, and such opinions change over time. To conclude that most voters take issues into account by choosing centrist rather than extreme positions is not very different from concluding that most voters choose the issue positions that most voters prefer, because that is how "centrist" is defined.

Nor are party identification, issue choices, and candidate preferences independent of one another. Voters are likely to assume that the parties and candidates they like will usually take the *positions* they like, especially when stands on issues are fuzzy. Issue voting is an important consideration, but the perception of issues is limited by the perception of parties and of candidates and by the distribution of opinions in the population as a whole.

There are some consistent and familiar differences between the issue positions of adherents of the two major parties, and these undoubtedly help to hold people to their respective parties. Democrats regularly show stronger support for government assistance to the aged and needy, aid to education, and school integration than do Republicans. The latter are more likely to believe in increased defense spending than are Democrats. Over time, distinct images of the parties have taken shape in voters' minds and now provide means by which they feel attachment to one or the other party; however, the differences are not great, for the reasons discussed earlier. Figure 15.4 shows that the Democratic Party has usually been perceived as the party of economic prosperity, and less clearly, as the party most likely to keep the peace.

These overall totals, however, conceal some important differences that are of growing importance in the 1980s. In 1983, with an apparent economic recovery well under way, polls began to show sharp differences between men and women in their perceptions of, and attachments to, the major political parties. Table 15.1 shows that, in overall totals, Americans were starting to see the Republican Party as the party of economic prosperity. It was viewed as being more likely to control inflation and insure recovery than the Democratic Party, but that was the view only of men, and not of women. The latter saw the Democrats as being more likely to achieve both goals. Men and women differed greatly in their perceptions of the parties on this issue. They differed less, but still significantly, on the question of which party would be most likely to keep the United States out of war, and, as a result, women were more strongly oriented to the Democratic Party than men. Such differences are quite new in American politics, and it is still too early to speculate about their long-range significance.

The Role of Campaign Financing. Campaign costs have mounted steadily, chiefly because of the high cost of increasingly necessary television exposure. Funding sources have become crucial determinants of who can become a candidate and how they will do in elections. The political parties have lost control of who gets nominated to run for office under their label, partly because the aspirant with the best funding has a great advantage in a primary campaign. In the final election, great expenditures are necessary— far more than a party can expect to provide by itself. Thus, candidates who have access to sources of contributions, whether individuals or political action committees, will stand a better chance of winning, and if they do win, they will know that they owed their success more to their contributors than to their political party organization.

Each succeeding campaign seems to cost about one-third more than the last one, counting both inflation and the expanded use of television advertising. We can only estimate the total costs involved, because only a portion is required to be reported to the Federal Elections Commission. Funds raised and spent by political action committees "independently" of a candidate's campaign (whether to promote one candidate, attack another candidate, or simply to promote an issue position—such as anti-abortion or gun control) do not fall under the reporting rules. Total spend-

Figure 15.4.   *Long-Term Trends in Images of the Parties*

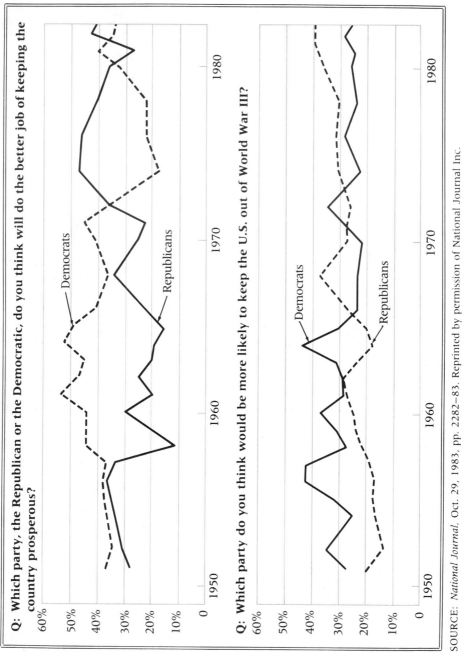

Q: Which party, the Republican or the Democratic, do you think will do the better job of keeping the country prosperous?

Democrats

Republicans

Q: Which party do you think would be more likely to keep the U.S. out of World War III?

Democrats

Republicans

SOURCE: *National Journal*, Oct. 29, 1983, pp. 2282–83. Reprinted by permission of National Journal Inc.

TABLE

15.1   **Images of the Political Parties, 1983**

	All Americans	Men	Women
Call themselves:			
Democrats	38%	32%	43%
Republicans	23	25	21
Which party is most likely to keep U.S. out of war:			
Democratic Party	40	38	41
Republican Party	27	32	23
Which party is better able to handle inflation:			
Democratic Party	32	26	38
Republican Party	41	51	33
Which party is better able to insure economic recovery:			
Democratic Party	36	32	39
Republican Party	40	49	32

SOURCE: New York Times–CBS News Poll, June 1983, reported in *The New York Times,* July 10, 1983, p. E5.

ing in the 1982 congressional campaigns, for example, was *reported* at $314 million, up from $240 million in 1980.[3] Spending that is not required to be reported would probably add another $50 to $75 million. Presidential elections, of course, are the most expensive of all, and sums approaching $200 million for that election alone are not beyond belief.

Campaign funding levels can be vital to the outcome of elections, although they are certainly not the only factor involved. The 1982 congressional elections are a good example. The Republicans lost twenty-six seats in the House, a solid defeat grounded in public unhappiness with the economic recession that was then under way, as well as the usual swing away from the party of the presidential incumbent. But from ten to twelve more seats might have been lost, converting defeat into disaster, if Republican candidates in closely-contested districts had not had great advantages in available campaign funds.

In 42 races where Republicans won with 55 percent of the vote or less, 29 Republican candidates had raised more than $50,000 more than their Democratic opponents by the crucial six-weeks-before-election point in their campaigns. In the 41 races in which Democrats won with 55 percent or less, 18 won despite having raised at least $50,000 less than their Republican opponent at the same point in the campaign. In other words, victory does not always go to the biggest spender, but the closer the race,

---

[3] *The New York Times,* January 11, 1983, p. 7.

the more important is the availability of extra funds. Democrats and Republicans alike agreed that the funding differences translated into between ten and twelve seats in 1982. The Republican proportion of the total vote was just 43.7 percent, a figure which, based on past results, would have meant the loss of forty-four seats instead of the twenty-six that actually changed hands.[4]

The importance of campaign funding makes the *source* of such funding equally important. There are three major sources: the candidates' personal wealth or independent contributors, the political parties, and political action committees (PACs). The law limits individual contributions to a candidate to $1,000 in each primary or general election, $5,000 by a PAC or state party committee, and $10,000 by national party committees to a House candidate or $17,500 to a Senate candidate. The parties are also authorized to pay campaign expenses for candidates, up to limits adjusted for inflation for House candidates and inflation plus state population for Senate candidates. In 1984, this translated into about $20,000 per House candidate and ranges from about $80,000 in small states to $1.3 million in California, the largest.

The parties must raise the money in the first place, in order to be this helpful, however. This is where the Republicans have achieved dramatic advantages. They not only appear able to draw on generally larger and wealthier sources, but their House and Senate campaign committees quickly adapted to the new legislation in a much more aggressive manner. They began direct-mail solicitations and built up contributor lists, so that they were able to draw in more than $190 million in contributions in 1981–82, according to reports of the Federal Election Commission. By contrast, the Democratic committees drew in only $28 million.[5] The Republican sources include many PACs and literally million of individuals, whereas the Democrats draw from fewer PACs and far fewer individuals.

The PACs have steadily assumed a greater role in campaign financing. In addition to being a major source of funds for both parties, they have become increasingly important as direct contributors to candidates, providing about 35 percent of all money raised by candidates in 1982. Almost one-fourth of the House of Representatives, including the Speaker, the minority leader, and other top leaders, raised more than half of their 1982 campaign money from PACs. Representative Robert Michel of Illinois, the House minority leader, led all House candidates with a total of $469,561 (68 percent of all his campaign funds) from PACs, which were primarily connected with corporations and trade associations in the oil, food, and insurance industries.[6]

Contributions from PACs tend to favor incumbents, particularly those

---

[4] *The New York Times*, November 9, 1982, p. 1.

[5] *National Journal*, October 29, 1983, p. 2261.

[6] All data in this and the following paragraph are drawn from *The New York Times*, January 19, 1983, p. 9.

with leadership positions. Of the 85 House candidates who received $150,000 or more from such committees, 72 were incumbents and only 8 were running against incumbents. The median member of the House (one with half of all members receiving more and half less) received $87,228 or 39 percent of all campaign funds from PACs. "We are evolving very quickly into the best Congress money can buy," *The New York Times* quoted Representative Mike Synar of Oklahoma as saying in 1983. But he added, "You don't buy a United States Congressman with a contribution, of course, but you buy access and access is the name of the game."[7] It is exactly this point about access that troubles both representatives and observers; the ease of raising money from PACs and the sense of obligation to listen to such contributors' views could make Congress the captive of such special interests. It certainly removes candidates and officeholders from any primary loyalty to their political parties.

The Effects of Party Reforms. Although there is considerable controversy about the effects of the post–1968 "reforms" in the Democratic Party's national convention delegate-selection procedures, there is wide agreement that the party as such has become less important. The new significance of binding primaries for choosing delegates has made the attributes of candidates and their access to funding sources early in the selection process crucial to obtaining the committed delegates that are needed for nomination. The party can be of little help in the primary election stage, and by the time of the national nominating conventions, one or another candidate has usually obtained the binding commitments of enough delegates to assure nomination. The former role of the parties of providing an arena for bargaining and compromise between factions and candidates no longer exists.

These changes gained much of their impetus from the recommendations of the post–1968 McGovern–Fraser Commission. The Commission developed several important new guidelines by broadly interpreting its mandate to provide for "full, meaningful, and timely" participation in the delegate selection process. It endorsed earlier standards of public notice, nondiscrimination, and openness for all meetings and delegate-selection activities. Perhaps more important, it required state parties to see that minorities, women, and young people (ages 18–30) were represented in nominating convention delegations in about the same proportions that they were found in that state's population. State parties were required to work in their states to see that all necessary changes in state legislation were made to assure that all of these reforms would be practical. (Changes in such state legislation had some spillover effects on Republican procedures, but for the most part, the Republican Party has not implemented similar reforms. It has, however, been obliged to follow state shifts to the primary as a means of selecting delegates.)

Primaries were not mandated by the McGovern–Fraser Commission,

---

[7] Ibid.

but they were widely perceived as a means of satisfying various participatory requirements. Besides, it seemed to some party organizations that it might be better to provide primaries so that the presidential-candidate enthusiasts would have a focus that was separate from the regular channels and decision-making tasks of the party. Primaries also bring money and attention to a state, particularly if they are held early in the delegate-selection process. In any event, the number of states holding primaries for the selection of delegates increased rapidly. In 1968, only 17 states held primaries (and some of these were not binding on the delegates chosen), electing about 40 percent of the delegates; in 1980, 35 states held primaries, electing almost 80 percent of the delegates. Table 15.2 traces these changes.

By 1984, however, the beginnings of a reaction seemed to be setting in. The number of states holding primaries was down to 24 for the Democrats (not including primaries in Puerto Rico and for the group known as ''Democrats abroad'') and 29 for the Republicans. In addition, the Democrats had established a new category of delegates. A total of 566, or about one-sixth of all delegates at the convention, were to be unpledged state, local, and national party leaders and elected officeholders. This presumably would give greater weight to concern for the party as such, and a more balanced view of where the national interest and/or the party's interest in winning an election might actually lie.

One of the main reasons behind these actions was the feeling that the proliferation of primaries was giving excessive weight to activist minorities within the party. The strategy for winning a primary, in which only a small fraction of the eligible electorate usually votes (26 percent on the average in 1980, with states ranging from 6 percent to 45 percent), is to mobilize a committed minority rather than seek to appeal to a broad base of voters. However, it is that very broad base that must be counted on to win the general election; without it, the party cannot win. Moreover, the skills, issue positions, and personality characteristics that are needed to mobilize such a committed minority might be quite at odds with those that are needed to govern the country if the candidate were finally to be elected. (This is often alleged to be the story of the Carter presidency.)

Finally, competition among the states pushes primaries earlier in a presidential nominating year, which forces the campaign to start earlier and makes it cost more. The campaign becomes ''front-loaded,'' because victory in the early primaries is necessary to develop media attention and momentum for collecting delegates later and obtaining the nomination. The need to achieve the vital ''name recognition'' in advance of such primaries forces candidates to invest heavily in travel and television time. Comparisons have been made between the cost per vote in the early primaries and those later in the year. In 1976 and 1980, the candidates spent $9.46 and $13.89 per vote in the January Iowa caucuses, $7.22 and $8.90 in the February New Hampshire primary, and $2.02 and $2.21 in the March Florida primary. By the time of the June California primary, the

**TABLE
15.2**   *Proportion of Delegates Selected in Primaries, 1952–80*

DEMOCRATS

YEAR	NUMBER OF PRIMARIES	CONVENTION TOTAL	DELEGATES SELECTED IN PRIMARIES		DELEGATES COMMITTED TO CANDIDATES BY PRIMARIES	
			Number	*Percent*	*Number*	*Percent*
1952	17	1230	570	.46	224	.18
1956	21	1372	690	.50	523	.38
1960	17	1521	686	.45	311	.20
1964	18	2316	1177	.51	943	.41
1968	17	2623	1276	.49	936	.36
1972	23	3016	1977	.66	1737	.58
1976	29	3008	2264	.75	1982	.66
1980	31	3331	2378	.71	2366	.71

Mean 1952–68: Selected 48.2%; Committed 30.6%
Mean 1972–80: Selected 70.7%; Committed 65.0%

REPUBLICANS

YEAR	NUMBER OF PRIMARIES	CONVENTION TOTAL	DELEGATES SELECTED IN PRIMARIES		DELEGATES COMMITTED TO CANDIDATES BY PRIMARIES	
			Number	*Percent*	*Number*	*Percent*
1952	15	1206	558	.46	290	.24
1956	18	1323	628	.47	572	.43
1960	15	1331	550	.41	468	.35
1964	17	1308	623	.48	462	.35
1968	16	1333	601	.45	480	.36
1972	22	1348	715	.53	555	.41
1976	28	2259	1501	.66	1219	.54
1980	33	1993	1502	.75	1374	.69

Mean 1952–68: Selected 45.4%; Committed 34.6%
Mean 1972–80: Selected 64.6%; Committed 54.7%

SOURCE: From *Consequences of Party Reform* by Nelson W. Polsby. Copyright © 1983 by Nelson W. Polsby. Reprinted by permission of Oxford University Press, Inc.

steady decline in expenditure per vote in the two election years brought the costs down to 68 cents and 23 cents.[8]

These effects of the expansion of primaries have led some informed observers to pull back from support of the primary system itself. In his

---

[8] *Congressional Quarterly Weekly Report,* December 26, 1981, p. 2566.

recent *The Crisis of American Leadership*,[9] presidential scholar James McGregor Burns argues that the primaries are peculiarly vulnerable to the mass media's impact. Because of the uncertainties and fluidity involved, the media can play an even greater role than usual in shaping public expectations and deciding what is a "victory" or "defeat" for one candidate or another. What is presented as undeniable one day on the basis of very limited hard evidence can be transformed into some quite different but equally conventional wisdom the next day. Primaries become media events, trivia contests in which meaningless events are blown way out of proportion, or "horse races" in which the media decide who is ahead and who is closing fast. The party is forced to stand by and watch while the media use its nominating process to form the basis of a half-year's entertainment.

The Role of the Mass Media, Particularly Television. Central to our analysis is the point that the structural needs of the media have come to dominate the needs of the political parties and perhaps even the American political process. These structural needs are quite commonplace; as big businesses, the media must earn an adequate return on their massive capital investment through providing an entertaining product, one that their market will pay for on a sustained basis. There is no intent on the part of owners, managers, or even reporters to undermine the parties or our political process. They do so, however, because of the very nature of the communications media whose capabilities they implement. These considerations suggest that it will be very difficult to reverse any of the trends that are visible, and that our politics may have to adapt more or less permanently to them.

The costs of covering a campaign are rising as rapidly as the costs of conducting a campaign. Estimates are that such independent big-city newspapers as the *Boston Globe* and the Baltimore *Sun* will have spent from $500,000 to $750,000 to cover the 1984 elections.[10] The big national newspapers like *The New York Times*, the *Los Angeles Times*, and *The Washington Post* are likely to have spent twice that sum. The major television networks each probably spends $150 million or more to cover the same elections. Television revenues from candidates bring in only about $30 million, because most of the more than $100 million invested in television time is paid to local stations. The remaining network investment must be justified on public service grounds, or in terms of the viewer attention it generates for advertisers in the news or immediately following broadcasts.

All of these factors converge to make it almost imperative for the media, and particularly television, to portray the campaigns in an exciting and entertaining light. Events lacking in drama must be given some, and

---

[9] James McGregor Burns, *The Crisis in American Leadership* (New York: Simon and Schuster, 1984).

[10] All data in this paragraph are drawn from *National Journal*, December 3, 1983, pp. 2521 and 2524.

races that do not seem close can be made to appear so by in effect pitting the leading candidate against "expectations" about his or her winning margin. These expectations, of course, are those of the media. One way or another, there must be a horse race with an uncertain outcome—over and over again. Human interest dimensions, personality quirks, and mistakes get played up far beyond the point that their merits would seem to justify. When there is nothing else to work with, the media often resort to open speculations about what might happen if one or another possibility should come to pass.

Neither expectations nor speculations have much basis in tangible or hard evidence. What evidence there is about how people actually feel about candidates in the early stages of a primary is sketchy and uncertain, and is perhaps more a product of the media's own actions in playing up certain candidates than anything else. Most people are uninformed about the candidates, and opinions are fluid and subject to change rapidly on the basis of little new evidence. What the media perceive as public opinion may be the other side of their own news judgments; the more the media present the race as between X and Y, the more that is the way the public sees it. When the public does tune in and act differently from media expectations, the media reverse themselves at once and all together, now declaring that a great upset has occurred and solemnly assuring readers and viewers that the world is now totally different from what it was only the week before. Volatility of opinion and of news presentations seems to be built into the new role of the media. What is left by the wayside is a continuing role for the political parties.

In his recent indictment of what television has done to the political process, the leading political scientist Austin Ranney listed five major effects:[11]

1. The sheer volume of political stories, which are often presented as being important when they are quite routine, results in confirmation of the public's perception that politics is dull, that politicians are all blowhards and hypocrites, and that it is better not to bother to vote.
2. TV domination of primaries and elections brushes the parties aside and makes it necessary for a candidate to be a TV success rather than a person who is capable of governing.
3. The constant search for scandals and wrongdoing, together with steady denigration of parties and politicians, also helps to drive people away from voting or other political activity.
4. The networks' need to have eye-catching new stories every night results in inflating politicians' rhetoric and peoples' expectations about what government can do. People expect more, officeholders

---

[11] Austin Ranney, *Channels of Power: The Impact of Television on American Politics* (New York: Basic Books, 1983).

have less time to try to fulfill those expectations, and once again people become frustrated with their government's performance.

5. All of these conditions mean that public life is much harder and less rewarding than before, and governments have less capacity to act. The vacuum is filled by non-elected bureaucrats, staff, and judges. Politicians retire sooner—with resultant lowering of experience and capability in government. Government is weaker in several ways, and more difficult to conduct.

However, Ranney concludes that in some important ways, this is merely an exaggeration of what the framers of the Constitution intended in the first place.[12] We might add that, after all, the framers were no friends of either political parties or popular democracy.

INTEREST GROUPS AND POLITICAL ACTION COMMITTEES

As the political parties have declined in importance in American politics, other forms of organized political influence have risen to fill the gap that has been left open. Interest groups, or pressure groups as they are sometimes known, have long been a part of the American political scene. They often try to help their friends and punish their enemies in electoral campaigns, but their primary focus is on lobbying at the legislative stage of policymaking or at the administrative stage of policy implementing. The newer participant, and the one that is most fully brought forth by the new campaign financing laws, is the political action committee. These are more often vehicles for collecting campaign funds and transferring them to candidates or causes, but they also engage in pressure tactics. The difference between an interest group and a PAC is not always clear, but it can be summarized as the difference between a membership organization with a concern for making itself felt in politics and a collection agency formed for political purposes. We shall look more closely at each in turn.

Between two-thirds and three-quarters of the American people belong to voluntary organizations to further interests they hold in common. Virtually all these interests involve stands on some political issues, either directly or indirectly. Table 15.3 shows the types of interests represented by the more than 13,000 voluntary associations that are national in their scope; many more are local or regional.

People tend to join groups to express interests that are stable and fairly strong. The doctor who joins the county medical society, the worker who joins a union, the factory owner who joins a trade association, and the hunter who joins the National Rifle Association all have other interests

---

[12] Ibid., p. 174.

TABLE
15.3   **Voluntary Associations of National Scope in the United States**

TYPE OF ORGANIZATION	NUMBER	PERCENTAGE
Business, trade, or commercial	3,494	19.8
Health and medical	1,704	9.7
Cultural	1,607	9.1
Public affairs	1,605	9.1
Social welfare	1,274	7.2
Scientific, engineering, technical	1,239	7.0
Hobby	1,210	6.9
Educational	1,100	6.2
Religious	864	4.9
Agricultural and commodity exchange	810	4.6
Athletic, sports	696	3.9
Legal, governmental, military	649	3.7
Fraternal, nationality, ethnic	469	2.7
Greek-letter societies	325	1.8
Labor	250	1.4
Veteran, patriotic	234	1.3
Chamber of Commerce	114	.6
Totals	17,644	99.9

SOURCE: *Encyclopedia of Associations*, Vol. 18, edited by Denise S. Akey (copyright © 1959, 1961, 1964, 1968, 1970, 1972, 1973, 1975, 1976, 1977, 1979, 1980, 1981, 1982, 1983 by Gale Research Company; reprinted by permission of the publisher), Gale Research, 1983.

that do not give rise to organizational membership, chiefly because they are not as important or continuous as these. Many people do not join organizations, in spite of stable and strong economic interests, because they enjoy the benefits of relevant pressure groups' activities anyway. Businesspeople benefit from the probusiness lobbying of the chamber of commerce even if they are not members; similarly, workers often win higher wages because employers want to *discourage* them from joining unions. One astute analyst has suggested that membership in interest groups is often dependent either on coercion (such as a requirement that lawyers join the state bar association in order to practice law) or on incidental benefits (such as a union pension plan or a malpractice insurance plan available only to members of a medical association).[13] It is chiefly middle-class and upper-middle-class people who join the interest groups that most actively try to influence governmental policy, for this class has solid economic and social roots and is likely to be conscious of its joint interests.

Some people have strong common interests, but are not brought together in a way that makes organization likely. This is true of the poor, the

---

[13] Mancur Olson, *The Logic of Collective Action* (New York: Schocken Books, 1968).

unemployed, the workers who work intermittently or are very poorly paid, and consumers. It cannot be taken for granted, therefore, that every interest will have its organized "watchdog." The oil and natural gas companies will lobby effectively through their trade associations, but the people who *buy* heating oil and gasoline are unlikely to organize at all.

Some interest groups represent stable and continuing concerns of the people who belong to them or support them, and so they remain active indefinitely or for long periods of time. Trade associations that represent businesspeople in the same industry, labor unions, farm organizations, medical and other professional associations, and churches are examples. Some voluntary groups spring up as a reaction to a political issue that arouses wide or passionate attention. Examples are "prolife" groups that oppose abortion and organizations that oppose nuclear power. Groups of these kinds survive as long as the issue they espouse remains controversial, which may be for a year or two or for decades or longer. Because such politically active groups are always concerned with controversial policies, they make claims that conflict with the claims of other groups.

Other kinds of interest groups are sometimes influential in contemporary government. Public-interest organizations try to protect the interests of people who are unorganized or have few financial resources with which to protect themselves, such as consumers, the poor, victims of environmental pollution, prisoners, and mental patients. Leading examples of public-interest groups are Ralph Nader's Center for the Study of Responsive Law, the League of Women Voters, Common Cause, Consumers Union, and public-interest law firms. Although such organizations represent interests shared by large numbers of people, they are not typically the concerns that many people feel intensely, so that legislators and administrators are tempted to pay less attention to them than to smaller groups with financial resources, skilled lawyers, and professional lobbyists at their disposal.

Local and state governmental organizations are an increasingly important kind of interest group, for they depend to a considerable extent on federal money and federal laws and regulations to carry on their functions. Individual cities and states lobby with Congress and executive agencies, as do organizations such as the Council of State Governments, the National League of Cities, and the Conference of Chief Justices.

Still another kind of organization exists to promote an ideological cause. Some examples are the John Birch Society on the far right, the Committee to Restore the Constitution almost as far in the same direction, and Americans for Democratic Action in the liberal center and moderate left. The Committee on the Present Danger lobbies for larger arms expenditures and a more militant stance toward the Soviet Union.

Interest groups play a part in all phases of the political process. They lobby to shape legislation, employ various tactics to influence executive and administrative actions, and appear before state and federal courts; they also play a role in election campaigns to try to elect sympathetic officials, thereby increasing their effectiveness in all the other governmental forums.

The Spurt in Political Action
Committees in the 1970s

The decline in the public support and financial resources of political parties has made it necessary for other institutions to perform some of their functions, especially in mobilizing public opinion behind policies and candidates and providing funds for campaigns. Interest groups have, accordingly, become far more active in elections, chiefly through political action committees (PACs).

Labor groups began forming such committees in the 1940s because of laws prohibiting unions from spending money in elections; the committees could do so from funds contributed by individual union members rather than from the union treasuries. Large gifts from individual corporate officials to the political parties were still possible until the 1974 election law amendments, so that corporations saw little need for political action committees before that time. But since the imposition of relatively small limits on individual contributions, corporations and other interest groups have vigorously been following the union lead, with results that are rapidly changing the electoral landscape.

The greatest increase in PACs after 1974 occurred in the corporate-sponsored category. Only 89 were in existence in 1974, as compared to 201 labor PACs and 318 formed by trade associations and medical or health-oriented groups. By 1980, there were 1,204 corporate PACs, as compared to 297 and 574 sponsored by the other two groups respectively. In 1983, there were 3,371 PACs in all, but about one-third of all contributions to congressional candidates came from the top 20 PAC contributors. The leader was Realtors PAC, which gave more than $2 million to congressional candidates. A majority of the top 20 contributors were labor groups, but the total contributions from corporate and trade associations' PACs were far greater.[14]

Perhaps a more important fact is that the best-known PACs, which are among the top fund-raisers, do not show up at all among the leading contributors to congressional candidates. This is because they engage in activities that are not connected to the campaigns of specific congressional candidates and therefore do not have to be reported as contributors to them. The leading fund-raisers are the National Congressional Club and the National Conservative Political Action Committee. From the beginning of 1981 to mid-October 1982, the Congressional Club, an organization that was created to help Senator Jesse Helms (R–N.C.), raised just over $9 million; NCPAC raised slightly less than $9 million, and both used their funds in a wide variety of ways to help conservative candidates and causes.

Some of the more successful committees concentrate on a single emotional issue and raise large amounts of money, often defeating candidates for their positions on that issue regardless of their records otherwise. Ex-

---

[14] All data in this and the next paragraph are drawn from *The New York Times,* January 11, 1983, p. 7.

amples of such single-issue groups are the Gun Owners of America, the National Rifle Association, PACs opposing abortion, and those advocating large increases in the arms budget.

Mailing lists and computers are crucial to the new financial politics. People who subscribe to a magazine with a particular ideological bent, contribute money to an ideological cause, or have particular economic, ethnic, or other traits can be identified by computers as likely prospects for related causes. Such pinpointing of prospects for PAC solicitations has been enormously successful, especially as employed by the developer of the technique, Richard A. Viguerie, who concentrates on raising money for conservative causes and has helped create more than a dozen new-right organizations. His computer stores more than 200 mailing lists that are broken down by issues and include 10 to 20 million contributors to right-wing causes.

It appears, then, that a major result of the changes we have described in political parties, nominating procedures, interest-group activities, and campaign financing has been sharply increased influence for groups with strong positions on a small set of issues and sharply reduced importance of identification with a political party. The influence of the single-issue, ideological, and economic groups comes much less from their numbers than from effective deployment of their financial resources.

While campaign contributions are unlikely to buy legislative votes or presidential support, they do make it easier to gain entry and to win a sympathetic hearing. On most issues, legislative and executive officials will not have strong personal positions or knowledge; thus, financial support is likely to make the official receptive to the information and arguments of those who supply it. That is why interest groups find it helpful to support incumbents. An officer of one major national corporation doubtless reflected these assumptions when he told an acquaintance who asked for a political contribution: "If you're an incumbent, we give $1,000, and if you beat an incumbent, we give $1,000 to retire your debt."[15]

Interest groups play a part in election campaigns in other ways as well. Some rate legislators according to their votes on issues of concern to the group. Environmental Action, Inc., publicizes its "Dirty Dozen" list of members of Congress who take antienvironmental positions, and the Consumer Federation of America lists "Consumer Heros" and "Consumer Zeros." Such ratings amount to indirect endorsements and denunciations, and some interest groups endorse candidates directly as well. Ratings and endorsements are not major influences on votes.

Lobbying in All Three Branches

Pressure groups that lobby for favorable legislation are most effective when they can be helpful to the legislators they try to influence. Buttonholing a member of Congress at a cocktail party is not likely to be very useful to a

---

[15] *The New York Times*, May 30, 1979, p. A23.

lobbyist, nor is an organized letter-writing campaign. The most effective lobbyists are those who regularly provide useful information to legislators and so come to be trusted. A legislator often needs accurate information about both technical matters and the strength of various groups' feelings about an issue; thus, the lobbyist who gains a reputation for accurate reporting on such matters wins goodwill and influence for his or her group.[16] In 1977 there were more than 5,000 persons engaged in lobbying with Congress, although many of them were not registered, because of loopholes in the 1946 Federal Regulation of Lobbying Act.[17]

Bringing pressure on legislators indirectly through the arousal of sentiment in their home districts, either among the public in general or among sympathetic groups, is a common and effective lobbying ploy. Lobbyists often help draft bills of interest to the groups they represent. Because a bill must hurdle many obstacles as it goes through subcommittees, committees, votes on the floor, and amendments, lobbyists who are trying to kill a proposal are usually in a better tactical position than those who are pushing for new legislation.

Like legislators themselves, lobbyists form alliances with one another when they can. Although business and labor groups are typically on opposite sides on bills to encourage or discourage collective bargaining or increase minimum wages, they work as allies on bills to restrict auto emissions or to restrict the importation of competing foreign products.

Many interest groups devote more attention to administrative than to legislative bodies, even though these efforts are less widely recognized and publicized. As we noted in Chapter 11, it is chiefly administrative rules and decisions that allocate tangible values. Some administrative agencies continuously reflect particular economic or social interests, as in the cases of the Commerce and Labor departments. Others do pretty much the same, while symbolically reflecting a different or wider range of interests, as in the case of regulatory commissions that are consistently sensitive to the interests of the industries they are supposed to control. A growing number of Washington, D.C. law firms specialize in such fields as radio, health, or environmental law and become practiced lobbyists before the appropriate governmental agencies for interest groups and corporations that hire them. In the 1970s, the number of trade and professional associations with headquarters in Washington exceeded the number in New York City for the first time. In 1977, 1,800 organizations, well over half of those with annual budgets of more than a million dollars, were located in the Washington metropolitan area to facilitate administrative and legislative lobbying.[18]

Interest groups can sometimes be more effective through court action

---

[16] For a good account of legislative lobbying, see Lester Milbrath, *The Washington Lobbyists* (Chicago: Rand McNally, 1963).

[17] Carol S. Greenwald, *Group Power* (New York: Praeger, 1977), p. 191.

[18] Hugh Heclo, "Issue Networks and the Executive Establishment," in Anthony King, ed., *The New American Political System* (Washington, D.C.: American Enterprise Institute, 1978), p. 97.

than through legislative or administrative lobbying. The National Association for the Advancement of Colored People has relied heavily on the courts to protect blacks' civil and economic rights. Environmental groups often resort to the courts as well. When possible, groups representing the disadvantaged have brought "class action suits," which is a way of protecting the interests of all people suffering the same infringement of their rights even if they are not actively associated with the lawsuit. The Supreme Court severely limited the use of such actions in a 1974 decision.[19] Interest groups also try to influence judicial policies by filing "friend of the court" briefs in cases that, although they are not party to, nonetheless affect their interests. Because the law places considerable emphasis on the protection of property rights and because it offers numerous procedural devices for blocking change, the courts are also a valuable recourse for business groups. Interest groups often have some leeway in the choice of the court in which they file an action and so can shop around for a sympathetic one. More generally, the courts provide an alternative channel to interest groups for winning benefits they are denied in the legislative, executive, or administrative arenas.

Popular Support and Opposition to Interest Groups

Although organized groups lobby and spend money to advance their objectives, their success depends heavily on how a much wider body of public opinion responds to their activities. They need either sympathizers or apathy, and they need to minimize popular opposition to their goals. In general, pressure groups try to avoid publicity and to work through ongoing governmental contacts when they are getting what they want and the issues are technical or complex. This strategy prevents potential opposition from being awakened to action. Groups that are losing under existing arrangements, on the other hand, usually gain more by publicizing an issue in the hope that a larger public will support them. Paper mills in Wisconsin are not likely to appeal for public support of their right to pollute rivers with contaminating chemicals as long as they are allowed to do so without interference, but environmental groups are sure to try to arouse as wide a public as possible to the dangers of pollution. "Fellow travelers" who are not themselves members of interest groups often make a critical difference in determining policy outcomes.

SUMMARY

Every government distributes or redistributes the benefits that people value and also tries to maintain its legitimacy—its public support and loyalty. Political parties and elections have always been the chief legitimizers of

---

[19] *Eisen* v. *Carlisle and Jacquelin*, 417 U.S. 156 (1974).

American government and its policies. Although they still serve that function, they are less effective legitimizers than they were twenty years ago, while some other political institutions are becoming much more effective.

Fewer people now identify themselves as Republicans or as Democrats, and the major parties have lost much of their historic role as raisers and spenders of funds in political campaigns. At the same time, more people call themselves independents, fewer vote on election day, fewer vote straight party tickets, and the lack of party discipline over public officials that has always been characteristic of American politics continues.

Single-issue groups and political action committees, especially on the right, have become more numerous and far more significant than they once were, in election financing, in lobbying, and in influencing public opinion. Interest groups act directly in election campaigns and in legislative, administrative, and judicial lobbying, largely filling the vacuum left by the reduced role of the parties.

We are left with some questions that go directly to the heart of the issues with which we began this book. What does the loss of functioning political parties mean for the prospect of democratic governance in the United States? Is democracy possible in a large-scale society without effective parties, and if not, does that mean that we are consigned to some form of despotism? Can or should the political parties be revived, or replaced with some new equivalent? Much depends on what voters want in politics, and how they act on election day, and that is the subject to which we now turn.

CHAPTER 16

American Elections: Stability and Realignment

Our first goal in this chapter is to develop a framework for understanding what elections *mean* in American politics—how they *fit*, in general terms, into the process of governing in the United States. This is no small task. For example, even though elections are clouded with mythology and symbolism, they are often thought to set specific directions for future policy. They seem to be the essence of democracy, and yet barely half of all eligible voters actually take the trouble to vote—a proportion well below that of all the other industrialized democracies of the world.

We shall try to set elections in a broad context, link them to social and economic changes under way, and then connect them to basic changes in governing institutions and new directions in public policies. Some elections are clearly more important than others in these respects, which has led to attempts to identify "critical elections" in which substantial realignments of voters take place. This means that new groups of voters turn out on election day, and/or substantial numbers of voters shift their allegiance from one political party to another, with the result being the placement of a new set of elites in power in government.

After we develop this general theory of the part played by elections in the American political economic system, we shall apply it to the present period. As we have noted, our times are distinguished by the decline of the political parties, to the point where some observers have termed it a period of "dealignment." Once we see recent history in terms of our general framework, we shall explore the key factors that will determine future electoral behavior and outcomes. Finally, we will take up the results of the election of 1984 in the light of all we have said about what is at stake in contemporary elections.

MEANING IN ELECTIONS: STABILITY
AND REALIGNMENT CYCLES

Elections mean different things to different people. A moment's reflection suggests that participation of some kind is a stabilizing feature of any political system. The fact that it is very hard to make specific links between electoral outcomes and particular public policies is just as obvious.

For most people, voting is the most potent of all symbols of popular rule and therefore a powerful ingredient in the legitimacy of a regime that holds public office. Whether a group of political participants wins or loses an election, the fact that it has supposedly been consulted evokes its support for the government. It may not like certain policies the government pursues, but it is far less likely to challenge its right to pursue them than would be the case if the government had not been elected. In this critical sense, elections lessen social tensions and inhibit potential civil strife. This is frequently the chief function they serve in the political system, although that hypothesis is debatable and not easily susceptible to rigorous testing. Provisions for compulsory voting in some countries, as well as social pressures to vote in order to prove that one is a "good citizen," doubtless reflect an awareness that people who vote are psychologically inoculated against fundamental resistance to the state.

It is even more clear that the use of elections in nondemocratic states reflects the same awareness. Some forms of election, such as the plebiscites of totalitarian countries, do not even offer the *possibility* of defeating unpopular candidates or policies; this amounts only to ratification of actions already taken. It is in such rigged elections, nonetheless, that legal and social pressure to vote has been strongest. The citizen who fails to vote is suspect as a potentially disloyal person and can expect the kind of ostracism that would await a member of a primitive tribe who refused to participate in a communal fertility rite or war dance. Sometimes elections are rigged to eliminate candidates who stand for a genuine alternative on controversial issues. The results are nevertheless publicized as mandates for the government and fervently accepted by many as exactly that.

Apart from their uses in promoting and symbolizing social solidarity, to what degree do elections provide policy guidelines for public officials to follow? They apparently do furnish a clear mandate on the occasional major issue on which the two major parties disagree, although historical examples warn against making this logical assumption without empirical evidence. In 1928, the Democratic platform favored repeal of the Eighteenth (Prohibition) Amendment, while the Republicans were "dry." A Republican victory did indeed delay repeal for four years, even though public sentiment increasingly favored repeal, and in 1932, both parties' platforms reflected that sentiment. In 1964, escalation of the Vietnam War, which was certainly a major issue, was favored by Barry Goldwater, the Republican candidate, and opposed by Lyndon Johnson, his Democratic opponent. Although Johnson won by a wide margin, he moved quickly after the election to escalate the war. This is by no means the only instance in which a major party disregarded what appeared to be a clear popular mandate; however, elections do in such instances provide a means for evaluating the performance of a regime. This can be an important factor in the following election, as it evidently was in 1968, but there is no guarantee that it will be.

Even when elections do offer a real choice, however, they are not a sufficient condition of democracy. Election mandates are almost always unclear, and it is always possible to justify departures from them on the ground that conditions have changed since election day. Even when elected officials have every intention of heeding the voice of the people as they understand it, election mandates typically furnish only the vaguest kind of guide to administrative officials and judges who have to make decisions in particular cases. Does the fact that the winning political party promised to hold down prices mean that it should institute wage-and-price ceilings when some economists forecast rising prices and others disagree? Should officials elected on such a platform plank institute price controls after prices have risen 6 percent? Eight percent? Fifteen percent? What difference should it make if the winning political party also promised to avoid unnecessary government intervention in the economy? Answers to such questions cannot be predetermined, or even guided very far, by the votes people cast in elections.

These reflections suggest that the signals given through elections vary widely, and that elections may have multiple meanings in any given year—meanings that would be quite different from those of other years. At a slightly higher level of analysis, however, we can see that elections play a crucial part in long-range trends of policy and institutional change. In the next sections, therefore, we offer a general perspective on the role of elections in American political history.

THE BACKGROUND OF ELECTORAL POLITICS IN THE UNITED STATES

The United States is different from all other industrialized capitalist countries of the world in several ways. Perhaps the most important of these differences is the fact that it has never known feudalism. No feudalism, no socialism, asserts Walter Dean Burnham, the best of the political scientists who study elections.[1] In a feudal society, there were *lords*, who had great landholdings and other assets, at the top of the social pyramid, and *serfs*,

---

[1] Walter Dean Burnham, "The 1980 Election: Earthquake, Realignment, Reaction, or What?" in Thomas Ferguson and Joel Rogers, eds. *The Hidden Election: Politics and Economics in the 1980 Election Campaign* (New York: Pantheon, 1981). The development of this point is the responsibility of the authors, however.

who had no property and no prospects of gaining any, at the bottom. Gradually, such societies developed a middle class of traders, merchants, and artisans. Ultimately, feudal society broke down and capitalism emerged, which was soon to become industrial capitalism. Burnham's point is that the lasting residue of feudalism is a social class-based kind of society, in which the former lords become a genuinely aristocratic upper class and the former serfs become a dispossessed working class with social-ist aspirations.

The American continent, however, was settled by the members of the new middle class that arose in the English seventeenth century. There never was a feudal society on this continent, and thus none of the great differences of wealth and sense of deprivation that led to a socialist tradi-tion elsewhere. The United States began as a *liberal* society, which stressed the middle-class values of individualism, property rights, and limited gov-ernment (all of which meant that individuals were to seek their goals in the private sphere and government was to be limited to the least possible interference). The Constitution that was established in 1787 set up a gov-ernment in which majorities would have a very hard time uniting for the purpose of doing *anything,* let alone redistributing property (the goal that the framers assumed would characterize the "have nots" of every age).

In the founding period, which was roughly 1770–1800, the basic character of the liberal society that was to develop was fixed. Liberalism was so thoroughly accepted as to be the unremarkable common sense or "natural" order of things. To be sure, there was the Hamilton-versus-Jefferson conflict over just how the nation should develop in economic terms. Their contending models of economic development—commerce and manufacturing versus the yeoman farmer—had echoes in the kind of government that should be encouraged (a strong and active national gov-ernment versus one that was more strictly limited on behalf of state and local predominance). But these differences all took place within the framework established by shared liberal values. *Nobody* disputed the basic principles of individualism, property rights, and limited government.

Three crucial implications for American political life immediately fol-low from these basic facts. One is that when *capitalism* and capitalist indus-trialization began to take hold in the new country, it found completely hospitable values and attitudes waiting for it. The liberal values are the same as capitalist values, and capitalism, too, was "natural" for Ameri-cans. Another important point is that *democracy*, which really arrived with Jefferson's presidency, had to adapt to the established liberal values; what people could do with their participation and votes in the expanding fran-chise was limited by the prior principles of individualism, property rights, and limited government. The latter meant, of course, that government action would always appear suspect, and thus a kind of anti-statism was built into American attitudes and practice. Historically, it is both practically very difficult and ideologically conflicting to attempt to use government to serve even strongly felt popular needs.

Finally, individualism and the Constitution became the dominating forces that have shaped American politics to this day. Because Americans think and act entirely in liberal-individualist terms, there has been little conscious sense of social class conflict in our elections. When the pressures of economic and social change affect Americans particularly strongly, what emerges instead of class conflict is a religious revival, nativism, or racism. The latter are individual ways of venting frustrations and anxieties, and can be shared widely and acted out vigorously. When the spasm is over, nothing has really been changed because the basic individualist assumptions have not been challenged.

Similarly, the Constitution and the limited, set-against-itself (separation of powers, and checks and balances) government it establishes remain unquestioned. The institutional changes we have made are all relatively minor, and they have been made within this basic framework. For these reasons, the government we have now is increasingly out-of-date and lacking in capacity to respond to the demands of the contemporary world. However, it takes great social and economic pressures and massive political mobilization to make even minor changes in its structure.

This system of social relations and its accompanying values and assumptions were essentially in place by the early decades of the nineteenth century, or before widespread electoral participation began. The country was developing in the capitalist image, expanding westward and building new industry, and attracting new population—all in splendid physical isolation. With these premises in mind, we can now proceed to look at particular elections.

We shall link key elections with the social and economic pressures that helped to make them important, and also with the institutional changes that followed them. Perhaps surprisingly, we shall see that these "critical elections" occurred at regular intervals of 32 to 36 years each.[2] Less surprisingly, they were associated with the economy's cycles of boom and bust in many ways, and the institutional changes that followed were closely linked to the basic electoral changes that occurred. In short, if there were no economic crisis, there would be no realignment; if there were no realignment, there would be no institutional change; if there were no institutional change, there would be no enduring policy change. Table 16.1 summarizes these relationships, and will provide relevant information throughout this discussion. Comparisons of the turnout rates for presidential elections will be particularly instructive, as will (for the later years) the data on unemployment and economic growth rates.

The Election of 1828. This was one of the first elections after the franchise was expanded by the new state constitutions that were drafted and ratified in the decade of the 1820s. The turnout of voters was more than double that of 1824, partly because of the outpouring of support for Andrew Jackson, who had been deprived of the presidency by the decision of

---

[2] Walter Dean Burnham, *Critical Elections and the Mainsprings of American Politics* (New York: Norton, 1970).

TABLE 16.1
Critical Elections and Economic Conditions in American Political History

YEAR OF CRITICAL ELECTION (1)	TURNOUT PERCENTAGE*		AVERAGE TURNOUT/YEAR SINCE LAST CRITICAL ELECTION		AVERAGE UNEMPLOYMENT RATES, PERIODS INDICATED		AVERAGE ANNUAL GROWTH IN GROSS DOMESTIC PRODUCT, PERIODS INDICATED	
	Nation (2)	South (3)	Nation (4)	South (5)	Boom (6)	Crisis (7)	Boom (8)	Crisis (9)
1828	57.3	42.6	27.2	27.4	—	—	—	—
1860	81.9	76.3	72.9	63.2	—	—	—	—
1896	79.5	56.9	78.7	66.6	— (1873–92)	11.8 (1892–99)	6.6 (1873–92)	2.9 (1892–99)
1932	56.9	24.3	60.1	28.4	4.9 (1899–1929)	18.3 (1929–37)	3.7 (1899–1929)	−0.5 (1929–37)
1936	61.0	25.0	—	—	—	—	—	—

SOURCES: Turnout data calculated from Walter Dean Burnham, "The 1980 Election: Earthquake, Realignment, Reaction, or What?" in Thomas Ferguson and Joel Rogers, eds., *The Hidden Election: Politics and Economics in the 1980 Presidential Campaign* (New York: Pantheon Books, 1981), p. 101.

Economic data from Samuel Bowles, David M. Gordon, and Thomas E. Weisskopf, *Beyond the Waste Land* (New York: Doubleday, 1983), p. 243.

NOTE: * Turnout calculated on a base that excludes all aliens.

the House of Representatives, despite his winning a plurality of the popular vote in the election of 1824. This increase was greatest in the new western and "border" states, where well over 60 percent of voters turned out; this was a considerably higher proportion than in the South.

The rising numbers of western residents also sought to break free of the grip of eastern creditors and other forms of eastern political economic domination. What followed this election was a surge of institutional changes, including the institution of the spoils system, the breaking down of the National Bank and other monopolies, and a new network of internal improvements. Most historians think that the provision of greater opportunity for individual capitalist ventures was the major result of the Jacksonian period's institutional changes at the state and national levels.

The Election of 1860. The social tensions leading up to the Civil War are too familiar to require comment. They were accompanied by analogous tensions between the industrialized capitalist economy of the North and the plantation and agricultural base of the South. Voting rates had risen steadily since 1828, and in 1860 were up about 10 percent over the average of the previous six presidential elections. Turnout set still-standing national and Southern records, as many urban workers and Midwestern small farmers went over to the new Republican Party and the Democrats fragmented.

The result, of course, was great expansion of the national government in order to fight the war, the far-reaching post-war constitutional amendments, and the groundwork of a national political system. Not incidentally, an entirely new political party system also resulted, one that lasted well beyond the end of Reconstruction in 1877 and into the early years of the ensuing period of transformation to a modern, urban, and industrialized world power.

The Election of 1896. As this transformation got fully under way, it quickly gave rise to serious social and economic dislocations and tensions. Workers struggled to form labor unions, to protect themselves against the hardships of the new capitalist accumulation process, and perhaps to gain a larger share of its rewards. The 1880s and 1890s saw a series of bloody and destructive strikes; this is still the most protracted and bitter period of capital versus labor conflict in our history. Farmers bore the brunt of the pressures of the crop-lien system and the contracting money supply, often losing their land and being forced into tenancy or sharecropping. Their response also was to organize, first in interest-group terms as the Alliance and then politically as the People's Party.

The farmers and some workers (now known as "populists") gained a foothold (including some electoral college ballots) in the election of 1892. Aided by the panic and depression of 1893, they appeared likely to do even better in 1896. The Supreme Court contributed to the growing class-based cleavage with a series of decisions defending corporations against state and national efforts at regulation, voiding the income tax, and enforcing the court injunctions that were increasingly the employers' best weapon against strikes. Among its most important decisions was the case of *Plessy* v. *Ferguson*[3] in May of 1896; this decision constitutionally endorsed Southern state laws requiring segregation of the races.

William Jennings Bryan used the inflation-promoting cause of free coinage of silver as the symbol of opposition to the hard-money gold standard of the Republican Party, and secured the Democratic nomination. With that in hand, and a platform that included much that appealed to the populists, he was able to gain the support of a majority fragment of their partisans. However, the resources and efforts of the Republicans were even greater, and in the first of the modern media-plus-organization campaigns, McKinley won.

Voting rates had remained high during the entire period from 1868 to 1896 in all the non-Southern regions of the country, as a result of the deep emotions and close contests involved. Even in the South, turnout reached 75 percent in 1876, but intimidation of blacks after that reduced proportions steadily. In the 1896 election, turnout nationally could (and did) increase only slightly, but in the South it declined to a post-war low of 56.9 percent. The economic conditions associated with this period also suggest reasons for high participation: growth was low in comparison with the norms of the period, and unemployment was high.

It is not an overstatement to say that the election of 1896 shaped the character of the American twentieth century. Under this umbrella, the Republican Party gained sixteen crucial years of national power, and the corporate-banking community used the opportunity to design its version of the role of government in the newly integrated national economy Immediately after the election, prosperity began to return. The War of 1898 captured popular attention, promoted nationalism, and gave the United States an imperial role. In this context, the Democratic renomination of Bryan in 1900 handed the election to McKinley and the newspaper hero of the Cuban campaign, Theodore Roosevelt.

With the basic issue of 1896 resolved, turnout was already sliding downwards. Reduction in turnout proportions got a major push from the enactment and enforcement of new Jim Crow laws in the South and immigrant-purging new voter registration requirements in the North. The Southern laws and accompanying practices, which drew on the Supreme Court's ruling in *Plessy* v. *Ferguson* and earlier decisions limiting constitutional protections only to things done directly by states, effectively eliminated blacks from voting opportunities. The new "good government"-oriented middle-class Progressives similarly instituted residence and literacy requirements in Northern cities as a way of breaking the power of the urban political machines.

As turnout dropped, institutional change began. The basic thrust of this change was toward greater integration between the larger corporations

---

[3] *Plessy* v. *Ferguson*, 163 U.S. 537. For the context and character of the other leading cases, see Arnold Paul, *Conservative Crisis and the Rule of Law* (New York: Harper & Row, 1963).

and banks of the private economy and the national government, particularly its executive branch. New legislation was drafted and enacted that appeared to respond to reformers' demands for government control over the corporations, but it actually reflected the corporations' and banks' needs for making the economy less competitive and more rational and predictable. The Federal Reserve Act, which was discussed at length earlier, is a good example.

Before it was over, the Progressive Era saw several such institutional changes that were designed to inject the national government into an economy-managing role that has been sometimes characterized as "the rise of the positive state."[4] This role was a double one, however, because it involved both serving the needs of business for greater economic stability, while also granting some portion of the demands of reform movements. The latter included remnants of the populist and labor movements of the nineteenth century, as well as socialists and progressives, all of whom were committed to the use of their votes to gain a larger share of power and income in the society. The combination of these forces resulted in institutional changes in this period that established the model for American institutional development for the rest of the twentieth century.

In short, the election of 1896 fixed the electoral lineup that endured for decades, and gave rise to the institutional changes and structure that we now know as "the liberal state." This required a shift away from the classical laissez-faire liberalism of the 1890s, and toward a new, interventionist way of using the national government on behalf of business-and-social-welfare that has come to be known as "corporate liberalism" or "welfare liberalism." These labels reflected the new version of liberal values and ideology that was coherent with the new institutional structure and practice; it has endured to the present stage of our history.

The Elections of 1932–36. When the Great Depression hit the country in 1929–31, economic problems and social tensions were restored to the highest levels they had been since the early 1890s. Unemployment was over 20 percent in some of these years, and business seemed to be locked into a standstill. As Table 16.1 indicates, the contrasts between the depression years and the more or less prosperous times of the 1899 through 1929 period were sharp.

Voting turnout had been declining steadily since 1896 throughout the country, and national rates dropped between 10 and 15 percent when the woman suffrage amendment became effective in 1920. Given past legal exclusion and continuing cultural discouragement, it was quite natural for women to vote at lower rates than men and thus for the overall proportions of voter turnout to drop a bit. The turnout decline was sharpest in the

---

[4] This is a widely used term emerging from the work of three leading historians of the period. See Gabriel Kolko, *The Triumph of Conservatism* (New York: Quadrangle, 1963); James Weinstein, *The Corporate Ideal in the Liberal State, 1900–1918* (Boston: Beacon Press, 1968); Robert Wiebe, *The Search For Order, 1877–1920* (New York: Hill & Wang, 1967).

South, where the continued (and now legal) disenfranchisement of blacks brought proportions down as low as 18.9 percent of the eligible electorate in 1924.

The election of 1932 saw only a slight change in these turnout patterns; in national terms, voting rates were up about 8 percent from the lows of 1920, but were still nowhere near the 1896 and previous levels. The outcome was primarily a rejection of the incumbent President Herbert Hoover, and not an affirmative endorsement of much of anything. It could not have been, because Franklin Roosevelt did not offer any sign of the New Deal that would follow. Indeed, he campaigned on a balanced-budget and otherwise conservative economic platform. However, the program that was actually implemented was a considerable extension of the Progressive Era model that moved the national government substantially further in the dual directions of simultaneously helping business prosperity and serving social welfare needs.

It was the election of 1936 that provided the ratification of these new directions. Turnout across the country was up another 5 percent. By 1936, people knew what FDR stood for, and his landslide victory that year confirmed millions of new Democratic loyalties that lasted for at least three decades. It also permitted him to go farther, first confirming the New Deal's basic policy departures before the Supreme Court, and then extending them through the implementation of new legislation and further personnel appointments. The positive state reached its fullest form, with the coming of World War II and the needs it brought for effective mobilization of all kinds of resources through the government.

THE POST–WORLD WAR II YEARS: FROM AFFLUENCE TO DISARRAY

As the world's leading economic and military power after World War II, the United States began to enjoy an unprecedented period of affluence that lasted until the early 1970s. During this time, as Table 16.2 demonstrates, economic growth rates averaged a healthy 4.7 percent and unemployment was relatively low. But something happened somewhere in the late 1960s and early 1970s to change both economic and political conditions in what may well prove to be a fundamental way. The economy, the political parties (as we have seen), and voter turnout all began to decline at about the same time. Soon the economic transformation began to be evident, although it was unaccompanied by the usual political changes. We have not yet reached the end of this process, but we can set the stage for analyzing our future prospects by looking closely at their early stages.

Voter turnout, which is detailed in Table 16.2, provides one dimension for this analysis. From the post-war low of 53.4 percent in 1948, which is not even five percentage points better than the first presidential election with full woman suffrage (1924), turnout rose steadily. Much of this in-

TABLE 16.2
Post–World War II Elections and Economic Conditions

ELECTION	TURNOUT PERCENTAGE		AVERAGE UNEMPLOYMENT RATES, PERIODS SHOWN		AVERAGE ANNUAL GROWTH RATES IN GROSS DOMESTIC PRODUCT	
	Nation	*South*	*Boom (1948–73)*	*Crisis (1973–81)*	*Boom (1948–73)*	*Crisis (1973–81)*
1960	65.4	41.4	4.8	6.9	4.7	1.5
1964	63.3	46.4				
1968	62.3	51.8				
1972	57.1	45.7				
1976	55.8	48.8				
1980	55.1	50.0				

SOURCES: Turnout data calculated from Walter Dean Burnham, "The 1980 Election: Earthquake, Realignment, Reaction, or What?" in Thomas Ferguson and Joel Rogers, eds., *The Hidden Election: Politics and Economics in the 1980 Presidential Campaign* (New York: Pantheon Books, 1981), p. 101.

Economic data from Samuel Bowles, David M. Gordon, and Thomas E. Weisskopf, *Beyond the Waste Land* (New York: Doubleday, 1983), p. 243.

crease occurred in the South, where the civil-rights commitments of the Democratic Party after 1948 began to attract new black voters and send whites steadily toward the Republican Party. In the country as a whole, however, turnout increased steadily after the war, peaking at its post-war high of 65.4 percent in 1960, partly because the Catholicism of John F. Kennedy brought out both supporters and opponents in large numbers.

National voter participation rates have declined steadily since 1960. Each of the last five presidential elections has seen a smaller proportion of voters at the polls, and the same ratio has held true in the lower-turnout midterm congressional elections. To some extent, the addition of 18-to-21-year-old voters (in time for the 1972 election) may be responsible. The youngest categories of voters traditionally vote with lower frequency than their elders, and we know that newly added groups take some time to participate in the same proportions as long-term voters. However, all adult voting categories have exhibited this continuing decline in turnout, with one important exception—black voters, in both the South and the North, have been voting with steadily *increasing* proportions. Were it not for this increase, the decline in turnout of the American electorate would be precipitate indeed.

Another dimension for analysis is the change in American economic circumstances. In earlier chapters, we saw that the dominance of the United States began to be challenged in the mid-1960s, and that the U.S. economy began to decline in comparison to both its own prior achievements and the achievements of other industrial capitalist countries in 1968. The affluence that was once taken for granted began to disappear for many people by the mid-1970s, as inflation and unemployment rose simultaneously. Economists and others began to describe the transformation to new forms of production and new patterns of occupations, and nearly everybody experienced some effects of the deep recession of 1981–82. Despite an apparent recovery shortly after, the economic prospects for the future seemed very uncertain.

This was also the period in which the major political parties began to fragment and lose their influence in the American political system. As we saw in the last chapter, the rise of the mass media, the increase in campaign spending based on direct private contributions to candidates, and a variety of changes in nominating practices all combined to reduce the role of parties. Parties no longer serve as important means of reaching accommodations, keeping candidates and officeholders together around agreed policy positions, or enabling government to operate in a coherent manner. They have by and large given way to special-interest groups, independent campaigns, and the overall dominance of the mass media, particularly television, in shaping political outcomes.

In addition to trying to understand what *was* happening in this period, attention might also be paid to two things that were *not* occurring. One is the "normal" critical election and realignment that historically was due in 1968 or 1972.[5] Such a realignment and confirmation of new directions would be vital for the sort of change in political institutions and practices that would be necessary to permit government action to cope with the drastically changed economic conditions that now faced the country. The latter cannot occur without such a critical election, and the failure to experience the combination of these two phenomena in this era is an important part of our current political economic stalemate.

Why did this "normal" critical election and realignment period not occur on schedule? Perhaps the cycle was only coincidental, and none should have been expected, or conditions are so different now that the timing of such a realignment period might be expected to be different. But, as we saw earlier and as Table 16.2 shows again, the economic conditions that apparently helped to bring about such decisive elections in the past were coming to a head in the late 1960s and early 1970s. To be sure, economists speak of a "missed recession" in the mid-1960s, which was the result of the boom generated by the Vietnam War.[6] In the post–World War II period, relatively mild recessions occurred at regular intervals, but skipped the 1960s. Ultimately, however, we had a much more serious set of economic difficulties throughout the late 1970s and early 1980s— conditions that should have forced some kind of political change.

---

[5] The best analysis of the missed realignment may be found in Kevin Phillips, *Post-Conservative America* (New York: Random House, 1982).

[6] Samuel Bowles, David M. Gordon, and Thomas E. Weisskopf, *Beyond the Waste Land* (New York: Doubleday, 1983), makes the argument about the missed recession.

Electoral analysts give some tentative reasons why the overdue critical realignment has not yet occurred. The best analysis suggests that a realignment process did in fact begin with the Republican candidacy of Barry Goldwater in 1964, but that it was short-circuited by the unique series of subsequent events.[7] This argument says that the basic realignment was (and is) of a conservative nature, not in the classic sense of conservatism, but in a new, populist ("New Right") version. In part, it consists of a reaction against the extension of the New Deal represented by the Great Society of Lyndon Johnson's late-1960s term in office. More specifically, it is a reaction against the social engineering of a new class of liberal intellectuals and the changes in lifestyles and social practices that occurred in the 1960s—many with the help of an activist Supreme Court. It is also, on the part of the substantial business component of this movement, a reaffirmation of the desire for freedom from government taxation and regulations that are intended to provide social services and help consumers.

This incipient realignment was prefigured by the political forces that secured the nomination for Barry Goldwater and wrested control of the Republican Party from the liberal, eastern Republican establishment. They were political interests and people from the Southwest and the West, and also white Southerners who were once New Dealers but had now turned against the Democratic Party because of its involvement in civil rights and other social programs. According to this analysis, two things happened to prevent this developing realignment from proceeding in the normal way.

One event was the Republican-authorized break-in at the Watergate headquarters of the Democratic National Committee. This incident led to an extensive cover-up that was managed from the White House itself, and eventually President Nixon was exposed as having known about, lied about, and obstructed justice by covering up the illegal acts involved. The resulting movement in Congress to impeach him had reached the point where action was quite likely, and Nixon resigned instead. The result of this scandal, nevertheless, was to cause many independents and some Republicans to vote against Republican Party candidates for the elections that immediately followed. Probably some Democrats were also discouraged from switching over, as they might otherwise have done. In any event, the developing conservative movement was deflected and at least delayed for a few years.

The other factor was the nomination of Jimmy Carter as the Democratic candidate in 1976. As the first Democratic candidate from the deep South in more than a century, Carter was able to hold a good share of the white Southerners, particularly those of fundamentalist religions, who might otherwise have continued their shift toward the Republican Party. Once again, the realignment that might have happened was delayed.

Thus, the United States is marking time. The basic alignments of 1932–

---

[7] Phillips, *Post-Conservative America,* is the source of this term and the best analysis of the New Right generally.

36, although still visible (particularly with respect to domestic economic issues), are disintegrating from age and the effects of changing conditions. But no clear alternative alignment—or policy program, or institutional change—has yet developed to take its place. The election of 1980 did not show the signs of realignment that many Republicans had hoped for, and was (like the election of 1932) more a rejection of the incumbent than the deliberate choice of a new and different policy direction. Although President Reagan clearly stood for a substantial, and even dramatic, shift in the role of government, voters did not see it that way in 1980. Turnout continued to decline, and many more people continued to call themselves Democrats than Republicans.

However, again like the 1932–36 combination of elections, this *could* mean that the really fundamental realignment was not going to be missed entirely but would simply arrive late—in 1984. It also could mean that no significant group of Americans was yet ready to realign its political allegiances in any fundamental way. Still another possibility was that the Reagan policies, when implemented over a period of four years, might generate such a reaction that the old New Deal coalition or something like it might be revived and represent the missing realignment of the 1970s in a new form.

What is really happening in the American electorate is certainly not yet clear. It may be too simple for subtle analysis to perceive; Americans may merely be withdrawing into privatistic lives and abandoning public affairs out of frustration, or some new and powerful shift may be building up. In the next section, we will explore some of the key forces at work and what they portend for the future.

THE KEY FACTORS IN ANY POTENTIAL REALIGNMENT

All of our analysis to this point has emphasized the importance of voter turnout. *Who* votes is crucial to the outcome of elections. Continuing alignments of voters mean continued dominance by particular parties and interests. In general, the better-educated and higher-income classes vote at much higher rates than the lower classes. In recent presidential elections, however, only a bare majority of eligible American voters have actually turned out at the polls, and the proportion has been dropping steadily since 1948, which means that those who do vote are enjoying more of whatever political influence can be generated through elections. At the same time, numbers of nonvoters might at any time enter the electoral process and potentially turn U.S. policy directions completely around.

We must investigate the turnout phenomenon, and the real prospects for a massive influx of nonvoters and the resulting dramatic change in our political system. The other question of great importance in the 1980s has to do with *which* voters will be newly mobilized to vote or to shift from one party to the other. Central to answering this question are the growing role of the New Right and the contrasting possibility that the Reagan administration programs will so polarize people that they will generate a class-based realignment from the left.

We shall build a framework for understanding the 1984 election by looking first at the circumstances that determine turnout and what this basic factor means for American politics, and then at these two polar possibilities for realignment. It is not simply a matter of which candidate or party wins the election; what matters for new policies and institutional change is whether they win with a lasting electoral realignment behind them that will enable such policy and institutional changes to be implemented over a long period of time.

Turnout. We shall look first at who does and does not vote, and why; then we shall explore the implications of the rising proportions of nonvoters in the United States since the 1960 election. The leading study of nonvoting was done by Professors Raymond Wolfinger of California-Berkeley and Steven Rosenstone of Yale in the late 1970s; it used survey data collected in regard to the 1972 election by the Center for Political Studies, the country's primary source for national election data collection and research. Published as *Who Votes?*, this study found that the single most determinative factor with regard to electoral participation was voters' education level.[8] Occupation and income were correlated with voting (the higher one's occupational status and the greater one's income, the more likely one is to vote), but they were not as significant as years of education. Thus, although we might expect better-educated people to also be higher-income people, it is the education, and not the income or status, that carries the most weight in causing people to vote. Even low-income people are likely to vote if they have had several years of education.

Table 16.3 is drawn from this study, and expands on the importance of education. Here we see that education plays a central role because it seems to generate a high sense of "citizen duty" and to inspire interest in politics. It also seems to lead to greater use of the mass media and greater information about what is going on in politics. With only two exceptions, the more years of education a particular segment of those surveyed had, the higher the proportion of them who are well informed, use the media more, feel a sense of civic duty in voting, and so on. Whatever the problems of the American educational systems, it appears that they are functioning effectively to produce greater involvement in the standard political activities.

Education, income, and occupation are closely linked, of course, and translate together into voting behavior. Table 16.4 reproduces another table from *Who Votes?* and shows these recurring patterns in a somewhat different way. Here, most occupations are grouped grossly into three classes, plus two small categories of "agriculture." What matters is the relationship between proportions of the labor force and percentages vot-

---

[8] Raymond Wolfinger and Steven Rosenstone, *Who Votes?* (New Haven, Conn.: Yale University Press, 1980).

TABLE 16.3
Relationship between Education and Civic Virtue in 1972

Years of Education	Percentage Who Express a High Sense of Citizen Duty[a]	Percentage Who Say They Are Very Interested in Politics	Percentage Who Use the Mass Media at a High Rate[b]	Percentage Who Are Well In-Formed About Politics[c]
0–4	42	16	11	5
5–7	41	22	26	8
8	44	27	33	17
9–11	39	28	31	14
12	50	34	35	17
1–3 college	52	47	53	32
4 college	56	55	68	37
5 + college	66	75	68	59

SOURCE: Raymond E. Wolfinger and Steven J. Rosenstone. *Who Votes?* (New Haven, Conn.: Yale University Press, 1980), p. 19 (Table 2.2). Data are taken from Center for Political Studies 1972 National Election Study.

[a] Respondents who disagreed with these statements: "It isn't so important to vote when you know your party doesn't have a chance to win." "So many people vote in the national election that it doesn't matter much to me whether I vote or not." "If a person doesn't care how an election comes out he shouldn't vote in it." "A good many local elections aren't important enough to bother with."

[b] Respondents who did at least three of the following: read about the campaign in the newspapers; listened to speeches or discussions about the campaign on the radio; read about the campaign in magazines; watched programs about the campaign on television.

[c] Respondents who knew at least five of the following six political facts: the number of terms a president can serve; the length of a term for a U.S. senator; the length of a term for a U.S. representative; the names of the House candidates in his district; the party controlling Congress before the election; the party controlling Congress after the election.

ing. The upper-middle-class makes up only 25 percent of the labor force, while the working-class totals 47 percent, a ratio of almost two-to-one. When voting rates are used to convert this ratio into political terms, however, the relationship becomes only a four-to-three advantage for the much more numerous working class.

These patterns of voting and nonvoting tend to be consistent ones. The same groups produce roughly similar turnout proportions in each presidential election and still smaller voting rates (but in the same relative ratios) in midterm congressional elections. When overall turnout declines over a period of time, as has been the case since 1948, nonvoting occurs in a similar pattern. That is, more people at the lower end of the socioeconomic ladder drop out than do those at the higher levels.

The phenomenon of low and declining turnout rates has led in recent years to much concern about the quality and future of American democracy. What does it mean that the United States has the lowest rate of voting participation of all the liberal democracies of the world? Why is participa-

TABLE
16.4   Occupations and Turnout in 1972

Occupation of Respondent	Percentage of Labor Force	Percentage Who Voted
Upper middle class:		
Professional and technical	15	86
Managers and administrators	10	79
Lower middle class:		
Clerks and salespeople	24	75
Working class:		
Skilled workers	13	64
Semiskilled and unskilled workers	23	53
Nondomestic service workers	11	63
Agriculture:		
Farmers and farm managers	2	79
Farm laborers and foremen	1	46
Total	99	—

SOURCE: Raymond E. Wolfinger and Steven J. Rosenstone, *Who Votes?* (New Haven, Conn.: Yale University Press, 1980), p. 23 (Table 2.3).

NOTE: This table is an analysis of data taken from the Center for Political Studies 1972 National Election Study.

tion declining still further? Arguments can take many forms, but there are only two major positions. One says that nonvoters are relatively uninformed, apathetic, and withdrawn from politics, and possibly are satisfied to let others run things. They probably should not vote—or at least their choice not to vote should be respected—and the system is kept more stable by their nonparticipation. A recent version of this argument says that it doesn't really matter very much that Americans don't vote at high rates because nonvoters do not hold different attitudes or preferences from those who do vote.

The other argument holds that everybody should vote in a democracy, either because it is the right thing to do as a citizen or because it gives people a stronger sense of having a stake in the system and thus makes them feel obligated to obey the laws that it produces. This position finds today's turnout levels to be a serious reflection on the United States and seeks to do everything possible to increase turnout. Favorite remedies include reducing registration requirements, having voting over a two-day period (perhaps on weekends or as a holiday), and of course massive education and exhortation campaigns. Most people who are on this side of the issue believe that outcomes would be different if the less advantaged voters turned out in proportions that were equal to the better educated and wealthier people. Some are concerned that, at some election, a large number of people who are typically nonvoters might turn out to vote and thus bring about undesirable changes in policy directions, or even in our form of government.

The *Who Votes?* study is a good example of the first position. The authors see nonvoting as a relatively permanent fixture of American society, because it is grounded in the way that people are differently exposed to education. By sorting out the causes of nonvoting carefully, they are able to argue persuasively that reducing registration requirements in all states to those of the most permissive state would add only a potential 9 percent to the voting electorate. Finally, they show from their 1972 data that the preferences of nonvoters were pretty much the same as those of people who vote regularly.

The other side is well argued by Arthur T. Hadley, whose *The Empty Polling Booth* is based on a special survey of nonvoters that was undertaken in 1976.[9] Hadley believes that nonvoters constitute a "time bomb" that is waiting to explode and change the course of American political history, and he advocates drastic changes in registration requirements and the handling of election day itself in order to bring people back into regular voting habits. One of the strengths of his work is the categorization of reasons for nonvoting that he was able to produce from the intense exploration involved in his study. His categories, with the percentages of nonvoters in each, are as follows:[10]

1. Positive Apathetics (35 percent)
2. Bypassed (13 percent)
3. Politically Impotent (22 percent)
4. Physically Disenfranchised (18 percent)
5. Naysayers (6 percent)
6. Cross-pressured (5 percent)

The first and largest category of "positive apathetics" are people who are quite like voters but who are simply too busy and too full of other alternatives in their lives to bother with voting. They might vote at any time, and if they did, they would probably follow dominant tendencies, just as Wolfinger and Rosenstone suggest. The "bypassed" category includes people of low income and education whom life has left behind, and who probably would not vote under most circumstances. The "politically impotent" category, however, includes people who are alienated and cynical about politics. They are the people who might, as Hadley fears, abruptly enter electoral politics again in support of an extremist candidate or cause.

The "physically disenfranchised" nonvoters are about one-third unable to vote because of health reasons. The rest were prevented by having moved recently, being out of town on election day, or other such reasons. With less stringent registration requirements, their votes would have been recorded. "Naysayers" are well-educated people who deliberately, and for reasons that are sufficient to them, refuse to vote, even though they are

---

[9] Arthur T. Hadley, *The Empty Polling Booth* (Englewood Cliffs, N.J.: Prentice-Hall, 1978).

[10] Ibid., Chapter 3, pp. 67–103.

TABLE   *Two-Party Data on Candidate Preference, Stratified by Turnout*
16.5   *Category Among Adult Population (1980)*

| | TWO-CANDIDATE VOTE | | |
CATEGORY OF ADULT	*Percentage for Carter*	*Percentage for Reagan*	*Lead*
Registered voters (71 percent of sample):			
Most likely to vote (top 25 percent)	47.1	52.9	5.8 R
Middle group (50 percent)	49.95	50.05	0.1 R
Least likely to vote (bottom 25 percent)	52.8	47.2	5.6 D
Adults by registration status:			
Registered (71 percent of sample)	49.4	50.6	1.2 R
Nonregistered (29 percent of sample)	59.4	40.6	18.8 D
Total adult population (100 percent)	52.3	47.7	4.6 D

SOURCE: Walter Dean Burnham, ''The 1980 Election: Earthquake, Realignment, Reaction, or What?'' in Thomas Ferguson and Joel Rogers, *The Hidden Election: Politics and Economics in the 1980 Presidential Campaign* (New York: Pantheon, 1981), Table 2, p. 103.

well informed about politics. The last small group of ''cross-pressured'' nonvoters are people with conflicting loyalties who solve their problem by not voting at all. Hadley's point is that there are only a few reforms that would really help to bring out nonvoters, such as post-card registration with 30-day registration requirements, making election day a holiday, and having easy absentee voting arrangements. The real remedy for nonvoting, he argues, is to develop credible and attractive political programs that make people feel that it is meaningful for them to take part in politics again.

A final point on the nonvoting issue was made by Walter Dean Burnham in a review of the 1980 election.[11] Using data from the CBS/New York Times poll, he argues convincingly that there were major differences in political preferences between voters and nonvoters in 1980. Table 16.5 is reproduced from this study. Whatever may have been the case in other elections, people who were not registered were far less favorable to Reagan than those who were. A similar difference in preferences is evident among registered voters, between those who are most and least likely to vote. These findings give great weight and importance to the argument that registering nonvoters is crucial to securing the election of candidates who are favorable to less advantaged people.

[11] Walter Dean Burnham, ''The Election of 1980,'' p. 100.

Which Voters Will Shape Future Directions? This question involves *both* the possibility of nonvoters turning out to vote in support of one candidate, party, or program *and* the possibility of major blocs of voters shifting from one party to the other. Each of these basic social processes historically has been involved in periods of realignment, and is likely to play a part in our long-overdue realignment of voters and parties. The realignment that was in its infancy in 1964 was a conservative one, and the New Right has certainly risen to a position as the most important new force in American politics in the 1980s. The only possible counterweight to the New Right is a class-based realignment from the left in which minorities and women would play a major role. We shall consider each in turn.

The New Right is composed of two overlapping groups of people. One is made up of a wide variety of fundamentalist religious groups, which include tens of millions of people who live mostly in the South and Midwest. The other is a national category that is coming to be known as "Middle American Radicals" (MARs), because of an intensive study by a Michigan sociologist that uses that term to describe about 25 percent of all Americans.[12] New Right supporters have been characterized as "populist conservatives" because they believe in majoritarian means of restoring previous social conditions and practices.[13] They are particularly concerned about such "social issues" as abortion, school prayer, and gun control. The Moral Majority, formed in 1979 by the Rev. Jerry Falwell, represents the religious side of this movement.

The MARs, according to the leading study, are lower-middle-class people who feel that they are being forced by government to pay for concessions that the rich have made to the militant minorities and poor. They pay in part through taxes, but also in part because it is their children who must be bused to distant schools, and their families that are being subjected to what they perceive as liberal social engineering. MARs were often New Deal supporters on economic issues, but they have become resentful of government assistance to those who do not appear to have worked as hard as themselves, as well as of the loss of the first war in America's history and with it the paramount world role that the country enjoyed for so long. Nationalism and strong anticommunism thus also form part of the New Right world view.

Most New Right supporters were either blue-collar Democrats or nonvoters in the 1950s. Their move to the right occurred in the 1960s, and their organized entry into electoral politics took place only in the 1970s. While they are clearly the major source of change in American politics today, it is not clear what their eventual impact will be; it could be to strengthen the right wing of the Republican Party and enable it, together with its business allies, to govern effectively for some time.

---

[12] Donald I. Warren, *The Radical Center: Middle Americans and the Politics of Alienation* (South Bend, Ind.: University of Notre Dame Press, 1976).

[13] Phillips, *Post-Conservative America.*

However, some business interests and the more moderate wing of the Republican Party do not support the social policies or the ultra-nationalistic foreign policy of the New Right. There could be a lengthy struggle for control of that party, with the New Right ultimately being forced into starting a new political party of its own. Whether it formed its own party or effectively forced the moderates out of the Republican Party, the New Right could be the trigger for extensive realignment of the American party and electoral systems.

The polar opposite possibility is for realignment to emerge from the mobilization of nonvoters, particularly urban minorities, with women, organized labor, and other progressives in a "rainbow coalition" of voters seeking greater equality and wider distribution of wealth and economic opportunities. In 1983, two well-experienced advocates for the poor and minorities, Frances Fox Piven and Richard E. Cloward, developed a thesis that they called "class-based realignment."[14] They called for efforts to energize people who were adversely affected by the vast array of Reagan administration cutbacks in social programs and to register them to vote. They urged social service workers to join in the registration drive, with the claim that the Reagan administration in effect had initiated a "class war" against the poor and the only alternative was to fight back on the same basis. The unemployed and the poor are the least likely of all people to vote, however, and the prospect seemed at best doubtful.

A stronger prospect for developing the "rainbow coalition" seemed to lie with efforts to get minorities to register and vote in much larger proportions than is their usual practice. In broad demographic terms, minorities are becoming an ever-larger share of the American population and their voting rates are quite low. They are also concentrated in the larger states that have big blocks of Electoral College ballots. Table 16.6 shows the proportions of blacks and Hispanics, and all minorities, in the major states in 1980 and as projected for the year 2000. These percentages represent *potential* strength only, of course, because each minority would have to vote at the same rates as whites to make the measures accurate. However, it is quite significant to note that both California and Texas will be about half minority in voting electorate by the year 2000.

The trouble with such analyses of potential minority voting strength is not just that it is still very difficult to imagine minorities rising above the cultural, educational, and other barriers to voting and thus reaching voting rates equal to whites. It is also the case that "minorities" may be just one word, but the interests and probable voting choices of minorities are far from unified. Indeed, minorities (like most other groups in American politics) have great difficulty in agreeing on any one program or strategy.

---

[14] Frances Fox Piven and Richard A. Cloward, "The American Road to Democratic Socialism," *democracy*, Summer, 1983, p. 65; Richard A. Cloward and Frances Fox Piven, "Toward a Class-Based Realignment of American Politics: A Movement Strategy," *Social Policy*, Winter 1983, pp. 3–14.

TABLE 16.6
Minority Percentages in Key Electoral College States, 1980 and 2000

	1980				2000			
	Elec. College Ballots	*Black*	*Hispanic*	*Total* Minority*	*Elec. College Ballots*	*Black*	*Hispanic*	*Total* Minority*
California	45	8.0	20.2	30.1	49	9.5	29.7	46.2
Florida	17	13.8	9.2	23.0	21	13.0	12.9	25.9
Illinois	26	14.5	5.6	20.1	23	16.8	9.5	26.3
Michigan	21	12.7	1.0	13.7	20	15.5	1.5	17.0
New Jersey	17	12.8	6.5	19.3	16	15.6	10.6	26.2
New York	41	14.5	9.2	23.7	36	19.0	12.6	31.6
Texas	26	12.5	22.8	35.3	30	12.4	32.8	45.6

SOURCE. U.S. Census Bureau projections, 1982.
* Includes Asian and others where applicable.

Blacks and Hispanics often disagree over candidates and policy priorities. Urban and Southern blacks disagree, and the black middle-class is often at odds with black lower classes. Hispanics have contrasting origins and interests; Cubans, Caribbean islanders, Puerto Ricans, and Mexican-Americans all have their distinct perspectives. Still, it seems clear that the registration and actual voting of new millions of minorities, if achieved, might greatly increase the chances of most Democratic presidential candidates.

With these two major possibilities at the forefront, political strategists made unprecedented efforts in 1984 to bring out the particular mix of voters and nonvoters that they thought would help their respective candidates. Political analysts, on the other hand, watched for the underlying trends that would indicate fundamental realignment and long-term consequences for the American political system. Given the policy changes initiated by the Reagan administration in its first term, and the possibility that these changes might be made permanent in a second term, the 1984 election loomed as potentially being one of the most important in twentieth-century American history.

THE ELECTION OF 1984

The first question arising from the record-setting Reagan electoral triumph of 1984 was whether the long-awaited realignment was finally at hand. Many Republicans naturally wanted to hope so, and some political observers argued that the massive Reagan victory signalled at least a "new natural majority" of voters in support of the Republican Party. It was certainly true that President Reagan drew strong support from nearly all definable groups of voters—blue collar and white collar, Catholics and Protestants, women and men, Easterners and Westerners. The old Democratic or New Deal coalition seemed gone forever.

But most of the evidence about voting in the 1984 election argues against the realignment thesis, and in favor of the "personal triumph" characterization that we employed in our earlier discussion in Chapter 10:

1. Turnout increased over that of the 1980 election by only three-tenths of 1 percent, and a new record was set for the number of people of voting age who did *not* vote; all prior realignments were distinguished by a surge in voter turnout.
2. Voters did not support the Republican Party as such, its programs, or its other candidates anywhere nearly as strongly as they supported Ronald Reagan. The Democrats actually gained a net of two seats in the Senate, a fact that almost by itself refutes the idea of realignment. These Democratic gains pose a real threat to continued Republican control of the Senate (now 53–47) past the election of 1986, when 22 Republican seats won in the election of 1980 will be at risk. If past precedents hold and/or the economy takes another downturn, the party in power is likely to suffer substantial mid-term losses.
3. The Republicans still trail well behind the Democrats in number of state governorships. Nor did the Republicans gain enough seats in the House that they could hope to develop a "working majority" through alliance with Southern conservative Democrats.

These ratios are not the mark of a realignment of voters behind the Republican Party or its candidates. At best, the 1984 election can be seen as endorsement of a presidential Republican Party (or rejection of the national Democratic Party), and perhaps as embodying the potential for creating a new national majority in response to the Reaganite Republican policies to be implemented during the President's second term. The election of 1984 did not represent an electoral realignment as that concept has been understood historically.

It now appears that the long-term implications of the 1984 election could follow one of three possible scenarios:

1. The first is somewhat analogous to the events following the election of 1936, which in fact *did* mark a realigning period. This is a policy imprint of major dimensions that has the effect of shaping national policy and also voting reactions for some time into the future. As Franklin Roosevelt did in his second term (to which he was elected in 1936), Reagan may have four or five Supreme Court appointments to make. Five Justices of the Supreme Court were over 75 years of age on election day 1984, and are thus likely to retire or die in office by 1988. FDR appointed five Justices during his second term in office, and the longevity of these new judges meant that there was an effective Roosevelt majority on the Court into the 1960s; his first four appointees served an average of 28 years on the Court. Together with potential executive leadership in other policy areas, such as tax re-

form, this appointing power could lead to Court decisions that would chart the course of American public policy for decades to come.

2. A "new natural majority" has in fact come into being, and in the future elections will not be shaped by the allegiances of large voting blocs of ethnic, religious, racial, class, or other groups. Instead, it is argued, the media's new dominance makes all voters equally subject to the appeals of candidates' personalities and the sophistication with which they poll opinion, appeal to valued symbols, and generally package their campaigns. This view sees the affluent middle class as the great bulk of the electorate, able to shape election results to serve its own economic interests.

3. The third possibility is even less clear or certain, but it is nevertheless an interesting historical analogy. This is the reverse analogue to 1964, the year in which the Goldwater candidacy—though defeated by the greatest popular-vote margin of the twentieth century—effectively ignited the New Right movement that eventually led to control of the Republican Party and the election of Ronald Reagan to the presidency. The argument is that there was an underlying polarization in the election of 1984, in which poor people, minorities, and to some extent women, formed the core of Democratic support, and that their vigorous effort to shape the Party and its programs in the future might help to spur a vast influx of current nonvoters to their future support. The polarization is a fact. As Table 10.5 (p. 291) showed, voters with incomes under $12,500 favored Mondale by a wide margin, whereas Reagan preferences increased sharply with rising income above that level. The "class based realignment" is at least possible, although it is hard to imagine the lower echelons mobilizing enough voters to win an election. But that is what most observers said about the New Right after the Goldwater defeat.

As a conclusion, it is hard to resist harking back to some of our earlier themes. The 1984 election was another in our continuing series of "marking time" or "status quo" elections—a personal triumph for Ronald Reagan but otherwise indecisive. The missing realignment is yet to occur, and meanwhile our political stalemate lingers on. There is no doubt about the economic transformation underway, or the need for a comprehensive economic renewal program to restore a viable, modern American sector of the new world economy. But neither leaders nor people seem to have seen, let alone decided upon, the institutional changes and new public policies that will add up to that sort of program. Without such political change—electoral, institutional, and programmatic—there will be no adequate economic change.

CHAPTER 17

Alternatives in American Politics: Forms and Forces

In this chapter, we will explore two kinds of alternatives to what we have seen as the structure and practices of American politics. The first are different *means* or forms of participation by which people seek to influence outcomes, such as civil disobedience, demonstrations, or riots. These forms of mobilizing and wielding power go well beyond the traditional means—the elections, interest-group activity, and lobbying—that we have examined so far. The second kind of alternatives are different *ends* or goals that people have in politics—goals that are out of the mainstream and that in some way stand opposed to accepted practices or purposes of the society. These contending forces impel people into action, whether in traditional or alternative ways, in search of changes in basic values, structures, or policy directions. They give politics its real dynamism, because they embody efforts to make a better future amidst changing circumstances.

As we take up these alternative forms and forces in order, we shall see that what is really at stake here is a potential redefinition of politics itself. The traditional means of participation are those that have been set up to allow people to participate within established assumptions about what kind of social order we shall have; they do not encourage change of any sort in government or society whatsoever. Instead, they assume the rightness of a capitalist, liberal society with the current distribution of wealth, status, and power; to employ other means is to challenge these basic assumptions about what should be. The traditional goals and purposes of American politics have also been consistent with the maintenance of this sort of society; to seek fundamentally different goals is to challenge the society's very foundation.

Together, the orthodox means and ends have fit with only one conception of what it means to be "political" or to engage in "politics," but if people seek other ends, or employ other means, they are in effect re-defining what it means to be political. For example, if some people see practically everything in their lives as being shaped by uses of power over which they have very little control, they may well come to resent what is being done to them. Their family relationships, work life, daily activities, and even their personal thoughts, are being shaped by the power and preferences of others. Conversely, however, they may realize that by think-ing and acting differently in these intimate dimensions of their lives—in terms of another, better, and more satisfying model of what could be—they could change the world in which they live, and thus reshape the power distribution and usage pattern of their society.

At the root of this process of change is the recognition that what seems to be merely personal is actually political. This is the same as redefining the meaning of "politics" and "political." The conditions of daily life lead to felt needs for change, which in turn lead to alternative forms of action and alternative goals. Acting differently in order to achieve a better life for oneself and others amounts to acting out that different definition of poli-tics. Not every use of alternative forms of political participation or every effort to obtain an alternative goal in politics involves such a major redefinition, of course; probably most are merely limited attempts to serve one's self-interest a little better. But these alternative forms and forces include both the ways that politics *can* be redefined and wholly new means and ends that replace the current ones. This is where *change* begins.

ALTERNATIVE FORMS OF POLITICAL PARTICIPATION

The alternative forms of participation span a wide range of activities. Some are as authorized and accepted as, although less formalized than, elections or interest-group actions. Others are discouraged or forcefully repressed, but nevertheless represent means by which some nonelites participate in politics and may influence policy. In general, although the alternative forms are frequently efforts to bypass the established channels, they exhibit many of the same class biases as do parties, elections, and interest-group activities.

One of the most obvious and accepted modes of communication and "pressure" from nonelites to decision-making elites is the simple act of writing a letter or signing a petition to be sent to an official or a newspaper. Legislators are sometimes said to "wait for the mail" before making up their minds on how to vote on an issue. But there are several problems with this assumption. One is that people tend to write or petition those they have reason to believe are on their side or at least on the fence. This means that letter writers favoring a proposal write to decisionmakers who favor it, and those against a proposal write to those who oppose it. The net result, even if the decisionmakers take their mail seriously, is no change in positions. Another problem is that decisionmakers become impervious to pressure campaigns organized by small interest groups.

Even more important is the fact that writing letters, and to a lesser extent, carrying and signing petitions, is more likely to be undertaken by people who are relatively well educated and upper class. Even within class and education levels, it is an act that is more likely to be undertaken by conservatives than by liberals. In an effort to find out why the 1964 Republican strategists thought there was a "hidden" conservative vote, the Michigan Survey Research Center compared the political preferences of those who wrote letters to officials or newspapers with those who did not.[1] The researchers found that only 15 percent of the population had ever written a letter to a public official and that two-thirds of *all* letters were written by a total of 3 percent of the population. The 3 percent was distinctly conservative in every ideological dimension; by "vote" of letter writers, Goldwater would have been elected by a comfortable majority. Thus, if decisionmakers took guidance, or if officials sought to measure the mood of the country, they would acquire a very skewed image from the views expressed in the mail to officials and newspapers.

Citizen Participation

Some alternative forms of participation are built into the process of administering and implementing laws. Juries, for instance, place a significant function in the hands of citizens and might well serve as a means of communicating citizens' dissatisfaction with law or with their circumstances. But juries are drawn from lists of voters or property owners (or, in the case of grand juries, from "blue-ribbon" panels) and thus reflect class orientations. Nevertheless, juries in many cases involving political figures and issues (Black Panthers, draft resisters, the Chicago 7 trial, and others) have refused to convict or been relatively lenient, suggesting that some potential prosecutions may have been discouraged by these results.

Advisory boards of citizens are required by law in many areas of governmental activity. Urban renewal, selective service, and other agencies deliberately engage citizens in the implementation of their programs, but they accomplish relatively little for ordinary citizens, because participants in these programs are drawn from the higher echelons of nonelites. Businesspeople, local leaders, and higher-status people generally dominate these positions. Only in the Community Action Agencies of the poverty program was there a real contest over who was to shape a governmental program. Lower-class citizens did begin to take part, and the result was first an amendment to the law that gave local governments control over the local aspects of such programs; then such controversy arose that the funding for many local units was sharply cut back or eliminated.

---

[1] These data are drawn from Philip Converse, Warren Miller, Jerold G. Rusk, and Arthur C. Wolfe, "Continuity and Change in American Politics: Parties and Issues in the 1968 Election," *American Political Science Review* 63 (1969), p. 333.

In general, formal participation by nonelites in policy-making bodies is bound to be largely ritual unless it is accompanied by a form of power that nonelites can assert, such as a strike, boycott, or disruption of programs that are important to elites. The chance to participate is often regarded as a concession, but it is more often a way of making sure that a low-status group will not resort to effective protest or resistance. Participation is so effective a way of diverting discontented people from disorder that it is often *required* of low-status groups in totalitarian settings such as prisons, mental hospitals, schools, and totalitarian states, where it serves as a form of pseudodemocracy.

A much less institutionalized form of participation that has arisen from time to time in American history, and particularly during the 1960s, is the protest demonstration, sit-in, disruption, or deliberate refusal to obey rules. Those who have been unable to make themselves heard through the established channels have resorted to these tactics, and often with great success, when their claims were consistent with generally shared values and not at extreme odds with the basic features of the political system. But when they have been unable to find allies or have been seen as dangerously at variance with established values or familiar political practices, rejection and repression have been very harsh. Successful protest-type activity requires allies, or at the very least inaction on the part of those who might oppose the protesters. It involves risks of a personal kind for the participants and is difficult to keep up for a long period of time without a supportive environment. Thus, it depends on achieving some tangible goal, usually from an existing political structure.

Another, even less institutionalized, alternative form of participation is the spontaneous riot. Although clearly grounded in the circumstances of ghetto existence, the riots of the 1960s and those in Miami in 1980 were spontaneous, in contrast to deliberate obstructive sit-ins or other protest tactics. Touched off by one or another form of provocation, riots may engage thousands of participants for days at a time. The immediate consequences are destruction of millions of dollars' worth of property and the deaths of many ghetto residents at the hands of police and national guard forces. Subsequently, governmental assistance to ghetto residents and other poor people may increase, as it did in the aftermath of the 1960s riots, but so too did popular support for repressive measures and for political candidates who stood for such action.

The 1960s and early 1970s, with the wholly unanticipated civil rights and anti-war movements, were a period of massive public involvement in politics. What this period produced in the way of public disturbances is summarized in Table 17.1. The data come from the U.S. Department of Justice, and may strike us in the 1980s as indicating a time of great upheaval. At the very least, the table suggests widespread use of alternative means to send a political message.

Patterns of participation in riots offer some insight into these alternative forms of participation. In the case of the widespread ghetto riots of 1967, for example, it is clear that substantial proportions of each community were involved. Supplemental studies undertaken for the National

TABLE
17.1   *Civil Disturbances and Related Deaths, 1967–73*

| | DISTURBANCES | | | RELATED |
YEAR	*Total*	*Major*[1]	*Other*[2]	DEATHS
1967	52	12	40	87
1968	80	26	54	83
1969	57	8	49	19
1970	76	18	58	33
1971	39	10	29	10
1972	21	2	19	9
1973	4	1	3	2

SOURCE: U.S. Department of Justice, Internal Security Division, cited in Nelson Polsby, *Consequences of Party Reform* (New York: Oxford University Press, 1983), p. 18.

NOTES: [1] Characterized by all of the following: (a) vandalism; (b) arson; (c) looting or gunfire; (d) outside police forces or troops used; (e) more than 300 persons involved, excluding police; (f) twelve hours or longer duration.

[2] Characterized by: Any three elements (a) through (d) in #1; duration of at least three hours; and more than 50 persons involved, excluding police.

Commission on Civil Disorders estimate that participants represented from 11 to 35 percent of residents of the riot areas in major cities (Detroit, Newark, New Haven) where riots occurred.[2] The composition of the rioters was roughly representative of the occupational makeup of the ghetto population, with a slight emphasis on the less skilled and the unemployed. Nearly all of those who were arrested during the riots were residents of the neighborhoods involved.[3] The riots were thus fairly broad-based actions by cross sections of the area populations. They were not caused by the "criminal elements," by "outside agitators," or by a tiny minority of militants. They were, it seems fair to say, genuine expressions of community protest of an essentially political kind. Certainly they were perceived as such by most blacks; indeed, several surveys have shown that while most blacks do not approve of rioting, they see it in many cases as necessary and helpful toward achieving black goals.[4] Younger blacks in particular tend to believe that violence will be necessary before such objectives are attained.

Eruptions in the black ghettos of a large number of major cities in the 1960s almost certainly helped keep welfare rolls high by frightening the

[2] Robert M. Fogelson and Robert B. Hill, "Who Riots? A Study of Participation in the 1967 Riots," *Supplemental Studies for the National Advisory Commission on Civil Disorders* (Washington, D.C.: U.S. Government Printing Office, 1968), p. 231.

[3] Ibid., pp. 236, 237.

[4] Opinion data in this section are drawn from Angus Campbell and Howard Schuman, "Racial Attitudes in Fifteen American Cities," in Fogelson and Hill, *Supplemental Studies*, pp. 48–52.

middle class into liberalizing eligibility and benefits, at least for a time.[5] But it is already clear that the riots have not significantly changed the social or economic conditions of the poor and/or black population. Each wave of riots in American history has produced commissions and recommendations for reform in employment practices, city services to the poor, housing, transportation, and racist attitudes, but such recommendations yield few lasting results.

Generating an Impact on Policy

Elections are an uncertain vehicle of political participation. Interest groups are highly specialized. The alternative forms of participation are erratic and even counterproductive. And yet needs, claims, and demands *are* introduced into the political arena by the actions of segments of citizens. At least to some extent, elites feel obliged, or are forced, to respond. Their response may be merely symbolic, negative, or marginal, but there is nevertheless often *some* response and sometimes one that is consistent with nonelite demands.

Frequently, a fully satisfactory "solution" is impossible because of perceived conditions, opposition from other segments of the public, or elites' priorities and preferences. These determinations are made by elites, of course. Their power, status, and legitimacy enable them to decide how to fit demands that are strongly pressed and supported by established values into the mix of policy and practice that characterizes the political system. Other demands can normally be deflected or dismissed. In this process, elites are aided by the screening effect of the greater participation and efficacy of the better-educated and higher-status citizens. They cushion or absorb much of the thrust of deviant, minority, or lower-class demands before such demands emerge into the national political arena and begin to induce elite response.

In many instances, at least some members of elites *want* to respond; they may even have been waiting for a chance to do so. Elites may support mass demands because they expect to benefit from doing so. Free universal public education is a case in point. Before the Industrial Revolution, free public education was an issue that divided Americans along economic class lines. It was a major plank in the platform of one of our earliest third parties, the Workingmen's Party, which gained considerable support among wage earners in Philadelphia between 1828 and 1832. The issue grew less and less controversial as industrial technologies required that a larger proportion of the work force be literate and possess elementary skills in arithmetic and what were called the "agricultural, industrial, and mechanic arts." Indeed, many states began establishing normal schools, state colleges, and universities around the middle of the nineteenth century, and

---

[5] Frances F. Piven and Richard A. Cloward, *Regulating the Poor* (New York: Random House, 1971).

the federal government helped them to do so in the Morrill Act of 1862. As industry and agriculture have required work forces with increasingly complex skills, elite support for education at all levels has also increased. To some degree, this trend has been further bolstered by the fact that methods of financing state universities provide a direct subsidy to the largely middle-class students who attend them.

Sometimes elites have even more pressing and immediate economic reasons to support mass demands. In the early years of the twentieth century, a growing number of states enacted minimum-wage laws. It was widely acknowledged that if workers were unable to live on their earnings, they should be entitled to a wage that would at least support their families at a subsistence level. This policy was supported both on a moral basis and because it was recognized that people could not work efficiently when undernourished. A chief reason for the enactment of the first federal minimum-wage law in 1938 was its support by some powerful industrial groups, especially New England textile manufacturers. Forced by unions of their workers to pay higher wages than their unorganized Southern competitors, the New England mill owners saw in the minimum wage a device to increase their competitors' labor cost to the level of their own, thereby improving their own competitive position.

Social security legislation, which is certainly a significant benefit to a large part of the public, has also enjoyed substantial elite support, for economic and other reasons. Growing worker demands for industrial pension plans, backed by the right to strike, put employers under strong pressure to make some concessions. Governmental old-age benefits that were financed by regressive payroll taxes paid chiefly by the workers and by consumers, represented an economical solution. Consequently, frequent improvements in the benefits and coverage of American social security legislation have been relatively uncontroversial since the basic federal law was enacted in 1935.

Elite Fear of Public Restiveness

This discussion has deliberately moved from a consideration of such routine channels of influence as voting and legislative bargaining to those that some regard as illegitimate, such as civil disobedience. The analysis and illustrations should make it obvious that there is no clear dividing line between legitimate and illegitimate tactics. Similarly, there is no clear empirical distinction, but only an analytically useful one, between people who feel relatively gratified and those who feel relatively deprived. It is the relatively deprived who are most likely to support political strikes, boycotts, riots, civil disobedience, or civil war as channels of influence.

It is tempting but misleading to classify people neatly as being either content or dissatisfied, as exhibiting a sense of gratification or a sense of deprivation, as perceiving the political system as legitimate or illegitimate, or as believing that they are efficacious or politically powerless. Test results do, of course, categorize people in these ways, but there is also clear evidence, some of which we have already cited, that people's feelings may vary over time, by issue, and according to the social context in which the question is presented to them. How stable and how consistent any individual or social group is in these respects is an empirical question, to be answered by observation and research. To take stability and consistency for granted is to underestimate human complexity and to guarantee that some of the most significant political phenomena will not be investigated or fully understood.

In spite of great inequalities in wealth, power, and dignity, the mass of the population rarely makes demands for basic changes in who gets what. People usually accept their lot, partly because of the legitimizing and symbolic actions discussed earlier and partly because it is rarely clear how to organize common action among people who share the same grievances. Only when conditions become desperate or intolerable is common protest action likely, not simply when people come to expect a better life; rising expectations alone do not bring serious political restiveness.

Sometimes public officials and the general public fail to recognize protest activities for what they are. A sharp increase in delinquent rent or tax payments, in truancy from school, or in welfare applications signals massive discontent, but because it is usually not organized or publicized, people see it only as individual delinquency, and not as political action, so that it is more likely to result in repression than in responsiveness to people's grievances.

In the face of disorder or civil disobedience, however, there is sure to be some kind of elite response. Sometimes there are significant concessions. All industrialized countries, for example, have established social security systems; almost all of them were instituted earlier and extend wider protection than the American system does. In Germany, Bismarck's highly elitist and authoritarian government provided extensive social security protections as early as the 1880s.

Similarly, the civil rights demonstrations and boycotts led by Martin Luther King in the late 1950s and early 1960s brought wider awareness of discriminatory practices and of denials of civil liberties. Figure 17.1 shows that Congress passed the civil rights laws of 1964 and 1965 when demonstrations were most frequent. Although it is impossible to prove a direct causal connection, this study and others make it reasonable to conclude that the demonstrations were responsible both for a rise in public concern about civil rights and for congressional actions, which continued for a time even after the demonstrations began to wane. But the *enforcement* of the voting rights and open-housing laws Congress passed in those years is itself responsive to public concern and so is likely to lapse with a decline in that concern.

Fear of mass restiveness or violence has been a major reason for the enactment of other governmental programs benefiting nonelites. For example, large-scale strikes, rural violence to protest the taking of land from farmers who could not make payments on their mortgages, and the spread

Figure 17.1. Number of Civil Rights Demonstrations and Passage of Civil Rights Laws

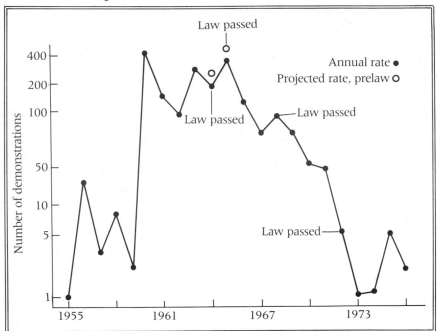

SOURCE: Reprinted by permission of the publisher from "Public Opinion, Demonstration, and the Passage of Antidiscrimination Legislation," by Paul Burstein, *Public Opinion Quarterly* 43, Fall 1979, p. 169.

of radical ideology helped win wide support for the New Deal reforms of the 1930s.

Although mass defiance is one of the few ways the poor and the disadvantaged have been able to achieve some political impact, the gains this tactic has won for them have usually been quite limited. While such legislative victories as those just mentioned are seen as major break-throughs, their administrative enforcement tends to become half-hearted after a time, and symbolic results are more common than tangible ones. As protest fades, established inequalities often reappear, and concessions may be withdrawn.

The rise and demise of the National Welfare Rights Organization (NWRO) offers some insight into the uses and limits of disruption as a political strategy for disadvantaged groups. Founded in 1966 to promote the rights of welfare applicants and recipients, the NWRO relied during its first few years on mobilizing the poor to demonstrate against specific griev-ances. Although it had little money in its treasury and only a skeletal organization, NWRO repeatedly forced welfare office staff members to grant applicants the benefits to which they were legally entitled by inform-ing them of their rights and helping them file claims, by staging demonstra-tions outside and inside the offices, picketing, demanding hearings, and encouraging a national campaign for special grants for hardship cases. This militancy not only won welfare rights for individuals and groups, but also contributed to support for the antipoverty program in general by reminding officials and the general public of the risks of disorder. The very success and prominence of the NWRO began to bring it legitimacy, substantial funds from private foundations and from the public treasury, and formal representation on governmental committees. By the early 1970s, it was functioning largely through the conventional lobbying channels of bureaucratic and legislative politics and abandoning its earlier reliance on demonstrations and disruption of established routines. As it became respectable, paradoxically, the NWRO lost its effectiveness and gradually faded from the scene. Its demise was due not only to its change in tactics and status, but also to the ebbing of black protest in general.[6]

Militance and Popular Support

The efficacy of civil disobedience and militance in winning benefits for the masses depends ultimately on how much popular support these tactics stimulate for their cause. When they serve dramatically to call attention to deprivations that are widely regarded as shocking and unfair, they are effective in rallying such support. Until the civil disobedience campaigns of the early 1960s and the riots of the middle 1960s, a large segment of the American people was blissfully unaware of the "other America" living in poverty and denied basic civil rights. Increasingly militant demonstrations against the Vietnam War awakened many Americans to the dubious grounds on which the Johnson administration had justified escalation of the war, its high toll in civilian and military casualties, and the corruption and unpopularity of the Saigon regime.

Civil disobedience and violence do, as we have seen, create a "backlash" and so damage the political position of those who engage in them. Militance unquestionably antagonizes some people and evokes repression. The historical record leaves no doubt, however, that it also wins support for righting genuine wrongs. If such real deprivations can be dramatically brought to public attention, then militant tactics are the most potent political device in the meager arsenal of tactics that are available to nonelites.

ALTERNATIVE FORCES
IN AMERICAN POLITICS

What people seek in politics is surely as important as how they seek it. As might be expected in a time of transformation, the 1980s are distinguished by the range of contrasting goals that people and groups are struggling to

---

[6] Cf. Frances F. Piven and Richard A. Cloward, *Poor People's Movements* (New York: Pantheon Books, 1977), pp. 264–362.

achieve. As conditions change, these forces will be the ones whose mobilization and determination will shape the American future. We shall look first at the radical, minority, and women's movements on the left, the "rainbow coalition" that some believe might emerge from today's polarization and realignment. Then we shall examine the currently better-organized and more powerful forces on the right, the business community and the New Right.

Radicalism is the belief that drastic change is necessary at the roots of the social order. Radicalism of the left seeks change toward more egalitarian (equal) distribution of wealth, status, and power, while radicalism of the right defends inequalities in these respects and seeks to restore the values and traditions that support them. Each form of radicalism also holds contrasting images of *human nature* and of the amount of coercive *order* necessary to maintain social harmony. According to the left radicalism on which we focus here, humans are essentially good and cooperative and should enjoy a maximum of civil liberties and individual freedom. In contrast, conservatives generally hold a pessimistic view of human nature as being selfish and aggressive, and in need of restraint.

Radicalism, which was in eclipse during the 1940s and 1950s as a result of war, repression, and general social mobilization in support of the cold war, was reborn in the mid-1960s. Blacks' struggles for basic civil rights quickly reignited similar undertakings by Chicanos, Puerto Ricans, American Indians, Asians, and other minorities. The efforts of white college students, which were directed at first to the civil rights movement, soon shifted to opposition to the Vietnam War and then to community organizing, citizen participation, and efforts to change universities. This collection of activities, so much in contrast with that of earlier decades, soon became known as the "New Left." Lacking a fundamental critique of American society, it lost much of its momentum with the end of the Vietnam War. But the more theoretical and dedicated radicals among its ranks moved on to develop fuller critiques and a variety of alternative models for the future. Some sought to make links with working people, and others to find new movements (antinuclear, environmental, minorities, feminist) that would join the effort toward large-scale social change.

The American left, however, remains characterized by division rather than coherence in either critique or program. Not counting radical demands made by nationalists in every major minority group, three major strains of radical thought currently pose serious opposition to American liberal orthodoxy: reformism, anticapitalism, and extreme individualism.

Reformism

This primary strain of radicalism best illustrates the nature and consequences of the radical commitment to equality. Much of the history of tension between radicalism and the dominant orthodoxy can be attributed to the conflict between the values of equality and property as they are understood by the respective ideologies. The argument has involved both the *definition* and the *priority* attached to equality. Radicalism of this kind defines equality in broad and steadily expanding terms, proceeding from equality of opportunity to equality in the actual conditions of people's lives. It gives full priority to equality, elevating it above all other political values when they come into conflict.

But it is easy to exaggerate the "radicalness" of this radical argument. For example, at no time in American history did any significant number of these radicals call for the abolition of private property as such or for drastic action to equalize the conditions of people's lives. They asked only for somewhat greater emphasis on equality in the context of competitive individualism and respect for property rights. Starting from the acknowledged principle of political equality, in the sense of voting rights and majoritarianism, they gradually caused restrictions that were inconsistent with such principles, such as those involving property, sex, and race, to be removed.

Increasingly in the twentieth century, however, sources of power other than government and other socially produced limitations appear to have prevented individuals from attaining their ends. Radicals, therefore, have sought to expand the implications of equality to legitimize government action to preserve opportunity and the provision of sufficient education and social status to enable individuals to compete more equally. Once again, there has been strong resistance on the part of those holding more restrictive definitions of equality. Thus, although equality is symbolically unchallenged, its political and socioeconomic effectuation has been tentative and controversial.

By contrast, attachment to property as a legitimate and paramount value has been widely shared and rarely challenged. No major American thinker, including Jefferson (supposed by some of his contemporaries to have been unsympathetic to the wealthy and propertied), has failed to support strongly the individual's right to whatever land, goods, and money he or she could amass. Hamilton and some other Federalists considered these to be the central goals of human motivations and sought to construct a government to serve these ends. Men like Adams and Jefferson believed that property gives people political independence, a stake in the society, and the capacity and right to judge—which in turn leads to wise public decisionmaking.

It should be clear that reformism historically affirmed other traditional values as well as property rights. The concepts of individualism, materialism, natural rights, limited government, and legalism were all taken for granted in the effort to expand and enhance equality. The same is true today: what this form of radicalism seeks is a reality that conforms to orthodox American rhetoric, and provides greater opportunity for individuals to compete more successfully and to amass larger amounts of the material rewards of the American system.

To some extent, reformists do see flaws and limitations in the existing values and would repair these deficiencies. Although the principle of limited government is still considered to be valid in the abstract because people should be free to attain their individual ends, it is seen as being much violated in practice. In this view, the worst violations are subsidies, price supports, and other financial benefits for those very economic interests that are most likely to use the principle of limited government as a defense against proposed policies that would benefit ordinary people. Individualism is considered to have humanistic and esthetic, as well as material, dimensions. Material aspirations, however, are still taken to be the primary motivation of "human nature" and the basic dynamic of social life. Racism is acknowledged and condemned, but the chief remedy proposed is laws to prevent discrimination. According to Robert Allen,

> Black liberation, however, will not come about solely through the activities of black people. Black America cannot be genuinely liberated until white America is transformed into a humanistic society free of exploitation and class division. The black and white worlds, although separate and distinct, are too closely intertwined—geographically, politically, and economically—for the social maladies of one not to affect the other. Both must change if either is to progress to new and liberating social forms.[7]

Reform ideology thus contains a profound ambivalence. On the one hand, it brusquely rejects the orthodoxy's claim that present policies must be appropriate because they are enacted by a system in which rules and widespread participation ensure outcomes that reflect a democratic consensus. Economic and social conditions, which are readily visible to all who are willing to look, completely rebut the claims of American orthodoxy and must be corrected. Concentrations of economic power must be prevented from continuing their exploitation, and ordinary citizens must recapture power over the circumstances of their lives. On the other hand, reformism holds that these goals can be achieved if more people become involved, reopen the political processes, and "throw the rascals out." By reforming certain aspects of politics, installing better people in office, and thus rearranging the priorities of government and society, the conditions of the mass of the people can be dramatically improved. In short, things are very bad, but it won't take much to set them right.

> The fight against this concentration of privilege—open and covert, legal and illegal—is, we believe, the most important political question of this decade. Its goal is a more equitable distribution of wealth and power; its enemy is the entire arrangement of privileges, exemptions, and free rides that has narrowed the opportunity of most Americans to control their own destiny. This fight for fairness is political; it can be won only by organizing a new political majority in America.[8]

This ambivalence has its roots in the acceptance of most of the orthodox political values "as is" and in the effects of orthodox political ideol-

---

[7] Robert L. Allen, *Black Awakening in Capitalist America: An Analytic History* (New York: Doubleday, 1970), p. 281.

[8] Jack Newfield and Jeff Greenfield, *A Populist Manifesto: The Making of a New Majority* (New York: Warner Paperback Library, 1972), p. 17.

ogy. By accepting the values of competitive individualism and materialism, reformists can say only that the "problem" is the unfair distribution of rewards—not the wrongness of the nature or workings of the economy as a whole. Because reformists think within the framework of American political ideology and are therefore convinced of the rightness and legitimacy of the political system as a whole, they can say only that there must be something temporarily wrong. If it were corrected through the sincere efforts of the people, the national government could again become the agent of the people and the instrument of economic opportunity for all. For these reasons, reformism remains principally a protest movement, demanding reform and opportunity *within* the existing system.

Anticapitalism

Although not yet primary, the anticapitalist version of contemporary radicalism has grown in proportion to the failure of reformist radicalism to achieve real success for more than a few sectors of the population. It holds that the traditional American values are not just in need of redefinition and reordering, but are themselves the cause of current problems. In particular, anticapitalist radicalism rejects individualism in the orthodox sense. These radicals argue that human nature is not necessarily competitive and self-aggrandizing; people can learn to share and to cooperate for the betterment of their mutual condition. When they do, a true sense of community will emerge, and justice in the form of roughly equal distribution of rewards will be available for all.

The key to achieving such results is seen as the abolition of the private ownership of productive machinery and resources and the profit-maximizing use that necessarily results. As long as such private ownership and profit orientation exist, masses of people *must* be exploited. Thus, anticapitalist radicalism must reject the value of property rights, not with regard to personal property or home ownership, but with regard to large private holdings of land, capital, securities, and other forms of wealth.

The concept of limited government must also be abandoned, because government must serve as a central planning agency on behalf of the society as a whole. In order to provide enough goods and services for qualitative improvement of the lives of millions of ordinary American citizens and to discharge obligations to the rest of humanity, it will be necessary to employ the society's productive resources in an efficient manner. Central planning is thus required to determine at least what is to be done where. Local organizations of workers or others may then assume responsibility for deciding how each goal will be reached and by whom.

Materialism is not entirely rejected, for it will be crucial to raise the material standard of living for most Americans as well as for other people in the world. This is a prerequisite to the opportunity to enjoy other aspects of life and to develop the creative, esthetic, and other human potential that exists in all persons. But materialism will not be the principal motivating force in people's lives, because they will not seek to amass things for themselves. They will be assured of enough to serve their needs and instead will work out of a commitment to bettering the lives of others.

Anticapitalist radical values are clearly fundamentally different from those held by most Americans. The ideology derived from such values sees the American system today as fundamentally irrational. Private ownership and the profit motive lead inexorably to exploitation, widespread misery, and a sharply stratified class system with a very few powerful individuals at the top. There is a continued need for manipulation of the masses by the ruling capitalist class and its agents. Because the ruling class controls the nation's wealth, it also controls the government and, through it, the educational system and the political process generally. The major means of manipulation is inculcation of the ideology we have been calling American orthodoxy which, once fixed in the minds of the people, makes social control possible with a minimum of conscious effort. Aspiring and competent people are induced to become agents of the ruling class because the ruling class controls the rewards and opportunities they seek.

In this self-reinforcing and self-perpetuating way, the system operates relatively smoothly. The problems that exist arise out of the characteristics of capitalism, but people recognize only their surface manifestations and not their causes. The financial problems of cities, for example, result not from the lack of a tax base or from too much spending on education or welfare, but rather from the vast sums that are spent to pay the interest and principal on loans from capitalist bankers. Because so many people are seen as being hopelessly trapped in the orthodox values and ideology, anticapitalist radicals face a serious dilemma. Either they must commit themselves to trying to transform the system through revolutionary action with the conscious support of only a minority of the people, or they must await a change of mind on the part of a decisive majority of the people, through events or persuasion or both. Understandably, this issue remains a subject of vigorous debate within this strain of radicalism.

Individualism

Reformist radicalism accepts orthodox values and ideology and asks that rhetoric be made reality. Anticapitalist radicalism requires sweeping value changes and a sharp rupture with orthodox ideology. But both of these strains have in mind an ideal social system, in which aggregations of people do certain things in accordance with specific principles, thereby producing a pattern of rewards for individuals. If the rewards or satisfactions are not just or desirable, the remedy is to change the way the social system operates. However, the individualist form of radicalism rejects the idea that a large-scale social system can provide what individuals really need; these needs include such nonmaterial things as an understanding of life and its meaning, harmony with nature and other people, love, and other forms of personal growth and fulfillment.

Thus, the individualist rejection of what it sees as a corruptly commercialized and destructive world is a personal, and not a social, form of radicalism. Emphasis on individualism is greatly expanded and turned inward, away from material acquisitiveness and from the great mass of other people. The more limited government is, the better, for each individual must seek his or her own solution; real help can come only from the very small number of other persons with whom one has established special relationships.

> It is plain that the goal of revolution today must be the liberation of daily life. . . . Revolutionary liberation must be a self-liberation that reaches social dimensions, not "mass liberation" or "class liberation" behind which lurks the rule of an elite, a hierarchy and a state. . . . Out of the revolution must emerge a self that takes full possession of daily life, not a daily life that takes full possession of the self. . . .

> If for this reason alone, the revolutionary movement is profoundly concerned with lifestyle. It must try to live the revolution in all its totality, not only participate in it. . . . The revolutionary group must clearly see that its goal is not the seizure of power but the dissolution of power—indeed, it must see that the entire problem of power, of control from below and control from above, can be solved only if there is no above or below.[9]

This form of radicalism can be reached by a direct route from American orthodoxy or from reformist radicalism because it does not require extensive value change. Its emphasis on individualism and withdrawal makes it intellectually accessible to those who tire of struggling against large and impersonal social forces and to those who conclude that all large-scale social organizations are equally destructive of human freedom and potential. Unless vast numbers of people suddenly embrace the same personalized form of radicalism, it poses no serious threat to the continued operation of the American system or its orthodoxy. Power and its capabilities in a society are unaffected by the withdrawal of a few persons, particularly when their withdrawal is consciously based on the conviction that social efforts toward change are by definition undesirable or impossible. Nevertheless, this form of radicalism is gaining adherents, perhaps because the other two forms of radicalism are frustrating and (in the case of anticapitalism) require greater value change than people can or want to achieve.

Summary

Table 17.2 summarizes these three viewpoints, all of which have run throughout American history. Reformism is probably the most conspicuous, for it has taken many forms and has led to changes in the character of capitalism itself. The Jacksonian, Populist, Progressive, and New Deal periods were all characterized by such protests and by the ultimate transformation of capitalism from one form to another. In effect, the dominant

---

[9] Murray Bookchin, *Post-Scarcity Anarchism* (Berkeley: Ramparts Press, 1971), pp. 44–7.

TABLE 17.2
Characteristics of the Major Strains of American Radicalism

Ideology	Attitude toward Basic American Values	Approach to U.S. Economic System	Major Goals
Reformist	Accepts all; seeks realization in practice, putting equality foremost	Accepts basic structure and dynamics; seeks greater opportunities for all and some redistribution of wealth and income	More humane welfare capitalism, with greater participation by all people
Anticapitalist	Rejects most, particularly individualism, but endorses greatly expanded equality and community	Rejects it as unjust and exploitative	Socialism, usually in decentralized egalitarian form, with all civil liberties
Individualist	Accepts all, but in original form, emphasizing freedom of individual and rights to property	Rejects it as too big, stifling to individuals, bureaucratic, and no longer true free enterprise	Individualist anarchist society via withdrawal or small-scale units

system was able to blunt, absorb, and convert such demands into forms that could serve its own needs because their basic nature was not antagonistic to the principles of capitalism. Direct challenges to capitalism itself were first made by late-nineteenth-century socialists, and have continued to the present. They have been notably unsuccessful to date, because of the strength of American orthodoxy and attacks on those who hold such views by governments and others. Individualist withdrawal began with the transcendental individualists' attacks on the commercial society in the early nineteenth century, and today it takes the forms of a kind of libertarian anarchism and of certain versions of countercultural withdrawal. Because it has never been a serious threat, it has never been repressed, as have direct challenges to capitalism.

Thus, radicalism is neither a single coherent system of thought nor the rallying point of a unified social movement. Instead, it is a collection of different (and sometimes conflicting) beliefs, whose adherents chiefly share the conviction that they are deprived, powerless, and victimized by the dominant system. Radicalism begins as a set of reactions against contemporary conditions and the values and ideology that rationalize and justify them. Ultimately, it takes the form of an alternative ideology.

People can and do move from one strand of radical thought to another. In the 1970s, radicals tended to shift from demands for participation and reform to rejection of the existing system. Such rejection takes the form either of calls for the replacement of capitalism or of withdrawal into highly individualistic anarchism or countercultural lifestyles. At any given moment, of course, some people are sincerely hoping and working for reforms that will make the system more just in their eyes, while others, who have despaired of this approach, are either attacking capitalism itself or abandoning politics and social life to find solace by themselves. The developing economic crisis spurs each of these various currents in radical thought.

Types of Feminism

Although women make up about 53 percent of the population, they suffer from some of the same forms of discrimination and bias as do racial minorities. Women are typically expected to take care of the housework or to fill low-status, low-wage jobs outside the home. Many people have been socialized to believe that women are less creative, less independent, and less capable than men of exercising independent judgment about business or governmental decisions. Men often seem to address women principally as sexual objects, to the point of oral or physical harassment and assault. The depths of women's resentment, fear, and anger may not be grasped even by normally sensitive men. Clearly, just as the problem in the case of minorities is starting to be recognized as a *white* problem, the feminist problem is at least as much a *male* problem as a *female* problem.

In the 1960s and 1970s, a growing feminist movement tried to counter these demeaning attitudes regarding the capabilities and roles of women, to work for equality for women, and to raise the consciousness of both men and women about gender roles. While many premises and goals were shared within this movement, there were differences of analysis and pre-scriptions among groups of feminists. We will distinguish these as equal rights feminism, radical feminism, and socialist feminism.

Equal Rights Feminism. This brand of feminism, of which the National Organization of Women (NOW) is an example, calls for the status and opportunity for women to be equal to those for men in every aspect of social, economic, and political life, but does not seek to otherwise change those systems. Women should be able to have a chance for professional careers or other jobs, just as men do, free of household or family respon-sibilities. To this end, NOW supports state- or employer-provided child-care facilities, the sharing of housework or hiring of outside help, and the rights of women to family-planning assistance and abortion. NOW also insists upon equality in the workplace. This means opening up tradi-tionally male occupations, such as the military, to women, "affirmative action" to employ qualified women, and above all equal compensation.

Equal rights feminism seeks the opportunity for women to compete equally with men for the rewards that society has to offer. These opportu-nities are to be ensured through expanded participation in politics by women to help obtain legislation to protect and advance such opportuni-ties. Although these goals do not fundamentally challenge the family or the socioeconomic system, they generate substantial reaction from men and often from other women as well. The idea of women having independent lives and needs clearly contains serious threats to others' self-conceptions.

Radical Feminism. This version of feminism sees the world in more clear-cut class terms, with the classes being males as the oppressors and females as the oppressed. The biological nature of males and females is more important than race or wealth or economics in any form. The fact that women are the reproducers of the species makes them objects to be owned as property or targets to be possessed. Men become obsessed with power and the manipulation of others, while women learn to be far more sensitive, intuitive, and emotionally developed. A strong separatist current flows within radical feminism; they believe that women are nicer people, and before all else, they should come to appreciate their qualities and enjoy one another.

The remedy that radical feminists see, therefore, focuses on the way that the society shapes sexual attitudes and seeks basic changes in such cultural concepts. Some believe that the society can be restructured from within by learning to accept homosexuality and bisexuality and/or by recognizing expanded and more flexible versions of the family than the traditional nuclear family. Others think that only a social revolution can accomplish liberation of women and that such an upheaval must focus on sexism and patriarchy *first* and economics or politics only secondarily. All radical feminists identify male domination as *the* problem, although their prescriptions then vary sharply.

Socialist Feminism. This approach to feminism combines the socialist critique of class-based exploitation with the feminist critique of male domination. It holds that neither can be eliminated without the other and that total social reconstruction must be accomplished. Socialists are charged with having failed to give sexism and racism equal status with the class struggle, but the socialist analytical framework is accepted as the only one that is comprehensive enough to include both an explanation and a prescription for the oppression of women. Sexism predated capitalism, but has grown together with it so that the two are now mutually supportive, and effective action to liberate women requires a strategy to deal with both at the same time.

Socialist feminists believe that they have much to offer a socialist movement. Paramount is the insight that the *personal* is *political*—that is, everyday life and intimate personal relationships are often shaped by the larger society, its values, social formations, power relationships, and the like. In turn, those everyday life and personal-identity factors *reproduce themselves* in people, thus preparing them to accept those same values, power relationships, and so forth in the future. If the personal-political link is recognized, therefore, it is within the power of every person to initiate the process of social change in his or her own life. And *only* in this way (accompanied, of course, by action to change the world) will the really desirable kind of change eventuate—a change that addresses both capitalism and patriarchy simultaneously not only for men, but for women as well.

The mainstream, or equal rights, feminists (who are clearly dominant within the movement) have gained some legitimacy from their moderation in contrast with the latter two, more radical, versions. Despite being charged with some such radical intentions, NOW and its supporters have achieved some real progress to which they are entitled to point with pride.

Accomplishments of the Feminist Movement

The most impressive accomplishments in changing women's roles have come in the economic marketplace. In the 1950s, women began working outside their homes in increasing numbers, and in the 1970s the trend became a floodtide. But the median earnings of women were far less than those of men, and in the 1980s men's incomes were rising at a more rapid rate. College enrollments of women have also spurted, with women outnumbering men in undergraduate colleges and making up one-quarter of the students in law and medical schools. In at least some social circles there is a new awareness of sexism in everyday language and in everyday assumptions about who should do what kinds of work; many cities and states have made it illegal to discriminate on the basis of sex in hiring or pay.

Still, the feminist movement has experienced serious setbacks as well as some successes, and it is not clear that significant gains can be expected in the future. Although a small number of women have become executives or have achieved high status in prestigious professions, most are still finding low-status, low-paying, dead-end jobs. Because child-care facilities are often inadequate or nonexistent, many women cannot go to school or seek work in industry. The opposition to equality has remained strong and seemed to be mounting as part of an upsurge of conservative lobbying. Many men also seem immune to the new awareness of sexism, although the feminist movement cannot be successful unless men's consciousness of the inequity and the pathology of inequality in gender roles is also raised.

Probably the most publicized goal of the feminist movement has been ratification of the Equal Rights Amendment (ERA), an objective it has found extremely difficult to achieve. The Equal Rights Amendment is a short, simple statement declaring that there shall be no discrimination on the basis of sex. It was sought as one of the early goals of NOW. In March 1972 the Congress passed the amendment and referred it to the states, with the usual stipulation that unless ratification by the necessary two-thirds of state legislatures occurred within seven years, the amendment would be void. Several states immediately ratified the amendment, some in such a hurry to be among the first to do so that charges later arose that they had not carefully considered its implications. But then a reaction set in, an active group of women began to oppose ratification, and the approval by states came only slowly and after protracted debate. In some states the amendment was defeated. Congress eventually extended the time limit for ratification, but the needed state approvals were not forthcoming.

The reasons for the opposition reflected some misconceptions, some consequences of changes and tensions within American society, and a good deal of symbolism. In what would have fit well with Justice Holmes's famous description of a "parade of imaginary horrors," opponents of the amendment dreamed up all manner of possible changes and disruptions of social life that would follow upon ratification. It was said that women would be forced into military combat roles, that all bathrooms would have to be "unisex," that alimony and child support would be abolished, that the traditional role of housewife would be altered beyond recognition, and so forth. What lay behind these exaggerated fears in many cases were feelings of pressure from changes in social values and practices, and particularly a sense of threat to the family from a variety of sources. The ERA seemed to its opponents to be a symbolic endorsement of all these changes and threats. To its supporters, on the other hand, the ERA seemed like simple justice.

Conservative Themes and the New Right

Any process of social change, particularly one with the media visibility of the equality-expanding efforts of the 1960s and early 1970s, is likely to produce a countering reaction. Such a backlash was already developing when the economic decline of the mid- to late-1970s set in, and the combined effect was soon certified by those same media as "the new conservative mood" of the country. The growing sense of military confrontation with the Soviet Union also was welcomed by some as helping to reduce the priority given to all other issues.

The "new conservatism" is actually a collection of several different types of reaction to previous changes and present conditions; some of them are not new at all and most are not conservative. (By "conservative," we mean a view that holds that people are fundamentally unequal in talent or wisdom and that the better-endowed should prescribe for the rest.) Two major themes seem to underlie much of this activity. One is an effort enjoying significant popular support to restore older values, particularly those surrounding the family. The other is the attempt by a defensive and profit-squeezed business community to reduce costs by eliminating regulation, increasing tax advantages, and rolling back the welfare state with its taxing, services, and minimum wage standards. We will touch briefly on some campaigns with popular appeal and on the business counterattack, before concluding with an assessment of the conservative intellectual component associated with these reactions.

Popular Movements. One cause that has enlisted substantial numbers of people working to limit abortions is the Right to Life movement. While opposition to abortion was led by the Catholic Church, many supporters from other faiths opposed abortions as well. Opposition took the form of:

1. Seeking the reversal of the Supreme Court's 1973 opinion holding that states could not constitutionally interfere with women's freedom of choice in early pregnancy or utterly forbid abortion in later pregnancy.
2. Attempting to prevent the use of public funds for abortions on the part of poor or welfare women.
3. Running candidates against, or otherwise taking electoral action to punish, officeholders who supported abortion rights.

In some states with third-party traditions, such as New York, a Right to Life party became a serious factor in state politics.

Related to the Right to Life movement are other campaigns that often draw support from the same or similarly minded people. One is the effort to block the expansion of homosexual rights, which has taken the form of electoral referenda in several communities. Gay men and lesbian women were in several instances able to win nondiscrimination ordinances or pledges so that they could be employed by governments or schools on an open and nondiscriminatory basis. In almost every case, however, counterpressure has been brought to bear, and where elections were forced, the principle of such homosexual rights was defeated. National visibility was gained for this campaign by the efforts of singer Anita Bryant. Another campaign with national visibility was that mounted against the Equal Rights Amendment and the feminist cause in general. As noted earlier, organized pressure was mounted on state legislatures by means of highlighting a variety of undesirable consequences said to follow from ERA ratification.

One factor underlying the wide appeal of each of these movements may be the sense that the traditional family unit is threatened. Although (or perhaps because) a relatively small and declining proportion of families consist of the stereotyped mother, father (both married only once—to each other) and two children, this model has great symbolic weight. Divorce, abortion, homosexuality, and feminism all seem to pose dangers to the ideal, and some people feel that their own self-worth, or perhaps their last refuge in a high-pressure world, is being undermined.

Another popular movement focuses on taxation. Known as the "tax revolt," it charges government at all levels with waste and corruption and particularly with profligate welfare expenditures. It took the form in 1978 of a statewide referendum, "Proposition 13," in California that reduced the state property tax, which was the principal source of state aid to local governments, by about 60 percent. In other states, different forms of tax or expenditure limitations were pressed, often successfully. At the national level, many state legislatures asked Congress to call a constitutional convention to propose a constitutional amendment to limit federal taxation.

The roots of the tax revolt are not difficult to understand. As our earlier analyses show, the tax system as a whole places its heaviest burden upon middle- and low-income groups, and in the 1970s these same people were squeezed even harder by prices that rose faster than most of their incomes.

At the same time, the welfare system must support two kinds of casualties of the economic system: millions of unemployed people (a 6 percent unemployment level has come to be regarded as "normal") and millions of the working poor. In effect, industry is relying on government, through the welfare system, to compensate for the inability of the economic system to provide jobs for all who are able and willing to work, and to provide incomes that are adequate to support a family.

Still, the stark reality to the individual taxpayer is an increasingly tight family budget, higher taxes, higher prices, and constant claims of governmental waste and fraud, especially in administering welfare programs. He or she is understandably troubled, resentful, and easy to persuade that the tax burden is due chiefly to welfare and governmental waste, which are easier targets than price increases for which specific people cannot be blamed or defense expenditures that the public is socialized to accept as being necessary for national security. In California, conservative groups played on these feelings, because the affluent are the chief beneficiaries of tax cuts of the Proposition 13 type, while they would be the chief losers if there were serious tax reforms that eliminated loopholes.

About two-thirds of the tax savings in California go to the corporations that own apartment houses and commercial property rather than to the individual homeowners who provided strong support for Proposition 13. Nor do the cutbacks in public services apply chiefly to welfare programs, which are funded largely by the federal government, although there would be some effect on them. Most cutbacks are felt in the budgets for schools, police and fire protection, health, and recreation—services of great value to the lower class and the middle class. Initially, however, surpluses in the state treasury cushioned some of the impact.

Businesses are not only principal beneficiaries of antitax campaigns, but also leading sponsors. In several instances, corporate financial support has combined with popular energies to bring about reductions in government expenditures and limitations on revenue raising.

A final category of popular movements—the fundamentalist religious groups—has a long history. These groups simultaneously advocate traditional religious values, laissez-faire economics, and vigorous anticommunism. Often supported by very wealthy individuals, themselves frequently self-made millionaires or more, such groups maintain a highly visible radio and television presence and appear to enjoy substantial popular followings.

Business Counterattacks. Although business often feels itself unappreciated, the sense among businesspeople that the corporate economy and free enterprise itself were under attack probably reached a height in the early 1970s. Consumer groups, ecology and environmental groups, muckraking journalists, and a veritable army of government regulators and inspectors seemed bent on eliminating profitability. Business reaction took several forms, from reconstructing public attitudes to extensive financial participation in electoral campaigns to active lobbying in Congress and the executive branch.

Perhaps the most immediately visible business response was the formation of a major new lobbying-and-educating arm in 1973, the Business Roundtable. The chief executives of the nation's largest corporations, who were already organized in the Business Council, a semiofficial body enjoying regular and close advisory contact with the highest officials in the executive branch, decided to form a more open organization to serve lobbying needs with Congress and educating functions with the public. In 1976, thirty-three of the forty-five leaders of the Business Roundtable were also members of the Business Council.[10] The Roundtable originally merged three other business committees that were engaged in lobbying or public education in order to generate more impact. It is supported by 150 member companies that supply a $2.5 million annual budget. According to a leading business journal, the Business Roundtable has, in the short time since its creation, become "business' most powerful lobby in Washington,"[11] credited with having blocked several proconsumer and prolabor bills in the mid- and late-1970s.

The public-education activities of business groups have also been extensive. The themes articulated by the Roundtable and in corporate "institutional" advertising are deregulation, increase in productivity, reduction of government services (and hence taxation and the general wage level), the need for new tax advantages (depreciation, investment incentives), and the imperative of controlling inflation by means of eliminating federal budget deficits. A vital new component of the business effort has been the funding of new "think tanks" to provide business-oriented answers to others' proposals and a rationale for the basic themes of the business campaign. Such independent organizations as the American Enterprise Institute in Washington, the Hoover Institute in Stanford, and several business policy centers at major universities have begun to receive support now totaling more than $20 million per year from corporations or their foundations.

Neoconservative Intellectuals

A number of intellectuals have been in the forefront of the New Right reaction, who have been inspired in part by the new corporate funding, but also in part (as befits the intellectual role) by critically reacting against the conventional wisdom. Many of them were mainstream liberals of the later 1950s or early 1960s who apparently came to believe that too much was being attempted by government. Their view of human nature and the limited possibility of its improvement led to the conviction that the policies of the late 1960s were romantic and impractical. Some even concluded that a new class of impractical elitist intellectuals was seeking to remake

---

[10] G. William Domhoff, *The Powers that Be* (New York: Vintage Books, 1979), p. 79.

[11] *Business Week*, 20 December 1976, p. 63.

the country against the interests and preferences of the majority of lower- and middle-class people. Such leaders of opinion as Irving Kristol, Daniel Patrick Moynihan, Edward Banfield, James Q. Wilson, Seymour Lipset, and others of similar age and experience mounted a campaign to relegitimate a conservative approach to social policy.

By the early 1980s, business seemed to be well on its way to repairing the policy damage wrought earlier. Economic decline made the business case appear more compelling, at least in the eyes of policymakers. The social policy advances of the 1960s and early 1970s were being criticized from all points on the political spectrum; they were not enough and/or badly administered—or they were badly conceived and/or far too much—depending on the source. The conflict produced a significant amount of debate and captured such attention as was allowed for domestic issues after foreign policy crises received their priority.

PART V

Political Change

CHAPTER 18

Power and Change: Prospects for the Future

What will emerge from the interplay of changing social and economic conditions and the political ideology, structure, practices, and goal-seeking that we have described? We think the outcome—our future—depends on three key factors:

1. The present distribution of power in the United States and the way that it sustains itself.
2. How changing social and economic conditions generate political effects and perceptions among people.
3. Which people or groups seek what ends through politics and how.

It would be foolish to try to predict what will happen in the future, when we cannot know what changes in domestic conditions or foreign relations will occur or what new forces will arise to seek new goals. But we *can* set up some parameters and state some possibilities. For example, we can sketch the present structure of power in the United States, and explore the ways in which it changes and/or manages to maintain its position. We can state some criteria about changing conditions, and indicate which kinds of effects and perceptions are more likely to create the prospects of certain kinds of change. And we can combine known conditions and present trends to develop some relatively plausible scenarios for the kinds of change that are most likely to occur. These three tasks are what we will discuss in this chapter.

Before we do so, however, we should touch base with an early theme of this analysis that will take on a stronger presence as we proceed. This is our initial point that the American political system represents neither extreme that its advocates and detractors hold out as characterizations; it is neither democracy nor despotism, but rather a much subtler set of relationships. We have seen far too much inequality and lack of opportunity to accept the description of the United States as a democracy, without some serious redefinition of that concept. But we have not seen Americans as being totally lacking in their capacity to affect outcomes, or as being wholly subject to the preferences of some fixed group of rulers.

Much depends on latent potential, on what people want and seek in politics, and on how far their determined efforts can bend or reshape the existing structures and practices of the political system. The vital importance of this fact is that the future directions of the American polity are open to the preferences of people in general; if enough people want something badly enough, the chances are that they can get it. The process will not be easy in most cases, but they can usually achieve the ends they seek if they work hard and effectively in or around the channels of American politics. That is the basic theme of this book: we live in a time when basic changes are on the agenda, and the question is only what direction they will take; and *that* question is almost completely up to the choices to be made by Americans, individually and collectively. Let us proceed to take up each of the three tasks outlined earlier, and then return to this question.

POWER DISTRIBUTION IN THE UNITED STATES

We have characterized the distribution of power in the United States throughout this book in terms of an establishment, or a generally continuing body of people who hold distinctive power as a result of their institutional positions, family ties, talents, or wealth. We also noted that in the 1980s there appeared to be cracks in this establishment, such that two major segments were contending with each other. One was the Sun Belt grouping of free-market advocates and defense suppliers who held a strong anticommunist ideology, and the other was an eastern, internationalist, financial interest with more flexible ideas about foreign relations.

What this division within the establishment means is that, at least on some issues, there are unusual openings for people to seek their goals. The more the external social and economic conditions create uncertainty and divisions among elites, the more ordinary citizens have an opportunity to affect outcomes. The question is whether they see their chances to do so, and how they will go about that effort. Let us think first about what it means to have such an establishment, with its traditions of holding together, and then about what this means for democracy.

The concept of an *establishment*, although vague and subject on occasion to overtones of conspiracy, has an expressiveness that justifies its use. For us the term encompasses individuals holding positions of power (in government *and* private affairs) who have come to share roughly the same values, interests, political ideology, and sense of priorities about what government should be doing. Most of all, it denotes a shared proprietary concern for the continued success of the enterprise—meaning the American system in its familiar social, economic, and political dimensions. Admission to the establishment is not easy, and it is never automatic. It is contingent first on possession of some distinct power resource. Among the many men and women with such resources, some are distinguished by their concern for the success of the enterprise, their willingness to play by the familiar rules, and their talent for finding and articulating the compromise or making the sacrifice that ensures conflict reduction. These are the crucial attributes. It is such people whom established leaders will invite into the loose and highly informal establishment. Members recognize one another not by labels or lapel pins, but by the orthodoxy they share—for example, the readiness with which they can negotiate with one another, even across class lines or occupational boundaries. Establishment types are "regular guys" who try to understand the other fellow's problems, avoid "rocking the boat" publicly, and instead do what they can to reach accommodations in which all end up better off than when they started. Mutual trust, mutual support, and mutual advantage knit the establishment together, but it is never so self-conscious and coherent as when challenges arise to the very system that has made possible this relaxed and congenial arrangement.

The establishment recognizes its antagonists on both the left and the right, uses their complaints to demonstrate its own middle-road propriety, but acts against them only when they "go too far." In part, this is because the establishment has loose margins at either side, some useful part-time members who move back and forth, and it prefers to act only at such late stages that practically all its members and supporters will concur that "something must be done." (This was true, for example, when conservatives took the lead in the late stages of undermining Senator Joseph McCarthy in the 1950s and again when liberals formed the cutting edge of prosecution of radicals and peace movement leaders in the 1960s.) Within the establishment itself, consensus is highly valued. Members may disagree on occasion, particularly over the *best* means by which to preserve the system in times of crisis, without risking their membership, unless their convictions lead them into taking antisystem, instead of system-preserving, actions.

Thus, our concept of establishment does not suggest that a unified upper social class totally and automatically dominates the nation's political structure, although great wealth and upper-class connections serve many as platforms from which they can achieve such a status. Nor do we see economic imperatives as being the sole determinants of establishment actions, although in the absence of compelling reasons to the contrary, they will often be the "natural" principles of behavior. We do not even envision much explicit consultation among establishment members about positions on issues, partly because none is necessary. Our concept of an establishment is not a tight ruling class, but neither is it the benevolent representative statesmen envisioned by some democratic pluralists. Our establishment ranges between the two, depending on the type of issue involved. On most routine issues and decisions, it may function much as the latter view suggests, but on fundamental questions or when the system itself is threatened, it acts in ways characteristic of the former.

Social background and shared responsibility for the management of public affairs are not the only factors operating to cause decisionmakers at this level to see issues from a single perspective. Most people in key positions are of roughly the same generation and thus they became politically "aware" at the same period in American history. All of us tend to be structured permanently by what was happening in politics at the time we happened to tune in to such matters. For one generation, Vietnam meant opposition to a callous and wasteful foreign policy. For many of their teachers, however, political socialization occurred during the early days of the cold war or the late years of World War II, when one did not question the need to defend the "free world" and to resist the spread of communism. For those who made up the establishment in the 1960s, the structuring experiences dated back to pre–World War II failures to contain Hitler, and their actions showed that they remembered those lessons. The analogy to Munich and the inevitable failure of appeasement was offered again and again as a rationale for American policy in Vietnam.

The image of international communism as a unified, monolithic force was shared by most decisionmakers. Thus, wherever trouble broke out in the world, including the United States, the guiding hand of Moscow was discerned. An oft-cited classic example is the allegation by Dean Rusk, made two years after the Chinese Revolution, while he was in charge of Far East operations for the State Department, that Mao Tse-tung was a Russian agent. Mao's regime, he asserted, was "a colonial Russian government—a Slavic Manchukuo on a large scale—it is not the government of China. It does not pass the first test. It is not Chinese."[1] The point is not that anyone can be wrong on occasion; it is that each generation shares a basic image of what is going on in politics and what is likely to happen that is created largely by the lessons its members have drawn from experiences at the outset of their careers. As a result, today's establishment shares an understanding of the world derived from the 1940s and before.

The Establishment View of the World

The convergence and rigidification of beliefs and principles of action among the top echelon of decisionmakers is further aided by some characteristic features of large-scale organizations. Once a position has been taken and the organization has become committed to it in terms of allocation of resources and the career investments of personnel, it is very difficult to modify its methods, purposes, or actions. Many large agencies of the national government, such as the FBI and the State Department, are now

---

[1] Dean Rusk, as quoted in Ronald Steel, *Pax Americana* (New York: Viking, 1967), p. 129. In 1961 Rusk became secretary of state, serving in that capacity until 1969.

committed to a view of the world, a set of procedures, and an understanding of how things should work that reflect and support the establishment's principles. They see, and report to their superiors, what is consistent with their expectations and career aspirations. One classic example of the triumph of organizational commitments over evidence is the experience of strategic bombing during World War II.[2] The Air Force and its supporters had insisted for years that bombing alone could destroy German war production, cripple the armed forces, and eliminate the German people's will to fight. The U.S. Air Force accordingly had been designed and trained for strategic bombing, which was carried out with high optimism and massive loads of explosives. However, according to the careful postwar Strategic Bombing Survey that was undertaken by the Air Force itself, strategic bombing never seriously affected war production, had little or no effect on the capacity of the armed forces or the will of the population, and incurred heavy losses in the bargain. Intelligence failures, equipment failures, and faulty analysis of the German economy and society were also to blame, but the chief explanation was simply the incapacity of bombing to accomplish the goals set for it. The same conclusion was arrived at by a similar official study in Japan at the end of hostilities there. The Vietnamese experience suggests that lessons about the limited capabilities of air power have still not been learned.

An establishment of relatively small size thus receives many self-confirming and supporting messages from its environment. Its approach to politics and its view of the world are validated by almost every trusted source—in bureaucratic memoranda, in the communications media, and at the country club. Attitudes and practices may, under such circumstances, become hardened. Supported by belief in the rightness of their actions, and even in the sacred nature of their responsibility to defend the system against those who would undermine it, members of the establishment may become highly resistant to basic change.

This does not mean, however, that they are insensitive or inflexible. Indeed, long-term stability is promoted by short-term flexibility (within limits) and adroit channeling of thrusts toward change—in part through judicious use of available coercive power. Although one major characteristic of the establishment is its shared basic beliefs and principles of political action, it would be a gross misinterpretation to see such agreement extending to rigidity of *membership* or of *specific policies*. Indeed, one of the most stability-producing features of American ideology and practice—of the American system, in other words—is its flexibility. By opening itself to new members, new ideas, and new policies, the American system incorporates thrusts toward change into its upper-level consensus. *Such new members, ideas, and policies must, however, accept the basic framework of political*

---

[2] This account is drawn from Herbert Wilensky, *Organizational Intelligence: Knowledge and Policy in Government and Industry* (New York: Basic Books, 1967), pp. 24–34.

values, ideology, structure, and style on which that system is based. To the extent that they do, of course, extrasystemic movements for change are effectively blunted. Popular movements lose their leaders and their platforms. New governmental policies include enough of their proposals to give the appearance of progress—and reasons for unusual political activity no longer exist.

Co-optation, Flexibility, and Stability

The process by which rising leaders with new ideas or programs are drawn into the establishment is known as *co-optation.* Many aspiring young men and women seek leadership positions and try to display their ideas and talents in such a way as to make themselves candidates for co-optation. Others find that their efforts on behalf of a particular constituency gain attention and produce opportunities to take on governmental responsibility and carry out some of the programs they have been urging. In both cases, establishment-arranged appointments to offices or aid in electoral advancement lead to rises in stature and responsibility. The sobering consequences of responsibility then combine with the real difficulties of achieving goals through the complex political process to induce the candidate to practice the skills of accommodation and mutual support that are the hallmark of the establishment. A candidate who demonstrates these skills and concern for the maintenance of the essential outlines of the system will rise further; one who does not will soon decide to leave government, thereby losing prospective establishment status.

Co-optation does not mean that new leaders give up their independence, ideas, or program entirely. They retain substantial proportions of each, but learn to adapt them to the framework of the established system so that they are compatible with it. They frequently do succeed in changing things, if they are skillful advocates of their causes, but not as much as they might originally have wished (and for reasons that they—and we—might rightly consider to be fully persuasive). The directions of public policy may shift in response to such initiatives after strenuous efforts by their new leaders, their supporters, and the new allies their establishment status has made available to them. When the process has run its course, some new policies have been instituted, the basic complaints against the system have been reduced, the establishment has absorbed new members, and the system has acquired new defenders. The basic outlines of the system have again survived. Flexibility in the short run, in other words, means permanence in the long run.

Other types of flexibility also contribute to the stability of the American political system. Many layers of government make for many alternative ways to achieve particular goals, and people who seek ends unacceptable to those in power may be directed from one government to another, from one type of approach to another, or from one branch, committee, or department to another. Demands that at first seem indigestible or extreme may be converted into another form and thereby rendered satisfiable. A minority group's demand for status and recognition may be salved by appointing a prominent leader to a visible position or by naming a public monument or park in the group's honor. If the group is not quieted by such costless tactics, then it may be diverted by channeling its claims into aggression against another minority religious or racial group. Some claims can be converted into economic demands or settled largely on such terms.

The materialistic orientation of the people and the abundance of the economy have made this a recurring tactic throughout American history. By merely increasing the size of the total economic product and directing the new surplus toward the demanding group, its claims could be satisfied without depriving those who were already advantaged of any of their possessions or expectations. In the history of labor-management conflicts, for example, an increase in total production and therefore total profits (or an increase in price to the consumer) made it possible to grant higher wages without reducing owners' returns. Workers, for their part, tended to be satisfied by higher wages and to abandon other goals, such as control over the means of production.

Flexibility is thus a means of absorbing, blunting, and deflecting thrusts toward change, but flexibility does not operate alone to promote stability. It functions in tandem with other factors to induce or compel behavior into the established channels. American political ideology emphasizes procedural regularity and insists on working through the means provided for the attainment of political goals. The "law-and-order" ethic legitimates action against those who do not follow such prescribed procedures. Under the conditions of the late twentieth century, the official agencies of law enforcement have a vast monopoly over the power that is necessary to compel obedience, and thus, there is a considerable array of inducements at work to direct political activity into forms that can be dealt with by the established order without serious threat.

Over the years, these factors have helped to render the American system stable—in itself a desirable characteristic for a political system to enjoy. Most people probably would assess the costs of this stability (in terms of lost opportunities, unfulfilled aspirations, poverty for some, and the like) as entirely tolerable. To many, stability is the highest priority in politics. Whether stability continues to be equally desirable today, measured against possibly greater costs and more challenging conditions, is a more acute and more controversial question. After an extended period of stability, however, unabsorbed pressures for change may build to explosive potential, or issues may arise that even the most flexible system will have difficulty containing.

Implications for Democracy

How is it that so many Americans can so firmly believe that the United States is a democracy, when the evidence so clearly points to rule by the establishment on behalf of the corporate-banking sector of the economy? Part of the answer must lie with the power of ideology and symbolism, described in Chapter 6. But part may also be found in the way democracy has come to be defined in the United States. We understand democracy entirely in terms that are compatible with capitalism and its associated structure of power; in other words, we know only *liberal democracy*. This is a kind of democracy that emphasizes the participation of citizens in elections and in communications to their government (writing letters, lobbying, and the like), stresses the availability of civil liberties, and endorses regular procedures for elite decisionmaking. Freedom means only the absence of government interference, and equality means only the opportunity to take part in economic and social life. It is a *procedural* definition of democracy, one that ignores as much about the world as does the pluralists' exclusive focus on governmental institutions.

A contrasting definition of democracy would be *substantive* in character—that is, it would emphasize the *content* of public policies, the *conditions* of people's lives, and the *quality* of their daily experiences. Substantive democracy would compare people's wants and needs with what the government was actually doing and measure the extent of democracy by what that government *did* rather than merely by the fact that people were able to vote for decisionmakers. Substantive democracy would focus on the conditions of people's lives and insist that equality should have social and economic dimensions and that people therefore should be roughly equal in wealth, status, and power, because only in that way can they be truly equal politically. Freedom would become the ability to do things, which would require the removal of constraints flowing from private power and vast development of people's human talents and potential. And substantive democracy would be concerned for people's relationships with other people, their sense of dignity, and their happiness.

If most Americans accepted the substantive definition of democracy, they would not so readily describe the United States as a democracy. It is crucial to governance by the few in the United States that most people accept the procedural definition of democracy, and it is a major ideological achievement that they have been led to do so. Definitions are by no means unimportant, and much intense political struggle takes place in a very quiet way over what definitions are to be inculcated in people. There *have* been advocates of the substantive definition of democracy in our history: some abolitionists, some black thinkers, some populists, some socialists, and some feminists. Part of the radical left today seeks to raise just this issue. Whether they can successfully put the question of change into the form of an effort to fully realize democracy in its substantive sense may be the real key to progressive change in the future.

THE ANALYSIS OF POLITICAL CHANGE: A FRAMEWORK

At the outset, we should recognize that there is often no direct, logical, or "rational" relationship between events or conditions and perceptions or consequences of them. The central theme of symbolic analysis of politics is the *gap* between perceptions or beliefs on the one hand and actual gains or losses in money, power, status, or tangible goods on the other. As political conflict escalates, this gap becomes wider.

The winner of symbolic victories may not be the winner of tangible victories. As an international war or "police action" escalates, the low- and middle-income citizens of the country that is victorious on the battlefield may find their taxes far more burdensome, their lives more regimented, and their sons and relatives killed or wounded. But they are "the winners." Defenders of civil rights who win a court decision guaranteeing that accused persons will be provided with lawyers and information about their procedural rights may later learn that actual practices in the stationhouse have changed little or not at all. Citizens, whose outcries against arbitrary rate increases and poor service by a public utility bring about legislation to protect consumer interests, have won a symbolic victory, but this form of political triumph rarely brings about lower rates or better service for long. The regulatory agency often makes it easier for the utility to raise rates.

Other disparities between perceived and real changes in policy consequences become evident as political conflict widens and intensifies. Benefits often come to be perceived as deprivations and vice versa. As international conflict grows hotter, the armed forces gain larger appropriations for weapons, new powers to draft soldiers, higher status, and more influence on governmental decisions. It is chiefly the poor and the lower middle class whose sons are drafted to fight, whose incomes are disproportionately taxed, and whose influence on governmental decisions is least. Rather than appearing as real benefits and losses for a specific group of people, however, these changes are perceived and publicized as "costs" of defense, or sacrifices the nation as a whole must valiantly assume to combat its enemies.

Even the identification of enemies and allies becomes confused and uncertain and may fail to correspond to observable reality as conflict escalates. Such confusion is not accidental; it is a consistent and systematic aspect of political conflict. It is important to create perceptions that induce people to fight, and to sacrifice if necessary, to serve a noble cause and to defeat an evil one. In international conflict, the belief is fostered that the country is uniting to defeat a common enemy. In fact, there are always internal divisions about whether and how seriously the fight should be waged and whether the enemy is really harmful or malevolent. These internal divisions partly reflect the differences in interest noted earlier. Escalation means that the more hawkish or militant groups are winning more support than their dovish rivals. As already noted, hawkish groups win support for their foreign counterparts as they win it for themselves, although this tacit cooperation is systematically masked by belief in the implacable hostility of the two countries.

As civil rights conflict escalates, the same ambiguities appear. Here the symbolic conflict is between believers in "the rights of minorities" and believers in "law and order." These symbols unite people on both sides and bolster political support. At the same time, there are tangible gains and losses for both supporters and opponents of civil rights that do not correspond to the symbolic definition of the situation. As civil rights conflict grows more intense, the more militant groups on both sides win tangible benefits and the less militant ones lose. White supremacists and civil libertarians win followings and money as public opinion is polarized. The police get larger appropriations for personnel and weapons, higher status and more influence for top police officials, and greater authority over others. The more militant black groups gain moral and financial support at the expense of the Urban League and white liberals. To make this point is to recognize both that there is competition for tangible benefits within groups of symbolic allies and that escalation benefits militants, whereas détente benefits moderates and compromisers. There is, then, a systematic link between symbol and fact, but it is a link that conceals or distorts the facts and thus can evoke political support for self-defeating policies.

Most political conflict is ritualistic. It is confined within narrow limits and pursued through mutually accepted routines; furthermore, it serves more to justify than to determine outcomes, for they are largely predetermined by long-standing differences in bargaining resources. Election campaigns (especially in a two-party system), the procedures of regulatory administrative agencies, and most international arms and trade negotiations are examples of such ritualized conflict. To the minor degree that they bring about policy changes, their functions are generally recognized and reported in the news. Insofar as they serve to promote wide public acceptance of leaders and of policy outcomes (that is, serve symbolic functions), news reports typically miss their significance.

Political leaders retain followings (which are, of course, what makes them leaders) by means of a number of devices that are basically symbolic in character. We ordinarily think of leaders as being people who point the way for others through unusual abilities, wisdom, courage, or force of personality, but leaders can often retain their positions, whether they have these qualities, by creating in their followers a belief in their ability to cope. We have just seen that ritualized conflict creates such a belief. Other common political actions do so as well. Leaders who are resolute and forceful and seem confident in a situation that makes most people anxious and uncertain reassure the public and create a following, whether their actions succeed or fail. Those who are bewildered want very much to believe that their political leaders can cope. President Kennedy's seemingly resolute action in the disastrous Bay of Pigs invasion of Cuba in 1961 and President Reagan's decisive action in Grenada in 1983 illustrate the point. Survey data show that presidential popularity consistently rises after such dramatic actions, whether they succeed or fail or are ambiguous in their consequences. Clearly, it is not the leader's skills, courage, and effectiveness that bring political success in such cases, but rather his or her dramaturgy and the anxieties of mass publics.

When is change likely to occur in the structure of policies of the American political system? What circumstances determine the form it will take?

Our approach is based on the premise that certain preconditions cause pressure to be exerted on the fundamental aspects of the political system. If they are strong enough, modifications of both mass and elite behavior follow, and—depending on the particular configuration of factors, forces, behavior, and events—political change of various kinds and directions then occurs. We shall take up three areas in which the preconditions of change are likely to be generated and then identify some of the major factors that determine the degree and kind of effect such conditions will have on the political system. We shall then consider four alternative types of political change that are possible in the United States and the prerequisites and processes associated with each of them.

The Preconditions of Change

In one sense political change is continuous. Governing elites regularly make adjustments in established policies or undertake major policy initiatives in response to changing conditions. Such changes may, and often do, result in alterations in domestic economic or social relationships or in international affairs. One example is the emergence of cold war foreign policy and the related evolution of massive defense and space programs. Another is the decision to institute a "war on poverty." But we term these changes *marginal* because their essential effect is to defend and to promote the established economic and political structures and the existing patterns of distribution of wealth and status within the society. We shall reserve the term *fundamental* for instances of substantial alteration in the economic or political power structures or in key governmental policies bearing on distribution of wealth and status. Fundamental change is drastic in character; it may come about, however, through either violent or relatively peaceful means.

Our approach to the analysis of political change should permit us to distinguish between these two types of change and to acknowledge the relative improbability of the more fundamental type. *Marginal* change is frequent, requiring few preconditions, but *fundamental* change is infrequent and is unlikely to occur without severe pressures on the central concerns of politics that are widely perceived and acted on by masses and elites alike. We would expect fundamental change only when the preconditions begin to disrupt or to seriously threaten the basic organization and operation of the economy, the class structure, existing control over the uses of government's coercive powers, or the established patterns of distribution of wealth and status. The more preconditions generate such effects, the more probable are changes in the structure and uses of political power, the character of political institutions, and the key policies of government. In short, the severity of dislocations in closely related policy areas determines the probability of fundamental *political* change; we shall consider three such areas in the order of their importance for political change.

Changes in the Level and Distribution of Economic Prosperity. The most powerful source of pressure on the political system is the state of the economic system, for the obvious reason that it affects first the very survival and then other avidly sought goals of people in all social settings. Despite its image of stability, American politics has always been highly sensitive to fluctuations and dislocations in the economy. When the economy is stable and unemployment limited, the political system is normally free of strain, even though distribution of economic rewards is very unequal, but if either inflation or recession occurs, pressures begin to build up, and distribution differences become salient and provocative. If a depression develops, pressures may become truly explosive.

Social Tensions and Underlying Value Changes. A second—and potentially quite independent—major source of pressure on the political system is the rise of tensions and open conflict among major segments of the society. Such conflict is often associated with, and normally exacerbated by, rapid changes in the level and distribution of economic prosperity or other major technological changes, but it can also be generated by noneconomic factors and can culminate in deep and widely felt animosities even during periods of economic affluence.

Deep social divisions exist within the United States, rhetorical calls for solidarity and assertions of consensus notwithstanding. The most visible, long-standing, and deeply rooted of these is race. The extent to which racism is entrenched in the psychological makeup, political values, and institutional practices of white America may never be fully understood, but white-black/brown/red tensions escalate with every new assertion of the right to equal status.

The tensions that are grounded in class consciousness are more likely to produce fundamental change than those that are created by the demands of relatively small and containable racial minorities. Suppose that most blue-collar workers and other wage earners—black and white, men and women—should come to perceive themselves as jointly exploited for the benefit of a small group of owners and managers who already hold the vast majority of the nation's wealth. Justice, in their eyes, entitles them to a much larger share of the economic product. Their numbers alone would ensure great impact, if their power could be organized and applied—although that is difficult.

Other sources of tension exist, although none compares with race and class as long-established antagonisms with continuing raw edges. Religious, regional, and rural-urban conflicts remain real and could exert pressure on the political system if particular issues again raise perceptions of deprivation or create frustrations. But new forms of tension that are not rooted in old divisions also exist. One is the general lack of a sense of personal satisfaction that seemed to pervade the United States in the 1970s. Despite such achievements as moon landings and the highest standard of living in the world, many observers saw Americans as lacking contentment, self-confidence, and a sense of purpose. Work seemed to be providing a less meaningful rationale for life and to be less a source of pride than in previous decades. Individuals seemed to be aware of their apparent powerlessness to affect the course of public events or even the private matters touching their own lives.

In the late 1960s and early 1970s, much of the pressure for change in the United States came from the new values developed by young people. Some of these changes emphasized egalitarianism, humanism, participation, and self-fulfillment through a wide variety of individual activities. Their contrast with the materialism, nationalism, conformity, and support for the economic and political status quo of their elders was so sharp that these values together came to be known as a "counterculture." Some young people went beyond the counterculture to join with left intellectuals and trade unionists in a sustained left political movement. Parallel pressures were generated by a growing women's liberation movement that pressed for change that reached deep into the personal relationships and public roles of men and women and potentially into the most basic societal values. All these movements ultimately provoked a vigorous backlash in the form of the New Right, a loose coalition of interests seeking to restore the values and government practices of the 1950s. Conditions, particularly the apparent return to the cold war and military preparedness of that period, seemed to give the latter group a greater prospect of success in the 1980s.

International Tensions and Events. The obvious interdependence of international and domestic affairs means that events overseas often spark economic and social tensions at home. Such developments may serve either to generate massive new pressure on the political system or to deflect already powerful pressures away from it.

The most obvious source of restructured domestic relationships is war or the immediately perceived threat of war. A relatively small, festering war in a distant place, such as Korea or Vietnam, is likely to create new social divisions or to exacerbate tension between left and right; at the same time, it promotes economic well-being and then inflation. A full-scale war or even a small war close to home tends to draw wider support and to eclipse all other issues that might otherwise divide people. More complex effects derive from the threat of armed conflict and from a posture and ideology that support constant readiness for nuclear war. This atmosphere creates underlying tensions while it legitimates many actions and diverts attention from others in the name of patriotism and national security.

However, war and the threat of war are only the most obvious sources of disruptive tensions and the prospect of political change. Sharp changes overseas—such as an oil embargo, nationalization, or severance of trade relations—may reverberate throughout segments of the U.S. economy and induce shortages, diplomatic pressure, or military intervention to restore American advantage. International developments of a noneconomic nature may also have an impact on American life. The increasing militance among American blacks during the 1950s and 1960s was due in part to the example of newly independent African and Asian nations whose nonwhite leaders acquired power and led their countries effectively and with great pride.

This brief analysis of some sources of intrasocietal tensions and conflicts that are sufficient to raise the possibility of fundamental political change is merely illustrative, and not comprehensive. No doubt there are many other causes of pressure on the political system, but our point is that substantial pressures must be generated from *some* source before established econopolitical relationships are likely to undergo change of a fundamental kind. If there are several such pressures, and if they converge or overlap in such a way as to be mutually reinforcing (rather than pitting different groups against one another in a self-canceling and immobilizing fashion), the prospect of such change is greater.

The Political Impact of the Preconditions of Change

Preconditions are thus necessary, but not sufficient, causes of fundamental change. What is crucial for our purposes is the manner in which such preconditions become translated into effects on the political system. Multiple sources of tension clearly exist; some of them are deep and others are worsening. But there have always been some such tensions, and fundamental political change has not occurred in more than a century. Depressions and severe social tensions have given rise to militant parties and movements that seek fundamental change, but they have failed to achieve their goals. (Sometimes, of course, depression and serious social tensions do not inspire action at all. They may send people into withdrawal, apathy, or destructive scapegoating; or, they may redouble support for the status quo through the helpless conviction that "happiness is just around the corner.") Social tensions must not only produce converging and mutually reinforcing perceptions of deprivation, but must also be translated into politics in particular ways before they are likely to generate fundamental change. We can identify several prerequisites, which if they are fulfilled, will make fundamental change more likely. Again, we do not see it as necessary or inevitable for all these political effects to be present in order for change to take place, but the prospect of change will increase as each is fulfilled. We shall frame the conditions as three basic questions.

1. How fully do existing dislocations, tensions, and underlying value changes disrupt established patterns of distribution and detach masses of people from their previous commitments to the dominant political values, ideology, and behavior? *For fundamental change to occur, there must be a decrease in the supportive attitudes of people toward their government; its legitimacy must be eroded, and a vacuum of authority must develop.* This is a long-term process, of course, and must be deep-seated enough to counteract the best efforts of the major socializing and interpreting agents (schools, mass media) of the existing system. It also requires visible, legitimate leadership, but leaders are not likely to arise until the trend of popular change is already under way. Thus, the impetus toward change in values must be self-generated. Social and economic conditions, international events, or personal experience must create perceptions of such serious personal deprivation that people will question the legitimacy of the established political values and practices. Such perceptions of contradiction or unworkability in the present system must be strong enough to survive explanations and diversions like the alleged failure of individuals, racial

antagonisms, symbolic appeals, anticommunism, and so forth. An extended and cumulating series of these perceptions are probably necessary to drive people to develop new priorities for political action and to seriously consider alternatives to the present system. Without deep doubts about established values, at the very least, proposals or movements for change will be ignored, dismissed, or resisted by the very people who constitute an almost irreplaceable component in the process.

2. How much (and what kind of) power can be mobilized by change-oriented elements within the society, and how does such power relate to elites' power resources? Almost by definition, those who feel personal deprivation in such a way as to commit themselves to fundamental change do not possess large or immediately effective power resources. A few wealthy, well-connected, or strategically located persons may identify with the causes of the deprived and serve as leaders or key supporters, but most persons with access to major power resources are probably either already members of the establishment or at least persuaded that the basic structures and values are acceptable and that only marginal change is required. *Fundamental change thus normally requires the mobilization of the latent power resources of the currently powerless.* Numbers become crucial. Regardless of how slight their individual power, if a substantial segment of the population becomes committed to unified action in support of fundamental change, their joint power is immense. Strategic location within the economy or society is also important. Effective strikes in vital service-providing fields (governmental functions, transportation, and the like) greatly multiply the power of relatively small numbers of people.

The most crucial factors for mobilizing the powerless into a potentially successful force for fundamental change are *organization* and *communication.* Organization means the emergence of groups of people whose commitment is so complete that they subordinate all economic and other personal goals and make single-minded efforts to awaken numbers of other people to the need for (and prepare them for the action necessary to) achieving fundamental change. Organization building requires a supportive environment for group members so that their commitments are regularly reinforced and new members are recruited. It also requires substantial agreement on (or at least only limited conflict over) the basic strategy by which change is to be accomplished.

The need for communication has both internal and external dimensions. There must be regular exchanges of information and effective coordination between the geographically (and perhaps in some ways ideologically) separated units of the growing organization, and there must be communication between the organizers and the people whom they seek to mobilize. Unless numbers of people can be brought to support the organized movement, or at least detached from their support of established ways and thus neutralized, the movement has little real prospect for success. It will either gradually become aware of its failure and dissipate or be forced into isolation and resort to indiscriminate terrorism or other desperate and self-destructive measures.

The task of mobilizing numbers of people into a unified, change-seeking force is very difficult. Previously inert individuals must acquire a sense of political efficacy and hope that is strong enough to impel them to action. Various means of attracting attention and reaching people in terms they can readily identify with and understand are necessary; action, deliberate self-sacrifice, rational persuasion, and blatant propaganda all play parts at various stages. As organization progresses, a series of minor skirmishes in which victories over established institutions or procedures are scored probably contributes to the awakening of self-confidence and determination. The bases of solidarity among people must be developed over time and against a background of deep-seated suspicions, divisions, prejudices, and misunderstandings. Without the development of such organization and its promotion of broad support, fundamental change seems unlikely.

3. How do established elites react to forces seeking fundamental change? Existing elites' behavior plays a vital role in the evolving process of change, because they hold the initiative and have a responsibility to act in response to events. They may act to promote divisions and hostility within the population and/or to isolate and discredit groups seeking change, thereby making mobilization difficult or impossible. They may appear to institute, or actually make, marginal changes in policies in order to reduce popular perceptions of deprivation, thereby undercutting (or, in some circumstances, promoting) the thrust toward fundamental change. They may introduce wholly new issues or appeals, such as space exploration, war, or the threat of war, which redirect attention or mobilize support for the existing order. They may also engage in active repression of change-seeking groups. If this is done with sophistication and restraint, it may help to solve their problem, but if handled crudely, it can provide the movement with substantial new constituencies.

In each case, it is clear that elite response shapes the opportunities and problems of change seekers. What determines how elites act? In part it depends on which segment of the establishment is currently dominant within the executive branch. The eastern upper class, the managers of the great corporations, and welfare-state liberals tend to react with modest policy changes, deflection, and sophisticated repression. Those who are newer to real power and more steeped in the ideology than the practice of American government, such as the southern and southwestern individualist-conservatives, are more likely to react by exaggerating the threat, appealing to popular fears and prejudices, and escalating open repression.

Neither set of behaviors by itself determines whether the movement for change will gain or lose momentum as a result. What it does, essentially, is to shape the degree of polarization in the society. When accompanied by the disaffection, tensions, and loss of legitimacy described earlier, and when there is a cohesive organization that is ready to act with substantial popular support, a highly polarized situation that is ripe for fundamental change may be created. What is then required is a spark—the fortuitous event that creates the opportunity for the movement to cross the threshold to real and sweeping impact of some kind. Then, if the existing organization has the skill (or the sheer determination, which may often overcome lack of skill or the absence of some important conditions) to apply its power decisively, the whole structure of power may be sharply altered. Violent revolution need not occur, although violence undoubtedly plays a major role in promoting change of a fundamental nature. Established elites are quite unlikely to release their grip on governmental power unless they are convinced that it is necessary or inevitable that they do so. Often the escalation of the stakes that results from serious and repeated mutual violence has created such conviction. A relatively low level of violence, if sustained and accompanied by credible threats of more to follow, has sometimes induced elites to acquiesce in, or even to institute, major changes that have been sought in a relatively peaceful manner. Once the process of change has reached this point, developments are no longer even crudely predictable. The outcome depends on such factors as key individuals' personalities and chance.

We can summarize these general observations about the politics of change in terms of a contrast between top-down and bottom-up processes of change. Thus far, we have been speaking chiefly of fundamental change and its prerequisites; marginal change is almost always possible, at the almost exclusive option of establishment elites. To be sure, there are limits within which such elites must select their policy options, but these are chiefly of their own making and only partially subject to popular preferences. In a fundamental change situation, however, elites have lost their predominance. They are either fragmented and beginning to contend with one another or struggling to maintain themselves against the demands of a newly powerful antagonist arising from outside their ambit. Clearly, we are dealing with two contrasting levels and processes of change. Change initiated from the top down by established elites occurs because of their perceptions and needs, or perhaps through gradual changes in their membership. Such changes are likely to affect only minor policies that are well within the established power system—or, in short, to be *incremental* changes. Only when a thrust from outside the establishment (that is, from below) begins to have an impact on elites' power and status does fundamental change become a possibility. The agency of change must be created by the previously powerless and must build on deep social tensions and/or value changes to force its way into the political arena. The more such thrust is generated from below, the more the system itself is the target, and the more likely is fundamental change.

DIRECTIONS OF CHANGE: THREE SCENARIOS

So far, we have said nothing about the *direction* that either marginal or fundamental change may take. Clearly, either may go to the left, in the direction of wider distribution of wealth, status, and power within the society, or to the right, toward more rigid insistence on the status quo or even narrower and more restrictive distribution. We shall reduce the many possibilities to a total of three, which are listed in the order of their likelihood:

1. A centrist marginal change, culminating in either decline, disintegration, and chaos *or* a corporatist system in which the major corporations dominate.
2. A New Right–forced realignment, in which the United States embarks on a program of domestic authoritarian-populism and a kind of Fortress America nationalism in foreign affairs.
3. A class-based realignment in which the elements of the "rainbow coalition" form the nucleus of an unprecedented left-oriented majority grouping of voters.

Marginal Change, Leading to Chaos or Corporatism. This scenario assumes that no major depression develops, but that economic conditions remain troublesome for many, such as when inflation remains a threat and unemployment rises above 6 percent. Class consciousness stays low, and radicals are irrelevant except as they are said to pose the threat of terrorism and therefore create the need for surveillance and concern. Threats of nuclear war continue, but no major land war is fought outside the Western hemisphere. In short, basic conditions create no major new dislocations and leave established elites well entrenched.

But the trend lines are inescapably down, meaning that pressure continues to build up to *do* something. The continued success of the great corporations seems to depend more and more on government assistance. This is the point on which the actual direction of the society turns. If government is employed to help the corporations in the way that the new generation of technocratic liberals and forward-looking businesses desire, the ultimate result will be *corporatism.* This term means an integrated system in which business, government, and labor act in partnership to run the country for the principal benefit of business. The needs of people come second, and their capacity to shape the actions of government lessens significantly.

If government is *not* employed to help the corporations in this unprecedented and systematic manner, then the economy's decline will pick up speed. Inflation will increase to new heights, while unemployment will also climb; both are the results of an inability to compete successfully in the world economy and business's determination to cut costs to the bone. A relative few soon will be doing quite well, but most people will suffer steady reductions in their standards of living. Tensions between races, classes, and various other groups will rise, and ultimately a general chaos will ensue. Out of this may come any number of possible new systems, or none at all.

New Right–Catalyzed Change to Populist Authoritarianism and Fortress America. This scenario assumes not only that a major depression is avoided, but also that a level of economic prosperity is attained that is sufficient to allow the populist-conservatives of the New Right to attend exclusively to noneconomic issues. In that way, the New Right can preserve its unity around the social issues (family, religion, schools, and abortion), anticommunism, and tax reduction. (If economic hardships press in on New Right voters, they will be tempted to emphasize the New Deal-type programs that they support, which will bring them back into alliance with Democratic Party elements and other working-class people.)

In time, the New Right will find that the Republican Party is unable or unwilling to fulfill its nostalgic aspirations for returning American values and practices to what they were in the early twentieth century. The New Right, which is deeply grounded in fundamentalist religious values and very well organized through the churches and its own direct-mail system, will then have to decide on its choices. Concentration on a religious fourth Great Awakening will not be enough, because the commitment to politics is too strong. The choice must be whether to take over the Republican Party or to begin a third party that is created in the image of New Right principles from the start.

In either case, a major realignment of voters and parties would follow. The New Right's movement out in search of the old values and the restoration of American national grandeur might be unsuccessful or very dangerous, perhaps provoking a nuclear war. At the least, it would mean a polarized reaction on the left, in which many people would seek to prevent it from attaining its goals by forming a strong opposition party. The center of the political spectrum would be likely to suffer the most, although there might at first be several fragmenting parties that try to consolidate the opposition. However, initiative would remain for some time with the New Right, as the best-organized and most powerful of the newer forces in American politics.

A Class-Based Realignment Around the Rainbow Coalition on the Left. This scenario assumes that economic conditions worsen considerably, perhaps even ending in a depression. Only such conditions can force the separate units of the reform-oriented center-to-left portion of the American spectrum into a viable coalition for any length of time. The polarization that occurred in the mid-1980s in reaction to President Reagan's cutbacks in social programs and deliberate upward redistribution of income might indicate that more such movement could occur, as we discussed in Chapter 16. The point is that some external force—such as a depression, a dramatic move to the right by the New Right, or continued polarizing pressure from the Reagan administration—is needed to bring the left together.

The one sign of self-generated capability to bring disparate groups together on the left is in the "backyard revolution"[3] of many different

---

[3] The phrase is Harry Boyte's. See his *The Backyard Revolution: Understanding the New Citizen Movement* (Philadelphia: Temple University Press, 1980). See also John Herbers, "Grass Roots Groups Go National," *The New York Times Magazine,* September 4, 1983, p. 22.

citizens' groups that began to act coherently together in the early 1980s. Taking the New Right's mastery of communications and cooperative efforts as a model, many different environmental, anti-nuclear power, antiwar, and neighborhood groups started to support candidates and practice a much more sophisticated brand of politics. Organized labor, however, despite its decline and continued vulnerability, still seemed more inclined to go its own way. We believe that no left-oriented movement can hope to be successful without a full commitment and real support from organized labor.

None of these scenarios has much merit as a potential description of directions in American politics without taking into account the profound changes in social and economic—and political—circumstances that are being wrought by the ongoing transformation in which we are all caught up. Amidst such a transformation, many possibilities become real that might otherwise deserve to be dismissed as fantasy or utopianism. We live in unprecedented times, and we must learn to think and act in unprecedented ways. Much that has been accepted as absolute in American politics for decades has been shown to be subject to change or just plain wrong in the 1980s. The plain, though not always welcome, fact seems to be that the future we get is the future we permit to happen to us—or the future we actively seek.

The Constitution of the United States of America

We the People of the United States, in Order to form a more perfect Union, establish Justice, insure domestic Tranquility, provide for the common defence, promote the general Welfare, and secure the Blessings of Liberty to ourselves and our Posterity, do ordain and establish this Constitution for the United States of America.

Article I

Section 1. All legislative Powers herein granted shall be vested in a Congress of the United States, which shall consist of a Senate and House of Representatives.

Section 2. The House of Representatives shall be composed of Members chosen every second Year by the People of the several States, and the Electors in each State shall have the Qualifications requisite for Electors of the most numerous Branch of the State Legislature.

No Person shall be a Representative who shall not have attained to the age of twenty five Years, and been seven Years a Citizen of the United States, and who shall not, when elected, be an Inhabitant of that State in which he shall be chosen.

Representatives and direct Taxes shall be apportioned among the several States which may be included within this Union, according to their respective Numbers, *which shall be determined by adding to the whole Number of free Persons, including those bound to Service for a Term of Years,* and excluding Indians not taxed, *three fifths of all other persons.*[1] The actual Enumera-

---

[1] Italics are used throughout to indicate passages that have been altered by subsequent amendments. In this case, see Amendment XIV.

tion shall be made within three Years after the first Meeting of the Congress of the United States, and within every subsequent Term of ten Years, in such Manner as they shall by Law direct. The Number of Representatives shall not exceed one for every thirty Thousand, but each State shall have at Least one Representative; and until such enumeration shall be made, the State of New Hampshire shall be entitled to chuse three, Massachusetts eight, Rhode-Island and Providence Plantations one, Connecticut five, New-York six, New Jersey four, Pennsylvania eight, Delaware one, Maryland six, Virginia ten, North Carolina five, South Carolina five, and Georgia three.

When vacancies happen in the Representation from any State, the Executive Authority thereof shall issue Writs of Election to fill such Vacancies.

The House of Representatives shall chuse their Speaker and other Officers; and shall have the sole Power of Impeachment.

Section 3. The Senate of the United States shall be composed of two Senators from each State, *chosen by the Legislature thereof,* [2] for six Years; and each Senator shall have one Vote.

Immediately after they shall be assembled in Consequence of the first Election, they shall be divided as equally as may be into three Classes. The Seats of the Senators of the first Class shall be vacated at the Expiration of the second Year, of the second Class at the Expiration of the fourth Year, and of the third Class at the Expiration of the sixth Year, so that one third may be chosen every second Year; *and if Vacancies happen by Resignation, or otherwise, during the Recess of the Legislature of any State, the Executive thereof may make temporary Appointments until the next Meeting of the Legislature, which shall then fill such Vacancies.* [3]

No Person shall be a Senator who shall not have attained to the Age of thirty Years, and been nine Years a Citizen of the United States, and who shall not, when elected, be an Inhabitant of that State for which he shall be chosen.

The Vice President of the United States shall be President of the Senate, but shall have no Vote, unless they be equally divided.

The Senate shall chuse their other Officers, and also a President pro tempore, in the Absence of the Vice President, or when he shall exercise the Office of President of the United States.

The Senate shall have the sole Power to try all Impeachments. When sitting for that Purpose, they shall be on Oath or Affirmation. When the President of the United States is tried, the Chief Justice shall preside: And no Person shall be convicted without the Concurrence of two thirds of the Members present.

Judgment in Cases of Impeachment shall not extend further than to removal from Office, and disqualification to hold and enjoy any Office of

---

[2] See Amendment XVII.

[3] Ibid.

honor, Trust or Profit under the United States: but the Party convicted shall nevertheless be liable and subject to Indictment, Trial, Judgment and Punishment, according to Law.

Section 4. The Times, Places and Manner of holding Elections for Senators and Representatives, shall be prescribed in each State by the Legislature thereof; but the Congress may at any time by Law make or alter such Regulations, except as to the Places of chusing Senators.

The Congress shall assemble at least once in every Year, and such Meeting shall be on the first Monday in December, unless they shall by Law appoint a different Day.[4]

Section 5. Each House shall be the Judge of the Elections, Returns and Qualifications of its own Members, and a Majority of each shall constitute a Quorum to do Business; but a smaller Number may adjourn from day to day, and may be authorized to compel the Attendance of absent Members, in such Manner, and under such Penalties as each House may provide.

Each House may determine the Rules of its Proceedings, punish its Members for disorderly Behavior, and, with the Concurrence of two thirds, expel a Member.

Each House shall keep a journal of its Proceedings, and from time to time publish the same, excepting such Parts as may in their Judgment require Secrecy; and the Yeas and Nays of the Members of either House on any question shall, at the Desire of one fifth of those Present, be entered on the Journal.

Neither House, during the Session of Congress, shall, without the Consent of the other, adjourn for more than three days, nor to any other Place than that in which the two Houses shall be sitting.

Section 6. The Senators and Representatives shall receive a Compensation for their Services, to be ascertained by Law, and paid out of the Treasury of the United States. They shall in all Cases, except Treason, Felony and Breach of the Peace, be privileged from Arrest during their Attendance at the Session of their respective Houses, and in going to and returning from the same; and for any Speech or Debate in either House, they shall not be questioned in any other Place.

No Senator or Representative shall, during the Time for which he was elected, be appointed to any civil Office under the Authority of the United States, which shall have been created, or the Emoluments whereof shall have been encreased during such time; and no Person holding any Office under the United States, shall be a Member of either House during his Continuance in Office.

Section 7. All Bills for raising Revenue shall originate in the House of Representatives; but the Senate may propose or concur with Amendments as on other Bills.

---

[4] See Amendment XX.

Every Bill which shall have passed the House of Representatives and the Senate, shall, before it become a Law, be presented to the President of the United States; if he approve he shall sign it, but if not he shall return it, with his Objections to that House in which it shall have originated, who shall enter the Objections at large on their Journal, and proceed to reconsider it. If after such Reconsideration two thirds of that House shall agree to pass the Bill, it shall be sent, together with the Objections, to the other House, by which it shall likewise be reconsidered, and if approved by two thirds of that House, it shall become a Law. But in all such Cases the Votes of both Houses shall be determined by Yeas and Nays, and the Names of the Persons voting for and against the Bill shall be entered on the Journal of each House respectively. If any Bill shall not be returned by the President within ten Days (Sundays excepted) after it shall have been presented to him, the Same shall be a Law, in like Manner as if he had signed it, unless Congress by their Adjournment prevent its Return, in which Case it shall not be a Law.

Every Order, Resolution, or Vote to which the Concurrence of the Senate and House of Representatives may be necessary (except on a question of Adjournment) shall be presented to the President of the United States; and before the Same shall take Effect, shall be approved by him, or being disapproved by him, shall be repassed by two thirds of the Senate and House of Representatives, according to the Rules and Limitations prescribed in the Case of a Bill.

Section 8. The Congress shall have Power To lay and collect Taxes, Duties, Imposts and Excises, to pay the Debts and provide for the common Defence and general Welfare of the United States; but all Duties, Imposts and Excises shall be uniform throughout the United States;

To borrow Money on the credit of the United States;

To regulate Commerce with foreign Nations, and among the several States, and with the Indian Tribes;

To establish an uniform Rule of Naturalization, and uniform Laws on the subject of Bankruptcies throughout the United States;

To coin Money, regulate the Value thereof, and of foreign Coin, and fix the Standard of Weights and Measures;

To provide for the Punishment of counterfeiting the Securities and Current Coin of the United States;

To establish Post Offices and post Roads;

To promote the Progress of Science and useful Arts, by securing for limited Times to Authors and Inventors the exclusive Right to their respective Writings and Discoveries;

To constitute Tribunals inferior to the Supreme Court;

To define and punish Piracies and Felonies committed on the high Seas, and Offences against the Law of Nations;

To declare War, grant Letters of Marque and Reprisal, and make Rules concerning Captures on Land and Water;

To raise and support Armies, but no Appropriation of Money to that Use shall be for a longer Term than two Years;

To provide and maintain a Navy;

To make Rules for the Government and Regulation of the land and naval Forces;

To provide for calling forth the Militia to execute the Laws of the Union, suppress Insurrections and repel Invasions;

To provide for organizing, arming, and disciplining, the Militia, and for governing such Part of them as may be employed in the Service of the United States, reserving to the States respectively, the Appointment of the Officers, and the Authority of training the Militia according to the discipline prescribed by Congress;

To exercise exclusive Legislation in all Cases whatsoever, over such District (not exceeding ten Miles square) as may, by Cession of particular States, and the Acceptance of Congress, become the Seat of the Government of the United States, and to exercise like Authority over all Places purchased by the Consent of the Legislature of the State in which the Same shall be, for the Erection of Forts, Magazines, Arsenals, dock-Yards, and other needful Buildings;—And

To make all Laws which shall be necessary and proper for carrying into Execution the foregoing Powers, and all other Powers vested by this Constitution in the Government of the United States, or in any Department or Officer thereof.

Section 9. The Migration or Importation of such Persons as any of the States now existing shall think proper to admit, shall not be prohibited by the Congress prior to the Year one thousand eight hundred and eight, but a Tax or duty may be imposed on such Importation, not exceeding ten dollars for each Person.

The Privilege of the Writ of Habeas Corpus shall not be suspended, unless when in Cases of Rebellion or Invasion the public Safety may require it.

No Bill of Attainder or ex post facto Law shall be passed.

No Capitation, or other direct, Tax shall be laid, unless in Proportion to the Census or Enumeration herein before directed to be taken.

No Tax or Duty shall be laid on Articles exported from any State.

No Preference shall be given by any Regulation of Commerce or Revenue to the Ports of one State over those of another: nor shall Vessels bound to, or from, one State, be obliged to enter, clear, or pay Duties in another.

No Money shall be drawn from the Treasury, but in Consequence of Appropriations made by Law; and a regular Statement and Account of the Receipts and Expenditures of all public Money shall be published from time to time.

No title of Nobility shall be granted by the United States: And no Person holding any Office of Profit or Trust under them, shall, without the Consent of the Congress, accept of any present, Emolument, Office, or Title, of any kind whatever, from any King, Prince, or foreign State.

Section 10. No State shall enter into any Treaty, Alliance, or Confederation; grant Letters of Marque and Reprisal; coin Money; emit Bills of Credit; make any Thing but gold and silver Coin a Tender in Payment of

Debts; pass any Bill of Attainder, ex post facto Law, or Law impairing the Obligation of Contracts, or Grant any Title of Nobility.

No State shall, without the Consent of the Congress, lay any Imposts or Duties on Imports or Exports, except what may be absolutely necessary for executing its inspection Laws: and the net Produce of all Duties and Imposts, laid by any State on Imports or Exports, shall be for the Use of the Treasury of the United States; and all such Laws be subject to the Revision and Control of the Congress.

No State shall, without the Consent of Congress, lay any Duty of Tonnage, keep Troops, or Ships of War in time of Peace, enter into any Agreement or Compact with another State, or with a foreign Power, or engage in War, unless actually invaded, or in such imminent Danger as will not admit of delay.

Article II

Section 1. The executive Power shall be vested in a President of the United States of America. He shall hold his Office during the Term of four Years, and, together with the Vice President, chosen for the same Term be elected as follows:

Each State shall appoint, in such Manner as the Legislature thereof may direct, a Number of Electors, equal to the whole Number of Senators and Representatives to which the State may be entitled in the Congress: but no Senator or Representative, or Person holding an Office of Trust or Profit under the United States, shall be appointed an Elector.

The Electors shall meet in their respective States, and vote by Ballot for two Persons, of whom one at least shall not be an Inhabitant of the same State with themselves. And they shall make a List of all the Persons voted for, and of the Number of Votes for each; which List they shall sign and certify, and transmit sealed to the Seat of the Government of the United States, directed to the President of the Senate. The President of the Senate shall, in the Presence of the Senate and House of Representatives, open all the Certificates, and the Votes shall then be counted. The Person having the greatest Number of Votes shall be the President, if such Number be a Majority of the whole Number of Electors appointed; and if there be more than one who have such Majority, and have an equal Number of Votes, then the House of Representatives shall immediately chuse by Ballot one of them for President; and if no Person have a Majority, then from the five highest on the List the said House shall in like Manner chuse the President. But in chusing the President, the votes shall be taken by States, the Representation from each State having one Vote; A quorum for this purpose shall consist of a Member or Members from two thirds of the States, and a Majority of all the States shall be necessary to a Choice. In every Case, after the Choice of the President, the Person having the Greatest Number of Votes of the Electors shall be the Vice President. But if there should remain two or more who have equal Votes, the Senate shall chuse from them by Ballot the Vice President.[5]

---

[5] See Amendment XII.

The Congress may determine the Time of chusing the Electors, and the Day on which they shall give their Votes; which Day shall be the same throughout the United States.

No Person except a natural born Citizen, or a Citizen of the United States, at the time of the Adoption of this Constitution, shall be eligible to the Office of President; neither shall any Person be eligible to that Office who shall not have attained to the Age of thirty five Years, and been fourteen Years a Resident within the United States.

The Case of the Removal of the President from Office, or of his Death, Resignation, or Inability to discharge the Powers and Duties of the said Office, the Same shall devolve on the Vice President, and the Congress may by Law provide for the Case of Removal, Death, Resignation or Inability, both of the President and Vice President, declaring what Officer shall then act as President, and such Officer shall act accordingly, until the Disability be removed, or a President shall be elected.

The President shall, at stated Times, receive for his Services, a Compensation which shall neither be encreased nor diminished during the Period for which he shall have been elected, and he shall not receive within that Period any other Emolument from the United States, or any of them.

Before he enter on the Execution of his Office, he shall take the following Oath or Affirmation:—"I do solemnly swear (or affirm) that I will faithfully execute the Office of President of the United States, and will to the best of my Ability, preserve, protect, and defend the Constitution of the United States."

Section 2. The President shall be Commander in Chief of the Army and Navy of the United States, and of the Militia of the several States, when called into the actual service of the United States; he may require the Opinion, in writing, of the principal Officer in each of the executive Departments, upon any Subject relating to the Duties of their respective Offices, and he shall have Power to grant Reprieves and Pardons for Offences against the United States, except in Case of Impeachment.

He shall have Power, by and with the Advice and Consent of the Senate, to make Treaties, provided two thirds of the Senators present concur; and he shall nominate, and by and with the Advice and Consent of the Senate, shall appoint Ambassadors, and other public Ministers and Consuls, Judges of the supreme Court, and all other Officers of the United States, whose Appointments are not herein otherwise provided for, and which shall be established by Law; but the Congress may by Law vest the Appointment of such inferior Officers, as they think proper, in the President alone, in the Courts of Law, or in the Heads of Departments.

The President shall have Power to fill up all Vacancies that may happen during the Recess of the Senate, by granting Commissions which shall expire at the End of their next Session.

Section 3. He shall from time to time give to the Congress Information of the State of the Union, and recommend to their Consideration such Measures as he shall judge necessary and expedient; he may, on extraordinary Occasions, convene both Houses, or either of them, and in Case of

Disagreement between them, with Respect to the Time of Adjournment, he may adjourn them to such Time as he shall think proper; he shall receive Ambassadors and other public Ministers, he shall take Care that the Laws be faithfully executed, and shall Commission all the Officers of the United States.

Section 4. The President, Vice President, and all civil Officers of the United States, shall be removed from Office on Impeachment for, and Conviction of, Treason, Bribery, or other high Crimes and Misdemeanors.

Article III

Section 1. The judicial Power of the United States, shall be vested in one supreme Court and in such inferior Courts as the Congress may from time to time ordain and establish. The Judges, both of the supreme and inferior Courts, shall hold their Offices during good Behavior, and shall, at stated Times, receive for their Services, a Compensation, which shall not be diminished during their Continuance in Office.

Section 2. The Judicial Power shall extend to all Cases, in Law and Equity, arising under this Constitution, the Laws of the United States, and Treaties made, or which shall be made, under their Authority;—to all Cases affecting Ambassadors, other public Ministers and Consuls;—to all Cases of admiralty and maritime Jurisdiction;—to Controversies to which the United States shall be a Party;—to Controversies between two or more States;—*between a State and Citizens of another State;*[6]—between Citizens of different States;—between Citizens of the same State claiming Lands under Grants of different states, *and between a State, or the Citizens thereof, and foreign States, Citizens, or Subjects.*[7]

In all cases affecting Ambassadors, other public Ministers and Consuls, and those in which a State shall be Party, the supreme Court shall have original Jurisdiction. In all the other Cases before mentioned, the supreme Court shall have appellate Jurisdiction, both as to Law and Fact, with such Exceptions, and under such Regulations as the Congress shall make.

The Trial of all Crimes, except in Cases of Impeachment, shall be by Jury; and such Trial shall be held in the State where the said Crimes shall have been committed; but when not committed within any State, the Trial shall be at such Place or Places as the Congress may by Law have directed.

Section 3. Treason against the United States, shall consist only in levying War against them, or in adhering to their Enemies, giving them Aid and Comfort. No person shall be convicted of Treason unless on the Testimony of two Witnesses to the same overt Act, or on Confession in open Court.

The Congress shall have Power to declare the Punishment of Treason,

---

[6] See Amendment XI.

[7] Ibid.

but no Attainder of Treason shall work Corruption of Blood, or Forfeiture except during the Life of the Person attainted.

Article IV

Section 1. Full Faith and Credit shall be given in each State to the public Acts, Records, and judicial Proceedings of every other State. And the Congress may by general Laws prescribe the Manner in which such Acts, Records, and Proceedings shall be proved, and the Effect thereof.

Section 2. The Citizens of each State shall be entitled to all Privileges and Immunities of Citizens in the several States.

A Person charged in any State with Treason, Felony, or other Crime, who shall flee from Justice, and be found in another State, shall on Demand of the executive Authority of the State from which he fled, be delivered up, to be removed to the State having jurisdiction of the Crime.

No Person held to Service or Labour in one State, under the Laws thereof, escaping into another, shall, in Consequence of any Law or Regulation therein, be discharged from such Service or Labour, but shall be delivered up on Claim of the Party to whom such Service or Labour may be due.[8]

Section 3. New States may be admitted by the Congress into this Union; but no new State shall be formed or erected within the Jurisdiction of any other State; nor any State be formed by the Junction of two or more States, or Parts of States, without the Consent of the Legislatures of the States concerned as well as of the Congress.

The Congress shall have Power to dispose of and make all needful Rules and Regulations respecting the Territory or other Property belonging to the United States; and nothing in this Constitution shall be so construed as to Prejudice any claims of the United States, or of any particular State.

Section 4. The United States shall guarantee to every State in this Union a Republican Form of Government, and shall protect each of them against Invasion; and on Application of the Legislature, or of the Executive (when the Legislature cannot be convened) against domestic Violence.

Article V

The Congress, whenever two thirds of both Houses shall deem it necessary, shall propose Amendments to this Constitution, or, on the Application of the Legislatures of two thirds of the several States, shall call a Convention for proposing Amendments, which, in either Case, shall be valid to all Intents and Purposes, as Part of this Constitution, when ratified by the Legislatures of three fourths of the several States, or by Conventions in three fourths thereof, as the one or the other Mode of Ratification may be proposed by the Congress; Provided that no Amendment which may be

---

[8] See Amendment XIII.

made prior to the Year One thousand eight hundred and eight shall in any Manner affect the first and fourth Clauses in the Ninth Section of the first Article; and that no State, without its Consent, shall be deprived of its equal Suffrage in the Senate.

Article VI

All Debts contracted and Engagements entered into, before the Adoption of this Constitution shall be as valid against the United States under this Constitution, as under the Confederation.

This Constitution, and the Laws of the United States which shall be made in Pursuance thereof; and all Treaties made, or which shall be made, under the Authority of the United States, shall be the supreme Law of the Land; and the Judges in every State shall be bound thereby, any Thing in the Constitution or Laws of any State to the Contrary notwithstanding.

The Senators and Representatives before mentioned, and the Members of the several State Legislatures, and all executive and judicial Officers, both of the United States and of the several States, shall be bound by Oath or Affirmation, to support this Constitution; but no religious Test shall ever be required as a Qualification to any Office or public Trust under the United States.

Article VII

The Ratification of the Conventions of nine States, shall be sufficient for the Establishment of this Constitution between the States so ratifying the Same.

Done in Convention by the Unanimous Consent of the States present the Seventeenth Day of September in the Year of our Lord one thousand seven hundred and eighty seven and of the Independence of the United States of America the twelfth. In witness whereof We have hereunto subscribed our Names.

AMENDMENTS TO THE CONSTITUTION

(Articles in addition to, and in amendment of, the Constitution of the United States of America, proposed by Congress, and ratified by the several States, pursuant to the Fifth Article of the original Constitution.)

Amendment I

[*Ratification of the first ten amendments was completed December 15, 1791*]

Congress shall make no law respecting an establishment of religion, or prohibiting the free exercise thereof; or abridging the freedom of speech, or of the press; or the right of the people peaceably to assemble, and to petition the Government for a redress of grievances.

Amendment II

A well regulated Militia, being necessary to the security of a free State, the right of the people to keep and bear Arms, shall not be infringed.

Amendment III

No Soldier shall, in time of peace be quartered in any house, without the consent of the Owner, nor in time of war, but in a manner to be prescribed by law.

Amendment IV

The right of the people to be secure in their persons, houses, papers, and effects, against unreasonable searches and seizures, shall not be violated, and no Warrants shall issue, but upon probable cause, supported by Oath or affirmation, and particularly describing the place to be searched, and the persons or things to be seized.

Amendment V

No person shall be held to answer for a capital, or otherwise infamous crime, unless on a presentment or indictment of a Grand Jury, except in cases arising in the land or naval forces, or in the Militia, when in actual service in time of War or public danger; nor shall any person be subject for the same offence to be twice put in jeopardy of life or limb; nor shall be compelled in any criminal case to be a witness against himself, nor be deprived of life, liberty, or property, without due process of law; nor shall private property be taken for public use, without just compensation.

Amendment VI

In all criminal prosecutions, the accused shall enjoy the right to a speedy and public trial, by an impartial jury of the State and district wherein the crime shall have been committed, which district shall have been previously ascertained by law, and to be informed of the nature and cause of the accusation; to be confronted with the witness against him; to have compulsory process for obtaining witness in his favor, and to have the Assistance of Counsel for his defence.

Amendment VII

In Suits at common law, where the value in controversy shall exceed twenty dollars, the right of trial by jury shall be preserved, and no fact tried by a jury, shall be otherwise re-examined in any Court of the United States, than according to the rules of the common law.

Amendment VIII

Excessive bail shall not be required, nor excessive fines imposed, nor cruel and unusual punishments inflicted.

Amendment IX

The enumeration in the Constitution, of certain rights, shall not be construed to deny or disparage others retained by the people.

Amendment X

The powers not delegated to the United States by the Constitution, nor prohibited by it to the States, are reserved to the States respectively, or to the people.

Amendment XI

[January 8, 1798]

The Judicial power of the United States shall not be construed to extend to any suit in law or equity, commenced or prosecuted against one of the United States by Citizens of another State, or by Citizens or Subjects of any Foreign State.

Amendment XII

[September 25, 1804]

The Electors shall meet in their respective states and vote by ballot for President and Vice President, one of whom, at least, shall not be an inhabitant of the same state with themselves; they shall name in their ballots the person voted for as President, and in distinct ballots the person voted for as Vice President, and they shall make distinct lists of all persons voted for as President, and of all persons voted for as Vice President, and of the number of votes for each, which lists they shall sign and certify, and transmit sealed to the seat of the government of the United States, directed to the President of the Senate;—The President of the Senate shall, in the presence of the Senate and House of Representatives, open all the certificates and the votes shall then be counted;—The person having the greatest number of votes for President, shall be the President, if such number be a majority of the whole number of Electors appointed; and if no person have such majority, then from the persons having the highest numbers not exceeding three on the list of those voted for as President, the House of Representatives shall choose immediately, by ballot, the President. But in choosing the President, the votes shall be taken by states, the representation from each state having one vote; a quorum for this purpose shall consist of a member or members from two thirds of the states, and a majority of all the states shall be necessary to a choice. And if the House of Representatives shall not choose a President whenever the right of choice shall devolve upon them, *before the fourth day of March next following,*[9] then the Vice President shall act as President as in the case of the death or other constitutional disability of the President.—The person having the greatest number of votes as Vice President, shall be the Vice President, if such number be a majority of the whole number of Electors appointed, and if no person have a majority, then from the two highest numbers on the list, the Senate shall choose the Vice President; a quorum for the purpose shall consist of two-thirds of the whole number of Senators, and a majority of the whole number shall be necessary to a choice. But no person constitutionally ineligible to the office of President shall be eligible to that of Vice President of the United States.

Amendment XIII

[*December 18, 1865*]

Section 1. Neither slavery nor involuntary servitude, except as a punishment for crime whereof the party shall have been duly convicted, shall exist within the United States, or any place subject to their jurisdiction.

Section 2. Congress shall have power to enforce this article by appropriate legislation.

Amendment XIV

[*July 28, 1868*]

Section 1. All persons born or naturalized in the United States, and subject to the jurisdiction thereof, are citizens of the United States and of the State wherein they reside. No State shall make or enforce any law which shall abridge the privileges or immunities of citizens of the United States; nor shall any state deprive any person of life, liberty, or property, without due process of law; nor deny to any person, within its jurisdiction the equal protection of the laws.

Section 2. Representatives shall be apportioned among the several States according to their respective numbers, counting the whole number of persons in each State, excluding Indians not taxed. But when the right to vote at any election for the choice of electors for President and Vice President of the United States, Representatives in Congress, the Executive and Judicial officers of a State, or the members of the Legislature thereof, is denied to any of the male inhabitants of such State, being twenty one years

---

[9] See Amendment XX.

of age, and citizens of the United States, or in any way abridged, except for participation in rebellion, or other crime, the basis of representation therein shall be reduced in the proportion which the number of such male citizens shall bear to the whole number of male citizens twenty one years of age in such State.

Section 3. No person shall be a Senator or Representative in Congress, or elector of President and Vice President, or hold any office, civil or military, under the United States, or under any State, who, having previously taken an oath, as a member of Congress, or as an officer of the United States, or as a member of any State legislature, or as an executive or judicial officer of any State, to support the Constitution of the United States, shall have engaged in insurrection or rebellion against the same, or given aid or comfort to the enemies thereof. But Congress may by a vote of two thirds of each House, remove such disability.

Section 4. The validity of the public debt of the United States, authorized by law, including debts incurred for payment of pensions and bounties for services in suppressing insurrection or rebellion, shall not be questioned. But neither the United States nor any State shall assume or pay any debt or obligation incurred in aid of insurrection or rebellion against the United States, or any claim for the loss or emancipation of any slave; but all such debts, obligations, and claims shall be held illegal and void.

Section 5. The Congress shall have power to enforce, by appropriate legislation, the provisions of this article.

Amendment XV

[*March 30, 1870*]

Section 1. The right of citizens of the United States to vote shall not be denied or abridged by the United States or by any State on account of race, color, or previous condition of servitude.

Section 2. The Congress shall have power to enforce this article by appropriate legislation.

Amendment XVI

[*February 25, 1913*]

The Congress shall have power to lay and collect taxes on incomes, from whatever source derived, without apportionment among the several States, and without regard to any census or enumeration.

Amendment XVII

[*May 31, 1913*]

The Senate of the United States shall be composed of two Senators from each State, elected by the people thereof, for six years; and each Senator shall have one vote. The electors in each State shall have the qualifications requisite for electors of the most numerous branch of the State legislatures.

When vacancies happen in the representation of any State in the Senate, the executive authority of such State shall issue writs of election to fill such vacancies: *Provided,* That the legislature of any State may empower the executive thereof to make temporary appointments until the people fill the vacancies by election as the legislature may direct.

This amendment shall not be so construed as to affect the election or term of any Senator chosen before it becomes valid as part of the Constitution.

Amendment XVIII

[*January 29, 1919*]

Section 1. After one year from the ratification of this article the manufacture, sale, or transportation of intoxicating liquors within, the importation thereof into, or the exportation thereof from the United States and all territory subject to the jurisdiction thereof for beverage purposes is hereby prohibited.

Section 2. The Congress and the several States shall have concurrent power to enforce this article by appropriate legislation.

Section 3. This article shall be inoperative unless it shall have been ratified as an amendment to the Constitution by the legislatures of the several States, as provided in the Constitution, within seven years from the date of submission hereof to the States by the Congress.[10]

Amendment XIX

[*August 26, 1920*]

The right of citizens of the United States to vote shall not be denied or abridged by the United States or by any State on account of sex.

Congress shall have power to enforce this article by appropriate legislation.

Amendment XX

[*February 6, 1933*]

Section 1. The terms of the President and Vice President shall end at noon on the 20th day of January, and the terms of Senators and Representatives at noon on the 3rd day of January, of the years in which such terms would have ended if this article had not been ratified; and the terms of their successors shall then begin.

---

[10] Repealed by Amendment XXI.

Section 2. The Congress shall assemble at least once in every year, and such meeting shall begin at noon on the 3rd day of January, unless they shall by law appoint a different day.

Section 3. If, at the time fixed for the beginning of the term of the President, the President elect shall have died, the Vice President elect shall become President. If a President shall not have been chosen before the time fixed for the beginning of his term, or if the President elect shall have failed to qualify, then the Vice President elect shall act as President until a President shall have qualified; and the Congress may by law provide for the case wherein neither a President elect nor a Vice President elect shall have qualified, declaring who shall then act as President, or the manner in which one who is to act shall be selected, and such person shall act accordingly until a President or Vice President shall have qualified.

Section 4. The Congress may by law provide for the case of the death of any of the persons from whom the House of Representatives may choose a President whenever the right of choice shall have devolved upon them, and for the case of the death of any of the persons from whom the Senate may choose a Vice President whenever the right of choice shall have devolved upon them.

Section 5. Sections 1 and 2 shall take effect on the 15th day of October following the ratification of this article.

Section 6. This article shall be inoperative unless it shall have been ratified as an amendment to the Constitution by the legislatures of three fourths of the several States within seven years from the date of its submission.

Amendment XXI

[*December 5, 1933*]

Section 1. The eighteenth article of amendment to the Constitution of the United States is hereby repealed.

Section 2. The transportation or importation into any State, Territory, or possession of the United States for delivery or use therein of intoxicating liquors, in violation of the laws thereof, is hereby prohibited.

Section 3. This article shall be inoperative unless it shall have been ratified as an amendment to the Constitution by conventions in the several States, as provided in the Constitution, within seven years from the date of the submission hereof to the States by the Congress.

Amendment XXII

[*February 26, 1951*]

Section 1. No person shall be elected to the office of the President more than twice, and no person who has held the office of President, or acted as

President, for more than two years of a term to which some other person was elected President shall be elected to the office of President more than once. But this Article shall not apply to any person holding the office of President when this Article was proposed by the Congress, and shall not prevent any person who may be holding the office of President, or acting as President, during the term within which this Article becomes operative from holding the office of President or acting as President during the remainder of such term.

Section 2. This article shall be inoperative unless it shall have been ratified as an amendment to the Constitution by the legislatures of three fourths of the several States within seven years from the date of its submission to the States by the Congress.

Amendment XXIII

[March 29, 1961]

Section 1. The District constituting the seat of Government of the United States shall appoint in such manner as the Congress may direct:

A number of electors of President and Vice President equal to the whole number of Senators and Representatives in Congress to which the district would be entitled if it were a State, but in no event more than the least populous State; they shall be in addition to those appointed by the States, but they shall be considered, for the purposes of the election of President and Vice President, to be electors appointed by a State; and they shall meet in the District and perform such duties as provided by the twelfth article of amendment.

Section 2. The Congress shall have power to enforce this article by appropriate legislation.

Amendment XXIV

[January 23, 1964]

Section 1. The right of citizens of the United States to vote in any primary or other election for President or Vice President, for electors for President or Vice President, or for Senator or Representative in Congress, shall not be denied or abridged by the United States or any state by reason of failure to pay any poll tax or other tax.

Section 2. The Congress shall have power to enforce this article by appropriate legislation.

Amendment XXV

[February 10, 1967]

Section 1. In case of the removal of the President from office or of his death or resignation, the Vice President shall become President.

Section 2. Whenever there is a vacancy in the office of the Vice President, the President shall nominate a Vice President who shall take office upon confirmation by a majority vote of both Houses of Congress.

Section 3. Whenever the President transmits to the President pro tempore of the Senate and the Speaker of the House of Representatives his written declaration that he is unable to discharge the powers and duties of his office, and until he transmits to them a written declaration to the contrary, such powers and duties shall be discharged by the Vice President as Acting President.

Section 4. Whenever the Vice President and a majority of either the principal officers of the executive departments or of such other body as Congress may by law provide, transmit to the President pro tempore of the Senate and the Speaker of the House of Representatives their written declaration that the President is unable to discharge the powers and duties of his office, the Vice President shall immediately assume the powers and duties of the office as Acting President.

Thereafter, when the President transmits to the President pro tempore of the Senate and the Speaker of the House of Representatives his written declaration that no inability exists, he shall resume the powers and duties of his office unless the Vice President and a majority of either the principal officers of the executive department[s] or of such other body as Congress may by law provide, transmit within four days to the President pro tempore of the Senate and the Speaker of the House of Representatives their written declaration that the President is unable to discharge the powers and duties of his office. Thereupon Congress shall decide the issue, assembling within forty-eight hours for that purpose if not in session. If the Congress, within twenty-one days after receipt of the latter written declaration, or, if Congress is not in session, within twenty-one days after Congress is required to assemble, determines by two-thirds vote of both Houses that the President is unable to discharge the powers and duties of his office, the Vice President shall continue to discharge the same as Acting President; otherwise, the President shall resume the powers and duties of his office.

Amendment XXVI

[*June 30, 1971*]

Section 1. The right of citizens of the United States, who are 18 years of age or older, to vote shall not be denied or abridged by the United States or by any state on account of age.

Section 2. The Congress shall have power to enforce this article by appropriate legislation.

Proposed Amendment (XXVII)—Equal Rights for Men and Women

[Passed by Congress on March 22, 1972, and submitted to the state legislatures for ratification]

Resolved by the Senate and House of Representatives of the United States of America in Congress assembled (two-thirds of each House concurring therein), That the following article is proposed as an amendment to the Constitution of the United States, which shall be valid to all intents and purposes as part of the Constitution when ratified by the legislatures of three-fourths of the several States [within seven years from the date of its submission by the Congress:][11]

Article

Section 1. Equality of rights under the law shall not be denied or abridged by the United States or by any State on account of sex.

Section 2. The Congress shall have the power to enforce, by appropriate legislation, the provisions of this article.

Section 3. This amendment shall take effect two years after the date of ratification.

Proposed Amendment (XXVIII)—Treatment of the District of Columbia

[Passed by Congress on August 22, 1978, and submitted to the state legislatures for ratification]

Article

Section 1. For purposes of representation in the Congress, election of the President and Vice President, and article V of this Constitution, the District constituting the seat of government of the United States shall be treated as though it were a State.

Section 2. The exercise of the rights and powers conferred under this article shall be by the people of the District constituting the seat of government, and as shall be provided by the Congress.

Section 3. The twenty-third article of amendment to the Constitution of the United States is hereby repealed.

Section 4. This article shall be inoperative, unless it shall have been ratified as an amendment to the Constitution by the legislatures of three-fourths of the several States within seven years from the date of its submission.

---

[11] In 1978 Congress extended the deadline for ratification of the ERA to June 30, 1982. As of publication of this text (January, 1985), the proposed amendment had not been ratified by the legislatures of three-fourths of the states.

Glossary

Anarchism Usually refers to the doctrine that government in any form is oppressive and should be abolished. It comes from a long-standing philosophical tradition, the core of which is an aversion to any kind of institutional management of people's lives. There are two main strands: communal and individual. The most common American version tends toward individualistic, or libertarian, anarchism; the main emphasis is the removal of all external restraints of any kind on the individual.

Annapolis Convention The precursor to the Constitutional Convention, it was called in 1786 by Alexander Hamilton. Its purported purpose was to discuss the economic problems merchants were encountering due to state and local particularism in credit laws, tariff policies, and so on. These conditions were perceived to be "chaotic" by the middle and upper classes.

Articles of Confederation The document on which the government of matters of general concern to the newly independent and embattled colonies was based prior to the framing of the Constitution. In it, each state had an equal vote.

Authoritarian A term, usually pejorative, used to imply that an entity is too controlling. When used in connection with a government, it implies that there is too much ordering of citizens' lives.

Authority That which is generally accepted as having the deciding voice—that is, governmental authority would be that person and/or institution that is accepted as the controlling voice of the government.

Business cycle An assumption that the economy will expand and contract in a regular, predictable fashion. It is a normal aspect of capitalist society and is assumed to be healthy as long as neither the expanding nor the contracting aspect of the cycle varies too widely from the norm.

Capital Money or property available for use in producing more wealth.

Capital gain Profit from the sale of capital.

Capitalism An economic system in which the major resources of the society are privately owned and production of goods and services is for private profit.

> **Capitalist countries** Those countries whose economic system is devoted to private profit and production or at least whose main emphasis is private profit.

Capitalist society A community or nation whose economy, social structure, politics, and cultural and ideological characteristics are consistent with and support the economic system of capitalism.

World capitalism The capitalist economic system that extends across national boundaries.

Caucus A group of like-minded and or interested persons who meet to devise common strategies and/or policies, in order to present as united a front as possible.

Change Alterations within the political system:

Fundamental Substantial alteration in the economic or political power structures or in key governmental policies bearing upon distribution of wealth and status.

Incremental Alteration in minor policies, well within established power systems. See also **incrementalism.**

Marginal Alteration whose essential effect is to defend and promote established economic and political structures and existing patterns of distribution of wealth and status within the society.

Political Alteration in the economic or governmental structures and/or policies.

Process of How alterations occur.

Theory of Beliefs regarding how, and what types, of alterations are possible and/or probable.

Class Socioeconomic status. Some definitions rely solely on objective indicators, such as income level, education level, and so forth. Others include qualitative and subjective measurements, such as power components, feelings of inferiority, superiority, and so forth. More radical and Marxist definitions derive their definitions of class from one's relationships to the means of production—that is, whether one owns the means of production or works for those who do.

Class consciousness Awareness of the arbitrary nature of socioeconomic status and of one's place within it.

Class system Existing patterns of distribution of socioeconomic status that make differences apparent.

Middle class Strictly speaking, those whose socioeconomic indicators place them above poverty and below wealth. However, it is often used in a mythical manner—for example, referring to the United States as a "middle class" nation, which somehow translates into "stable and affluent," as almost everyone prefers to define themselves.

Ruling class Major owners of key banks and corporations.

Working class Those who sell their labor power.

Communism A belief system that theorizes eliminating class distinctions and private-profit enterprise, so that everyone shares in basic necessities and no one is in need. Also a pejorative term used in the United States to denigrate beliefs and/or nations that disagree with and/or challenge American ideas, making "communism" something to be feared and destroyed by "anti-Communists."

Community control An approach to government in which local groups, from neighborhoods to cities, direct those policies and programs that affect them—for example, school board policy, zoning, and police practice.

Competitive sector   That portion of the American economy that is composed mostly of retail or service-providing small businesses, in which real competition still exists and market principles apply.

Conceptual framework   That set of underlying premises and assumptions that provide the basis for organizing data, argument, research, and so on.

Conservative   A term used in a variety of ways in the American polity. Originally, it was a distinctive ideology based on tradition and a notion of an organic society moving through time with societal interests paramount. In the United States (so strongly liberal in the classic mold), conservatives can be either those who believe in the original tradition or those who believe in classical, laissez-faire liberalism.

   Fiscal conservative   One who prefers that the government refrain from spending ("excessive spending") and the manipulation of the economy.

Constituency   A group to which a representative is responsible, most often the people living in the geographical area from which he or she is elected.

Context of understanding   The assumptions, perceptions, and expectations about a particular subject area or problem that are derived from orthodox American political values and ideology and the specific beliefs supplementing them.

Co-optation   The process by which a dissenter or protester becomes a supporter by being given a share of the "pie" and/or a position of status so that his or her criticisms are eroded (almost subconsciously).

Corporate-banking sector   The portion of the American economy that is composed of the largest, often multinational, productive and financial institutions, which are not subject to the competitive "market," because of their size and position.

Cost of living   A statistical measure of the amount required to sustain human life—that is, the cost of the basic necessities, such as food, shelter, clothing, transportation, and so on.

Crisis   A point at which a problem becomes critical; it can be "real," "imagined," and/or "manufactured," or all three, depending upon the point of view.

   Fiscal crisis   The financial condition in which tax revenues and other state or governmentally collected monies cannot meet the loan and bond obligations (and similar forms of long-term debt obligations), with the result that the mutually supportive transfer of money between banks and governmental entities is in danger of collapsing.

   Legitimacy crisis   A situation in which the general populace loses confidence in the leaders and/or major institutions of a society, threatening withdrawal of popular support and obedience. See **legitimacy.**

   Population crisis   The condition, asserted and advertised by some, that the number of people on earth is outstripping the capacity of the earth to support human life in terms of such basics as food and space. Those who argue that the way in which the earth's resources are distributed causes the problem also say that this crisis is ideologically based and is therefore "imagined."

   Social Security crisis   A threatened bankruptcy of the Social Security System, projected from the current trend of money being paid out of the system at a greater rate than it is being replenished. Because of better health and medical care, more elderly people are living longer and drawing benefits indexed to inflation; at the same time, worker and employer taxes are contributing less money to the system because of the recessionary trend in the economy.

Third World debt crisis   A situation in which major Western banks are carrying billions of dollars in loans to Third World countries while worldwide economic and internal domestic conditions make it increasingly difficult for such countries to even pay interest on such debts, much less repay any principal; in fact, they have been borrowing more money in order to pay the service fees on the previous loans. Any major default on the part of one of these Third World nations could bring the international financial system tumbling down in a financial version of the "domino" theory.

Culture   The pattern of beliefs and institutions characteristic of a particular community or population.

Currency   Paper money issued by national governments and supposedly backed by them.

Devaluation   A national policy by which the currency value relative to other nations' is deliberately lowered.

Exchange rate   The value of the basic unit of currency of one nation relative to that of another.

Fixed exchange rate   A ratio established and agreed to by nations for currency-exchange purposes.

Floating exchange rate   The ratio that fluctuates according to the buying and selling of currency by those speculating on the value of national currency.

Deflation   The economic condition in which money buys more. See **inflation.**

Democracy   In popular terms, the "people rule." When examined more closely, it covers many different ideas and is used when someone wishes to label a certain practice, institution, or policy as "good."

Liberal democracy   The version of democracy peculiar to the United States, defined by classical liberalism and its institutions. It is based on the individual and the belief that the pursuit of individual satisfaction (usually in terms of material things) within strictly prescribed processes and rules (a constitution) will mechanically result in a good society.

Procedural democracy   Democracy defined by open electoral processes, with little concern for outcomes or substantive policy results.

Substantive democracy   Democracy that requires rough equality in power and decision-making ability among all the members of the community, as well as open processes. It asserts that democracy (people in control of their public decisions) requires more than simple "political" processes; it must extend to social, economic, and cultural matters as well.

Democratic pluralism   The generally accepted view of the American political process, in which negotiation and compromise among many factions and groups result in a product that is a reasonable approximation of both democracy and the public interest.

Demography   The study of such characteristics of human populations as geographic distribution, size, growth, age distribution, birth rates, and death rates.

Depression   An extended period of decline in gross national product, industrial production, and employment.

Détente   An uneasy truce between the United States and the Soviet Union.

Developed countries   Those nations whose economic base is industrial and technologically advanced. This definition carries an ideological bias, so that economic imperialism can be promoted as aiding the "development" of "undeveloped countries" in order to enable them to grow up in the image of "developed" countries.

Distribution   The manner in which resources (national, world, and so forth) are shared and/or used.
>   **Maldistribution**   When some have more or less than their fair share.
>   **Redistribution**   To alter the present patterns of resource usage and consumption.

Due process   The term covering the notion that governmental practices and implementation must be carried on by established procedures in a fair, reasonable, depersonalized, impartial, and neutral manner.

Economists   Those who study and attempt to make policy for the economy.
>   **Conservative economists**   Those who favor a return to a position of governmental hands off the economy.
>   **Liberal economists**   Those who accept Keynesian notions of government/economy partnership, in order to control and ameliorate the effects of business cycles; they assume that government can, and should, control the economy.
>   **Radical economists**   Those who perceive government as the servant of the major units of the economy; usually Marxian, they maintain that capitalism is irrational and to the detriment of the people.
>   **Supply-side economists**   Those who argue that the major problems with the economy will be solved by "freeing" capital for investment, in order to produce new goods and services. This is in opposition to the Keynesian concern for maintaining demand.

Egalitarianism   The belief system that emphasizes equality, of all forms, above all other concerns.

Elite   Those who hold more of the resources of power than others do.
>   **Governing elite**   Those members of the upper class in public positions.
>   **Nonelites**   Those not in power and status positions.
>   **Power elite**   Those who have influence and power and can shape governmental events and policies for their benefit.

Empiricism   The way of thinking that bases truth only on tangible evidence, that which can be discovered through the use of the senses. The belief that there is a tangible world "out there" that can be discovered and defined.

Entitlements   The benefits and services that people are eligible for, once the conditions specified by the enabling legislation have been met—for example, when a person reaches a certain age, he or she is entitled to a certain amount of Social Security income.

Establishment   The group of people holding positions of power (in government and private affairs) who have come to share roughly the same values, interests, political ideology, and sense of priorities about what government should be doing and a shared proprietary concern for the continued success of the American system in its familiar social, economic, and political dimensions.

Executive agreement   An agreement made by the President, without senatorial ratification, with the head of a foreign state.

Fascism A governmental system in which economic and governmental spheres are merged and social control of all aspects of an individual's life is achieved, usually accompanied by police-state apparatus to ensure compliance at all levels and to repress any and all dissent.

Federal Reserve System The institutions and practices of the federal banks and management personnel (the Federal Reserve Board) that make and enforce national fiscal and monetary policy.

Federalism The division of powers between constituent units (the states) and a single central unit (the national government), such that each has defined powers and is supreme in its own allotted sphere.

Federalist Party The label for the group that, at the time of the drafting, ratification, and initial implementation of the U.S. Constitution, supported ratification and a subsequent policy of increasing use of national powers and centralization. Among the Federalists were James Madison, Alexander Hamilton, George Washington, and John Adams—but not Thomas Jefferson, a bitter enemy of the Federalists.

Fiscal year A twelve-month period for which a government or organization plans its revenues and expenditures.

Framers Those men who drafted the body of the U.S. Constitution, in convention, in Philadelphia in 1787. Most of them remain unknown, but names such as Madison, Hamilton, Adams, and Franklin generally evoke the image of "framers."

Freedom In American ideology, the absence of restraint on an individual. Because total absence of restraint would lead to chaos, it also usually implies only those restraints necessary and includes a procedure by which those restraints can be tested, with full coverage afforded by the Bill of Rights.

Full employment Originally, that proportion of the work force minus only those workers normally changing jobs or temporarily displaced by the advent of new technologies. The definition of full employment has shifted to include that proportion of unemployment that will maintain price stability and hold inflation down. In other words, full employment is achieved at higher and higher levels of unemployment.

Government The ongoing structure, institutions, and practices generally perceived to be public, carrying authority and granted legitimacy by its citizens.

Gross national product (GNP) The total value of the goods and services a nation produces during a specified period of time.

Growth rate The proportion of increase or decrease in the gross national product from one year to the next.

Hegemony Conformity. Usually refers to ideological conformity, so that all agree, or at least publicly state that they agree, on goals, policies, and so on. The "party line."

Humanism The values based in the desire to improve the welfare and well being of human beings as the end goal of any activity.

Ideology That collection of beliefs that people in a society hold about how their government works, or should work, and why.

Imperialism One nation's interference in the affairs of another through military dominance, economic capability, cultural arrogance, and/or any combination of these, resulting in one nation dominating the other for its own benefit.

Incrementalism   The process, especially in budgeting, by which policy changes by inching forward one small step at a time.

Incumbent   Current officeholder.

Industrialized countries   Those whose economy is based on industry, as opposed to those based primarily on agricultural or raw materials.
  Industrial capitalist countries   Those that are industrialized and capitalist; usually means the "free world"—that is, the United States, Canada, Western Europe, and so on.

Inflation   A general rise in the prices of goods and services, resulting in the real, or purchasing power, value of money being reduced.

Infrastructure   Underlying but necessary building blocks.

Institutions   Identifiable, long-standing structures and/or associations.
  Economic institutions   Those structures involved with the production of goods and services, such as corporations and trade unions.
  Political (public) institutions   Those structures, such as Congress, the President, and political parties, that have open accountability and responsibility.
  Private institutions   Those structures, such as churches, the family, and corporations, with no governmental character.

Interest   A concern and/or need.
  Public interest   That which is of concern to *all* members of the polity.
  Special interest   That which concerns a certain segment and/or group and/or institution, often assumed to be in contrast to the public interest, though it is advertised to be congruent with it by the special interest.

Investment guaranty contract   Insurance underwritten by the U.S. government for private enterprise involved in ventures in foreign nations, so that the risks of such economic involvement are lessened.

Judicial review   The power of the Supreme Court to declare acts of Congress unconstitutional and thus void; in other words, overseeing of the "political" branches by the "legal" branch of the government.

Laissez-faire   Denotes the proponents and policies associated with the belief that the government should not interfere with the economy. The belief that the government is best that governs least, especially with regard to property and economics.

Law and order   A catch phrase denoting the American ideological belief in the need for prescribed rules to which everyone must adhere, so that anarchy or chaos will not prevail. It became a political slogan covering repression of dissent and protest by terming dissenters lawless (thus criminal) and thus capable of bringing on anarchy.

Left   Those who lean toward support of a wider distribution of power, wealth, and status within the society.

Legalism   Belief in procedural regularity and written rules for conduct *and* procedure as the best method of dispute settlement of *any* kind.

Legitimacy   1. The quality of a government by virtue of which it is regarded as lawful or as entitled to compliance with its orders. 2. A status conferred by people generally upon the institutions, acts, and officials of their government by believing that their government is the right one, that it works properly and for desirable ends, so that they place their trust in it and grant it their obedience.

Liberal   Another word for the American ideology, but used popularly only for those on the left side of the American ideology.
> **Liberal/capitalist**   The peculiar interlocking combination of political and economic ideologies extant in the United States.
> **Liberal economist**   See **economists.**

Libertarian anarchism   See **anarchism.**

Logrolling   The exchanging of votes by legislators: "You vote for my locally oriented bill, and I'll vote for yours."

Masses   Those who hold little power—nonelites. See **elites.**

Median (in statistics)   The middle value in a distribution, with an equal number of values above and below it.

Military-industrial complex   The popular term for the interlocking and interchanging people and interests between the armed forces and the large private contractors and industries that benefit from arms and related production and require military protection for foreign investments.

Multinationals   Economic entities that operate in several nations and move easily through national boundaries, faithful only to themselves.
> **Multinational banks**   The financial institutions servicing and dealing with the multinational corporations.
> **Multinational corporations**   Multinational industries and productive enterprises—for example, the oil companies.

National economic planning   The newest move to institute extensive government planning and controls to keep the economy running smoothly.

National income   The sum of the income residents of a nation receive in profits, interest, pensions, and wages.

National security   Originally, military supremacy over the Soviet Union and other Communist countries and now becoming expanded and controversial as interference in other countries takes on multiple dimensions.

National security managers   American policymakers who specialize in foreign affairs.

Nationalization   The taking over by the government or other public bodies of the management and interest in a previously privately owned and managed enterprise.

Norm   A prescribed standard of acceptability, desirability, or typicality.

Organization of Petroleum Exporting Countries (OPEC)   The Third World organization of heads of state of those nations with oil resources and holding shares in multinational oil corporations, whose purpose is to unify and increase their bargaining power relative to the multinational American-dominated oil companies.

Pluralist   See **democratic pluralist.**

Policy   An established set of rules, written or unwritten, and procedures, either formal or informal.
> **Fiscal policy**   Rules regarding government management of its own finances.
> **Foreign policy**   Rules regarding relations with other nations.
> **Incomes policy**   Rules regarding wages and prices.

Monetary policy   Rules regarding the money supply.

Public policy   Usually official (though it can be informal) governmental rules and procedures regarding a certain subject area or areas.

Policy planning groups   Those institutionalized entities, such as the Council on Foreign Relations, Business Roundtable, Trilateral Commission, and so forth, to which the planners and managers of major policy proposals and national decisions belong.

Political consciousness   Awareness of, critical involvement in, and/or challenge of present ideological constraints and circumstances.

Political economy   The conceptual approach that sees economic, political, and social life as an integrated whole, interpenetrating and mutually supportive.

Political participation   Involvement in the public arena and its processes, in varying degrees of passivity or activity and self-consciousness, including the act of withdrawal, which grants others the right to act in one's stead.

Political science   That branch of study devoted to public institutions and relationships.

Political socialization   The process by which children become imbued with the values and assumptions supportive of the present governmental arrangements—schools, family, television, and so on—and of nationalism and patriotism.

Politics   The process by which power is employed to affect whether and how government will act on any given matter.

Population crisis   See **crisis.**

Populist   One critical of big government and big business and supportive of the "little people."

> **Populist conservative**   Term coined by Kevin Phillips to describe many members of the "New Right" who are socially conservative but economically liberal—those who challenge the status quo on behalf of the "common person," but want to return to traditional American values (home, family, patriotism) and plan to do so through the electoral process.

> **Radical populist**   One who challenges the status quo on behalf of the "common person," but who emphasizes equality, democracy, and community as the alternative.

Pork barrel   A piece of legislation that enriches a certain district and/or area, such as a defense contract, a highway project, or a new building.

Poverty   An arbitrarily defined line below which a family of four would be unable to procure the fundamental necessities—that is, adequate food, shelter, and clothing. The annual dollar amount fluctuates depending upon the political viewpoint and/or the agency that is defining the poverty standard.

> **Feminization of poverty**   The term used to describe the fact that an increasing proportion of those falling below the poverty threshold are women and children. By one account, by the year 2000, if present trends continue, the entire poverty population will be women and young children.

Power   The possession of those resources, ranging from money and prestige to official authority to moral persuasion, that causes others to modify their behavior and conform to what they perceive the possessor of the resources prefers.

Power structure The relatively permanent distribution of power among people and institutions that serves to set the general direction of public opinion and public policy.

Pragmatic A philosophy associated with William James, based on the "possible." The current American variant reduces it to what is possible in present terms, usually meaning a continuation of what presently exists and acceptance of all those boundaries and constraints.

Private enterprise The American ideological term for ownership, management, and receipt of the profits of production and other property uses inhering in individuals for individual benefit.

Productivity The rate at which hours or days of labor input result in tangible output, meaning products or services that can be sold.

Protectionism Belief in the use of governmental policy to shelter internal product prices from competitive pressure from the same or similar products from other localities.

Public interest See **interest**.

Radicalism The belief in the need for drastic change at the roots of the social order.
    Radical economist See **economist**.
    Radical populist See **populist**.

Rationing A public policy of controlling production and consumption and enforcing it through controlling the amounts available to individuals and other entities by issuing certificates for the purchase of such commodities in limited quantities and requiring that such certificates be presented before purchase is allowed.

Real income The amount of money received, adjusted to take account of increases or decreases in prices: income adjusted to reflect change in purchasing power.

Real wages See **wages**.

Reality The "facts" and "laws" of the universe. Different ways of thinking pose different versions of what is "real" or "reality." American liberal empiricism's reality is the tangible world outside ourselves that can be discovered, measured, and defined through the use of the scientific method.
    Reality testing Examining for truth or actual existence.

Recession A decline in economic activity, less severe and shorter than a depression; a temporary period of increase in unemployment and decline in investment and production.

Republic A form of government in which the public has a voice but does not rule absolutely—not strict majority rule, but tempered, checked, and balanced in a variety of ways.

Revolution A destruction of the old order and replacement with a new one. Debate continues on what deserves the name, ranging from seizure of governmental power to total transformation of values, institutions, culture, and so on.

Right Those who lean toward insistence upon the status quo and/or even narrower and more restrictive distribution.

Separation of powers The division of specific national governmental powers among the institutions of the national government.

Social legislation   Those statutes enacted to further policies designed to promote the health and well-being of the populace.

Socialism   A philosophy, with many variants, centering on human beings as social beings (as opposed to self-sufficient individuals) whose minimal material needs can and should be met through cooperative and communal efforts, thus allowing social relationships to grow and develop.

Socialist countries   Those nations in opposition to the capitalism of the United States and its allies and/or that claim to be so. The term "socialist" is used in a variety of ways and for various countries by different people at different times, depending upon the immediate issue at hand.

Spoils system   The filling of governmental posts and bureaucratic positions by an incumbent (usually newly elected) as rewards for service rendered to the officeholder; supposedly replaced by the Civil Service system.

State   The combined governmental units and practices of a nation.

Status quo   The present structure and distribution of power and resources.

Strategic Arms Limitation Talks (SALT)   Ongoing, but presently stalled, negotiations between the United States and the Soviet Union regarding halting and/or limiting production and stockpiling of weapons of war.

System   A related and connected series of institutions, practices, and/or policies that are mutually beneficial and reinforcing.
　　Class system   A society in which people occupy and possess differentiated material and status positions.
　　Economic system   The private enterprise connections.
　　Econopolitical system   The combined governmental and economic enterprises.
　　International monetary system   The connections among world currencies that allow international trade to occur.
　　Political system   The public enterprise connections.
　　"The" system   A general term covering the institutionalized status quo.

Tariff   The taxes one has to pay in order to import articles.

Third World   A term referring to the "undeveloped" countries, those not firmly within the Western or the Soviet blocs, such as nations in Africa, the Middle East, and Central and South America.

Trade war   A condition in which a government formulates policies that are used to increase the advantage of its home industries, and a competing government retaliates with its own import/export restrictions.

Transformation   A fundamental change under way in the economic system, analogous to the shift from an agricultural to an industrial nation, forcing changes in all other aspects of the political economy.

Trilateral Commission   An international group of leading financiers and corporate executives, initiated by David Rockefeller of the Chase Manhattan Bank, which makes studies and proposals for economic coordination among capitalist countries.

Tunnel vision   The total acceptance of an ideology, so that one sees only within its confines and interprets everything within its terms.

Wages   Payment for services rendered.

Marginal wages   Just enough payment to maintain life, sometimes a little more, but only so that the worker is in constant fear of any major or unforeseen expense.

Real wages   The purchasing power of the payment.

Warren Court   The term denoting the Supreme Court while Earl Warren was chief justice; actually came into widespread usage only as the Court's civil-liberties decisions became more liberal and more controversial.

Welfare capitalism   The "humanizing" of capitalism through social services and income support for masses of people.

Welfare state   A term, often used pejoratively, to describe a government that aids its citizens through various programs supplementing income, such as unemployment compensation and Medicare.

Workers   Those who must sell their labor power in order to survive.

Blue-collar workers   Manual laborers; the term "blue collar" is derived from the dominant color of working clothes.

Marginal workers   Those who do not make enough to be secure and/or are part-time or temporary laborers, seasonal workers, and so on, so that survival is a constant problem.

World Bank   The financial institution, created by the United Nations and dominated by the United States, that provides loans to developing nations, more affluent countries allowing their money to be loaned and used by less affluent ones.

World view   The comprehensive and consistent manner of perceiving people and the natural world and their interrelationship, underlying and leading to more specific values, beliefs, ideologies, and so on.

Zero growth   The concept of limiting population and industrial and other kinds of expansion or increase to as close as possible to a 0.0 percent growth rate for the world.

Bibliography

The selections that follow have been drawn from a vast and ever-changing literature on American politics. We have sought to identify additional reading that will fill out each chapter. Sometimes the selections contrast sharply with our interpretation; at other times, they extend it beyond the point that we consider supported by available evidence; or they represent reflections or methods worth examining. In no case, of course, can our selections be taken as a comprehensive bibliography. They are a beginning.

CHAPTER 1 Politics as Political Economy: Designing an Approach

Abernathy, William J., Kim B. Clark, and Alan M. Kantrow. *Industrial Renaissance.* New York: Basic Books, 1982.

Bluestone, Barry, and Bennett Harrison. *The Deindustrialization of America.* New York: Basic Books, 1982.

Carnoy, Martin, and Derek Shearer. *A New Social Contract: The Economy and Government After Reagan.* New York: Harper & Row, 1983.

Crozier, Michael J., Samuel P. Huntington, and Joji Watanuki. *The Crisis of Democracy.* New York: New York University Press, 1975.

Dahl, Robert A. *Dilemmas of Pluralist Democracy.* New Haven: Yale University Press, 1982.

Lasswell, Harold. *Politics: Who Gets What, When, How.* New York: McGraw-Hill, 1936.

Laxalt, Paul, and Richard S. Williamson, eds. *A Changing America: Conservatives View the 80s from the United States Senate.* South Bend, Ind.: Regnery/Gateway, 1980.

Lipset, Seymour Martin, and William Schneider. *The Confidence Gap: Business, Labor, and the Government in the Public Mind.* New York: Free Press, 1983.

Naisbitt, John. *Megatrends: Ten New Directions Transforming Our Lives.* New York: Warner Books, 1982.

Schell, Jonathan. *The Fate of the Earth.* New York: Knopf, 1982.

Schumpeter, Joseph A. *Capitalism, Socialism, and Democracy.* 3rd ed. New York: Harper Torchbooks, 1950.

Thurow, Lester. *The Zero-Sum Society.* New York: Basic Books, 1980.

Toffler, Alvin. *The Third Wave.* New York: Wm. Morrow & Co., Inc., 1980.

CHAPTER 2 Political Economy: Analysis and Evaluation

Best, Michael, and William E. Connolly. *The Politicized Economy.* Lexington, Mass.: D. C. Heath, 1976.

Croly, Herbert. *The Promise of American Life.* New York: Dutton, 1963.

Friedman, Milton. *Capitalism and Freedom.* Chicago: University of Chicago Press, 1962.

Gilder, George. *Wealth and Poverty.* New York: Basic Books, 1980.

Greenberg, Edward S. *Serving the Few: Corporate Capitalism and the Bias of Government Policy.* New York: Wiley, 1974.

Hartz, Louis. *The Liberal Tradition in America.* New York: Harcourt, Brace, 1955.

Kolko, Gabriel. *The Triumph of Conservatism: A Reinterpretation of American History, 1900–1916.* New York: The Free Press, 1963.

Kristol, Irving. *Two Cheers for Capitalism.* New York: Basic Books, 1978.

Mills, C. Wright. *The Power Elite.* New York: Oxford University Press, 1956.

———. *The Sociological Imagination.* New York: Oxford University Press, 1959.

Nash, George H. *The Conservative Intellectual Tradition in America Since 1945.* New York: Basic Books, 1976.

Rossiter, Clinton. *Conservatism in America: The Thankless Persuasion.* New York: Knopf, 1962.

Skowronek, Stephen. *Building a New American State: The Expansion of National Administrative Capacities, 1877–1920.* New York: Cambridge University Press, 1982.

Tsongas, Paul. *The Road From Here: Liberalism and Realities in the 1980s.* New York: Knopf, 1981.

Weinstein, James. *The Corporate Ideal in the Liberal State.* Boston: Beacon Press, 1968.

CHAPTER 3 Political Economy I: The Economic Context

Bartlett, Bruce. *Reaganomics: Supply-Side Economics in Action.* Westport, Conn.: Arlington House, 1981.

Bowles, Samuel, David M. Gordon, and Thomas E. Weisskopf. *Beyond the Waste Land: A Democratic Alternative to Economic Decline.* New York: Doubleday Anchor, 1983.

Donovan, John C. *The Cold Warriors: A Policy-Making Elite.* Lexington, Mass.: D. C. Heath, 1974.

Dye, Thomas R. *Who's Running America? The Reagan Years.* 3rd ed. Englewood Cliffs, N.J.: Prentice-Hall, Inc., 1976, 1979, 1983.

Galbraith, John Kenneth. *Economics and the Public Purpose.* Boston: Houghton Mifflin, 1973.

Klare, Michael. *Supplying Repression*. Washington, D.C.: Institute for Policy Studies, 1980.

Marchetti, Victor, and John D. Marks. *The CIA and the Cult of Intelligence*. New York: Knopf, 1974.

Mermelstein, David, ed. *The Economic Crisis Reader*. New York: Vintage Books, 1975.

Novak, Michael. *The Spirit of Democratic Capitalism*. New York: Simon and Schuster, 1982.

Pirages, Dennis, and Paul Ehrlich. *Ark II: Social Response to Environmental Imperatives*. San Francisco: W. H. Freeman, 1974.

Reich, Robert. *The Next American Frontier*. New York: Times Books, 1983.

Reich, Robert, and Ira Magaziner. *Minding America's Business: The Decline and Rise of the American Economy*. New York: Harcourt Brace Jovanovich, 1982.

CHAPTER 4   Political Economy II: The Social Pyramid

Bell, Daniel. *The Cultural Contradictions of Capitalism*. New York: Basic Books, 1976.

Bottomore, T. B. *Classes in Modern Society*. New York: Vintage Books, 1966.

Dolbeare, Kenneth M. *American Public Policy: A Citizen's Guide*. New York: McGraw-Hill, 1982.

Eisenstein, Zillah, ed. *Capitalist Patriarchy and the Case for Socialist Feminism*. New York: Monthly Review Press, 1979.

Evans, Sara. *Personal Politics: The Roots of Women's Liberation in the Civil Rights Movement and the New Left*. New York: Knopf, 1979.

Hayden, Tom. *The American Future: New Visions Beyond Old Frontiers*. Boston: South End Press, 1980.

Lampman, Robert J. *The Share of Top Wealth-Holders in National Wealth*. Princeton, N.J.: Princeton University Press, 1962.

Marable, Manning. *How Capitalism Underdeveloped Black America*. Boston: South End Press, 1983.

Newfield, Jack, and Jeff Greenfield. *Populist Manifesto: The Making of a New Majority*. New York: Warner Paperback Library, 1972.

CHAPTER 5   Political Economy III: Managing the Agenda

Auerbach, Jerold S. *Unequal Justice: Lawyers and Social Change in Modern America*. New York: Oxford University Press, 1976.

Brownstein, Ronald, and Nina Easton. *Ruling Class: Portraits of the President's Top One Hundred Officials*. New York: Pantheon, 1982.

Crawford, Alan. *Thunder on the Right: The "New Right" and the Politics of Resentment*. New York: Pantheon, 1980.

Domhoff, G. William. *The Bohemian Grove and Other Retreats*. New York: Harper & Row, 1974.

———. *Fat Cats and Democrats*. Englewood Cliffs, N.J.: Prentice-Hall, 1972.

———. *The Higher Circles: The Governing Class in America*. New York: Random House/Vintage Books, 1970.

———. *The Powers That Be: Processes of Ruling Class Domination in America.* New York: Random House/Vintage Books, 1978.

———. *Who Really Rules?* San Francisco: Goodyear, 1968.

———. *Who Rules America?* Englewood Cliffs, N.J.: Prentice-Hall, 1967.

Dye, Thomas R. *Who's Running America? The Reagan Years.* 3rd ed. Englewood Cliffs, N.J.: Prentice-Hall, Inc., 1976, 1979, 1983.

Ferguson, Thomas, and Joel Rogers. *The Hidden Election: Politics and Economics in the 1980 Presidential Campaign.* New York: Random House/Pantheon, 1981.

Goulden, Joseph C. *The Superlawyers.* New York: Dell Publishing Co., 1971.

McConnell, Grant. *Private Power and American Democracy.* New York: Knopf, 1966.

Melone, Albert P. *Lawyers, Public Policy and Interest Group Politics.* Washington, D.C.: University Press of America, 1979.

Merkle, Judith. *Management and Ideology.* Berkeley: University of California Press, 1980.

Shoup, Lawrence, and William Minter. *Imperial Brain Trust: The Council on Foreign Relations and United States Foreign Policy.* New York: Monthly Review Press, 1977.

Viguerie, Richard A. *The New Right: We're Ready to Lead.* Falls Church, Va.: The Viguerie Company, 1980.

Weinstein, James. *The Corporate Ideal in the Liberal State, 1900–1918.* Boston: Beacon Press, 1968.

CHAPTER 6   Ideology and Symbolism

Apter, David, ed. *Ideology and Discontent.* New York: Free Press, 1964.

Banfield, Edward. *The Unheavenly City Revisited.* Boston: Little, Brown, 1974.

Campbell, Angus, Philip Converse, Warren Miller, and Donald Stokes. *The American Voter.* New York: Wiley, 1960.

———. *Elections and the Political Order.* New York: Wiley, 1966.

Devine, Donald. *The Political Culture of the United States.* Boston: Little, Brown, 1972.

Edelman, Murray. *Political Language.* New York: Academic Press, 1977.

———. *The Symbolic Uses of Politics.* Urbana: University of Illinois Press, 1964.

Girvetz, Harry. *The Evolution of Liberalism.* New York: Collier Books, 1963.

Goldwater, Barry. *The Conscience of a Conservative.* Shepherdsville, Ky.: Victor, 1960.

Hartz, Louis M. *The Liberal Tradition in America.* New York: Harcourt Brace Jovanovich, 1955.

Kristol, Irving. *On the Democratic Idea in America.* New York: Harper & Row, 1972.

Rossiter, Clinton. *Conservatism in America: The Thankless Persuasion.* New York: Vintage Books, 1955.

Steinfels, Peter. *The Neoconservatives: The Men Who Are Changing America's Politics.* New York: Simon and Schuster, 1979.

Warren, Donald. *The Radical Center: Middle Americans and the Politics of Alienation.* South Bend, Ind.: University of Notre Dame Press, 1976.

Whitaker, Robert W., ed. *The New Right Papers.* New York: St. Martin's Press, 1982.

CHAPTER 7   The Constitution

Bailyn, Bernard. *The Ideological Origins of the American Revolution.* Cambridge, Mass.: Harvard University Press, 1967.

Beard, Charles. *An Economic Interpretation of the Constitution.* New York: Macmillan, 1913.

Brown, Robert. *Charles Beard and the Constitution.* Princeton, N.J.: Princeton University Press, 1956.

Corwin, Edward S. *The Constitution and What It Means Today.* 13th ed. Princeton: Princeton University Press, 1973.

————, and Jack W. Peltason. *Understanding the Constitution.* New York: Holt, Rinehart & Winston, 1973.

Farrand, Max. *The Records of the Federal Convention of 1787.* 4 vols. New Haven: Yale University Press, 1911–1937.

Hamilton, Alexander, John Jay, and James Madison. *The Federalist Papers.* Introduction and Commentary by Garry Wills. New York: Bantam Books, 1982.

Neustadt, Richard. *Presidential Power and the Politics of Leadership.* New York: Wiley, 1960.

Wood, Gordon S. *The Creation of the American Republic.* Chapel Hill: University of North Carolina Press, 1969.

CHAPTER 8   The Judicial Branch

Abraham, Henry J. *The Judicial Process.* New York: Oxford University Press, 1980.

Alper, Benedict S., and Laurence T. Nichols. *Beyond the Courtroom: Programs in Community Justice and Conflict Resolution.* Lexington, Mass.: D. C. Heath and Company, 1981.

Auerbach, Jerold S. *Justice Without Law?* New York: Oxford University Press, 1982.

Cronin, Thomas E., Tania Z. Cronin, and Michael E. Milakovich. *U.S. v. Crime in the Streets.* Bloomington, Ind.: Indiana University Press, 1981.

Goldman, Sheldon, and Thomas P. Jahnige. *The Federal Courts as a Political System.* 2nd ed. New York: Harper & Row, 1976.

Goldman, Sheldon, and Austin Sarat, eds. *American Court Systems: Readings in Judicial Process and Behavior.* San Francisco, Cal.: W. H. Freeman & Company, 1978.

Jacob, Herbert. *Justice in America.* 2nd ed. Boston: Little, Brown, 1972.

Horowitz, Donald. *The Courts and Social Policy.* Washington, D.C.: Brookings Institution, 1977.

Lieberman, Jethro K. *The Litigious Society.* New York: Basic Books, 1981.

Murphy, Walter F., and C. Herman Pritchett, eds. *Courts, Judges, and Politics.* New York: Random House, 1979.

Rodgers, Harrell R., and Charles S. Bullock III. *Law and Social Change: Civil Rights Laws and Their Consequences.* New York: McGraw-Hill, 1972.

Scheingold, Stuart A. *The Politics of Rights: Lawyers, Public Policy, and Political Change.* New Haven, Conn.: Yale University Press, 1974.

Schubert, Glendon. *The Judicial Mind Revisited.* New York: Oxford University Press, 1974.

————. *Judicial Policy-making.* New York: Scott Foresman, 1974.

CASE STUDY   Legal Politics: The Abortion Case

Gordon, Linda. *Woman's Body, Woman's Right: A Social History of Birth Control in America*. New York: Grossman Publishers, 1976.

Milbauer, Barbara, in collaboration with Bert Obrentz. *The Law Giveth: Legal Aspects of the Abortion Controversy*. New York: Atheneum, 1983.

Paige, Connie. *The Right to Lifers: Who They Are, How They Operate, Where They Get Their Money*. New York: Summit Books, 1983.

Rubin, Eva R. *Abortion, Politics, and the Courts: Roe v. Wade and Its Aftermath*. Greenwood, Conn.: Greenwood Press, 1982.

Woodward, Bob, and Scott Armstrong. *The Brethren: Inside the Supreme Court*. New York: Simon & Schuster, 1979.

CHAPTER 9   The Congress

Barone, Michael, and Grant Ujifusa. *The Almanac of American Politics: 1984*. Washington, D.C.: The National Journal, 1984.

Davidson, Roger H., and Walter J. Oleszek. *Congress and Its Members*. Washington, D.C.: Congressional Quarterly Press, 1981.

Fenno, Richard F., Jr. *Congressmen in Committees*. Boston: Little, Brown, 1973.

————. *Homestyle: House Members in Their Districts*. Boston: Little, Brown, 1978.

————. *The Power of the Purse*. Boston: Little, Brown, 1966.

Foley, Michael. *The New Senate: Liberal Influence on a Conservative Institution, 1959–1972*. New Haven, Conn.: Yale University Press, 1980.

Green, Mark. *Who Runs Congress?* 3rd ed. New York: Bantam, 1979.

Jackson, John E. *Constituencies and Leaders in Congress*. Cambridge, Mass.: Harvard University Press, 1974.

Mayhew, David R. *Congress: The Electoral Connection*. New Haven, Conn.: Yale University Press, 1974.

Oleszek, Walter J. *Congressional Procedures and the Policy Process*. Washington, D.C.: Congressional Quarterly Press, 1978.

Weatherford, J. McIver. *Tribes on the Hill*. New York: Rawson, Wade, 1981.

CHAPTER 10   The Presidency

Barber, James David, ed. *Choosing the President*. Englewood Cliffs, N.J.: Prentice-Hall, 1974.

————. *The Presidential Character*. 2nd ed. Englewood Cliffs, N.J.: Prentice-Hall, 1977.

Bernstein, Carl, and Bob Woodward. *All the President's Men*. New York: Warner Books, 1975.

Cronin, Thomas E. *The State of the Presidency*. 2nd ed. Boston: Little, Brown, 1980.

Fisher, Louis. *President and Congress: Power and Policy*. New York: The Free Press, 1972.

Goldstein, Joel K. *The Modern American Vice Presidency: The Transformation of a Political Institution*. Princeton, N.J.: Princeton University Press, 1982.

Hargrove, Edwin C. *The Power of the Modern Presidency*. New York: Knopf, 1974.

Heclo, Hugh, and Lester M. Salamon, eds. *The Illusion of Presidential Government*. Boulder, Colo.: Westview Press, 1981.

Kessler, Frank. *The Dilemmas of Presidential Leadership: Of Caretakers and Kings*. Englewood Cliffs, N.J.: Prentice-Hall, 1982.

Koenig, Louis W. *The Chief Executive*. 4th ed. New York: Harcourt Brace Jovanovich, 1981.

Mueller, John E. *War, Presidents, and Public Opinion*. New York: John Wiley, 1973.

Neustadt, Richard. *Presidential Power*. New York: New American Library, 1960.

Pious, Richard M. *The American Presidency*. New York: Basic Books, 1979.

Reedy, George E. *The Twilight of the Presidency: An Examination of Power and Isolation in the White House*. New York: World Publishing Co., 1970.

Rossiter, Clinton. *The American Presidency*. 2nd ed. New York: New American Library, 1964.

Schlesinger, Arthur M. *The Imperial Presidency*. Boston: Houghton Mifflin, 1973.

Wise, David. *The Politics of Lying*. New York: Random House, 1973.

CHAPTER 11   The Bureaucracy

Barnet, Richard. *The Economy of Death*. New York: Atheneum, 1970.

Halperin, Morton H. *Bureaucratic Politics and Foreign Policy*. Washington, D.C.: The Brookings Institution, 1974.

Heclo, Hugh. *A Government of Strangers: Executive Politics in Washington*. Washington, D.C.: The Brookings Institution, 1977.

Lindblom, Charles E. *The Intelligence of Democracy*. New York: Free Press, 1965.

Melman, Seymour. *The Permanent War Economy*. New York: Simon & Schuster, 1974.

Pressman, Jeffrey, and Aaron Wildavsky. *Implementation*. Berkeley: University of California Press, 1973.

Rourke, Frances E., ed. *Bureaucracy, Politics, and Public Policy*. 2nd ed. Boston: Little, Brown, 1976.

Simon, Herbert A. *Administrative Behavior*. 3rd ed. New York: Free Press, 1976.

————. *Politics and Markets*. New York: Basic Books, 1977.

Wilson, James Q. *The Politics of Regulation*. New York: Basic Books, 1980.

CHAPTER 12   The Budgetary Process: Working Together

Ippolito, Dennis. *Congressional Spending*. Ithaca, N.Y.: Cornell University Press, 1981.

Pfiffner, James P. *The President, The Budget, and Congress: Impoundment and the 1974 Budget Act*. Boulder, Colo.: Westview Press, 1979.

Wildavsky, Aaron. *The Politics of the Budgetary Process*. 3rd ed. Boston, Mass.: Little, Brown and Company, 1979.

CHAPTER 13   The Impact of Economic and
Social Problems

Braverman, Harry. *Labor and Monopoly Capital.* New York: Monthly Review Press, 1974.

Huber, Joan, and William Form. *Income and Ideology: An Analysis of the American Political Formula.* New York: The Free Press, 1974.

Jacobs, Paul, Saul Landau, and Eve Pell. *To Serve the Devil, Volume I: Natives and Slaves.* New York: Random House, 1971.

Piven, Frances Fox, and Richard A. Cloward. *The New Class War: Reagan's Attack on the Welfare State and Its Consequences.* New York: Pantheon Books, 1982.

Rubin, Lillian B. *Worlds of Pain.* New York: Basic Books, 1976.

CHAPTER 14   Public Opinion and Attitude Change

Abel, Elie, ed. *What's News.* San Francisco: Institute for Contemporary Studies, 1981.

Apter, David E., ed. *Ideology and Discontent.* New York: The Free Press, 1964.

Chaffee, Steven H., ed. *Political Communication.* Beverly Hills: Sage Publications, 1975.

Epstein, Edward Jay. *News From Nowhere: Television and the News.* New York: Random House, 1973.

Erikson, Robert S., and Norman R. Luttbeg. *American Public Opinion: Its Origins, Content, and Impact.* New York: John Wiley, 1973.

Free, Lloyd A., and Hadley Cantril. *The Political Beliefs of Americans.* New York: Simon & Schuster, 1968.

Gitlin, Todd. *Inside Prime Time.* New York: Pantheon Books, 1983.

Graber, Doris A. *Mass Media and American Politics.* Washington, D.C.: Congressional Quarterly Press, 1980.

Green, Philip, and Sanford Levinson, eds. *Power and Community: Dissenting Essays in Political Science.* New York: Random House, 1970.

Hamilton, Richard F. *Class and Politics in the United States.* New York: Wiley, 1972.

Katz, Elihu, and Paul Lazarsfeld. *Personal Influence.* New York: Free Press, 1955.

Klapper, Joseph T. *The Effects of Mass Communication.* New York: Free Press, 1960.

Lane, Robert E., and David O. Sears. *Public Opinion.* Englewood Cliffs, N.J.: Prentice-Hall, 1964.

Lipset, Seymour Martin, and William Schneider. *The Confidence Gap: Business, Labor and Government in the Public Mind.* New York: The Free Press, 1983.

Patterson, Thomas E., and Robert D. McClure. *The Unseeing Eye: The Myth of Television in National Politics.* New York: G. P. Putnam's Sons, 1976.

Ranney, Austin. *Channels of Power: The Impact of Television on American Politics.* New York: Basic Books, 1983.

Sears, David O., and Richard E. Whitney. *Political Persuasion.* Morristown, N.J.: General Learning Press, 1973.

Sperlich, Peter W. *Conflict and Harmony in Human Affairs: A Study of Crosspressures and Political Behavior.* Chicago: Rand McNally, 1971.

Truman, David. *The Governmental Process.* New York: Knopf, 1951.

Welch, Susan, and John Comer, eds. *Public Opinion*. Palo Alto, Cal.: Mayfield, 1975.

Wise, David. *The Politics of Lying*. New York: Random House, 1973.

CHAPTER 15   Political Parties in the 1980s

Abramson, Paul, John H. Aldrich, and David W. Rohde. *Continuity and Change in the 1980 Elections*. Washington, D.C.: Congressional Quarterly Press, 1982.

Barber, James D., ed. *Choosing the President*. Englewood Cliffs, N.J.: Prentice-Hall, 1974.

Burns, James McGregor. *The Crisis in American Leadership*. New York: Simon & Schuster, 1984.

Chambers, William N., and Walter Dean Burnham, eds. *The American Party Systems: Stages of Political Development*. 2nd ed. New York: Oxford University Press, 1975.

Crotty, William S., and Gary C. Jacobson. *American Parties in Decline*. Boston: Little, Brown, 1980.

Greenwald, Carol S. *Group Power*. New York: Praeger, 1977.

King, Anthony, ed. *The New American Political System*. Washington, D.C.: American Enterprise Institute, 1978.

Ladd, Everett Carl, Jr. *Transformations of the American Party System*. 2nd ed. New York: W. W. Norton, 1978.

Milbrath, Lester. *The Washington Lobbyists*. Chicago: Rand McNally, 1963.

Nie, Norman H., Sidney Verba, and John R. Petrocik. *The Changing American Voter*. Cambridge, Mass.: Harvard University Press, 1976.

Olson, Mancur. *The Logic of Collective Action*. New York: Schocken Books, 1968.

Petrocik, John R. *Party Coalitions: Realignment and the Decline of the New Deal Party System*. Chicago: University of Chicago Press, 1981.

Polsby, Nelson W., and Aaron B. Wildavsky. *Presidential Elections*. 5th ed. New York: Scribner's, 1980.

Pomper, Gerald, et al. *The Election of 1980: Reports and Interpretations*. Chatham, N.J.: Chatham House, 1981.

Ranney, Austin, ed. *The American Elections of 1980*. Washington, D.C.: American Enterprise Institute, 1981.

————. *Channels of Power: The Impact of Television on American Politics*. New York: Basic Books, 1983.

Sorauf, Frank J. *Party Politics in America*. 4th ed. Boston: Little, Brown, 1980.

Sundquist, James L. *Dynamics of the Party System*. Washington, D.C.: Brookings Institution, 1973.

CHAPTER 16   American Elections: Stability
and Realignment

Bowles, Samuel, David M. Gordon, and Thomas E. Weisskopf. *Beyond the Waste Land*. New York: Doubleday, 1983.

Burnham, Walter Dean. *Critical Elections and the Mainsprings of American Politics.* New York: Norton, 1970.

Ferguson, Thomas, and Joel Rogers, ed. *The Hidden Election: Politics and Economics in the 1980 Election Campaign.* New York: Pantheon, 1981.

Hadley, Arthur T. *The Empty Polling Booth.* Englewood Cliffs, N.J.: Prentice-Hall, 1978.

Kolko, Gabriel. *The Triumph of Conservatism.* New York: Quadrangle, 1963.

Paul, Arnold. *Conservative Crisis and the Rule of Law.* New York: Harper & Row, 1963.

Phillips, Kevin. *Post-Conservative America.* New York: Random House, 1982.

Pomper, Gerald, et al. *The Election of 1980.* Chatham, N.J.: Chatham House Publishers, 1981.

Rusher, William A. *The Making of the New Majority Party.* New York: Sheed and Ward, 1980.

Warren, Donald I. *The Radical Center: Middle Americans and the Politics of Alienation.* South Bend, Ind.: University of Notre Dame Press, 1976.

Weinstein, James. *The Corporate Ideal in the Liberal State, 1900–1918.* Boston: Beacon Press, 1968.

Wiebe, Robert. *The Search for Order: 1877–1920.* New York: Hill & Wang, 1967.

Wolfinger, Raymond, and Steven Rosenstone. *Who Votes?* New Haven, Conn.: Yale University Press, 1980.

CHAPTER 17 Alternatives in American Politics: Forms and Forces

Allen, Robert L. *Black Awakening in Capitalist America: An Analytic History.* New York: Doubleday, 1970.

Baxter, Sandra, and Marjorie Lansing. *Women in Politics.* Ann Arbor: University of Michigan Press, 1980.

Boles, Janet K. *The Politics of the Equal Rights Amendment.* New York: Longman, 1979.

Bookchin, Murray. *Post-Scarcity Anarchism.* Berkeley: Ramparts Press, 1971.

Freeman, Jo. *The Politics of the Women's Movement.* New York: McKay, 1975.

Garcia, Chris F., and Rudolph O. de la Garza. *The Chicano Political Experience.* North Scituate, Mass.: Duxbury, 1977.

Goodwyn, Lawrence. *The Populist Moment.* New York: Oxford University Press, 1977.

Jencks, Christopher, et al. *Inequality.* New York: Basic Books, 1972.

Kirkpatrick, Jeane. *The Politics of the Women's Movement.* New York: McKay, 1975.

Lowi, Theodore. *The End of Liberalism: Ideology, Policy and the Crisis of Authority.* 2nd ed. New York: W. W. Norton, 1978.

Newfield, Jack, and Jeff Greenfield. *A Populist Manifesto: The Making of a New Majority.* New York: Warner Paperback Library, 1972.

Piven, Frances F., and Richard A. Cloward. *Poor People's Movements.* New York: Pantheon Books, 1977.

———. *Regulating the Poor.* New York: Random House, 1971.

CHAPTER 18   Power and Change: Prospects
for the Future

Bowles, Samuel, David M. Gordon, and Thomas E. Weisskopf. *Beyond the Waste Land: A Democratic Alternative to Economic Decline.* New York: Doubleday Anchor, 1983.

Boyte, Harry. *The Backyard Revolution: Understanding the New Citizen Movement.* Philadelphia: Temple University Press, 1980.

Carnoy, Martin, and Derek Shearer. *Economic Democracy: The Challenge of the 1980s.* White Plains, N.Y.: M. E. Sharpe, 1980.

Cohen, Joshua, and Joel Rogers. *On Democracy.* New York: Penguin Books, 1984.

Dolbeare, Kenneth M. *Democracy at Risk: The Politics of Economic Renewal.* Chatham, N.J.: Chatham House, Inc., 1984.

————. *Political Change in the United States: A Framework for Analysis.* New York: McGraw-Hill, 1974.

Gross, Bertram. *Friendly Fascism: The New Face of Power in America.* New York: M. Evans, 1980.

Harrington, Michael. *Decade of Decision: The Crisis of the American System.* New York: Simon and Schuster, 1980.

Hart, Gary. *A New Democracy: A Democratic Vision for the 1980s and Beyond.* New York: Quill, 1983.

Heilbroner, Robert. *An Inquiry Into the Human Prospect.* New York: W. W. Norton, 1975.

Piven, Frances F., and Richard Cloward. *The New Class War: Reagan's Attack on the Welfare State and Its Consequences.* New York: Pantheon Books, 1982.

Wilensky, Herbert. *Organizational Intelligence: Knowledge and Policy in Government and Industry.* New York: Basic Books, 1967.

Wolfe, Alan. *America's Impasse: The Rise and Fall of the Politics of Growth.* Boston: South End Press, 1981.

Index